# The Boke of the Cyte of Ladyes

MEDIEVAL AND RENAISSANCE
TEXTS AND STUDIES

VOLUME 457

# The Boke of the Cyte of Ladyes

Christine de Pizan

*translated by*
Brian Anslay

*edited by*
Hope Johnston

ARIZONA CENTER FOR MEDIEVAL

ACMRS

AND RENAISSANCE STUDIES

Tempe, Arizona
2014

THE ARIZONA CENTER FOR
# MEDIEVAL &
# RENAISSANCE
STUDIES

Published by ACMRS (Arizona Center for Medieval and Renaissance Studies)
Tempe, Arizona
© 2014 Arizona Board of Regents for Arizona State University.
All Rights Reserved.


Library of Congress Cataloging-in-Publication Data

Christine, de Pisan, approximately 1364-approximately 1431.
The boke of the cyte of ladyes / Christine de Pizan ; translated by Brian Anslay ;
edited by Hope Johnston.
    pages cm -- (Medieval and Renaissance texts and studies ; volume 457)
English and French.
Includes bibliographical references and index.
ISBN 978-0-86698-508-6 (alk. paper)
1. Imaginary conversations. 2. Women--History--Early works to 1800.
3. Women--Conduct of life--Early works to 1800. 4. Feminism--Early works
to 1800. I. Anslay, Brian, translator. II. Johnston, Hope, editor. III. Christine, de
Pisan, approximately 1364-approximately 1431. Livre de la cité des dames.
IV. Christine, de Pisan, approximately 1364-approximately 1431. Livre de la cité
des dames. English. V. Arizona Center for Medieval and Renaissance Studies.
VI. Title.
PQ1575.L56E5 2014
843'.2--dc23
                                                                    2014047091

∞
This book is made to last. It is set in Adobe Caslon Pro,
smyth-sewn and printed on acid-free paper to library specifications.
*Printed in the United States of America*

# TABLE OF CONTENTS

## The Fyrst Parte
### *La premiere partie*

---

[1] maniere : rubric in text reads *navierre*
[2] Lilie then Cenobie in *L* table; order here reflects order in text
[3] [Archemise] : *omitted*

---

[4] Rommai[n]e : *Rommaire*
[5] Cyr[c]es : *Cyrtes*
[6] orcharde[s] : *Orcharde*
[7] dit [de] Ysis : *dit Ysis*
[8] planter plantes : *planter planter plantes*

---

⁹ taindre : *traindre*
¹⁰ *omitted*
¹¹ Dydo, then Gay Cirile in *L* table; order here reflects order in text

## The Seconde Parte
### *La seconde partie*

---

[12] com[m]ence : *comence*
[13] D[r]ipetrue : *Dipetrue*
[14] C[l]audyne : *Caudyne*

---

[15] [X]ancippe : *Pancippe*

---

[16] emp[er]eur : *empeur*

---

[17] joliveté (60), Claudine (61), Juno (62) in *L* table; order here reflects order in text

## The Thyrde Parte
*La tierce partie*

# ABBREVIATIONS

*Catholic Encyclopedia*  The Catholic Encyclopedia, ed. Charles G. Herbermann et al., 17 vols. (New York and London: Appleton, 1907-22) http://www.newadvent.org/cathen/

*Città*  Christine de Pizan, *La Città delle Dame*, ed. Earl Jeffrey Richards, trans. Patrizia Caraffi, Biblioteca Medievale 2, 2nd ed. (Milan: Luni, 1998)

Curnow  Christine de Pizan, "The *Livre de la cité des dames* of Christine de Pisan: A Critical Edition," ed. Maureen Cheney Curnow, 2 vols. (Ph.D. diss., Vanderbilt University, 1975)

EJR  Christine de Pizan, *The Book of the City of Ladies*, trans. Earl Jeffrey Richards (New York: Persea, 1982; rev. ed. 1998)

*FW*  Giovanni Boccaccio, *On Famous Women*, ed. and trans. Virginia Brown, I Tatti Renaissance Library 1 (Cambridge, MA, and London: Harvard University Press, 2001)

Lange  Christine de Pizan, "*Livre de la Cité Des Dames*, Kritische Textedition auf Grund der sieben überlieferten 'manuscrits originaux' des Textes," ed. Monika Lange (Ph.D. diss., University of Hamburg, 1974)

*LA*  Jacobus de Voragine, *Legenda aurea*, trans. William Caxton, ed. F. S. Ellis, 7 vols. (London: Dent, 1900)

*Letters and Papers*  Letters and Papers, Foreign and Domestic, of the Reign of Henry VIII, ed. J. S. Brewer, J. Gairdner, and R. H. Brodie, 2nd ed., 22 vols. (London: HMSO, 1920)

*MED*  Middle English Dictionary, ed. Hans Kurath, Sherman M. Kuhn, and Robert E. Lewis, 20 vols. (Ann Arbor: University of Michigan Press, 1952-2001)

*ODB*  Oxford Dictionary of Byzantium, ed. A. Kazhdan, 3 vols. (New York: Oxford University Press, 1991)

| | |
|---|---|
| *ODMA* | *Oxford Dictionary of the Middle Ages*, ed. R. Bjork, 4 vols. (Oxford: Oxford University Press, 2010) |
| *OED* | *Oxford English Dictionary*, prepared by J. A. Simpson and E. S. C. Weiner, 2nd ed., 10 vols. (Oxford: Oxford University Press, 1989) |
| *Oxford DNB* | *Oxford Dictionary of National Biography*, ed. H. G. C. Matthew and Brian Harrison, 61 vols. (Oxford: Oxford University Press, 2004) |
| *PL* | *Patrologia Latina*, ed. Jacques-Paul Migne, 221 vols. (Paris: Imprimerie Catholique, 1844-65); repr. ProQuest, *Patrologia Latina Database*, accessed 2013 http://pld.chadwyck.com |
| RBG | Christine de Pizan, *The Book of the City of Ladies*, trans. Rosalind Brown-Grant (New York and London: Penguin Classics, 1999) |
| *STC* | A. W. Pollard & G. R. Redgrave, *A short-title catalogue of books printed in England, Scotland, & Ireland and of English books printed abroad, 1475-1640*, 2nd ed. rev. and enl. by W. A. Jackson, F. S. Ferguson and K. F. Pantzer, 3 vols. (London: Bibliographical Society, 1976-91); record numbers accessed via English Short Title Catalogue (ESTC), http://estc.bl.uk/ |

# ACKNOWLEDGEMENTS

This project benefitted from the generosity of numerous individuals. Deep thanks go to Helen Cooper, Rosalind Brown-Grant, Sylvia Huot, and Daniel Wakelin for reading my work in detail at an early stage and for providing useful feedback. Earl Jeffrey Richards offered encouragement and loaned me a rare copy of Monika Lange's unpublished critical edition of *Le Livre de la cité des dames*. I am grateful as well to Ardis Butterfield, Anne E. B. Coldiron, Stephanie Downes, Martha Driver, A. S. G. Edwards, Kate Harris, David Kelsall, Wai Kirkpatrick, Patricia McGuire, David McKitterick, Linda Merman, Thomas O'Donnell, James Simpson, Joanna Snelling, Alexander Wilkinson, and Georgianna Ziegler for their assistance. I would also like to thank D. Thomas Hanks, Dianna Vitanza, and my other colleagues at Baylor University for supporting my research on Christine de Pizan. Many thanks should go as well to Roy Rukkila, Leslie MacCoull, and Todd Halvorsen at the Arizona Center for Medieval and Renaissance Studies for improving the edition so skillfully; any missteps are entirely my own. Finally, the foundation for this book's construction has been my family, and I am more grateful to them than I can say in any language.

# INTRODUCTION

*The Boke of the Cyte of Ladyes* (1521) is the earliest surviving English translation of Christine de Pizan's *Le Livre de la cité des dames* (1405), and, perhaps more remarkably, the only time that the work appeared in print in either France or England before the twentieth century.[1] *The City of Ladies* stands out as a landmark defense of women by a female author who commanded the respect of the most influential men and women of her time.[2] Her career stands out because it is so singular: few women pursued academic studies with comparable tenacity, and none attained the international fame that she did as a young widow when her courtly poetry first caught the attention of patrons. She wrote prolifically over the next twenty years and became an authority on moral, religious, and political issues. English readers took a strong interest in her work during her lifetime and for more than a century afterward.[3]

---

[1] The St. Andrews French Vernacular Book Project found no evidence of the book's publication in French before 1601; see *French Vernacular Books*, ed. Andrew Pettegree, Malcolm Walsby, and Andrew Wilkinson, 2 vols. (Leiden: Brill, 2007).

[2] Charity Cannon Willard's *Christine de Pizan: Her Life and Works* (New York: Persea, 1984) is the authoritative account of the author's life. Françoise Autrand has published another biography more recently, *Christine de Pizan: Une Femme en politique* (Paris: Fayard, 2009). Two excellent modern English translations are available: *The Book of the City of Ladies*, trans. Rosalind Brown-Grant (New York and London: Penguin Classics, 1999); trans. Earl Jeffrey Richards (New York: Persea, 1982; rev. ed. 1998). A general discussion of the book's content will refer to the book by its modern English title, the *City of Ladies*, and the same holds true for character names. When the focus turns to either the French or the English version, specifically, this will be signaled through language use, i.e., the *Cité des dames* or *Cyte of Ladyes*. All quotations come from Anslay's English text; if a matter of translation is being discussed, the corresponding Middle French text will be provided, too. Chapter numbers follow the order in Anslay's text.

[3] Concerning the circulation of Christine's writing in England during her lifetime and in the decades following her death, see P. G. C. Campbell, "Christine de Pisan en Angleterre," *Révue de littérature comparée* 5 (1925): 659–70; Stephanie Downes, "A 'Frenche Booke Called the Pistill of Othea': Christine de Pizan's French in England," in *Language and Culture in Medieval Britain: The French of England, c.1100-c.1500*, ed. Jocelyn Wogan-Browne et al. (Woodbridge: York Medieval Press, 2009), 457–68; James C. Laidlaw, "Christine de Pizan, the Earl of Salisbury and Henry IV," *French Studies* 36 (1982): 129–43.

The central viewpoint of the *City of Ladies*, that women are as worthy as men, remained a minority opinion when Brian Anslay translated her arguments into English and Henry Pepwell put them in print with backing from Richard Grey, third earl of Kent. The Printer's Prologue observes the custom "of people lewde theyr prowesse to dyspyse," but he suggests that those with a more noble spirit, inclined toward "the furtheraunce of all gentylnesse," will gladly learn about women's virtue for their own moral development, which will spur them in turn "to sprede theyr royall fame." The topic of women's education and ability to rule coincided with a public interest in the royal household, where Anslay served as an administrator. At the time of the book's publication, Catherine of Aragon had one daughter but no sons and after twelve years of marriage, this was a source of increasing anxiety for the king. Mary was reaching the age when decisions needed to be made about her education, and the future for which it would prepare her. Her humanist program of studies would set an important precedent for her sister Elizabeth and other noblewomen in England. However, Henry VIII's desire for a male heir ultimately culminated in the annulment of his first marriage and England's division from the Roman Catholic church in 1534, with such profound cultural ramifications that literary scholars increasingly view the Reformation as a decisive turning point from the Middle Ages to the Renaissance in English society.[4] *The Cyte of Ladyes* therefore provides an interesting opportunity to study material of topical interest to readers in the sixteenth century.[5]

Its place within the history of the book is noteworthy, too, since the transition from manuscript to print increased the potential audience for Christine's ideas considerably. Only five copies of the *Cyte of Ladyes* remain more or less intact, plus a fragment in the Bagford Ballad collection, a far smaller number than the twenty-seven surviving manuscript copies of the *Cité des dames*. The small number of printed copies is misleading, though, and reflects the poor survival rate for early printed books rather than the number of copies in circulation at the time of its publication: by 1521, production capacity had reached six hundred copies or more per edition.[6] This means that the pro-feminine arguments

---

[4] For the views on this transition by the foremost scholars in the field, see *Cultural Reformations: Medieval and Renaissance in Literary History*, ed. Brian Cummings and James Simpson (Oxford and New York: Oxford University Press, 2010).

[5] For a discussion of the book's contemporary context, see Robert Costomiris, "Christine de Pisan's Boke of the Cyte of Ladyes in its Henrician Setting," *Medieval Perspectives* 18 (2003 [2011]): 79-93, and Mary Beth Long, "A Medieval French Book in an Early Modern English World: Christine de Pisan's *Livre de la Cité des Dames* and Women Readers in the Age of Print," *Literature Compass* 9 (2012): 521-37.

[6] Writing about the preceding period in print history, Jonathan Green, Frank McIntyre, and Paul Needham state that "if some 18–20 million books were printed in the fifteenth century (as sensible assumptions about print runs and observation of recorded

and stories found a much greater number of readers than previously believed. Additionally, a robust import trade meant that readers in London could also acquire copies of Christine's writing printed in Paris, Lyons, or Rouen if they so desired; the export demand for English books would be much smaller since few people outside of England had cause to learn what was a provincial vernacular during the late medieval and early modern period.[7] The audience for the *Cyte of Ladyes* was therefore paradoxically both larger and more limited than the readership of manuscript copies of the *Cité des dames*.

The present edition makes Anslay's Middle English translation available for study alongside the Middle French text of Ms. London, British Library Royal 19.A.xix (*L*). The French text is potentially of interest in its own right because scholars believe that the scribe copied it from a very early version of the work, creating an opportunity to see how Christine revised certain passages between its composition in 1405 and its presentation to Isabeau of Bavaria in 1414 as part of the Queen's Manuscript, or *manuscrit de la reine*, Ms. London, British Library Harley 4431 (*R*). Anslay's translation shares structural similarities with *L*, and it seems plausible that he consulted the manuscript as he worked given its provenance as part of the royal collection after ca. 1461 and his administrative position in the royal household. Annotations identify certain places where

---

editions seem to suggest), of which 450,000–550,000 still exist today (as ongoing census projects show), then the average survival rate of incunables would like somewhere around 2–3 percent"; from "The Shape of Incunable Survival and Statistical Estimation of Lost Editions," *Papers of the Bibliographical Society of America* 105 (2011): 141–75, at 144. See also Andrew Wilkinson, "Lost Books Printed in French before 1601," *The Library*, 7th ser., 10 (2009): 188–205. For print-run estimates, see Lotte Hellinga, *William Caxton and Early Printing in England* (London: British Library, 2010), 9, 122, 160; Philip Gaskell, *A New Introduction to Bibliography* (Winchester: St. Paul's Bibliographies and New Castle, DE: Oak Knoll Press, 1995), 160–63; Ronald B. McKerrow, *An Introduction to Bibliography for Literary Students* (Winchester: St Paul's Bibliographies and New Castle, DE: Oak Knoll Press, 1994), 130–33.

[7] Elizabeth Armstrong, "English Purchases of Books from the Continent 1465–1526," *English Historical Review* 94 (1979): 268–90; Lotte Hellinga, "Importation of Books Printed on the Continent into England and Scotland before c. 1520," in *Printing the Written Word: The Social History of Books, circa 1450–1520*, ed. Sandra Hindman (Ithaca and London: Cornell University Press, 1991), 205–24. See also Cynthia J. Brown, "The Reconstruction of an Author in Print: Christine de Pizan in the Fifteenth and Sixteenth Centuries," in *Christine de Pizan and the Categories of Difference*, ed. Marilynn Desmond, Medieval Cultures 14 (Minneapolis and London: University of Minnesota Press, 1998), 215–35. On the status of English as a vernacular, see Christopher Cannon, *Middle English Literature: A Cultural History* (Cambridge and Malden, MA: Polity, 2008), 37, 70–71; David Wallace, "Chaucer's Italian Influence," in *Cambridge Companion to Chaucer*, ed. Piero Boitani and Jill Mann, 2nd ed. (Cambridge: Cambridge University Press, 2003), 36–57, at 36.

Anslay departs from Christine's original text, sometimes deliberately, at other times inadvertently. A close examination of the texts in tandem will reward the curious reader with discoveries of many additional small variations; the implications of these divergences would be well worth considering in future studies. The texts by a female author and a male translator cross boundaries from French into English, manuscript into print, and one century into the next, advancing a polemical stance with regard to gender that would remain avant-garde more than a hundred years after Christine composed it.

## About the *City of Ladies*

The book consists of three parts narrated by three allegorical virtues, sent by God to defend women's reputation. Reason, Rectitude (or in Anslay's English, *Ryghtwysenesse*), and Justice will stand as their champions, and together they help the author's persona build a stronghold where the good reputation of women will be safe forever. The central image of an ideal city comes from Augustine's *De civitate Dei* (*City of God*, AD 413–436), a defense of Christianity by a venerated *auctor*. Christine's decision to situate her narrative collection in a Christian context represents one of the key ways that the *City of Ladies* differs from Giovanni Boccaccio's *De claris mulieribus* (*On Famous Women*, ca. 1361–1362).[8] She rewrites seventy-four of his hundred and six stories with calculated alterations to advance her ideological project.[9] His sequence is broadly chronological and focuses predominantly on pre-Christian *exempla*; she integrates material thematically, with a crowning collection of saints' lives once the Virgin Mary arrives to rule as the sovereign of the allegorical city. Boccaccio follows classical tradition when he admonishes his reader to emulate virtue and shun vice, thereby obtaining moral profit through the experience of reading,

---

[8] The Four Church Fathers are Ambrose (AD 340–97); Augustine (AD 354–430); Gregory (ca. AD 530–604); and Jerome (ca. AD 340–420). Augustine of Hippo, *De civitate dei*, trans. Marcus Dods (Buffalo, NY: Christian Literature Publishing, 1887; New Advent, 2009), http://www.newadvent.org/fathers/1201.htm; Lori J. Walters, "La réécriture de saint Augustin par Christine de Pizan: *De la Cité de Dieu* à la *Cité des dames*," in *Au champ des escriptures: IIIe Colloque international sur Christine de Pizan*, ed. Eric Hicks, Études Christiniennes 6 (Paris: Champion, 2000), 197–215; Charity Cannon Willard, "Raoul de Presles's Translation of Saint Augustine's *De civitate Dei*," in *Medieval Translators and Their Craft*, ed. Jeanette Beer (Kalamazoo: Western Michigan University, 1989), 329–46.

[9] A considerable amount of scholarship compares the work of Boccaccio and Christine de Pizan, including criticism by Angeli, Brownlee, Brown-Grant, Caraffi, Casebier, Doreste and Picón, Dulac, Franklin, Kellogg, Kolsky, Phillippy, Quilligan, and Stecopoulos with Uitti. See bibliography for publication details.

whether the actions in a given story commend or condemn its heroine. [10] Christine declares unequivocally that only virtuous women will be welcome in her city, but critics have noted that in some cases their actions are difficult to reconcile within the moral parameters of "virtue." Christine's city might aspire to heavenly ideals, but it also has its darker *arrondissements* where one would not wish to linger for too long.

The frame narrative begins in a place where the author spends a great deal of time, at a desk in her study, where her fictional self sets aside her work at the end of the day to relax with a little light reading. She laughs when she happens to see a slim volume that a friend lent to her, Matheolus' *Lamentations*, which her persona believes to be an encomium of female virtue. It turns out to be quite the opposite. The vitriolic treatise, written late in the thirteenth century, received a new lease on life when Jean Le Fèvre translated it into French and added his own response styled as a defense of women, called *Le Livre de Leësce* (ca. 1380–1387). Critics are divided as to whether it is a rebuttal in good faith, or if it is a disingenuous rhetorical exercise. [11] Alcuin Blamires argues that Christine knew the intricacies of the existing pro-feminine rhetoric and incorporated its strongest points in crafting her own defense of women. [12] Positive depictions of women were far outweighed by the number of texts dating from antiquity through Christine's day about the evils of marriage (*misogamy*) and the inferiority of women to men in general (*misogyny*). [13] Matheolus himself might be dismissed by the narrator as an intellectual lightweight, but she explains that the harm lies in the preponderance of negative writing by philosophers, theologians, and poets over more than

----

[10] *FW*, Dedication, 4–5.

[11] Renate Blumenfeld-Kosinski, "Jean Le Fèvre's *Livre de Leësce*: Praise or Blame of Women?" *Speculum* 69 (1994): 705–25; Karen Pratt, "The Strains of Defense: The Many Voices of Jean Le Fèvre's *Livre de Leësce*," in *Gender in Debate from the Early Middle Ages to the Renaissance*, ed. Thelma S. Fenster and Clare A. Lees (New York and Basingstoke: Palgrave, 2002), 113–33. Alcuin Blamires takes a less ironic view but acknowledges that the effectiveness of defenses can be compromised by facetiousness; see *The Case for Women in Medieval Culture* (Oxford: Clarendon Press, 1997), 5–7, 37. Jill Mann reads *Leësce* as a "vigorous defence of women"; see *Geoffrey Chaucer* (London: Harvester Wheatsheaf, 1991), 2, 34.

[12] Blamires, *Case for Women in Medieval Culture*, 3, 5, 25, 36, 39–41, 47, 91, 95, 103–6, 108–9, 122–23, 142–44, 149–50, 156, 165, 176, 179–82, 190, 199, 219–30, 232, 234, 236.

[13] Renate Blumenfeld-Kosinski, "Christine de Pizan and the Misogynistic Tradition," *Romanic Review* 81 (1990): 279–92; Rosalind Brown-Grant, "Christine de Pizan as a Defender of Women," in *Christine de Pizan: A Casebook*, ed. Barbara K. Altmann and Deborah L. McGrady (New York and London: Routledge, 2003), 81–100; Glenda McLeod and Katharina Wilson, "A Clerk in Name Only—A Clerk in All but Name: The Misogamous Tradition and 'La Cité des Dames'," in *The City of Scholars: New Approaches to Christine de Pizan*, ed. Margarete Zimmermann and Dina De Rentiis (Berlin and New York: Walter de Gruyter, 1994), 67–76.

a millennium. Her persona concludes, miserably, in a lament of her own that "the wytnesse of many is for to byleve" (I.1).

Reason, Rectitude, and Justice arrive shortly after this in a scene reminiscent of the Annunciation to Mary, brightening her dark study with the declaration that they will help the narrator build a fortified city in the Field of Letters to defend the honor of virtuous women.[14] The frame narrative consists of a series of questions posed by the author's persona, who wishes to know the truth about assertions that have been made by misogynists, and the replies that she receives from Reason in Part I, Rectitude in Part II, and Justice in Part III. They support each point with narratives demonstrating women's fortitude, fidelity, and mental acuity; the running disputation represents the allegorical construction process, and the stories provide building material and a population for the City of Ladies. Together, they build a case that the advancement of civilization requires collaborative effort between the sexes, and that distrust between men and women lessens their collective potential. *The City of Ladies* concerns more than the fame of any given woman, including the author herself; it extrapolates the principle of joint interest from personal to public space, and the stories prove not only women's inherent self-worth, but also their value to society as a whole.

Christine locates the foundation of the *City of Ladies* within the ideological concept of *translatio imperii et studii*, which maintained that the ascent of civilization could be traced from Troy in Asia Minor across the Mediterranean to Western Europe, building upon the idea in Vergil's *Aeneid* that the hero fled the destruction of Troy to fulfill his destiny in the foundation of Rome. Sylvia Federico remarks that "its narrative is one of old empires lost, and more importantly, of new empires won."[15] Various Troy narratives coexisted in the West and remained in circulation throughout the Middle Ages. As early as the seventh century, the Franks appropriated the foundation myth, developing an account of how Hector's son, Francion, gave rise to France and its royal line; by the tenth century, English historiographers began to relate how a descendant of Aeneas, named Brutus, founded Britain.[16] Christine refers to Hector, the forefather of France's originary myth, in several of her works, but importantly, she incorporates legendary women

[14] Jacqueline Cerquiglini-Toulet, "Fondements et fondations de l'écriture chez Christine de Pizan: Scènes de lecture et Scènes d'incarnation," in Zimmermann and De Rentiis, *City of Scholars*, 79–96; V. A. Kolve, "The Annunciation to Christine: Authorial Empowerment in *The Book of the City of Ladies*," in *Iconography at the Crossroads*, ed. Brendan Cassidy (Princeton: Princeton University Department of Art and Archaeology, 1993), 172–96.

[15] Sylvia Federico, *New Troy: Fantasies of Empire in the Late Middle Ages* (Minneapolis and London: University of Minnesosta Press, 2003), xv.

[16] Susan Reynolds, "Medieval *Origines Gentium* and the Community of the Realm," *History* 68 (1983): 375–90, at 376.

into the traditional narrative.[17] Reason creates a history for the City of Ladies even as she foretells its success, invoking associations with dominant foundation stories: "Haste thou not redde that the Kynge Troys founded the grete cyte of Troye by the helpe of Appolo, Mynerve, and Neptune . . . ?" She alludes in turn to Cadmus and the tragic history of Thebes (I.4), noting that both men were reputedly assisted by pagan gods, but "for al that, those cytees by space of tyme were overthrowne and ben tourned into ruyne." Reason allocates twice as much space to her recollection of the formidable status that the Amazon Empire achieved, noting that it too perished, as all "worldely lordshyppes" must. The old "femenyne royalme" exists only as a story, but the new city, made of stories, strives to progress beyond its achievements. Christine adds a sense of divine purpose to the endeavor when, in lieu of Troy's three pagan gods, she invokes Reason, Ryghtwysnesse, and Justyce as Christian virtues described in Trinitarian terms: "amonge us .iii. ladyes that thou seest here we be as one selfe thynge, and we may none of us do without other" (I.6). Reason declares that the time has come for Christine to deliver her own people "out of the handes of Pharao" as Moses once did (I.3), quarrying a foundation from both classical and Christian history.

Despite its military metaphors and sharp rejection of misogynist thinking, men are not always enemies. Quite the contrary: the book envisions a mutually beneficial partnership between the sexes, and the heroines overcome physical and ideological barriers for the sake of men as well as women. Hypsicratea (II.14), Triaria (II.15), and Antonina (II.29) are exemplary wives who follow their husbands into battle. Drypetina (II.8), Hypsipyle (II.9), and Claudine (II.10) reflect the greatness of their warrior heritage when they put themselves at risk for the sake of their fathers. Camilla's father (I.23) fled with little except his infant daughter when an uprising deposed him, and she returns his unconditional love when she grows up by returning her family to power in their native land with an alliance of supporters.[18] Even the Amazons, who banish all men from their territory, demonstrate love for their sons in the story of Thamaris (I.17). The encounter between Theseus and Hippolyte concludes with their marriage (I.18), and the chaste Penthesilea proves herself worthy of remembrance with Hector when she avenges his death at the cost of her own life (I.19). The female heroes achieve greatness without denigrating men as a whole, as misogynists did with women.

---

[17] Lorna Jane Abray, "Imagining the Masculine: Christine de Pizan's Hector, Prince of Troy," in *Fantasies of Troy: Classical Tales and the Social Imaginary in Medieval and Early Modern Europe*, ed. Stephen D. Powell and Alan Shepard (Toronto: Centre for Reformation and Renaissance Studies, 2004), 133–48.

[18] Earl Jeffrey Richards, "Where are the Men in Christine de Pizan's City of Ladies? Architectural and Allegorical Structures in Christine de Pizan's *Livre de la cité des dames*," in *Translatio Studii: Essays by His Students in Honor of Karl D. Uitti for His Sixty-Fifth Birthday*, ed. Renate Blumenfeld-Kosinski, Kevin Brownlee, Mary B. Speer, and Lori J. Walters (Amsterdam and Atlanta: Rodopi, 2000), 221–44.

In contrast with this respectful approach to male bloodlines, the patriarchal kingdom in which Christine lived and wrote took a far less favorable view of female leadership and the role of women in determining hereditary rights. The statute decreeing male succession, known as Salic law, ostensibly dated from the fifth century and argued that the royal crown was not private property but a public dignity, similar to the priesthood, reserved for men alone.[19] The motive for reviving the law in the fourteenth century was to discount English claims to the French crown through the mother of Edward III. Christine, unsurprisingly, had little love for the English during the Hundred Years' War, but neither was she one to discount female agency in matters of state. She encouraged Isabeau of Bavaria to take a stronger role in settling the struggle for control between the Armagnac and Burgundian factions after mental illness incapacitated her husband, Charles VI.[20] Her last known work is a poem celebrating Joan of Arc's historic victory over the English in 1429, taking great pleasure in the fact that a girl achieved what numerous men could not do.[21] While Christine argues forcefully against prevailing stereotypes of female weakness, it would be anachronistic to consider her a feminist, and some of the views that she expresses sit uncomfortably with modern readers.[22] Her parting admonition at the end of Part III

[19] Marilynn Desmond, *Reading Dido: Gender, Textuality, and the Medieval Aeneid*, Medieval Cultures 8 (Minneapolis and London: University of Minnesota Press, 1994), 207–9; Craig Taylor, "The Salic Law, French Queenship, and the Defense of Women in the Late Middle Ages," *French Historical Studies* 29 (2006): 543–64.

[20] Tracy Adams, "Christine de Pizan, Isabeau of Bavaria, and Female Regency," *French Historical Studies* 32 (2009): 1–32, and eadem, "Recovering Queen Isabeau of France (*c.* 1370–1435): A Re-Reading of Christine de Pizan's Letters to the Queen," *Fifteenth Century Studies* 33 (2008): 35–54; Charity Cannon Willard, ed., *The "Livre de la Paix" of Christine de Pizan* ('S-Gravenhage: Mouton, 1958), 17–27. See also Deborah McGrady, "What is a Patron? Benefactors and Authorship in Harley 4431, Christine de Pizan's Collected Works," in Desmond, *Categories of Difference*, 195–214.

[21] Christine de Pizan, *Le Ditié de Jehanne d'Arc*, ed. and trans. Angus J. Kennedy and Kenneth Varty, Medium Ævum Monographs n. s. 9 (Oxford: Society for the Study of Mediæval Languages and Literature, 1977); Nancy Bradley Warren, "Christine de Pizan and Joan of Arc," in *History of British Women's Writing, 700-1500: Volume One*, ed. Liz Herbert McAvoy and Diane Watt (New York and Basingstoke: Palgrave Macmillan, 2012), 189-97; and eadem, "French Women and English Men: Joan of Arc, Margaret of Anjou, and Christine de Pizan in England, 1445–1540," *Exemplaria* 16 (2004): 405–36. For a reassessment of the poem's meaning, see Françoise Michaud-Fréjaville, "'Fors nature': Dieu, le roi Charles et la Pucelle, ou Faut-il changer notre titre du *Ditié* de Jeahnne d'Arc?" *CRMH* 25 (2013): 545–58.

[22] Sheila Delany, "Rewriting Woman Good: Gender and Anxiety of Influence in Two Late-Medieval Texts," in *Chaucer in the Eighties*, ed. Julian N. Wasserman and Robert J. Blanch (Syracuse, NY: Syracuse University Press, 1986), 75–92; eadem, "'Mothers to Think Back Through': Who Are They? The Ambiguous Example of Christine de Pizan," in *Medieval Texts and Contemporary Readers*, ed. Laurie A. Finke and Martin B. Shichtman

exhorts them to be demure and obedient through all the stages of their life as virtuous daughters, wives, and widows, in a manner befitting their respective rank in society, whether they are of high, middle, or modest standing. Even strong heroines such as Semiramis (I.15), Zenobia (I.20), Artemisia (I.25, II.16), and Fredegunde (I.13, I.22) step into a leadership role only after the death of their husbands. It would therefore be premature to rally citizens in the City of Ladies with a cry of *liberté, égalité, fraternité*. The author maintains that women should be recognized for the valuable contributions they have made and continue to make within a hierarchical civilization.

She notably departs from social tradition when she challenges the standard custom of foreclosing academic opportunities for girls. In the voice of Reason, she argues:

> yf it were the custome to put the lytel maydens to the scole, and that sewyngly were made to learn the scyences as they do to the man chyldren, that they sholde lerne as parfytely, and they sholde be as wel entred into the subtyltes of al the artes and scyences as they be. (I.27)

Cornificia (I.28) illustrates this point because her parents sent her to school in disguise with her brother as a practical joke, yet she proved so proficient in her academic studies according to Reason that she eclipsed her brother's accomplishments. Proba (I.29) wins praise for recrafting Vergil's poetry as a revelation of Christian truth, a feat not entirely unlike Christine's own process of rewriting Boccaccio's pagan examples to reveal the goodness of women as a whole, within a much more overtly Christian framework. Christine maintains that scholarly learning should be held in higher regard than cleverness expressed in deeds because establishing one's place in the Field of Letters offers the prospect of enlightening others in perpetuity (I.43). She complements the enduring model of women from classical antiquity to offer examples closer to her own day. She notes how Giovanni Andrea (1275–1347) fostered his daughter's aptitude for legal study and draws a parallel between their relationship and the academic encouragement she received from her own father, Tommaso da Pizzano (ca. 1315/20–1387), when she was a girl (II.36).[23] Christine, in turn, would provide instruction

---

(Ithaca and London: Cornell University Press, 1987), 177–97; and eadem, "History, Politics, and Christine Studies: A Polemical Reply," in *Politics, Gender, and Genre: The Political Thought of Christine de Pizan*, ed. Margaret Brabant (Boulder, CO and Oxford: Westview Press, 1992), 193–206. For a cogent reply, see Christine Reno, "Christine de Pizan: 'At Best a Contradictory Figure?'" in Brabant, *Politics, Gender, and Genre*, 171–91.

[23] For a brief account of Christine's education within a humanist context, see Sarah Gwyneth Ross, *The Birth of Feminism: Woman as Intellect in Renaissance Italy and England* (Cambridge, MA and London: Harvard University Press, 2009), 19–30. See also Karen Green, "Christine de Pizan: Isolated Individual or Member of a Feminine Community of Learning?" in *Communities of Learning: Networks and the Shaping of Intellectual Identity*

for her son in *Les Enseignements moraux* (ca. 1399) and *L'Epistre Othéa* (ca. 1400), as well as writing a mirror for princes, *Le Livre du corps de policie* (ca. 1406), and a military guidebook, *Le Livre des fais d'armes et de chevalerie* (1410), showing by example that women can be adept not only as students but as instructors, too.[24]

During Anslay's lifetime, the topic of female education drew considerable interest during the development of northern humanism. Catherine of Aragon commissioned Juan Luis Vives to write *De institutione feminae Christianae* (1523) with her daughter Mary in mind, but for the benefit of women more generally; to this end she asked Sir Thomas More to translate it into English, and the task was undertaken by a humanist tutor named Richard Hyrde, who served as an instructor for female members of More's family.[25] The *Instruction of a Christen Woman* proved so popular that it went through eight editions between ca. 1529 and 1592.[26] It advocates academic study by women in general as a moral occupation to stave off idle fantasies, and as a means to enrich their conversations with

---

in Europe, 1100–1500, ed. Constant J. Mews and John N. Crossley (Turnhout: Brepols, 2011), 229–50. On the depiction of daughters, see Leslie Abend Callahan, "Filial Fili- ations: Representations of the Daughter in the Works of Christine de Pizan," in Hicks, *Au Champ des escriptures*, 481–91. On the career of Christine's father, see Charity Cannon Willard, "Christine de Pizan: The Astrologer's Daughter," in *Mélanges à la mémoire de Franco Simone: France et Italie dans la culture européenne*, ed. J. Beck and Gianni Mombello (Geneva: Slatkine, 1980), 95–111; Edgar Laird, "Christine de Pizan and Controversy Concerning Star-Study in the Court of Charles V," *Culture and Cosmos* 1 (1997): 35–48.

[24] See Bernard Ribémont, "Christine de Pizan et la figure de la mère," in *Chris- tine de Pizan 2000: Studies on Christine de Pizan in Honour of Angus J. Kennedy*, ed. John Campbell and Nadia Margolis (Amsterdam and Atlanta: Rodopi, 2000), 149–61.

[25] Diane Valeri Bayne, "*The Instruction of a Christian Woman*: Richard Hyrde and the Thomas More Circle," *Moreana* 45 (1975): 5–15; Elizabeth McCutcheon, "The Education of Thomas More's Daughters: Concepts and Praxis," in *East Meets West: Homage to Edgar C. Knowlton, Jr.*, ed. Roger L. Hadlich and J. D. Ellsworth (Honolulu: Department of European Languages and Literature, University of Hawaii, 1988), 193–207. More's eldest daughter became an esteemed scholar in her own right; see John Archer Gee, "Marga- ret Roper's English Version of Erasmus' *Precatio Dominica* and the Apprenticeship behind Early Tudor Translation," *Review of English Studies* 13 (1937): 257–71; Jaime Goodrich, "Thomas More and Margaret More Roper: A Case for Rethinking Women's Participation in the Early Modern Public Sphere," *Sixteenth Century Journal* 39 (2008): 1021–40.

[26] *STC* 24856–24863: Berthelet, [1529?], [1531?], 1541, 1547; Powell, 1557; Wykes, [1567?]; Waldegrave, 1585; Danter, 1592. See Elizabeth Patton, "Second Thoughts of a Renaissance Humanist on the Education of Women: Juan Luis Vives Revises his *De institutione feminae Christianae*," *American Notes & Queries* 5 (1992): 111–14; Betty S. Travitsky, "Reprinting Tudor History: The Case of Catherine of Aragon," *Renaissance Quarterly* 50 (1997): 164–74. For a modern English translation of the work, see Juan Luis Vives, *The Education of a Christian Woman*, ed. and trans. Charles Fantazzi (Chicago and London: University of Chicago Press, 2000).

men. Not all humanists took such a repressive view.[27] Hyrde observes in a preface to *A Devoute Treatise upon the Pater Noster* (ca. 1524), which is a translation of Erasmus' *Precatio dominica in septem portiones distributa* (1523) by Margaret More Roper, that some women receive a superior education to men who wish they could claim the same.[28] The idea that girls should be educated at school as boys are, then apply their knowledge for the public good, remained a controversial subject with respect to higher education into the early twentieth century; Virginia Woolf discusses the disparity in opportunities for young men and women in a lecture series delivered in 1928 for the two all-women's colleges of Cambridge University at the time, Newnham and Girton, and it became the basis for *A Room of One's Own* (1929); in it, she famously asks her audience what would have happened if Shakespeare had had a sister. The answer emerging from ongoing research is that certain privileged girls would learn alongside their brothers, but Woolf's point rings true. Talented girls belonging to a slightly lower rank in society lacked a social framework to provide them with the kind of schooling available to non-aristocratic boys such as Chaucer and Shakespeare. Even in the unusual cases where women enjoyed sufficient wealth, leisure, and paternal support to pursue academic studies, their writing would be for a private audience rather than for public consumption.

One last character in the *City of Ladies* worth special note is Zenobia, who is praised for being "unyversall in all the vertues" of public duty and private life (I.20). Elsewhere in medieval literature, her narrative appears in collections of stories that are predominantly about men. Boccaccio's *De casibus virorum illustrium* (ca. 1360) speaks in book eight of the respect she commanded as leader, holding her own until the Roman emperor Aurelian seized victory on the battlefield and led Zenobia away as a captive; it is among the small number of vignettes that Chaucer selects for the Monk in the *Canterbury Tales* (ca. 1387–1395), and Lydgate translated Boccaccio's collection in its entirety for English readers as the *Fall of Princes* (ca. 1431–1439). For Christine, Zenobia not only surpassed "all

---

[27] Prudence Allen, *The Concept of Woman: The Early Humanist Reformation, 1250–1500* (Grand Rapids, MI: W. B. Eerdmans, 2006), 2:659–760; Susan Groag Bell, "Christine de Pizan (1364–1430): Humanism and the Problem of a Studious Woman," *Feminist Studies* 3–4 (1976): 173–84; Pamela Joseph Benson, *The Invention of the Renaissance Woman: The Challenge of Female Independence in the Literature and Thought of Italy and England* (University Park, PA: Pennsylvania State University Press, 1992), 157–81; Maria Dowling, *Humanism in the Age of Henry VIII* (London: Croom Helm, 1986), 219–47; Hilda L. Smith, "Humanist Education and the Renaissance Concept of Woman," in *Women and Literature in Britain, 1500–1700*, ed. Helen Wilcox (Cambridge: Cambridge University Press, 1996), 9–29.

[28] Hope Johnston, "Desiderius Erasmus, *A deuoute treatise vpon the Pater noster*," EEBO Introduction Series, http://eebo.chadwyck.com/intros/htxview?template=basic. htx&content=roper.htm.

other knyghtes of the worlde" in her life but "also she passed all other ladyes in noblesse," and when she had time to rest, "then ryght dylygently she toke hede to the scole and desyred to be taught in phylosophy" (I.20). Her erudition applied to "Latyne and the Grekysshe letters," two of the languages that humanists sought to master, and one of the English humanists, Sir Thomas Elyot, invokes this association of the heroine with learning in his *Defense of Women* (1540).[29] Christine explains, in her version, that Zenobia delayed marriage because she wished to remain a virgin, but Elyot says that she married late because she wanted to pursue her education first. Yet her role in the debate between Candidus and Caninius is relatively small. She stands at a remove from their academic sparring, demurely inviting them into her home after her defeat and imprisonment by Aurelian; her personal experience comes as an afterword to their intellectual debate, when she has no further pages to turn. By contrast, the queen actively pursues knowledge in the *City of Ladies* with a view to the future as she orchestrates the studies of her children, through whom her noble lineage would continue. She does not specify whether these are sons or daughters: both would be worthy of education. Imperial might is paired with studious achievement in a female hero who is also an attentive mother. She stands as a moral example for her life, rather than her fall. Christine omits her defeat, consistent with Reason's promise that the inhabitants of the new City would never be ousted by enemies. Instead, they look forward to the Christian life everlasting exemplified in Book III by martyrs who are never defeated. Even Zenobia, a pre-Christian character, embodies hope as remains for the reader *in medias res*, writing "all her hystoryes" by her own hand (I.20).

## About the Author

Christine de Pizan (ca. 1364–1430) was born in Venice, and as an adult she would continue to assert her Italian identity through her writing, aligning herself with the homeland of Dante, Petrarch, and Boccaccio.[30] Her father, Tommaso

---

[29] *STC* 7657.5, 1540; *STC* 7658, 1545. For discussion, see Benson, *Invention of the Renaissance Woman*, 183–203; Constance Jordan, "Feminism and the Humanists: The Case of Sir Thomas Elyot's *Defence of Good Women*," in *Rewriting the Renaissance: The Discourses of Sexual Difference in Early Modern Europe*, ed. Margaret W. Ferguson, Maureen Quilligan, and Nancy J. Vickers (Chicago and London: University of Chicago Press, 1986), 242–58; Greg Walker, *Persuasive Fictions: Faction, Faith and Political Culture in the Reign of Henry VIII* (Aldershot: Scolar Press and Brookfield, VT: Ashgate, 2006), 178–203.

[30] See Thérèse Moreau, "I, Christine, an Italian Woman," in *Displaced Women: Multilingual Narratives of Migration in Europe*, ed. Lucie Aiello, Joy Charnley, and Mariangela Palladino (Newcastle upon Tyne: Cambridge Scholars, 2014), 71–90.

da Pizzano, trained and taught in Bologna as a physician and astrologer. The king of Hungary had offered him a position, which he declined, instead moving his family to Paris in 1368 to join Charles V's court.[31] Autobiographical details in her writing recount how he encouraged her interest in academic study as a girl, and her experience is consistent with the findings of Holt Parker that girls were more likely to receive academic training if their father had a strong intellectual background.[32] According to Christine, her mother was the one to delay her progress, wanting the girl to concentrate upon acquiring skills expected of young ladies. Christine would in time write a conduct manual, *Le Livre de Trois Vertus* (1405), as a sequel to the *Cité des dames*, which offers advice to women of different social rank through the various stages of their lives. Though the story of Cornificia praises her for setting aside women's work, Christine also emphasizes the value of domestic endeavors for the prosperity of a household.

At fifteen she married a university-trained notary and royal secretary named Etienne Castel, and they had three children before his death in 1390. She never remarried.[33] The sudden loss of Christine's husband left her with legal and financial entanglements, a reversal described in *Le Livre de la mutacion de Fortune* (1403), through her situation began to improve after 1392 when Philippe de Mézières purchased property that her father had left to her.[34] Scholars believe that she trained as a scribe and might have copied texts as a source of income; paleographical studies indicate that she copied parts of her presentation manuscripts in her own hand.[35] She also renewed her pursuit of scholarship once she

---

[31] Suzanne Solente, *Christine de Pisan: Extrait de l'histoire littéraire de la France*, vol. 40 (Paris: Klincksieck, 1969), 1–2. For family background, see Nikolai Wandruszka, "Familial Traditions of the *de Piçano* at Bologna," in A. J. Kennedy et al., eds., *Contexts and Continuities: Proceedings of the IVᵗʰ International Colloquium on Christine de Pizan (Glasgow, 21–27 July 2000)* (Glasgow: University of Glasgow Press, 2002), 3:889–906 and "The Family Origins of Christine de Pizan: Noble Lineage between City and *Contado* in the Thirteenth and Fourteenth Centuries," in Hicks, *Au champ des escriptures*, 111–30.

[32] Jacqueline Cerquiglini-Toulet, "Christine de Pizan and the Book: Programs and Modes of Reading, Strategies for Publication," *Journal of the Early Book Society for the Study of Manuscripts and Printing History* 4 (2001): 112–26; Holt Parker, "Women and Humanism: Nine Factors for the Woman Learning," *Viator* 35 (2004): 518–616.

[33] See Anne Marie West, "'Doulce chose est que mariage': Exemplarity and Advice in the Works of Christine de Pizan" (Ph.D. diss., Florida State University, 2009), 40–146.

[34] Willard, *Christine de Pizan, Her Life and Works*, 16, 19–20, 23, 33–35, 40. See also Bernard Ribémont, "Christine de Pizan, la justice et le droit," *Moyen Âge* 118 (2012): 129–68.

[35] RBG, xxv; Solente, *Christine de Pisan*, 9; Willard, *Life and Works*, 39–40, 45–47 regarding her work as a copyist. Regarding paleographical analyses and manuscript descriptions, see bibliography for relevant publications by Aussems, Ouy and Reno, Parussa, and Willard.

was a widow, and she engaged three scholars in an epistolary debate known as *La Querelle de la Rose* (ca. 1400–1404) about the misogynistic content of Jean de Meun's *Roman de la Rose*, an extremely popular thirteenth-century poem. Jean Gerson, chancellor of the University of Paris, gave Christine his intellectual support, and through her early courtly poetry she secured financial support from patrons in the highest tiers of society.[36] She interweaves autobiographical details through her writing, including *Le Livre du chemin de long estude* (1402), describing her acquisition of knowledge in the guise of an allegorical journey led by Sibyl, a female embodiment of enlightenment.[37] *Le Livre de l'advision Cristine* (1405) provides additional information about the life of the female author.[38] She pursued her career assiduously, as her record shows. Between 1399 and 1415, she wrote prolifically in both poetry and prose, assembling collections of proverbs, conduct manuals, political commentaries, allegories, religious meditations, a universal history, and a biography of Charles V.[39] All told, some two hundred

---

[36] *Le Débat sur le Roman de la Rose*, ed. Eric Hicks (Paris: Champion, 1977); Eric Hicks, "Situation du débat sur le *Roman de la Rose*," in *Une Femme de lettres au moyen âge: Études autour de Christine de Pizan*, ed. Liliane Dulac and Bernard Ribémont (Orléans: Paradigme, 1995), 51–67; Christine McWebb and Earl Jeffrey Richards, "New Perspectives on the Debate about the *Roman de la rose*," in L. Dulac et al., eds., *Desireuse de plus avant enquerre: Actes du VI<sup>e</sup> Colloque international sur Christine de Pizan (Paris, 20–24 juillet 2006)* (Paris: Champion, 2008), 103–16. See also Deborah McGrady, "Reading for Authority: Portraits of Christine de Pizan and Her Readers," in *Author, Reader, Book: Medieval Authorship in Theory and Practice*, ed. S. B. Partridge and E. Kwakkel (Toronto: University of Toronto Press, 2012), 154–77, esp. 155–57.

[37] Andrea Tarnowski, "The Lessons of Experience and the *Chemin de long estude*," in Altmann and McGrady, *Christine de Pizan: A Casebook*, 181–97. On the importance of the sibyls in Christine's writing, see Maureen Quilligan, *Allegory of Female Authority: Christine de Pizan's Cité des Dames* (Ithaca and London: Cornell University Press, 1991), 105–16; Jessica R. Weinstein, "Sibylline Voices of Christine de Pizan" (Ph.D. diss., Rice University, 2006), 6, 11–34.

[38] Christine de Pizan, *Le Livre de l'advision Cristine*, ed. Christine Reno and Liliane Dulac (Paris: Champion, 2001). For discussion, see Liliane Dulac and Christine Reno, "Le *Livre de l'advision Cristine*," in Altmann and McGrady, *Christine de Pizan: A Casebook*, 199–214. See also Roberta Krueger, "Christine's Anxious Lessons: Gender, Morality, and the Social Order from the *Enseignemens* to the *Avision*," in Desmond, *Christine de Pizan and the Categories of Difference*, 16–40, regarding the subject of education in Christine's early works.

[39] For a concise overview of Christine's writing, see EJR, xxv–xxx, and Marilynn Desmond, "Christine de Pizan: Gender, Authorship and Life-Writing," in the *Cambridge Companion to Medieval French Literature*, ed. Simon Gaunt and Sarah Kay (Cambridge: Cambridge University Press, 2008), 123–35.

manuscripts preserve Christine de Pizan's writing in Middle French, including twenty-seven copies of the *Cité*.[40]

However, the work that survives in the greatest number of copies is *L'Epistre Othéa* (ca. 1400), in which the goddess of wisdom offers moral and religious lessons to Hector in his youth, using a hybrid style that defies easy classification. Brief stanzas capture part of a classical myth in poetry, followed by two prose glosses for each, and illuminations provide yet another interpretive element.[41] When she wrote *Othéa*, her son Jean Castel was about the same age as the adolescent Hector and living away from home at the time. He moved to England after John Montagu, third earl of Salisbury (ca. 1350–1400), sought out Christine during a visit to Paris and offered her eldest son a position in his household. It should have been an auspicious career opportunity, given Salisbury's close ties to Richard II; however, when Henry Bolingbroke returned from exile to depose the king and become Henry IV, his supporters executed Salisbury in 1400, and the king himself took custody of Christine's son.[42] Paul Strohm suggests that his attempts to have Christine join the English court might have been motivated by a "desire for legitimacy, for the adherence of established figures, for the celebration of poets."[43] She sent "livres," which could mean books or money, to England for two years while her son lived there. James Laidlaw makes a convincing case that she dedicated a copy to Henry IV, not Charles VI, when she makes an appeal to the 'king'." She simultaneously petitioned Louis of Orléans through *Le Débat des deux amans* (ca. 1400) and *Le Dit de la rose* (1402) to accept her son into his service. Ultimately another patron, John the Fearless, offered the youth a secure living in Burgundy.[44]

She might have harbored little love for "le mal païs d'Angleterre, | où muable y sont les gents" [that terrible land of England, where the people are fickle], but

---

[40] Fifteenth-century manuscripts also preserve early translations of her writing in Flemish and Portuguese; see Angus J. Kennedy, *Christine de Pizan: A Bibliographical Guide* (London: Grant & Cutler, 1984); *Supplement I* (London: Grant & Cutler, 1994); *Supplement II* (Woodbridge: Tamesis, 2004); Edith Yenal, *Christine de Pizan: A Bibliography*, 2nd ed. (London: Scarecrow, 1989). For a catalog and scholarly analysis of her manuscripts, see Gilbert Ouy, Christine Reno, and Inèz Viellela-Petit, *Album Christine de Pizan* (Turnhout: Brepols, 2012).

[41] Marilynn Desmond and Pamela Sheingorn, *Myth, Montage, and Visuality in Late Medieval Manuscript Culture: Christine de Pizan's Epistre Othéa* (Ann Arbor: University of Michigan Press, 2003). On its English reception, see Downes, "A 'Frenche Booke Called the Pistill of Othea'," 457–68.

[42] Laidlaw, "Christine de Pizan, the Earl of Salisbury and Henry IV," 129–43; Anthony Goodman, "Montagu, John, Third Earl of Salisbury (c. 1350–1400)," *Oxford DNB* 38:741–42.

[43] Paul Strohm, *Hochon's Arrow: The Social Imagination of Fourteenth-Century Texts* (Princeton: Princeton University Press, 1992), 91–92.

[44] Willard, *Life and Works*, 165–67.

the political climate in France was hardly in better shape.[45] She demonstrates a sustained interest in contemporary political issues and concern about good governance in a time of deep conflict.[46] Charles VI came to the throne as a minor and only wrested control from his guardians in his twenties; he suffered bouts of insanity as an adult, and a power struggle between the Armagnac and Burgundian factions led to civil war some decades before the War of the Roses would embroil the English monarchy in similar turmoil. Christine wrote *Le Livre des fais d'armes et de chevalerie* (1410), a war manual, comissioned for the dauphin, but she also wrote *La Lamentacion sur les maux de la France* (1410) and *Le Livre de la Paix* (1413) with hopes that Queen Isabeau might heal the country's division. Escalating violence eventually drove the author to seek refuge in Poissy, where her daughter was a nun, and while there she wrote one last poem, *Le Ditié de Jehanne d'Arc* (1429).[47] Scholars assume that she died not long afterward.

French manuscripts of Christine's writing circulated in England during her lifetime and continued to do so after her death. For much of the Middle Ages, French equaled or exceeded English in importance as a vernacular language of Britain; as Elizabeth Salter remarks, "a view of English culture which relied exclusively upon writing in the English language [. . .] would be an impoverished one indeed."[48] What critics call the "French of England" has attracted increasing attention in recent years, including important studies by Ardis Butterfield, who argues that English and French were "both in use in a relationship lasting several hundred years."[49] English authors wrote in French, and French scribes

---

[45] Christine de Pizan, *Autres Balades*, XXII, ll. 24–25, in *Oeuvres poétiques de Christine de Pisan*, ed. Maurice Roy, 3 vols., Société des anciens textes français 23 (Paris: Firmin Didot, 1886–1896), 1:232–23.

[46] Renate Blumenfeld-Kosinski, "Christine de Pizan and the Political Life in Late Medieval France," in Altmann and McGrady, *Christine de Pizan: A Casebook*, 9–24; Kate Langdon Forhan,*The Political Theory of Christine de Pizan* (Aldershot: Ashgate, 2002); Claude Gauvard, "Christine de Pizan et ses contemporains: L'Engagement politique des écrivains dans le royaume de France au xive et xve siècles," in Dulac and Ribémont, *Une Femme de lettres*, 105–28; Stephen H. Rigby, "The Body Politic in the Social and Political Thought of Christine de Pizan: Part I, Reciprocity, Hierarchy and Political Authority," *CRMH* 24 (2012): 461–83, and eadem, "The Body Politic in the Social and Political Thought of Christine de Pizan: Part II, Social Inequality and Social Justice," *CRMH* 25 (2013): 559–79. Charity Cannon Willard, "Christine de Pizan: From Poet to Political Commentator," in Brabrant, *Politics, Gender and Genre*, 17–32.

[47] See n. 20, above.

[48] Elizabeth Salter, *English and International: Studies in the Literature, Art and Patronage of Medieval England*, ed. Derek Pearsall and Nicolette Zeeman (Cambridge: Cambridge University Press, 1988), 1.

[49] Ardis Butterfield, *The Familiar Enemy: Chaucer, Language, and Nation in the Hundred Years War* (Oxford: Oxford University Press, 2009), 11. See also Butterfield, "Chaucerian Vernaculars," *Studies in the Age of Chaucer: The Yearbook of the New Chau-*

worked in England; the international book trade readily supplied reading material from mainland Europe, in both manuscript and print.[50] Henry IV's desire to entice Christine to England and her son's placement with the earl of Salisbury are consistent with this wider cultural phenomenon; the first Lancastrian king had been living in France before his return to overthrow the last of the Plantagenet line, and the first Yorkist king, Edward IV, was born on 28 April 1442 in Rouen, France. English readers might not have perceived Christine's writing as being quite as "foreign" as native English speakers would view the French language today. The female author was truly an international writer: Italian by birth, deeply rooted in France, with an avid following in England during and after her lifetime.

## About the Translator

Few biographical details for Brian Anslay (*d.* 1536) can be pinned down with certainty, including the date of his birth. Records in the International Genealogical Index indicate that he was probably the son of William Robert Annesley and Mabel Anne English, born in the village of Ruddington, near Nottingham.[51] The family was well established in the area and would remain so for many years. When Christine was writing, at the beginning of the fifteenth century, Henry IV's *Calendar of Inquisitions Post Mortem* records that Sir Hugh de Annesley left an estate in Ruddington to an eight-year-old heir by the same name; much later, in 1542, royal documents identify Gervaise Annesley as the lord

---

*cer Society* 31 (2009): 25–51. For essays on English reception of French literature, see Wogan-Browne et al., *Language and Culture in Medieval Britain: The French of England, c.1100–c.1500*. Anglo-Saxon and Anglo-Norman both arrived from foreign origins, as did Latin before them. Calvert Watkins notes that the native Celtic languages "are the only branch of Indo-European threatened with extinction" despite recent efforts to revive Welsh: *The American Heritage Dictionary of Indo-European Roots*, ed. Calvert Watkins, 2nd ed. (New York: Houghton Mifflin Harcourt, 2000), xli.

[50] James Simpson, "Chaucer as a European Writer," in *The Yale Companion to Chaucer*, ed. Seth Lerer (New Haven and London: Yale University Press, 2006), 55–86, at 56; J. J. G. Alexander, "Foreign Illuminators and Illuminated Manuscripts," and Margaret Lane Ford, "Importation of Printed Books into England and Scotland," in *Cambridge History of the Book in Britain*, ed. Lotte Hellinga and J. B. Trapp, vol. 3 (Cambridge: Cambridge University Press, 1999), 47–64; 179–201 respectively. See also Scot McKendrick, "A European Heritage: Books of Continental Origins Collected by the English Royal Family from Edward III to Henry VIII," in *Royal Manuscripts: The Genius of Illumination*, ed. Scot McKendrick, John Lowden, and Kathleen Doyle (London: British Library, 2011), 43–65.

[51] "Bryan Annesley" was probably born about 1486; see International Genealogical Index, http://familysearch.org/pal:/MM9.2.1/MQVB-R1Q.

of "Riddingtone."[52] Brian Annesley first appears in Tudor records among the attendants of Henry VII's funeral on 11 May 1509; he also received livery for the coronation of Henry VIII and Catherine of Aragon on 24 June of the same year, listed among a smaller group of attendants assigned specifically to the "Queen's Chamber" and was old enough to hold a man's rank, as yeoman, at that time.[53] Her staff even then formed a subset of the overall household administration, ultimately answerable to the king. Anslay is referred to in the prologue as a "Yoman of the seller with the eyght Kynge Henry," which is corroborated by a record from 1528 that he was rewarded with land in Bradwell by the Sea, Essex, as "yeoman for the mouth in the office of the King's cellar." In addition to his duties related to the cellars, he delivered valuables for the crown in 1532, and in addition to the land in Essex, he obtained a desirable lease from the queen's dower of Fasterne Great Park and the woodward of Braden Forest, Wiltshire, in 1534.

Anslay and his wife, Anne Polsted, settled not far from court in Darenth, Kent, close to others affiliated with royal business. William Thynne, the 1532 editor of Chaucer's *Works*, worked as a clerk in the kitchens during Anslay's tenure in the cellar administration, and the Thynnes' home in Erith, Kent, was about six miles from where the translator lived.[54] It seems plausible that they might have known each other professionally, if not personally. The same could be true by extension for the senior court official who wrote the introduction to Thynne's edition and supplied medieval manuscripts to John Leland; Sir Brian Tuke started his career in the spicery of Henry VII before 1506, and through a series of promotions became Master of the Posts, then the king's French secretary, and finally his treasurer by 1528.[55] The kitchen offices might not strike the modern reader as a likely venue for literary scholarship, but Anslay's bureaucratic post would have meant that he crossed paths with other men who shared his interest in medieval writing. His involvement with the wine trade raises the likelihood that he acquired a working knowledge of French and Italian much in the same way that scholars believe that Chaucer first became familiar with

---

[52] *Calendar of Inquisitions Post Mortem*, vol. 18, *1–6 Henry IV (1399–1405)*, ed. J. L. Kirby (London: HMSO, 1987), 299. It records that he held 1 messuage and 3 ½ bovates of land; a "messuage" is defined by the *OED* as "a dwelling house together with its outbuildings and the adjacent land assigned to its use." A "bovate" is defined as the amount of land an ox could plough in a year, "varying in amount from 10 to 18 acres." The reference to Gervaise Annesley occurs in *Letters and Papers*, 17:594.

[53] *Letters and Papers*, 1:17, 41.

[54] Robert Costomiris, "Some New Light on the Early Career of William Thynne, Chief Clerk of the Kitchen of Henry VIII and Editor of Chaucer," *The Library*, 7th ser., 4 (2003): 3–15; Sydney Lee, "Thynne, William (*d.* 1546)," rev. A. S. G. Edwards, *Oxford DNB* 54:750–51; Greg Walker, *Writing Under Tyranny: English Literature and the Henrician Reformation* (Oxford and New York: Oxford University Press, 2005), 29–72.

[55] P. R. N. Carter, "Tuke, Sir Brian (*d.* 1545)," and James P. Carley, "Leland, John (*c.* 1503–1552)," *Oxford DNB* 55:523–24 and 33:297–301 respectively.

these languages as the son of a vintner.[56] A letter from 1533 addresses him as "Master Ansley, Yeoman of the Cellars," which could simply be a title of professional courtesy, but the term would also be applied to men trained at university. His name does not appear among records of Cambridge and Oxford alumni, but records from the time are not comprehensive. He is able to correct a mistaken reference to Cato Uticensis (I.10), suggesting that he knew at least some Latin.

Other Annesley family members found secure employment in the Tudor household: Hugh Annesley found favor with Henry VII and was granted "the office of keeper of the beds in Windsor castle" on 20 October 1486.[57] Thomas Annesley is identified as a yeoman of the cellar in Henry VII's funeral procession, then elevated to the rank of gentleman in the coronation lists; Brian Anslay carries no title in the first, but he is identified as a yeoman in the second, raising the possibility that he followed a path of advancement in his wake.[58] Ralph Annesley is listed as a groom of the cellar, and a younger Thomas Annesley served as a page in the buttery. The relationship between the Annesleys remains unclear, if connections existed at all; however, it seems to be more than a coincidence that so many men with the same surname worked as royal functionaries during the Henrician era and would continue to do so through the end of the sixteenth century.

His will, dated 8 March 1536, does not specify the extent of his wealth at the time of his death; it does not mention any books, but this is not unusual for the time period. He enjoyed sufficient luxury to bequeath clothes of costly fabrics to other men in his family: "To my brother John a doblet of crymsyn sattyn. To my brother Robert of Charluton a doblet of yellowe velvet, and to my cosyn Hugh my tawney cote gardeid with velvet and a mark in money. To Edmund Wright my newe rede cote and 10s."[59] He names "Maister Nicolas Statham of

---

[56] Derek Pearsall, *The Life of Geoffrey Chaucer: A Critical Biography* (Oxford and Cambridge, MA: Blackwell, 1992), 11–23.

[57] *Calendar of Patent Rolls*, vol. 1, *1485–1494*, ed. H. C. Maxwell Lytle, J. G. Black, and R. H. Brodie (London: PRO, 1914; repr. Nendeln, Liechtenstein: 1970), 26.

[58] The younger Thomas may or may not have been the same man named by John Graynfyld [Grenville] to Arthur Plantagenet, Lord Lisle in a letter dated 1 May 1536 saying that he "begs favor for Thos. Anseley," again asking Lisle in a letter dated 21 May 1536 to "be good to one Anseley." Thomas was seeking to have a pardon for the man who killed his brother John in Calais overturned, but his bid was ultimately unsuccessful. John Annesley held the Cluniac priory in Lenton, Nottinghamshire, about five miles from Ruddington.

[59] Ms. London, PRO, PROB 11/25/360. See Kathleen Ashley, "Material and Symbolic Gift-Giving: Clothes in English and French Wills," in *Medieval Fabrications: Dress, Textiles, Clothwork, and Other Cultural Imaginings*, ed. E. Jane Burns (New York: Palgrave Macmillan, 2004), 137–46; Ann Rosalind Jones and Peter Stallybrass, "The Currency of Clothing," in *Fashion: Critical and Primary Sources*, ed. Peter McNeil, vol. 1 (Oxford and New York: Berg, 2009), 315–41.

Soton" as co-executor with his wife, directing that his estate be divided equally between his wife and children. Anslay's younger son followed closely in his footsteps during the reign of Elizabeth I, and a memorial in St. Margaret's Church, Lee, Kent, is dedicated with a poem to "Nicholas Anseley, esquier, Sergiant of her Maiesties's sellar."[60] Sir Brian, the elder son, became a subject of intrigue when two of his daughters sought to gain control of his property by having him declared insane; the youngest, named Cordelia, wrote to Robert Cecil in October 1603 with a request that her "poore aged and daylye dyinge ffather" be allowed to live out his life in dignity. She prevailed and had a monument in the same church dedicated to his memory.[61] Shakespeare scholars have suggested that the case was well enough known that contemporaries might have drawn a connection between it and the plot of *King Lear*.[62] If true, Cordelia's letter provides an interesting literary coda for the translator's family.

No evidence exists that the translator, printer, or patron offered a copy of the *Cyte of Ladyes* to the royal library; it is not listed among surviving inventories, but early documentation of the royal collection is far from complete, and printed books were less likely to be kept at the time than manuscripts. According to Leland, the main part of the king's book collection could be found in

---

[60] Personal correspondence of Linda Merman, Senior Local Studies Assistant, Lewisham Archives, 30 September 2006. In a catalog entry dated 1796, Daniel Lysons reports that among other monuments in St. Margaret's parish church, "on the south wall of the chancel is an inscription to the memory of Nicholas Ansley, or Annesley, Esq. who died in 1593: above is an upright figure (in brass) of the deceased, in armour, kneeling at a desk." See D. Lysons, "Lee," *The Environs of London: volume IV: Counties of Herts, Essex & Kent* (1796), 500–13, http://www.british-history.ac.uk/report.aspx?compid=45488; drawing of memorial in *Gentleman's Magazine* 82 (1812): 520; *The Mirror of Literature, Amusement, and Instruction 20* (1825): 153 republishes Lysons's account, incorrectly identifying Sir Brian as the son of Nicholas. The Kent Archaeological Society provides transcriptions of three Annesley memorials based upon a survey of St. Margaret's by Joseph and Charles Perkins Gwilt on 22 August 1830. Another antiquarian, F. W. Cock, came into possession of the Gwilt manuscript, which Leland L. Duncan copied by hand in 1919; Frank Bamping transcribed Leland's records in 2001. His text can be found on the Kent Archaeological Society's website at http://www.kentarchaeology.org.uk/Research/Libr/MIs/MIsLee/MIsLee.htm.

[61] William Shakespeare, *King Lear*, ed. Grace Ioppolo (New York and London: Norton, 2008), 160–62.

[62] Geoffrey Bullough, "*King Lear* and the Annesley Case: A Reconsideration," in *Festschrift Rudolf Stamm zu seinem sechzigsten Geburstag am 12. April 1969*, ed. Eduard Kolb and Jorg Hasler (Bern: Francke, 1965), 43–49; John W. Hales, *Notes and Essays on Shakespeare* (London: G. Bell, 1884), 271–72; John Knowles, "How Shakespeare Knew King Leir," *Shakespeare Survey* 55 (2002): 12–35.

his three favorite palaces: Greenwich, Whitehall, and Hampton Court.[63] A post-mortem inventory of Greenwich Palace notes only that the library was furnished with seven desks and 329 (unnamed) books; the record for Hampton Court is even less specific, reporting that the library contained a great number of books, also unnamed. Other times, books might be described by the color and material used for their bindings without reference to their contents: Catherine's post-mortem inventory mentions "three books covered withe red lether, garnyssid withe golde foyle, and tyed with a grene reabande" and "seevyntene other bookys, smalle and greate, lockid in a cheste."[64] However, royal inventories do list tapestries depicting scenes from the City of Ladies, which no longer survive.[65] A copy of the *Cyte of Ladyes* became part of the Thynne family library by the 1540s when the nephew of the editor, Sir John Thynne, purchased Longleat, where it has remained ever since. It bears the name of William Brereton, a courtier who was charged and executed on the grounds of adultery with Anne Boleyn.[66] A reference to the "castle of Ladiez" appears in an account of royal festivities held at Kenilworth Castle during the reign of Elizabeth I, in 1575, as one of the books belonging to a guest named "Captian Cox."[67] The description of the event was printed twice, attesting to contemporary interest in it, though critics have questioned the veracity of the letter and whether such a man in fact existed.[68] The list of some sixty books, including medieval romances, provides useful insights about the popular reading tastes of Elizabethans, and it suggests that Christine's work lived on in the English cultural memory for a long time.

---

[63] James P. Carley, ed. *The Libraries of King Henry VIII*, Corpus of British Medieval Library Catalogues 7 (London: British Library, 2000), lxiii.

[64] James P. Carley, *The Books of King Henry VIII and His Wives* (London: British Library, 2004), 23, 27, 120.

[65] Susan Groag Bell, *The Lost Tapestries of the* City of Ladies: *Christine de Pizan's Renaissance Legacy* (Berkeley: University of California Press, 2004), 2, 6, 36–39.

[66] Sydney Lee, "Thynne, William (*d.* 1546)," rev. A. S. G. Edwards, *Oxford DNB* 54:750–51.

[67] *Captain Cox, His Ballads and Books; or, Robert Laneham's Letter*, ed. Frederick J. Furnivall (London: Ballad Society, 1871), v; A. H. Bullen, "Cox, Captain, of Coventry (*fl.* 1575)," rev. Elizabeth Goldring, in *Oxford DNB* 13:831.

[68] *Robert Langham, A Letter*, ed. R. J. P. Kuin (Leiden: Brill, 1983); H. R. Woudhuysen, "Langham, Robert (*c.* 1535–1579/80)," *Oxford DNB* 32:481–82. *STC* 15190.5 (1575); *STC* 15191 [ca. 1585]. It was printed a third time in 1784.

## *The Cyte of Ladyes* as a Translation

Critics who have compared Anslay's translation to the *Cité des dames* agree that his work follows the Middle French text closely. Jennifer Summit remarks in her book about the transmission of literature by women ca. 1380–1589 that the *Cyte of Ladyes* "is unusually faithful to Christine's original."[69] Omissions and extrapolations, commonly found in earlier medieval translations, became less common later in the period as translators began striving for accuracy with a minimum of editorial intervention. The topic of humanist translation theory seems to have occupied intellectuals on the continent before academics in England, where humanism found its footing at a later date.[70] Modern studies have directed their attention primarily toward the vernacular translation of Latin texts and the implied transfer of authority from clerical to lay audiences across economic strata, reaching an expanded audience without formal training, including women.[71] Early printers William Caxton and Robert Copland translated French literary works into English themselves for publication, using both language and medium to capitalize upon an interest in vernacular translations.[72] Five of Chris-

[69] Jennifer Summit, *Lost Property: The Woman Writer and English Literary History, 1380–1589* (Chicago and London: University of Chicago Press, 2001), 63.

[70] Petrarch and Boccaccio, influential Italian Renaissance writers, wrote nearly contemporaneously with canonical English medieval writers such as Langland, Gower, and Chaucer. Regarding vernacular translation in France, see Nadia Margolis, "From Chrétien to Christine: Translating Twelfth-Century Literature to Reform the French Court during the Hundred Years War," in *Shaping Courtliness in Medieval France*, ed. Daniel E. O'Sullivan and Laurie Shepard (Woodbridge: D. S. Brewer, 2013), 213–25. Regarding old and new attitudes to translation in England, see Massimiliano Morini, *Tudor Translation in Theory and Practice* (Aldershot and Burlington, VT: Ashgate, 2006), 15–19, 21–24. See also Nicholas Watson, "Theories of Translation," in *The Oxford History of Literary Translation in English*, vol. 1: *to 1550*, ed. Roger Ellis (Oxford: Oxford University Press, 2008), 71–91. For an anthology of early English writing about writing, see *The Idea of Vernacular: An Anthology of Middle English Literary Theory, 1280–1520*, ed. Jocelyn Wogan-Browne, Nicholas Watson, Andrew Taylor, and Ruth Evans (Exeter: University of Exeter Press, 1999).

[71] Gretchen A. Angelo suggests that translators gave the spoken language gravitas with anti-feminine attitudes; see "Creating a Masculine Vernacular: The Strategy of Misogyny in Late Medieval French Texts," in *The Vulgar Tongue: Medieval and Postmedieval Vernacularity*, ed. Fiona Somerset and Nicholas Watson (University Park, PA: Pennsylvania State University Press, 2003), 85–98. For a nuanced study of English translation, see Alastair Minnis, *Translations of Authority in Medieval English Literature: Valuing the Vernacular* (Cambridge: Cambridge University Press, 2009).

[72] See Anne E. B. Coldiron, "William Caxton," in *The Oxford History of Literary Translation in English*, 1, ed. Ellis, 160–69; Robert Copland, *Poems*, ed. Mary C. Erler (Toronto: University of Toronto Press, 1993), 4, 9, 18, 20–21; Brenda M. Hosing-

tine's books appeared in print as English translations, two of them translated by the printers: *The Morale Proverbes of Cristine*, trans. Anthony Woodville (Caxton, 1478); *Fayttes of Armes and of Chyvalerie*, trans. Caxton (Caxton, 1489); *The Cyte of Ladyes*, trans. Anslay (Pepwell, 1521); *The Body of Polycye*, anon. trans. (Skot, 1521); *The .C. Hystoryes of Troye*, trans. Robert Wyer (Wyer, [1549?]).[73] The demand for French literature in translation during the early years of printing provides one context for understanding why the *Cyte of Ladyes* came to be published in England.

Anslay's changes to Christine's text can be divided, broadly speaking, into three categories. The first would be instances where Anslay deliberately alters his source for his own purposes. The second reflects decision-making by Anslay as a translator and editor. The third kind of change seems to be unintentional, for example misreading of minims, misunderstanding vocabulary, or losing track of syntax. Earl Jeffrey Richards remarks that in the case of the *Cyte of Ladyes*, the English version is almost "a calque of the original, with occasional mistakes," which can raise difficulties of its own, as he points out: "Anslay's fidelity—excessive, in my view—to the letter of Christine's work [is] evidenced in the awkwardness of his grammar."[74] His word-for-word rendering of long, complex sentences sometimes feels as though the translator decided to shift the responsibility for discerning meaning to the shoulders of the reader. Yet as Jane H. M. Taylor notes with respect to the anonymous French translation of Boccaccio's *Des Cleres et nobles femmes* (1401), even when a person seeks to hew as closely as possible to the original text, following the source text virtually word-for-word, vocabulary choices reveal insights about the translator's perspective on the content; specifically, she examines dittology, or *binômes synonymiques*, a linguistic practice linking two words as one unit.[75] Christine adds binomials extensively as an editor of her own writing in later redactions of the *Cité des dames*, as seen in these representative examples:

ton, "Translation, Early Printing, and Gender in England, 1484–1535," *Florilegium* 23 (2006): 41–67.

[73] Brown, "Reconstruction of an Author in Print," 215–18, 228–29; Martha W. Driver, "Christine de Pisan and Robert Wyer: The .C. *Hystoryes of Troye*, or *L'Epistre d'Othea* Englished," *Gutenberg-Jahrbuch* 72 (1997): 125–39.

[74] Summit, *Lost Property*, 63; Earl Jeffrey Richards, "Finding the 'Authentic' Text: Editing and Translating Medieval and Modern Works as Comparable Interpretive Exercises (Chrétien's *Charrette*, Christine de Pizan's *Cité des Dames*, and Diderot's *Neveu de Rameau*)," *L'Esprit Createur* 27 (1987): 111–21, at 116–17.

[75] Jane H. M. Taylor, "Translation as Reception: Boccaccio's *De mulieribus claris* and *Des cleres et nobles femmes*," in *Por le soie amisté: Essays in Honour of Norris J. Lacy*, ed. Keith Busby and Catherine M. Jones (Amsterdam and Atlanta: Rodopi, 2000), 491–507.

| | |
|---|---|
| redargue | redargue et reprent |
| parfaire | parfaire et achever |
| les voies | les voies et les manieres |
| de prouece | de vaillance et de prouece |
| la plus noble | la plus riche et la plus noble |

Doublets appear frequently in English works, too, but Anslay does not seem inclined to expand her use of a single word into two, perhaps because she already uses dittology extensively.[76]

Any number of individual cases would invite interpretive skirmishes, if one looks at word choice closely. How did Athena's *chouette* [owl] become a *chough* [type of crow] in Anslay's version (I.34)? The most immediate answer would be that the words look similar, and the black plumage of a chough, at a stretch, could work for the allegory about knights and scholars needing to work in the dark of night. A lack of familiarity with the correct terminology for wild birds is not hard to imagine since an Englishman who managed the royal cellars probably did not need to know the French names for birds unless they were destined for the dinner table.[77] The chough is native to the British Isles, not the continent, making the use of *chough* instead of *chouette* interesting from the standpoint of regional knowledge. But an attentive reader would also take note that choughs are notoriously noisy, consistent with the stereotype of overly talkative, shrewish women. In I.39, he also turns "yraigne" [spider] into "flee" [flea] in the description of Minerva's transformation of Arachne. Being cursed from human to spider would be a misfortune worthy of retelling as a warning about pride, but turning into a flea is an even worse metamorphosis for the worse since the persistent, biting pest offers few redeeming qualities and inspires less fascination than spiders with their clever, useful, and artistic webs. Were the changes of the creature names owing to faulty vocabulary, ignorance of the myth, or an intentional change? Instances such as these are interesting enough to merit a second or third consideration. The replacement of *chough* for *chouette* could be a mechanical mistake (group 3), an editorial substitution of a native bird (group 2), or an intentional departure from Christine's view of women (group 1).

A key concern in studies about translations of female writing is the potential for manipulation by the men who stand as gatekeepers between author and

---

[76] For example, David Fowler notes that "[John] Trevisa is famous for his tendency to use two English words for one Latin word"; see *The Life of Times of John Trevisa, Medieval Scholar* (Seattle and London: University of Washington Press, 1995), 140. See also J. Beal, *John Trevisa and the English Polychronicon*, MRTS 437 (Tempe: ACMRS, 2012).

[77] His occupational knowledge of French might also explain why his descriptions of swordplay and naval maneuvers feel awkward at times.

reader.[78] Researchers are finding evidence that gender issues associated with medieval texts are more complicated than once thought; though John Lydgate is not a great champion of women in his writing, he was sponsored by female patrons and shows an awareness of the women reading his work, as Julia Boffey has shown.[79] She draws attention to annotations in a copy of extracts of Lydgate's *Fall of Princes*, Harley 2251, made by John Shirley, who did not share the author's misogynistic outlook:

> "Holdith your pees"; "Ye have no cause to say so"; "Ye had better be pees for ye have no thank"; "be pees or I will rende this leef out of your booke." To read the manuscript is effectively to recreate an ambiance conducive to the parrying of pro- and anti-feminist remarks.[80]

Helen Swift argues, similarly, that critics who are tempted to make assumptions about the perspectives of literary writers based on their sex run the risk of over-simplifying a complex range of viewpoints.[81] So, too, with Anslay it becomes necessary to take an assessing look at the details, without losing sight of the larger context. Associating Minerva with a clamoring bird and a biting pest is hardly flattering. He narrows the assertion by Reason that women possess sufficient intelligence to rule, omitting her comment "et moult grant de telles y a" ["there are many such women," EJR, 31]. He uses the double entendre of good/goods in a chapter claiming that men admire virtue in a woman and pursue them romantically for "le grant bien d'elles," turning it into a suggestion that men pursue widows for their "grete welthe" (II.64). His habit of choosing masculine pronouns would be worth studying more comprehensively, and details within the chapters attest to an awareness of male readers first signaled in the book's prologue. Yet he writes to provide an alternative viewpoint from the standard

---

[78] Diane Bornstein, "Anti-Feminism in Thomas Hoccleve's Translation of Christine de Pizan's *Epistre au Dieu d'Amours*," *English Language Notes* 19 (1981): 7–14; Jane Chance, "Gender Subversion and Linguistic Castration in Fifteenth-Century Translations of Christine de Pizan," in *Violence Against Women in Medieval Texts*, ed. Anna Roberts (Gainesville, FL: University Press of Florida, 1998), 161–94; Anne E. B. Coldiron, *English Printing, Verse Translation, and the Battle of the Sexes* (Farnham and Burlington, VT: Ashgate, 2009), 21–68; Dhira Mahoney, "Middle English Regenderings of Christine de Pizan," in *The Medieval Opus*, ed. Douglas A. Kelly (Amsterdam: Rodopi, 1996), 405–27; Summit, *Lost Property*, 61–71.

[79] Julia Boffey, "Lydgate's Lyrics and Women Readers," in *Women, the Book and the Worldly*, ed. Lesley Smith and Jane H. M. Taylor (Cambridge: D. S. Brewer, 1995), 139–49.

[80] Boffey, "Lydgate's Lyrics," 141.

[81] Helen J. Swift, *Gender, Writing, and Performance: Men Defending Women in Late Medieval France, 1440–1538* (Oxford: Clarendon Press, 2008), 184. Helen Solterer shares a similar opinion in *The Master and Minerva: Disputing Women in French Medieval Culture* (Berkeley and Los Angeles: University of California Press, 1995), 135.

misogynist fare. The easiest way to suppress Christine's voice would be to leave her arguments untranslated and unprinted, relegating the case for women all the more swiftly to obscurity.

Anslay asserts his own identity early in the book when Reason promises that she and her sisters will refresh the author with water from a pure wellspring; the yeoman of the cellar tweaks this to read "thou shalt receive of us thre **wyne** and water" (I.4). Another moment of self-assertion when Ryghtwysnesse refutes the misogamous claim that it is better to hire a male servant than marry a wife, saying that no servant could equal the devotion of a woman who loves her husband: "Je croy que on ne trouveroit point de tel serviteur" (II.13). Anslay writes that "one shal not fynde but fewe suche servauntes," intimating that some men, such as himself, are indeed devoted in their sworn service to men or to women. He also changes Christine's chastisement of knights for failing to uphold the good name of women by rephrasing the accusation into a rallying appeal: "Yet what shall these nobles and knyghtes say to this thynge, so moche agaynst ryght, that saythe evyll generally of all women?" (I.38). He extends Christine's argument that women can be discreet into a moral lesson applicable to men as well, adding "for dyscrecyon and secretenesse are to be commended in ony person" (II.25). One act of discretion, perhaps, is Anslay's decision to omit Christine's barbed criticism of contemporary clergy members (I.10). A study of what Anslay changes therefore requires studying what is not there. Purchasers of the printed book would also find Anslay's voice brought to the fore through a mistaken reading of the manuscript, where the frame narrative indicates a shift between narrators: "*Christine*. Et je dis à elle: 'Ha, dame! [. . .]'" (I.38). Punctuation and capitalization in *STC* 7271 produce a different effect: "Christine and I sayd to her. Ha madame [. . .]" (sig. Nn1v). Elsewhere, a reference to Christine becomes "my lady Christine" (II.53). Such instances cast a shadow of male presence and a patrilineal worldview, but it does not displace female authority entirely.

Addresses to Christine's French audience remain intact for the most part in Anslay's translation for English readers. The importance of the wool trade would give readers cause to take an interest in Minerva's instruction of humanity in the skills of shearing, carding, spinning, and weaving wool, which Anslay details in full.[82] The production of linen, another cloth trade, was less common in England than on the continent. Christine describes how Arianne developed the techniques required, step by step: "cultiver, ordener, roir, teiller, cerancer et filer à la conoille, et faire toilles," but Anslay only writes the "maner of werkes to make

---

[82] Discovery of olive oil, also attributed to her, was far more central to Mediterranean culture; her gift of it was the deciding factor in how she came to be the patron of Athens. Curiously, Christine leaves out her competition with other gods for the honor, though it can be found in Boccaccio's *De mulieribus claris*. See H. David Brumble, *Classical Myths and Legends in the Middle Ages and Renaissance* (Westport, CT: Greenwood Press, 1998), 218–22.

lynnen clothe" (I.39). His rubric erroneously reports that Arachne developed "the crafte to shere sheepe, to dresse the wolles, and to make clothe," despite describing a few chapters earlier how Minerva developed these skills. He distinguishes between French and English when glossing *ita*, writing, "that is to say in Frensshe *ouy*, and in Englysshe *ye*" (I.33). Similarly, he changes the translation of a Greek phrase, given by Christine in French, while Anslay writes, "which was to say in Englysshe" (II.2). She does not denigrate the English in this work, as she does in certain others, obviating the question of whether they remain intact in the *Cyte of Ladyes*. He does, however, change Christine's boast that the best artisans work in Paris, making Anastasia's achievement all the greater; he writes instead that she was as adept as "ony werkeman in the towne of Parys," without privileging Parisian artists over the rest of the world (I.41).

Anslay acts in an editorial capacity in several places. Christine's persona expresses her eagnerness to read the *Liber Lamentationum Matheoli* because she has heard that it praises women, which Christine Reno argues is intentional irony.[83] The English translation reports that Matheolus does *not* speak reverently toward women; the narrator seems to be laughing in delight at the prospect of setting him straight, which might be true behind the scenes, but it is not how Christine sets the stage for her narrator's disillusionment and restoration to clear reason. As noted before, he corrects a reference to Cato Uticensis (I.10). He specifies that there were nine muses, not numbered in Christine's original (I.30), and he adds the name Genesis when she says that Sarah's story can be found in the first book of the Bible (II.38). His translations sometimes forge interconnections between different parts of the text that are not explicitly stated in the original. In the first chapter, Christine describes how her persona recalls the many negative comments by men against women "si comme personne en letargie" ["as if I were in a stupor," EJR, 4]. Anslay writes, "as a persone halfe from hymselfe," which notably uses a male pronoun, and also eludes the chastisement of Reason that Christine must be out of her mind to think that the misogynists are right about women (I.2). The original text claims that Cornificia went to school because "ses parens" [parents, or relatives] thought it would be a good joke; Anslay reports, instead, that "her fader" made the decision, putting the blame at his feet instead of asserting that the mother thought it would be laughable to send a girl to school, while also alluding to the chapter in Part II discussing how some fathers are enlightened enough to encourage their daughters in academic pursuits. He says that Orithyia agreed to a "small peas" with the Greeks (I.18), rather than the perpetual alliance Christine says that they forged, since it apparently would be broken a generation later when Orithyia's daughter, Penthesilea, battles mightily with the Greeks on the side of the Trojans (I.19). He also quietly removes

---

[83] Christine Reno, "Christine de Pizan: Feminism and Irony," in *Seconda miscellanea di studi e ricerche sul Quattrocento francese*, ed. Jonathan Beck and Gianni Mombello (Chambéry: Centre d'Etudes Franco-Italiens, 1981), 125–33.

Rectitude's promise at the outset of Part II that they shall finish soon; with more than half of the book to go, they would have quite a lot of work ahead of them, as the translator would know quite well as a fellow laborer in the endeavor.

Some of the changes made by Anslay undermine Christine's unconventional but deliberate narrative decisions. As already noted, Thamaris exacts vengeance upon Cyrus for a beloved son, "un sien filz" [a son of hers], as a reigning Amazon queen, but Anslay reports instead that the leader of an all-female society seeks retribution "for one of her maydens" harmed in the past by the tyrant (I.17). The departure from Christine's account means that the English version fails to make the key point that Amazons loved their sons as well as their daughters. Another example of an unexpected twist lost in the translation occurs in the story of Florence (II.51). When her husband the emperor rides off to war, his brother makes unwanted sexual advances toward Florence; Christine states that she put an end to it by imprisoning her brother-in-law, but freeing him as soon as news arrives of her husband's return. The villain turns the emperor against his wife with his lies, and she flees from a death sentence, a pattern repeated when another would-be lover frames her for the murder of a child. Anslay dutifully recounts the travails of Florence, but he envisions the hapless empress in the initial scene as the one locked away unjustly during her husband's absence, rather than the other way around. This mars the symmetry in Christine's narrative arc, which consistently associates confinement with sin and virtue with freedom. When Florence receives her miraculous vision of the Virgin, and knowledge of a healing salve, she is sleeping in the open; the villains, by contrast, find themselves confined to bed, imprisoned by bodies struck down with disease in divine retribution for their lust. Her just imprisonment of the brother-in-law, and his merciful release from prison, foreshadows the fact that only Florence can free them physically and spiritually through the process of confession, repentance, absolution, and holy anointment. Readers of Anslay's translation still find this lesson in the story's conclusion, but they miss the parallel between the secular beginning, when the empress acts as regent, and sacred ending, when she acts in the name of the Virgin and the Son.

A common kind of sort of discrepancy between the French and English versions of the text can be put down to what Curnow describes as mechanical mistakes.[84] Minims cause bedevilment on occasion, such as when Anslay reads *vuit* as *vint*. He seems to misread the "m" in the name of the Cumaean sibyl as "ni," resulting in a reference to "Cunyana" at the beginning of Part II. He occasionally runs into trouble with lobe closure of o/e, mistaking *louer* for *lever*; c/t graph confusion might explain other interpretations, for instance when *craire* replaces *taire*. The resulting words, despite similarities in French, differ markedly in English:

---

[84] Curnow, *"The Boke of the Cyte of Ladyes,* an English Translation," 125.

| *Cité* | *Cyte* | Chap. |
|---|---|---|
| empty (*vuit*) | come (*vint*) | I.3 |
| praise (*louer*) | lift (*lever*) | I.9 |
| keep quiet (*taire*) | believe (*craire*) | I.10 |

The ripple of disruption can also be felt in u/n misreadings, though it is difficult without seeing Pepwell's manuscript copy to know whether the confusion originated with Anslay, or if a compositor reversed letters when he did not recognize the names of legendary characters: *Theseus* to *Thesens*, and *Mausole* to *Mansole*. Other instances are sufficiently ambiguous to make one wonder if Anslay capitalized on the possibility for creative misreadings. "Errer" and "hier" sound enough alike for one to assume their confusion was a mistake, but the replacement of "errer" with "hier" changes the reading in interesting ways. Christine, in the original version, declares that she cannot err with the virtues by her side, while Anslay writes that they will help the narrator accomplish what she could not "yestereven" (*hier*) on her own, stepping back from an assertion of infallibility (I.4). In another instance, Raison says that some wrongful opinions about women arise from the wretched character (*vilté*) of the men who slander them, but Anslay converts this more narrowly to men of "grete age" (*vieillesse*) who are bitter about their impotence. The substitution remains grounded in the author's material, alluding to a point already made, but here it mitigates the accusation of vicious motives writ large. Additional examples of such alterations receive mention in the annotations.[85] *The Cyte of Ladyes* remains very close to the original text, as Richards and Summit have both surmised, yet the changes, small perhaps, raise multiple interpretive possibilities for future scholars to consider.

## Bibliographical Discussion

### 1. Editorial history of the *City of Ladies*

*The City of Ladies* captured popular interest when Richards published a modern English translation with Persea in 1982 (rev. ed., 1998). Penguin issued a new English translation by Brown-Grant in 1999 that has also been marketed as part of their Great Ideas series since 2005. Additional translations into Dutch, French, German, and Italian testify to the book's modern appeal. The Middle French text has been surprisingly difficult to obtain. Monika Lange (University of Hamburg, 1974) and Maureen Cheney Curnow (Vanderbilt University, 1975) both edited the *Cité des dames* for their Ph.D. dissertations, but regretta-

---

[85] Annotations do not reflect orthographical variations, and instances where words and phrases remain the same but in a different syntactic order. Scribal corrections are not noted; rather, the text silently presents the text as corrected by the manuscript proofreader.

bly, neither has been published. Curnow uses Ms. Paris, Bibliothèque Nationale de France fr. 607, the Duke's Manuscript (*D*), as her base text; Brown-Grant bases her translation upon Curnow's edition. Of the extant editions, Lange's is the most difficult to obtain. She uses London, Ms. British Library Harley 4431, the Queen's Manuscript (*R*). Richards also selects *R* as the base text for his Middle French edition, published in parallel with a modern Italian translation by Patrizia Caraffi (Milan: Luni, 1997; second ed., 1998). He offers selected variants from the following editions as being illustrative of the text's evolution: *D*; Ms. Paris, Bibliothèque Nationale de l'Arsenal 2686; Ms. Paris, Bibliothèque Nationale de France fr. 1178. An XML student edition of *R* is available online through the *Making of the Queen's Manuscript* site, with modern diacritical marks provided throughout, but no modern punctuation; it remains very much a transcription of the manuscript text. This is the source for variants from *R* provided in this edition.

Lange and Curnow both provide discussions of the textual history of the *Cité des dames*, but they arrive at different conclusions. Curnow approaches her discussion of the work's textual history by separating the manuscripts into four groups, ranked by their perceived authority: she chooses the Duke's Manuscript from Group I as her base text; *L* falls on the other end of the spectrum, in Group IV, which she characterizes as sharing "willful omissions" and deterioration from the five manuscripts of her Group I, dating from the author's lifetime.[86] In fact, Christine supervised seven of the *Cité* manuscripts including Ms. Paris, Arsenal 2686 and Ms. Bibl. nat. fr. 24293, which Curnow places in her "corruptted" Group IV. Lange interprets the variations as signs of authorial revision over time; from this view, the lacunae in *L* and Anslay's translation are not omissions but passages yet to be written.[87]

Five key changes lead Lange to extrapolate a chronological progression for the text's evolution. In the earliest redactions Arthemise first appears in I.25, but later her chapter shifts to I.21. Christine also divides II.53 in two (II.53 and II.54) and relocates the Juno chapter from its original placement after Claudine, as II.62, to follow the three *Decameron* tales instead as II.60. Later versions rephrase the title of II.64 and add a second Belisaire example in II.29, which is absent from all early redactions.[88] Furthermore, Lange observes that the table of contents falls out of step with the reorganized text; she theorizes that the table

---

[86] Curnow groups the manuscripts based on what she perceives as graduated levels of authority. Group I: Ms. Brussels, Bibliothèque Royale 9393, Ms. BL 4431, Mss. BnF fr. 607, 1178, 1179. Group IV divides into two subgroups: (a) BnF fr. 24293, Ms. London, BL Royal 19.A.xix, Ms. Paris, Arsenal 2686, Ms. Paris, BnF fr. 826; (b) Ms. Munich, BS Gall. 8, MS. Vienna, ON Vindob. 2605, Ms. Paris, Arsenal 3182; see "*Cité des dames*," 334–39, 520–78, 585–89. The rest of the manuscripts are in Groups II and III.

[87] Lange, "*Cité des dames*," xxxix, lx.

[88] Lange, "*Cité des dames*," lxv-lxvi.

continued to list the old order for a while and was only later updated to reflect the actual contents. So, for example, the Juno chapter follows the Claudine chapter in both the table and text of Arsenal 2686. In BnF fr. 24293, the table still lists the Juno as chapter II.62, but the text it shifts forward to II.60. This is true the text has shifted it forward to join the in both the table and text; this is also true for BnF fr. 1179 and KB 9393, but in the final redaction the table and text both list the Juno chapter after the three *Decameron* chapters. She charts this progression of table (Ta) and text (Te) order to show a progressive sequence:[89]

| LANGE SCHEMA | Arthemise | | | | II.53 | | II.53–54 | | Juno II.62 | | II.64 | | | |
|---|---|---|---|---|---|---|---|---|---|---|---|---|---|---|
| | I.25 | | I.21 | | | | | | | | version a | | version b | |
| | Ta | Te | Ta | Te | Ta | Te | Ta | Te | Ta | Te | Ta | Te | Ta | Te |
| Arsenal 2686 | x | x | | | x | x | | | x | x | x | x | | |
| BnF fr. 24293[88] | (omitted entirely) | | | | x | x | | | x | | x | x | | |
| BnF fr. 1179 | | | x | x | x | | | | x | x | x | x | | |
| KB 9393 | | | x | x | x | | | | x | x | x | | | x |
| BnF fr. 607 | | | x | x | x | | | | x | | x | | | x |
| BnF fr. 1178 | | | x | x | | | x | x | | | | | x | x |
| BL Harley 4431 | | | x | x | | | x | x | | | | | x | x |

As Richards has observed, Lange's work deserves far greater recognition than it has received to date; her detailed analysis of the manuscript witnesses demonstrates the high standard of her scholarship.[91]

Using the same metric, Lange proceeds to evaluate all other extant MSS to establish a redaction history for the *Cité des dames*. Richards concurs with her finding that *F* and *L* present a redaction that pre-dates Arsenal 2686, but the basis for this conclusion might require rethinking. Lange lists Juno as following Claudine in both the table and text of *L*, but the chapter within the text has in fact shifted forward to join the three *Decameron* stories, where it also appears in

---

[89] Lange's table reproduced from "*Cité des dames*," lxv.

[90] Lange, lxiii: "Die Hs Paris, Bibl. de l'Arsenal 2686 bietet das Arthemise-Kapitel als 25. des ersten Buches, sodass auf das 'exemple' der Witwe Veronice die Taten der Witwe Arthemise folgen. Die Hs Paris, Bibl. Nat. fr. 24293 lässt das Kapitel sowohl in der 'Table' wie im Text aus und die übrigen fünf Handschriften reihen es als das 21. des ersten Buches ein." [In Ms. Paris, Bibl de l'Arsenal MS 2686, Arthemise is the 25th chapter of the first book, so that the deeds of the widow Arthemise follow the 'exemple' of the widow Veronice. Ms. Paris, Bibl Nat. fr. 24293 omits the chapter both in the table and in the text, and the other five manuscripts organize it as the 21st one of the first book.]

[91] Earl Jeffrey Richards, "Editing the *Livre de la cité des dames*: New Insights, Problems and Challenges," in Hicks, *Au champ des escriptures*, 789–816.

the *Cyte of Ladyes*. Her argument for locating the *Cyte of Ladyes* between Ms. Arsenal 2686 and Ms. Bibl. nat. fr. 24293 hinges on the Juno chapter, and by the same logic it would seem that the text of *L* belongs to the same phase, making it somewhat later than Arsenal 2686.[92] Both Lange and Richards use Arsenal 2686 as a control text, since it is apparently the earliest of the manuscripts dating from Christine's lifetime.

## 2. Henry Pepwell and the *Cyte of Ladyes*

Bibliographers consider Henry Pepwell's entry into the printing business as part of a change from foreign to native practitioners in the London book trade.[93] He began printing as well as selling books by 1518, and the combined venture was a success judging from the report that he was worth £40 in the 1523–1524 lay subsidy rolls.[94] In 1526, Pepwell became a warden of the Stationers' Company and he seems to have set aside his modest printing business some years earlier.[95] Only sixteen printed works are attributed to him between 1518 and 1539, including several assumed to have been printed for him off-premises, perhaps overseas.[96] Peter Blayney remarks that Pepwell "seems to have found his real métier in importation and retail bookselling."[97]

Almost half of the slim printing output attributed to him is made up of grammar books. All were standard reading materials at St. Paul's School, meaning he had a reliable source of demand before he invested time or money in his printing venture. These were hard-used by young students and survive mostly in fragments. Pepwell's inventory also included a number of religious service books and devotional writings. Most of the texts Pepwell chose to print were proven best-sellers. *The Dyetary of Ghostly Helthe* (*STC* 6833), issued by De Worde in 1520, was popular enough to warrant a second edition by Pepwell (*STC* 6834) the following year. He printed it again ca. 1523 (*STC* 6835), the only text Pepwell is known to have printed twice.

The reference to Henry VIII in the *Cyte of Ladyes's* prologue is echoed by a visual reference to him in a decorative capital "H." It appears to show a youthful

---

[92] Lange, *"Cité des dames,"* lxvi–lxviii.

[93] C. Paul Christianson, "The Rise of London's Book-Trade," in *Cambridge History of the Book in Britain*, 3:128–47, at 145.

[94] E. Gordon Duff, "Notes on Stationers from the Lay Subsidy Rolls of 1523–4," *The Library*, 2nd ser., 9 (1908): 257–66, at 261.

[95] E. Gordon Duff, "The Booksellers at the Sign of the Trinity: Part II, 1518–1539," *Bibliographica* 1 (1895): 174–93, at 175.

[96] Alexandra Gillespie, "Pepwell, Henry (*d.* 1539/40)," *Oxford DNB* 43:637–38.

[97] Peter W. M. Blayney, *The Stationers' Company and the Printers of London, 1501–1557*, 2 vols. (Cambridge: Cambridge University Press, 2013), I:182; for further discussion of Pepwell's career, see 128–29, 213–14, 236, 273, 317 in same volume.

| Copy of Pynson "T" | Copy of Pynson "H" | Pepwell "T" |
|---|---|---|
| *.XII. Frutes of the Holy Ghoost* | *Boke of the Cyte of Ladyes* (Pep- | *Boke of the Cyte of Ladyes* (Pep- |
| (Copland, 1535), *STC* 13608 | well, 1521), Folger Shakespeare | well, 1521), Folger Shakespeare |
| Trinity College, Cambridge | Library STC 7271, sig. C5v | Library STC 7271, sig. C3v |
| C.7.12[2], sig. a2v | | |

By permission of the Master and Fellows of Trinity College, Cambridge and the Folger Shakespeare Library

Henry VIII, whose profile is not unlike the one found in De Worde's corona-tion woodcut (Hodnett 883), and a painted depiction of the king's procession to parliament in 1512.[98] The capital "H" seems to have been used first by Richard Pynson, royal printer, then copied by Pepwell and others in subsequent years. Pynson also used a distinctive capital "T" with a dimidiated rose and pomegran-ate. Pepwell, however, decided against using Pynson's "T" and chose to use a ver-sion that is more stylistically consistent with the "H," in effect creating a matched pair. They are used together like bookends on either side of Part 2, chap. 13, where Ryghtwysnesse begins to discuss "the grete love of women to theyr hus-bandes," naming them among the first citizens to enter the walled city (sig. C3v). Suitably, Pepwell uses the combined royal emblems at this juncture.

As the longest of Pepwell's works, the *Cyte of Ladyes* unsurprisingly suffered some errors during the imposition process; furthermore, each copy has expe-rienced its own wear and tear over the centuries. British Library C.13.1.18 is complete and bound in the correct order, with some marginalia; King's Col-lege, Cambridge M.29.9 is complete but with misplaced folios, seemingly due to irregularities in the printed signatures. The copy at Longleat House, while also complete, mixes quires from two different parts of the book. Folger Shake-speare Library *STC* 7271 wants the last leaf, which is supplied in facsimile, and Corpus Christi College Oxford Δ.3.7 lacks the entire first quire as well

---

[98] Christopher Lloyd and Simon Thurley, *Henry VIII: Images of a Tudor King* (Oxford: Phaidon Press, 1990), 19; Edward Hodnett, *English Woodcuts, 1480–1535* (Oxford: Oxford University Press, 1973). On Pepwell's type, see Joseph J. Gwara, "Three Forms of w and Four English Printers: Robert Copland, Henry Pepwell, Henry Wat-son, and Wynkyn de Worde," *Papers of the Bibliographical Society of America* 106 (2012): 141–230.

as sig. Mm3–Mm4 and the colophon leaf.[99] It would be impossible to read the Oxford, Cambridge, or Longleat copies sensibly, cover to cover, because their mispagination interrupts a continuous reading of the text. Christine gave careful thought to the organization of her *exempla*, but the discontinuity of certain narratives might not have concerned early readers if they saw the volume as a compilation of stories rather than as a single work to be read straight through. Someone interested in the story of Dido, for instance, might not have been particularly worried about accidents of foliation that may have befallen Fredegunde. Four of the five copies have been rebound, and the fifth, at King's, has been rebacked; it is therefore possible that errors were introduced at a later stage, but a close look at the signatures suggests that at least some of the confusion probably originated in Pepwell's shop.

Judging by his dated colophons, the *Cyte of Ladyes* was finished on 26 October, and less than a month later on 16 November he put the finishing touches to his compilation of devotional treatises, which constitutes his second longest book. Double letters are used in the *Cyte of Ladyes* for signatures through the end of Part I, continuing with single letters through Parts II and III. The woodcut of three women approaching a fourth seated at her desk recurs before each division of the book. The devotional compilation uses a woodcut image of the Arms of Christ, surrounded by words of pardon, three times as decoration between individual treatises; although its attribution to Pepwell is uncertain, the xylographic text is similar to the lettering found in his second Trinity device (Ronald B. McKerrow, *Printers' and Publishers' Devices in England and Scotland, 1485–1640* [London: Bibliographical Society, 1999], 52). The collection of short devotional works is correctly signed; "F.j." could be an exception, but alternatively it might have been intentional since it marks the beginning of a new treatise. Pepwell's printing endeavor was operating at an unprecedented level of activity late in 1521, as far as can be judged from his surviving materials; the *Cyte of Ladyes* becomes all the more impressive for its stylistic consistency and overall accuracy.

Most of the aberrations in the *Cyte of Ladyes* were corrected, although some were of such little consequence that it seems they were left as is. Omitting the running title from H.iij. does not affect the assembly of the book, nor does the

---

[99] Variations across the surviving copies have caused confusion, particularly the imperfect book at CCC Oxford. Dibdin classifies it with reservations under "de Worde" in his revised edition of *Typographical Antiquities* (London: Bulmer, 1810–1819), 2:378. Duff also accepts the premise that De Worde printed a separate edition ("Booksellers: Part II," 182), citing Hazlitt. Unfortunately, Duff's reference is somewhat obscure; Hazlitt's *Hand-Book*, collections, notes and supplements appear to contain only one entry for the *Cyte of Ladyes*, and that is attributed to Pepwell. The known relationship between de Worde and Pepwell on other projects might have led to conjecture that Pepwell was copying de Worde, again. On Pepwell and de Worde, see Blayney, *Stationers' Company*, I:73, 124.

lack of a signature on S.iij. pose any trouble in a quire of four leaves; Pepwell's standard practice of signing the third folio in his 4s was a stylistic convention, and since folios two and three were conjoined there was little danger of S.iij. going astray. Other mistakes were apparently caught in the process of proof-reading: he compensated for mistakes on the third folios of Hh and R by adding a fourth signature with the correct letter to signal the proper placement of the conjoined leaves. Two other mistakes were caught and changed: the Folger and Longleat copies sign G.j. as "G.ij.," but it was changed to read correctly in the other three copies; likewise, only the Longleat copy preserves Mm.iij. signed incorrectly. This might mean that the Longleat copy, which has the earliest known provenance, is also most likely one of the earlier copies from the print run. Only two quiring mistakes appear to have escaped notice: the incorrect signature of Ff.iij. as "Ee.iij.," and the omission of a signature on E.iij. in the second part of the book. That "Ee.iij." appeared twice and "E.iij." was omitted seems interesting as far as the practice of setting signatures is concerned.

## Signature Irregularities

Ff   Ff.iij. signed "Ee.iij."
Gg   "Gg.j" signed "Gg.ij." in Folger copy only
Hh   Hh.iij. signed "Ii.iij."; conjugate page signed "H.iiij."
Mm   Mm.iij. is signed "Oo.ij." in Longleat copy only
E    E.iij. unsigned
H    Running title is omitted from H.iij.
R    R.iij. signed "R.iij."; conjugate page signed "R.iiij." without running title
S    S.iij. unsigned

The signatures of Ff.iij. and Hh.iij., however, proved troubling for the binder of the King's College copy. His mantra must have been to keep like with like: he placed the missigned "Ii.iij." in quire Ii and *both* of the folios signed "Ee.iiij." in quire Ee, although unfortunately in the wrong order: the actual Ff.iij. precedes the true Ee.iij. The "skilful Bibliographer" who changed the penciled value on the fly leaf has tried to untangle the resulting confusion with corresponding marks in pencil to guide the reader through the text. A different conundrum appears in the Corpus Christi College copy, in which Mm.iij. is lacking. Whoever was originally responsible for assembling the book may have remembered that Mm.iij. was missigned "Oo.ij."; in any case, "Oo.iij." is supplied twice: once in lieu of Mm.iij. and again in its proper place in quire Oo. In the Longleat copy, one finds a different problem again, and the transfer of four quires from Part II (D-G) between Mm and Nn in Part I defies an easy, logical explanation. The absence of a signature seems to have been less troublesome than the presence of ones that were incorrect. "E.iij." is omitted from a quire of six, without further

signatures in the quire; nevertheless, quire E is assembled correctly in all five surviving copies of the *Cyte of Ladyes*.

## 3. Codicological Notes

### The Boke of the Cyte of Ladyes
English; printed in London, 26 October 1521
Paper, quarto, 190 folios

**Begins**: ¶Here begynneth the boke of the Cyte of Ladyes / the whiche boke is deuyded in to .iij. partes.

**Ends**: ¶Here endeth the thyrde and the last partye of the boke of the Cyte of Ladyes. ¶Imprynted at London in Poules chyrchyarde at the sygne of the Trynyte by Henry Pepwell. In þe yere of our lorde. M.CCCCC.xxj. The .xxvj. day of October. And the .xij. yere of the reygne of our souerayne lorde kynge Henry the .viij.

**Collation**:
38 quires as follows:

Part 1:
Aa$^4$, Bb$^6$, Cc$^4$, Dd$^6$, Ee$^4$, *Ff$^6$, *Gg$^4$, *Hh$^6$, Ii$^4$, Kk$^6$, Ll$^4$, Mm$^6$, Nn$^4$, Oo$^6$, Pp$^6$

Parts 2 & 3:
A$^6$, B$^4$ C$^6$, D$^4$, *E$^6$, F$^4$, G$^6$, *H$^4$, I$^6$, K$^4$, L$^6$, M$^4$, N$^6$, O$^4$, P$^6$, Q$^4$, *R$^6$, | *S$^4$, T$^6$, U$^4$, X$^6$, Y$^4$, Z$^4$

* Quires with irregular signatures discussed above.

**Presentation of Text**:
In three parts, each prefaced with a separate table of contents; abbreviated running title "Cyte of La." at the bottom of signed pages; 30 lines of single-column black-letter type to the page, with standard abbreviation and punctuation.

### Decoration:

Woodcuts

*Above:* (l) title page, recto: factotum of two women, city; (r) colophon page, recto: factotum of two women, all with blank banderoles. *Below:* (l) Hodnett 2281: Justyce with tankard measure, Ryghtwysnesse with ruler, Lady Reason with mirror below diamond-paned windows, on tiled floor, approaching author in widow's garb, at lectern with books; (r) McKerrow 48: Pepwell's second Trinity device with barbed Tudor roses.

**<u>Binding</u>:**
BL, CCC Oxford, Folger, and Longleat have modern binding; King's copy bound in plain white leather, with offset ink on back cover; rebacked by Gray, April 1939.

**<u>Marginalia</u>**

*British Library:* Writing on upper right corner of title page, perhaps numbers, with evidence of cropping; same page, bottom right corner, cropped signature, seems to be Gough's. Table of contents, character names are copied in margins by a cursive hand. Printer's prologue, "Unto my lorde / the gentyll Erle of Kente" underscored. Manicule points to "leest re=|wardes of his lorde" (sig. Bb 3r). Above rubric of chapter iii, "Xine" written out "cristine" in a modern hand (sig. Bb 5r). Manicule points to capital "W," chapter v (sig. Cc 2v). "Reason; Ryghteusnes; Justice" one above other in right margin next to rubric of chapter vi (sig. Cc 3r). Manicule at "But falsely they measure" (sig. Cc 3 v). "Not" in margin at "I am not Saynt Thomas"; manicule at "Nor my feble wytte can not" (sig. Cc 4v). Sketched greyhound appears in the space between chapters vii and viii (sig. Dd 1r). Manicule at "and cursed as it showeth" (sig. Dd 2v); another at "Matheo=|lus" (sig. Dd 3r). Sketched lion or royal leopard between the title and main text of chapter x (sig. Ee 1r). Table of contents, Part II, "agaynst them þᵗ say þᵗ it is not good þᵗ women lerne letters" and "þᵗ wyfe of Barnabo the Geneuoys" both underscored (sig. Pp 5v). Manicule points to "Sybelle" (sig. A 1v). Manicule at "here xpine speketh to ryghtwysnes," caret after name: "the auctors name wᶜʰ was a woman" (sig. B 2v). Manicule at "so grete loue to her fader" (sig. B 4r). Rubric underscored: "Of the worshypfull quene hester" (sig. G 3v). Above printer's device "this is S.B. his booke | lent to my <unclear>."

*King's College, Cambridge*: Title page, shelfmark in black ink upper right corner; "S" penned beneath woodcut (sig. Aa 1r); old shelfmark in black ink upper, right corner (sig. Aa 2r). "X" at "made the sygne of the crosse"; "credence" in margin, underscored, keyed to word "faythe" in text, also underscored (sig. Bb 3v). Cancellation of second "euer" at "For who was euer that housband þᵗ ~~euer~~" and "H" in margin, two lines later, at "haue leue to saye so many vylanyes"; "X" in margin, four lines from the bottom: "Nowe come agayne to thyselfe" (sig. Bb 4v). Star in margin next to "sygnyfyenge" (sig. Bb5v). Modern hand has pencilled "pick axe?" at "py|coys" (sig. Dd 1r). Inserted note about mispagination corresponds with symbols penciled into book by same hand.

*Corpus Christi College, Oxford:* Top of first extant page reads "The booke of the Citie of Ladies" with "Liber C.C.C. Ox | ex testament | M. Br. Twine" in outside margin, underscoring in text: "opened this boke and I saw by þᵉ intytula=|cyon that it called hym Matheolus" (sig. Bb 1r); another mark of ownership, "Briannvs Twine" (sig. Bb 6v). Underscoring "dawnynge of the daye" (sig. Ii 4r). Pen trials

(sig. Oo 1v); doodles (sig. Oo 4r). In margin of woodcut beginning of Part II, "Brianus twine posidet hunc librum" (sig. Pp4v). Sig. E 6v marginalia impaired by cropping, inscription "Brian Twyne his boke" legible. Facing page in upper right corner, cropped, reads "By me | Brian | Twy"; more doodling, writing at bottom of sig. F 1r. Sig. F 4v pen trials; in same unconfident hand, bottom margin of G 1r, "DEe of ABC" bottom margin. More pen trials, sig. T 1v, T 5v.

*Folger Shakespeare Library*: Foliation of unsigned pages in pencil, modern hand; on sig. U3r pen trial, upper right corner.

*Longleat*: Title page, "William Brereton" in black ink, light brown ticking within diamond floor pattern.

## Provenance

William Brereton (*ca.*1487x90–1536), as previously noted, owned a copy of the book before it went to Sir John Thynne (1512/13–1580), builder of Longleat, where the book has remained ever since. Brian Twyne (1581–1644), a fellow of Corpus Christi College, Oxford, bequeathed 350 volumes containing 750 works to the college, including its copy of the *Cyte of Ladyes*. Another copy was bequeathed to King's College, Cambridge by Jacob Bryant (1715–1804), a fellow and private tutor of the Marlboroughs.[100] C. H. Hartshorne's survey of rare books in Cambridge includes a chapter on King's College Library, reprinting the opening stanza of the printer's prologue and citing the following comment made by an unnamed "skilful Bibliographer":

*Cyte of Ladyes. Pepwell, 1521.* 4to. Some insane person had written on the fly leaf, with a pencil, "Worth 100*l.* !" I took the liberty to write with a pencil, "pro 100 *l.*, lege 2*l.*, 12*s.* 6*d*"'[101]

W. C. Hazlitt records that antiquarian James West (1703–1772) paid £1 17*s.* for his copy in 1773, which in turn passed to Richard Gough (1735–1809), George Steevens, King George III, and the British Library; James Bindley (1739–1818) reportedly paid £3 19*s.* for an imperfect copy, probably the one acquired in turn by Frederick Startridge Ellis (1830–1901), Henry Huth (1815–1878), Sir Leicester Harmsworth (1870–1937), and finally the Folgers.[102] Modern scholars have "rediscovered" Christine de Pizan and rejoined the *querelle des femmes*

---

[100] Seymour de Ricci, *English Collectors of Books and Manuscripts, 1530–1930* (Cambridge: Cambridge University Press, 1930), 69.

[101] C. H. Hartshorne, *Book Rarities in Cambridge* (London: Longman, 1829), 205–6, 214; note subsequently erased from book.

[102] W. C. Hazlitt, *Hand-Book to the Popular, Poetical, and Dramatic Literature of Great Britain* (London: J. R. Smith, 1867), 104; Furnivall, *Captain Cox*, xliii; Folger Shakespeare Library catalog.

through feminist criticism, but for book historians at least the *Cyte of Ladyes* was never entirely forgotten.

## Editorial Principles

The goal of the present book is to make the *Cyte of Ladyes* accessible to readers with an academic interest in the work. Capitalization in both the English and French texts is regularized according to modern conventions; punctuation and paragraph breaks are provided in an effort to improve the text's readability. Abbreviations have been expanded silently in both texts, and letters that were used interchangeably have been replaced with their expected modern forms: *i/j*, *v/u*, *vv/w*. Roman numerals are retained, through consistent with the previous rule, *i* replaces *j*. The reader will encounter double letters where a single letter is used today (*soo, goo, doo*) and single letters where doubling is now the norm (*thre, fle, se; al, wel, wyl*). Silent regularization occurs when spelling differentiates between the meaning of two words in modern usage (*the/thee, to/too, of/off*). Letters and words supplied by the editor appear in square brackets. Proper nouns are spelled here as they are in the *Cyte of Ladyes*. Instances of c/t and n/u confusion result in mutations of certain names (Mansole for Mausole; Cancre for Tancre), showing a lack of familiarity it would seem with the original stories, but in fact one finds "Mansole" in other manuscript copies of the *Cité des dames* and *Des Cleres et nobles dames* as well. Where the English text seems to be faulty, the words in question have been assessed in their immediate context and checked in the *OED* for arrested variants and early modern usage. A glossary provides a brief list of English words that are now obscure.

The Middle French text remains as close to *L* as possible to facilitate the comparison of Anslay's translation with the original readings in the royal manuscript available to him. Indeed, the edition preserves some fairly straightforward scribal errors that he follows faithfully. For example, on fol. 98r b the text should read "**dons** esperituelx" [spiritual gifts]; the *L* scribe writes "**dont** esperituelx," which Anslay translates as "of whens they be spyrytuall" (sig. G1v). The edition does not systematically document erasures and corrections in the manuscript; rubric headings missing within the text are supplied by the table, and vice versa. Unless otherwise noted, variants come from the XML student edition of *R* available from the *Making of the Queen's Manuscript* project, version 27 January 2010. The most extensively revised passages can be found among the textual annotations.

Lange's analysis identifies *F* as the closest extant version to *L*, but the manuscript is problematic as a witness because it appears that the scribe was working from an incomplete exemplar. Part I wants the end of chap. 11, chap. 12, and the first portion of chap. 13, and Part III is missing the last eleven chapters of the book. A preliminary comparison with *L* turns up numerous places where phrases may or may not have been omitted from *F*, but it is difficult to reconstruct with certainty: (i) which of the variants and lacunae are an accurate representation of

an early redaction; (ii) which are copied faithfully from a flawed exemplar; (iii) which were introduced by the *F* scribe, whose work does not appear to be subject to correction by a supervisory hand; (iv) which departures between *L* and *F* can be attributed to errors by the *L* scribe. References to *F* are therefore made sparingly.

The scribal hand of *L* is of a professional standard, but it does not distinguish clearly between c/t n/u, especially when joined by ligature, a practice that occurs frequently enough in other Middle French manuscripts to merit note on a regular basis among modern editorial principles.[103] The ambivalent scribal practice is usually resolved here with *ct* (e.g., *faicte* rather than *faitte*), which seems to be the more common form found among headwords in Huguet's *Dictionnaire de la langue française*, and in Vérard's 1497 edition of the *Trésor* (e.g., *Droicture* rather than *Droitture*). The scribe tends to use the singular forms of *le quel*, *du quel*, etc. but combine their plural forms: *lesquelz, desquelz*, etc. For consistency, they are combined in both cases. *Tousjours* appears as one word in the manuscript, and here; the scribe's practice of separating *pour quoy* is also maintained. Word division otherwise proceeds from consultation of critical editions of Christine's Middle French texts. The facing-page format should help facilitate comparative study. As Fredson Bowers points out, a scholarly edition should be "constructed for easy and agreeable reading," and the text at hand strives toward such a goal.[104]

[103] Richards, "Editing the *Livre de la cité des dames*," 796–98.

[104] Fredson Bowers, "Notes on Theory and Practice in Editing Texts," in *The Book Encompassed: Studies in Twentieth-Century Bibliography*, ed. Peter Davidson (Winchester: St. Paul's Bibliographies and Newcastle, DE: Oak Knoll Press, 1998), 244–57.

## Hereafter Foloweth the Prologue of the Prynter

The kyndly entente of every gentylman
Is the furtheraunce of all gentylnesse,
And to procure in all that ever he can
For to renewe all noble worthynesse.
5    This dayly is sene at our eye expresse
Of noble men that do endyte and rede
In bokes olde, theyr worthy myndes to fede.

So nowe of late came in my custodye
10    This foresayd boke by Bryan Anslay,
Yoman of the seller with the eyght Kynge Henry,
Of gentylwomen the excellence to say;
The whiche I lyked, but yet I made delay
It to impresse, for that it is the guyse
15    Of people lewde theyr prowesse to dyspyse.

But then I shewed the foresayd boke
Unto my lorde the gentyll Erle of Kente
And hym requyred theron to loke,
With his counsayle to put it into prente;
20    And he forthwith, as ever dylygente
Of ladyes abrode to sprede theyr royall fame,
Exhorted me to prynte it in his name.

And I, obeyenge gladly his instaunce,
Have done my devoyre of it to make an ende;
25    Prayenge his lordshyp, with others that shall chaunce
On it to rede, the fautes for to amende
If ony be, for I do fayne intende
Gladly to please, and wylfully remytte
This ordre rude to them that have fresshe wytte.

*Thus endeth the prologue*

# Le Livre de la cité des dames

Ms. London, British Library Royal 19.A.xix, fol. 4r

### Cy commence la table des rubriches du livre de la cité des dames,

*lequel dit livre est parti en troys parties:*

## Here Begynneth the Boke of the Cyte of Ladyes,

*The whiche boke is devyded into .iii. partes:*

❖ The fyrst parte telleth howe, and by whom, the walle and the cloystre aboute the cyte was made;

❖ The seconde parte telleth howe, and by whom, the cyte was buylded within and peopled;

❖ The thyrde parte telleth howe, and by whom, the hyghe battylmentes of the towres were parfytely made, and what noble ladyes were ordeyned to dwell in the hyghe palayces and hyghe dongeons.

And the fyrst chapytre telleth howe, and by whom, and by what movynge the sayd cyte was made.

Title page of the *Cyte of Ladyes*
Folger Shakespeare Library STC 7271, sig. Aa1r
By permission of the Folger Shakespeare Library

*Chapitre 1*      Ci commence *Le Livre de la cité des dames*, duquel le
premier chapitre parle pour quoy et par quel mouvement
le dit livre fu fait [fol. 3r a]

Selon la maniere que j'ay plus en usaige et a quoy est disposé l'excercice de ma
vie, c'est asavoir en la frequentacion d'estude de lettres, un jour comme je fusse
seant en ma celle avironnee de pluseurs volumes de diverses matieres, mon entendement a celle heure aucques travallié de recueillir la pesanteur des sentences
de divers aucteurs par moy longue piece estudiez, dreçay mon visage ensus du
livre, deliberant pour celle fois laissier en paix c[h]oses[1] subtilles et m'esbatre
a[2] regarder aucune joyeuseté des ditz des pouetes. Et comme adonc [fol. 4r b] en
celle entente je cherchasse entour moy d'aucun petit livret, entre main[s] me
vint d'aventure un livre estrange, non mie de mes volumes, mais qui avec autres
livres m'avoient[3] esté bailliez si comme en garde. Adonc, ouvert cellui: je vi en
l'intitulacion qu'il se clamoit *Matheolus*. Lors, en soubz riant pour ce que oncques
ne l'avoie veu, et maintes foys ouy dire avoye qu'entre les aultres livres cellui parloit bien[4] a la reverence des femmes, me pensay qu'en maniere de soulas le vise-
teroye. Mais regardé ne l'os moult long espace quant je fus appellee de la bonne
mere qui me porta pour prendre la reffection du soupper dont l'eure estoit venue;
donc,[5] proposant le veoir l'endemaine, le laissay a celle heure.

　　Le matin ensuivant rassise [fol. 4v a] en mon estude, si que j'ay de coustume,
n'oubliay pas mettre a effect le vouloir qui m'estoit venu de visiter ycellui *Livre
de Mettheole*. Adonc pris a lire et proceder un pou avant, mais comme la matiere
ne me semblast pas[6] moult plaisant a gens qui ne se delittent en mesdit, ne aussi
de nul prouffit a aucun edefice de vertu et de meurs, veu encore les paroles et
matieres deshonnestes de quoy il touche, visetant un pou ça et la et veue la fin,
le laissay pour entendre a plus hault estude et de plus grant utilité. Mais la veue
d'icellui dit livre, tout soit il de nulle auctorité, ot engendré en moy nouvelle
pensee qui fist naistre en mon courage grant admiracion, pensant quelle peut
estre la cause ne dont [fol. 4v b] ce peut venir que tant de divers hommes, cler[c]s et
aultres, ont esté et sont si enclins a dire de bouche, et en leurs tractiez et escrips,
tant de deableries et de vituperes de femmes et de leurs condicions—et non mie
seulement un ou deux, ne cestui *Matheolus*, qui entre les livres n'a aucune reputacion et qui traicte en maniere de trufferie—mais generaulment aucques en tous
traictiez, philosophes, pouetes, tous orateurs, qui longue chose seroit nommer

---

[1] c[h]oses : *closes* main[s] : *main* cler[c]s : *clers*
[2] a] et
[3] mais qui] qui
[4] parloit bien] parloit
[5] venue donc] ja venue par quoy
[6] proceder . . . semblant pas] proceday . . . semblast

*Chapter 1*     Here begynneth the fyrste chapytre whiche telleth howe, and by whome, the Cyte of Ladyes was fyrst begon to buylde
[Bb1r]

After the maner that I have moche in usage, and to that thynge whiche the excercyse of my lyfe is moost dysposed, that is to knowe in the hauntynge of studye, on a day as I was syttynge in my lytell cell, dyvers bokes of dyvers matters aboute me, myne entente was at that tyme to travayle and to gather into my consayte the wayenge of dyvers sentences of dyvers auctours by m[e]¹ longe tyme before studyed. I dressed my vysage towarde those foresayd bokes, thynkynge as for that tyme to leve in peas subtyll thynges and to dysporte me for to loke upon some pleasaunt boke of the wrytynge of some poetes. And as I was in this entente, I serched aboute me after some praty boke, and of adventure came a straunge boke into my handes that was taken to me to kepe: I opened this boke, and I sawe by the intytulacyon that it called hym *Matheolus*. Then in laughynge bycause I had not sene hym, and often tymes I had herde speke of hym that he sholde not speke well of the reverence of women, I thought that in maner of solace I wolde vysyte hym. And yet I had not loked longe on hym but that my good moder that bare me called me to the refeccyon of [Bb1v] souper wherof the houre was come. Purposynge to se hym in the mornynge, I lefte hym at that tyme.

And in the morowe folowynge, I sate me agayne to my study as I dyde of custome; I forgate it not [and]² put my wyll to effecte that came to me the nyght before to vysyte the foresayd *Boke of Matheolus*. And then I began to rede and to prosede in hym, but as me semed the matter was not ryght pleasaunt to people that delyted them not in evyll sayenge, nor it was of no profyte to ony edyfyenge of vertue, seynge the wordes and the matters dyshonest of whiche it touched, vysytynge here and there, and so came to the ende, I lefte hym and toke hede of more hygher matters and of more profyte. Yet the syght of this foresayd boke, howe be it that he was of none auctoryte, it engendred in me a newe thought, whiche made grete mervayle to growe in my courage and thynkynge. What myght be the cause and wherof it myght come that so many dyvers men, clerkes and others, have ben and ben enclyned to say by mouthe and in theyr treatyse and wrytynges so many slaundres and blames of women and of theyr condycyons? And not onely one or twayne, nor this Matheolus, whiche amonge others hath no maner of reputacyon and treateth in maner of scorne, but generally in all treatyses of phylos[o]phres,³ poetes, and all rethorycyens—whiche sholde be longe to

---

¹ m[e] : *my*
² [and] : *in*
³ phylos[o]phres : *phylosphres*

leurs noms — semblent[1] que tous parlent par une mesme bouche et tous accordent
une semblable conclusion, determinant les meurs femmenins enclins et plaines
de tous vices.[2]

Ces choses pensant a par moy tres perfondement, je pris a [fol. 5r a] examiner
moy mesmes et mes meurs comme femme naturelle, et semblablement discu-
toye des autres femmes que j'ay hantees tant princesses, grandes dames comme
moyenes[3] et petites a grant foison, qui de leur grace m'ont dit de leurs privetez et
estroictes penseez, asavoir[4] mon a jugier en conscience et sans faveur se ce puet
estre vray ce que tant de notables hommes, et uns et autres, en tesmoingnent.
Mais non obstant que pour chose que je peusse[5] congnoistre, tant longuement y
sceuse viser ne epluchier, je ne aperceusse[6] telz jugemens estre vrais encontre les
naturelz meurs ou[7] condicions femmenines. J'arguoie fort contre les femmes, disant que trop fort seroit que tant de si renommez hommes, si sollemnelz [fol. 5r b]
cler[c]s[8] de tant hault et grant entendement, si cler veans en toutes choses comme
il sembloit,[9] en eussent parlé mençongeusement et en tant de lieux que a peine
trouvoie volume moral qui qu'en soit l'aucteur que avant que je l'aye tout leu, que
je ne[10] voye aucuns chapitres ou certaines clauses au blasme d'elles. Ceste seule
raison, brief et court, me faisoit conclure que, quoy que mon entendement pour
sa simplece et ignorance ne sceust congnoistre les grans deffaultes,[11] et semblablement des aultres femmes, que vraiement toutevoie couvenoit il que ainsi fust, et
ainsi m'en raportoye plus au jugement d'aultrui que ad ce que moy mesmes en
sentoye et savoye.

En ceste pensee fus je [fol. 5v a] si comme personne en letargie et me venoient
au devant moult grant foison de ditz et proverbes de[12] grant foison d'aucteurs ad
ce propos que je ramentevoie en moy mesmes, l'un aprés l'aultre, comme ce[13] fust
une fontaine resordant. Et en conclusion de tout, je determinoie que vile chose
fist Dieux quant Il fourma femme, en m'esmerveillant comment si digne ouvrier
daigna oncques faire tant abhominable ouvrage qui est vaissel au dit d'iceulx si

---

[1] qui longue chose seroit nommer leurs noms semblent] desquieulx les noms dire
seroit longue chose semble

[2] vices] les vices

[3] dames comme moyenes] dames moyennes

[4] asavoir] savoir

[5] je peusse] je y peusse

[6] ne aperceusse] ne apperceusse ne congneusse

[7] ou] et

[8] cler[c]s : *clers*

[9] il sembloit] il semble que ceulx fussent

[10] ne] n'y

[11] deffaultes] deffaultes de moy mesmes

[12] fus je . . . et proverbes de] fus tant et si longuement fort fichee que il sembloit que
je feusse si come personne en letargie et me venoient au devant moult

[13] ce] se ce

reherce all theyr names—speketh as it were by one mouthe and accordeth all in semble conclusyon, determynynge that the condycyons of women ben fully [Bb2r] enclyned to all vyces.

These thynges thynkynge in me ryght depely, I began to examyne myselfe and my condycyons as a woman naturall. And in lykewyse I dyscuted of other women whos companye I haunted, as well of pryncesses and of grete ladyes as of meane gentyll women ryght grete plentye, whiche of theyr graces have tolde me theyr pryvytees and strayte thoughtes, to knowe by my jugement in conscyence and without favoure yf it[1] myght be trewe that so many notable men of one and other wytnesseth. Yet notwithstandynge that for thynges that I myght knowe, as longe as I have sought and serched, I coude not perceyve that suche jugementes myght be trewe agaynst the naturall condycyons or maners of women.

I argued strongly agaynst these women, sayenge that it sholde be too grete a thynge that so many famous men, so solempne clarkes of soo hyghe and grete understandynge, so clerely seynge in all thynges, as it semed, that sholde have spoken or wryten lyengly, and in so many places, that of payne I founde ony morall volume whatsoever the auctoure were that or I had redde it to the ende but some chapytres or certayne clauses were of blamynge of theym. This onely shorte reason made me to conclude that myne understandynge for his symple-nesse and ygnoraunce, ne coude not knowe my grete defautes, and semblably of other women, that alwaye it accorded that it was so truely. And soo I reported me more to the jugement [Bb2v] of other then to that I felte or knowe of myselfe.

Thus in this thought was I as a persone halfe from hymselfe, and there came before me ryght grete foyson of dyttyes and proverbes of many dyvers auctours to that purpose that I remembred in myselfe one after another as it were a welle spryngynge. And in conclusyon of all I determyned that God made a foule thynge when He fourmed woman, in mervayllynge howe soo worshypfull a werkeman deyned ever to make one soo abhomynable werke, whiche is the vessell as by sayenge of them

---

[1] it : *it it*

comme le retrait et heberge de tous maulx et de tous vices. Adonc moy estant en ceste pensee, me sourdi une grant desplaisance et tristece de courage, en desprisant moy mesmes et tout le sexe femmenin, si comme se ce fust monstre en nature, [fol. 5v b] et disoie telz paroles en mes regrais:

"Ha Dieux, comment puet ce cy estre? Car se je n'erre en la foy, je ne doy mie doubter que ton infinie sapience et tres perfaicte bonté ait riens fait que[14] tout ne soit bon. Ne fourmas Tu toy mesmes tres singulierement femme, et dés lors lui donnas toutes telles inclinacions qu'il te plaisoit que elle eust? Et comme[nt][15] pourroit ce estre que Tu y eusses en riens failli? Et toutevoyes voy cy tant de grandes accusacions: voire toutes jugees, determinees, et concluses contre elles. Je ne sçay entendre ceste repugnance.

"Et s'il est ainsi, beau sire Dieux, que ce soit vraye qu'en[16] sexe femmenin[17] tant d'abhominacions habondent si que tesmoingnent maint, et Tu dis toy mesmes que le tesmoingnage de pluseurs fait [fol. 6r a] a croire, par quoy je ne doy doubter que ce ne soit vray. Helas, Dieux, pour quoy ne me feis Tu naistre au monde en masculin sexe a celle fin que mes inclinacions fussent toutes a te mieulx servir, et que je n'errasse en riens, et fusse de si grant perfection comme homme masle se dit estre? Mais puis que ainsi est que ta debonaireté ne se est de tant estendue vers moy, espargne doncques ma negligence en ton service, beau sire Dieux, et ne te desplaise, car le servant qui moins reçoit de guerrerdons de son seingneur, moins est obligié a son service."

Telz paroles et plus assez tres longuement en triste pensee disoie a Dieu en ma lamentacion, si comme celle qui par ma foulour me tenoie tres mal contente de ce qu'en corps femmenin m'ot Dieux fait naistre[18] [fol. 6r b] au monde.

*Chapitre 2*     **Cy dit Christine comment troys dames lui apparurent, et comment celle qui estoit devant l'arraisonna premiere et la reconforta d'un desplaisir que elle avoit**

En celle doulente pensee ainsi que je estoie, la teste baissee comme personne honteuse, les yeulx pleins de larmes, tenant ma main soubz ma joe acoudee sur le pommel de ma chaiere, soubdainement sur mon giron vi descendre un ray de lumiere si comme se le soleil fust. Et je, qui estoie en lieu obscurre[19] ou quel a celle heure soleil rayer ne peust, tressailli adoncques si comme se je fusse reveillee de somme, et dreçant la teste pour regarder dont telle lueur venoit, vi devant moy

[14] que] qui
[15] comme[nt] : *comme*
[16] qu'en] que ou
[17] femmenin: *feminenin*
[18] naistre] estre
[19] estoie en lieu obscurre] en lieu obscur estoie

and the draught and herbegage of al evyll and of all vyces. Then I, beynge in this thought, there sprange in me a grete dyspleasa[u]nce[1] and sorowe of courage in dyspraysynge myselfe and all womenkynde so as yf that sholde be shewed in nature, and I sayd suche wordes in my complayntes:

"Ha, Lorde God, howe may that be? For if I arre not in the fayth, I ought not doubt that Thyne infynyte wysdome and veray parfyte goodnesse had nothynge made but that all were good. And fourmest not Thou Thyselfe woman ryght syngulerly, and then Thou gave her all suche inclynacyons that pleased Thee that she sholde have? And howe maye that be that Thou sholde have fayled in ony thynge? And alway se here so many grete occasyons thus juged, determyned, and concluded ayenst them. I cannot understande this repugnaunce.

"And yf it be so, good Lorde God, that it be true that womankynde haboundeth in so many abhomynacyons as many men wytnesseth, and Thou sayest Thyselfe that the wytnesse of many is for to byleve, [Bb3r] by the whiche I ought not doubte but that it sholde be true. Alas, good Lorde, why haddest Thou not made me to be borne into this worlde in the masculyne kynde, to that entente that myne enclynacyons myght have ben al to have served Thee the better, and that I sholde not have arred in ony thynge and myght have ben of so grete perfeccyon as they say that men be? Yet syth it is so that Thy debonayrnesse stretcheth not so moche towarde me, then spare my neglygence in Thy servyce, good Lorde God, and be not dyspleased for that servaunt that receyveth leest rewardes of his lorde, leest is bounde to his servyce."

Suche wordes and mo ynowe I sayd ryght longe in my sorowfull thought to God and in my lamentacyon so as she that, by my foly, helde me ryght evyll contente of that that God made me to be borne into this worlde in kynde of woman.

*Chapter 2*    **Christine telleth howe .iii. ladyes appered to her, and howe she that wente before reasoned with her fyrste and comforted her of the dyspleasure that she had**

As I was in this sorowfull thought, the heed downecast as a shamfull persone, the eyes full of teeres, holdynge myne hande under my cheke, lenynge on the pomell of my chayre — sodeynly I sawe come downe upon my lappe a stremynge of lyght as it were of the same. And I, that was [Bb3v] in a derke place in whiche the sone myght not shyne at that houre, sterte then as thoughe I had ben waked of a dreme. And dressynge the heed to beholde this lyght fro whens it myght come, I sawe before me

---

[1] dyspleasa[u]nce : *dyspleasannce*

tout en estant trois dames couronnees de tres souveraine reverence, desquelles la resplendeur de leurs cleres faces [fol. 6v a] enluminoit moy mesmes et toute la place. Lors se je fus esmerveillee, nul nel demant, considerant sur moy le huis clos et elles la venues. Doubdant que ce fust aucune fantausme[1] pour me tempter, fis en mon front le signe de la crois, remplie de tres grant paour.

Adonc celle qui premiere des troys estoit, en soubsriant, me prist ainsi a araisonner:

"Fille chiere, ne t'espovente. Car nous ne sommes mie cy venues pour ton contraire, ne faire aucun encombrier, ains pour toy consoler comme piteuses de ta turbacion et te giter hors de l'ignorance, qui tant aveugle ta mesmes cognoiscence que tu deboutes de toy ce que tu sces de certaine science pour donner foy au contraire ad ce[2] que tu ne sens,[3] ne vois, ne cognois autrement fors par pluralité [fol. 6v b] d'oppinions estranges. Tu ressembles le fol dont la truffe parle, qui en dormant au molin fu revestu de la robe d'une femme et au ressembler[4] pour ce que ceulx qui le moquoyent lui tesmoingnoient que femme estoit, crut mieulx leurs faulx dis que la certaineté de son estee.[5]

"Comment, belle fille, et qu'est[6] ton sens devenu? As tu doncques oublié que le fin or s'espreuve en la fornaise, que[7] ne se change ne muet de sa vertu,[8] ains afine[9] de tant plus est martellé et demené en diverses façons? Ne sces tu que les tres meilleures choses sont les plus debatues, et les plus arguees? Se tu veulx viser[10] mesmement aux plus haultes choses qui sont les ydees, c'est assavoir les choses cellestielles, regardes se les tres plus grans philosophes [fol. 7r a] qui ayent esté, que tu argues contre ton mesmes sexe, en ont point determiné faulx et au contraire du vray, et s'ilz repugnent l'un l'autre et reprenent si comme tu mesmes l'as veu ou *Livre de Methaphisique*, la ou Aristote redargue[11] leurs opinions et recite semblablement de Platon et de autres. Et notes de rechief se saint Augustin et autres docteurs de l'Eglise ont point repris mesmement Aristote en aucuns pars, tout soit il dit le 'prince des philosophes,' et en qui philosophie naturelle et morale fu souverainement. Et il semble que tu cuides que toutes les paroles des philosophes soient articles de foy, et qu'ilz ne peussent errer!

---

[1]  fantausme] fantasie
[2]  science pour donner foy au contraire ad ce] science et ajoustes foy a ce
[3]  sens] scez
[4]  ressembler] resveiller
[5]  estee] estre
[6]  et qu'est] qu'est
[7]  que] qui
[8]  sa vertu] ses vertus
[9]  affine] plus affine
[10]  viser] aviser
[11]  redargue] redargue et reprent

standynge thre ladyes crowned of ryght soverayne reverence, of the whiche the shynynge of theyr clere faces gave lyght unto me and to all the place there as I was, mervayllynge, neyther man nor woman with me consyderynge the dore close upon me — and they thyder came; doubtynge leest it had ben some fantasye for to have tempted me, made the sygne of the crosse in my forehede, ful of drede.

And then she whiche was the fyrst of the thre, in laughynge, began thus to reason with me: "Dere doughter, drede thee nought, for we be not come hyder for nothynge that is contrary unto thee, nor to do thee to be encombred, but for to comforte thee as those that have pyte of thy trouble, and to put thee out of the ygnoraunce that so moche blyndeth thyne understandynge; and that thou puttest fro thee that thou knowest of very certayne scyence, to gyve faythe to the contrary to that whiche thou felest not, ne seest not, ne knowest otherwyse than by pluralyte of straunge opynyons. Thou resemblest the fole of the whiche was made a jape, whiche was slepynge in the mylle and [was]¹ clothed in the clothynge of a woman. And to make resemblaunce those that mocked hym wytnessed that he was a woman, and so he byleved more theyr false saynges than the certaynte of his beynge.

"Howe [Bb4r] is it, fayre doughter, and where is thy wytte become? Hast thou forgoten nowe howe the fyne golde proveth hym in the fornayse, that he chaungeth not his vertue but is more plyaunt to be brought into dyvers facyons? And knowest thou not that the moost mervayllous thynges be moost debatous and most arguous? Yf thou wylte advyse thee in the same wyse to the moost hyghe thynges that ben, that is to knowe the celestyall thynges, beholde yf these grete phylosophres that hath ben (that thou arguest agaynst thyne owne kynde) have determyned false and to the contrary of trouthe, and as they repugne one agaynst another as thou thyselfe hast sene in the *Boke of Metaphisike*, whereas Arystotle reproveth theyr opynyons and reherseth the same wyse of Plato and of others. And note this agayne if Saynt Austyne and other doctours of the chyrche have done so the same wyse Arystotle in some partyes, al be it that he be called the 'Prynce of Phylosophres,' and in whome phylosophye naturall and morall was soveraynely. And it semeth that [thou]² trowest that al the wordes of phylosophres ben artycles of the fayth of Jhesu Cryst, and that they maye not arre!

---

¹ [was] : *whas*
² [thou] : *that trowest*

"Et des poetes dont tu parles: ne sces tu pas bien que ilz ont [fol. 7r b] parlé en plusieurs choses en maniere de fable, et se veulent aucune fois entendre au contraire de ce que leurs dis demonstrent? Et le puet on prendre par la rigle[1] de gramaire qui se nomme *antifrasis,* qui s'entent comme[2] tu sces si comme on diroit 'tel est mauvais,' c'est a dire qu'il est bon, et aussi par le contraire.[3] Si te conseil que tu faces ton proffit de leurs dis, et que tu l'entendes ainsi quelque fust leur entente es lieux ou ilz blasment les femmes. Et par aventure que cellui homme qui se nomma Matheolus en son livre l'entendi ainsi, car maintes choses y a lesquelles qui a la lettre tenir les vouldroit, ce seroit pure heresie. Et la vituperacion que dit non mie seulement lui mais d'aultres—et mesmement le *Rommant de la Rose,* ou plus grant foy est [fol. 7v a] adjoustee pour cause de l'auctorité de l'aucteur—de l'ordre de mariage qui est saint estat digne et de Dieu ordonné—c'est chose clere prouvee[4] par l'experience que le contraire est vray du mal qu'ilz proposent et dient estre en cellui[5] estat a la grant charge et coulpe des femmes. Car qui fu oncques[6] le mary qui tel maistrise souffrist avoir a sa femme que elle eust loy de tant lui dire de villenies et d'injures comme yceulx mettent que femmes dient? Je croy que quoy que tu en aies veu en escript, que oncques nul[7] de tes yeulx non[8] veis. Si sont mençonges pures trop[9] mal coulourees.

"Si te dis en concluant, chiere amie, que folie[10] t'a meue a la present oppinion. Or te reviens a toy mesmes et repren ton sens: ne[11] plus ne te troubles pour telx fanfelues, [fol. 7v b] car saiches que tout mal dit si generaument des femmes empire les diseurs, et non[12] mie elles mesmes."

---

[1] la rigle] une figure
[2] comme] si comme
[3] et aussi par le contraire] aussi a l'opposite
[4] clere prouvee] clere et prouvee
[5] cellui] ycellui
[6] qui fu oncques] ou fu oncques trouvé
[7] nul] de nul
[8] non] n'en
[9] pures trop] trop
[10] folie] simplece
[11] et repren ton sens: ne] reprens ton sens: et
[12] et non] non

"And as to these poetes of whiche thou spekest, knowest not thou well that they have spoken in many thynges in manere of fables, and do entende so moche to the contrary of that that theyr sayenges sheweth? And it maye be taken after the rewle of grammere the whiche is named *antyphrasys*, the whiche entendeth thus [Bb4v] as thou knowest well, as one sholde say syth 'one is a shrewe' that is to saye that he is good, and so by the contrary. So I counsayle thee that thou do thy profyte of theyr sayenges and thou understande it so, whatsoever be theyr entente in suche places whereas they blame women. And peradventure this same man that is Matheolus in his boke understode the same, for there be many thynges whoso taketh them after the letter, it sholde be pure heresye and shame to hym that sayth it; and not onely to hym, but to others. And the same wyse of the *Romaunce of the Rose* on whome is put grete faythe bycause of the auctoryte of the maker, of the ordre of maryage, whiche is an holy estate and worshypfull and ordeyned of God: this thynge proveth clerely by experyence that the contrary is true of the shrewdenesse that they purpose and s[a]yth[1] to be in that estate, to the grete charge and blame of women. For who was ever that housbande that ever suffred suche maystrye of his wyfe, that she sholde have leve to saye so many vylanyes and injures as they put upon women that they sholde saye? I byleve whatsoever thou hast sene in wrytynge, thou sawest it never at the eye. So they be pure lesynges ryght shrewdely coloured.

"Thus I say in concludynge, my lefe frende, that folye caused thee this presente opynyon. Nowe come agayne to thyselfe, and take thy wytte, and trouble thee no more for suche fantasyes. For knowe wel that all this evyll saynges generally of women hurteth the sayers and not the women." [Bb5r]

---

[1] s[a]yth : *syth*

*Chapitre 3*        **Ci dit Christine comment la dame qui l'ot araisonnee lui**
**devisa quelle estoit sa proprieté et de quoy elle servoit, et**
**lui anonça comment elle edifieroit une cité a l'aide d'elles**
**trois dames**

Ces paroles me dist la dame renommee, a la presence de laquelle je ne sçay lequel
de mes sens fu plus entrepris: ou mon ouye en escoutant ses dignes paroles, ou
ma veue en regardant sa tres grant beaulté, son atour, son reverent port, et sa tres
honnouree contenance—et semblablement des autres si que ne savoye laquelle
regarder, car si fort s'entre ressembloient les trois dames que a peine congneust
on l'une de l'autre excepté que la desraine, tout ne fust [fol. 8r a] elle de maindre
auctorité que les autres: elle avoit la chiere si fiere que qui es yeulx la regardat si
hardi ne fust que[1] grant paour n'eust de mesprendre, car ades sembloit que elle
menaçast les malfaicteurs.

Si estoie devant elles en estant levee de mon siege[2] pour leur reverence, les
regardant sans mot dire comme personne si surprise[3] que mot ne scet sonner. Et
moult grant admiracion en mon cuer avoie, pensant qui pouoient ycelles estre, et
moult voulentiers, se j'osasse, enqueisse leurs noms et de leur estre; et quelle estoit
la signifiance des septres differenciez que chascune d'elles en sa main destre
tenoit, qui tous estoient de moult grant richece; et pour quoy furent la venues?
Mais comme je me reputasse non digne [fol. 8r b] d'araisonner en telx demandes
si haultes dames comme elles m'apparoient, n'osasse nullement, ains continuoie[4]
ades sur elles mon regart, demue[5] espoventee et demie asseuree par les paroles
que ouies avoye qui m'orent gictee[6] de ma premiere pensee.

Mais la tres saige dame qui m'ot araisonnee, qui congnut en esperit ma pensee
comme celle qui voit en toutes choses, respondi a ma cogitacion, disant ainsi:

"Chiere fille, saches que la providence de Dieu, qui riens ne laisse vague ne
vuit, nous a establies, quoy que nous soiens choses celestieles, estre et frequenter
entre les gens de ce bas monde afin de mettre en ordre et tenir en equité les
establissemens fais par nous mesmes selon le vouloir de Dieu en divers offices,
auquel Dieu toutes .iii. sommes filles et de lui nees.

"Si est mon office: [fol. 8v a] de radrecier les hommes et les femmes quant ilz
sont desvoyez, de le[s][7] remettre en droicte voye. Et quant ilz ont erreur,[8] se ilz
ont entendement qui me sache veoir, je viens a eulx coyement en esperit, tout

---

[1] que: *qui*
[2] levee de mon siege] levee
[3] surprise] entreprise
[4] continuoie] continuant
[5] demue] demie
[6] gictee] gicté hors
[7] le[s] : *le*
[8] ont erreur] errent

*Chapter 3*  Christine sayth howe that the lady that reasoned with her devysed what was her propryete and wherof she served, and tolde her howe she sholde buylde a cyte with the helpe of these .iii. ladyes

This famous lady sayenge these wordes to me, with the presence of whome I cannot say whiche of my wyttes was moost undertaken—in myne herynge, in herkenynge of her worthy wordes; where that my syght was in beholdynge her grete beaute, her attyre, her reverent porte, and her ryght worshypfull countenaunce—and the same wyse of the others, and wyst not whiche of them to beholde; for soo moche these thre ladyes resembled eyther other that of payne I myght knowe that one from that other, but that I sholde have ben deceyved. And she of the lesse auctoryte than that other had her chere so fyerse that whome her eyen behelde was not so hardy but that he sholde be undertaken with grete drede, for it semed that she manased the evyll doers. Soo I was before them, standynge up from my syege for theyr reverence, beholdynge them without faynynge of ony worde as that persone that was so overtaken that coude not sowne a worde. And I had grete mervayle in my herte thynkynge who they myght be and ryght gladly yf I had durste I wolde have asked theyr names and theyr beynge; and what [Bb5v] was the sygnyfyenge of the dyfferent septres that eche of them helde in theyr ryght handes, whiche were of ryght grete rychesse; and wherfore they were come thyder? Yet when I had thought me not worthy to reason with them in suche demaundes, soo hyghe ladyes as they appered unto me, I durst in no manere but contynued my syght upon theym halfe aferde, and halfe assured by the wordes that I had herde them saye, whiche hathe cast me out of my fyrst thought. Yet that ryght wyse lady that had reasoned with me, whiche knewe my thought in spyryte as she that hath syght in all thynges, answered to my thought saynge thus:

"Dere doughter, knowe ye that the provydence of God that nothynge leveth vayne ne cometh not us to estable, thoughe that we knowe celestyall thynges, to be and to haunte amonge the people of this bace worlde to that entente to put in ordre and to holde in equyte the stablementes made by ourselfe after the wyll of God in dyvers offyces, to the whiche God we thre ben doughters and of Hym borne.

"So it is myne offyce to redresse men and women when they are out of the waye, to put them agayne in the ryght waye. And I come to them pryvely in spyryte,

celeement,[1] et les presche et sermonne, en demonstrant leur erreur et ce en quoy ilz faillent, et leur assigne les causes. Et puis je leur enseigne la maniere de suivre ce qui est affaire, et comment fuiront ce qui est a laissier.

"Et pour ce que je sers de demonstrer clerement et faire veoir en conscience et de fait a un chascun et chascune ses propres taches et deffaulx, me vois tu tenir en lieu de ceptre cestui resplendissant miroir que je porte en ma main destre. Si saches de vray qu'il n'est quelconques personne qui s'y mire, quelque la creaturee soit, qui clerement ne se [fol. 8v b] cognoisse. O, tant est de grant dignité mon miroir: sans cause n'est il pas avironné de riches pierres precieuses, si que tu le vois, car par lui les essences,[2] qualitez, proporcions, et mesures de toutes choses sont congneues, ne sans lui ne puet riens[3] estre bien fait.

"Et pour ce que tu desires semblablement savoir quelx sont les offices de mes autres suers que tu vois cy, afin que le tesmoingnage de nous te soit plus certaine, chascune en sa personne respondra de son nom et de sa proprieté. Mais le mouvement de nostre venue te sera cy[4] endroit par moy declairié: je te notifie que, comme nous ne facions riens sans bonne cause, n'est mie en vain nostre apparicion cy endroit. Car quoy que nous ne soions pas communes en plusieurs [fol. 9r a] lieux, et que nostre congnoissance ne viengne a toutes gens, neant moins toy—pour la grant amour que tu as a l'inquisicion de choses vrayes par long et continuel estude, par quoy tu te rens ycy solitaire et soubstraicte du monde—tu as deservi et dessers estre de nous, comme chiere amie, visitee et consolee en ta perturbacion et tristece, et que tu soies faictes cler veant es choses qui contaminent et troublent ton courage en obscurté de pensee.

"Autre cause de nostre venue [y a][5] plus grant et plus especiale que tu seras par nostre relacion: si saches que pour fors clourre du monde la semblable erreur ou estoies[6] encheue, et que les dames et toutes vaillans femmes puissent d'or enavant avoir aucune retrait et closture de deffence contre tant de [fol. 9r b] divers assaillans, lequelles dictes dames ont par si long temps esté delaissiees, descloses comme champ sans haye, sans trouver champion aucun qui pour leur deffence comparust souffisamment, non obstant les nobles hommes qui par ordenance de droit deffendre les deussent, qui par negligence et non chaloir les ont souffertes fouler; par quoy n'est merveille se leurs envieux anemis et l'oultrage des villains, qui par divers dars les ont assaillies, ont eu contre elles victoire de leur guerre par faulte de deffence. Ou est la cité si forte qui tost ne fust prise, se resistance n'y

---

[1] en esperit, tout celeement, et] en esperit et
[2] essences] exausses
[3] ne puet riens] rien ne peut
[4] cy] or
[5] [y a] : *space*] y a
[6] estoies] tu estoies

all covertely, and I preche them and teche them in shewynge theyr erroure; and that in whiche they fayle, I assygne them the causes. And after, I teche theym the manere to folowe that that is to do, and howe they sholde flee that that is to be lefte.

"And for that I serve to showe clerely and make to se in conscyence [Bb6r] theyr dedes to every man and woman, and theyr propre tatches and defautes, thou [s]eest[1] me holde instede of a septre this bryght glasse or myroure that I bere in my ryght hande. Knowe this for trouthe that there is no persone that loketh in this myroure but he maye knowe, every creature, what he is clerely. O my myroure, it is of so grete dygnyte that it is not without grete cause that he is so envyronned of so ryche precyous stones as thou seest it, for by hym these beynges, qualytees, proporcyon, and measures of al thynges ben knowne, ne without hym may nothynge be well made nor done.

"And for that that thou desyrest to knowe also the offyces of myne other two systers that thou seest here, to that entente that the wytnessynge of us may be to thee more certayne, eche of them in theyr owne persone shall answere of theyr name and of theyr propryete. Yet the cause and the movynge of our comynge shall be declared by me ryght here. I make thee to understande that as there shall be done nothynge without good cause, our apperynge is nothynge here in vayne. For thoughe that we be not comunely in many places and that the knowlege of us cometh not unto all people, neverthelesse for the grete love the whiche thou haste for to enquyre after thynges by veray longe and contynuall studye, by the whiche thou doest yelde thyselfe here solytarye. And thou withdrawest thee out of the worlde, thou haste deserved and thou deservest to be vysyted and to be comforted [Bb6v] of us in thy trouble and sorowe as ryght a dere frende, and that thou be made clerely seynge those thynges that defoule and trouble thy courage in the derkenesse of thought.

"Also there is a gretter cause of our comynge and a more specyal that thou shalte knowe by our revelacyon: so understande to that entente that this erroure myght be destroyed, we wolde that these ladyes and all worshypfull women myght have from hensforthe some manere of place to come to or a cloystre of defence agaynst all those that wolde assayle them, for the defaute of whiche all these foresayd ladyes and famous women have longe tyme be[n][2] lefte unclosed as a felde without hedge, without fyndynge of ony champyon that for theyr defence myght compare suffycyently, notwithstandynge these noble men that by ordenaunce of ryght ought to defende theym, whiche by neglygence and no force hathe suffred them to be defouled; by the whiche it is no mervayl thoughe theyr envyous enemyes and the outrage of vylaynes assaylled them by dyvers craftes and have had the vyctory agaynst them in theyr warre for defaute of defence. Where is that cyte so stronge that myght not sone be taken yf there be not founde

---

[1] [s]eest : *feest*
[2] be[n] : *be*

estoit trouvee? Ne si n'est si juste[1] cause qui par constumance ne fust gaingnee de cellui qui plaide sans partie?

"Et les simples debonnaires dames, a l'exemple de [fol. 9v a] pacience que Dieu commande, ont souffert amiablement les grans injures qui tant par bouche de pluseurs, comme par mains escrips, leur ont esté faictes a tort et a pechié, eulx raportant a Dieu de leur bon droit. Mais or est temps que leur juste cause soit mis hors des mains de Pharaon. Et pour ce entre nous trois dames que tu vois cy, meues par pitié, te sommes venues annoncier un certain edefice fait en la maniere de la clousture[2] d'une cité fort maçonnee et bien edifiee, qui a toy faire[3] est predestinee et establie par nostre aide et conseil, en laquelle n'abitera fors toutes dames de renommee et femmes dignes de los. Car a celles ou vertu ne sera trouvee, les murs de nostre cité seront fors clos."

*Chapitre 4* **Ci dit encore comment la dame devise a Christine de la cité qui lui estoit commise a faire, et que elle estoit establie[4] a lui aidier a bastir la muraille et la closture d'environ; et puis lui dit son nom** [fol. 9v b]

"Ainsi belle fille, t'est donnée la prerogative entre les femmes de faire et bastir la Cité des Dames, pour laquelle fonder et perfaire tu prendras et puizeras en nous trois eaues[5] comme en fontaines cleres, et te livrerons assez matiere plus fort et plus durable que nul marbre saellé a cyment ne pourroit estre: si sera ta cyté tres belle, sans pareille, et de perpetuelle duree au monde.

"N'as tu pas leu que le roy Tros fonda la grant cité de Troye par l'aide d'Appollo, de Minerve, et de Neptunus, que les gens de lors reputoient dieux? Et aussi comment Cadmus fonda Thebes la cité par la ministracion[6] des dieu[x]?[7] Et toutevoyes icelles cités par [fol. 10r a] espace de temps decheirent et sont tournees[8] en ruine. Mais je te prophetize comme vraye sebille que ja[9] ceste cité que tu, a nostre aide, fonderas ne sera adnichillee ne decherra, ains durera en prosperité

---

1 ne si n'est si juste] ne si
2 fait en la maniere de la clousture] en maniere de
3 faire] a faire
4 establie] commise
5 eaues] eaues vives
6 la ministracion] l'admonnestement
7 dieu[x] : *dieu*
8 sont tournees] tournees si comme
9 ja] a

resystence, nor so unjuste a cause but it myght be goten by contynuaunce of hym that pledeth without party?

"Ryght so these symple and debonayre ladyes, to the ensample of pacyence whiche God commaundeth, hath suffred frendely these grete injuryes that so moche, by the mouthe of so many and theyr handes wrytynge, [Cc1r] have suffred so moche wronge; thus they reporte them to God of theyr good ryght. Yet nowe it is tyme that theyr juste cause be put out of the handes of Pharao. And therfore bytwene us thre ladyes that thou seest here, moved by pyte, we be come to tell thee of a certayne buyldynge made in the manere of a cloystre of a cyte strongely wrought by masons' handes and well buylded, whiche is predestynate to thee for to make and to stable it by our helpe and counsayle, in the whiche shall none enhabyte but onely ladyes of good fame, and women worthy of praysynges. For to them where vertue shall not be founde, the walles of our cyte shall be strongely shytte."

*Chapter 4*          **Christine telleth howe the lady devysed to her the cyte that was commytted to her to make, and that she was stabled to helpe her to begyn the walles and the cloystre aboute; and after, tolde her her name**

"Thus, fayre doughter, the prerogatyve is gyven to thee amonge al other women to make and fortefye the Cyte of Ladyes, for the whiche thou shalte take upon thee to make the foundement and parfytely conclude hym. And thou shalte receyve of us thre wyne and water as of a clere welle. And we shall delyver to thee mater ynoughe, more stronger and more durable than ony marbre; [Cc1v] and as for cyment, there shal be no better than thou shalte have. So shall thy cyte be ryght fayre, without pere, and of perpetuall durynge to the worlde.

"Haste thou not redde that the Kynge Troys founded the grete cyte of Troye by the helpe of Appolo, Mynerve, and Neptune, whiche the people at that tyme trowed theym as goddes? And also howe Cadmus founded the cyte of Thebes by the mynestracyon of goddes? And for al that, those cytees by space of tyme were overthrowne and ben tourned into ruyne. But I prophecye to thee as verray sybylle that never this cyte whiche thou shalte founde shall be brought to nought,

et tousjours mais,[1] malgré tous ses envieux anemis. Et quoy que elle soit par mains assaulx combatue, si ne sera elle point prise ne vacueue.[2]

"Jadis fu commencié le royaume de Mazonie[3] par l'ordennance et emprise de plusieurs femmes[4] de grant couraige qui servitude desprisierent, si comme les hystoires te ont tesmoingné; et long temps[5] par elles le maintindrent soubz la seingneurie de pluseurs roynes, moult nobles dames que elles mesmes eslirent[6] qui bien et bel[7] les gouvernerent, et par grant vigueur maintindrent la seingneurie. Et neant moins, [fol. 10r b] tout fussent ycelles de grant force et poissance, et que ou temps de leur dominacion grant partie de tout Orient conquistrent, et toutes les terres voisines espoenterent, et mesmement les redoubtoit[8] le païs de Grece, qui adonc estoit la fleur des contrees du monde. Et[9] non pour tant, a chief de temps deffailli[10] la poissance d'ycellui royaume par telle maniere que, si que il est de toutes mondaines seigneuries, il n'en est demouré ou temps d'ore fors seulement le seul nom.[11]

"Mais trop plus fort edefice sera par toy basti en ceste cité que tu as a faire, pour laquelle encommencier suis commise par la deliberacion d'entre nous trois dames ensemble, et[12] te livrer mortier durable et sans corrupcion a faire les fors fondemens et les gros [fol. 10v a] murs tout a l'environ; lever haulx, larges, et a grosses tours et fors chastiaulx fossoies, bastides, et braies[13] tout ainsi qu'il apertient a cité de fort[14] deffence. Et par nostre divise tu les asserras en perfont pour plus durer, et puis les murs sus si[15] hault esleveras qu'ilz ne craindront tout le monde.

"Fille, si t'ay ores dit les causes de nostre venue. Et afin que plus adjoustes foy a mes ditz, te vueil orendroit mon nom aprendre par le son duquel seulement pourras savoir[16] que tu as en moy, se ensuivre veulx mes ordenances, amenistraresse en ton oeuvre faire telle que errer ne pourras: je suis nommee Dame Raison. Or, avises doncques se tu es en bon conduit. Si ne t'en dis plus a ceste fois."

---

[1] tousjours mais] tousjours
[2] si ne sera elle point prise ne vacueue] elle ne sera point prise ne vaincue
[3] de Mazonie] d'Amasonie
[4] femmes] dames
[5] long temps] lonc temps aprés
[6] que elles mesmes eslirent] qui elles mesmes eslisoient
[7] bel: *belles*
[8] redoubtoit] redoubterent ceulx du
[9] et] mais
[10] deffailli] failli
[11] le seul nom] le nom
[12] et] a
[13] et braies] et vrayes
[14] fort] fort et durable
[15] si] tant
[16] savoir] apprendre et sçavoir

ne shall not fall but alway endure in prosperyte, maulgre all his envyous enemyes. Thoughe that he be fought withall by many dyvers assaultes, so she shal never be taken ne overcome.

"Somtyme the royalme of Amosonye was begonne by the ordynaunce and entrepryse of dyvers women of grete courage whiche despysed bondage so as the hystoryes bereth wytnesse. And longe tyme by them it was mayntayned under sygnyouryes of dyvers quenes ryght noble ladyes the whiche they chose themselfe, and governed ryght fayre and well, and by grete strengthe maynteyned the lordshyp. And neverthelesse, thoughe they were of grete myght and puyssaunce, and that in the tyme of theyr domynacyon conquered grete parte of the Oryent, and all the landes nyghe them put them in drede—and in the same wyse the countre of Grece doubted them, whiche [Cc2r] that tyme was the f[l]oure[1] of all countrees of the worlde—and not for that, within processe of tyme the puyssaunce of the royalme, by the same manere as it is of all other worldely lordshyppes, there is not byden in this tyme as nowe but onely the fame.

"But this cyte shal be of moche more stronger buyldynge that thou hast to make, for the whiche to begyn I am commytted by the delyberacyon amonge us all thre ladyes togyder to delyver thee morter durable and without corrupcyon to make the stron[ge][2] foundementes and the grete walles all aboute, and to lyfte up the hyghe, large, and grete towres and stronge castelles dyked, bastyled, and barred as moche as it perteyneth to a cyte of grete defence. And by our devyse thou shalte set it in grete depnesse to endure the longer, and after thou shalte lyfte up the walles so hyghe that all the worlde shal drede them.

"Doughter, thus I have nowe tolde thee the causes of our comynge to the entente that thou take the more credence to my sayenge. Nowe I wyll that thou lerne my name, by the sowne of that whiche onely thou shalte knowe that thou hast in me, if thou wylte folowe myne ordynaunces, a mynystresse in thy nede to do that thou myght not yestereven. I am named Dame Reason: nowe advyse thee, then, yf thou be in good conduyte. So I say no more to thee at this tyme."

---

[1] f[l]oure : *foure*
[2] stron[ge] : *stron*

*Chapitre 5*    **Ci dit Christine[1] comment la seconde dame lui dist son nom, et de quoy elle servoit, et comment elle lui aideroit a maçonner la Cité des Dames** [fol. 10v b]

Quant la dame dessus dicte ot sa parole achevee, ains que loisir eusse de respondre, la seconde dame encommença en tel maniere: "Je suis appellee Droicture, qui en[2] ciel plus qu'en terre ay ma demeure. Mais comme ray et resplendeur de Dieu, et messagiere de sa bonté, je frequente entre les justes personnes et leur amonneste tout bien a faire, rendre a chascun ce qui est sien selon leur pouvoir, dire et soustenir verité, porter le droit des povres et des innocens sans[3] grever autrui par usurpacion,[4] soustenir la renommee des accusez sans cause. Je suis escu et deffense des serfs de Dieu. J'empesche la poissance[5] des mauvais; je fais[6] donner loier aux travaillans, et meriter [fol. 11r a] les bien faicteurs. Dieu manifeste par moy a ses amis ses secrez: je suis leur avocate ou ciel.

"Ceste ligne replandissant qu'en lieu de septre tenir me vois en ma destre,[7] c'est la rigle droicte qui depart le droit du tort, et demonstre la difference d'entre bien et mal: qui la suit ne se forvoye. C'est le baston de paix qui reconsilie les bons et ou ilz s'apuient, qui bat et fiert les mauvais. Que t'en diroi je?[8] Par ceste ligne sont toutes choses limitees, car infinies sont les dignitez d'elle. Si saches qu'elle te servira, et bien besoing en aras a l'edifice mesurer de la cité qui a faire t'est commise,[9] pour laquele dicte cité massonner; et au[10] par dedens faire les haulx combles,[11] les palais compasser, les maisons, et toutes les rues, les [fol. 11r b] places,[12] et toutes choses couvenables l'aidier et[13] peuplier. Je suis venue en ton aide avec ma seur Raison, et ceste haute noble dame qui yci est.[14] Si sera tel mon office. Or ne t'esmaies pour la grant largece et long circuit de la closture et des murs,[15] car a l'aide de Dieu et de nous, bien et bel la peuplieras et edifieras sans riens vague y laissier[16] de belles et fortes mansions et heberges."

---

[1]  Christine] *omitted*
[2]  en] ou
[3]  sans] ne
[4]  usurpacion] exurpacion
[5]  poissance] puissance et rigueur
[6]  fais] fois
[7]  ma destre] ma main dextre
[8]  diroi je] diroie
[9]  commise] commise et bien besoing en aras
[10]  et au] au
[11]  combles] temples
[12]  les rues, les places] les mansions, les rues, et les places
[13]  et] a
[14]  avec ma seur Raison, et ceste haute noble dame qui yci est] *omitted*
[15]  des murs] de la muraille
[16]  laissier] delaissier

*Chapter 5*    Here Christine telleth howe the seconde lady tolde her her name, and wherof she served, and howe she sholde helpe her to make the masonry of the Cyte of Ladyes [Cc2v]

Whan the lady abovesayd had accheved her worde, or that I had laysoure to answere, the seconde lady began to answere in this manere: "I am called Ryght-wysnesse, whiche hathe my dwellynge more in heven than in erthe. But as a sone beme and a lyghtnynge or a shynynge of God and messangere of His goodnesse, I haunte amonge the juste persones and counsayle them to do all thynge well, and to yelde to every man that that is his, and after to say and sustayne trouthe to bere the ryght of the poore people and innocentes, to greve others by usurpa-cyon, and sustayne the renowne of them that ben accused without cause. I am the shelde and defence of the servauntes of God. I call on the punycyon of evyll folkes; I make to gyve and alowe to the travayllers, and I rewarde the good doers. And God maketh open His secretes by me to His frendes: I am theyr advocate in heven.

"This shynynge lyne that thou seest me holde instede of a septre in my ryght hande is the ryght rewle that departeth the ryght from the wronge, and it sheweth the dyfference bytwene good and evyll: whoso foloweth it shall not goo out of the waye. This is the staffe of peas that reconsyleth the good, and whereupon they lene them; he smyteth and beteth the evyl doers. What sholde I more saye to thee? By this lyne all thynges are lymytted and the dygnytees of hym ben infynyte. Soo understande that he shall serve thee wel, and thou [Cc3r] shalte have nede of hym to measure the buyldynge of the cyte that is commytted to thee to make; and of the sayd cyte to make the stonewerke and to make within the hyghe towres and the hyghe palayces, to compace the housynge and all the mansyons, the stretes and places, and all thynges covenables to helpe thee; and to put suffycyent people within the foresayd cyte. Thus am I come in thyne helpe with my syster Reason and this noble lady whiche thou seest here. Boholde, this is myne offyce! Nowe dysmaye thou not of the grete largenesse and longe cyr-cuyte of the closynge of the walle, for by the helpe of God and of us thou shalte buylde it and people it ryght well and fayre, without levynge of ony voyde thynge, with fayre mansyons and strong herbegages."

*Chapitre 6*    Ci dit Christine[1] comment la tierce dame lui dist qui
elle estoit et de quoy elle servoit, et comment elle lui
aideroit a faire les haulx combles des tours de sa cité, et la
peupleroit de nobles dames[2]

Aprés parla la tierce dame, qui dist ainsi: "Christine, amie chiere,[3] je suis Justice,
la tres singuliere fille de Dieu, et mon essence procede de sa [fol. 11v a] personne
purement. Ma demeure est ou ciel, en terre, et en enfer: ou ciel, pour la gloire
des saints et des ames beneurees; en terre pour departir et donner sa porsion a
un chascun, du bien ou du mal, qu'il a desservi; en enfer pour la punicion des
mauvais. Je ne flechis nulle part, car je n'ay ami ne anemi, pour quoy affeccion,[4]
voulenté, pitié ne me convaint, ne cruaulté ne me muet. Mon office seulement
est de jugier, departir, et faire la paye selon la droicte desserte d'un chascun. Je
soubstiens toutes choses en estat, ne sans moy riens ne seroit estable. Je suis en
Dieu, et Dieu est en moy, et sommes comme une mesmes chose.

"Qui me suit ne puet faillir, et ma voye est seure. J'enseingne a tout homme
et femme de sain entendement qui me veullent[5] croire de chastier, cognoistre, [fol.
11v b] et reprendre premierement eulx[6] mesmes; faire a aultrui ce que il voudroit
que on leur feist; departir les choses sans faveur, dire verité, fuir et hair mençonge, debouter toutes choses vicieuses.

"Cestui vaissel de fin or que tu me vois tenir en ma main destre, fait en guise
d'une ronde mesure: Dieu mon Pere le me donna, et sert de mesurer a un chascun sa livree de tel merite[7] comme il doit avoir. Il est seigné a la fleur de lis de
la Trinité, et a toutes portions il se rent juste—ne nul de ma mesure ne se puet
plaindre. Mais les hommes de terre ont autres mesures que ilz dient deppendre et
venir de la mienne, mais faussement; mainteffois soubs umbre de moy mesurent,
ne tousjours n'est mie leur mesure juste, ains est trop large aux aucuns et [fol. 12r a]
trop estroicte aux autres.

"Assez te pourroie tenir long compte des proprietes de mon office, mais a
brief dire je suis especiale entre les Vertus, car toutes se refierent en moy. Et entre
nous trois dames que tu voys cy sommes comme une mesme chose: ne ne pouons l'un[8] sans l'autre. Et ce que la premiere dispose, la seconde ordonne et met a

---

[1] dit Christine] dit
[2] de sa cité, et la peupleroit de nobles dames] et des palais, et lui amenroit la Royne
accompaignée de haultes dames
[3] amie chiere] amie
[4] pour quoy affeccion] ne escalourgiant
[5] veullent] veult
[6] eulx] soy
[7] merite] mesure
[8] pouons l'un] pourriens l'une

*Chapter 6*     Here Christine telleth howe the thyrde lady tolde her
what she was and wherfore she served, and howe she
wolde helpe her to make the hyghe bataylmentes of the
towres of her cyte and to people it with noble ladyes

After this spake the thyrde lady whiche sayd ryght thus: "Christine, ryght dere
frende, I am Justyce, the synguler doughter of God, and my beynge procedeth
purely of His propre persone. My dwellynge is in heven, in erthe, and in helle:
in heven, for the glorye of sayntes and of blessyd [Cc3v] soules; in erthe, for to
departe and gyve every man his porcyon, other of good or of evyll as he hathe
deserved; in helle, for the punycyon of evyl people. I bowe not to no parte for
there is no frende, no fere of grete wyl, pyte nor prayer, thretnynge nor cruelte
that moveth me. Myne offyce is onely for to juge, departe, and to make the payment after every mannes ryghtfull deservynge. I susteyne all thynges in estate,
and without me there may no thynge be stablysshed. I am in God, and God is in
me, and we be as one selfe thynge.

"He that foloweth me maye not fayle, and my waye is sure. I teche to every
man and woman holsome understandynge yf he byleve me. And I teche hym
to chastyce, to knowe and to reprove hymselfe: fyrst to do to another that that
he wolde sholde be done to hym, to departe thynges without favoure, to saye
trouthe, to fle and hate lesynges and to put away all vycyous thynges.

"This vessell of fyne golde that thou seest in my ryght hande made after the
guyse of a rounde measure, God my Fader gave it me, and it serveth to measure
to every man his lyveray of suche meryte as he ought to have. It is marked with
the floure deluce of the Trynyte, and he yelded hym juste to porcyons; there maye
noo man complayne of my measure. But these men of the worlde have other measures whiche they saye dependeth and cometh of myne, but falsely they measure,
often tymes under shadowe of me. And there theyr measure is not alwaye juste:
other it is too large to some, or [Cc4r] too lytel to some others.

"I myght holde longe tale ynoughe of the propryetees of myne offyce, but
shortly for to say I am an especyall amonge other vertues, for al they referre them
to me. And amonge us .iii. ladyes that thou seest here, we be as one selfe thynge.
And we may none of us do without other: and that the fyrst dysposeth, the seconde
ordeyneth and putteth it to werke, and then I that am the thyrde perfourmeth it

euvre, et puis moy la troisiesme parachieve[1] la chose et la termine. Si suis par le voloir de nous troys establie a ton aide pour perfaire[2] ta cité, et sera mon office de faire les haulx combles, des tours, des mansions, et des heberges[3] qui tous seront faiz de fin or reluisant. Et la te peupleray de tres dignes dames, et seront celles qui aront la prerogative et l'onneur[4] entre les autres [fol. 12r b] femmes comme les plus excellentes. Et la te rendray[5] par ton meismes aide parfaicte fortifiee et closes de fortes portes que je yray quere ou ciel et les clefs entre tes mains te livreray."

## *Chapitre 7*    Dit[6] Christine comment elle parla au[x][7] .iii. dames

Les[8] paroles dessus dictes finees que j'os de toutes les .iii. dames escoutees par grant entente, et qui de moy orent fortraicte entirrement la desplaisance que ains leur venue eue avoye, soubdainement me gitay a leurs piez—non mie seulement a genoulx, mais toute estendue pour leur grant excellence—baisant la terre d'environ leurs piez, les aourant comme deesses de gloire commençay a elles ainsi mon oroison:

"O, dames de souveraine digneté, lueurs des cieulx et enluminement de la terre, fontaines [fol. 12v a] de paradis, et la joye des beneurez, dont est venue a vostre haultece telle humilité que daingnié avez descendre de voz pontificaulx sieges et resplendissans trosnes pour venir ou tabernacle troublé et obscur de la simple et ignorant estudiante? Qui pourra rendre graces souffisentes a tel benefice! Et qui ja avez, par la pluie et rousee de vostre doulce parole sur moy descendue, percee et atrempee la secheresse de mon entendement, si qu'il se sent des maintenant prest de germer et gitter hors plantes nouvelles, disposees a porter fruit de proffitable vertu et delictable saveur.

"Comment sera fait en[9] moy tel grace que je recepvray don selon vostre parole de bastir et faire orendroit au monde nouvelle cité? Je ne suis mie saint Thomas l'Apostre, qui au roy de [fol. 12v b] Inde par grace divine fist ou ciel un riche palais. Ne mon foible sens ne scet ne congnoist l'art, ne les mesures ne estudié ne l'ay, ne la pratique[10] de massonner; et se ces choses par possibilité de

---

[1] parachieve] parcheve
[2] perfaire] parfaire et achever
[3] des mansions, et des heberges] et des souveraines mansions et heberges
[4] tres dignes dames . . . l'onneur] de dignes dames avec la haulte Royne qui je t'i amenray, et ycelle sera l'onneur et la prerogative
[5] Et la te rendray] Et ainsi te rendray ta cité
[6] Dit] Ci dit
[7] au[x] : *au*
[8] Les] Ces
[9] en] a
[10] ne l'ay, ne la pratique] ne a la science, ne la pratique

and bryngeth it to ende. Thus am I stabled to helpe thee by the wyll of us thre perfytely to make thy cyte. And myne offyce shall be to make the hyghe roffes of thy towres, of the mansyons and of the herbegages whiche shall be of fyne golde shynynge bryght. And I shall people it of ryght worthy ladyes, and they shal be suche that shall have the prerogatyve and the honoure amonge these other women as the moost excellen[t]es.[1] And there I shall yelde thee by thyne owne helpe parfyte fortefyenge and closynge of stronge gates, the whiche I shall go seke in heven, and I shall delyver unto thee the keyes with myne owne handes."

*Chapter 7*      **Here Christine telleth howe she spake to[2] the .iii. ladyes**

These wordes abovesayd ended, whiche I had herkened by grete entente of these .iii. ladyes, whiche had drawne fro me entyerly the dyspleasaunce that I had before theyr comynge, [Cc4v] sodaynly I fell downe at theyr feete, not onely on knees but all flatte for theyr grete excellence, kyssynge the erthe aboute theyr feete, worshyppynge theym as goddesses. I began myne oryson of praysynge of them in this wyse:

"O, lady of soverayne dygnyte! Lanternesse of heven, gyvynge lyght to all the erthe! Welles of paradyse, and the joy of them that ben blessyd! Wherof is come to your hyghnesse suche humylyte that ye have vouchedsaufe to come frome your hyghe syeges and shynynge trones into the troubled tabernacle and darke of a symple and an ygnoraunt studye, whiche maye not yelde covenable thankynges to suche a benefyce? And whiche have by the rayne of the dewe of your swete wordes fallen upon me departed and tempered the drynesse of myne understandynge, so that it feleth hym nowe redy to burgyn and put out newe plantes, dysposed to bere fruyte of profytable vertue and delectable smellynge.

"Howe shal it be done in me suche grace that I shall receyve the gyfte after your worde, to make and fortefye nowe ryght in this worlde suche a newe cyte? I am not Saynt Thomas the Appostle that made by devyne grace in heven a ryche palays to the kynge of Ynde. Nor my feble wytte can not, ne knoweth not the crafte, ne measures, ne the studye, nor the pratyke of buyldynge. And yf these thynges by possybylyte of connynge were nowe in myne understandynge, where

---

[1] excellen[t]es : *excellences*
[2] to : *to to*

science estoient ores en mon entendement, ou seroit prise force souffisante a mon
foible corps femmenin pour mettre a oeuvre si grant chose? Mais toutevoyes,
mes tres redoubtes dames, combien que l'admiracion de ceste nouvelleté me soit
estrange, sçay je bien que riens n'est impossible quant a Dieu, et ne doye doubter
que quelconques choses qui soyent par le conseil et aide de vous .iii. entreprises
ne soient bien et bel terminees. Si loue Dieu de toute ma poissance et vous, mes
dames, qui tant honnouree m'avez qu'establie [fol. 13r a] suis a si noble comission,
laquelle reçoy par tres grant leesce. Et voy cy vostre chamberire, preste d'obeir: or
commandez selon voz plaisirs."[1]

*Chapitre 8*      **Dit[2] Christine comment par le commandement et aide
                  de Raison elle commença a fouir en terre[3] pour faire [les
                  fondemens][4]**

Adonc respondi Dame Raison et dist: "Or sus, fille, sans plus attendre, alons au[5]
Champ des Escriptures. La sera fondee la Cité des Dames en païs plain et fertile,
la ou tous fruis et doulces rivieres sont trouvees, et ou la terre habonde de toutes
bonnes choses. Pren la pioche de ton entendement et fouis fort et fay grant fosse
tout par tout ou tu verras les traces de ma ligne, et je t'aideray a porter hors la terre
a mes propres espaules."
      Adonc pour obeir a son commandement me dreçay [fol. 13r b] appertement,
me sentant par la vertu d'elles trop plus forte et plus legiere que devant n'estoie. Si
ala devant et moy aprés et nous venues au[6] dit champ, pris a fossoier et fouir selon
son signe a tout la pioche d'inquisicion. Et fu mon premiere ouvrage fait ainsi:
      "Dame, bien me souvient que cy devant m'avez dit appliquant au propos de ce
que plusieurs hommes ont tant blasmees et blasment generaument les condicions
des femmes, que *l'or plus est en la fournaise, plus s'affine*; qui est a entendre, que plus
sont blasmees a tort, et plus croite[7] le merite de leur gloire. Mais je vous pry, dictes
moy pour quoy ce est, et dont vient la cause, que tant de divers aucteurs ont parlé
contre elles en leurs livres, puis que je [fol. 13v a] sens des ja de vous[8] que c'este a
tort: ou se Nature les y encline, ou se par haine le font, et dont sourt celle chose?"

---

    [1]  selon voz plaisirs] je obeiray et soit fait de moy selon voz paroles
    [2]  Dit] Ci dit
    [3]  en terre] la terre
    [4]  [les fondemens] : *omitted*] les fondemens
    [5]  au] ou
    [6]  au] ou
    [7]  croite] croist
    [8]  des ja de vous] de vous des ja

sholde be taken suffycyent strengthe in my feble woman's body to put so grete a thynge [Dd1r] to werke? Yet nevertheles, my ryght redoubted ladyes, howe be it that the mervayllynge of these newe tydynges be straunge to me, I knowe well that there is nothynge impossyble as to God. And I ought not doubte that what thynges that ever be taken on hande by the counsayle and helpe of you thre, but that they be wel and fayre ended. Thus worshypped be God with al my power — and you, my ladyes, that so moche have worshypped me that I am stabled to so noble a commyssyon, the whiche I receyve with grete gladnesse. And se here your chamberere redy to obey: nowe commaunde after your pleasure."

*Chapter 8*     **Here Christine telleth howe, by the commaundement of Dame Reason, she began to dygge the erthe to make the foundement**

Reason, the noble lady, then answered and sayd: "Nowe ryse, doughter, without more abydynge; go we into the Felde of Scryptures. There shall be founded the Cyte of Ladyes in a playne countre and fruytefull, there where all fruytes and swete waters ben founde and where the grounde haboundeth of all good thynges. Take the pycoys of thyne understandynge and dygge strongly, and make a grete dyke aboute where thou seest the trace of my lyne; and I shall helpe thee to bere out the erthe upon myne owne sholders."

And then for [Dd1v] to obeye to theyr commaundemente I dressed me lyghtly, felynge myselfe by the vertue of them more stronge and more lyght than I was before. So she wente before and I after, and we came into the foresayd felde. I began to dyke and dygge after her sygne with the picoys of inquisycyon, and my fyrst worke was done in this wyse:

"Madame, me thynketh well that ye have sayd to me before applyenge to the purpose of that that many men have so moche blamed and blameth generally the condycions of women, that *the golde the more it is in the fornayce, the more it fyneth hym*, whiche is to understonde that the more they be blamed wrongfully, the more encreaseth theyr meryte of theyr praysynge. Yet I pray you, tell me wherfore it is and whens cometh the cause that so many dyvers auctours have spoken agaynst them in theyr bokes, syth that I fele nowe that it is of wronge: whether that Nature enclyne them, or yf they doo it for hate? And whens ryseth the cause?"

Lors elle respont ainsi:[1] "Fille, pour te donner voye d'entrer plus en perfont, je porteray hors ceste premiere hottee. Saches que ce ne vient mie de Nature, ains est tout au contraire, car il n'est ou monde nul si grant ne si fort liam comme est cellui de la grant amour que Nature par voulenté de Dieu met entre homme et femme. Mais diverses et differenciees sont les causes qui ont meu et meuvent plusieurs hommes a blasmer les femmes, et mesmement les aucteurs en leur livres ainsi que tu l'as trouvé.

"Car les aucuns l'ont fait en bonne entencion, c'est assavoir pour retraire les forvoiez hommes de la frequentacion de aucuns femmes qui sont vicieuses[2] et dissolues dont ilz sont assotez,[3] [fol. 13v b] ou pour les garder qu'ilz ne s'en assottent. Et afin que tout homme fuye vie lubre et luxurieuse, ilz ont blasmés generaulment toutes femmes pour leur cuidier faire de toutes abhominacion.

"Dame,"[4] dis je adoncques, "pardonnez moy se je romps ycy vostre parole. Doncques ont il[z][5] bien fait, puis que bonne entencion les y a meuz? Car l'entencion, dist on, juge l'omme."

"C'est mal pris belle fille," dit elle, "car ignorance grasse ne fait mie a excuser. Se on te occioit en bonne entente et par fol cuidier, seroit ce donc bien fait? Mais ont en ce qui[6] qu'ilz soient usé de mauvais droit, car faire grief et prejudice a une partie pour cuidier secourir a un[7] autre n'est pas equité, et de blasmer tous les meurs femmenins au contraire de verité, si que je te monstreray par l'experience, [fol. 14r a] non obstant le feissent[8] en entente de retraire les folz de folie. Et ainsi[9] que se je blasmoye le feu, qui est element tres bon et tres neccessaire pour tant se aucuns s'i bruslent; et aussi l'eaue pour se ce[10] on s'i noie; et semblablement se pourroit dire de toutes bonnes choses de quoy on puet et bien et mal user — toutevoies, ne les doit on mie[11] blasmer pour tant se les folz en abusent, et ces poins as tu te mesmes touchié[12] autre part en tes dictiez.

"Mais yceulx qui ainsi ont parlé abondamment, quelque fust leur entente, ilz ont pris leur propos sur le large pour seulement venir a leur entente. Tout ainsi que fait cellui qui se fait taillier longue et large robe en[13] meismes la grant piece de

---

[1] elle respont ainsi] celle respont
[2] qui sont vicieuses] vicieuses
[3] sont assotez] peuent estre assottées
[4] Dame] Dames
[5] il[z] : *il*
[6] ce qui] ce faisant qui
[7] un] une
[8] non obstant le feissent] poson que ilz l'ayent fait
[9] Et ainsi] est aussi
[10] se ce] ce se
[11] mie] pas
[12] as tu te mesmes touchié] toy mesmes assez bien touchié
[13] en] a

Than she answered thus: "Doughter, for to gyve thee waye to goo in more deper, I shall bere out this fyrst to be borne out. Knowe that it cometh not of Nature, but it is all the contrary. For there is in the worlde no man so grete, ne so stronge, as he is of the grete love that Nature by the wyll of God putteth bytwene man and woman. But the causes ben dyvers and indyfferent that hath moved and moveth many dyvers men to blame women, and the same wyse the auctours in theyr bokes as that thou hast founde. [Dd2r]

"For some have done it in good entente; that is to knowe, for to drawe agayne these men that be out of the waye by the hauntynge of dyvers women that ben vycyous and lyght, wherof they be assotted, other to kepe them that they be not assotted. And to the entente that every man sholde fle the lyfe that is lecherous and foule, they have blamed all women generally for theyr trowynge to do of al abhomynacyons."

"Madame," sayd I then, "pardon me yf I yelde you here your worde. Then have they done well, syth that good entente hathe moved them? For it is sayd that the entente jugeth the man."

"Fayre doughter, that is evyll taken," sayd she. "For ygnoraunce maketh not one to excuse hym yf he slewe a man in good entente, and by his folysshe trowynge, then sholde it be well done? Yet whatsoever they be, as in that they have used of evyll ryght for why to do grevaunce and prejudyce to one partye to trowe to socoure another, it is no ryght—and to blame al the condycyons of women to the contrary of trouthe so as I shal shewe thee by experyence, not-withstandynge they sholde do it in the entente to withdrawe these foles from folye. And also that yf I blame the fyre, whiche is ryght a good element and ryght necessary, bycause that some men were brente therin? And also the water, for that some men ben drowned in it? And the same wyse yf one sholde saye of all good thynges whiche a man may use bothe wel and evyll, no man ought to blame them, thoughe these foles abuse them! And these poyntes thou haste touched thyselfe in thy [Dd2v] sayenges.

"Yet they that so hath spoken habundauntly, whatsoever was theyr entente, they have taken theyr purpose upon the large onely to come to theyr entente, so as he dothe that maketh hym to cutte a longe and a large gowne of a pece of

drap, qui riens ne lui coste et que nul ne lui contredit: si prent et s'atribue l'autrui droit a son usage. Mais si comme tu as autreffois [fol. 14r b] assez bien dit, se yceulx eussent quis les voies[1] de retraire les hommes de folie et de les garder que ilz ne s'i enlaçassent par blasmer la vie et les meurs de celles, lesquelles se demonstrent vicieuses et dissolues; comme il ne soit chose en ce monde qui plus face a fuir, a droicte verité dire, que fait la mauvaise femme dissolue et perverse, si comme monstre,[2] qui est chose contrefaicte et hors de sa propre condicion naturelle, qui doit estre simple, coye, et honneste. Je consens bien que souverainement aroient edifié bon et bel ouvrage; mais de blasmer toutes, ou tant en y a[3] de tres excellentes? Je te promet que ce ne vint oncques de moy, et qu'en ce tres grandement faillirent et faillent tous ceulx qui les en suivent. Si gettez hors ces ourdes pierres braçonneuses et noires de ton ouvrage, car ja ne serviront [fol. 14v a] ne seront[4] mises ou bel edifice de ta cité.

"Aultres hommes ont blasmé femmes pour autres causes, car aux aucuns est venu par leurs propres vices, et les autres y ont esté meuz par le deffault de leur mesmes corps; les autres par pure envie; aucuns aultres pour delectacion que de leur propre condicion ont de mesdire. Autres, pour monstrer que ilz ont beaucop veu d'escriptures, se fondent sur ce que ilz ont trouvé en livres, et dient aprés les aultres et alleguent les aucteurs.

"Ceulx a qui il est venu de leurs propres vices sont hommes qui ont usé leur joenece en vie dissolue et habondé en plusieurs amours de diverses femmes. Si sont ruses par divers[5] cas qui leur sont avenus et ja sont envieillis en leurs pechiez, sans repentence. Mais ilz[6] ont [fol. 14v b] regrait a leurs folies passees et vie dissolue que ilz ont menee en leurs temps, car[7] Nature est refroidiee en eulx qui ne sueffre a la voulenté du courage mettre a effect ce que l'appetit, sans poissance, vouldroit. Si ont dueil quant ilz voyent que la vie que ilz souloient appeller 'bon temps' est faillie pour eulx, et que les joeunes, qui sont ores comme ilz souloient estre, ont le temps, ce leur semble. Si ne scevent comment evaporer[8] et mettre hors leur tristece fors par blasmer les femmes, par les cuidier faire aux autres desplaire. Et voit on communement telx vieillars parler lubrument et deshonnestement, ainsi que tu le pues veoir proprement de Matheolus, qui confesse lui mesmes que il estoit vieillart plein de voulenté [fol. 15r a] et non poissance. Si pueux par lui bien esprouver vray ce que je te dis, et croy fermement que semblablement est il de mains aultres.

---

[1] les voies] les voyes et les manieres
[2] monstre] monstre en nature
[3] y a] a
[4] ne serviront ne seront] ne seront
[5] divers] maint
[6] Mais ilz] et
[7] que ilz ont menee en leurs temps, car] qu'en leur temps ont menee, mais
[8] evaporer] et apporter et mettre

cloth that cost hym nought, and no man saythe the contrary: so he taketh and graunteth the ryght of another to his usage. Yet as thou haste sayd other tymes ynowe, if thou sholde have sought the wayes to withdrawe these men from folye and to kepe them that they laboure not in vayne, to blame the lyfe and the condycyons of theym, the whiche sheweth them vycyous and lyght, as there is nothyng in the worlde that maketh one more to fle (to say the ryght trouthe) as dothe a shrewde woman, lyght and cursed as it showeth, whiche is a thynge counterfayte and out of her propre condycyon naturall, whiche ought to be symple, pryvy, and honest, I consente well that they sholde have buylded soveraynely a good and fayre worke. But to blame *all* where there ben so many ryght excellent? I promyse thee that it came never of me, but that they fayled and fayle gretely, and al they that foloweth them. So cast out these foule stones, ragged and blacke, out of thy werke: for they shall never serve, ne shal not be put in good buyldynge of thy cyte.

"Other men have blamed women for other causes, for to some it is come of theyr owne vyces, and some be moved for the defaute of theyr owne ladyes, others for pure envye; some others for delectacyon that [Dd3r] of theyr propre condycyon hath to saye shrewdely; other for to showe that they have sene ynoughe of scrypture, and so they grounded them on that that they have founde in bokes and speketh after those others and aledge them for auctours.

"Those the whiche it is come of theyr propre vyces ben men that have used theyr youthe in the dyssolute lyfe and habounded them in many dyvers loves of dyvers women. Thus they are borne up by dyvers causes whiche taketh no hede of themselfe and waxeth olde in theyr synnes without repentaunce. Yet take they sorowe to theyr passed folyes and dyssolute lyfe that they have ledde in theyr tyme, for Nature is waxed colde in them whiche suffreth theym not to put theyr courage to effecte after theyr wyl that the appetyte wolde without puyssaunce. So they have sorowe when they se that the lyfe that they were wonte to calle theyr good tyme is faylled from them, and that the yonge men that ben nowe have the tyme as they were wonte to have. Thus they knowe not howe to put away theyr sorowe but to blame women by theyr trowynge to do dyspleasaunce to others. And one saythe communely suche olde men speke foule and dyshonestly, soo as thou mayst se them and properly of Matheolus, whiche confesseth hymselfe that he was olde, full of wyll, and no power. And thou mayst prove it true by hym that I have sayd to thee, and byleve it stably that it is in the same wyse of others.

"Mais ces vieillars ainsi corrompus, qui sont comme la meselerie qui garir ne puet, ne sont mie des bons preudeshommes ancians que j'ay parfois en vertu,[1] en laquel bouche[2] selon le courage sont toutes paroles de bon exemple, honnestes, et discretes, et qui[3] heent tout meffait et tout mesdit. Et ceulx ne blasment[4] ne diffament femmes ne hommes, mais oil bien tous vices en general, conseillent a les fuir et suivre[5] droicte voye.

"Ceulx qui ont esté meuz par le deffault de leur propre corps sont aucuns impotens et difformés de leurs membres qui ont l'entendement agu et malicieux; et le dueil de leur [fol. 15r b] impotence n'ont sceu autrement vengier que par blasmer celles de qui joye vient a plusieurs, par cuidier[6] destourner le plaisir a aultrui dont[7] ilz ne peuent en leur personne user.

"Ceulx qui par envie les ont blasmés sont aucuns meschans hommes qui ont veu et cogneu[8] plusieurs femmes de plus grant entendement et plus nobles de meurs que ilz ne sont.[9] Et, pour ce, leur grant envie les a meuz a blasmer toutes femmes, cuidant reprimer et apeticier la gloire et los d'elles. Tout ainsi que a fait, ne sçay quel homme en son[10] dictié que il claime et intitule 'de philosophie' ou quel moult il se travaille de prouver comment il n'apartient que quelconques femmes soit par homme[11] moult honnourés, et dit que ceulx qui si grant compte en font pervertissent [fol. 15v a] le nom de son livre: c'est assavoir, que de *philosophie* font *philosopholie*.[12] Mais je te promet et affie que lui mesmes par la deduction pleine de mençonges du proces que il y tient en fait une droit phisopholie.[13]

"Ceulx qui par Nature sont mesdisans, n'est merveille, quant ilz blasment chascun, se ilz mesdient des femmes. Et toutevoyes te promez je qu'a homme qui mesdit voulentiers[14] de femme vient de tres grant vilté de courage, car il fait contre Raison et contre Nature: contre Raison, en tant que il est tres ingrat et mal cognoiscent des grans benefices que femme[15] lui a fais, si grans que il ne pourroit

---

[1] que j'ay parfois en vertu] que je parfais en vertu et sagece. Car tous les vieulx ne sont pas de tele corrumpue voulenté, et dommage seroit

[2] bouche] bouche des bons

[3] qui] yceulx

[4] ceulx ne blasment] ne blasment

[5] mais oil bien . . . suivre] les vices heent et les blasment en general sanz nullui encoulper ne chargier, conseillent fuyr le mal, suivre les vertus, et aler

[6] par cuidier] et ainsi ont cuidié

[7] dont] lequel

[8] cogneu] apperceu

[9] ne sont] ne sont si en ont eu dueil et desdaing

[10] son] un sien

[11] soit par homme] soient par hommes

[12] philosopholie] phisofolie

[13] en fait une droit phisopholie] fait du contenu de son livre une droite phisofolie

[14] a homme qui mesdit voulentiers] a tout homme qui voulentiers mesdit

[15] benefices que femme] biens que femmes

"But these olde men thus defouled, whiche be as the lyfe [Dd3v] of a mesell that may not be heled, [are not][1] of the good auncyent men that I have made perfyte in vertue, in the mouthe of whome after theyr courage all the wordes ben of good ensamp[l]e,[2] honest and dyscrete, and whiche hateth all evyll doynge and evyll sayenge. And they defame not ne blame nother men ne women but hateth all vyces in generall, counsaylynge to fle them and folowe the ryght waye.

"Those that have ben moved by defaute of theyr owne body ben some impotent and dyfformed of theyr membres that have sharpe and malycyous understandynge. And the sorowe of theyr impotencye can none otherwyse advenge them but to blame them of whome cometh joye to many, by trowynge to tourne away the pleasaunce of others when they may not use it in theyr owne persone.

"Those that have blamed them by envye ben some myschevous men that have sene and knowne dyvers women of gretter understandynge and more noble of condycyon than they be that blameth them. And therfore theyr grete envye hath moved them to blame all women, trowynge to withdrawe and to make lesse theyr worshyp and praysynge. All this that he hath done, I wote not what man in his sayenge that he claymeth tytle of 'phylosophy' in whiche he travayleth hym moche to prove howe it perteyneth not that every woman be worshypped moche by man, and sayth that they that maketh so moche of them chaungeth wrongfully the name of his boke; that is to say, of *phylosophye* maketh *phylosopholy*. [Dd4r] But I promyse thee and afferme that he hymselfe, by the bryngynge forthe of that processe full of lesynges that he holdeth, maketh a ryght phylosopholy.

"Those that of nature are evyll sayers, it is no mervayle whan they blame every man thoughe they saye evyll of women. And alwayes this I promyse thee, that a man that saythe evyll wylfully of women, it cometh of ryght grete age of courage, for he dothe agaynst reason and agaynst kynde. Agaynst reason, insomoche that he is ryght unkynde and evyll knowynge of the grete benefeytes that women hath done to hym, so grete that he may not yelde them agayne, and by so

---

[1] heled, [are not] of : *heled of*
[2] ensamp[l]e : *ensampre*

rendre, et par tant de fois et continuelment a neccessité que elle lui face; contr[e][1] Nature en ce que il n'est beste mue quelconques [fol. 15v b] ne oisel qui naturelment n'aime chierement son per, c'est la femmelle. Si est bien chose desnaturee quant homme raisonnable fait au contraire.

"Et si comme il n'est si digne ouvrage, tout[2] soit fait de bon maistre, que aucuns (non obstant que petit y sachent) n'aient voulu et ne veulent[3] contrefaire, sont maint que[4] se veulent mesler de dictier, et leur semble que ilz ne pouent mesprendre, puis que autres ont dit en livres ce qu'ilz veulent dire, et commencent ainsy a mesdire.[5] J'en sçay aucuns d'yceulx qui[6] se veullent entremettre de parler en faisant dictiez d'eaue doulce sans sel[7] telz comme qui font[8] balades sans sentement, parlant des meurs des femmes ou de seigneurs ou d'aultre gent, et ilz ne scevent pas eulx [fol. 16r a] mesmes cognoistre ne aviser leurs chetives inclinacions et deffaulx. Et[9] les simples gens qui sont ignorans comme eulx dient que c'est le mieulx fait du monde."

*Chapitre 9*     Comment[10] Christine fouissoit en terre, qui est a entendre les questions qu'elle faisoit a Raison, et comment Raison lui respondoit

"Or t'ay preparé et ordonné grant ouvrage, si penses de fouir[11] en terre selon la pourtraiture de mon signe."

Et adonc moy, pour obeir a son commandement, frappay sus a tout mon pic en tel maniere: "Dame, dont vint a Ovide, qui est reputé entre les pouetes comme le plus souverain (non obstant que assez de clers dient, et mon jugement le consent[12] toutevoies soubz vostre correccion que trop [fol. 16r b] plus fait a louer Virgile, et de plus grant efficace me semblent ses dis) qui les femmes tant blasma[13]

---

[1] contr[e] : *contra*

[2] tout] tant

[3] aucuns . . . ne veulent] aucuns n'ayent voulu et veulent

[4] que] qui

[5] commencent ainsy a mesdire] comme ce me dire

[6] d'yceulx qui] d'yceulz

[7] d'eaue doulce] de eaue

[8] qui font] quieulx ou

[9] de seigneurs . . . et deffaulx. Et] des princes, ou d'autre gent, et eulx mesmes ne se scevent congnoistre ne corriger leurs chetifs meurs et inclinacions. Mais

[10] Comment] Ci dit comment

[11] de fouir] a continuer de fouyr

[12] comme le plus souverain . . . consent] le plus souverain quoy que plusieurs et moy mesmes m'y consens

[13] et de plus grant efficace me semblent ses dis qui les femmes tant blasma] que il tant blasma femmes

often tymes and contynuelly that she dothe to hym of necessyte. Ayenst kynde, in that that there is no dome beest ne byrde but naturally it loveth derely theyr fader and moder. So it is a thynge out of kynde whan a reasonable man dothe the contrary.

"And so as there is so worthy a werke al be it that it be made by a good mayster but some, notwithstandynge that they can but lytell, they wyll counterfeyte. There ben many that medle them of endytynge, and they seme that they may not do amysse syth that others have sayd in theyr bokes that that they wolde say. And as that men saythe, I knowe some of theym that wyll entremete and medle for to speke in makynge of dyttyes of fresshe water without salte: suche ben theyr wrytynges and theyr balades without understandynge or felynge, and spekynge of the condycyons of women or of lordes [Dd4v] or of other peo[p]le,[1] and they cannot knowe themselfe nor advyse theyr caytyvous inclynacyons and defautes. And the symple people, whiche ben ygnoraunt as they, saye that it is the beste done thynge in the worlde."

## Chapter 9     Here Christine telleth howe she dygged in the erthe, whiche is to understande the questyons that she made to Reason; and howe Reason answered her

"Nowe I have arayed and ordeyned grete worke; so thynke thou to dygge in the erthe after the pourtrayenge of my sygne."

And then, to obeye her commaundement, I smote with all my myght in this manere: "Madame, whens came it to Ovyde — that is of reputacyon amonge poetes as one of the moost soverayne, notwithstandynge that dyvers clerkes say and my jugement accordeth to the same, always under your correccyon, that Vyrgyle was more to prayse and his wrytynges of more spedefulnesse than

---

[1] peo[p]le : *peole*

en plusieurs de ses dictiez, si comme ou livre que il fist que il appelle *De l'art d'amours*, et aussi en autres[1] de ses volumes?"

*Response*: "Ovide fu homme soubtil en l'art et science de poesie, et moult ot grant entendement.[2] Toutevoies, son corps laissa couler en toute vanité et delit de ch[a]r,[3] non mie en une seule amour mais abandonné a toutes femmes se il peust, ne il ne garda mesure ne loyaulté a nulle. Tant[4] comme il pot en sa joeunesce hanta celle vie de laquel chose, a la perfin, il en[5] ot le guerdon et la paye qui a tel cas affiert: c'est assavoir, diffamme et perte de biens et de membres. Car pour sa grant lubrieté, tant [fol. 16v a] de fait comme de parole, conseillant aux jounes mener semblable vie que il mennoit, il en fu envoié[6] en exil.

"*Item*, comme il avenist aprés que par faveur d'aucuns joeunes poissans Rommains,[7] il fust rappellé de l'exil et ne se gardast mie aprés de rencheoir[8] ou mesfait dont la coulpe l'avoit ja aucunement pugny, fu par ses demerites chatiez et disserviez[9] de ses membres. Si est au propos que cy dessus te disoie, car quant il vid que plus ne pourroit mener la vie ou tant se souloit delicter, adonc prist fort a blasmer les femmes par ses soubtilles raisons et par ce s'efforça de les faire aux autres desplaire."

"Dame, bien dictes. Mais je vis un livre d'un autre auteur ytalien, je croy du païs ou des marches de Toscane, qui [fol. 16v b] s'appelle Ceco d'Ascoli, qui en un chappitre en dit abhominacions merveilleuses plus que nul autre, telles[10] que ilz ne font a reciter de personne qui ait entendement."

*Response*: "Se Ceco d'Ascoli dist mal de toutes femmes, fille, ne t'en esmerveilles, car toutes les abhominoit et avoit en haine et desplaisance, et semblablement par son orrible mauvaistié les vouloit faire desplaire et hair a tous hommes. Si en ot le loyer selon son merite, car par la desserte de son criminel vice fu ars en feu deshonnestement."

"Un autre petit livre en latin vi, dame, qui se nomme *Du Secret des femmes*, qui dit de la composicion de leurs corps naturel moult de grans deffaulx."

*Response*: "Tu pueux cognoistre [fol. 17r a] par toy mesmes sans nulle autre preuve que cellui livre fu fait a voulenté et fainctement coulouré, car se tu l'as

---

[1] en autres] en cellui que il nomma *De Remede d'amours*, et en autres
[2] grant entendement] grant et vif entendement en ce a quoy il s'occupa
[3] ch[a]r : *cher*
[4] ne garda mesure ne loyaulté a nulle. Tant] ne il n'y garda mesure ne loyauté ne tenoit a nulle. Et tant
[5] il en] on
[6] comme de parole . . . en fu envoié] en lui mesmes comme de parole en conseillant aux autres mener par semblable vie que il menoit, il en fu mené
[7] Rommains] Rommains, ses aderans
[8] de rencheoir] d'encheoir
[9] chatiez et disserviez] chastrez et difformez
[10] telles] et teles

his—whiche blamed women so moche in many of his dyttyes as in the boke that
he made whiche is called the *Crafte of Love*, and also in other of his volumes."

*Answere*: "Ovide was a subtyll man in the crafte and scyence of poetrye and
had grete understandynge, all be it he lete his body slyppe into all vanyte and
delyte of flesshe—not onely in one love, but habandoned hymselfe to al [Dd5r]
women so as he myght. Nor he kepte not measure, nor trouthe to no woman,
but haunted this lyfe in his youthe as lpnge as he myght. For the whiche at the
last he had the rewarde and payment that unto suche a case perteyneth, that
is to knowe sclaundre, losse of goodes, and membres. Wherfore for his grete
voluptuousnesse, as well in dede as in worde, counsayllynge the yonge folke to
lede the same lyfe, he was sente into exyle.

"Also as it happened after that, by favoure of some yonge puyssaunt
Romaynes, he was called agayne fro exyle. And he kepte hym not after frome fallynge agayne in his evyll doynge wherof he was somwhat punysshed before. And
then he was chased and dyssevered frome his membres by his owne deserte. Thus
it is to the purpose that I sayd to thee above, for when he sawe that he myght not
lede the lyfe in the whiche he was wonte to delyte hym so moche, then he toke on
hym strongly to blame women by his subtyll reasons, and by that enforced hym
to dysprayse them to others."

"Madame, ye say wel. But I have sene a boke of another auctoure Italyen, I
suppose of the contray[1] or of the marches of Costane, whiche calleth hym Ceco
d'Astoly, that sayth in a chapytre mervayllous abhomynacyons more than ony
other, suche as be not to reherce of no persone that hathe understandynge."

*Answere*: "Thoughe Ceco d'Astoly saye evyll of all women, doughter, mervayle thee not, for he had all women in hate and dyspleasaunce. [Dd5v] And the
same wyse, by his horryble shrewdenesse, he wolde make them to dysplease and
to be hated of al men. So he was alowed after his meryte, for by the deservynge
of his cursed vyce he was brente in the fyre ryght dyshonestly."

"Another lytell boke in Latyne I sawe also, madame, that nameth hym the
*Secrete of Women*, whiche speketh of the makynge of theyr bodyes naturall many
grete defautes."

*Answere*: "Thou mayst knowe by thyselfe without ony other prove that that
boke was made at volentees and fayntly coloured as thou hast redde, whiche is

---

[1] contray : *contrary*

leu, ce t'est[1] chose manifeste que il est traictié tout de mençonges. Et quoy que aucuns dient que ce fu Aristote, ce[2] n'est mie a croire que tel philosophe se fust chargié de si faictes bourdes. Car par ce que les femmes peuent clerement par espreuve savoir que aucunes choses[3] qu'il touche ne sont mie vraies, ains pures bourdes, peuent elles conclure que les autres particularites dont il traicte sont droittes mençonges. Mais ne te souvient il que il dist a son commencement que ne sçay quel pape escomenia tout homme qui le liroit a femme, ou lui bailleroit a lire?"[4] [fol. 17r b]

"Dame, bien m'en souvient."

"Sces tu la malicieuse cause pour quoy celle bourde fu donnee a croire aux hommes bestiaulx et nyces au commencement de ce livre?"

"Dame, non, se ne le me dites."

"Ce fu afin que les femmes n'eussent cognoissance de ce livre et de ce qu'il contient. Car bien savoit celui qui le fist que se elles le lisoient ou ouoyent lire que bien saroient que bourdes sont, si le contrediroient et s'en moqueroient. Si voult l'aucteur qui le fist abejauner et frauder les hommes qui le liroient par celle voye."

"Dame, il me souvient qu'entre les autres choses que il dist, quant il a asses parlé de l'impotence, imperfeccion, et foiblece[5] qui est cause de former le corps femmenin ou ventre de la mere, que Nature [fol. 17v a] est aussi comme toute honteuse quant elle voit qu'elle a formé tel corps comme chose imperfaicte."

"Ha, la tres grant folie! Avises, doulce amie, l'aveuglement hors de toute raison qui mut a ce dire. Et comment Nature, qui est chamberiere de Dieu, est elle doncques plus grant maistresse que son maistre,[6] Dieu tout poissant, qui ou voult de sa pensee avoit très oncques la fourme d'omme et de femme quant vint a sa saincte voulenté de fourmer Adam du limon de la terre ou champ de Damas? Et puis quant il[7] l'ot fait, il le mena en paradis terrestre, qui estoit et est la plus digne place de ce bas monde. La endormi Adam, et de l'une de ses costes, afin que il amast la femme comme[8] sa propre char, fourma le corps de la femme. Si [fol. 17v b] n'ot pas honte le Souverain Ouvrier de faire et fourmer corps femmenin; et Nature s'en hontoioroit? Ha, la somme des folies de ce dire!

"Voire, et comment fut elle fourmee? Je ne sçay se tu le nottes: elle fu formee a l'ymage de Dieu. O, comment ose bouche mesdire de[9] si noble emprainte! Mais

---

[1]  leu ce t'est] veu ce te peut estre

[2]  ce] il

[3]  aucunes choses] aucune chose

[4]  lui bailleroit a lire] ou a lire lui bailleroit

[5]  l'impotence, imperfeccion, et foiblece] de l'impotence et foiblece

[6]  son maistre] son maistre dont lui vient tele auctorité

[7]  et puis quant il] et il

[8]  afin que il amast la femme comme] en signifiance que elle devoit estre coste lui et non mie a ses piez comme serve, et aussi que il l'amast comme

[9]  de] de vaissel qui porte

an open thynge to thee that it is drawne all of lesynges. And thoughe that some men saye that it was Arystotyll, that is not to byleve that suche a phylosophre was so charged with so false tales for by that that these women maye clerely prove and knowe that some thynges that he toucheth be not true but verye fables, thus they may conclude that these maters that he treateth of be very lesynges. But remembrest thou it not that he saythe at his begynnynge that I wote not what pope cursed every man that sholde rede it to ony woman, or take it them to rede?"

"Madame, I remembre it wel."

"Than knowest not thou the malycyous cause wherfore this jape was gyven to be byleved of bestyall men and nyce at the begynnynge of that boke?"

"Madame, nay, but yf ye tell it me."

"It was to the entente that women sholde not have no knowlege of that boke nor of that conteyned in hym. For he that made it knewe wel that yf they redde it or herde it redde, that they sholde [Dd6r] knowe well that it was but tryfles, so they sholde have spoken ayenst hym and mocked hym. Thus wolde the auctoure that made it mocke and begyle the men that sholde rede it by this way."

"Madame, I am remembred that amonge these other thynges that he hath sayd, when he hath spoken ynoughe of the impotence, imperfeccyon, and feblenes whiche is cause of mysshapynge of woman's body in the wombe of the moder, that Nature is ashamed when she sawe that she had fourmed suche a body as a thynge imperfyte."

"Ha, the grete foly, swete frende, and the grete blyndnesse out of all reason that moveth or styreth ony man to say it! And howe Nature, whiche is the chambryere of God, is she more maystres than her mayster, Almyghty God, whiche had the shap of man and woman in His thought when it came to His wyll to fourme Adam of the slyme of the erthe in the Felde of Damas? And when He had made hym, He brought hym into paradyse terrestre whiche was and is the worthyest place of this lowe worlde. And there Adam slepte, and of one of his rybbes to that entente that he sholde love woman as his owne flesshe, fourmed the body of the woman. So the moost Soverayne Werkeman had no shame to make and fourme the body of woman; and sholde Nature be ashamed therof? Ha, the grete some of folyes to saye that it is trewe!

"And howe was she fourmed? I wote not yf thou notest it: she was fourmed after the ymage of God. O, howe durste the mouthe say so evyl of so noble a

aucuns sont si folz que ilz cuident quant ilz oient parler que Dieu fist homme a son ymage, que ce soit a dire du corps materiel. Mais non est, car Dieu n'avoit pas lors pris corps humain; ains est a entendre de l'ame qui est esperit intellectuel et qui durera sans fin a la semblance de la Deité, laquelle ame Dieu crea et mist aussi bonne et aussi[1] noble et toute pareille au[2] corps femmenin [fol. 18r a] comme au[3] masculin. Mais encore a[4] la creacion du corps, la femme fu doncques faicte du Souverain Ouvrier. Et en quel place fut elle faicte? En paradis.[5] De quoy[6] fust ce? De vil matere? Non, mais de la tres plus noble que[7] oncques eust esté cree: c'estoit le corps[8] de quoy Dieu la fist."

"Dame, selon ce que[9] j'entens de vous, femme est moult noble chose. Mais toutevoyes dit Tulles que homme ne doit servir nulle femme, et que cellui qui le fait s'aville, car nul ne doit servir plus bas que[10] lui."

*Response*: "Eureux est cil qui sert a la Vierge, qui est pardessus tous les angelz, et cellui ou celle est le plus hault en qui plus a de vertus."[11]

"Dist[12] un des Catons, qui fut grant orateur, que se cest[13] monde fust sans femme, nous conversissions [fol. 18r b] avec les dieux."

*Response*: "Or pues tu bien veoir[14] la folie de cellui que on tint a sage, car par achoison de femme, homme regne avec Dieu. Et s'aucun veult dire[15] que il en fu bannis par femme pour cause de Dame Eve, je dy que trop plus hault degré a acquis par Marie qu'il ne perdi par Eve, quant humanité est conjoincte a la Deité, ce qu'il ne seroit mie se le mesfait de Eve ne fust avenu. Si se doit lever[16] homme et femme de celle mesprison, et qui[17] telle honneur lui est ensuivie: car de

---

[1]  et aussi] aussi

[2]  au] en

[3]  au] ou

[4]  encore a] a ancore parler de la creacion

[5]  paradis] paradis terrestre

[6]  De quoy] Dequelle chose

[7]  noble que] noble creature qui

[8]  le corps] le corps de l'omme

[9]  ce que] que

[10]  que] de

[11]  Response: Eureux . . . de vertus] Response: Cellui ou celle en qui plus a vertus est le plus hault; ne la haulteur ou abbaissement des gens ne gist mie es corps selon le sexe, mais en la perfeccion des meurs et des vertus. Et cellui est eureux qui sert a la Vierge qui est pardessus tous les anges

[12]  Dist] Dame ancore dit

[13]  se cest] se ce

[14]  pues tu bien veoir] peus tu veoir

[15]  avec Dieu. Et s'aucun veult dire] avecques Dieu. Et se aucun me dit

[16]  lever] louer

[17]  et qui] par laquelle

prynte! But some be so grete foles that they trowe when they here say that God [Dd6v] made man after His ymage, that it be to say of materyall body. But it is not so, for God had not then taken the body of man, but it is to understande of the soule whiche is a spyryte understandynge, the whiche shal endure without ende to the lykenes of the Deite, the whiche soule God made and put as good and as worthy and all even to the body of woman as of man. But yet as to the makynge of the body, the woman was made of the moost Soverayne Werkeman. And in what place was she made? In paradyse terrestre. Wherof came the 'foule matere' that she was made of? Nay, it was of the moost noble matere that ever was made: that was of the body that God made."

"Madame, after that that I fele of you, woman is ryght a noble thynge. But yet Tullyus sayth that a man sholde never serve a woman, and he that dothe it defouleth hymselfe for none ought to serve that that is lower than hymselfe."

*Answere*: "He is happy that serveth the Vyrgyne that is above al the aungelles, and he or she that is moost hyghe ought to serve her in whom all vertue habound-eth."

"Also, madame, one of the Cathons sayth, whiche that was a grete clerke, that yf the worlde had ben without [women][1] we sholde have ben conversaunt with goddes."

*Answere*: "Nowe mayst thou well se the foly of hym that men helde so sage, for by the encheson of woman men reygneth with God. And yf ony wolde saye that man was banysshed by woman by the cause of Dame Eve, I saye that he hathe goten more hyghe degre by Ou[r]e[2] [Ee1r] Lady Mary than he lost by Eve insomoche that the manhode is joyned to the Godhede, and that had not ben yf the trespace of Eve had not ben. So bothe man and woman ought to lyfte up themselfe from that defaute, and he that worshyppeth woman worshyppeth hymselfe. For of so moche as mannes nature fell more lower by suche a creature

---

[1] without [women] we : *without we*
[2] Ou[r]e : *oue*

tant comme[1] nature humaine trebucha plus bas par creature, a elle esté relevee plus hault par creature.[2] Et de converser avec les dieux comme dit cellui Caton se femme n'estoit, il dist plus vray que il ne cuidoit car il estoit payen. [fol. 18v a] Et entre eulx de celle loy entendoient aussi bien dieux estre en enfer comme ou ciel: c'est assavoir les deables, que ilz appelloient dieux d'enfer. Si n'est mie bourde que avec yceulx dieux conversassent les hommes se Marie ne fust."

*Chapitre 10*     **Encore de ce mesmes altercacions et responses**

"Encore[3] dit ycellui Caton Uticensis que la femme qui plaist a l'ome naturelment ressemble a la rose qui plaisant est a veoir, mais l'espine est dessoubz qui point."

*Response*: "De rechief dit plus vray qu'il ne cuida ycellui Caton, car toute bonne, honneste[4] femme et de belle vie doit estre et est une des plus plaisans choses a veoir qui soit. Et toutevoyes y est[5] l'espine de paour de mesprendre et de [fol. 18v b] componction ou courage de telle femme qui ne s'en part, et ce la fait tenir coye, et rassise,[6] et en cremeur. Et c'est ce qui la garde."

"Pluseurs aucteurs ont tesmoingné que femmes sont par nature lecherresses."[7]

"Fille, tu as par maintes fois ouy recorder le proverbe qui dit: *Ce que Nature donne, nul ne puet tollir*. Si seroit moult grant merveille que naturelment elles y fussent tant enclines. Et que toutevoyes elles fussent pou ou nyant trouvees es lieux ou se vendent friandises[8] et lecheries, comme es tavernes et autres lieux ad ce ordennez. La sont cler semmees, et se aucun vouloit[9] respondre que honte les en garde, je dis que ce n'est mie vray que autre chose les en garde fors leur [fol. 19r a] condicion, qui n'y est mie encline. Et poson que enclines y fussent, et que honte leur donnast tel resistence contre inclinacion naturele, que ceste vertu et constance leur doit tourner a grant louenge.

"Et ad ce propos, ne te souvient il mie que[10] n'a pas moult que si comme[11] tu estoies a un jour de feste a la porte de ton hostel devisant avecques une honnourable damoiselle, ta voisine, et tu avisas un homme yssant d'une taverne qui aloit,

---

[1] comme] que
[2] trebucha ... creature] trebuche ... Createur
[3] Encore] Encore de rechief
[4] bonne, honneste] bonne et honneste
[5] y est] est
[6] coye et rassise] quoye rassise
[7] Pluseurs ... lecherresses] Dame, est il vray aucuns aucteurs ont tesmoignié que femmes sont par nature lecharresses et curieuses en leurs mengiers?
[8] friandises] les friandises
[9] vouloit] veult
[10] mie que] que
[11] que si comme] si que

as woman, by woman she is lyfte up agayne more hygher. And to be conversaunt with goddes, as Caton sayth yf woman had not be, he sayd more truer than he wende for he was a paynyme, and amonge them of that lawe they understode as well goddes to be in helle as in heven, that is to knowe the devylles whiche they called theyr goddes of helle. So it is no jape that men sholde have ben conversaunt with *those* goddes yf Our Lady Mary had not ben."

## *Chapter 10*      Also of the same altrycacyons and answeres

"Also the same Caton sayth yet that the woman that pleaseth a man naturally resembleth the rose whiche is pleasaunt to se, but the thorne is under and prycketh."

*Answere*: "This Caton sayth more trewer agayne than he wende, for every good honest woman and of good lyfe ought to be and is one of the pleasauntest thynges that is to se. And alwayes there is the thorne of drede to do amysse and a compunccyon in her courage whiche that parteth not fro [Ee1v] her. And that maketh her to holde her pryve and sytteth styll; and that is it that kepeth her."

"Many auctours bereth wytnesse, madame, that women ben by nature synful."

"Doughter, thou hast herde speke of a proverbe that sayth that *that Nature gyveth may not be taken away.* So it sholde be too grete a mervayle yf they sholde be so enclyned to synne naturally. For the women that loveth her worshyp, Nature styreth them never to come in suche places whereas that synne that is sayd of them is used, as in tavernes and other places to that or for that ordeyned. And yf ony man wolde answere and saye that shame kepeth them, I say that is not true. For it is another thynge that kepeth them whiche is theyr naturall condycyon, whiche is not so enclyned therto. And I put case that they were so enclyned, and that shame gave them suche resystence contrary to theyr naturall inclynacyon, that that vertue and constaunce sholde tourne them to grete worshyp and praysynge.

"And to that purpose, remembrest thou not that not longe ago, that as thou were in a festfull day at the gate of thyne house, devysynge one and other with a worshypfull damoysell thy neyghboure, and thou sawest a man come out of a

devisant a un aultre: 'J'ay, dit il, tant despendu a la taverne que[1] ma femme ne buvra huy mais de vin.' Et que adonc tu l'appellas et lui demandas la cause pour quoy elle n'en buvroit point?[2] Et il te dist, 'Pour ce, dame: car elle a une telle maniere que toutes les fois que je viens de la taverne, elle me demande combien [fol. 19r b] j'ay despendu. Et se plus y a de .xii. deniers, elle veult recompenser par la sobriece de sa bouche en ce que j'ay trop despendu, et dit que se tous .ii. voulions largement despendre, nostre mestier ne pourroit fournir a la despense.'"

"Dame," dis je adoncques, "de ce moult bien me souvient."

Et elle a moy: "Par assez de exemples peux tu cognoistre que par nature sont femmes sobres, et celles qui ne le sont se desnaturent. Ne plus lait vice ne pourroit[3] estre en femme que gloutonnie, car cellui vice attrait infinis aultres.[4] Mais tu les pueux bien veoir a tres grans tourbes et a grans presses par ses eglises aux sermons et aux pardons, tenans pate[r]nostres[5] et heures."

"Tout en est plain voire, dame," dis je. "Mais ces hommes dient que elles [fol. 19v a] y vont cointtes et jolies pour monstrer leur beaulté, et attraire les hommes a leur amour."

*Response*: "Ce seroit chose a croire, amie chiere, se on ne veoit ne mes[6] les joeunes et jolies. Mais se tu y prens garde, pour une joeune que tu y verras, .xx. ou .xxx. vieilles de simple habit et honnesté voit[7] on converser les lieux de devocion. Et se devocion est es femmes, semblablement n'y deffault mie charité. Car qui visete les malades, les reconforte, seceures[8] aux povres, cerche les hospitaux, ensevelist les mors? Il me semble que ce sont les oeuvres des femmes, lesquelles[9] sont les traces souveraines que Dieu commande a suivre."

"Dame, trop bien dites. Mais un aucteur dit que femmes ont par nature chetif courage et sont[10] [fol. 19v b] comme l'enfant, et pour ce conversent voulentiers les enfans avecques elles, et elles avec les enfans."

*Response*: "Fille, se tu prens garde a la nature de l'enfant, de sa condicion,[11] il aime amiableté et doulceur. Et quel chose est en ce monde plus doulce et plus amiable que est femme bien ordonnee? Ha, mauvaises gens dyaboliques qui veulent pervertir le bien et la vertu de benignité, qui est en femme par nature, en mal et en reproche! Car se femmes aiment les enfans, il ne leur vient mie par

---

[1] J'ay, dit il, tant despendu a la taverne que] J'ay tant despendu en la taverne. Ma femme
[2] buvroit point] buveroit
[3] pourroit] peut
[4] vice attrait infinis aultres] vice ou qu'il soit attrait plusieurs autres
[5] pate[r]nostres : *patenostres*
[6] ne veoit ne mes] n'y veoit ne mais
[7] simple habit et honnesté voit] simple abit y voit
[8] seceures] secuert
[9] lesquelles] lesquelles oeuvres
[10] et sont] et que elles sont
[11] nature de l'enfant de sa condicion] condicion de l'enfant de sa nature

taverne that wente talkynge with another sayenge: 'I have spente thus moche at the taverne, and my wyfe shall drynke no wyne tonyght.' And then thou called hym to thee, and asked the cause why? And he sayd to thee, 'For this cause, madame: for she hathe suche a condycyon that every tyme that I come from the taverne, she asketh [Ee2r] me howe moche I have spente. And yf it be more than .xii. pens, she wyll recompence me by the sobernes of her mouthe and that that I have spente too moche, and sayth that yf we bothe sholde spende so largely, oure crafte sholde not fournysshe us to our dyspence.'"

"Madame," sayd I then, "of that I remembre me well."

And then she sayd to me, "Thou mayst knowe by ensamples ynowe that by nature women ben sobre. And those that be not, they go out of kynde; for there may not be a more lewder vyce in a woman than glotony, for that vyce draweth to hym many other vyces. But thou mayst well se of them grete companyes and grete prese in theyr chyrches at sermons and at pardons, holdynge theyr beedes in theyr handes, sayenge theyr prayers."

"Madame," sayd I, "that is trouthe. But these men say that they go fresshe and joly to showe theyr beaute and to drawe these men to theyr love."

*Answere*: "That sholde be a thynge for to byleve, dere frende, yf one sawe none there but yonge women and fresshe. But thou shalte se there for one yonge woman, .xx. or .xxx. olde of symple habyte to go and haunte the places of devocyon. And yf devocyon be amonge women, it sholde folowe in the same wyse that charyte fauteth not there, for they vysyte the syke and comforte them; they renne to pore people, and sercheth hospytalles, and bury the deed bodyes. Me semeth that these be the werkes of women, the whiche ben the soverayne traces that God commaundeth us to folowe."

"Madame, ye say wel. But there is an auctour sayth that women by nature have yll courage and be as chyldren. [Ee2v] And for that cause, chyldren ben conversaunt with them, and they with the chyldren."

*Answere*: "Doughter, yf thou take hede to the nature of a chylde of his condycyon, he loveth frendlynesse and swetnes. And what thynge is there in the worlde more swetter and more amyable than is a woman well set in ordre? Ha, the cursed people of the devylles condycyon, that wolde have the welthe and vertue of mekenesse and benygnyte that is in women tourne to evyll and into

vice d'ignorance, ains leur vient de la doulceur de leur condicion. Et se elles sont comme l'enfant en benigneté, de ce sont souverainnement bien conseillees, car si que recorde l'Euvangile, ne dist pas Nostre Sire [fol. 20r a] a ses apostres lors que ilz contendoient entr'eulx qui seroit le plus grant;[1] et il appella un enfant, et lui mist la main sur le chief, et dist,[2] 'Je vous di certainement que cellui qui se tendra petit et humble comme l'enfant sera le plus exaucié, [c]ar[3] qui se humilie est eslevez, et qui se eslieve est abaissiez'."[4]

"Dame, hommes me font un grant harnois d'un proverbe en latin que ilz tant reprochent aux femmes qui dit *Plourer, parler, et filer*[5] *mist Dieux en femme.*"

*Response*: "Certes, doulce amie, ceste parole est vraye, combien que qui le cuide ou die, ce ne leur soit point de reproche. Et de bonne heure pour celles qui par parler, plourer, et filer ont esté sauvees, mist Dieux [fol. 20r b] en elles ycelles condicions. Et contre ceulx qui tant leur reprochent la condicion de plourer, je dis que se Nostre Sauveur Jhesucrist, a qui nulle pensee n'est muciee et qui tout courage voit et cognoist, eust sceu que les larmes des femmes venissent seulement par fragilité et simplece, la dignité de sa tres grant haultesse ne se fust pas[6] enclinee a rendre lui mesmes larmes des yeux de son digne corps glorieux par compassion quant il vit plourer Marie Magdaline et Marthe sa seur pour la mort de leur frere, Lazar, que il resuscita.

"O, quantes grans graces fist Dieux a femmes pour cause de leurs larmes! Il ne desprisa mie celles de la dicte Marie Magdaleine, ains [fol. 20v a] les accepta tant que Il lui en pardonna ses pechiez. Et par les merites d'ycelles[7] elle est ou ciel glorieusement.

"*Item*, Il ne debouta mie celles de la femme vesve qui plouroit aprés son filz[8] mort que on portoit en terre. Et Nostre Sire, qui plourer la vid, lui[9] qui est fontaine de toute pitié, meu de compassion pour les larmes d'ycelle, lui ala demander: 'Femme, pour quoy pleures tu?' Et adonc[10] lui resuscita son enfant.

"Aultres grans graces qui longues seroient a dire[11] fist Dieux a maintes femmes pour leurs larmes, et tous les jours fait car je tiens que a cause des larmes de leur devocion soient sauvees pluseurs d'elles et d'autres pour qui elles prient.

---

[1] entr'eulx qui seroit le plus grant] ensemble lequel seroit le plus grant d'entre eulx
[2] sur le chief, et dist] sus le chief, en disant
[3] [c]ar: *quar*
[4] abaissiez] humiliez
[5] et filer] filer
[6] pas] jamais
[7] d'ycelles] d'icelles larmes
[8] son filz] son seul filz
[9] lui] comme cellui
[10] adonc] tantost
[11] a dire] a dire si comme on peut veoir en la Sainte Escripture

reproffe! For thoughe women love chyldren, it cometh not of them by the vyce of ygnoraunce, but it cometh of the swetnesse of theyr condycyon. And yf they be as chyldren in benygnyte, of that and in that they be well counsaylled. For so as the gospell recordeth, ne sayd not Our Lorde to His appostles when they stryved amonge theym whiche sholde be moost grete, and He called a chylde and layde his hande on his heed, and sayd, 'I saye you certaynly that he that wyl holde hym lytell and meke as a chylde shal be moost hye. For who that meketh hym shall be enhaunced, and he that enhaunceth hym shall be put lowe.'"

"Madame, men dothe me grete hurte of one proverbe in Latyne that they reprove women by often tymes, whiche sayth *wepe, speke, and spynne God hath put in woman.*"

*Answere*: "Forsothe swete frende, that worde is true, howe be it that he that trowed or sayd that in reprove. It was for them a good happe whiche by spekynge, wepynge, and spynnynge have ben saved: thus God put in them suche condycyons. And agaynst [Ee3r] them that so moche reproveth them in the cond[yc]yon[1] of wepynge, I saye yf that Our Savyour Jhesu Cryst, to whome no thought is hydde and whiche seeth every courage, had knowen that the teeres of women had come onely of fragylyte and symplenesse, the dygnyte of His grete hyghnesse had not ben so enclyned to yelde Hymselfe teeres of the eyen of His worshypfull and gloryo[u]s[2] body by compassyon when He sawe Mary Magdaleyne and Martha her syster wepe for the dethe of theyr broder Lazare, whiche He raysed from the dethe. O, howe many grete graces God hath done to women bycause of theyr teeres? He dyspraysed not the teeres of the foresayd Mary Magdaleyne but accepted them insomoche that He pardoned her of her synnes, and by the merytes of them she is in heven gloryously. Also, He put not awaye those teeres of the wydowe whiche wepte for her deed sone that one bare to the erthe. And Our Lorde whiche is the welle of all pyte, moved of compassyon for the teeres of her, wente to aske her, 'Wherfore wepest thou?' And then anone He raysed the chylde to the lyfe.

"Other grete graces, whiche sholde be longe to telle, God hathe done to many women for theyr wepynge and alwaye dothe. Wherfore I suppose that bycause of theyr wepynge and theyr devocyon many of them ben saved, and others also whiche they pray for. Ne was not Saynt Austyne, the gloryous

---

[1] cond[yc]yon : *condyon*
[2] gloryo[u]s : *gloryons*

"Ne fu saint Augustin, le glorieux docteur [fol. 20v b] de l'Eglise, convertis a la foy pour cause des larmes de sa mere? Car la tres bonne dame sans cesser plouroit, priant a Dieu que il lui pleust enluminer le cuer de son filz, qui estoit paien et incredule de la lumiere de la foy. Donc saint Ambroise, a qui la saincte dame aloit souvent requerir que il priast Dieu pour lui, l[ui]¹ dist: 'Femme, je tiens que ce soit chose impossible que tant de larmes soient perdues.' O benoit Ambroise! Tu ne tenoies pas que ce fussent frivoles que larmes de femmes. Et ce² puet respondre aux hommes qui tant les reprochent, que a cause des larmes d'une femme est ce saint luminaire ou front de Saincte Eglise qui toute l'esclaire et enlumine, c'est assavoir [fol. 21r a] monseigneur saint Augustin. Si ne parlent plus non hommes en cest endroit.

"Semblablement le parler mist Dieux voirement en femme: il en soit leuez,³ car se parler n'y eust mis, muetes fussent. Mais en contre ce que dit le proverbe, que ne sçay qui fist⁴ a volenté en leur reproche, se language de femme eust esté tant reprouvable et de si petite auctorité comme aucuns veulent dire, Nostre Sire Jhesucrist n'eust jamais daingnié vouloir que si digne mistere que fu cellui de sa tres glorieuse Resurrection fust premierement annoncié par femme, si comme il mesmes le commanda a la benoicte Magdaleine, a qui premierement s'apparut le jour de Pasques, que elle [fol. 21r b] le deist et nonçast a ses⁵ apostres et a Pierre. O benoit Dieux, Tu soies louez, qui avec autres infinis dons et graces que tu as faictes et donnees au sexe femmenin, voulx que femme fust porterresse de si haultes et dignes⁶ nouvelles! Bien se deussent tous envieux taire se bien y avisassent.⁷

"De bonne heure pour elle fu si grant parlerresse ycelle femme cananee, qui ne faisoit que crier et se debatre⁸ aprés Jhesucrist, alant par les rues de Jheru-salem, disant: 'Aies mercy de moy,⁹ car ma fille est malade.' Mais que faisoit le benoit Dieu, il en qui toute misericorde habondoit et abonde, et a qui souffisoit une toute seule parole venant du cuer pour avoir mercy? Il sembloit que il se delictast [fol. 21v a] en pluseurs paroles de¹⁰ la bouche de celle femme, tousjours perseverant en sa priere. Mais pour quoy le faisoit il? C'estoit pour esprover sa constance, car quant il l'ot comparee aux chiens, ce sembloit un pou rudement pour ce que elle estoit d'estrange loy et non pas de celle de Dieu. Elle n'ot pas

---

¹ l[ui] : *li*

² ce] se

³ leuez] louez

⁴ dit le proverbe, que ne sçay qui fist] dit le dit proverbe, que ne sçay qui trouva

⁵ a ses] aux

⁶ dignes] si dignes

⁷ avisassent] *R continues; see annotations for extended passage*

⁸ faisoit que crier et se debatre] **finoit** de crier et braire

⁹ de moy] de moy, Sire

¹⁰ de] yssans de

doctoure of the chyrche, converted to the fayth bycause of wepynge of his moder? For that same good lady wepte without [Ee3v] seasynge, praynge to God that it myght please Hym to enlumyne the herte of her sone, whiche was at that tyme a paynyme and out of the byleve from the lyght of the faythe, wherfore this good lady wente often tymes to requyre Saynt Ambrose that he sholde pray to God for hym."

And then my Lady Reason sayd to me: "I suppose," sayd she, "that it sholde be a thynge impossyble that so many teeres of a woman sholde be lost. O, blessyd Saynt Ambrose! Thou trowed not that so many teeres of a woman sholde be set at nought. And that may be answere to men that reprove women, that bycause of theyr wepynge of a woman is that holy lyght in the fronte of holy chyrche, whiche clereth and enlumyneth all the chyrche: that is to knowe, Saynt Austyne. Soo lette men speke no more of that as nowe.

"The same wyse, truely, God put the spekynge in woman: worshypped be He, for yf speche had not ben put in theym, they had ben dome. Yet contrary to that that the proverbe, whiche I knowe not who made it at his pleasure in the reproffe of women, yf language of the woman had ben so moche reprovable and of so lytell auctoryte as some men wolde saye, Our Lorde Jhesu Cryst had never vouchedsaufe that so worshypfull a mystery as that was of His gloryous Resur-reccyon whiche was fyrst announced by woman, as He Hymselfe commaunded to the blessyd Mary Magdaleyne, to whome He appered fyrst on Ester Day that she sholde tell it and announce it to His dyscyples and to Peter. O blessyd Lorde Jhesu, loued be Thou whiche with other infynyte [Ee4r] gyftes and graces that Thou hast done and gyven to womankynde woldest that woman sholde be the berer of so hyghe and worshypfull tydynges! Wel ought these envyous men to be styll yf they advyse them well.

"It was a good happe that the woman of Cananee was so grete a speker, whiche dyde nought elles but crye after Our Lorde Jhesu Cryst, goynge by the stretes of Jherusalem, sayenge, 'Have mercy on me, Lorde, for my doughter is syke!' But what dyde Our Lorde God, He in whom al mercy habounded and haboundeth, and to whom it suffysed one onely worde comynge from the herte to have mercy? It semed that He delyted in many wordes of the mouthe of that woman, alway perseveraunt in her prayer. But wherfore dyde He it? It was to prove her stedfastnesse. For when He herde her lyken herselfe to dogges that semed a lytell rudely for that she was of a straunge lawe and not of Goddes law,

honte de parler bien et sagement, en disant: 'Sire, c'est bien voir. Mais[1] de la table du seigneur se vivent les petis chiennetz.' O tres sage femme, qui t'aprist a ainsi parler? Tu gaingnas ta cause par ton lengage[2] yssu de bonne voulenté. Et bien ypparu, car Nostre Seigneur tesmoingna de sa bouche, se tournant adoncques vers ses apostres, disant qu'il[3] n'avoit trouvé tant de foy en tout Israel, et lui ottroya sa requeste. [fol. 21v b] He, qui pourra sommer souffisamment cest honneur en[4] sexe femmenin, que les envieux veulent desprisier, considerant que ou cueur d'une petit femmelete de la lignee des paiens, Dieu trouva[5] plus de foy qu'en tous les evesques, les princes, les prestres, et le peuple[6] des Juifs qui se disoient estre le diggne peuple de Dieu?

"En telle maniere parla aussi longuement et a grant plait bien pour elle la femme Samaritaine, qui estoit venu[7] traire de l'eaue ou elle trouva Jhesucrist seant tout lassé. O benoite Divinité, conjointe ad ce digne corps, comment souffroies Tu celle saincte bouche ouvrir a tenir resne de paroles de salut a celle povre petite[8] femmellete pecherresse, qui [fol. 22r a] mesmement n'estoit de ta loy? Vraiement, Tu monstroies bien que point ne desdaingnoies le devot sexe des femmes. Dieux, a quans coups noz pontificaux d'aujourd'ui daingneroient tenir parole,[9] mesmes de son sauvement, a une si simple[10] femmellete?

"Ne parla pas moins sagement la femme qui se seoit au sermon de Jhesucrist, qui si fu embrasee de ses sainctes paroles, si comme[11] on dit que femmes ne se peuent[12] taire, de bonne heure parla a celle fois,[13] lors que elle se leva par grant voulenté et dist:[14] 'Benoit soit le ventre qui Te porta, et les mamelles que Tu suceas.'

"Ainsi que tu pues entendre, belle doulce amie, Dieux a demonstré que voirement il a[15] mis languaje en femme pour [fol. 22r b] en estre servi. Si ne leur

---

[1] Mais] Mais des mietes de la table
[2] lengage] prudent lengage
[3] adoncques vers ses apostres, disant qu'il] vers ses appostres que il
[4] en] ou
[5] trouva] trouvast
[6] le peuple] tout le peuple
[7] Samaritaine qui estoit venu] de Samaritaine qui estoit venue au puis
[8] povre petite] petite
[9] parole] parolles
[10] si simple] petite
[11] si comme] que si comme
[12] peuent] scevent
[13] celle fois] celle fois la parolle que sollempneement est recordee en l'euvangile que elle dit
[14] et dist] disant haultement
[15] il a] a il

she had no shame to speke well and wysely in sayenge: 'Lorde, it is true that the lytell dogges eteth the crommes that falleth from the table of theyr lorde.' O ryght wyse woman, who hathe tought thee to speke so? Thou gatest thy cause by thy language yssued of good wyll. And well it semed, for Oure Lorde bare wytnesse of His owne mouthe retournynge than unto His appostles, sayenge to theym that He had not founde suche fayth in Israell, and graunted unto her request and desyre. Ha, who maye somme suffysauntly the worshyp in the kynde of woman, the whiche the envyous men wyll [Ee4v] so dysprayse, consyderynge that in the herte of a lytell woman of the kyn[d]red¹ of paynymes God founde more faythe than in all the bysshoppes and prynces or preestes, or in the people of Jewes that called themselfe the worthy people of God?

"In suche a manere spake also longly and with grete pleatynge, and wel for her the woman Samarytane that was come to drawe of the water where she founde Jhesu Cryst syttynge all wery. O, Thou blessyd Godhede conjoyned to the worshypful body, howe myght Thou suffre Thy holy mouthe to open and to holde the rayne of wordes of helthe to this poore and lytel woman synner, the whiche was not of that lawe? Truely, Thou shewed well that Thou dysdayned not the devoute kynde of women.

"Ne spake not wysely the woman that sate at the sermone of Our Lorde Jhesu Cryste, whiche was so embraced with His holy wordes? So as one saythe that women may not byleve so soone, yet she spake at that tyme; and then she rose with a grete wyll, and sayd: 'Blessyd be that wombe that bare Thee and the pappes that Thou sowked.'

"Thus thou mayst understande, fayre swete frende, that God hathe shewed that truely He loveth language to be well served. So that ought not to be reproffe

---

¹ kyn[d]red : *kynred*

doit estre reprochié ce dont maint bien vient et pou de mal, car petit voit[1] on grant prejudice venir a cause de leur langage.

"Quant est du filer, voirement a Dieu voulu que ce leur soit naturel car c'est office neccessaire au service divin et a l'aide de toute creatures raisonnable, sans lequel ouvrage les offices du monde seroient maintenus en grant ordure. Si est grant mauvaistié de rendre en reproche aux femmes ce qui leur doit tourner a tres grant gré, honneur, et los."

*Chapitre 11*          **Demande Christine a Raison pour quoy ce est que femmes ne sient en siege de plaidorie, et response**

"Tres hault et honnoree dame, voz belles raisons satiffient tres grandement ma pensee. Mais encore me dites, s'il vous [fol. 22v a] agree, la verité pour quoy ce est que les femmes ne tiennent plaidoierie en cours de justice, ne cognoiscent des causes, ne ne[2] font jugemens? Car ces hommes dient que c'est pour ne sçay quel femme qui en siege de justice se gouverna mausagement."

"Fille, ce sont frivoles et choses controuvés[3] de ce que on dit d'ycelle. Mais qui vouldroit demander les causes et raisons de toutes choses trop[4] y aroit a respondre, combien que Aristote ou *Livre des Problemnes* rende raison de maintes choses et ensement ou *Livre des Proprietes des Choses* sont contenues les essences de pluseurs actions naturelles. Mais quant a ceste, belle amie, semblablement se pourroit demander pour quoy n'ordenna Dieux [fol. 22v b] que les hommes feissent les offices des femmes, et celles des femmes feissent les hommes? Mais la response si est que tout ainsi comme[5] un sage seigneur bien ordonné establist sa maisiné a faire en divers offices l'un une chose, l'autre une autre; et ce que l'un fait, l'autre ne fait mie. Semblablement Dieux a establi homme et femme pour le servir[6] et pour aussi aidier, conforter, et compaignier l'un l'autre, chascun en ce qui lui est establi a faire, et a chascun sexe a donné tel nature et inclinacion comme a faire son office lui appartient et compete, combien que nature humaine

---

[1]  petit voit] pou souvent voit
[2]  ne ne] ne
[3]  controuvés] controuvees par ruse
[4]  toutes choses trop] *after this phrase, F wants rest of chap. 11; chap. 12; beginning of chap. 13*
[5]  combien que Aristote ... l'un l'autre] ne Aristote, combien qui l'en declaire maintes ou *Livre de ses problemes* et en cellui *Des Proprietez* n'y souffiroit mie. Mais quant a ceste question, belle amie, semblablement se pourroit demander pour quoy n'ordena Dieux aussi bien que les hommes feissent les offices des femmes que elles font, et les femmes ceulx des hommes. Si peut a ceste question estre respondu que tout ainsi que
[6]  servir] servir en divers offices

to them wherof so moche welthe cometh and so lytell evyll, for no man seeth grete prejudyce come of theyr language.

"And as to spynne, truely, it is Goddes wyll that it be kyndely to them, for that offyce is necessary to Goddes servyce and to the helpe of every creature reasonable, without [Ff1r] the whiche worke the offyces of the worlde sholde be maynteyned in grete foulenesse and unclennesse. So it is grete shre[w]denesse[1] to put that into the reproffe of woman that ought to tourne them to grete honoure and praysynge."

## Chapter 11    Christine demaundeth of Reason wherfore it is that women sytteth not in the syege of pleadynge

"Right hyghe and worshypfull lady, your fayre reasons satysfyeth ryght gretely my thought. But yet tell me, yf it please you, the trouthe: wherfore is that that these women holde noo pleadynge in the courte of justyce, nor they knowe not the causes, ne dothe no jugement? For these men saye that it is for they can not, and that woman that sytteth in the place of justyce governeth her shrewdely."

"Doughter, these ben but japes and thynges contryved of that that one lyst to say of women. But he that wolde demaunde the causes and reasons of al thynges, it sholde be too moche to answere, howe be it that Arystotle in his *Boke of Problemes* yeldeth reason of many thynges, and in the same wyse in the *Boke of Propryetees of Thynges* ben conteyned the beynges of dyvers accyons naturalles. But as to that, fayre frende, the same wyse yf it be demaunded why God ordeyned not that these men sholde do the offyces of women, and the women [Ff1v] the offyces of men? But the answere is this that as a wyse lorde well ordeyned stablyssheth his meyne to do dyvers offyces: one one thynge, another another thynge, as so that that one dothe another dothe not. The same wyse God hath ordeyned man and woman to serve and also to helpe, comforte, and holde company one with another, every of them in that he is ordeyned to do, and hathe gyven to every kynde suche nature and inclynacyon as to do his offyce competently perteynynge

---

[1] shre[w]denesse : *shredenesse*

abuse souventeffois en ce que il[1] doit faire. Il a donné aux hommes corps fort
poissant et hardi d'aler, [fol. 23r a] de venir, de parler.[2] Et pour ce, les hommes
qui ont celle nature apprennent les lois et le doivent faire[3] pour tenir le monde
en ordre de justice et sont tenus que ou cas que aucuns ne vouldroient[4] obeir aux
lois establies par raison de droit, que ilz les feissent obeir par force de corps et par
poissance d'armes; et ce ne pourroient mie faire les femmes. Car[5] combien que
Dieux leur ait donné entendement, et moult grant[6] de telles y a, toutevoyes pour
l'onnesteté ou elles sont enclines, ce ne seroit point chose couvenable que elles se
alassent monstrer en jugement[7] comme les hommes, car il y a assez qui le face:[8]
a quoy faire envoieroit on trois hommes lever un fardel que deux peuent [fol. 23r b]
ligierement porter?

"Mais se aucuns vouloient dire que femmes n'ayent entendement souffisant
pour aprendre les loys, le contraire est manifeste par l'esperience[9] qui appert et
est apparue de plusieurs femmes, si que sera dit cy aprés, qui ont esté tres grandes
philosophes et ont aprises de trop plus soubtilles sciences et plus haultes que ne
sont loys[10] escriptes et establissemens d'ommes. Et de rechief qui vouldroit pro-
poser que elles n'eussent sens naturel en fait de policie et de gouvernement? Je
te donne exemple de pluseurs grans maistresses qui ont esté les temps passez,
mesmement en ton temps,[11] afin que tu mieulx congnoisces ma verité, qui sont
demourees vesves, le [fol. 23v a] bel gouvernement qu'ilz[12] ont eu et ont en tous leurs
affaires aprés la mort de leurs maris donne manifeste experience que femme qui
a entendement est couvenable en toutes choses."

---

[1] nature humaine abuse souventeffois en ce que il] l'espece humaine abuse souvent
en ce que elle
[2] parler] parler hardiement
[3] le doivent faire] faire le doivent
[4] aucuns ne vouldroient] aucun ne vouldroit
[5] et ce ne pourroient mie faire les femmes. Car] laquelle excecucion ne pourroient
mie faire les femmes. Lesquelles
[6] et moult grant] moult grant a
[7] jugement] jugement baudement
[8] face] fait
[9] par l'esperience] par preuve de experience
[10] loys] les lois
[11] mesmement en ton temps] Et mesmement t'en ramentevray aucunes de ton temps
[12] le bel gouvernement qu'ilz] dont le bel gouvernement qu'elles

to hym, howe be it that mannes nature abuseth often tymes in that that he ought to do. He hath gyven to men body stronge power and hardy to go and come, and speke, and for that these men that have that nature lerneth the lawes, and ought to put them in the execucyon to holde the worlde in the ordre of justyce. And they be bounde that, in case that ony wolde not obey to the lawes establed by ryght and reason, that they sholde make them to obeye by force of theyr bodyes and by puyssaunce of armes; and that the women may not do. For howe be it that God hath gyven them understandynge, yet they may not use it in that manere for theyr honeste, for it were not convenyent that they sholde goo sewe them in jugement as these men done for there ben ynowe that dothe it. For what nedeth thre men to lyfte up a fardell that twayne may lyghtly bere it away?

"Yet yf some men wolde saye that women have not suffycyent understandynge for to lerne the lawes, the contrary is made open by experyence. And it appereth of many women, as it shall [Ff2r] be sayd hereafter, the whiche have ben ryght grete phylosophres and have lerned more subtyll scyence and more hygher than the lawes wryten by men. And also who wolde purpose that they have not naturall wytte in dede of polycye and of governaunce? I gyve thee ensample of many grete maystresses that have ben in tyme past, and also in thy tyme, to the entente that thou sholdest knowe the better my trouthe of them that have ben wydowes whiche have kepte good governaunce in all theyr doynges after the dethe of theyr housbandes, whiche gyveth open experyence that a woman that hath understandynge is covenable in all thynges."

### Chapitre 12    Dit[1] de l'empereris Nicole, et aprés d'aucunes roynes et princeces de France

"Je te pri, dis moy ou fu oncques roy de plus grant savoir en fait de policie, de gouvernement, et de souveraine justice tenir, et mesmement de haulte magnificence de vivre, que il est leu de la tres noble emperis Nicole? Car non obstant que es contrees grandes et lees et diverses que elle dominoit eussent esté pluseurs roys de grant renommee appellez *pharaons*, desquelz descendue elle estoit,[2] ceste dame fu celle qui premierement [fol. 23v b] commença a vivre en son regne selon lois et policie mondaine,[3] et destruisi et mist afin les rudes manieres de vivre des lieux que elle seigneurissoit. Et[4] dient les aucteurs qui d'elle parlent que elle amenda la rudece des autres. Elle demoura heritiere des dessus diz pharaons non mie de petit pays mais du royaume d'Arabé, de cellui d'Ethiope, et de cellui d'Egipte, et de l'isle Meronnee, qui est moult longue, et moult large, et habondante de tous biens, et est close du fleuve du Nil, que elle gouverna par merveilleuse prudence. Que te diroye de ceste dame de tous biens? Et elle[5] fu tant sage et de tant grant gouvernement que mesmes la Saincte Escripture parle [fol. 24r a] de sa grant vertu. Elle mesmes institua loys et tres[6] droiturieres pour gouverner son peuple. Elle abonda en grant noblece et combleté de richeces pres que autant que tous les hommes qui oncques furent. Elle fu perfonde et experte es escriptures et sciences. Et tant ot[7] hault courage que marier ne se daigna ne voult que homme se acostast a elle."

### Chapitre 13    Dit d'une royne de France qui fu nommee Fridegonde

"De dames de sage gouvernement assez te pourroye dire. La royne de France Fredegonde qui ot esté femme du roy Charles,[8] non obstant fust elle cruelle oultre loy naturelle de femme, toutevoyes aprés la mort de son mary gouverna le royaume de France par grant savoir, voire qui estoit pour lors [fol. 24r b] en moult

---

   [1] Dit] Ci dit
   [2] descendue elle estoit] elle estoit dessendue
   [3] mondaine] ordenee
   [4] seigneurissoit. Et] seignourissoit et amenda les rudes usages des ethiopiens bestiaulx. Si fait ceste dame de tant plus a louer; ce
   [5] dame de tous biens? Et elle] dame? Elle
   [6] loys et tres] lois tres
   [7] ot : *hot*
   [8] gouvernement . . . Charles] gouvernement des temps ancians assez te pouroie dire si comme cy aprés vendra ad ce propos ce que je t'en diray. En France fu la royne Fredegonde, laquelle fu femme du roy Chilperich. Celle dame

*Chapter 12*         **Here it speketh of the Empresse Nychole, and after of**
                     **dyvers noble quenes and pryncesses of Fraunce**

"Tell me, I praye thee, where was ever that kynge of grete understandynge in
the dede of polycye of governaunce to kepe soverayne justyce, and also of hyghe
magnyfycence in lyvynge that is reede of the ryght noble Empresse Nychole?
For notwithstandynge that in these countrees grete, large, and dyvers that she
had the rewle of had ben kynges of grete fame called *pharaons*, of whom she was
descended, this lady was she that fyrste began to lyve in her royalme after [Ff2v]
lawes and worldely polycy, and she destroyed the rude maners of lyvynge of those
countrees that she had in governaunce. And these auctours saye that speketh of
her that she amended the rudenesse of her people. And she was herytoure of the
foresayd Pharaons, not onely of the lytell countre but of the royalme of Arabee,
of Ethyope, and of Egypte, and of the Ile Maromye whiche is ryght longe and
large and habundaunte of all manere of goodes, whiche is closed with the flode
of Nyle, whiche she governed by mervayllous prudence. What shall I saye more
of this lady whiche had all this welthe, but that she was so wyse and of suche governaunce that Holy Scrypture speketh of her grete vertue? She herselfe ordeyned
lawes and ryghtes to governe her people. She habounded in grete noblesse and
rychesse more than ony man in those dayes, and she was profounde and experte
in scryptures and in scyences. And she had so hyghe a courage that she dysdeyned to be maryed, ne wolde that no man sholde have knowlege of her body."

*Chapter 13*         **Of the quene of Fraunce whiche was named Fredegonde**

"Of ladyes of wyse governaunce I myght telle thee ynoughe. The Quene of
Fraunce Fredegonde that had ben the wyfe of Kynge Charles, notwithstandynge she was cruell out of naturall [Ff3r] lawe of woman, yet after the dethe of
her housbande she governed the royalme of Fraunce by grete prowesse, whiche

grant balance[1] car un petit filx sans plus lui estoit demourré heritier du pere, lequel[2] on nommoit Clotaire. Si avoit grant division entre les barons pour cause du gouvernement et ja estoit sourse grant guerre sur[3] le royaume. Mais celle dame, tenoit continuelment son enfant entre ses braz, assembloit les barons a conseil[4] et leur disoit: 'Seigneurs, voy cy vostre roy. N'aies pas[5] en oubli la loyaulté qui tousjours a esté es François, et ne le vueillez desprisier pour tant s'il est enfant car a l'aide de Dieu il croistra. Et quant il sera en aage, il congnoistra ses bons amis et les guerdonnera selon leurs dessertes, si ne le vueilliez desheriter a tort et a pechié. Et quant a moy, je vous fais certains que a ceulx qui bien et [fol. 24v a] loyaument se maintidront, je les guerdonneray si grandement qu'a tousjours[6] leur en sera de mieux.' Et ainsi ceste royne apaisoit les barons, de laquel chose par son sage gouvernement tant fist que elle tira son filz des mains de ses anemis;[7] le nourrist elle mesmes tant qu'il fu grant, et par elle fu revestu de la couronne et de l'onneur du royaume, ce qu'il n'eust oncques esté se la prudence d'elle ne fust.

"Et semblablement se puet dire de la tres sage et en tous cas bonne la noble royne Blanche, mere de saint Louis, qui tant noblement et prudemment gouverna le royaume de France tant que son filz fu menre d'aage, que oncques mieulx par homme ne fu gouverné. Et mesmement quant il fu grant, par l'espreuve de son sage [fol. 24v b] gouvernement estoit elle[8] tousjours chief du conseil: ne riens n'estoit fait sans elle, et mesmes en guerre suivoit son enfant.[9]

"Infinies d'aultres ad ce propos te pourroie dire, que je laisse pour briefté. Mais puis que nous sommes entrez a parler des dames de France, sans aler histoires plus loings querre,[10] tu veis en ton temps la noble royne de France Jehanne,[11] vesve du roy Charles .iiii.e du nom,[12] se tu en as memoire: avises les grans biens que renommee tesmonigne de celle noble dame,[13] tant en notable ordonance de sa court comme en maniere de vivre et en souveraine justice tenir. Oncques ne fu parlé de nul prince qui mieulx la tenist et gardast en sa terre de ce qui lui appartenoit que celle dame faisoit. Et bien lui [fol. 25r a] ressembla sa noble fille, qui fu mariee au duc d'Orliens, filz du roy Philippe, laquelle en sa vesveté ou elle

---

[1] balance] balance et peril
[2] lequel] que
[3] sur] sus
[4] les barons a conseil] a conseil les barons
[5] N'aies pas] Ne metez pas
[6] tousjours] tousjours mais
[7] *F rejoins narrative here*
[8] de son sage gouvernement estoit elle] du sage gouvernement d'elle fu
[9] mesmes en guerre suivoit son enfant] mesmement en guerre suivoit son filz
[10] histoires plus loings querre] plus loings histoires querre
[11] royne de France Jehanne] royne Jehanne
[12] du nom] de cellui nom
[13] noble dame] dame

was at that tyme in ryght grete balaunce, for there was lefte her a sone without
mo herytours of his fader, the whiche was called Clotharye. So there was grete
devy[s]yon[1] amonge the lordes bycause of governaunce, and upon that there fell
grete warre to the royalme. Yet this lady helde contynually her sone bytwene
her armes, and she called and assembled theyr lordes in a counsayle, and sayd:
'Lordes, se here your kynge. Ye have not forgoten the trouthe whiche alwayes
hath ben in Fraunce: and nowe dyspyse hym not, thoughe he be a chylde, for
by the helpe of God he shall encrease. And when he shall come to age, he shal
knowe his good frendes and shall rewarde them after theyr desertes. So I pray
you, dysheryte hym not wrongfully. And as for me, I make you certayne that he
shall rewarde them that well and truely maynteyneth hym, that they shall be the
better ever after.' And so this quene appeased the lordes, thrughe the whiche
sadde governaunce she dyde so moche that she drewe her sone out of his enemyes
handes and nourysshed hym herselfe tyl that he was of age. And by her he gate
the crowne and the worshyppe of the royalme, whiche had never ben done but by
the grete prudence of her.

"And in the same wyse one maye saye of the ryght wyse and in all cases
good, the noble Quene Blaunche, moder unto Saynt Lowes, whiche [Ff3v] so
nobly and prudently governed the royalme of Fraunce tyll her sone were rype of
age, whiche was never better governed by man. And also whan he was come to
his age by the proffe of her wyse governaunce, she was alway chyefe of his counsayle, and no thynge was done without her. And also she sewed her sone alwaye
in batayle and in warre.

"Other without nombre I myght tell thee to this purpose, whiche I let passe
for shortnesse of tyme. Yet syth that we be entred to speke of ladyes of Fraunce
without goyenge ferther to seke straunge storyes, thou sawest in thy tyme the
noble Quene of Fraunce Jane, wedowe of Kynge Charles the Fourth, yf thou
have it in mynde: advyse [thee] the[2] grete welthe that the fame of this noble
lady wytnesseth, as moche in notable ordynaunce of her courte as in manere of
lyvynge and in soverayne justyce. It was never spoken of prynce that maynteyned
and kepte better in his londe that was pertaynynge to hym than this lady dyde.
And the noble lady that was wedded to the duke of Orlynaunce, sone of Kynge
Phylyp, resembled her wel. The whiche in her wydowhode, in the whiche she

---

[1] dev[y]son: devyfyon
[2] [thee] the : *the*

fu par long temps maintint justice en son païs si droitturierement que plus ne pourroit estre fait.

"*Item*, la royne de France Blanche feu femme du roy Jehan maintint sa terre et gouverna par grant ordre de droit et de justice. Et que puet on dire de la vaillant et sage ducesse d'Anjou, fille jadis de saint Charles de Blois, duc de Bretaingne? Feu femme du jeusne frere aprés lui du roy Charles de France, lequel duc fu puis appellé[14] roy de Cecille? Comment tint elle[15] soubz grant verge de justice les terres et païs, tant de Provence comme d'ailleurs [fol. 25r b] que elle gouverna et tint en sa main pour ses tres nobles enfans tant comme ilz furent petiz? Ou fu oncques la clameur ou plaincte ouye de injustice ou tort fait que feist ceste noble dame?

"Semblablement[16] la contesse de la Marche, dame et contesse de Vandosme et de Castres, grant[17] terrienne qui encores est en vie: que puet on dire de son gouvernement? Ne veult elle savoir comment et par quelle maniere sa justice est maintenue, et elle mesmes comme bonne et sage ne s'en prent elle[18] garde curieusement. Et que t'en diroye? Assez de grandes, de moyennes,[19] et petites pareillement se puet dire de ce qui leur apertient et qui prendre y veult garde. Il me semble que on puet veoir que ces nobles [fol. 25v a] dames en[20] leur vesveté ont soustenu et soustiennent en aussi bonne jurisdicion et juste droit[21] leurs seigneuries que faisoient leurs maris a leurs vivans, et autant[22] sont amees de leurs subgiez, et mieulx telles y a. Car n'est point de doubte ne[23] desplaise aux hommes que il est moult de femmes qui ont meilleur entendement et meilleur indicative[24] que n'ont tout plain d'ommes est il, et desquelles se leurs maris les creussent ou eussent pare[i]l[25] sens, grant bien et proffit pour eulx seroit.[26] Mais se les femmes communement ne se meslent du fait de jugier, ne de[27] prononcier les causes des parties ne jugier, ce[28] ne leur puet chaloir, car tant ont elles moins de charge a leurs

---

[14] Feu . . . appellé] Et feu femme de l'ainsné frere aprés lui du sage roy Charles de France, lequel duc fu puis

[15] elle] celle dame

[16] Ou fu oncques . . . Semblablement] *R see annotations for revised passage*

[17] grant] tres grant

[18] ne s'en prent elle] s'en prent

[19] Et que t'en diroye? Assez de grandes, de moyennes] Que t'en diroye? Je t'asseure que foison de grandes, moyennes

[20] de ce qui . . . dames en] lesquelles qui prendre y veult garde on peut veoir qu'en

[21] bonne jurisdicion et juste droit] bon estat

[22] autant] qui autant

[23] ne] n'en

[24] il est . . . indicative] quoy qu'il soit des nices femmes que il en est maintes qui ont meilleur entendement et plus vive consideracion et indicative

[25] pare[i]l: *parel*

[26] pour eulx seroit] seroit pour eulx

[27] ne de] ou

[28] ne jugier ce] de ce

was longe tyme, maynteyned justyce in her countre so ryghtfully that no man myght do better.

"Also the Quene of Fraunce, Dame Blaunche, whiche was wyfe to Kynge Johan maynteyned her londe and governed by grete ordre of ryght and justyce. And what myght one saye of the worshypfull and wyse lady, the duchesse of Anjou? Sometyme doughter to the holy Charles [Ff4r] de Bloys, duke of Brytayne, and after was wyfe to the yonger brother of the kynge of Fraunce, the whiche duke was called syth kynge of Cecyl: how helde she under the rodde of justyce the londes and countrees, as well of Provance as of other that she governed, and helde in her honde for the ryght noble chyldren whyle that they were yonge? Where was ever clamoure or playnte harde of wronge done that this noble lady sholde do?

"In the same wyse the countesse de la Marche, lady and countesse of Vandome and of Castres, whiche yet is on lyve: what myght one saye of her governaunce? Wolde it not be knowne howe and in what manere her justyce was maynteyned, and she herselfe as a good and wyse lady toke hede therto curyously? And what sholde I say more? One myght say ynoughe of grete ladyes, meanes, and lesse in the same wyse, howe they dyde that that was perteynynge to them whoso wyl take hede. It semeth me that one myght se that these noble ladyes in theyr wydowhode have susteyned and suffycyently well kepte jurysdyccyon and ryght in theyr lordeshyppes as theyr housbandes dyde that tyme lyvynge, and as well loved of theyr subjectes, and better. For be it no doubte nor dyspleasaunce to men that there ben many women that have better understandynge than some of these men have, of the whiche yf theyr housbandes had byleved them that they had had suche understandynge as they had, it myght have tourned theym to grete profyte. Yet thoughe these women communely [Ff4v] medle them not of the dede of jugement ne pronounce the causes of partyes, it is to theym no force for by so moche they have the lesse charge to theyr soules and to theyr bodyes.

ames et corps. Et combien que ce soit [fol. 25v b] chose neccessaire pour punir les mauvais et faire droit a un chascun, assez d'ommes sont en telz offices que[1] devroient vouloir que oncques n'y eussent sceu ne que leurs meres. Car se tous y vont la droitte voye, ce scet Dieux; de laquelle chose quant fraude y est,[2] la punicion n'est pas petite."

## *Chapitre 14*    Dit encore[3] altercacions et argumens de Christine a Raison

"Certes,[4] bien dites, et moult sont consonnantes voz raisons en mon courage. Mais toutevoyes quoy que il soit de leur entendement,[5] c'est chose prouvee que femmes ont le corps foible, tendre et non poissant en fais[6] de force, et par nature sont couardes. Et c'est une chose que moult a petice[7] le degré et auctorité du sexe femmenin, par le jugement des [fol. 26r a] hommes.[8] Car ilz veulent dire que de tant comme une corps[9] est plus imperfait en quelque chose, de tant est reprimee et apeticee de sa vertu, et par consequent il en fait moins a louer."

*Response*: "Fille chiere, ceste consequence n'est point bonne et ne fait a soustenir. Car sans faille on voit souvent que quant Nature s'est restrainte a quelconque corps que elle a fourmé, donner si grant perfeccion[10] a un autre: ains la fait d'aucunes choses imperfait ou defformé ou de beaulté, ou de aucune impotence, ou foiblece de membres, que il advient que elle le recompense d'aucun aultre trop plus grant don que elle ne lui atollu. Exemple: si comme il est dit du tres grant philosophe [fol. 26r b] Aristote, qui estoit tres lait de corps, un oeil plus haulte[11] que l'autre et d'estrange phisonnomie; mais s'il ot aucune defformité de corps, vrayement Nature le recompensa moult grandement en entendement retentive et sentement, si comme il appert par ses auttentiques escriptures, si lui valu trop plus celle recompensacion de si grant engin que se il eust eu le corps propre ou semblable de Absalon.

---

[1] que] qui
[2] fraude y est] faulte y a
[3] Dit encore] Ancore
[4] Certes] Certes, dame
[5] leur entendement] l'entendement
[6] fais] fait
[7] Et c'est une chose que moult a petice] Et ycestes choses par le jugement des hommes appetissent moult
[8] par le jugement des hommes] *R omits phrase*
[9] une corps] un corps
[10] a quelconque . . . perfeccion] de donner a quelque corps que elle ait formé aussi grant perfection comme
[11] haulte] bas

And howe be it that it is a thynge necessary for to punysshe the evyll doers and to do ryght unto every man, there ben men ynowe and suche offycers that they myght wysshe that they had never knowne more than theyr moders. For yf they go all the ryght waye, God knoweth; of the whiche if there be ony fraude, theyr punycyon is not lytell."

## Chapter 14     Of altercacyons and argumentes of Christine to Dame Reason

"Certes, madame, ye say ryght wel, and your reasons ben ryght well sownynge in my courage. But yet thoughe it be so of theyr understandynge, is that proved that women have feble bodyes, tendre, and not myghty in the dedes of strengthe, and by nature they ben cowardes? And this is one thynge that maketh moche lesse the degree and auctoryte of the kynde of woman by the jugement of men. For they wyll saye that insomoche as a body is more imperfyte in every thynge, so moche is it is abredged and made lesse of his vertue, and by that that thou folowest it, it is the lesse for to prayse."

*Answere*: "Dere doughter, thys [Ff5r] folowynge is not good, nor to be susteyned. For without fayle one seeth often tymes that when Nature hathe restrayned ony thynge frome a body that she hathe fourmed, she rewardeth that body in some other thynge of as moche valoure, as thus: if a woman be imparfyte of shap or of beaute, or of impotencye, or feblenes of membres, it is sygne that she recompenseth her with some other thynge that is more worth than that she hath berafte her. Ensample: as it is sayd of the grete phylosophre Arystotle, whiche was ryght lewde of shap, one eye hygher than that other and of straunge vysage; yet thoughe he had ony deformyte of body or of shap, truely Nature recompensed hym ryght gretely in understandynge retentyfe and felynge as it appereth by this autentyke wrytynges, so that recompensynge of so grete wytte was of more valoure than thoughe he had a body lyke unto Absolon.

"Pareillement se puet dire du grant empereur Alixandre qui fu tres lait, petit, et de chetif cors,[1] et toutevoies ot il en son courage si grant vertu comme il apparu,[2] et ainsi est il de mains aultres. Si te promet, belle amie, que le grant et fort corps ne fait mie le vertueux et poissant courage, [fol. 26v a] ains vient d'une vigueur et vertueuse maniers[3] qui est don de Dieu, qui[4] concede a Nature empraindre es unes creatures raisonnables plus que es autres, et est son giste mucié en l'entendement et ou courage, et non mie en la force du corps ou des membres. Ce veons nous[5] souvent par ce que assez de grans hommes et de fors membres veons qui sont lasches,[6] faillis, et recreans, et d'aultres petiz et foibles de corps qui sont hardis et vigoureux. Et semblablement est des autres vertus.

"Mais quant a la hardiesse et telle force de corps, Dieux et Nature ont assez fait pour les femmes qui leur en a donné impotence car a tout le moins sont elles par cellui agreable deffault excusees [fol. 26v b] de non faire les orribles cruaultes,[7] les murtres, et les grans griefs et extorsions,[8] lesquelles a cause de force on a fait et fait on continuelment au monde. Si n'en aront mie la punicion que telz cas requierent; et bien seroit et aroit esté pour les ames de plusieurs des plus fors que ilz eussent passé leur pellerinage en ce monde en corps femmenin et foible. Et vraiement je di et reviens a mon propos, que se Nature n'a donnee grant force de membres a corps femmenin,[9] que elle l'a bien recompensé en ce que inclinacion y a mise tres vertueuse, c'est d'amer son Dieu, et estre cremeteuse naturelment[10] de faillir contre ses commandemens, et celles qui sont autres se desnaturent.

"Mais avises toutevoies, [fol. 27r a] fille[11] chiere, comment il semble que Dieu tout de gré ait voulu demonstrer[12] aux hommes quoy que ilz dient que pour tant si[13] femmes n'ont mie toutes si grant force et hardiece corporele que ont communement hommes,[14] que ilz ne doivent mie croire[15] que ce soit pour ce que du sexe femmenin soit forclose toute force et hardiece corporelle. Il appert par ce que en plusieurs femmes a demonstré grant courage, force, et hardiece de toutes fortes choses emprendre et achever semblablement que firent les grans hommes

---

[1] cors] corsage
[2] apparu] y paru
[3] et vertueuse maniers] vertueuse naturelle
[4] qui] que il
[5] veons nous] nous appert
[6] de fors membres veons qui sont lasches] fors de membres voyons
[7] orribles cruaultes] cruaultez orribles
[8] griefs et extorsions] et griefs extorcions
[9] femmenin] de femme
[10] cremeteuse naturelment] cremeteuse
[11] fille] amie
[12] demonstrer] monstrer
[13] quoy que ilz dient que pour tant si] que pour tant se
[14] communement hommes] hommes communement
[15] croire] dire ne croire

In the same wyse one maye say of the grete Emperoure Alexandre that was but lytell of body, yet had he grete vertue in his courage as it appered, and so it is by many others. So I promyse thee, fayre love, that the grete and stronge body causeth not the vertuous and myghty courage, but it cometh of a vertuous strengethe and maners that is gyven of God, whiche graunteth to Nature to leve to some creatures reasonables more than to some others: for it is a gyfte hyd in the understandynge and in courage, and not onely in the strengthe of body nor of membres. Thus we knowe often tymes by that the grete men ynowe and [Ff5v] of stronge membres we se they be latches, faylynge, and recrayed, and of others that have ben lytell and feble of body that ben hardy and full stronge. And the same wyse it is of other vertues.

"But as to the hardynes and suche strengthe, God and Nature hathe done ynoughe for women in that that He hath gyven them impotencye for at the leest they ben agreably excused by that defaute, insomoche that they do not these horryble crueltees, the wronges, and the grete greves and extorcyons, the whiche are done to the worlde bycause of strength, so they shal not have suche punysshmentes as suche case requyreth. And it sholde have ben ryght good for the soules of man that they myght have passed the pylgrymage of this worlde in the feble body of woman. And truely I saye and come agayne to my purpose, that yf Nature had not gyven grete strengthe of membres to a woman's body, that she recompenseth her ryght well in that that there is gyven to her a more vertuous inclynacyon; that is, to love God and to be dredefull naturally to do contrary to His commaundementes. And those that do otherwyse dothe out of kynde.

"But always advyse thee, dere doughter, howe it semeth that God lyst to showe all degrees to men thoughe that they say that for as moche as women have not all so grete strengthe and hardynesse corporall as communely these men have, that they ought not byleve that it is for that that al bodely strengthe and hardynesse be shytte fro the kynde of woman. It appereth by that that in many women there is shewed grete courage, [Ff6r] strengthe, and hardynesse to undertake all maner of stronge thynges and to accheve them lyke as dyde these

sollemnelx conquereurs et chevalereux dont si grant mencion est faicte es escriptures, si que je te rementenray cy aprés par exemple.

"Belle fille,[1] or t'ay preparé grant et large [fol. 27r b] fosse et tout descombré de
la terre que j'ay portee hors a grans hottees sur mes espaules. Et des or est temps
que tu assies ens les grosses et fortes pierres des fondemens des murs de la Cité
des Dames. Si pren la truelle de ta plume, et t'apreste de fort ouvrer et maçonner[2]
par grant deligence. Car voy cy une grant et large pierre que je vueil qui soit la
premiere assise ou fondement de ta cité, et saches que Nature propre la pourtray
par les signes d'astralogie pour estre alouee en ceste oeuvre. Si te tray un pou
arriere, et je la gitteray sus."[3]

## Chapitre 15     Dit de la royne Semiramis

"Semiramis fu femme de moult grant vertu en fait de grant et vigoireux[4] courage
es entreprises et excercite [fol. 27v a] du fais des armes, laquelle y fu si tres excellente que les gens de lors qui estoient paiens disoient[5] pour la grant poissance que
elle avoit sur terre et sur mer, que elle estoit suer du grant dieu Jupiter et fille de
l'ancien dieu Saturnus, que ilz disoient estre dieux de terre et de la mer. Cest[e][6]
dame fu femme du roy Ninus, qui nomma la cité de Nynive de son nom, et fu si
grant conquereur que a l'aide de sa femme Semiramis, qui semblablement comme
lui chevauchoit en armes, il conquist la grant Babiloine et toute la grant terre
d'Assire, et autre païs maint.

"Avint que la dame estant encore assez en[7] joeune aage, Nynus son mary fu
occis d'une saiette a l'assault d'une cité. [fol. 27v b] Mais les obseques et sollemnitez
faictes couvenablement du dit roy, ne delaissa pas[8] la dame l'excercite des armes,
ains plus que devant par tres grant courage prist par[9] vigureuse force a gouverner
et seigneurir les royaumes et terres que son mary et elle avoient de leur propre
et conquises[10] a l'espee, lesquelx royaumes et terres elle garda moult notablement

---

[1]  fille] fille et chiere amie
[2]  ouvrer et maçonner] maçonner et ouvrer
[3]  gitteray sus] te gitteray jus
[4]  de grant et vigoireux] de fort et vertueux
[5]  disoient] distrent
[6]  Cest[e] dame: *Cest dame*
[7]  que la dame estant encore assez en] ou temps que la dame estoit ancore en assez
[8]  et sollemnitez faictes couvenablement du dit roy, ne delaissa pas] sollempnellement
faictes si qu'il appartenoit du dit Ninus ne delaissa pas
[9]  par] en
[10]  de leur propre et conquises] tant de leur propre comme conquises

grete men and solempne conquerours of whom there is made so grete mencyon in wrytynges, as I shall remembre thee hereafter by ensample.

"Fayre doughter, nowe I have ordeyned and arayed for thee a pytte grete and large, and I have borne out upon my sholdres ryght grete burdens of rubrysshe of the erthe. And it is tyme that thou sette in these grete and stronge stones for the foundement of the walles of the Cyte of Ladyes. Nowe take thy truell and thy plumbe with thy lyne, and make thee redy to werke strongly the masonry by grete dylygence. For se here a grete and a large stone, whiche I wyll that it be the fyrste set in the foundement of thy cyte. And knowe it that Nature herselfe hathe pourtrayed it by the sygnes of astrologye for to be alowed in this werke. Nowe drawe thee a lytell abacke, and I shall cast hym on."

## Chapter 15 Of the Quene Semyramys

"Semyramys was a woman of ryght grete vertue in dede, of grete and vyctoryous courage in undertakynge of entrepryses and in hauntynge of dedes of armes, the whiche was so excellent that the people there (the whiche were paynymes) sayd that for the grete myght and strengthe that she hadde bothe upon the lande and upon the see, that she was syster unto the grete god [Ff6v] Jupyter and doughter to the auncyent god Saturnus, whiche they called the god of the lande and of the see. This lady was the wyfe of Kynge Nynus that named the cyte of Nynyve of his name. And he was so grete a conqueroure that by the helpe of his wyfe Semyramys, whiche lykewyse as he rode alway with hym in harnoys, he conquered the grete Babylone and all the lande of Assyrye, and other countrees many.

"It happened that the lady beynge yet ynoughe in yonge age, Nynus her housbande was slayne with an arowe at the assaulte of a cyte. Yet when the obsequyes and solompnytees was covenably done of the foresayd kynge, the lady never lefte the excercyse of armes but more than before by ryght grete courage toke upon her to governe by strengthe the lordshyppes, royalmes, and landes whiche her housbande and she had conquered with the swerde, whiche landes and royalmes she kepte ryght notably by grete discyplyne of chevalrye. So and in suche

par[1] grant discipline de chevalerie. Si et en tel maniere excercita et acompli tant de notables oeuvres que nul homme en vigueur et force ne la surmonta.

"Celle dame en qui habondoit tres hardi courage ne redoubtoit nulle peine, n'estoit espoventee par nulz perilz, ains se exposoit a tous par telle excellence que [fol. 28r a] elle surmonta tous ses adversaires qui l'avoient cuidiee debouter en sa vesveté des contrees acquises. Par quoy elle fu tant crainte et doubtee en armes que elle ne garda mie tant seulement les contrees ja conquestees,[2] mais avec ce a tres grant armee ala sus la terre d'Ethioppe que elle combati par grant force et la subjugua et adjoingny a son empire. De la s'en ala a grant poissance en Ynde et fort assailli les Yndois, auxquelx oncques homme n'avoit approchié pour leur faire guerre. Si les vainqui et subjugua, puis ala plus avant sur les autres contrees tant que, a brief parler, aucques tout Orient conquist et mist a sa subjeccion avecques ces[3] conquestes, qui furent grandes et poissantes. [fol. 28r b] Ceste Semiramis[4] enforça et reffist la cité de Babiloine, qui avoit esté fondee par Nembroth et les geans, et estoit assisse ou champ de Semmaar, grande et de merveilleuse force et circuite. Mais encore plus l'enforça ceste dame de plusieurs deffenses, et fist faire au tour larges et parfons fossez.

"Semiramis estoit une fois en sa chambre avironnee de ses damoiselles, qui lui pignoient son chief. Adonc avint que nouvelles lui vindrent que un de ses royaumes s'estoit rebellé contre elle; si se leva a cop[5] et jura par sa poissance que jamais l'autre trece de son chief, qui estoit a trecier, ne seroit trecee jusques ad ce que elle eust vengee celle injure et eust remise la terre[6] en sa subgeccion. Si fist prestement armer [fol. 28v a] ses gens en grant multitude et ala sus les rebelles, et par merveilleuse force et vigueur les mist en sa subgecion et tellement espoventa yceulx et tous ses autres subgiez que oncques puis pié ne s'en osa[7] rebeller. Duquel fait tant noble et courageux par long temps donna tesmoingnage une grande statue d'un[8] ymage faicte d'arain doree richement eslevee sus un hault pillier en Babiloine, qui representoit une princesse tenant une espee et avoit l'un des costez de son chief trecié, et l'autre non. Ceste roine fonda et edefia de nouvel plusieurs citez et fortes placez, et perfist plusieurs autres grans fais et acompli tant que de nul homme n'est point [fol. 28v b] escript plus grant corage ne plus de fais merveilleuse et dignes de memoire.

"Bien est vray que plusieurs lui donnent blasme, et a bon droit lui fust donné se de nostre loy eust esté, de ce que elle prist a mary un filz que elle avoit eu de

---

[1] par] et par
[2] conquestees] conquises
[3] ces] ses
[4] Semiramis] Dame Semiramis
[5] a cop] tantost
[6] eust remise la terre] que la terre fust remise
[7] pié ne s'en osa] ne s'en osa pié
[8] d'un] d'une

manere she haunted and accomplysshed so many of notable werkes that no man in vygure and in strengthe surmounted her.

"This lady, in whom habounded ryght hardy courage, ne doubted no payne ne was not aferde of no perylles but put herselfe to all thynges by suche excellence that she overcame all her adversaryes that had trowed to put her in her wydowhode out of all her conquestes. By the whiche she was so dredde and doubted in armes that she kepte not onely the countres before conquered but with a ryght grete armye [Gg1r] wente upon the lande of Ethyope, whiche she overcame by grete strengthe and put it under subjeccyon, and joyned it to her empyre. From thens she wente with a grete puyssaunce into Inde and assayled strongly the men of Inde, to whom there was never man approched to make them warre. So she overcame them and put them under her subjeccyon, and syth she wente ferther upon theyr countrees so moche that to say shortly that she conquered all the Oryent whiche is called the Eest parte of the worlde, whiche were ryght grete and myghty. This Semyramys enforced and made agayn[1] the cyte of Babylone, whiche was founded by Nembroche and the gyauntes and was set in the Felde of Semyaar, grete and of mervayllous strengthe and cyrcuyte. And so this lady made it more stronger of dyvers defenses, and lete make aboute large and depe dykes.

"Semyramys was in a tyme in her chambre and maydens aboute her, kemynge her heed. It happened that tydynges came that one of her royalmes began to rebell agaynst her. So she lyfted up herselfe and sware by her puyssaunce that the other tresse of her heed sholde never be tressed whiche was untressed, tyll the tyme that she had venged her of that injury and put agayne that londe into her subjeccyon. So she made anone all her men to arme them in a grete multytude and wente upon these rebelles, and by mervaylous strengthe put them under subjeccyon. And thus they and all her other subjectes dradde her that never [Gg1v] syth they durste not move a fote to rebell. Of the whiche noble dede and couragyous longe tyme after gave wytnesse a grete ymage made of brasse gylte rychely lyfte up upon an hyghe pyller in Babylone, whiche represented a pryncesse holdynge [a][2] swerde in her hande and one of the sydes of her heed tressed, and the other not. This quene founded and edyfyed of newe dyvers cytees and stronge places and accomplysshed many other grete dedes, so moche that there was never wryten of no man of so grete courage ne of more mervaylous werkes worthy to be had in mynde.

"It is trouthe that many blameth her, and so she ought of ryght yf she had ben of our lawe, of that that she toke her owne sone to housbande that she had goten

---

[1] agayn : *agaynst*
[2] holdynge [a] swerde : *holdynge swerde*

Nynus son seigneur. Mais les causes qui la murent ad ce furent deux principales:
l'une qu'elle ne vouloit mie qu'en son empire eust autre dame couronnee que elle,
laquel chose eust esté se son filz eust espousee autre dame; l'autre estoit qu'il lui
sembloit que nul autre homme n'estoit digne de l'avoir a femme fors son propre
filz. Mais de ceste erreur, qui trop fu grande, ycelle noble dame fait aucunement
[fol. 29r a] a excuser pour ce que adonc n'estoit encore point de loy escripte, ains
vivoient la gent a l[o]y¹ de Nature ou il loisoit a un chascun² de faire sans mesprendre tout ce que le cuer lui aportoit. Car n'est pas doubte que se elle pensast
que mal fust ou que aucun blasme lui en peust encourir, que elle avoit bien si
grant et si hault courage, et tant amoit honneur, que jamais ne le feist.

"Mais or est assise la premiere pierre³ ou fondement de nostre cité. Si
nous couvient d'ores en avant asseoir ensuivant pierres a quantité pour avancier
nostre edeffice."

## *Chapitre 16*     Dit des Amazonnes

"Une terre siet vers la fin de Europe selon la grant mer⁴ qui enceint tout le monde.
[fol. 29r b] Ycelle terre est appellé Siche ou Sichie. Avint jadis que celle contree fut
per force de guerre despoillee de tous les jouvenceaulx⁵ hommes masles habitans
en ycelle contree. Quant les femmes du lieu virent que tous avoient perdus leur
maris, et freres, et parens, et ne leur estoit demouré que les viellars et les petiz
enfans, elles s'assemblerent par grant courage et prisdrent conseil entre elles, et
en conclusion delibererent que dela en avant par elles maintendroient leur seigneurie sans subgeccion d'ommes, et firent un tel edit que homme quelconque
ne seroit souffert entrer en leur jurisdicion; mais pour avoir lignee, elles yroient
es contrees voisines a certaines [fol. 29v a] saisons de l'annee et puis retourneroient
en leur païs. Et se elles enfantoient masles, les envoieroient a leurs peres; et se
femmelles estoient, les nourriroient. Pour perfurnir ceste ordennance establirent
des plus nobles dames d'entre elles deux que a roynes couronnerent, dont l'une fu
appellee Lampheto, l'autre Marpasie.

"Ceste chose faicte, tantost chacierent hors de leurs païs tous les masles qui
leur estoient demourez. Et aprés s'armerent et a grant bataille toute dames et
pucelles⁶ alerent sur leurs anemis et toute la terre gasterent par feu et par armes,
ne il ne fu nul qui a elles peust resister; et a brief parler, moult bien vengirent la

---

¹ l[o]y: *lay*
² un chascun] chacun
³ pierre] partie
⁴ mer] mer océanne
⁵ jouvenceaulx] principaulx
⁶ dames et pucelles] de dames et de pucelles

of Nynus her lorde. But the causes that moved her to that were .ii. pryncypally: that one, that she wolde not have had in her empyre none other lady crowned save onely herselfe, the whiche sholde have ben if her sone had wedded ony other lady; that other cause was that her semed no man worthy to have her to his wyfe save onely her owne sone. Yet was this cause the gretter thrughe whiche she was somwhat excused in that that she was not of our lawe for the people lyved after the lawe of Nature, where one durste doo to another without mysse takynge that whiche his herte perceyved or desyred. For it is no doubte that if she had thought that it had ben evyll or that ony blame sholde fall to her therof, but that she had so grete and soo hyghe courage and loved so moche worshyp she [Gg2r] wolde never have done it.

"Nowe is the fyrst stone set in the foundement of our cyte. Nowe it is convenyent from hensforthe to set sewyngly stones to the quantyte for to avaunce our buyldynge."

## *Chapter 16*     Of the Amozones

"A lande there is towarde the ende of Europe after the grete see that holdeth in all the worlde, whiche lande is called Syche or Sychye. It happened somtyme that that countre by force of warre was despoyled of all the yonge men dwellynge in that countree. And when the women of that place sawe that they had lost theyr housbandes, theyr bretherne, and theyr kynnesmen, and there was none lefte but olde men and chyldren, they assembled by grete courage and toke counsayle bytwene them and advysed the conclusyon that from that tyme forth they wolde maynteyne theyr lordshyppes without ony subjeccyon of men, and made suche a commaundement that no maner of man sholde entre into theyr jurysdyccyon. Yet for to have lygnage, they sholde go into the nexte countre by a certayne season of the yere, and then sholde they tourne home agayne into theyr countre. And yf they were delyvered of ony sones, they sholde sende them unto theyr faders. And yf they [Gg2v] were mayde chyldren, they wolde nourysshe them themselfe to perfourme theyr ordynaunce. Then they chose .ii. of the moost noble ladyes amonge them to be crowned quenes, of whiche one was called Lampheto, that other Marpasye.

"This done, they chased out of theyr countre all the mankynde that was lefte, bothe yonge and olde. And after that they armed them and with a grete batayle all of ladyes and of maydens went upon theyr enemyes and wasted all theyr lande by fyre and by arm[e]s,[1] and there was none that myght resyst them. And to speke shortely, they avenged the dethe of theyr frendes full notably. And by this

---

[1] arm[e]s : *armrs*

mort de leurs amis.[1] Et par celle [fol. 29v b] voye commencierent les femmes de
Siche a porter armes qui furent puis appellés Amazones, qui vault autant a dire
comme desmamellees pour ce que elles avoient une telle maniere que aux nobles
d'entre elles, quant petites filletes estoient, leur cuisoient par certain artefice la
mamelle senestre pour ce que elle ne leur encombrast a porter l'escu; et aux non
nobles estoient[2] la destre pour plus aisé traire de l'arc.

"Si s'alerent tant delictant en ycellui mestier d'armes que elles acrurent
par force moult leur païs et leur regne, tant que par tout ala leur hault renommee si que je t'ay cy devant touchié. Ycelles deux roynes Lampheto et Marpasie
s'estendirent en divers [fol. 30r a] païs, chascune menant moult grant host, et tant
y firent que elles conquistrent grant partie de Europe et de la region d'Aise, et
pluseurs royaumes subjuguerent et adjousterent a leur seigneurie villes et cités, et
maintes en fonderent,[3] et mesmement en Aise la cité de Ephese, qui est et long
temps a esté de grant renommee.

"De ces .ii. roynes, Marpasie morut la premiere en une bataille. Donc en
son lieu les Amazonnes couronnerent une sienne fille, vierge, noble, et belle qui
nommee fu Sinoppe. Ceste tant ot grant et hault courage que jour de sa vie
ne se daigna couppler a homme, ains remaint vierge tout son aage. Si n'avoit
autre amour ne autre cure fors seulement [fol. 30r b] en l'excercite d'armes. La
estoit toute sa plaisance par[4] telle ardeur que elle ne pouoit estre saoulee de terres
assaillir et conquerre. Par elle fu sa mere si grandement vengee que tous ceulx de
la contree ou occise ot esté mist a l'espee et toute gasta la terre, et mainte autre
grant contree[5] conquist."

## *Chapitre 17*      Ci dit[6] de la royne d'Amazonie Thama[ri]s[7]

"Ainsi comme tu pueux ouir commencerent et maintindrent par moult long
temps les Amazonnes leur seigneurie moult vigoureusement, desquelles furent
roynes par succession l'une de l'autre moult vaillans dames, qui a toutes nommer
de renc pourroit tourner aux lisans a annuy, si souffira dire d'aucunes principales.
Royne [fol. 30v a] d'ycelle terre fu la preux, vaillant, et sage Thamaris, par lequel
sens, cautelle, et force fu vaincu et pris Cirrus le fort et poissant roy de Perse, qui
avoit ja conquis[8] la grant Babiloine et mesmement une grant partie du monde.

---

[1] amis] ennemis
[2] estoient] ostoient
[3] en fonderent] fonderent
[4] par] et par
[5] et mainte autre grant contree] et avec ce mainte autre contree
[6] Ci dit de] De
[7] Thama[ri]s: *Thamans*
[8] avoit ja conquis] qui tant avoit fait de merveilles et conquis

way began the women of Syche or of Sychye to bere armes, the whiche syth were called *Amozonnes*, that is as moche to say as 'unpapped' for that they had suche a manere that the noble women, when they were lytell maydens, theyr lyfte pappes were cutte off by a certayne crafte for that they sholde not be combred to bere the shelde. And to them that were not gentylwomen, theyr ryght pappes were cut away to shote the more easely.

"So they wente so moche, delytynge in the crafte of armes, that they encreased by for[c]e[1] ryght moche theyr countre and theyr royalmes insomoche that theyr fame wente all aboute, as I have here before touched to thee. Then they wente into dyvers countrees, eche of theym ledynge a grete hoost, and dyde so moche that they conquered a grete parte of Europe and of the countre of Ay[s]e,[2] and put under subjeccyon many dyvers [Gg3r] countres and joyned them to theyr lordshyppes, and founded many cytees and townes, and in lykewyse in Ayse in the cyte of Ephese, whiche is and longe tyme hathe ben of grete renowne.

"Of these two quenes, Marpasye dyed fyrst in a batayle. Then the Amozones crowned her doughter in her place, a noble mayde and a fayre whiche was named Synoppe, whiche had so grete courage and hyghe that all the dayes of her lyfe she dysdeyned not to be coupled to no man but remayned styll a mayde al her lyfe. So she had none other love nor charge but onely in the excersyse of armes, and in that she had so grete pleasunce that she myght not be satysfyed to assayle and conquere landes and royalmes. And by her her moder was gretly venged, insomoche that those of that countre were slayne and put to the swerde, and wasted all the lande and conquered."

## Chapter 17      Of the Quene of Amozonye Thamaris

"Thus, as thou mayste here howe the Amozones began and maynteyned longe tyme theyr lordshyppes ryght worshypfully, of the whiche they made quenes by successyon one after another yf ryght worshypful ladyes, whiche to name by rowe it myght tourne the reders to grete noyaunce. So it shall suffyse to speke of the pryncypalles, of whiche there was one called Thamarye ryght hardy, wyse, and sage by whos wytte, cautele, [Gg3v] and strengthe Cyrrus the strong and myghty kynge of Perse was overcome and taken, whiche had conquered the grete Babylone and in the same wyse a grete parte of the worlde. So he wolde after many

---

[1] for[c]e : *forte*
[2] Ay[s]e : *Ayfe*

Si voult[1] aprés maintes autres conquestes que il ot[2] faictes aler sur la terre et royaume d'Amazonie, en esperance de la mettre semblablement soubz sa seigneurie.

"Donc il avint que comme ycelle sage royne Thamaris sceut par ses espies
comment ycellui roy[3] Cirrus venoit sur elle a si tres grant force de gens que
souffire deust a conquerir tout le monde, s'avisa que impossible seroit a tel host
desconfire par force d'armes, si lui couvenoit user [fol. 30v b] de cautelle. Adonc a
loy de vaillant chevetaine, quant elle sceut que ja estoit Cyrrus[4] entrez bien avant
en sa terre, laquelle chose elle avoit souffert tout de gré et[5] passer avant sans nul
contredit, fist armer toutes ses damoiselles, et par moult belle ordenance les mist
en diverses embusches sur montaignes et en bois par ou Cyrrus ne pouoit passer
par aultre part.

"La moult coyement Thamaris a tous ses hosts attendi tant que Cyrrus
et toute sa gent[6] aprés lui se fussent fichiez es destrois estranges et obscurs
entre roches, forests, et estroictes voies,[7] par ou aler lui convenoit. Adonc la
dame, quant vid son point, fist haultement [fol. 31r a] sonner sa buisine. Si se
trouva esbahy Cirrus, qui garde ne s'en donnoit, quant il se vid assailli de toutes
pars. Car par dessus les haultes montaingnes leur boutoyent[8] les dames sur eulx
grandes roches qui a tas les acravantoient, ne aler avant ne avancier ne se pouoient pour la diversité du païs. Et si leur estoit une des embusches au devant, qui
les occioit au fueur que ilz yssoient des destrois ne reculer aussi ne peussent,
pour l'autre embusche qui derriere eulx assise[9] estoit. Si furent la tous mors et
acravantes, et Cyrrus pris, et par le commandement de la royne laissié vif lui et
ses barons, que elle fist aprés la desconfiture amener [fol. 31r b] devant elle en un
paveillon que fait ottendre.

"Et la[10] pour la grant yre que elle avoit a lui pour cause d'un[11] sien filz qui avoit
esté occis, qu'envoyé avoit au devant de Cyrrus, ne le voult prendre a mercis ains
fist a tous ses barons trenchier les testes devant lui. Et puis aprés lui dist: 'Cirrus,
qui par ta cruaulté oncques ne fus saoulé de sang d'ommes, or en pourras[12] boire

---

[1] voult] volt cellui Cirus

[2] ot] avoit

[3] comme ycelle sage royne Thamaris sceut par ses espies comment ycellui roy] celle
sage royne comme elle sceut par ses espies que

[4] que ja estoit Cyrrus] que Cirus estoit ja

[5] et] a

[6] sa gent] ces gens

[7] estranges et obscurs entre roches, forests, et estroictes voies] et obscurs passages
entre roches et forests espesses

[8] boutoyent] lançoient

[9] qui derriere eulx assise] qui derriere eulx pareillement

[10] Et la] la

[11] pour cause d'un] pour un

[12] pourras] peus

other conquestes that he had done goo upon the lande of Amozones in hope to have put them under his subjeccyon, wherof it happened as this same wyse.

"The quene knewe by her spyes that this same Kynge Cyrrus wolde come upon her with so grete strengthe of people that ought suffycyently to conquere all the worlde. She advysed her that it sholde be impossyble to dyscomfyte theyr hoost by strengthe of armes, so it was convenyent to laboure by cautele. And then she wente, this worshypfull capytayne, when she knewe that Cyrrus was entred before into her londe, the whiche she suffred and lete hym passe before into her londe without ony gaynesaynge. She made arme all her damoyselles, and by ryght good ordynaunce put them in dyvers busshmentes upon the mountaynes and in the woodes where that Cyrrus myght passe none other way.

"There abode this Thamarys ryght stylly with all her hoostes unto the tyme that Cyrrus and his people were come into the strayte wayes in forestes, and amonge the craggy roches where thrughe he must nedes passe. And then the lady, when that she sawe tyme, made hastely to blowe a trompette. And then this Cyrrus was ryght sore abasshed, whiche toke no hede to hymselfe, and sodeynly sawe hym assayled in every [Gg4r] parte. For these ladyes that were upon the mountaynes threwe downe grete roches upon them whiche myght go nother forwarde ne backewarde for the dyversyte of the countre. And some of the busshmentes were before, whiche slewe the people downe ryght fervently that wolde have yssued out of the strayte passages and myght not gather them togyder for that other busshment that was behynde them. So they were smyten asondre with stronge roches to the dethe all the people, and Cyrrus taken, and by the commaundement of the quene lefte alyve and his barons with hym, whom she made to come before her into a pavylyon after the dyscomfyture.

"And for the grete wrathe that she had to hym for one of her maydens that he had slayne by the way before, she wolde have no mercy of Cyrrus nor of his barons but made to smyte off theyr hedes before hym. And after that she sayd to hym: 'Cyrrus, whiche by thy crueltees were never satysfyed with the blode of man, nowe thou mayst drynke at thy wyll.' And then she made to smyte off his

a ta voulenté.' Et adonc sa teste que elle ot faicte tranchier fist gitter en une tine, en laquelle avoit faicte recueillir le sang de ses barons.

"Belle fille et ma chiere amie, ycestes choses je te ramentois pour ce que il affiert a la matiere dont je te parloie, non obstant que bien les [fol. 31v a] saches et que toy mesmes les aies recitees autre fois en ton *Livre de la mutacion de fortune* et mesmement en ton *Epistre de Othea*.[1] Si t'en diray encores ensuivant."

*Chapitre [18][2]*     **Ci dit comment[3] le fort Hercules et Thezeus son compagnon alerent en Grece a grant host et grant naviere sus[4] les Amazones, et comment les deux pucelles Manalippe et Ypolite les abatirent chevaulx et tout en un mont[5]**

"Que t'en diroye? Ja orent tant fait a la force de leurs corps et par proece d'armes[6] les dames d'Amazonie que par tout païs furent craintes et redoubtees; et jusques en la terre de Grece, qui assez longtaine en estoit, en alerent les nouvelles. Et comment ycelles dames ne cessoient d'envair terres et[7] tout aloient [fol. 31v b] gastant païs se tost ne se rendoient a elles,[8] et comment il n'estoit force qui peust resister a la leur.[9] De ce fu Grece espoventee, doubtant que la force d'ycelles s'estendist quelque fois jusques a eulx.[10]

"Adonc estoit en Grece en la fleur de sa joeunece Hercules le merveilleux et le fort, qui en son temps fist plus de merveilles de force[11] que oncques ne fist homme de mere nez, dont il soit mencion en hystoires. Car il se combatoit aux geans, aux lyons, aux serpens, et monstres merveilleux et de toute avoit la victoire.[12] Et a brief parler, tant fu fort que oncques de force homme ne l'ataingny excepté Sampxon le Fort. Cellui Hercules [fol. 32r a] dist que il ne seroit pas bon d'atendre que les Amazonnes venissent sur eux: si estoit trop le meilleur de les aler premierement envair. Lors fist pour ce faire[13] armer navire et assembla grant

---

[1] ton *Epistre de Othea*] *l'Epistre Othea*

[2] [18] : *xxviij*

[3] Ci dit comment] Comment

[4] alerent en Grece a grant host et grant navierre sus] vindrent de Grece a grant navire sur

[5] mont] mont, et comment a la fin les ii chevaliers orent victoire sur les ii pucelles non obstant la grant force dont elles estoient

[6] corps et par proece d'armes] corps

[7] et] et conquerre et que par

[8] païs se tost ne se rendoient a elles] païs et contrees se tost a elles ne s'en rendoient

[9] peust resister a la leur] a la leur resister peust

[10] s'estendist quelque fois jusques a eulx] s'estendist a la fois jusques en celle terre

[11] force] force de corps

[12] toute avoit la victoire] tous avoit victoire

[13] Lors fist pour ce faire] Lors pour ce faire fist

heed and cast it into a basyne, into the whiche she had made to gather the blode of his lordes.

"Fayre doughter and my dere frende, these thynges I brynge in remembraunce for that affermeth the matter that I have tolde thee of notwithstandynge that thou knowest them well and thyselfe hast rehersed them another tyme in thy boke of the *Mutacyon of Fortune*, and in the same wyse in thyne *Epystle of Othea*. So I shall say to thee more yet hereafter folowynge." [Gg4v]

## Chapter 18     Howe the stronge Hercules and Theseus wente upon the Amozones, and howe the .ii. ladyes Menalope and Ypolyte had almoost overcome them

"What sholde I say more of the strengthe of theyr bodyes, or by the prowesse of armes of these ladyes of Amozonye?—whiche by all countrees were dredde and doubted anone to the londe [of] Grece[1] whiche was farre thens. And the tydynges wente howe these ladyes seased not to destroy landes and wasted the countres yf they wolde not yelde theym ryght soone unto theym, and howe they [were unable][2] to withstande theyr enemyes. Of this all Grece was aferde, doubtynge that the landes of theym sholde stretche in shorte t[y]me[3] unto theyr countre.

"Then there was in Grece in the floure of his youthe Hercules, the mervayllous stronge man whiche in his tyme dyde more mervaylles of strength than ever man dyde that was borne of woman, of whome is made mencyon in hystoryes. For he fought with gyauntes and lyons, with serpentes and monstres ryght mervayllous, and had of all them the vyctory. And to saye shortely, he was so stronge that never man was lyke hym in strength excepte Sampson le Forte. This Hercules sayd that it were not good to abyde tyl these ladyes of Amozonye came upon them, but it were moche better to go upon them fyrst. Then for that they lete ordeyne [Hh1r] a grete navye of shyppes and assembled a grete company of yonge

---

[1]  to the londe [of] : *to the of londe*
[2]  [were unable] : *see note*
[3]  t[y]me : *tnme*

foison de nobles jovenceaulx pour la aler a grant effort. Quant Theseus le vaillant
et le preux, qui roy estoit d'Athenes, sceut ceste[1] nouvelle dist que sans lui n'yroit
il mie. Si assembla son host avec[2] cellui d'Ercules, et[3] a grant gent se mirent en
mer tyrant vers le païs d'Amazonie.

"Et quant aucques en furent approchiez, Hercules, non obstant sa tres
mervelleuse force et souveraine hardiece,[4] et qui si grant host de vaillant gent
avoit avec[5] lui, n'osa oncques prendre [fol. 32r b] port par jour ne descendre sur
terre: tant ressongnoit la force d'ycelles, qui seroit une merveilleuse chose a dire
et croire[6] se tant d'ystoires ne le tesmoignoient que homme qui oncques par poissance de creature ne pot estre vaincu redoubtast force de femmes. Si attendi Hercules, lui et son host, tant que nuyt obscure fut venue. Et adonc, quant il fu l'eure
que toute chose mortelle doit prendre repos et somme, saillerent hors yceulx,
entrerent ou païs[7] et par les villes commencirent[8] a bouter feu, et occire celles
qui de leur venue garde ne se donoient. En peu d'eure, grande y fu la criee. Si[9]
ne furent pas lentes a courir aux armes communement toutes et[10] qui [fol. 32v a]
mieulx mielx prisdrent comme tres hardies a courir a grans tourbes vers la marine
sur leurs anemis.

"Adonc regnoit sur les Amazones la royne Orthia, qui fu dame de moult
grant vaillance et qui mainte terre avoit conquise. Et ceste fut mere a la vaillant[11]
royne Panthassillee, dont cy après mencion sera faicte. Ceste Orthia avoit esté
couronnee après la chevalereuse royne Anthioppe, qui les Amazonnes avoit maintenues[12] en grant discipline de chevalerie, et moult avoit esté preux en son temps.

"Si oy ceste Orthia les nouvelles comment les Grieux sans deffier s'estoient
par nuit embatus sur sa[13] terre qui tout aloient occiant. Adonc se elle fut ayree contre eulx, [fol. 32v b] nul nel demande, et bien leur cuide chier vendre son maltalant.

---

[1] ceste] celle
[2] avec] avecques
[3] et] et ainsi
[4] et souveraine hardiece] et hardiece
[5] avec] avecques
[6] la force d'ycelles, qui seroit une merveilleuse chose a dire et croire] la grant force et
hardiece d'icelles, laquelle chose seroit merveilleuse chose a dire et forte a croire
[7] saillerent hors yceulx] yceulx saillirent hors des nefs ou païs entrerent
[8] commencirent] pristrent par tout
[9] occire . . . la criee. Si] faire grant occision sur celles qui garde ne s'en donnoient et
qui despourveues furent prises si y fu grande la criee en petit d'eure. Et
[10] aux armes communement toutes et] communement toutes aux armes et au plus
tost qu'elles porent
[11] vaillant] preux
[12] maintenues] maintenues et gouvernees
[13] sa] leur

lusty men for to go thyder in grete haste. When Theseus the worshypfull and wyse man whiche was kynge of Athenes knewe this tydynges, he sayd that he sholde not go without hym. And so he assembled a grete hoost with this hoost of Hercules; and when they were all assembled, they put them into the see towarde the countre of Amozonye.

"And when they approched the countre Hercules, notwithstandynge his mervaylous strengthe and hardynesse and his grete host of people, durste not take the porte by day, ne to come downe upon the lande. So moche the strengthe of these Amozones was blowen aboute in dyvers countrees that it were mervayle to say and byleve yf there were not soo many hystoryes brynge wytnesse of them, that there hathe ben so many worshypfull men overcome by women. So Hercules and his hoost abode tyll the darke nyght was come. And then, when the houre was come that every mortall creature ought to take his rest and slepe, he and his hoost lepte a lande and entred into the countre, and began to sette fyre in cytees and townes, and slewe all the women that toke no hede of theyr comynge. In the meanetyme, grete was the crye amonge the people. Then they were not slowe to renne to theyr harnoys al maner of women as those that were moost hardyest to renne amonge the people towarde the seesyde upon theyr enemyes.

"And then there reygned upon these Amozones [Hh1v] the Quene Orthya, the whiche was a lady of ryght grete worthynesse and conquered many landes. And this was the moder of the worshypfull Quene Pantasylya, of whom shall be made mencyon hereafter. This Quene Orthya was crowned after the chevalrous Quene Anthyoppe, the whiche maynteyned the Amozones in grete dyscyplyne of armes and of chevalrye, and was passynge wyse and hardye in her tyme.

"Soo this Quene Orthya herde this tydynges howe the Grekes were come in by nyght, fyghtynge on the lande, and alway sleynge the people. Then it was to deme that she was wrothe and thought to be avenged upon theyr male talent, and

Et tantost, fort menaçant ceulx que[1] de riens elle ne craingnoit,[2] commanda a armer toutes ses batailles. La veissiez les dames embesoingnees de courir aux armes et elles assembler autour de leur royne; ja estoit le jour cler venus.[3]

"Mais entendis que celle armee[4] se faisoit et que la royne entendoit a mettre ses hostz et ses batailles[5] en ordonnance, deux vaillans pucelles de souveraine force et chevalerie, hardies et preux sur toutes[6] riens dont l'une estoit appellee Manalippe et l'autre Yppolite, et parentes estoient prouchaines a la royne,[7] n'attendirent pas les conrois de [fol. 33r a] leur dame, ains au plus tost que porent estre[8] armees — les lances es poins, les escus de fort elephant pendus au col, montees sur les courans destriers — s'en vindrent plus fort courant que elles porent de vers le port et par grant ardeur comme surprises d'yre et de maltalent, les lances baissees brochierent[9] contre les plus parans des Grieux, c'est assavoir Manalippe vers Hercules, et Yppolite a Theseus. Mais se elles orent yre bien ypparu, car non obstant la grant force, hardiece, et grant courage d'yceulx, si fort les hurterent et par si viguoureuse encontre les damoiselles que chascune abati son chevalier, cheval et tout en un mont, et elles autressi de l'autre part [fol. 33r b] cheurent. Mais le plus tost se releverent et a bonnes espees leur coururent sus.

"O, quel honneur dorent avoir ces damoiselles, quant par elles deux femmes estoient abatus deux les plus vaillans chevaliers qui fussent en tout le monde! Et ceste chose ne seroit mie creable que elle peust estre vraye se tant de aucteurs auttentiques ne le tesmoingnoient; lesquelx aucteurs mesmes[10] eulx esmerveillant de ceste aventure, en excusant par especial Hercules considerant son oultrageuse[11] force, dient que ce pot tenir a son cheval qui trebucha du grant hurt du cop, car ne cuident pas que se a pié fust eust esté trebuchiez.

"Honteux furent les deux [fol. 33v a] chevaliers d'estre par les pucelles abatus. Non obstant ycelles se combatirent aux espees a eulx par grant vigueur[12] et longuement en dura la bataille, mais au desrain, et quel merveille car ne deust pas estre la couple pareil, la furent[13] prises par eulx les damoiselles. De ceste prise

---

[1]  que] qui

[2]  craingnoit] craint

[3]  ja estoit le jour cler venus] qui a l'adjournant ot tous ses conrois prests

[4]  armee] assemblee

[5]  hostz et ses batailles] osts, batailles

[6]  toutes] toute

[7]  estoient prouchaines a la royne] parentes bien prochaines a la royne estoient

[8]  porent estre] estre porent

[9]  brochierent] brochent

[10]  ne le tesmoingnoient lesquelx aucteurs mesmes] ne l'eussent en leurs livres tesmoignié lesquieulx aucteurs mesmement

[11]  son oultrageuse] sa desmesuree

[12]  les pucelles . . . vigueur] les ii pucelles. Non pour tant ycelles se combatirent a eulx a bonnes espees par grant vertu

[13]  pareil, la furent] pareille furent

anone manasynge them that she dredde not, commaunded to make redy all her batayle. There one myght see all the ladyes busy to renne to theyr harnoys and assembled them aboute theyr quene; and by this tyme was the clere daye come. And then this quene armed herselfe and abode to put in ordre her bataylles and her hostes.

"Then were there .ii. worshypful maydens of soverayne strength of cheval-rye and hardynesse and wyse above many others, of whiche that one was called Manalyppe and that other Ipolyte, and they were ryght nyghe kynne to the quene. And they abode not onely the comynge of theyr quene, but as fast as they myght be armed—theyr speres in theyr handes, theyr sheldes of stronge elemphant hangynge upon theyr neckes, mounted upon theyr well rennynge coursers—wente ryght fast rennynge towarde the porte [Hh2r] and with grete hete as those that were supprysed with wrathe, berynge lowe theyr speres bare thrughe the best of the Grekes, that is to knowe Manalyppe towarde Hercules, and Ipolyte to Theseus.[1] But whether they had wrathe or no it apered wel for notwithstandynge the grete strengthe, hardynesse, and grete courage of them, so strongly these maydens hurte them and by so grete encountre, eche of theym bete theyr knyght, and they also fell on the other syde. But as soone as they myght, they recovered themselfe and ranne upon them with good swerdes.

"O, what worshyp ought these ladyes to have that by suche .ii. women were beten .ii. of the best knyghtes that were in all the worlde! And this thynge sholde not be credyble to be trewe but that so many antentyke doctours bereth wytnesse of it. These same doctours mervayllynge themselfe of this adventure, in excusy-nge specyally Hercules consyderynge his outragyous strengthe, sayth that he was beholdynge to his hors that lepte from the grete hurte of the stroke, for they trowed not yf they had ben on fote but they sholde have ben throwne downe.

"These .ii. knyghtes were ashamed to be thus beten of these .ii. maydens. Notwithstandynge, these maydens fought with theyr swerdes ayenst these .ii. knyghtes strongly and the batayle endured longe, yet at the last and what mervayle that these maydens were taken, for there ought not to be lyke strokes bytwene

---

[1] Theseus : *Thesens* here and elsewhere emdended silently

se tindrent si grandemens honnourez Hercules et Thezeus qu'ilz ne[1] voulsissent
tenir l'avoir d'une cité. Si se retrairent[2] en leur navire pour eulx reffreschir et
desarmer, et bien leur semble qu'ilz y ont grandement[3] esploitié. Les dames
moult honnourerent, et quant si belles et si avenantes desarmees les virent, adonc
doubla leur joye, car oncques n'orent pris proie qui tant leur [fol. 33v b] fust agreable, et a grant plaisir les regardoient.

"Ja venoit la royne sur les Gregois a grant host quant les nouvelles lui vindrent des deux damoiselles qui prises estoient. De ce fu dolente a merveilles; mais
pour doubte que pis en faissent aux damoiselles que prises tenoient se sur eulx
alast, s'arresta a tant et leur manda par deux de ses baronnesses que ilz voulsissent
mettre a tel reançon les damoiselles[4] comme il leur plairoit, et elle leur envoieroit.

"Hercules et Thezeus moult recevrent a grant honneur les messagieres et
courtoisement respondirent que se la royne vouloit faire paix a eulx, et promettre
elles[5] et ses baronnesses que [fol. 34r a] jamais contre les Grieux ne s'armeroient
ains seroient leurs bonnes amies, et que autressi pareillement leur promettroient,
que ilz rendroient les damoiselles tout quitement sans vouloir autre reançon fors
les armeures seulement. Car ce vouloient ilz bien avoir pour honneur et remembrance a tousjours mais d'ycelle[6] victoire que eue avoient sur les damoiselles.

"La royne, pour le desir que avoit d'avoir ces .ii. pucelles[7] que elle moult
chieres tenoit, fu contrainte de faire paix aux Grie[u]x.[8] Si fu tant la chose pour-
parlee et entre eulx acordee que la royne, toute desarmee, a moult belle com-
pagnee de dames et pucelles[9] en si riches atours que oncques pareil n'orent veu
les [fol. 34r b] Grieux, ala devers eulx pour les festoier et creanter la paix, et la fu
faicte moult grant joye. Mais non pour tant a Thezeus moult anuioit de rendre
Ypolite, car ferus en estoit[10] de grant amour. Si en pria et requist tant Hercules
pour lui a la royne[11] que elle ottroya que a femme la prensist et en son païs la
menast. Grandes y furent faictes les nopces,[12] puis s'en partirent les Grieux; et
ainsi en amena Theseus Ypolite, qui puis en ot un filz qui fut nommé Ypolitus,

---

[1] ne] n'en
[2] retrairent] retrayrent a tant
[3] qu'ilz y ont grandement] que grandement ont
[4] damoiselles] pucelles
[5] elles] elle
[6] mais d'ycelle] d'ycelle
[7] pour le desir que avoit d'avoir ces .ii. pucelles] pour le desire de ravoir ses .ii.
damoiselles
[8] Grie[u]x: *Griex*
[9] pucelles] de pucelles
[10] a Thezeus moult anuioit de rendre Ypolite, car ferus en estoit] moult anuyoit a
Theseus de rendre Ypolite car ja l'amoit
[11] requist tant Hercules pour lui a la royne] requist Hercules a la royne tant pour lui
[12] nopces] rïotes

them. Of this pryse they thought them gretely honoured: Hercules and Theseus were gladder than and they had taken a cyte. [Hh2v] So they helde them in theyr shyppes with them to refresshe them and to unarme them, and thought that they had well employed theyr wyll. And when they sawe them unarmed, and that they were so fayre and so semely, then doubled theyr joye for they toke never pray that was to them so agreable. And so they kepte them with grete joy and pleasaunce.

"Then came the quene upon the Grekes with a grete hoost. And when the tydynges came to her that these two maydens were taken, she was mervayllously sorowful. Yet for doubte that they sholde do ony harme to these ladyes that were taken yf she wente upon them, she rested as then and sente to them by .ii. of her baronnesses, and badde them to put theyr fynaunce for these .ii. ladyes as moche as it pleased them, and she wolde sende it unto them.

"Hercules and Theseus receyved these messageres with grete worshyp and answered theym courtoysly and yf the quene wolde make a small peas with them, and bothe she and her baronnesses sholde promyse that they sholde never arme them agaynst the Grekes but to be theyr good frendes, and the Grekes wolde promyse them in the same wyse that they wolde yelde home these .ii. ladyes all quyte without havynge ony other raunsome, save theyr harnoys onely, for that they wolde have for worshyp and remembraunce forever of this vyctory that they had upon these ladyes.

"Then the quene, for the desyre that she had to have these .ii. damoyselles agayne whom that she loved so moche, [Hh3r] was constrayned to make a peas with the Grekes. Soo was this matter entreated and accorded bytwene them that the quene came to them all unarmed, with ryght a fayre company of ladyes and maydens in so ryche araye that they sawe never suche before. The Grekes mette with them, and feested them and made sure the peas bytwene them, and there was moche joy made. Yet not for that it noyed gretely Theseus to delyver Ipolyte, for he was smyten with grete love. Soo Hercules prayed and requyred the quene so moche for hym that she graunted Theseus to take Ipolyte unto his wyfe, and so sholde lede her into his countre. And then were the weddynges made worshy-pfully, and after that the Grekes departed. And Theseus ledde home Ypolyte, whiche had a sone afterwarde that was called Ipolytus, whiche was a knyght of

qui fu chevalier[1] de grant elicte et moult renommé. Et quant en Grece fut sceu que paix avoient,[2] oncquez plus grant joye ne fu menee, car riens n'estoit que tant redoubtassent." [fol. 34v a]

*Chapitre 19*    **Dit de la royne Pantasselle, et comment elle ala au secours de Troye**

"Long temps vesqui ceste royne Orthia et en grant prosperité ot tenu le regne d'Amazonie et moult acreu leur poissance, et ja fu moult envieillie quant elle trespassa. Si couronnerent aprés elle[3] sa noble fille, la tres vaillant Pantassellee qui sur toutes porta la couronne de sens, de pris, de prouece, et de vaillance.[4] Ceste ne fu oncques lassee de porter armes ne de combatre. Par elle fu plus que oncques mais leur seigneurie accreue, car nul temps ne reposoit. Si estoit tant crainte de ses anemis que nul ne l'osoit attendre. Ceste dame fu de si hault courage que oncques ne se daingna coupler a homme et vierge fu toute sa vie.

"En son temps fu la grant guerre [fol. 34v b] des Grigois aux Troyens. Et pour la grant renommé qui adonc flourissoit par tout le monde de la tres grant vaillance et chevalerie de Hector de Troye comme du plus preux du monde, et du plus excellent en toutes graces; aussi[5] comme c'est usage que voulentiers chascun aime son semblable, Panthassellee qui estoit la souveraine des dames du monde, et qui tant de grans biens oyoit continuelment dire du preux Hector, l'ama honnourable[ment][6] de tres grant amour, et sur toute riens le desira a veoir. Et pour cellui desir acomplir, se parti de son regne a grant conroye et a moult noble compagnie de dames et de damoiselles[7] de grant proece et moult richement [fol. 35r a] armees.

"Si prist[8] son chemin vers Troye, dont la voye n'estoit pas petite mais tres longtaine, mais riens ne semble long ne travaillable[9] a cuer qui bien aime quant desir le porte. A Troye arriva la noble Panthassellee, mais tart estoit, car ja trouva Hector mort qui par Achilles avoit esté occis en agait en la bataille, et aucques toute perie la fleur de la chevalerie troyenne.

---

[1] fut nommé Ypolitus, qui fu chevalier] nommé fu Yypolitus qui chevalier fu
[2] avoient] avoient aux Amasones
[3] aprés elle] aprés elle les Amasones
[4] de prouece, et de vaillance] de vaillance et de proece
[5] aussi] ainsi
[6] honorable[ment] : *honorable*
[7] damoiselles] pucelles
[8] Si prist] et prist
[9] travaillable] agreable

grete worshyp and a chosen man amonge many. And when it was knowne in Grece that the[1] peas was made, they had never gretter joye for there was never noo thynge that they doubted more."

## Chapter 19    Of the Quene Pantassylea, howe she wente to the socours of Troye

"Longe tyme lyved this noble Quene Orthya and in grete prosperyte helde the lande of Amozonye, and moche encreased theyr puyssaunce; and she was ryght olde when she dyed. [Hh3v] Then they crowned after her her noble doughter, the ryght worshypfull Pantassylle, whiche above all others bare the crowne of wytte, of pryce, of wysdome and worthynesse. This lady was never wery to bere armes ne to fyght, and by her theyr lordshyp was encreased more than ever it was, for she rested never tyme. So she was so moche dredde of her enemyes that there durst none abyde her. This lady was of so hyghe courage that she dysdeyned never to be coupled to man but was a mayde all her lyfe.

"In her tyme was the grete warre of the Grekes agaynst the Troyans. And for the grete fame that floured thrughe all the worlde of the ryght grete worshyp and knyghthode of Ector of Troy as of the moost manly of the worlde, and of the moost excellent in al graces; as it is the usage that gladly every frende wolde desyre to vysyte his lyke, Pantassylle whiche was the chyefe of all ladyes of the worlde, and whiche that herde saye contynuelly so grete goodnesse of this worshypful Ector, she loved hym worshypfully of ryght grete love, and above all thynges she desyred to se hym. And for to fulfyll this desyre, she departed from her royalme in grete haste with ryght a noble company of ladyes and damoyselles of grete prowesse and ryght rychely armed.

"So she toke her way towarde Troy, whiche was not lytell but ryght ferre off, yet it thought not longe nor travaylable to the herte that loveth wel. And when they came to the porte of Troy, there aryved this noble Pantassylle, [Hh4r] and yet it was too late, for there she founde Ector deed whiche was slayne by Achylles lyenge awayte for hym in the batayle, in whom perysshed the floure of all knyghthode of Troy.

---

[1] that the : *that that the*

"A grant honneur fut receue du roy Priant de Troye et de la royne Hecuba et de tous les barons Panthassellee,[1] mais tant ot le cuer de ce que vif n'avoit trouvé Hector que riens resjoir ne la pouoit. Mais le roy et la royne qui sans cesser dueil menoient pour la mort de leur filz Hector lui distrent que puis [fol. 35r b] que vif ne lui pouoient monstrer, que mort lui monstreroient.

"Si la menerent au temple, ou sa sepulcure orent fait faire la plus noble qui oncques fut faicte dont mencion soit faicte en histoires.[2] La en une riche chapelle toute d'or et de pierres precieuses devant le maistre autel de leurs dieulx seoit le corps de Hector en une chaiere qui se estoit en basmee et conrees que il sembloit visiblement que il fust tout vif, l'espee nue tenant en sa main, sembloit encore que son fier visage menaçast les Grigois. Si estoit vestus d'un garnement grant et large, tout tyssu d'or, bandé de pierres precieuses,[3] qui trainoit tout par terre et couvroit les parties d'embas qu'il [fol. 35v a] avoit toutes plongieez en fin basme, qui a merveilles rendoit grant odeur.[4] La tenoient les Troyens ce corps en aussi grant honneur comme ce feust un de leurs dieux, a grant luminaire de cire et a moult grant clarté; ne nul ne pourroit somer la richece qui la estoit.

"La menerent la royne Panthasellee, laquelle aussi tost que la chappelle fut ouverte et que elle vit le corps, elle s'agenoilla, le saluant tout ainsi que se vif fust, puis s'approcha, et en le regardant ou visage ententivement prist a dire telx parolles en plorant:[5]

"'Ha, fleur et excellence de la chevalerie du monde! Le sommet, le comble, et la consommacion de toute vaillance! Qui se pourra d'or en [fol. 35v b] avant aprés vous jamais vanter de proece, ne ceindre espee puis que ores est estaintee la lumiere et exemple de si grant haultece? Helas, de quel heure fut oncques né le bras tant maudit[6] qui osa par son oultrage despoillier le monde de tant grant tresor?

"'O tres noble prince, pour quoy m'a Fortune tant esté[7] contraire que pres de vous n'estoie quant le traitire qui ce fist agaittoit vostre personne? Ja ce ne fust avenu, car bien vous en eusse gardé;[8] et se ores fust vif, bien cuideroie sur lui vengier vostre mort et la grant yre et douleur que mon cuer sent de ainsi vous veoir, sans poissance[9] de parler a moy, que je tant desiroye. Mais puis que[10]

---

[1] A grant honneur . . . Panthassellee] Panthassellee fu receue a grant honneur a Troye du roy Priant de la royne Hecuba, et tous les barons

[2] la plus noble qui fut faicte dont mencion soit faicte en histoires] la plus riche et la plus noble qui oncques feust faicte dont mencion soit en histoires

[3] d'or, bandé de pierres precieuses] de fin or bandé et pourfillé de pierres precieuses

[4] rendoit grant odeur] grant odeur rendoit

[5] a dire telx parolles en plorant] tielx parolles a dire tout en plourant

[6] maudit] maudit ne escommenie

[7] tant esté] esté tant

[8] en eusse gardé] en gardasse

[9] sans poissance] sans vie ne puissance

[10] Mais puis que] Mais puis que Fortune l'a ainsi consentu et que

"Then this Quene Pantassylle was receyved with grete worshyp of Kynge Pryamus and of the Quene Eccuba his wyfe, and of all theyr lordes, but yet she had her herte alway on that that she sawe never Ector on lyve, whiche caused her that there myght nothynge rejoyce her. Yet the kynge and the quene whiche without seasynge sorowed for the dethe of theyr sone Ector sayd to her that syth they myght not shewe hym to her on lyve, that they wolde showe hym to her deed.

"Then they ledde her into the temple, where they had made his sepulture the most noble and most ryche that ever ony hystory made mencyon of, for it was made in a chapell ryght ryche all of golde and precyous stones before the hyghe awter of theyr goddes. And there sate the body of Ector in a chayre, whiche was so bawmed and covered that it semed vysybly that it was on lyve, holdynge a swerde in his hande, semynge alway that his fyers vysage manased the Grekes; clothed in a garment grete and large, all of tyssue, embrowdred with precyous stones, traylynge on the erthe and covered the partyes bynethe whiche were plunged in fyne bawme, whiche yelded mervayllous swetnes. There the Troyans helde this body in grete worshyp as it had ben one of theyr goddes, with lyght of waxe clerely brennynge; and there was rychesse without nombre. And thyder they led this Quene Pantassylle, [Hh4v] the whiche as sone as the chapel was opened and sawe the body of Ector, kneled her downe, saluynge hym as he had ben on lyve. And after she wente nere, and in beholdynge the vysage, she began to saye suche wordes, wepynge:

"'Ha, floure and excellence of all knyghthode of all the worlde! The grounde and the endynge of all worthynesse! Who maye nowe from henseforthe avaunte hym after you of ony prowesse, or to stretche a swerde, syth that nowe is quenched the lyght and ensample of soo grete hyghnesse? Alas, what houre was borne the arme so cursed that durst by his outragyous courage despoyle the worlde of so grete a treasoure?

"'O ryght noble prynce, wherfore is my fortune so contrary that I had not ben so nyghe you when the false traytoure that slewe you made suche awayte upon your persone? If I had ben there, I wolde have wayted upon your persone myselfe; yet and [h]e[1] were on lyve, he wolde byleve your dethe sholde be revenged.

"'Ha, what grete wrathe and sorowe that myne herte feleth to se you thus without puyssaunce to speke to me, whom I desyred so moche to se. Nowe syth

---

[1] [h]e : *ye*

[fol. 36r a] autrement ne puet estre, je jure par tous les haulx dieux que nous creons et promez bien et affie a vous, mon chier seigneur, que tant que vie me pourra durer,[1] vostre mort sur Grieux sera par moy vengé.'

"Ainsi agenoillee devant le corps, parloit si hault Panthassellee que grant tourbe de barons, de dames, et de chevalerie[2] qui la estoient la pouoient ouir. Et elle et tous[3] plouroient par pitié, ne partir de la ne se pouoit. Toutevoies au desrain, baissant la main dont il tenoit l'espee, se parti disant: 'O digneté de chevalerie, quel deviez vous en vostre vivant estre quant la representacion de vostre corps mort vous tesmoingne de si grant excellence!'[4] Et a tant s'en parti, plourant moult tendrement. [fol. 36r b]

"Au[5] plus tost que elle pot s'arma et a tout son host sailli de la cité a moult noble conroy contre les Grieux qui estoient au siege. Et a brief parler de ce que elle y fist, sans faille tant y fist d'armes elle et sa route que se longuement vesquist, ja n'en retournast[6] pié en Grece. Elle abati Pirrus, qui avoit esté filz de Achilles et moult estoit vaillant chevalier de sa main, et tant le bati et navra que a pou ne fu occis. Et a moult grant peine lui fu de sa gent rescoux, et comme mort en fu portez, ne ja ne cuidoient Grieux que il en rechapast, dont grant dueil menoient. Et se elle portoit[7] haine au pere, bien le monstra au filz.

"Toutevoiez, pour abregier le conte,[8] quant tant y ot fait d'armes [fol. 36v a] par plusieurs journees, Panthassellee avec sa route[9] que les Grieux estoient oncques au bas,[10] Pirrus qui de ses plaies fu respassez ot a merveilles honte et dueil dont par elle ot esté abatus et si foulez. Si ordenna aux gens de son host, qui moult estoient de grant proece, que ilz n'entendissent en la bataille a nulle autre chose fors a enclorre Panthassellee entre eulx[11] et soubstraire des siennes, car par sa main vouloit[12] que elle fust occise, et leur promist que se ce[13] pouoient faire, grant guerdon leur en donneroit. A ceste chose acomplir mirent longuement peine la gent Pirrus ains que avenir y puissent, car trop la redoubtoient aprochier

---

[1] vie me pourra durer] vie ou corps me pourra durer
[2] chevalerie] chevaliers
[3] Et elle et tous] Et tous
[4] excellence] haultece
[5] Au] Et au
[6] n'en retournast] des Grieux ne retournast
[7] menoient. Et se elle portoit] menoient car ce estoit toute leur esperance. Mais se Panthassellee porta
[8] pour abregier le conte] pour abregier le conte, quoy que ses fais fussent merveilleux, au derrain
[9] Panthassellee avec sa route] avec sa route la tres preux Panthassellee
[10] oncques au bas] auques du tout au bas
[11] Panthassellee entre eulx] entr'eulx Panthassellee
[12] vouloit] vouloit il
[13] ce] tant

it maye none other wyse be, I swere by al the hyghe goddes that we byleve on and promyse well and afferme to you, my dere lorde, that whyle my lyfe shall endure, youre dethe shall be venged by me upon the Grekes.'

"Thus knelynge before the body, Pantassylle spake so hyghe that the grete company of lordes and ladyes of the chevalrye that were there myght here her. [Hh5r] She and all wepte for pyte and coude full evyll departe from thens, yet at the last kyssynge the hande with whiche he helde the swerde, she departed, saynge: 'Worthynesse of knyghthode, whiche semed you well in your lyfe when the representacyon of your body bereth you wytnesse of so grete excellence.' And anone she departed, wepynge ryght tenderly.

"And as soone as she myght, she armed her and lepte out of the cyte with her hoost ryght nobly arayed agaynst the Grekes that were at the syege. And to saye shortely of that that she dyde there, without fayle yf she had lyved longe she wolde have done many mervaylles of armes. So she wolde not tourne homewarde but wolde fyght with Pyrrus, that was the sone of Achylles and was a ryght manly knyght of his hande. And so moche she bete hym and wounded hym that he was almost slayne, and with grete payne he was rescowed of his people, and as a deed man was borne out of the felde. And the Grekes trowed never that he sholde escape, wherfore they made moche sorowe. And yf she hadde hate to the fader, she shewed it well to the sone.

"Neverthelesse, to make shorte the tale, when she had done there so moche of armes by dyvers journeys with her people that the Grekes were undernethe, Pyrrus that was amended of his woundes had mervayllous shame and sorowe that he was thus beten soo foule of this woman. So he ordeyned his people of his hoost, whiche were of ryght grete prowesse, that they sholde attende to none other thynge in the batayle [Hh5v] save onely to enclose Pantassyllee bytwene them and to put her from her people, for he wolde that she were slayne by his owne hande. And he promysed them yf they myght do thus, to gyve them grete gyftes. This thynge to accomplysshe, the people of Pyrrus put grete payne longe tyme or they myght happen to do it, for they dred soo moche to come nyghe her

pour les grans cops que elle departoit.[1] Mais non pour tant [fol. 36v b] a la perfin
comme ceulz qui a autre chose ne tendoient tant y exploitierent, une journee ou
elle avoit tant fait d'armes que souffire peust pour une journee[2] a peines a Hector, et par raison lassee deust estre, que ilz l'encloierent entre eulx et separerent
de sa bataille, et les dames tant empresserent que secourre ne la porent. Et la,
non obstant que par vertu merveilleuse se deffendist, toutes lui desrompirent ses
armes et un quartier[3] du heaume lui orent abatu. La fu Pirrus, lequel quant la
teste lui vit nue par ou[4] paroient ses blons cheveux si grant cop sur le[5] chief lui
donna que la teste et le cervel lui pourfendi. Et ainsi fina la preux[6] Panthassellee,
dont grant perte fu aux Troiens [fol. 37r a] et grant dueil[7] a tout son païs, qui grant
dueil en demeuerent,[8] car oncques puis sur les Amazones pareille ne regna. Si en
porterent le corps a grant doulour en sa terre.

"Et ainsi, comme tu pueux ouir, commença et se maintint le royaume des
femmes en haulte poissance, qui dura par l'espace de plus de viij[c] ans, si comme
tu peux toy mesmes notter et veoir[9] par le devis des histoires du[10] nombre du
temps qui peut courir depuis leur commencement jusques aprés la conqueste du
grant Alixandre qui conquist le monde, ou quel temps il appert que encore duroit
le regne et seigneurie des Amazones. Car l'istoire de lui fait mencion comment
il ala en ycelui [fol. 37r b] reaume, et comment il fu de la royne et des dames
receu. Si fu cellui Alixandre moult grant temps aprés la destruccion de Troye,
et mesmement plus de iiij[c] ans aprés la fondacion de Romme, qui long temps fu
aprés la dicte destruccion. Pour quoy se tu veulx prendre le loisir de concorder
les histoires ensemble, et ca[l]culer[11] les temps et le nombre, tu trouveras par
moult grant[12] espace avoir duré cellui royaume et la seigneurie des femmes, et
pueux notter qu'en toutes les seinggneuries qui ont au monde esté qui par l'espace
d'autant de temps aient duré, on ne trouvera point plus de notables princes, ne en
plus grant quantité, ne qui plus de notables fais aient fait, que furent et que [fol.
37v a] firent des roynes et des dames d'ycellui royaume."

---

[1] car trop la redoubtoient aprochier pour les grans cops que elle departoit] car pour
les tres grans coups qu'elle donnoit
[2] peust pour une journee] deust pour un jour
[3] quartier] grant quartier
[4] par ou] ou
[5] le : *le le*
[6] preux] tres preux
[7] dueil] marrement
[8] et grant dueil a tout son païs, qui grant dueil en demeuerent] et grant marrement a
tout son païs, ou merveilles grant dueil fu fait, et a bon droit
[9] notter et veoir] veoir
[10] du] le
[11] ca[l]culer: *carculer*
[12] grant] lonc

for the grete strokes that she gave. Yet not for that, to come to the conclusyon, they applyed it as those that toke no hede to other thynge and sawe in a journay where she dyde mervayllous dedes of armes that it myght nere hande suffyse to Ector yf he had ben on lyve, that by reason she ought to be wery. And there they enclosed her amonge them and departed her from her batayle, and so sore oppressed her ladyes that they myght not socoure her. And that not withstandynge, by ryght mervayllous vertue and strengthe she wolde have defended her. And then they brake her harnoys and smote off a quarter of her helme. Then Pyrrus, when he sawe the heed bare by whiche her yelowe heere appered, gave her so grete a stroke that he clefte in sondre the heed and the brayne. And thus ended the worshypfull Pantassylle, of whom it was grete losse to the Troyans and grete sorowe to all her countre, whiche made grete sorowe and lamentacyon, for never syth there reygned none suche upon the Amozones. And thenne they bare the bodye home into her owne countre.

"And thus, as thou mayst here, began the royalme of women and was [Hh6r] maynteyned by grete puyssaunce, whiche endured by the space of .viii. hondred yeres as thou thyselfe mayst note, and se and rede by the hystoryes of nombre whiche may renne syth theyr begynnynge tyll after the conquest of grete Alexandre that conquered al the worlde, in whiche tyme it appered that then endured the reygne and lordshyp of the Amozones. For the hystory of hym maketh mencyon howe he wente into that royalme and howe he was receyved of the quene and of the ladyes. So was this Alexandre longe tyme after the destruccyon of Troye, and that same wyse more than .iiii. hondred yeres after the foundacyon of Rome, whiche was longe tyme after the sayd destruccyon of Troy. Wherfore yf thou wylte take the leysoure to brynge togyder the hystoryes and to calcule the tymes and the nombre, thou shalte fynde that this royalme and the lordeshype of women endured ryght a longe space. And thou mayst note that in al the lordeshyp that hath ben in the worlde whiche by the space of so moche tyme hath endured, one shall not fynde more notable prynces, nor in more quantyte, ne that hath done more n[o]table[1] dedes than were done by the quenes and the ladyes of that realme."

---

[1] n[o]table : *natable*

## *Chapitre 20*      Dit de Cenobie, royne des Palmurines

"Ne furent pas des femmes preux seulement celles d'Amazonie, car ne doit mie[1] estre moins renommee la vaillant Cenobie, royne de Palmurenes, dame de tres noble sang yssu des Ptholomees, roys d'Egipte. De ceste dame fut apparant tres son enfance le grant courage et l'inclinacion chevalereuse que elle avoit. Et aussitost que aucques fu enforcie, nul ne la pot garder que elle ne delaissast la demeure des villes fermees, et des palais, et chambres royaulx pour habiter es bois et es forests, ou quel lieu çeinte d'espee et de dars par grant [fol. 37v b] diligence bersoit[2] la sauvagine, et puis des cerfs et des bisches se prist a combatre aux lions, aux hours, et a toutes autres fieres bestes que elle assailloit sans paour et vainquoit mervelleusement. Ceste dame ne tenoit point a peine de gesir au bois sans riens doubter, sus la terre dure, par froit et par chault, ne lui grevoit tracer par les destrois des forests, gravir par sus montaingnes, fouir par vallees courant après les bestes.

"Ceste pucelle desprisoit tout amour charnele, et long temps reffusa mariage comme celle qui garder virginité voloit.[3] Mais a la perfin, contrainte par ses parens, prist a espoux le roy des Palmurenes. De grant [fol. 38r a] beaulté souverainement de corps et de viaire[4] estoit la noble Cenobie, qui pou de conté de sa beaulté faisoit. Et de tant fu Fortune favourable a son inclinacion que elle lui consenti avoir mary asses correspondent a ses meurs. Cellui roy qui rechevalereux[5] estoit ot vouloir de conquere par force d'armes tout Orient et les empires d'environ.

"En cellui temps Valerien Auguste,[6] qui tenoit l'empire de Rome, estoit pris de Sapore, roy des Persans. Son grant host assembla le roy des Palmurenes, si ne fist pas grant force Cenobie sa femme[7] de garder la frescheur de sa beaulté ains se[8] disposa de souffrir le travail[9] d'armes avec son mary, vestir le harnois, et estre [fol. 38r b] participant avec[10] lui en tous labours en l'excercite de chevalerie.

"Le roy, qui nommé estoit Odonet, establi Herode son filz d'une autre femme[11] pour mener une partie de son host en l'avant garde contre le dit Sapoure,

---

[1]  mie] pas
[2]  bersoit] bersayoit
[3]  voloit] vouloit toute sa vie
[4]  souverainement de corps et de viaire] de corps et de viaire souverainement
[5]  rechevalereux] tres chevalereux
[6]  Valerien Auguste] Valerien
[7]  si ne fist pas grant force Cenobie sa femme] adont Cenobie qui pas ne fit grant force
[8]  ains se] se
[9]  le travail] travail
[10]  et estre participant avec] estre participant avecques
[11]  Herode son filz d'une autre femme] establi un filz qu'il avoit eu d'une autre femme, qui nommez estoit Herode

*Chapter 20*     Of Cenobye, quene of Palmurenes

"There were not worshypfull women onely of these Amozones, for the valyaunt Cenobye ought not to be of lesse fame and worthynes that was quene of Palmurenes, a lady of noble bloode [Hh6v] yssued of Ptholomees, kynges of Egypte. Of this lady was apperynge all her youthe the grete courage and knyghtly inclynacyon that she had for as soone as she was strengthed, there myght no man kepe her but that she wolde leve the dwellynge in the townes closyd, in palayces or in royall chambres, but to enhabyte the woodes and forestes, in whiche places she had her swerde gurde about her and dartes by grete dylygence to sle the wylde beestes, as hertes and hyndes, and after that began to fyght with lyons, with beres, and with many other wylde beestes. And she assayled them without drede, and overcame them mervayllously. This lady helde it for no payne to lye in the woodes, doubtynge nothynge upon the harde erthe, in hote and in colde. Ne it greved her not to trace the strayte passages of the forestes grave upon the mountaynes, dyke in the valays, rennynge after the bestes.

"This lady dyspr、praysed all carnall love, and longe tyme refused maryage as she that wolde kepe her vyrgynyte. Yet at the last, constrayned by her kynne, she toke to housbande the kynge of Palmurenes. Of grete beaute and soveraynly of body and of vysage was this noble Cenobye, whiche set but lytell by her beaute. And Fortune was so favourable to her inclynacyon that she consented to have an housbande corespondent ynoughe to her cond[yc]yons.[1] This kynge, whiche was a knyghtly man, hadde grete luste to conquere by strengthe of armes all the Oryent and the empyres aboute hym.

"In this [Ii1r] same tyme, Valeryan Auguste that helde the empyre of Rome was taken of Sapore, kynge of Perce. This kynge of Palmurenes assembled his grete hoost, and Cenobye made no grete force of the fresshnes of her beaute but dysposed her to suffre the travayle of armes with her housbande, and to were harnoys, and to be partycypant with hym in all labours in the exercyse of knyghthode.

"This kynge, that was named Ordonet, stabled Herode (his sone of another woman) to conduyte one parte of his hoost, takynge hede agaynst the sayd Sapore

---

[1] cond[yc]yons : *condyons*

roy des P[er]sans,[1] qui adonc occupoit Mesopotame; puis ordenna que de l'autre part yroit sur lui Cenobie sa femme a tout grant chevalerie, et il yroit d'autre part[2] a tout la tierce partie de l'ost.[3] Si se porterent en telle ordennance.

"Mais que t'en diroye? La fin de ceste chose fu telle,[4] si que tu pueux veoir par les histoires: que ycelle dame Cenobie tant vigoureusement,[5] et par tel hardiece et vertu, que plusieurs batailles contre cellui roy de Perse gaingna et ot la [fol. 38v a] victoire, et tant que par sa proece Mesopotame mist en la subgecion de son mary Sapore, assegie[6] en sa cité et le prist par force avec ses concubines, et grans tresors y conquist.[7]

"Aprés celle victoire avint que son mary fu occis par un sien parent pour envie de regner. Mais la dame de noble courage[8] prist la possession de l'empire pour ses enfans, encore petis, et se mist en siege royal comme empereris, prist le gouvernement par grant vertu et cure. Et a tout dire, tellement le gouverna et par si grant sens et discipline de chevalerie que Galerien et aprés lui Claudien, empereurs de Romme, quoy que ilz occupassent une partie d'Orient pour les Rommains, n'oserent [fol. 38v b] oncques entreprendre contre elle aucune chose.[9] Et semblablement les Egipciens, ne les Arabiens, ne ceulx d'Armenie ains tant redoubterent sa poissance et sa grant fierté que ilz furent tous contens de garder les termes de leurs contrees.

"Ceste dame[10] estoit de ses princes tres honnouree, de son peuple obeye et amee, de ses chevaliers crainte et doubtee, car quant elle chevauchoit en armes, qui souvent avenoit, point ne parloit a ceulx de son host fors le fer au dos[11] et le heaume au chief, ne en bataille point ne se faisoit porter en chariot,[12] non obstant que les roys de lors[13] s'i feissent porter en celle guise, mais[14] tousjours estoit montee sur le poingnant destrier,[15] [fol. 39r a] et aucune fois pour espier ses anemis chevauchoit mescogneue devant ses gens.

---

[1] P[er]sans : *Presans*

[2] d'autre part] d'autre lez

[3] l'ost] son ost

[4] La fin de ceste chose fu telle] Tele fu la fin de ceste chose

[5] vigoureusement] vigueureusement s'i porta et si courageusement, et par

[6] assegie] a la parfin assegia

[7] conquist] conquesta

[8] Mais la dame de noble courage] Mais riens ne lui val, car la dame de noble courage bien l'en garda; car, comme vaillant et preux

[9] contre elle aucune chose] aucune chose contre elle

[10] Ceste dame] Ceste dame tant sagement se savoit maintenir qu'elle

[11] fors le fer au dos] qu'elle ne fust de fer vestue

[12] chariot] cueurre

[13] lors] lors tous

[14] mais] ains

[15] le poingnant destrier] le destrier

kynge of Perce, whiche that tyme occupyed Mesopotame. After, he ordeyned that on that other parte sholde go upon hym Cenobye his wyfe with another grete parte of his hoost, and he hymselfe sholde go in that other parte with the thyrde parte of his hoost. Soo they departed in suche ordynaunce.

"But what shall I saye? The ende of this matter was suche so as thou mayst se by the hystoryes that this Lady Cenobye so myghtely and by suche hardynesse and vertue gate dyvers bat018ylles agaynst this kynge and had the vyctorye, and by her prowesse put Mesopotame under the subjeccyon of her housbande, and besyeged S[a]pore[1] the kynge of Perce in his owne cyte, and toke hym by strengthe with his concubynes, and there she conquered grete haboundaunce of rychesse.

"After this vyctorye it happened that her housbande was slayne by one of his owne kynnesmen for envye that he reygned upon hym. Yet this lady by noble [Ii1v] courage toke the possessyon of the empyre for her chyldren whiche were yet but yonge, and put herselfe in the see royall as empresse, and toke therof the governaunc[e][2] by grete vertue and charge. And to say all, so she governed by so grete wytte and dyscyplyne of knyghthode that Galeryan and Claudyan, emperoures of Rome, though[3] that they occupyed a parte of the Oryent for the Romaynes, durste never undertake ony thynge agaynst her. And the same wyse the Egypcyans, ne the Arabyens, ne those of Armony but doubted her puyssaunce and her grete fyersenesse, and helde theym contente to kepe that they had and medle no ferther.

"This lady was worshypped of her prynces, and of her people obeyed and loved, and of her knyghtes dred and doubted. For when she rode with her people as ofte tymes it happened, she wolde never speke to them of her hoost but her harnoys on her backe and her helme on her heed, nor to no batayle made her armure to be ledde in charyot, notwithstandynge other kynges used that guyse. And alway she rode upon a well-rennynge courser, and often tymes she wolde ryde unknowne to espye her enemyes before her folke.

---

[1] S[a]pore : *sopore*

[2] governaunc[e]: *governaunct*

[3] though : *thought*

"Ceste noble dame Cenobie, avec ce que elle passoit en discipline et art de
chevalerie tous les chevaliers du monde[1] en son temps, autressi passoit toutes
autres dames en nobles et bonnes meurs et honnesté de vie. Tres sobre de son vivre
estoit souverainement. Mais non obstant[2] souventeffois faisoit de grans convis et
de grans mengiers a[3] ses barons et a estrangiers, et la estoit tenue toute magnificence et royal largece en toutes choses, et grans dons et beaulx leur donnoit, et
moult savoit gent bel attraire a s'amour et benivolence. Ceste estoit de souveraine
chasteté, car non pas [fol. 39r b] seulement des autres hommes se gardoit, mais mesmement avec son mary ne vouloit gesir fors pour avoir lignee. Et ce monstroit elle
manifestement par ce que point n'y couchoit quant elle estoit enseinte.[4] Et afin
que tous les[5] semblans de dehors se confermassent a ceulx[6] de dedens, elle n'avoit
cure que nul[7] homme luxurieux ne de vilx meurs frequentast a sa court, et vouloit
que tous ceulx qui sa grace vouloient avoir feussent vertueux et bien morigines; et[8]
portoit honneur aux gens selon leur bonté, vaillance,[9] et vertus, et non mie pour
richece ou lignee, et moult amoit gens de pesans meurs et esprouvez[10] en chevalerie. Elle vivoit a royal [fol. 39v a] coustume d'empereris par grant magnificence et
coust d'estat selon la maniere de Perse, qui estoit la plus pontifical coustume qui
fust entre les roys: estoit[11] servie en vaisseaulx d'or et de pierres precieuses, aournee
de tous paremens, assembloit grans tresors de son propre, sans extorsion faire,[12] et
si largement en donnoit ou il estoit raisonable que oncques ne fut veu prince de
greingneur, largece, ne de plus grant magnificence.
     "Avec ces dictes choses, le comble de ses vertus que je t'ay a dire en toute
somme elle fu tres apprise en lettres, en celles des Egipciens, et en celles de
leur langage. Et quant elle estoit a repos, adonc diligement vaquoit a l'estude
et [fol. 39v b] voult estre aprise par Longin le philosophe, qui fu son maistre et
l'entroduise en philosophie; sceut le latin et les lettres greques, par l'aide desquelles elle mesmes toutes les histoires soubz brieves paroles ordena et mist
moult curieusement, et semblablement voult que ses enfans, que elle nourrissoit

---

[1] monde] monde qui feussent
[2] obstant] obstant ce
[3] convis et de grans mengiers a] assemblees ou mengiers avecques
[4] estoit enceinte] ançainte estoit
[5] les] ses
[6] confermassent a ceulx] correspondissent et confermassent aux meurs
[7] nul : *nulle*
[8] et] elle
[9] vaillance] et vaillance
[10] esprouvez] les esprouvez
[11] estoit] elle estoit
[12] tresors de son propre sans extorsion faire] tresors de ses revenues et du sien propre
sans extorcion faire a nullui

"This noble Lady Cenobye, with that that she passed all other knyghtes of the worlde that tyme in dyscyplyne and crafte of knyghthode, also she passed all other ladyes in noblesse and good condycyons of honest lyfe, and ryght sobre soveraynely in all her demeanynge. Yet notwithstandynge, she made often tymes grete feestes unto [Ii2r] her barons and to straungers, and all magnyfycence was holden with her, and royall largesse in all thynges, and grete gyftes and fayre, and coude well drawe people to her love and benyvolence. She was alway of a soverayne chastyte for she kepte her not onely from other men, but in the same wyse she wolde not lye with her housbande but for havynge of yssue. And that she shewed openly by that that she wolde not lye with hym after that she felte her with chylde. And to that entente that all that appered outwarde sholde afferme that that was inwarde, she wolde never that ony vycyous man sholde haunte her courte, and she wolde that al they that wolde desyre to stande in her good grace were vertuous and well condycyoned. And she dyde grete honoure to people after theyr worthynesse and vertues, and not onely for theyr rychesse or byrthe, and she loved moche those men that were of sadde condycyons and proved in knyghthode. She lyved after a royall custome of an empresse by grete magny-fycence and cost of estate after the maner of Perse, whiche was those dayes the moost pontyfycall custome that was amonge kynges. She was served in vessell of golde and of precyous stones; she was garnysshed of all good araye, and also she gathered grete treasoures of her owne without doynge of extorcyon. And she gave ryght largely where that it was reasonable, for there was never prynce of gretter largesse nor of more gretter magnyfycence. [Ii2v]

"And with these sayd thynges, one of the hyghest of her vertues that I shall saye to thee was lerned in letters: in those of Egypte, and of her owne language. And when she had rest, then ryght dylygently she toke hede to the scole and desyred to be taught in phylosophy by a phylosophre that was named Longyne. She knewe the Latyne and the Grekysshe letters, by the helpe of whiche she ordeyned and put ryghte curyously all her hystoryes under ryghte shorte wordes, and the same wyse she wolde that her chyldren that she nourysshed were lerned

en grant discipline, fussent[1] introduis en science. Si nottes et avises, chiere amie, se tu as point vue de nul prince ou chevaliers[2] plus universel en toutes les vertus."

## *Chapitre 21*[3]     Dit[4] de Lilie, mere du vaillant chevalier Tierris

"Et combien que la noble dame Lilie ne fust en la bataille en propre personne,[5] ne fait elle bien a louer comme tres preux [fol. 40r a] de ce que elle fist en amonnestant Tierris son filx, le tres vaillant chevalier, de retourner en la bataille, comme tu orras? Cil Tierris fu en son temps un des plus grans princes du palais a[6] l'empereur de Constantinoble, de tres grant beaulté estoit et esprouvé en vaillance de chevalerie, et avec ce par le tres bon nourrissement et amonicions de sa mere, moult vertueux et excellemment morigniez estoit.

"Avint que un prince nommé Odouacre courut sur[7] les Romains pour les destruire et toute Ytalie.[8] Et comme les diz Rommains alassent requerre au dit empereur de Constantinoble aide, il leur envoya cellui Tyerris comme le plus souverain de sa chevalerie a tout grant host de gent. Si avint [fol. 40r b] que comme il se combatist en bataille ordonnee contre ycellui Odouacre, la mal fortune de la bataille tourna contre lui tellement que par paour fu contraint de fouir vers la cité de Ravenne. Quant sa vaillant et sage mere, qui bien se prenoit garde de la bataille, vid son filz fuir, elle ot douleur a merveilles considerant que plus grant reproche ne puet estre en chevalier que fuir en bataille.

"Adonc la grant noblece de son courage lui fist oublier toute pitié de mere en tel maniere que mieulx amast veoir la mort de son filz honnourablement que ce qu'il encourust tel honte. Si acouru tantost au devant de lui et lui pria tres chierement que il ne se voulsist deshonnourer par [fol. 40v a] tel fuite, ains rassemblast sa gent et retournast a la bataille. Mais comme cellui ne feist force des parolles, adonc la dame, surprise de grant courroux, leva sa robe par devant et lui dist, 'Vraiement, beau filz, tu n'as ou fuir se tu ne tournes de rechief ou ventre dont tu yssis.'

"Adonc fu Thierris si honteux que il laissa la fuiete et assembla[9] sa gent, et retourna en la bataille, en laquelle pour l'enflambement qu'il avoit de la honte des paroles de sa mere se combati si vigoureusement que il desconfist ses anemis

---

[1] fussent] ne fussent
[2] vue de nul prince ou chevaliers] vue ne leu de quelconques prince ou chevalier
[3] *R chapter order* Arthemise I.21; Lilie I.22; Fredegonde I.23; Camille I.24; Veronice I.25
[4] Dit] Ci dit
[5] fust en la bataille en propre personne] fu en propre personne en la bataille
[6] a] de
[7] sur] sus
[8] Ytalie] Ytalie se il peust
[9] et assembla] rassembla

in scyences. Nowe take good hede, ryght dere frende, yf thou have ought sene of ony prynce or knyght more unyversall in all the vertues."

## Chapter 21     Of Lylye, moder of the good knyght Thyerrys

"And howe that the noble Lady Lylye was not in batayle in propre person, is she not to be praysed as ryght a noble and worshypfull lady? In that that she, counsayllynge her sone Thyerrys, the ryght noble knyght, made hym to tourne agayne into the batayle, as thou shalte here. This Tyerres was in his tyme one of the grete prynces of the palays of the emperour of Constantynoble, and was ryght a fayre man and ryght wel proved in the worthynesse of knyghthode. And with that, by the ryght good nourysshynge and counsayllynge of [Ii3r] his moder, was ryght vertuous and excellently manered.

"It happened that a prynce named Odonatre wente upon the Romaynes for to destroye them and all Italy. And as these Romayns wente to requyre the foresayd emperoure of Constantynoble of his helpe, he sente to them this knyght Tyerres as for the best knyght of chevalry with ryght a grete hoost of people. So it happened as he fought in batayle ordeyned agaynst this Odonatre, the fortune of the batayle tourned agaynst hym in suche wyse that for drede he was constrayned to fle towarde the cyte of Ravenne. And when this worshypful and wyse moder whiche toke good hede of the batayle sawe her sone fle, she had grete and mervayllous sorowe, consyderynge that there myght be no gretter reproffe to a knyght than to fle in batayle.

"Anone, the grete noblesse of her courage made her to forgete all moderly pyte in suche maner that she had lever to se the dethe of her sone worshypfully than there sholde falle to hym suche a shame. So she ranne anone before hym and prayed hym ryght tenderly that he sholde not dyshonoure hym by suche fleynge, but that he sholde assemble agayne his hoost and tourne to the batayle; yet he toke noo charge of these wordes. And then the good moder, supprysed with grete wrathe, lyfted up her gowne before and sayd to hym: 'Truely, fayre sone, thou hast no place to fle to but thou tourne agayne into the wombe fro whens thou camest.'

"Then was this Thyerres so ashamed that he lefte [Ii3v] his fleynge and assembled his people agayne, and tourned agayne to the batayle, in the whiche for the hete that he had of the shame of the wordes of his moder, he fought so strongly that he dyscomfyted his enemyes and slewe Odonatre. And so all Italye

et occist Adouacre. Et ainsi fu delivré toute Ytalie par le sens de celle dame, qui
en peril estoit d'estre toute perdue; si me semble [fol. 40v b] que l'onneur de celle
victoire doit plus estre[1] a la mere que au filz."

## *Chapitre 22*     Parle encore de la royne Fredegonde

"De celle royne de France Fredegonde, dont cy devant t'ay parlé, fut autressi
grande la hardiece de ce que elle fist en bataille. Car si que je t'ay ja touchié
comme elle fust demouree vesve du roy Childerich[2] son mary, aiant Clotaire son
filz a mamelle, et le royaume fust assailli de guerre, elle dist aux barons:[3]
    "'Seigneurs, ne vous espoventez point[4] pour la multitude de noz anemiz qui
sur nous sont venus, car j'ay pourpensé un barat par quoy nous vaincrons mais que
croire me vueilliez. Je lairay ester toute paour femenine [fol. 41r a] et armeray mon
cuer de hardiece de homme a celle fin de croistre le courage de vous et de ceulx
de nostre host, par pitié de vostre joeune prince. Si yray devant a tout, lui entre
mes bras, et vous me suivrez; et ce que j'ay ordené a faire a nostre connestable,
semblablement vous ferez.'
    "Les barons respondirent que elle commandast, et de bon cuer en tout
laboureroient.[5] Elle fist bien et bel ordenner tout l'ost, puis se mist devant bien
montee, son filz entre ses bras, les barons aprés, et les batailles par bel ordre
ensuivant des chevaliers les suivoient.[6] Et ainsi chevauchierent vers leurs anemis
tant que la nuit fut venue. Et adonc entrerent en une forest. [fol. 41r b] Si couppa
le connestable une haulte branche d'un arbre, et tous les aultres firent autressi,
et tous leurs chevaulx couvrirent de may et a pluseurs pendirent campanelles et
clochetes, comme on fait aulx chevaux qui vont en pasture.[7] Et en celle maniere
serrez ensemble le petit pas chevauchierent pres des[8] heberges de leurs anemis, et
tenoient haultes branches et fueillues[9] de may en leurs mains. Et tousjours aloient[10] la royne devant par hardi courage, amonnestant par promesses et doulces

---

[1] estre] estre attribuee
[2] Childerich] Chilperich
[3] dist aux barons] parla aux barons en tel maniere
[4] espoventez point] espovantez
[5] laboureroient] l'obeiroient
[6] par bel ordre ensuivant des chevaliers les suivoient] des chevaliers ensuivant aloient aprés
[7] pasture] pastures
[8] le petit pas chevauchierent pres des] chevaucherent pres de
[9] et fueillues] fueillues
[10] aloient] aloit

was delvyered of theyr enemyes by the wytte of this lady, where it was lyke to be utterly destroyed. So me semeth that the honoure of this vyctory came more of the moder than of the sone."

## Chapter 22    Of the Quene of Fraunce Fredegonde

"Of the Quene of Fraunce Fredegonde, of whom I spake before, was also of grete hardynesse of that that she dyde in batayle. For as I have touched howe that she was lefte wedowe of Kynge Chylderyke her housbande, havynge Clotharye her sone at her pappes, and the royalme was assayled with werre, she sayd to her barons:

"'Lordes, ne drede you not for the multytude of our enemyes that ben come upon us, for I have thought before a wyle by the whiche we shall overcome them, yf ye wyll byleve me. I shall leve al femynyne drede, and I shall arme myne herte with the hardynesse of a man to that entente to encreace the courage of you and of all our hoost, by pyte of your yonge prynce. So I shall go before, havynge hym in myne armes, and ye shall folowe me. And that we have ordeyned our conestable to do, ye shal do the same.' [Ii4r]

"And the barons answered and bad her to commaunde them, and with ryght good herte they wolde laboure it. And then she lete make and well ordeyned her hoost. Syth she put her before wel horsed, her sone bytwene her armes, the barons after and al the bataylles sewynge by fayre ordre. And so they rode towarde theyr enemyes so longe tyll the nyght was come. And then they entred into a forest, so the conestable cutte downe an hyghe braunche of a tree, and all the remenaunt dyde the same wyse, and covered al theyr horses with may and tyed belles aboute some of theyr neckes, as men dothe to horse that gothe in pastures. And in this maner they rode togyder an easy pace tyll they came nyghe the lodgynges of theyr enemyes; and they helde hyghe braunches and bowes of maye in theyr handes. And alway the quene wente before with hardy courage in warnynge theym by promyses and fayre wordes for to do wel, holdynge the lytell

paroles de bien faire, tenant le petit roy entre ses bras,[1] dont tous avoient grant pitié et plus courageux estoient de garder son droit. Et quant [fol. 41v a] assez pres de leurs anemis leur sembla estre, ilz s'arresterent.[2]

"Quant l'aulbe du jour commença a crever, ceulx qui faisoient le gait de l'ost des anemis, qui les apercevrent, pristrent[3] a dire l'un a l'autre, 'Voy cy trop grant merveille: car hersoir n'apparoit[4] bois ne forest pres de nous, et voy cy un tres grant et tres espes bois!'

"Les autres qui regardoient ceste chose disoient que il couvenoit que le bois y fust de pieça car il ne pouoit estre autrement, mais que ilz avoient esté si bestes[5] que aperceu ne l'avoient. Et que il fust voir que bois fust,[6] les companes des chevaulx et bestes qui paissoient les en pouoient faire certains. Et ainsi comme[7] ceulx devisoient, qui jamais ne pensassent la tricherie, [fol. 41v b] soubdainement ceulz de l'ost de la royne gitterent jus leurs branches, et adonc[8] ce qui sembloit a leurs anemis estre bois leur apparut chevaliers armez. Si leur coururent sus; mais ce fu si soubdainement que les anemis n'orent loisir de eulx armer, et tous estoient en leurs lis. Si se fichierent par les heberges, et tous les occirent et pristrent, et ainsi orent victoire par le sens de Fridegonde."

## Chapitre 23    Ci dit de la vierge Camille

"Des femmes preux chevalereuses,[9] asses te pourroie dire: la vierge Camille ne fut pas moins vaillant des susdictes. Fille fu ceste Camille du tres ancien roy des Voulques nommé Mathabius. Trés qu'elle fut nee, sa mere morut,[10] [fol. 42r a] et tost aprés son pere fu desherité par ses propres gens qui contre lui se rebellerent, et a tant le menerent que il fut contraint a fuir pour garentir sa vie; si n'en emporta[11] nulle autre chose fors Camille sa fille, que il amoit de grant amour.

"Et quant il vint a passer une grant riviere, qu'il lui couvenoit traversier a non,[12] moult fu a grant meschief pour ce que il ne savoit trouver conseil de passer

---

1 ses bras] ses bras les barons aprés
2 s'arresterent] s'arresterent et se tindrent quoy
3 apercevrent, pristrent] apperceurent prirent
4 n'apparoit] n'avoit
5 bestes] nices
6 fust] estoit
7 Et ainsi comme] Et adont si comme
8 adonc] lors
9 femmes preux chevalereuses] preux et chevalereuses
10 morut] mouru d'elle
11 n'en emporta] n'emporta
12 a non] a no

kynge bytwene her armes, of whiche they all had grete pyte and had the more courage to kepe his ryght. And when they thought that they were nyghe ynoughe theyr enemyes, they rested them.

"When the dawnynge of the daye began to appere, those that made watche of the hoost of the enemyes perceyved it and began to saye one to another: 'Se here a grete mervayle, for yesternyght there appered no woode nor forest nyghe us, and se nowe—a ryght grete and a thycke woode!'

"The others that beholde this thynge sayd that it must nedes be that [Ii4v] the woode had ben there longe tyme before for it myght be none otherwyse, but that they have ben so beestysshe that they have not perceyved it. And that it was to se that it was a woode, the belles of the hors that pastured myght have made them certayne. And so as they devysed, they thought never on the trechery. Sodeynly the quene's hoost cast away theyr braunches: and then that that semed to theyr enemyes a wode, it appered knyghtes armed. So they ranne upon them, and this was done so sodaynly that theyr enemyes had no leysoure to arme them for they were all in theyr beddes. So they wente into theyr lodgynges, and slewe and toke theym all that they coude fynde. And thus they had the vyctory by the wytte of this good Quene Fredegonde."

## Chapter 23    Of the mayde Camylle

"Of women of worshyp and of knyghthode I myght tell thee ynoughe: the noble mayde Camylle was noo lesse worthy than those before sayd. This Camylle was doughter of the ryght auncyent kynge of Voulques, named Machabyus. And when she was borne her moder dyed, and anone after her fader was dysheryted by his owne people that rebelled agaynst hym. And soo moche they troubled hym that he was constrayned to fle for savynge of his lyfe.

"Soo he bare nothynge with [Kk1r] hym save onely his yonge doughter whom he lo[ved][1] of so grete love. And when he came to passe over a grete ryvere that he myght not chose but he must nedes passe it, he was in grete myschyefe for that that he coude fynde no counsayle to helpe his lytel doughter to passe. And when

---

[1] lo[ved]: *lo=*

la fillete. Mais quant assez y ot songié, il prist de grans escorces d'arbres[1] et en fist un vaisselle si comme une petite nasselete. Si mist sa fille dedens et a tout bonnes hars de yerre lya la nasselete a son braz, puis se mist en la riviere; et en nouant, travioit tout [fol. 42r b] bellement celle escorce aprés lui, et ainsi passa lui et sa fille oultre l'iaue.[2] Es bois se vesqui cellui roy, car autre part n'osoit aler de paour de l'agait de ses anemis.

"Sa fille nourrissoit de lait des bestes[3] sauvages tant que elle fut enforcie et aucques grande, et des bestes qu'il occioit vestoit lui et la pucelle; n'avoient autre lit, ne autre couverture. Quant elle fut aucques grande, elle se prist a guerroier fort les bestes sauvages[4] et a les occire a fondes et a pierres; et couroit si legierement aprés que nul levrier ne peust mieulx. Et ainsi le continua tant que elle fut en aage perfait, ou quel se trouva de merveilleuse force et hardiece.[5]

"Et donc[6] bien informee du pere du [fol. 42v a] tort que lui avoient fait ses subgiez, elle, se sentant de grant vigueur et tres courageuse, se parti de la et prist les armes. Et a brief parler, tant fist et tant esploita que a l'aide d'aucuns siens parens, elle mesmes estant en personne es fieres batailles, fist tant par force d'armes que elle reconquesta son païs, ne[7] puis ne fina de poursuivre fais de chevalerie.[8] Mais tant fut de grant courage que oncques mary ne daigna prendre, ne se coupler a homme. Et ceste[9] Camille fut celle vierge qui ala au secours de Turnus contre Eneas quant il fu descendus en Ytalie."[10]

## *Chapitre 24*    Ci dit de la royne Vironice de Capadoce

"Une royne fu en [fol. 42v b] Capadoce qui nommee estoit Veronice, noble de sanc et de courage comme celle qui estoit fille du grant roy Mitridates, qui seigneurissoit une grant partie d'Orient, et femme du roy Ariaraces[11] de Capadoce. Ceste dame demoura vesve, en laquelle vesveté un frere de son mary l'assaillist[12] de guerre pour elle et ses enfans desheriter. Et comme il avenist durant cellui

---

[1] prist de grans escorces d'arbres] prist et esracha des arbres grans escorces

[2] travioit tout bellement celle escorce aprés lui et ainsi passa lui et la fille oultre l'iaue] conduisoit aprés lui la nasselette et ainsi oultre l'eaue passa lui et sa fillete

[3] de lait des bestes] du lait des biches

[4] fut aucques grande, elle se prist a guerroier fort les bestes sauvages] fu parcreue elle se prist fort a guerroier les bestes

[5] force et hardiece] force, legiereté, et hardiece

[6] donc] adont

[7] ne] et

[8] chevalerie] chevalerie tant qu'elle en ot souveraine renommee

[9] Et ceste] Ceste

[10] Ytalie] Ytalye si que les histoires font mencion

[11] Ariaraces] Anares

[12] son mary l'assaillist] son feu mary l'assailli

he had thought ynoughe, he toke grete ryndes of trees and made a vessell as it were a lytell bote. So he put his lytell doughter within and bounde the vessell with good ropes to his arme, and after put it in the ryvere; and he, swymmynge, trayled easely this vessell after hym. And so he and his doughter passed over the water into the woodes, and there he lyved longe, for he durste not go none other waye for drede of his enemyes.

"He nourysshed his doughter with the mylke of wylde bestes unto the tyme that she was well strengthed, and with the skynnes of the beestes that he slewe he covered bothe hym and his doughter; and they had none other bedde ne other coverynge but skynnes of bestes. And when she was waxed moche, she began to warre with wylde bestes and to sle them with her slynges and stones. And she wolde renne after so lyghtly that there myght no greyhounde do better. And thus she contynued tyl she came to her parfyte age, in whiche she founde herselfe of a mervayllous strengthe and hardynesse.

"And then she was en[f]ourmed[1] of her fader of the wronge that he had of his subgectes. She, felynge herselfe of grete strengthe and ryght couragyous, departed from thens and toke her to armes. [Kk1v] And to saye shortely, she dyde so moche and applyed her purpose that with the helpe of some of her kynnesmen, she beynge alwaye in her propre persone in batayles, dyde so moche by strengthe of armes that she conquered agayne all her countre, and never lefte after to pursewe the dedes of chevalrye. And she was of so hyghe courage that she deyned never to have housbande, ne to be coupled to man. And this same Camylle was the mayden that came to the socoure of Turnus agaynst Eneas when he was come downe into Italye."

## Chapter 24     Of the Quene Veronycle of Capadoce

"There was a quene in Capadoce that was named Veronycle, noble of blode and of courage as she that was doughter to the grete Kynge My[t]rydaces[2] that ruled a grete parte of the Oryent, and wyfe of Kynge Aryaraces the Capadocyan. This lady contynewed in her wedowhode, in the whiche wedowhode one of the bretherne of her housbande assayled her with warre to dysheryte her and her chyldren.

---

[1] en[f]ourmed : *ensourmed*
[2] My[t]rydaces : *Mycrydaces*

contens que en une bataille l'oncle occeist deux des filz de la dame et ses propres neveux,[1] elle en fu si tres durement dolente que celle grant ire fist fouir d'elle toute paour.[2] Si s'arma elle mesmes, et a grant host ala contre son serouge, et [fol. 43r a] tant y exploitta qu'en la parfin de sa propre main l'occist, et fist[3] passer son chariot sur lui, et vainqui la bataille."

## *Chapitre 25*      Ci dit de[4] la noble royne Archemise

"Que dirons nous moins que des aultres dames preux de la noble et tres excellent Archemise, royne de Care? Laquelle[5] demouree fu vesve du roy Mansole son mary, que elle ama de si grant amour que pour sa mort fu aucques au cuer partir et comme il ypparu, si que il te sera devisé en temps et lieu[6] cy aprés.

"Il lui[7] demoura moult grant païs en gouvernement, mais du gouverner ne s'esbahy mie car force en vertu, sagece[8] de meurs, et prudence [fol. 43r b] en gouvernement estoit toute en lui.[9] Si ot avec ce si grant hardiece en fait de chevalerie, et tant bien en garda la discipline, que plusieurs[10] victoires que elle ot la majesté de son nom par grant renommee tres hault esleva. Car en son vesvage avec ce que moult notablement gouvernoit le païs, elle se arma par plusieurs fois, et en especial en deux moult notables fais: l'un fu pour garder son païs, l'autre fu pour garder loyaulté[11] et foy promise.

"Le premier fu que[12] quant le dit roy Mansole son mary fu mort; ceulx de Rodes, qui marchissoient asses pres au[13] royaume de celle dame, orent grant envie et [fol. 43v a] desdaing que une femme eust seigneurie sur le royaume de Carie. Et pour ce en esperance de le[14] mettre hors et gaingnier la terre vindrent sur elle a grant armee et a foison navire, et adrecierent leur chemin devant la cité de Dalicarnase, qui siet sur la mer en un hault lieu appellé Ycare, qui moult est forte place.

---

   [1] des filz de la dame et ses propres neveux] de ses nepveus, c'est assavoir le filz de la dame
   [2] paour] paour femenine
   [3] de sa propre main l'occist, et fist] l'occist de sa propre main fist
   [4] Ci dit de] De
   [5] Laquelle] Laquelle quant
   [6] te sera devisé en temps et en lieu] devisé te sera en temps et en lieu
   [7] Il lui] A ceste dame
   [8] sagece] et sagece
   [9] lui] elle
   [10] plusieurs] par plusieurs
   [11] garder loyaulté] tenir loyauté d'amistié
   [12] que] tel que
   [13] au] du
   [14] le] l'en

And as it happened durynge this stryfe that the uncle slewe the .ii. sones of this lady and his owne nevewes, she was so utterly moved with sorowe that this grete wroth made all drede to fle from her. So she armed herselfe and with a grete hoost wente agaynst her brother-in-lawe. [Kk2r] And so she plyed her entente that at the last she slewe hym [by]¹ her owne hande and made her charyot to go over hym, and overcame the batayle."

## *Chapter 25*     Of the noble Archemyse, quene of Carye

"What shall we saye lesse of the noble and the ryght excellent Archemyse than of other worshypfull ladyes, whiche was quene of Carye? The whiche abode wedowe longe after her housbande Kynge Mansole, the whiche she loved of so grete love that it myght never departe from her herte, as it appered, so as it shall be devysed to thee in tyme and place hereafter.

"Her housbande lefte her many fayre and grete countrees in governaunce, yet to governe she never was abasshed for strengthe in vertue, sadnesse of condycy-ons, and pruden[c]e² in governaunce was all in her. So she had with that so grete hardynesse in dede of knyghthode, and so well kepte the dyscyplyne of cheval-rye, that she had the vyctory of many dyvers batoylles. And thus the hyghnesse of her name was gretely lyfte up by grete praysynge, for in her wedowhode with that that ryght nobly she governed the countres, she armed her by dyvers tymes, and in especyall .ii. notable dedes: that one was to kepe her countre, that other was to kepe trouthe and faythfull promyse. [Kk2v]

"The fyrst was when the foresayd Kynge Mansole her housbande was deed; those of the Rodes, whiche marched ryght nyghe the royalme of this lady, had grete envye and dysdayne that a woman sholde have the lordshyp of the royalme of Carye. And for that in hope to put her out and to gete the lande, they came upon her with a grete armye and a grete multytude of shyppes, and made [theyr]³ waye towarde the cyte of Dalycarnase whiche stode upon the see in an hyghe place called Icare, whiche was ryght a stronge place.

---

¹ hym [by] her : *hym her*
² pruden[c]e : *prudente*
³ [theyr] : *her*

"Si a celle cité deux ports, dont l'un est dedens la cité aussi comme mucié et couvert, et a l'entree tres estroicte, et y pouoit on aler et entrer du palais sans estre veu de ceulx de dehors,[1] ne mesmement de ceulx de la cité. L'autre port communal est coste les murs de la cité.

"Quant la preux et sage Archemise sceut par ses espies que ses [fol. 43v b] anemis venoient, elle fist armer ses gens—dont assez en avoit assemblés—et entra en ce petit port en[2] navire que la avoit fait venir. Mais ains que elle partist, ordena a ceulx de la cité, et a aucuns bons et feaulx, en qui bien se fioit que elle laissoit[3] pour ce faire, que quant elle leur feroit certain signe que leur devisa, que ilz feissent a ceulx de Rodes signe d'amour et que ilz les appellassent de dessus les murs, et leur deissent que ilz leur rendroient la cité, et que ilz venissent hardiement; et tant feissent, se ilz pouoient, que de leurs nefs les feissent saillir et entrer dedens la marchié de la ville. Et ceste chose [fol. 44r a] ordennee, la dame a tout son host s'en yssi hors du petit port, et ala par un destour en la haulte mer sans que les anemis s'en donnassent garde.[4]

"Et comme elle eust fait son signe, et eust congneu par le signe de ceulx de la cité que les anemis estoient entrez dedens, tantost elle retourna par le grant port et prist le navire de ses anemis, et entra dedens la cité, et fist les Roddais assaillir[5] de toutes pars par ses embuches: et elle avec son host leur fut devant,[6] et ainsi tous les occist, et desconfist[7] et ot la victoire.

"Plus grant vaillance fist Archemise, car elle entra aprés es [fol. 44r b] nefs de ses anemis a tout son host et ala a[8] Roddes, et fist lever hault signe[9] de victoire, comme se ce[10] feusent leurs gens qui retournassent victorieux. Et quant ceulx du païs ainsi les virent, cuidans que ce fussent les leur, furent moult esjoïs et laissierent leur port overt. Et Archemise entra dedens et ordenna gens pour eux tenir saisiz du port et ala droit au palais, et le[11] prist et occist tous les princes. Et ainsi furent pris ceulx de Rodes, qui garde ne s'en donnoient, et la dame se tint saisie de la cité et tost aprés se rendi a elle[12] toute l'isle de Roddes. Et aprés ce que elle ot mis toute l'isle en[13] servage et soubz treu, elle [fol. 44v a] la laissa garnie de

---

[1]  de dehors] dehors
[2]  en ce petit port en] ou petit port ou
[3]  laissoit] y avoit commis et laissiez
[4]  garde] de garde
[5]  les Roddais assaillir] forment assaillir les Rodes
[6]  devant] au devant
[7]  et desconfist] desconfit
[8]  a] en
[9]  signe] le signe
[10]  se ce] se
[11]  le] la
[12]  elle] lui
[13]  elle ot mis toute l'isle en] mise l'ot toute a son

"So there were to this cyte two gates, of whiche that one was within the cyte as it were hydde and covered and at the entrynge ryght strayte. And there myght one go and entre into that palays without seynge of them without and of them of the cyte also. That other comune gate was nyghe the walles of the cyte.

"And when this worshypfull and wyse Archemyse knewe by her spyes that her enemyes were come, she made her people to go to harnoys — of whom there were assembled ynowe — and entred in that lytell gate into the shyppes that she ordeyned to come thyder. Yet or she departed, she ordeyned to them of the cyte whiche were good and trewe, in whom she trysted wel to do suche thynges as she commaunded them that when she sholde make a certayne sygne that she devysed to them, that they sholde make to them of the Rodes a sygne of love, and that they sholde call them upon the walles and sholde saye to them that they wolde delyver to theym [Kk3r] the cyte, and that they sholde come boldely; and that they sholde do soo moche yf they myght to make them lepe out of theyr shyppes and to entre into the marketplace of the cyte. And this thynge ordeyned, the lady and her hoost yssued out at the lytell gate and wente a lytell waye into the hyghe see, so that her enemyes toke no hede of them.

"And as she had made her sygne and knewe by the sygne of them of the cyte that the enemyes were entred in, anone she retourned by the grete gate and toke the shyppes of her enemyes, and entred into the cyte, and made to assayle the men of the Rodes in every parte by her busshmentes. And she and her hoost were before them and so slewe them al, and dyscomfyted them and had the vyctory.

"And yet more worshypfully dyde this noble Archemyse, for she wente after into the shyppes of her enemyes with all her hoost and wente to the Rodes, and made to lyfte up an hyghe sygne of vyctorye, as thoughe it had ben theyr people that sholde come agayne vyctoryously. And when those of that countre sawe this, trowynge that it had ben theyr people, they were passynge joyfull and lete open theyr porte. And Archemyse came in and ordeyned people to kepe the porte, and then wente streyght to the palays and toke and slewe all the prynces. And thus those of the Rodes were taken whiche toke no hede of themselfe, and the lady kepte her seased in the foresayd cyte and anone after all the hole Ile of Rodes yelded theym unto her. [Kk3v] And after that she had put all the yle in servage and under trybute, she lefte it garnysshed with good kepers and so retourned

bonnes gardes et s'en retourna; mais ainçois que elle partit, elle fist faire en la cité deux ymages d'arain, desquelz l'un representoit la personne de Archemise comme vainquerresse, et l'autre la cité de Rodes comme vaincue.

"L'autre fait nottable entre les autres que ceste dame fist[1] fu tel que comme il fust ainsi que Xerces le roy de Perse fust venus contre les Macedoniens,[2] et ja fust toute la terre reemplie de ses gens de cheval et de pié et de son grant host, et le rivage plein et occupé de ses nefs et de ses vaissiaulx comme cellui qui cuidoit toute Grece destruire; adonc les Greux [fol. 44v b] qui aliance d'amistié avoient a ceste royne Archemise, lui envoierent requerre son aide a laquelle[3] aide n'envoya mie tant seulement,[4] ains comme tres chevalereuse y ala en propre personne a tres grant ost.

"Et si bien y tint son lieu que, a le faire brief, tantost se mist en bataille contre Xerces et le desconfist. Et quant sur terre l'ot desconfist, elle entra[5] en ses nefs et fu au devant de son navire et coste la cité de Salemine lui donna la bataille. Et ainsi comme ilz se combatoient a effort, la vaillant Archemise estoit entre les premiers barons et chevetaines[6] de son host, et les reconfortoit[7] par moult grant hardement, en disant: [fol. 45r a] 'Or avant, mes freres et mes bons[8] chevaliers: faictes tant que l'onneur en soit nostre. Si desservez loz et gloire, et mes grans tresors ne vous seront espargniez.' Et a tout dire, tant y[9] esploita que pareillement que elle avoit fait sur terre, desconfist Xerces par mer, et s'en fuy honteusement. Et si avoit gens innombrables, car si que tesmoingnent plusieurs historiographes, il avoit si tres grant host que plusieurs rivieres tarirent par ou ilz passoient.[10] Et ainsi celle vaillant dame ot ceste[11] noble victoire, et s'en retourna glorieusement a tout le dyademe de honneur en son païs."

---

[1] entre les autres que ceste dame fist] qu'entre les autres de ses fais fist ceste dame
[2] venus contre les Macedoniens] venu contre les Lacedemoniens
[3] a laquelle] au quel
[4] mie tant seulement] mie
[5] entra] rentra
[6] chevetainies] chevetains
[7] reconfortoit] reconfortoit et donnoit cuer
[8] et mes bons] et bons
[9] y] bien
[10] plusieurs rivieres tarirent par ou ilz passoient] par ou ilz passoient les rus des fontaines et des rivieres tarissoient
[11] celle vaillant dame ot ceste] celle vaillant dame ot celle

home. Yet or she departed, she lete make two ymages of brasse in the cyte, of whyche that one represented the perso[n]e[1] of Archemyse as overcomer, and that other the cyte of Rodes as overcome.

"Another notable dede amonge others that this lady dyde was this, that when it was so that Exerse, the kynge of Perse, was come agaynst the Macedonyes and all the lande was full of his hoost, bothe on horsebacke and on fote, and the ryvage ful of people and of his shyppes as he that trowed to destroye all Grece, than the Grekes whiche had made alyaunce with this Lady Archemyse sente to her to requyre her of her helpe, to the whiche helpe she sente not onely but lyke a chevalrous lady came in propre persone with ryght a grete hoost.

"And so well she kepte her place there that, to saye shortely, anone she put her in batayle agaynst these men of Perse and dyscomfyted them. And when she had dyscomfyted them upon the lande, she entred into the shyppes and was before al others with her navye, and nyghe the cyte of Salemyne she gave them batayle. And as they fought strongly, this worshypfull Archemyse was amonge the fyrst lordes and capytaynes of her hoost, and comforted them with grete boldenesse, sayenge: 'Nowe forthe, my bretherne and good knyghtes, and laboure so that the worshyp maye be ours. And deserve ye this daye praysynge [Kk4r] and worshyp, and my grete treasoure shall not be spared unto you.'

"And to saye all, she dyde so moche that in lykewyse as she dyscomfyted them on the londe, she dyscomfyted them on the water, and Exerses fledde shamefully. And thus she had people innumerable, for as many wryters of hystoryes bereth wytnesse, she had so grete an hoost that dyvers ryvers taryed theym as she passed. And so had this worshypfull lady this noble vyctorye, and retourned worshypfully into her countre with the dyademe of grete worshyp."

---

[1] perso[n]e : *persoue*

## *Chapitre 26*   Ci dit de la hardiece de Cleolis

"Hardie femme et sage fu Cleolis la noble [fol. 45r b] Rommaine,[1] non obstant ne fust en fait de guerre ou de bataille. Car comme il advenist une fois que les Rommains, pour certaines couvenances creantees entre eulx a[2] un roy qui ot esté leur adversaire, couvenist que pour certificacion d'ycelles lui fussent envoyees en hostage la noble pucelle Cleolis et autres vierges de noble lignee de Romme.[3] Quant une piece ot esté celle Cleolis ou dit ostage, elle se pensa que moult estoit grant amenrissement de l'onneur de la cité de Romme que tant de nobles vierges fussent tenues comme prisonniers d'un roy estrange. Si arma Cleolis son courage de grant hardiece, et fist tant par belles parrolles et par promesses[4] que elle deceut cauteilleusement [fol. 45v a] ceulz qui en garde les avoient; et s'en parti par nuit, et en mena ses compaignes, et tant alerent que elles arriverent sus la riviere du Tybre. La en la praerie trouva Cleolis un cheval qui paissoit. Adonc elle qui par aventure n'avoit [o]ncques[5] chevauché monta desus, et sans nulle freour ne avoir paour de la perfondeur de l'eaue, mist une de ses compaignes derriere elle et passa oultre, et puis ainsi toutes, l'une aprés l'autre, revint querre et les passa saines et sauves, et a Romme les mena et rendi a leurs parens.

"La hardiece de ceste vierge fu moult prisié de ceulx de Romme, et mesmement le roy qui en ostage la tenoit l'en prisa et en eut grant soulas. Et les Rommains, afin que de ce fait [fol. 45v b] fust remembrance[6] a tousjours mais, firent faire l'ymage de Cleolis qui fut fait en guise d'une pucelle montee sur un cheval. Et mistrent cel ymage en un hault lieu sur le chemin par ou on aloit a un temple, et y demoura par long temps.

"Mais ores sont assez souffisement achevees[7] les fondemens de nostre cité. Or nous couvient lever le hault mur[8] tout a l'environ."

---

[1] Cleolis la noble Rommaine] la noble rommaine Cleolis

[2] a] et

[3] de noble lignee de Romme] de Romme de noble lignee

[4] par promesses] promesses

[5] [o]ncques: *vncques*

[6] remembrance] memoire

[7] ores sont assez souffisement achevees] des or sont achevez

[8] couvient lever le hault mur] lever sus la haulte muraille

*Chapter 26*       Of the hardynesse of Cleolis

"Also Cleolis, the noble Romayne, was ryght an hardy woman and a wyse, not-withstandynge it was not in the warre nor in batayle. For as it happened ones that the Romaynes, by certayne covenauntes made bytwene them and a kynge that had ben theyr adversary, it was accorded that by certyfycacyon of the cove-nauntes there was sente to that kynge to be in hostage the noble mayden Cleolis and other ma[y]dens[1] of noble lygnage of Rome. And when this Cleolis had ben a grete whyle in the foresayd hoostage, she thought that it was a grete hurte to the worshyp of the cyte of Rome that so many of noble maydens sholde be holden as prysoners of a straunge kynge. Soo this Cleolys armed her courage [Kk4v] with grete hardynes, and dyde so moche by fayre wordes and fayre promyses that she deceyved wysele them that had them in kepynge, and departed from thens by nyght, and ledde her felowes and wente so longe tyll they aryved upon the rever of Tybre. And there this Cleolys founde in the medowes an horse pasturynge. And then she whiche happely never rode before mounted upon this horse, and without ony maner of drede of the depnesse of the water, put one of her felawes behynde her and passed over, and after all the others, one after another; and so they passed over saufe. And this Lady Cleolys ledde them to Rome and brought them to theyr frendes.

"The hardynesse of this mayde was gretely praysed of them of Rome, and the same wyse the kynge that had them in hostage praysed her gretely and had therof grete solace. And the Romayns, to that entente that there sholde be a remembraunce had of this dede from thensforthe, they made make the ymage of Cleolys whiche was made in the guyse of a mayde syttynge upon an horse. And they put this ymage in an hyghe place upon the waye by whiche they wente to a temple, and there it abode longe tyme.

"Now we have accheved ynoughe as for the foundement of our cyte. Nowe we must lyfte up the hyghe walles all aboute." [Kk5r]

---

[1]   ma[y]dens : *mandens*

*Chapitre 27*     [*Item*, **Demande Christine a Raison se Dieux voult oncques anoblir aucuns entendemens de femmes de la haultece des sciences, et response de Raison**][1]

Ces choses de moy ouïes, respondis a la dame qui parloit: "Sans faille, dame, voirement monstra Dieux grans merveilles en la force d'ycelles femmes dont vous contez. Mais encore [fol. 46r a] me faictes sage, se il vous plaist, se[2] a cellui Dieu qui tant leur a fait de graces a point pleu[3] de honnourer le sexe femmenin de[4] privilegier aucunes d'elles de vertu de hault entendement et grant science, et se elles ont point l'engin abille ad ce? Car ce desire je[5] savoir pour ce que hommes maintienent qu'entendement de femme soit de petite comprehencion."[6]

*Response*: "Fille, par ce que ja t'ay dit cy devant pueux tu cognoistre[7] le contraire de leur oppinion. Et pour le te exposer plus au[8] plain, te donray preuve par exemples.[9] Je te dis de rechief, et ne doubtes le contraire, que se coustume estoit de mettre les petites filles a l'escole, et que suivantment on leur[10] fait apprendre [fol. 46r b] sciences[11] comme on fait aux filx, que elles apprendroient aussi parfaictement et entendroient les subtillettes de tout[e]s[12] les ars et sciences comme ilz font. Et par aventure plus de telles y a, car si que j'ay touchié cy devant, de tant comme femmes ont le corps plus delié que les hommes et moins habile[13] a pluseurs choses faire, de tant ont elles l'entendement plus agu[14] ou elles s'appliquent."

"Dame, ne vous desplaise;[15] souffrez vous sur ce point, s'il vous plaist. Certainement hommes ne souffreroient jamais passer pour vraye ceste question se plus a plain n'estoit solue. Car ilz voudroient dire que on voit communement les hommes savoir trop plus[16] que les femmes ne font." [fol. 46v a]

*Response*: "Fille, sces tu[17] pour quoy ce est que moins scevent?"

"Dame, non, se ne le me dites."

---

[1]  *L reverses rubrics for chaps. 27, 28*
[2]  se] s'il a point pleu
[3]  a fait de graces a point pleu] fait de graces
[4]  de] par
[5]  ce desire je] je le desire moult
[6]  comprehencion] reprehensive
[7]  cognoistre] congnoistre estre vray
[8]  au] a
[9]  exemples] exemple
[10]  on leur] on les
[11]  sciences] les sciences
[12]  tout[e]s: *touts*
[13]  les hommes et moins habile] les hommes, plus foible, et moins abile
[14]  plus agu] plus a delivre et plus agu
[15]  Dame ne vous desplaise] Dame que dites vous? Ne vous desplaise
[16]  savoir trop plus] trop plus savoir
[17]  Fille, sces tu] Scez tu

*Chapter 27*   Christine demaundeth of Reason yf ever God lyste to
make a woman so noble to have ony understandynge of
the hyghnesse of scyence

These thynges of me ryght well herde, I answered to the lady that spake to me:
"Madame, truely without fayle, God shewed grete mervaylles in the strengthe
of these foresayd ladyes of the whiche ye have touched. Yet I praye you to make
me wyse, yf it please you, to the whiche God hathe gyven them soo many graces
it pleased [Hym][1] to worshyp the kynde of woman to gyve pryvylege to ony of
them of the vertue of hyghe understandynge and of grete scyence, and yf they
have abyle wytte to that? For that I desyre to knowe for that that men maynteyne
and say that the understandynge of women is but of lytell takynge."

*Answere*: "Doughter, by that that I have sayd heretofore thou mayst knowe
the contrary of theyr opynyon, and for to expounde it more playnly I shal gyve it
thee fyrst by ensamples. I saye to thee agayne, and doubte never the contrary, that
yf it were the custome to put the lytel maydens to the scole, and that sewyngly
were made to lerne the scyences as they do to the man chyldren, that they sholde
lerne as parfytely, and they sholde be as wel entred into the subtyltes of al the
artes and scyences as they be. And peradventure there sholde be mo of them, for
I have touched heretofore by howe moche that women have the body more softe
than the men have and lesse habyle to do dyvers thynges, by so moche they have
the understandynge more sharpe there as they apply it."

"Madame, be not [Kk5v] dyspleased; suffre me upon this poynte, yf it please
you. Certaynly, men wolde never suffre this questyon to passe for trouthe but yf
it were openly assoyled. For they wolde saye that one sayth comunely these men
to understande moche more than the women dothe."

*Answere*: "Doughter, knowest thou wherfore it is that they understande lesse?"

"Madame, naye, but yf it please you to tell it me."

---

[1] pleased [Hym] to : *pleased to*

"Sans faille, c'est pour ce que elles ne frequentent pas tant de diverses choses ains se tiennent en leurs hostieulx, et leur souffist de faire leurs mainages.[1] Et il n'est riens qui tant aprengne creature raisonnable que fait l'experience[2] de pluseurs choses diverses."

"Dames, et puis que elles ont l'entendement abille a concevoir et aprendre si que ont les hommes, pour quoy n'apprennent elles plus?"

*Response*: "Pour ce, fille: car il n'est pas neccessité a la chose publique que elles se meslent de ce qui est commis aux hommes a faire,[3] si que je t'ay[4] cy devant dit; il souffist que elles [fol. 46v b] facent le commun office a quoy elles sont[5] establies. Et de ce que on juge par l'experience de ce que on voit[6] moins savoir les hommes que les femmes que leur entendement soit mendre, regarde[7] moy les hommes ruraux de plat païs ou habitans es montaignes. Tu les me trouveras en assez de contrees qu'ilz semblent tous bestiaulx, tant sont simples. Et toutevoies n'est mie doubte que Nature les a perfais a[8] toutes choses, en corps et en entendement, aussi bien que les plus sages[9] et les plus expers qui soient es citez et es bonnes villes, mais tout ce tient a faulte d'aprendre.

"Non obstant si que je t'ay dit que d'ommes et[10] de femmes [fol. 47r a] les uns ont meilleur entendement que les autres, et qu'il ait esté de femmes de grant science et de hault entendement, je t'en diray et au propos que je te disoie de l'entendement des femmes semblable a cellui des hommes."

*Chapitre 28*  **Commence a parler d'aucunes dames qui furent enluminees de grant science, et premierement de la noble royne[11] Cornifie**

"Cornifie, la noble pucelle, fut de ses parens envoyé a l'escole par maniere de troufferie et de ruse avec Cornificien son frere quant petis enfans estoient.[12] Mais celle fillette, par merveilleux engin, tant frequenta l'estude[13] que elle prist a sentir

---

[1] leurs mainages] leur mainage
[2] l'experience] l'excercite et experience
[3] aux hommes a faire] a faire aux hommes
[4] t'ay] t'ay ja
[5] elles sont] sont
[6] voit] les voit
[7] les hommes que les femmes que leur entendement soit mendre, regarde] communement que les hommes, leur entendement estre mendre, regardes
[8] a] de
[9] sages] sages hommes
[10] et] ou
[11] royne] pucelle
[12] quant petis enfans estoient] en l'aage de leur enfance
[13] l'estude] les letres

"Without fayle, it is for that they haunte not so many dyvers places, ne so many dyvers thynges; but they holde them within theyr houses, and it suffyseth them to do theyr busynesses. And there is nothynge that techeth a creature reasonable so moche as dothe the experyence of many dyvers thynges."

"Madame, and syth that they have the understandynge abyle to conceyve and to lerne as the men have, wherfore lerne they not more?"

*Answere*: "For that, doughter, for it is no nede to that comune thynge that they medle them of that whiche is commytted to man to do, as I have sayd to thee before. It suffyseth that they do comune offyce to the whiche they are ordeyned.

"And that that one jugeth by the experyence of that that the women can lesse than men, it is no mervayle, as it is sayd before, though theyr understandynge be lesse. Make thee a beholdynge of the people of the lowe countre, or of the hyghe mountaynes: thou shalte fynde countrees ynowe that the people seme as bestes, they be so symple. And yet it is no doubte that Nature hath made them as parfyte in all thyse thynges, as in body [Kk6r] and understandynge, as well as the wysest people and the moost experte of those that ben in good cytees or in good townes; and that is for defaute of lernynge.

"Notwithstandynge as I have sayd to thee before that of men and women some have better understandynge[1] than some, for there hath ben women of ryght grete connynge and of grete understandynge I shall tell thee, and to our purpose that I tolde thee of the understandyng of women that they have as sharpe wytte to lerne as men have."

## *Chapter 28*    Of women that were enlumyned of grete scyences; and fyrst of the noble mayde Cornyfye

"Cornyfye, the noble mayde, was sent to the scole by her fader in maner of scorne or of jape with her brother Cornyfycyen when they were yonge chyldren. But this lytell mayde, by mervayllous wytte, haunted the scole so moche that she began

---

[1] understandynge : *undestrandynge*

le doulz goust de savoir par [fol. 47r b] apprendre. Si ne fust mie legiere chose
a lui tollir celle plaisance, a laquelle toutes autres oeuvres femmenines laissiés,
s'appliqua de tout en tout et tant par espace de temps s'i occupa que elle fu tres
souveraine pouete. Et non pas tant seulement en celle science, mes[1] sembloit que
elle fu nourrie du lait et de la doctrine de parfaicte philosophie. Car elle voult
sentir et savoir de toutes sciences que elle apprist souverainement, en tant que son
frere, qui tres grant pouete estoit, passa en toute excellence de clergie. Et ne lui
souffist mie tant seulement le savoir se elle ne mist l'entendement a oeuvre et les
mains a la plume en compillant pluseurs tres notables [fol. 47v a] livres, lesquelx
livres et dictiez estoient ou temps de saint Gregoire en tres grant pris. Et dont il
mesmes fait mencion de laquel chose Bocace l'Ytalien, qui fu grant pouete, en
louant ceste femme dist en son livre: 'O! tres grant honneur a femme qui a laissié
toute oeuvre femmenine, et a appliquié et donné son engin aux estudes des tres
haulx clers!'

"Dist oultre cellui Bocace, certifiant le propos que je te disoie de l'engin des
femmes: 'Or soyent, dist il, honteuses les paresceuses femmes[2] qui se deffient
d'elles mesmes et de leur entendement, lesquelles ainsi que se elles feusent nees
es montaingnes sans savoir que est bien ne[3] honneur, se descouragent et [fol. 47v
b] dient que ne sont a autre chose bonnes ne proffitables fors pour les hommes
acoler,[4] et porter, et nourrir les enfans. Et Dieu leur a donné le bel entendement pour elles appliquier, se elles veulent, en toutes les choses que les glorieux
et excellens hommes font. Se elles veulent estudier, les choses ne plus ne moins
leur sont communes comme aux hommes, et peuent par labour honneste acquerir
nom perpetuel, lequel avoir[5] est agreable aux tres excellens hommes.' Fille chi-
erre, si pueux[6] veoir comment cellui aucteur Bocace tesmoigne ce que je t'ay dit,
et comment il loue et appreuve science en femme."

*Chapitre 29*      **Ci dit de Probe la Rommaine**

"De grant excellence en science autressi fut Probe la Rommaine,[7] femme de
Adelphe, et fut crestienne. Ceste ot tant noble engin, et tant ama et frequenta
l'estude, que elle sceut souverainement les .vii. ars liberaulx et fut souveraine
pouete. Et par si grant labour d'estude hanta les livres des pouetes, et par especial

---

[1] en celle science, mes] en la science de poesie fu tres flourissant et experte, ains
[2] Or soyent, dist il, honteuses les paresceuses femmes] *R omits*
[3] que est bien ne] bien et qu'est
[4] les hommes acoler] acoler les hommes
[5] avoir] a avoir
[6] si pueux] peus
[7] excellence en science autressi fut Probe la Rommaine] excellence autresi fu Probe
de Romme

to fele the swete droppes of understandynge to lerne. So it was no lyght thynge to take away this pleasaunce from her, to the whiche all other women's werkes put aparte, she applyed her in that she myght. And thus she occupyed her so well by the space of tyme that she was ryght a soverayne poete. And not onely in that scyence, [Kk6v] but it semed that she was nourysshed with the mylke and with the doctryne of parfyte phylosophye, for she wolde fele and knowe of all maner of scyences that she lerned soveraynly insomoche that she passed her broder, whiche was ryght a grete poete in all excellent clargye. And it suffysed her not onely the connynge, but she put the understandynge to werke it and her handes to the penne in compylynge many ryght notable bokes, the whiche bokes and dyttyes were in the tyme of Saynt Gregory of grete pryce, of whom Bocace the Italyen whiche was a grete poete maketh mencyon, in praysynge this woman sayth in his boke: 'O, ryght grete worshyp to that woman that hath lefte woman's werkes, and applyeth and gyveth her wytte to the studye of ryght hyghe connynge!'

"And this Bocace sayth forthermore, certefyenge the purpose that I sayd to thee of the wyttes of women: 'Nowe ben they ashamed,' sayth he, 'as these slowe women that so myssetrusteth of theyrselfe and of theyr understandynge, so as thoughe they were borne in the mountaynes without understandynge what is welthe or worshyp, and so dyscourageth themselfe and sayth that they be not good to other thynge nor profytable but to take men aboute the necke, and to bere and nourysshe chyldren. And God hathe gyven them fayre understandynge, yf they wolde applye it in all thynges that these gloryous and excellent men dothe. For yf they wolde studye, the thynges be nother more ne lesse but also comune [Ll1r] to women as to men, and may by honest laboure gete them name perpetuall, the whiche havynge is agreable to all worshypfull men.' Ryght dere doughter, thus mayst thou se howe this auctoure Bocace bereth wytnesse of that that I have sayd to thee, and howe he prayseth and proveth scyence in woman."

## *Chapter 29*    Of Probe the Romayne

"Of grete excellence in scyence also was Probe the Romayne, wyfe of Adelphe, and was crystened. This woman had so notable wytte, and she loved and haunted the scole soo moche that she coude soveraynly the .vii. scyences lyberales and was ryght a soverayne poete. And by so grete laboure in studyenge she haunted

de Virgile et ses dictiez, que a tous propos lui estoient en memoire. Lesquelz livres et lesquelz dictiez comme une fois elle les veist[1] par grant entente de son engin et de sa pensee, et si comme elle se prenoit garde de la signifiance d'yceulx, en son entencion lui vint que on pourroit selon les ditz livres toute d'escripre l'Escriture [fol. 48r b] et les hystoires du Viel Testament et du Nouvel par vers plaisans et plains de substance. Laquelle chose pour certain, ce dit l'aucteur Bocace, n'est pas sans admiracion que si haulte consideracion peust entrer en cervel de femme, mais moult fu chose plus merveilleuse, ce dist il, de le mettre a execucion.

"Car adoncques elle,[2] moult desireuse d'acomplir sa pensee, mist la main a l'oeuvre, et maintenant par *Bucoliques*, et puis par *Georgiques*, ou par *Eneydes* qui sont livres ainsi appellez que fist Virgille la dicte[3] femme couroit, c'est a dire visetoit et lisoit, et maintenant d'une partie les vers tous[4] entiers prenoit, et maintenant de l'autre aucunes petites parties touchoit par [fol. 48v a] merveilleux arteffice et soubtiveté a son propos. Si ordenneement[5] vers entiers faisoit et les petites parties ensemble mettoit, couploit,[6] et lioit en gardant la loy, l'art, et les mesures des piez et conjonction des vers sans y faillyr[7] que nul homme ne peust mieulx. Et par telle[8] maniere des le commencement du monde fist le commencement de son livre, ensuivant[9] de toutes les hystoires de l'Ancien Testament et de Nouvel vint jusques a l'envoiement du saint Esperit aux apostres, les livres de Virgile a tout ce concordans si ordennement que qui n'aroit cognoiscence de ceste composicion cuideroit que Virgile eust esté prophete et euvangeliste ensemble. Pour [fol. 48v b] lesquelz choses ce dist mesmes Bocace grant recommendacion et louange affiert a ceste femme, car il appert manifestement que elle eust pour vray congnoiscence entiere et plainere des sains livres et des saints volumes[10] de la divine Escripture, laquel chose par[11] souvent n'avient mesmement a maint grans clers et theologiens de nostre temps. Et voult celle tres noble dame que sa dicte oeuvre faicte et composee par son labour fust appellee *Centonias*.[12]

"Et non obstant que le labour d'ycelle oeuvre pour sa grandeur deust souffire a la vie d'un homme a y vaquer, ne s'en passa mie a tant ains fist plusieurs aultres

---

[1]  veist] leust
[2]  elle] la dicte femme
[3]  la dicte] ycelle
[4]  tous] tout
[5]  Si ordenneement] ordeneement
[6]  couploit] et couuploit
[7]  faillyr] faillir ordenoit tant magistraument
[8]  telle] tel
[9]  ensuivant] et ensuivant
[10]  pour vray congnoiscence entiere et plainere des sains livres et des saints volumes] vraye congnoiscence et plainiere des sains livres et volumes
[11]  par] pas
[12]  Centonias] Centomias

the bokes of poetes, and in especyall of Vyrgyle and of his dyttyes, that to all purposes she had them all in mynde. The whiche, as in a tyme she sawe by grete entente of her wytte and of her thought, and as she toke hede of the sygnyfyenge of them, it came to her entencyon that one myght after the foresayd bokes dyscryve all the scrypture and the hystoryes of the Olde Testament and of the Newe by pleasaunt verses and full of substaunce, the whiche thynge for certayne that the auctoure Bocace saythe is not without mervayle that so hyghe consyderacyon myght entre in the brayne of woman; and ryght [Ll1v] a grete mervayle, as he sayth, to put it in execucyon.

"For she, ryght gretely desyrynge to fulfyll her thought, put the hande to the werke and somtyme she ranne by the *Bucolyques*, or by *Eneydos*, or by the *Georgykes*, whiche were the bokes that Vyrgyle made whiche ben so named; that is to say, she vysyted and redde, and nowe of one parte she toke the hole verse, nowe of others some lytell partes she touched by mervayllous crafte and subtylte to her purpose, and so ordynately made hole verses and the letell partes put togyder and coupled, and redde in beholdynge the lawe, the crafte and the measure of fete and the joynynge togyder the verses without faylynge in ony parte that no man myght do better. And by suche manere after the begynnynge of the worlde, she made the begynnynge of her boke, in sewynge all the hystoryes of the Olde Testament and of the Newe, and so came to the sendynge of the Hol[y][1] Ghost to the apostles, accordynge all with the bokes of Vyrgyle soo ordynately that who had not knowynge of this makynge wolde have wende that Vyrgyle had ben a prophete or an evangelyst togyder. For the whiche the foresayd Bocace sayth grete recommendacyon and lowynge of this woman, for it appereth openly that she had very knowlege and playne of holy bokes and holy volumes of Devyne Scrypture, the whiche boke was knowne of many grete clerkes and devynes of our tyme. And this noble lady wolde that this foresayd werke, made and compounded by grete laboure,[2] [Ll2r] sholde be called *Centonyas*.

"And notwithstandynge that the laboure of werke as for the gretnesse ought suffyse to the lyfe of a man, yet she lefte not tyll she had made many dyvers other

[1] Hol[y] : *Holn*
[2] laboure : *laboure laboure*

livres excellens et tres louables. Un [fol. 49r a] entre les autres en fist en vers appellé aussi *Centonie*, pour la cause de cent vers qui y sont contenus et prist les ditz de Omerus le pouete et les vers par quoy on puet conclurre a la louenge d'ycelle que non pas tant seulement les lettres latines savoit, mais les greques aussi sot[1] perfaictement. De laquel femme et de ses choses, ce dit Bocace, doivent estre en grant plaisir d'oïr aux femmes."

## *Chapitre 30*     Ci dit de Sapho, soubtille[2] femme poete et philosophe

"N'ot pas moins de science que Probe la sage Sapho, qui fut une pucelle de la cité de Milicene. Ceste Sapho fu de tres grant beauté de corps et de vis en contenant,[3] maintien, et parole [fol. 49r b] tres agreable et plaisant; mais sur toutes les graces dont elle fut douee passa celle de son hault entendement, car en pleuseurs ars et sciences fut tres experte et perfonde. Et ne savoit pas tant seulement lettres et escriptures par autrui faictes, ains d'elle mesmes trouva maintes choses nouvelles et fist pleuseurs livres et dictiez, de laquelle dit le poete Bocace par doulceur de lengage poetique[4] ces belles paroles:

"'Sapho, amonnesté de vif engin et d'ardant desir par continuel estude, entre les gens[5] bestiaulx et sans science hanta la haultece de Pernazus la montaingne, c'est assavoir d'estude perfaicte, par hardement et osement beneur[é];[6] s'acompaigna entre les muses non [fol. 49v a] reffusé, c'est assavoir entre les ars et les sciences. Et s'en entra en la forest de lauriers pleine de may, de verdure, de fleures de diverses couleurs, odourans de grant souefveté, et de pleuseurs herbes ou reposent et habitent gramaire, logique, et la noble Rethorique, Geometrie, Arismetique. Et tant chemina que elle vint et arriva en la caverne et perfondeur de Appolin, dieu de science, et trouva le ruissel et conduit de Castolio, la fontaine, et de la harpe prist le plestren et la touche: si en faisoit grans melandies avec les nimphes, menant la dance, c'est a entendre avec les ruilles d'armonie et d'acort de musique.'

"Par ces choses que Bocace dist d'elle doit estre entendu la perfondeur de son entendement, et les livres que elle fist de si perfonde [fol. 49v b] science[7] que les sentences en sont fortes a savoir et entendre, mesmes aux hommes de grant engin et estude selon le tesmoing des anciens. Et jusques aujourd'uy durent encore ses

---

[1] grecques aussi sot perfaictement] grecques sceut parfaitement
[2] Sapho : *Saphophe* soubtille] Sapho la tres soubtille
[3] contenant] contenance
[4] lengage poetique] poetique lengage
[5] gens] hommes
[6] beneur[é] : *beneur*
[7] perfonde science] parfondes sciences

bokes ryght worshypfull and excellente. One amonge all other she made in verses and to be called also *Centonye*, bycause of an hundred verses that ben conteyned therin also. She toke the bokes of Omerus the poete and the verses by whiche one myght conclude to the praysynge of her, whiche knewe not onely the Latyne letters but also the Grekes as parfytely. Of the whiche lady and of her thynges that she dyde, Bocace sayth that it ought to be grete pleasaunce to all women to here."

*Chapter 30*    Of Sapho, poete and phylosophre

"And of lesse connynge then Probe was not the noble Sapho, whiche was a mayde of the cyte of Mylycene. This Sapho was of ryght grete beaute of body and of vysage, and in manerly countenaunce and in speche ryght agreable and pleasaunt. And above all other graces that were gyven her, she passed of hyghe understandynge, for she was experte profoundely in many dyvers artes and scyences. And she knewe not onely letters and wrytynges made by others, but of herselfe she founde many newe thynges, and made many dyvers bokes and dyttyes, of whom speketh [Ll2v] the poete Bocace these fayre wordes of poetyke language:

"'Sapho, garnysshed of quycke understandynge and of brennynge desyre by contynuel study amonge the beestysshe people and without connynge, haunted the hyghnesse of the mountayne of Pernaso; this is to understande, the parfyte studye by veray hardynesse and boldenesse. She accompanyed herselfe with the .ix. muses not refused; that is to saye, amonge the craftes and scyences. And so entred in the forest of lawryere, full of braunches of vertue, and floures of dyvers colours, smellynge of grete swetnesse of dyvers herbes where they rest them and dwell: Grammer, Logyke, and the noble Rethoryke, Geometry, and Arysmetryke. And so moche she wente that she came and aryved in the cave and depnesse of Appolyne, god of scyence and connynge, and founde the sprynge and conduyte of Castolyo, the welle, and toke the wrest of the harpe and touched it: so she made grete melodyes with the nymphes, ledynge the daunce, this is to understande with the rules of Armony and cordes of Musyke.'

"By these thynges that Bocace sayth of her ought to be understande the depnesse of her understandynge, and the bokes that she made of so depe scyence that the sentences ben strong to knowe and understande to men of grete wytte. And the scole after the wytnesse of auncyent men endureth unto this day, and

escrips et dictiez, moult notablement composés et fais,[1] qui sont lumiere et exemple a ceulx qui sont venus aprés de parfaictement dictier et faire. Elle trouva plusieurs manieres de faire chançons et dictiez, lay et plaintes plourables, et lamentacions estranges d'amours, et autre[2] sentement moult bien faictes et par bel ordre, qui furent nommees de son nom, *Saphice.*

"Et de ces dictiez reco[r]de[3] Crasse[4] que quant Platon le tres grant philosophe qui fu maistre d'Aristote fu trespassé, on trouva le livre des dictiez Sapho soubz son chevet. A brief parler, de ceste[5] dame fut en science de si tres grant excellence qu'en la cité ou elle conversoit, afin que elle fut de tous tres honouree et qu'a tousjours fust en souvenance, on fist a sa semblance un ymage d'arain dedié ou nom d'elle eslevé haultement. Si fu celle dame mise et comptee entre les grans poetes renommez, desquelz (ce dit Bocace) les honneurs des dyademes et des couronnes des roys, et les mittres des evesques, ne sont point greingneurs, ne de ceulx qui ont victoires les couronnes et chapiaulx de lauriers et de palme.

"Leonce,[6] qui fu femme greque, fust elle[7] autressi si tres grant philosophe que elle osa par pures et [fol. 50r b] vrayes raisons reprendre[8] le philosophe Theophraste, qui en son temps tant estoit renommez."

## *Chapitre 31* [Ci dit de la pucelle Manthoa][9]

"Se les sciences sont propices et couvenables aux femmes[10] a apprendre, saches de vray que semblablement ne leur sont mie les ars vees. Et jadis[11] en l'anciene loy des payens les gens usoient de devinemens[12] de ce qui estoit a avenir par le vol des oisiaulx, et par les flammes du feu, et par les entrailles des bestes mortes; et ce estoit une propre art ou science que ilz tenoient en grant digneté. En celle art fu souveraine maistresse une pucelle qui fut fille de Thyrisie, qui estoit le tres grant prestre de la cité de Thebes—si que nous dirions evesque, car es [fol. 50v a] autres loys les prestres estoient mariez. Ceste femme qui nommee estoit Manthoa, qui

---

[1] composes et fais] fais et composez
[2] autre] d'autre
[3] reco[r]de : *recode*
[4] Crasse] Orace
[5] de ceste] ceste
[6] Leonce] De femmes de grant science te pourroie dire assez. Leonce
[7] fust elle] fu
[8] reprendre] reprendre et redarguer
[9] *L repeats chap. 30 rubric*
[10] propices et couvenables aux femmes] sciibles aux femmes et couvenables
[11] ne leur sont mie les ars vees. Et jadis] leur sont les ars non veez, si que tu orras: jadis
[12] de devinemens] d'endevinemens

her wrytynges and dyttyes ryght notably compounded and made b[e][1] the lyghtes and ensamples to them that cometh after [Ll3r] parfyte wrytynge and endytynge. She founde many dyvers maners of makynge of songes and dyttyes, playes and wepynge complayntes, and straunge lamentacyons of love ryght well and in fayre ordre, whiche were named after her name, *Saphyse*.

"And of these dyttyes recordeth Crassus that when Plato the grete phylosophre whiche was mayster to Arystotle was deed, one founde the bokes of the wrytynges of Sapho under his bolster of his heed. And to say shortely of this lady, she was of so grete excellence of connynge that in the cyte where she was conversaunt, to the entent that she was moost worshypfull and that she sholde be alwaye in remembraunce, one made to her lykenesse an ymage of brasse halowed in the name of her lyfte of a grete hyght. So was this lady named and counted amonge all other poetes of renowne, of the whiche as Bocace saythe the worshyppes of dyademes and of crownes, and of mytres of bysshoppes be not gretter, ne them that hathe vyctores and chaplettes of lauryere and palme.

"Leonte that was a Greke was a grete phylosophre also, whiche durste reprove the phylosophre Theophrast by pure and trewe reasons, whiche was so gretely named in his dayes."

## Chapter 31    Of the mayde Manthoa

"If the scyences ben easy and covenable to women to lerne, knowe it for trouthe that the [Ll3v] same wyse the craftes are not unsene to them. And somtyme in the olde lawe of paynymes, the people used many dyvers dyvynacyons of that that was to come by the flyght of byrdes, and by the flambes of fyre, and by the entrayles of deed beestes. And that was a propre arte or a connynge, whiche they helde in grete dygnyte. In this tyme a mayden was a grete maystresse, whiche was doughter of Thyryfye whiche was the gretest preest of the cyte of Thebes, so as we calle hym a 'bysshop,' for in that other lawes the bysshoppes were maryed. This woman that was named Manthea, whiche floured in the tyme of Kynge

---

[1] b[e] : *by*

florissoit ou temps du roy Edippus,[1] fu de si cler et de si grant engin que elle sceut toute l'art de piromancie, qui est a deviner par le feu, de laquelle art usoient ou tres ancien temps. Ceulx de Caldee qui la trouverent et autres dient que Nambroth le geant la trouva. Si n'estoit en son temps nul homme qui mieux cogneust les mouvemens des flammes du feu, les couleurs, le son qui du feu yst. Et aussi tant clerement congnoissoit les vaines des bestes, les gousiers des thoreaux, et les entrailles du toutes bestes,[2] que on creoit que par ses ars souventes fois contraingnoit les esperis a parler [fol. 50v b] et donner respons de ce que elle vouloit savoir. Ou temps de ceste dame fu destruitte Thebes pour achoison des enfans du roy Edippus.[3] Si s'en ala celle demourer en Aisie et la fiet un[4] temple au dieu Appollo, qui puis fist[5] en grant renommee. Elle fina sa vie en Ytalie, et du nom de ceste dame pour son auctorité fu nommee une cité du païs et encores est Manthoa, de laquelle Virgile fut nez."

*Chapitre 32*     **Ci dit de Medee, et d'une autre royne nommee Circes**

"Medee, de laquelle assez d'ystoires font mencion, ne sceut pas moins d'art et de science que celle devant dicte. Elle fu fille de Othes, roy de Colcos et de Perse. Moult belle, haulte, et droicte fu de corsage [fol. 51r a] et assez[6] de viaire, mais de savoir elle passa et exceda toutes femmes. Elle savoit de toutes herbes les vertus, et tous les enchantemens que faire se peuent, et de nulle art qui estre peust sceue elle n'estoit ignorante. Elle faisoit par vertu d'une chançon que elle savoit trobler et obscurcir le ciel,[7] mouvoir les vens des fousses et cavernes de la terre, commouvoir les tempestes en l'air, arrester les fleuves, confire venin,[8] composer feux sans labour pour ardoir quelconques choses que elle vouloit; et toutes semblables choses savoit faire. Ceste fut celle qui par l'ar[t][9] de son enchantement fist conquerre a Jason la toison d'or.

"Circes autressi fu [fol. 51r b] royne d'une contree sur la mer, qui siet sur les entrees d'Ytalie. Ceste dame sceut tant de l'art d'enchantement qu'il n'estoit chose que elle voulsist faire que par vertu de son enchantement ne feist. Elle savoit

---

[1] florissoit ou temps du roy Edippus] flourissoit ou temps de Edippus, roy de Thebes

[2] du toutes bestes] des bestes

[3] destruitte Thebes pour achoison des enfans du roy Edippus] destruite pour le contens des filz de Edippus le roy

[4] fiet un] fist au

[5] puis fist] fu puis

[6] belle, haulte, et droicte fu de corsage et assez] belle de corsage haulte et droite et assez plaisant

[7] le ciel] l'air

[8] venin] poisons

[9] l'ar[t] : *l'ar*

Edyppus, was of so clere and grete wytte that she knewe al the crafte of pyro-mancye, whiche is for to dyvyne by the flambes of fyre, the whiche arte used in the olde tyme those of Caldee whiche founde it, and others sayth that Nem-broche the gyaunt founde it. So there was in her tyme no man that knewe the movynges of the flambes of fyre, the colours, and the sowne that came out of the fyre but she. And also she knewe clerely the vaynes of beestes, the throtes of boles, and the entraylles of all beestes, that one wolde byleve that by these craftes often tymes the spyrytes were constrayned to speke and to gyve answere of that that one wolde knowe.

"In the tyme of this lady, Thebes was destroyed thrughe the encheson of the .ii. sones of Kynge Edyppus. Then wente this lady to dwelle in Asye and there she made a temple of the god Apollo, the whiche was [Ll4r] syth in grete renowne. She ended her lyfe in Italye, and of the name of this lady for her grete auctoryte there was named a cyte of the countre and yet is Manthoa, in the whiche Vyrgyle was borne."

*Chapter 32*  Of Medea, and another quene named Cyrces

"Medea, of whome hystoryes ynoughe maketh mencyon, coude as moche of crafte and connynge as she before reherced. She was the doughter of Othes, kynge of Coloos, and of Perce. She was ryght fayre of body and of vysage, but in connynge she passed all other women in her tyme. She knewe the vertues of every dyvers herbe, and all maner enchauntementes that myght be made, and of ony crafte that myght be lerned she was not ygnoraunt. By the vertue of a songe that she coude, she wolde make the ayre to trouble and the skye to waxe darke, move the wyndes out of the pyttes and caves of the erthe, to make the tempestes to ryse in the ayre, to make waters and grete ryvers to stande styll, to make venyme, to make fyres without laboure to brenne ony maner thynge that she wolde; and all suche maner of thynges she coude do. This was she that made Jason to conquere the golden fleece by enchauntement.

"Cyrces also was a quene of a countree upon [Ll4v] the see, whiche stode upon the entryes of Italye. This lady coude so moche of the crafte of enchauntement that there was nothynge that she wolde do but she wolde do it by the vertue of

par un buvrage¹ que elle donnoit transmuer corps d'ommes en figures de bestes sauvages et d'oysiaulx. Pour laquel chose tesmoingnier est escript en l'istoire de Ulixes que quant il s'en retournoit aprés la destruccion de Troye, cuidant raler en son païs de Grece, Fortune et orage de temps transporta ses nefs tant ça et la par maintes tempestes, que a la perfin arriverent au port de la cité de ceste royne Circes. Mais comme le sage Ulixes [fol. 51v a] ne voulsist mie descendre sans le congié et licence de la royne d'ycelle terre, envoia ses chevaliers par devers elle pour savoir se il lui plairoit qu'ilz descendissent. Mais celle dame, tantost reputant que ilz fussent ses anemis, abuvra les ditz chevaliers de son buvrage, par quoy tantost furent en pors convertis. Mais Ulixes ala tantost vers elle et tant fist que ilz furent remis en leur propre fourme. Et semblablement dyent aucuns de Diomedes (que estoit un autre prince de Grece) que quant il fut au port Circez² arrivés, que elle fist ses chevaliers muer en oysiaulx, qui encores sont lesquelx oisiaulx sont assez grans et d'autre fourme que autres oisiaux, et sont moult³ [fol. 51v b] fiers. Et les appellent ceulx de la contree *Dyomedes*."

### *Chapitre 33*　　Demande Christine a Raison se il fu oncques femme qui de soy trouvast aucune science non par avant sceue; et elle lui respont de Nicostrate, qui trouva le latin⁴

Je, Christine, qui ces choses entendoie de Dame Raison, lui repliquay sur ce pas en tel maniere: "Dame, je voy bien que assez et a grant nombre trouverez femmes apprises en sciences et ars. Mais je vous⁵ demande se nulles en savez qui par vertu de sentement et de soubtilleté d'engin⁶ ayant d'elles mesmes trouvees aucunes nouvelles ars et sciences neccessaires, bonnes, et couvenables qui par avant n'eussent esté trouveez, ne [fol. 52r a] cogneues? Car n'est mie si grant maistrise de suivre et apprendre aprés⁷ autre aucune science ja trouvee et commune⁸ comme est trouver de soy mesmes chose nouvelle et non acoustumee."

*Response*: "Ne doubtes pas du contraire, chiere amie, que maintes notables et grans sciences et ars ont esté trouvees par engin et soubtivetté de femmes tant en speculacion d'entendement, lesquelles se demonstrent par escript,

¹ par un buvrage] par vertu d'un beuvrage
² Circez] de Circes
³ oisiaux, et sont moult] oysiaulx ne sont, et sont moult
⁴ et elle lui respont de Nicostrate, qui trouva le latin] *omitted*
⁵ Mais je vous] Mais vous
⁶ d'engin] d'engin et d'entendement
⁷ aprés : *appres*
⁸ commune] congneue

her enchauntement. And by a drynke that she wolde gyve, she wolde chaunge the bodyes of men into the fygures of wylde bestes and byrdes. And to wytnesse the same thynge, it is wryten in the hystory of Ulyxes that when he retourned after the destruccyon of Troy, trowed to go agayne into his countree, of grete fortune and woodnesse of tempestes hurled his shyppes here and there by many dyvers troubles, that at the laste they aryved at the porte of the cyte of this Lady Cyrces. Yet this wyse Ulyxes wolde not take the lande without lycence of the quene of the lande: he sente certayne of his knyghtes to her for to knowe yf it pleased her that they myght take the lande. Then this lady trowed that they had ben her enemyes, gave them drynke of that drynke that she made and anone they were transfourmed into hogges. But Ulyxes wente anone to her and dyde so moche that they were put agayne into theyr owne shap. And in the same wyse, some men saye of Dyomede that was another prynce of Grece, that when he aryved at the porte of this Lady Cyrces that she made his knyghtes to be transfygured into byrdes, whiche be yet ryght grete and of other shappe than other byrdes ben, and they ben ryght fyerse. And those of that countree calle them *Dyomedens*." [Mm1r]

## Chapter 33    Christine asketh of Reason yf there was ever woman that founde ony thynge of her[s]elfe[1] that was not knowne before; and she tolde her of Nycostrate, otherwyse called Carmentis

I, Christine, whiche understode these thynges of Dame Reason, replyed upon that in this manere: "Madame, I se wel that ye myght fynde ynowe and of grete nombre of women praysed in scyences and in crafte. But knowe ye ony that by the vertue of theyr felynge and of subtylte of wytte have founde of themselfe ony newe craftes and scyences necessary, good, and covenable that were never founde before, nor knowne? For it is not so grete maystry to folowe and to lerne after ony other scyence founde and comune before, as it is to fynde of theymselfe some newe thynge not accustomed before."

*Answere*: "Ne doubte ye not the contrary, my dere frende, but many craftes and scyences ryght notable hathe ben founde by the wytte and subtylte of women as moche by speculacyon of understandynge, the whiche sheweth them by

---

[1] her[s]elfe : *herfelfe*

comme en ars qui se demonstrent en oeuvres manuelles et de labour. Et de ce
donray asses exemples.[1]

"Et premierement te diray de la noble Nicostrate, que ceulx d'Ytalie appellerent Carmentis. Ceste dame fu fille du roy d'Archade nommé Pallent. Elle [fol.
52r b] estoit de merveilleux engin et douee de Dieu d'especiaulx dons de savoir.
Grant clergece estoit es lettres greques, et tant ot bel et sage langage, et venerable
faconde, que les poetes de lors qui d'elle escriprent faingnirent en leurs dictiez
que elle estoit aimee de[2] dieu Mercurius, et un filz que elle ot de lui qui fu en son
temps[3] de moult grant savoir, dirent que elle l'avoit eu d'ycellui dieu.

"Ceste dame, par certaines mutacions qui avindrent en la terre ou elle estoit,
se transporta de son païs son filz et grant foison peuple qui la suivi avec elle a
grant navire, en la terre d'Ytalie, et arriva sur la[4] fleuve du Tybre; la descendi. Si
monta sur un hault mont que elle nomma du nom de son pere le mont Palentin,[5]
[fol. 52v a] sur lequel mont la cité de Romme fu depuis fondee. La celle dame avec
son filz et ceulx qui suivi l'avoient fonda un chastel, et com[m]e celle dame[6] eust
trouvé les hommes d'ycellui[7] païs comme tous bestiaulx, escripst certaines lois
ou[8] elle leur enjoingnoit a vivre par ordre de droit et de raison selon justice; et fu
la premiere qui en celle contree—qui puis fu tant renommee, et dont toutes les
loys de droit vindrent[9] et ysserent—qui premierement y establi lois. Ceste noble
dame sceut par inspiracion divine et par esperit de prophecie, dont avec les autres
graces que elle avoit singuliere especiauté lui ne[10] estoit donnee, comment celle
terre [fol. 52v b] devoit estre, le temps avenir, anoblie de excellence et de renommee sur tous les païs du monde. Si lui sembla que ce ne seroit pas chose honneste
que quant la haultece de l'empire de Romme vendroit, qui tout le monde devoit
seingnorir, que ilz usassent de lettres et de caratheres estranges et mendiees[11]
d'autre païs. Et afin aussi que elle monstrast sa sapience et l'excellence de son
engin aux siecles avenir, tant fist et estudia[12] que elle trouva propres lettres du
tout differenciés des autres nacions, c'este assavoir *l'a. b. c.* et l'ordenance du latin,

---

[1] exemples] exemple

[2] de] du

[3] ot de lui fu en son temps] avoit eu de son mari qui en son temps fu

[4] la] le

[5] le mont Palentin] Palentin

[6] com[m]e celle dame: *come celle dame*] comme elle

[7] d'ycellui] du

[8] ou] es quelles

[9] de droit et de raison selon justice; et fu la premiere qui en celle contree—qui puis
fu tant renommee, et dont toutes les loys de droit vindrent] *skips from* de droit *to* de droit
vindrent

[10] ne] en

[11] mendiees] mendres

[12] estudia] tant estudia

wrytynge, as in craftes that sheweth theym in werkynge of handes and of laboure. And of these I shall gyve thee ensamples.

"And fyrst I shal tell thee of Nycostrate, whiche those of Italye called Carmentes. This lady was doughter of the kynge of Archadye named Pallent. She was mervayllous wytty, and gyven of God to her of specyall gyftes of understandynge. She was a grete clarke [Mm1v] in the letter of Grece and had so moche fayre and wyse speche, and worshypfull faconde, that the poetes beynge that tyme that wrote of her fayned in [theyr][1] wrytynges that she was love[d][2] of the god Mercuryus, and that she had a sone by the foresayd god, whiche was of grete understandynge.

"This lady, by certayne chaunce that happened in the countre where she was, wente out of her countre, her sone and grete foyson of people that folowed and wente with her, and with a grete navye came into Italye, and aryved upon the water of Tybre; and there she descended out of her shyppes. So she wente up upon an hyghe hylle that she named the Mounte Palentyne after her fader, upon the whiche mounte the cyte of Rome was founded syth. This lady, with her sone and those that folowed her, founded a fayre castell there. And as this lady had founde the men of that countre al bestysshe and rude, she ordeyned and wrote certayne lawes by the whiche she enjoyned them to lyve by ordre of ryght and reason after justyce. And she was the fyrst that in this countre whiche was syth of so grete renowne—and of whom all the lawes of ryght come of—the fyrst that establed the lawes there. This lady knewe by inspyracyon devyne that by the spyryte of prophecye, amonge other graces that she had synguler specyalte was gyven to her, howe this countre ought to be in tyme to come moost noble of excellence and of renowne above all the countres of the worlde. So it semed her that it sholde be no honest thynge that when [Mm2r] the hyghnesse of the empyre of Rome that all the wor[l]de[3] ought to lordeshyp and governe, that they sholde use of letters and carectes straunge and begged of other countrees. And to that entente also that she wolde shewe her wysdome and excellence of wytte to the worlde to come, she dyde soo moche by her study that she founde propre letters dyfferenced from all other nacyons of the worlde, that is to knowe the *A. B. C.*, and the ordenaunce of Latyne by puttynge togyder of the same letters with the

---

[1] [theyr] : *her*

[2] love[d] : *love*

[3] wor[l]de : *worde*

l'assemblee d'ycelles, la difference des voyeux,[1] et toute l'entré de la science de [fol. 53r a] gramaire, lesquelles lettres et science elle bailla et apprist aux gens, et volt que communement fust sceue.

"Si ne fu pas petite science, ne pou prouffitable, que ceste femme trouva, ne dont petit gré lui doye estre sceu. Car pour la soubtiveté de la dicte science, et pour la grant utilité et bien qui au monde en est en suivi, on peut dire que oncques chose plus digne ne fu trouvee au monde. Et de ce benefice n'ont pas esté ingraz les Ytaliens, et a bon droit, a qui ceste chose fu tant merveilleuse que ilz ne reputerent mie seulement celle[2] femme plus que homme, mais deesse, pour laquel chose mesmes en sa vie l'onnorerent de honneurs [fol. 53r b] divines. Et quant elle fut morte, ilz lui edefient en son nom un temple,[3] et fu fait au pié de la montaigne ou elle avoit demouré. Et pour donner a celle dame perpetuele memoire, pristrent plusieurs noms de la science que elle eut trouvee, et aussi donnerent nom d'elle a plusieurs de leurs choses si comme eux mesmes de celle contree: pour la science du latin qui par celle dame fu la trouvé, se appellerent[4] par grant honneur *Latins*. Et qui plus est, pour ce que *ita* en latin, qui veult dire en françois *oil*, est la souveraine affirmacion d'icellui langage latin, ne leur souffist mie encore que ycelle contree fust appellee terre Latine, ains vouldrent que tout le païx de oultre les mons [fol. 53v a] — qui moult est grant et large, et ou a maintes diverses contrees et seigneuries — fust appellez *Ytallie*. De ceste Dame Carmentis furent nommez dictiez *carmen* en latin. Et mesmes les Rommains qui depuis grant temps vindrent nommerent une des peires[5] de la cité de Romme *Carmentele*, lesquelz noms pour quelconques prosperité que les Rommains ayent puis eue,[6] ne pour haultece de quelconques de leurs empereurs ne changerent puis si comme il appert jusques au jour d'ui qu'encores durent.

"Et que veulx tu plus, belle fille? Puet on plus grant[7] solemnité dire d'omme ne de mere? Mais ne cuides mie que ceste ait esté seule au monde par qui sciences plusieurs et diverses ayent esté trouvees."

---

[1] la difference des voyeux] et la difference des voyeux et des mutes

[2] celle] ceste

[3] edefient en son nom un temple] ediffierent un temple que ilz dedierent en son nom

[4] fu la trouvé, se appellerent] se appellerent fu la trouvee

[5] grant temps vindrent nommerent une des peires] vindrent lonc temps aprés nommerent une des portes

[6] puis eue] eue

[7] plus grant] greigneur

dyfference of vowelles, with all the entrynge of the scyence of grammere, the whiche letters and scyences she toke and taught them to her people, and wolde that it sholde be knowne communely.

"So it was no lytell scyence, nor lytell profytable, that this woman founde. For the subtylnesse of the sayd scyence, and for the grete profyte and welthe that is come to the worlde by it, one myght say that there was never worthyer thynge founde to the worlde. And of that benefyse the Italyens have not ben unkynde, and of good ryght, to whom this thynge was so mervayllous that they had her not onely in reputacyon more than man, but a goddesse, for the whiche they honoured her with devyne worshyppes. And when she was deed, they edyfyed and founded a tymple in her name, and it was made and buylded at the foote of the foresayd mountayne where she dwelled. And to gyve to this lady a perpetuall memorye forevermore, they toke many of them theyr names as after [Mm2v] the scyences that she had founde, and also they gave the name of her to dyvers of theyr thynges, so as themselfe of that countre for the scyence of Latyne whiche that was founde there by that lady, they call themselfe *Latynes* in grete worshyp. And that more is for that that *ita* in Latyne (that is to say in Frensshe *ouy*, and in Englysshe *ye*) the soverayne affyrmacyon of this language is Latyne. And yet it suffyseth not them that this countre was called the lande of Latyne, but they wolde that all the countres over the mountaynes whiche is grete and large, and where there were many dyvers countres and lordshyppes, all was called *Italye*. Of this Lady Carmentys, dyttyes were called *carmen* in Latyn. And also the Romaynes that came a grete whyle syth named one of the gates of the cyte of Rome *Carmentele*, the whiche names for what maner prosperyte that the Romaynes had syth, nother for no hyghnesse of emperours they chaunged never syth; so as it appereth unto this day, it endureth yet.

"And what wylte thou more, fayre doughter? May there ony man saye more worshyp of ony man borne of woman? Yet thou trowest not that this crafte be onely to the worlde, by whiche many scyences and dyvers have ben founde." [Mm3r]

*Chapitre 34*   **Dit**[1] **de Minerve qui trouva maintes sciences, et la maniere de faire armeures de fer et d'acier** [fol. 53v b]

"Minerve, si que toy mesmes en as ailleurs escript, fu une pucelle de Grece et fut surnommee Pallas. Ceste pucelle fut de tant grant excellence en engin que la fole gent de lors, pour ce que ilz ne savoient pas bien dequelz parens elle estoit, et lui veoient faire des[2] choses qui oncques n'avoient esté en usage, distrent que elle estoit deesse venue du ciel; car de tant que moins cognoissoient sa venue,[3] de tant leur fu plus merveillable le grant savoir d'elle sur toutes femmes en son temps.

"Ceste fu soubtille et de grant entendement non mie seulement en une chose, mais souverainement[4] en toutes. Elle trouva par sa soubtiveté [fol. 54r a] aucunes lettres greques que on appelle *karatheres*, par lesquelles on puet mettre une grant narracion de choses en escript en l'espace de bien pou de lettres et de brieve escripture; desquelles abreviations[5] encores usent les Grieux, qui fu moult belle invencion et soubtiveté[6] a trouver. Elle trouva nombre[7] et maniere de compter et d'assembler sommes. Elle avoit l'esperite tant[8] enluminé de savoir que elle trouva plusieurs ars et ouvrages a faire qui oncques n'avoient esté trovez: l'art de la laine et de faire draps trouva toute, et fu la premiere qui oncques s'avisast du berbis tondre de laine, charpir, pignier, carder a divers outilz, nettoier, amolier a broches de fer, filer a la conoille puis les outilz a faire le drap, et comment [fol. 54r b] il seroit tyru.[9]

"*Item*, elle trouva l'usage de faire l'uile des fruis de terre—des olives et d'aultres fruis—presser et en tirer la liqueur.

"*Item*, elle trouva l'art et usage[10] de faire chars et charetes a porter choses aisiement d'un lieu en aultre.

"*Item*, plus fist ceste dame et qui plus semble merveillable, pour ce que c'est loins de nature de femme que elle de telle chose se avisast, car elle trouva l'art et la maniere de faire harnois[11] et les armeurs de fer et d'acier, de quoy les chevaliers et les gens d'armes usent en bataille, dont[12] ilz cueuvrent leurs corps que celle[13]

---

[1] Dit] Ci dit
[2] des] de
[3] sa venue] sa venue si que dit Bocace
[4] souverainement] generaument
[5] abreviations] desquelles aujourd'uy
[6] soubtiveté] soubtive
[7] nombre] nombres
[8] Elle avoit l'esperite tant] soubz briefté. Et a tout dire, tant avoit l'esperit
[9] tyru] tissu
[10] usage] usages
[11] harnois] le harnois
[12] dont] et dont
[13] que celle] qu'elle

*Chapter 34*     Of Mynerve that founde many scyences, and the maner
                 to make armoure of iron and steele

"Minerve, so as thou haste wryten in other places, was mayden of Grece, and
her surname was Pallas. This mayde was of so grete excellence in wytte that the
lewde people of that countree for that that they knewe not well of what kynrede
she was of, and they sawe her do thynges that had not ben before in usage, sayd
that she was a goddesse comen frome heven. For by so moche as they knewe not
frome whens she came, the more was to them mervaylable the grete connynge of
her above all women in her tyme.

"This lady was subtyll and of grete understandynge not onely in one thynge,
but soveraynely in all thynges. She founde by her subtylnesse certayne lettres
Grekeysshe that some call them *carectes*, by the whiche one myght put a grete tale
of dyvers thynges in wrytynge in the space of ryght fewe lettres and of shorte
wrytynge, the whiche abrevyacyons useth the Grekes yet, whiche was ryght
a fayre invencyon and a subtyll to fynde. She founde nombre and maner of a
compte, and to put togyder sommes. She had the spyryte soo moche enlumyned
of understandynge that she founde many craftes and werkes to make that had
never ben founde before.

"*The crafte of wolle and to make clothe*: and she founde fyrst that ever was
advysed to shere shepe, to tose wolle, to kembe, and to carde it with dyvers
instrumentes to make it clene, to make it softe with roddes of yron, to spynne
at the dystaffe, and after instrumentes [Mm3v] to make the clothe, and howe it
sholde be woven.

"Also she founde the c[r]afte[1] and usage to make oyle of fruytes of the erthe,
of olyves and of other fruyte, to presse it and to drawe the lycoure.

"Also she founde the crafte and the usage to make cartes and charyottes to
bere thynges easely from one place to another.

"And yet dyde this lady more, and that semed more mervaylable for that that
it is ferre fro the nature of woman that she sholde advyse her of suche thynges, for
she founde the crafte and the manere of makynge of harnoys and armure of yron
and of stele, the whiche the knyghtes and men of armes useth in batayle, with

---

[1] c[r]afte : *cafte*

ballia premierement a ceulx d'Athenes, a qui elle apprist l'usage de ordener host
et batalles, et la maniere de combatre en ordre et arrengeniee.

"*Item*, elle trouva premierement fleustes et flaiolz, trompes, et instrumens
de bouche.

"Ceste dame avec la grant vertu d'entendement que elle avoit fu tout son temps
vierge. Et pour la grant chasteté dont elle estoit distrent les poetes en leurs fictions
que Vulcan le dieu du feu avoit lenguement luittié a elle, et que finablement elle
vainqui[1] et le surmonta, qui estoit a dire que elle surmonta l'ardeur et conc[u]-
piscence[2] de la char, qui donne grant assault en joeunesse. Les Atheniens orent en
si grant reverence ceste pucelle que ilz l'aourient comme deesse. Et l'appelloient
deesse d'armes et de chevalerie pour ce que premiere en trouva l'usage, et aussi
l'appelloient deesse de savoir pour la grant science qui en elle abandoit.

"Aprés sa mort lui firent a Athenes edifier un temple consacré en son nom,
et en cellui temple [fol. 54v b] asseirent son ymage qui estoit en la fourme[3] et semblance d'une pucelle, ou quel ymage signifierent sapience et chevalerie. Si avoit
cel ymage les yeulx terribles et crueulx, pour ce que chevalerie est ordonné pour
excecuter rigueur de justice; et aussi signifioit que on cognoit pou souvent a quel
fin tend l'entencion du sage. Elle avoit la teste heaulmee, qui segnefioit que chevalier doit avoir force en vigueur; et aussi signifioit que les consaulx des sages
doivent estre couvers et secrez.[4] Elle estoit vestue d'un haubert, qui signifioit la
poissance de l'estat de chevalerie; et nottoit aussi que le sage doit estre[5] tousjours
armez contre leurs mouvemens de Fortune, soit ou bien ou mal.[6] Elle tenoit
[fol. 55r a] une hasce ou une lance tres longue, qui estoit a dire que le chevalier
doit estre le baston de justice; et segnefioit autressi que le sage fiche ses dars de
moult loingnes. Elle avoit pendu ou col une targe ou un escu de cristal, qui signifioit que le chevalier doit tousjours estre esveillié et veoir cler[7] sur la deffense
du païs et du peuple; aussi signifioit que au saige toutes choses sont apportes[8] et
manifestes. Ou milieu de celle targe avoit pourtrait la teste d'une serpent que on
nommoit *Gorgon*, qui signifioit que chevalier doit estre cautilleux et agaitant sur
ses[9] anemis comme le serpent; estoit aussi a dire que le sage est avisé de toutes

---

[1]  vainqui] le vainqui

[2]  conc[u]piscence : *concipiscence*

[3]  fourme] figure

[4]  en vigueur; et aussi signifioit que les consaulx des sages doivent estre couvers et
secrez] ou adurcy et constant courage es fais des armes; et aussi signiffiot que les conseulz
des sages sont couvers, secres, et muciez

[5]  doit estre] estoit

[6]  ou mal] ou el mal

[7]  cler] par tout

[8]  toutes choses sont apportes] sont toutes choses appertes

[9]  ses] les

whiche they cover theyr bodyes. And that she toke it fyrst to them at Athenes, to whome she taught the usage of ordeynynge hoostes in batayle, and the maner of fyghtynge in ordre and arowe.

"And she founde fyrst pypes, shalmes, and trompes, and instrumentes of mouthe.

"This lady, with the grete vertue of understandynge that she had, was alwaye a vyrgyn. And for the gret chastyte that she was of, the poetes sayd in theyr sayenges that Wulcan the god of fyre had longe wrestled with her, and fynally she overcame hym and surmounted hym; that is as moche to saye, that she overcame the brennynge and the concupyscence of the flesshe, whiche gyveth grete defaute in youthe. The people of Athenes had her in grete reverence,[1] and called her goddesse of armes and of knyghthode bycause that she founde fyrst the usage. And also they called her goddesse of connynge, for the grete scyence that habounded in her.

"After her dethe they [Mm4r] made to her a temple in Athenes consecrate in her name. And in that temple they set her ymage whiche was in the shap and semblaunce of a mayden, the whiche ymage sygnyfyed wysdome and knyghthode. And so this ymage had the eyen terryble and cruell, for that that knyghthode is ordeyned to execute the rygure of justyce; also it sygnyfyed that one knewe lytel often tymes to what ende entendeth the entencyon of a wyse man. She had the heed helmet, whiche betokened that a knyght ought to have strengthe in vertue; and also it sygnyfyed that the counsayles ought to be coverte and secrete. She was clothed with an hawberke, whiche betokeneth the puyssaunce of the state of knyghthode; and it betokened also that the wyse man ought to be alway armed agaynst the mo[v]ynges[2] of Fortune, be it well or evyll. She helde a shafte or a longe spere, whiche was to say that a knyght ought to be the staffe of justyce; and it sygnyfyed also that the wyse man pycketh his darte of a grete lengthe. She had hangynge at her necke a targe or a shelde of crystall, whiche betokened that the knyghtes ought to be alwaye wakynge, and to se clere upon the defence of the countre and of the people; also it sygnyfyed that unto the wyse man al thynges ben brought and made open. In the myddes of this targe there was also pourtrayed the heed of a serpent the whiche was named Gorgon, the whiche heed betokened and sygnyfyed that a noble and worthy knyght ought to be subtyl, and wyly, and watchynge upon his enemyes as dothe the [Mm4v] serpent; it was also to understande that the wyse man ought to be advysed of all malyces

---

[1] reverence : *reverrnce*

[2] mo[v]ynges : *monynges*

malices[1] de quoy on lui pourroit nuire. Mirent aussi [fol. 55r b] coste celle ymage, comme pour la garder, un oisel qui vole par nuit que on nomme *chuete*, qui signifioit que chevalier doit estre aussi bien de nuit que de jours[2] tout prest pour la deffence civille se mestier est; aussi segnefioit que le sage vueille a tout heure sur ce qui lui est propice a faire.

"Ceste dame fu par long temps tenue en si grant reverence, et tant ala sa grant renommee, qu'en plusieurs lieux establirent temples en son nom, et mesmement long temps aprés que les Rommains estoient en leur grant poissance mistrent leur[3] ymage avec leurs autres dieux."

*Chapitre 35*     **Ci dit de la royne Ceres, qui trouva[4] l'art de labourer les terres et maintes autres ars** [fol. 55v a]

"Ceres, qui fu es tres anciens aages royne du royaume des Siculiens, et[5] prerogative de trouver par soubtilleté d'engin premierement la science et usage du cultivement des terres, et des outilz qui y apertienent. Elle enseigna a ses subgiez a domter et aprivoisier les bueufs, et a les acoustumer a estre acouplés au jouch; trouva aussi la charue et leur monstra la maniere comment fendroient et partiroient la terre,[6] et tout le labour qui y apertient. Et aprés leur enseigna agiter semence sur celle terre et couvrir; et aprés, quant celle semence fu parcreue et multepliee moultra,[7] comment ilz soyeroient les blefs, et par batre de fleyaulx les ostreroient des espis. Puis enseigna a le mouldre entre pierres dures par engin, et comment moulins feroient, et puis[8] de la [fol. 55v b] farine aprist a confire et faire[9] pain. Et ainsi ceste dame aprist et enseigna aux hommes, qui avoient acoustumé comme bestes a vivre de glans et de blef sauvage, de pommes et de ceneles, a user de plus couvenable[10] pasture. Encore fist plus ceste dame, car les gens de lors qui avoient a coustume de demourer ça et la, par bois et par lieux sauvages, vagans comme bestes, fist assembler a grans tourbes, et leur aprist a faire villes et cités, maisons, es quelles ilz demourassent ensemble.

---

[1]  malices] les malices
[2]  chevalier doit estre aussi bien estre de nuit que de jours] le chevalier doit aussi bien estre de nuit que de jour
[3]  leur] son
[4]  trouva : *trouvart*
[5]  et] ot
[6]  la terre] la terre avec ferremens
[7]  moultra] monstra
[8]  puis] aprés
[9]  faire] a faire
[10]  couvenable] couvenables

thrughe whiche he myght be noyed. Also they put a byrde in the one syde of this ymage as for kepe it whiche fleeth by nyght that men calleth a *choughe*, whiche betokeneth that a knyght ought to be as well by nyght as by daye all redy for the defence comune if nede be; also it sygnyfyed that the wyse man sholde wake at every houre upon that that is to hym easye to doo.

"This lady was by longe tyme holden by so grete reverence, and so moche wente her renowne that in many places were stabled and made temples in her name, and in the same wyse longe tyme after that the Romaynes were in theyr grete puyssaunce put her ymage amonge theyr other goddes."

## Chapter 35     Of the ryght noble Quene Seres

"Ceres, whiche was in the ryght olde dayes quene of the royalme of Syculyens, had a prerogatyve to fynde by subtylte of wytte fyrst the scyence and usage of the tyllynge of the erthe, and of the toles that perteyneth therto. She taught to her subjectes to put togyder and to make tame the oxen and accustome them to be coupled in the yoke. She founde also the ploughe and shewed them the maner howe they sholde cleve and departe the erthe, [Mm5r] and al the laboure that therto perteyneth. And after she taught them to cast the sede upon the erthe and to cover it; and after, when the sede was growne and multyplyed, she shewed theym howe they sholde repe the corne, and with betynge of flayles to put it out of the eres. After she taught them to grynde it bytwene .ii. harde stones by crafte, and howe they sholde make mylles. And she taught them after to make brede of the mele. And also this lady taught to the people that lyved customably as beestes with acornes, and hawthorne buryes, and wylde apples, to use more covenable fedynges. Yet this lady dyde more, for the people of that countre that had it of custome to dwelle here and there, in woodes and in wylde places and voyde as beestes, made them to assemble by grete companyes, and taught them to make townes and cytees and howses, in the whiche they sholde dwelle togyder.

"Et ainsi par ceste dame fu ramené le siecle de bestialité a vie humaine et raisonnable. De ceste Ceres faingnirent les poetes la fable comment sa fille lui fut ravie par Pluto, le dieu d'enfer. Et pour l'autorité de son savoir et le grant bien que elle avoit [fol. 56r a] procuré au monde, l'aourerent les gens de lors et l'appellerent deesse des blés."

### Chapitre 36     Ci dit de Ysis, qui trouva l'art de faire les courtillages et de planter plantes

"Ysis semblablement fu[1] de si grant savoir en[2] fait de labour que elle ne fut pas tant seulement nommee royne d'Egipte, mais tres singuliere et especiale deesse des Egipciens. De ceste Ysis parle la fable que Jupiter l'ama, et comment il la tresuma[3] en vache, et puis comment elle revint[4] en sa premiere fourme, qui sont toutes signifiances de son grant savoir si que tu as toy mesmes touche[5] en ton *Livre de Othéa*. Elle trouva aucunes manieres de lettres abrigiees que elle aprist aux Egipciens, et leur donna fourme de leur language trop long [fol. 56r b] abrigier. Ceste fut fille de Ynachus, roy des Grieux, et suer de Phoroneus, qui moult fu sages. Et se transporta celle dame par aucun accident de Grece en Egipte avec son dit frere. La leur aprist, entre les autres choses, l'usage des courtillages et de faire plantes[6] de divers estoz. Elle donna et ordenna certaines lois bonnes et droicturieres, et aprist[7] aux gens d'Egipte, qui vivoient rudement et sans justice[8] ne ordenance, a vivre par ordre de droicture. Et a brief parler, tant y fist que vive et mort l'orent en tres grant reverence, et par tout le monde ala sa renommee tant qu'en toutes parties lui furent establis temples et oratoires. Et mesmes a Romme ou temps de leur haultece firent[9] edifier un temple en son nom, ou ilz ordenerent [fol. 56v a] sacrefices et oblacions et grans solempnitez en la maniere que on avoit acoustumé de lui faire en Egipte. Le mary de ceste noble dame fut[10] Apis, qui selon l'erreur des anciens[11] fu filz du dieu Jupiter et de Nyo[b]e,[12] fille de Phoroneus, dont les histoires anciennes et les poetes font asses mencion."

---

1 fu] fu une dame
2 en] ou
3 tresuma] tourna
4 revint] redevint
5 touche] as touchié
6 plantes] plantes et antés
7 et aprist] apprist
8 sans justice] sanz loy de justice
9 firent] firent les Rommains
10 fut] fu nommé
11 anciens] payens
12 Nyo[b]e : *Nyode*

"And thus, by this lady the worlde was brought out of the beestysshnesse into the reasonable lyfe of man. Of this Ceres, the poetes fayned the tale howe her doughter was ravysshed by Pluto, god of helle. And for the auctoryte of her understandynge, and the grete[1] welthe that she had procured to the worlde, the people of thens worshypped her and called her goddesse of corne." [Mm5v]

### Chapter 36     Of the noble Quene Ises, that founde fyrste the crafte to make orchardes and to plante plantes

"The same wyse was Isys of so grete understandynge in the dede of labour that she was not onely named quene of Egypte, but ryght sy[n]guler[2] and specyall go[d]desse[3] of Egypcyens. Of this Isys speketh the fable that Jupyter loved her, and howe he transfourmed her into a cowe, and after howe she came into her fyrst fourme, whiche by sygnyfyenge of her grete understandynge, soo as thou haste touched her thyselfe in thy *Boke of Othea*. She founde dyvers maners of letters abreged that she tought the Egypcyans, and gave them fourme of theyr longe language to abrege it. This was the doughter of I[n]achus,[4] kynge of Grekes, and syster of Phoroneus, whiche was ryght a wyse man. And this lady wente out of Grece for dyvers thynges that fell, and wente into Egypte with her brother. There she taughte amonge other thynges the usage of orchardes and to graffe trees on dyvers stockes. And she gave and ordeyned certayne lawes and ryghtfull, and she tought the people of Egypte whiche lyved rudely without ordynaunce of justyce to lyve by ryght ordre. And to speke shortely, she dyde so moche that, lyvynge and deed, they had her in grete reverence, and her renowne wente thrughe the worlde insomoche that in dyvers places were made temples and oratoryes in her name. And also at Rome in the tyme of theyr hyghnesse, they made a temple in her name where they ordeyned sacrefyses and offerynges and grete solempnytees [Mm6r] in the maner as they of Egypte were accustomed to doo for her. The housbande of this lady was named Aprys, whiche after the arroure of auncyent people was sone of the god Jupyter and of Nyo[b]e,[5] doughter of Phoroneus, of whome the olde hystoryes and poetes maketh mencyon ynoughe."

---

[1] grete : *gretete*
[2] sy[n]guler : *syguler*
[3] go[d]desse : *goodnesse*
[4] I[n]achus : *Iuachus*
[5] Nyo[b]e : *Nyode*

*Chapitre 37*        Ci dit du[1] grant bien qui est venu au siecle par ycelles dames

"Dame, j'ay grant admiracion de ce que ouy dire vous ay, que tant de bien soit advenu[2] au siecle par cause d'entendement de femme. Et ces hommes communement dient que leur savoir est comme chose sans nul pris, et que elles[3] n'ont servi au monde ne servent fors de porter enfans et de filer."

*Response*: "Or puez tu bien cognoistre la grant ignorance dont il [fol. 56v b] leur vient,[4] ne graces n'en rendent a nullui. Et aussi tu pueux veoir clerement comment Dieux, qui riens ne fait sans cause, a voulu monstrer aux hommes que il ne desprise point[5] le sexe femmenin ne que le leur quant il lui a pleu conceder qu'en cervele de femme ait si grant entendement que non mie seulement soient abillez a aprendre de[6] retenir les scien[ce]s,[7] mais trouver d'elles mesmes toutes nouvelles voire sciences de si grant utilité et proffit au monde que riens n'est plus neccessaire.

"Si que pueux[8] veoir d'ycelle Carmentis dont or ains te parlay qui trouva les lettres latines, auxquelles Dieu a esté tant propice[9] et tant a multipliee la science que trouva celle dame que aucques toute [fol. 57r a] la gloire des lettres hebraiques et greques ont effaciee,[10] et que pres que toute Europe qui contient moult grant partie et espace de la terre use de ces lettres. Desquelles sont fais et composez si comme infinis livres et volumes de toutes facultes ou sont mis et gardez en perpetuelle memoire les fais des hommes, et les nobles et excellens gloires de Dieu, les sciences et les ars.[11] Si puez conclurre que les biens que celle femme a fais sont infinis car par celle sont hommes, quoy que ilz ne le recognoiscent, tirés hors d'ignorance et mis en cognoiscence. Par elle ilz ont l'art d'envoier leurs corages et entencions[12] si loins que ilz veulent, et de[13] notifier et faire savoir

---

[1] Ci di du] Du

[2] advenu] venu

[3] sans nul pris, et que elles] de nul price, et est un reproche que on dit communement quant on raconte de quelque folie de dire, c'est savoir de femme. Et, a brief dire, l'oppinion et dit des hommes communement est que elles

[4] bien cognoistre la grant ignorance dont il leur vient] congnoistre la grant ingratitude de ceulz qui ce dient, et ilz sont comme ceulx qui vivent des biens et ne scevent dont ilz leur viennent

[5] desprise point] desprise

[6] de] et

[7] scien[ce]s : *sciens*

[8] pueux] tu peus

[9] propice] favorable

[10] greques ont effaciee] grecques, qui tant furent en grant pris ou effaciee

[11] les ars] les ars et que on ne die que ycestes choses te die par faveur ce sont les propres paroles de Bocace, desquelles la verité est nottoire et magnifeste

[12] leurs corages] les secres de leurs pensees

[13] et de] de

*Chapter 37*　　　Of the grete welthe that is come to the worlde by dyvers ladyes

"Madame, I have grete mervayle of that that I have herde you saye that so moche good sholde come to the worlde bycause of the understandynge of woman. And these men saye comunely theyr understandynge is as a thynge withoute pryce, and that they have not served ne serveth to the worlde but for to bere chyldren and spynne."

*Answere*: "Nowe mayst thou well knowe the grete ygnoraunce, and they yelde no thankynges to them from whom they come! And also thou mayst se clerely howe God, whiche nothynge dothe without cause, hath wyll to showe to men that He dyspraseth not the woman kynde, ne thoughe that He consydereth that in the brayne of woman there is so grete understandynge that not onely they ben abyle for to lerne and to withholde the scyences, but to fynde of themselfe all newe scyences of soo grete utylyte and profyte unto the worlde that [Mm6v] nothynge is more necessary so as thou mayst se of this Carmentes, of whome I have spoken to thee, that founde the letters of Latyne, to the whiche God hath ben so gracyous and so moche multyplyed the scyence that this lady founde, whiche hathe defaced as amonge us all the letters of Ebrue and of Grewe, and that nyghe Europe—whiche conteyneth a grete partye and space of the erthe—useth of these letters, of the whiche there be made and compounded infynyte bokes of volumes of al facultees where be put and kepte in perpetuall memorye the actes and dedes of men, and the nobles and excellent praysyngees of God, and all maner scyences and craftes. So mayst thou conclude that the welthe that this woman hath done is infynyte for by this lady, thoughe that they wyl not knowe it, these men are drawne out of ygnoraunce and put into knowynge. By her they have the crafte to sende theyr courages and entencyons as ferre as they wyll, and have knowlege and understandynge agayne of all thynges that pleaseth them,

par tout ce qu'il leur plaist; et semblablement savoir les choses passees, [fol. 57r b] et presentes, et aucunes a avenir. De rechief par la science d'ycelle[1] femme puent hommes faire[2] accors et joindre amistiés a plusieurs personnes longtaines de eulx, et par responses que ilz donnent les uns aux aultres, eulx entre cognoistre sans s'entreveoir. Et a brief parler, tout le bien qui vient de lettres ne pourroit estre raconté, car ilz descripsent et font entendre et cognoistre Dieu, les choses celestieles, les cieulx,[3] la mer, la terre, toutes personnes, et toutes choses. Ou fu oncques homme qui plus grant bien feist?"[4]

## *Chapitre 38*     **Encore de ce mesmes**

"Et autressi,[5] ou fu oncques homme par qui au monde plus de bien avenust[6] qu'il fait par celle noble royne Ceres, dont je t'ay a devant[7] dit? Qui pourra jamais acquerir nom de plus grant louenge comme de [fol. 57v a] ramener les hommes vagues et sauvages, habitans es bois comme bestes cruelles sans loy de justice, demourer es villes et citez et les apprendre a user de droit et leur avoir pourchacié vitaille de meilleur pasture que glans et que pommes sauvages, c'este assavoir fremens et blez, par laquelle ont les hommes le corps[8] plus bel et plus cler,[9] et les membres plus fors et plus muables, comme c'estoit[10] viande plus confortative et plus couvenable a nature humaine. Et la terre pleine de chardons, d'espines, et de buissons mal composee et pleine d'arbres sauvages avoir apris de la embelir et nettoier par labour et semer de semence. Laquelle, par la coultiveure, devint de sauvage en franche et domestique ou proffit publique.[11] Et ainsi par celle dame nature [fol. 57v b] humaine recut ce proffit que le rude et sauvage siecle fu mué en civil et citoien. Et les engins[12] vagues et pareceux, estans comme es[13] cavernes d'ignorance, mua, attray et ramena a la haultece de contemplacion et a excercitacions couvenables, et ordenna aucuns hommes es champs pour faire les labours,

---

[1] d'ycelle] de celle

[2] hommes faire] faire hommes

[3] celestieles, les cieulx] celestes

[4] Ou fu oncques homme qui plus grant bien feist?] Je te demande, ou fu oncques homme qui plus de bien feist?

[5] autressi] pareillement

[6] avenust] avenist

[7] a devant] cy devant

[8] fremens et blez, par laquelle ont les hommes le corps] fourmens et blez par laquelle pasture les hommes ont le corps

[9] cler] cler et plus net

[10] c'estoit] ce soit

[11] publique] commun et publique

[12] engins] engins des hommes

[13] comme es] es

and the same wyse to knowe thynges passed, and present and some that are to come. And also by the scyence of this woman men may make accorde and joyne frendshyppes with persones ferre fro them, and by answeres that they gave that one to that other, they fele and knowe theyr wyll without seynge. And to say shortely, all the welthe that cometh of letters may not be tolde, for they dyscryve and make to understande and knowe God and celestyall thynges, the hevens, the see, the erthe, al persones, [Nn1r] and all thynges. Where was there ever man that ever dyde more good?"

## Chapter 38      Of the same

"And also, where was there ever man by whom more welthe happened to the worlde than dyde by this noble Quene Ceres, of whome I have spoken of to thee before? Whiche may not gete a name of gretter praysynge as to brynge the wylde men, dwellynge in wodes as beestes without lawe of ryght, to dwelle in cytees and townes, and to teche them to use the ryght way and to have pourchaced vytayle of better redynge than acornes and wylde apples; that is to knowe, whetes and cornes, by the whiche these men have the body more fayre and more clere, and the membres more stronge and more movynge, as it were mete more comfortatyfe and more covenable to mannes nature. And the lande full of thystles, of thornes, and of busshes evyll set togyder and full of wylde trees, she taught to clense by laboure and to sowe the sede, the whiche by the labourynge of the grounde there as it was wylde it becometh free and tame to the comune profyte. And so by this lady mannes nature receyveth that profyte by the whiche the wylde and rude worlde was chaunged into the guyse of good cytees and townes, and the slaw-strynge wyttes and slowe, beynge in the caves of ygnoraunce, were [Nn1v] chaunged and brought agayne into hyghnesse of contemplacyon and exersyses covenables. And she ordeyned some men to laboure the feldes, by the whiche so

par lesquelx tant de citez et de villes¹ sont reemplies et soustenues ceulx² qui font les autres oeuvres neccessaires a vivre.

"Ysis, semblablement, es courtillages: qui pourroit sommer le grant bien que elle procura au siecle de donner maniere d'eslever plantes, d'arbres,³ et de toutes bonnes herbes, tant bonnes et tant couvenables⁴ a la nourriture de l'omme?

"Minerve aussi, qui porvey de son savoir nature humaine de maintes choses tant neccessaires [fol. 58r a] comme de vestemens de laine, qui avant ne se vestoient fors de piaux de bestes, osta de la peine que ilz avoient de porter toutes leurs⁵ choses neccessaires entre braz d'un lieu a autre par leur trouver la maniere de faire chars et charettes pour leur secours. Et aux nobles et chevaliers, trouver et donner l'art et l'usage de faire harnois pour couvrir leur corps pour plus grant seurté en guerre, trop plus bel, plus fort, et plus couvenable que devant ne l'avoient, qui estoit seulement de cuir de bestes."

*Christine.* Et je dis⁶ a elle: "Ha, dame! Or aperçoy par ce que vous dites plus que oncques mais la tres grant ingratitude et descognoiscence d'yceulx hommes qui tant mesdient des femmes. Car non obstant que il me semblast que assez cause souffisant y avoit [fol. 58r b] de non les blasmer par ce que femme est a tout homme mere, et les autres biens que on voit manifestement que generaument femmes font a hommes, vrayement voy cy droit comble de benefices et a souveraine largece que ilz ont receu et reçoivent d'elles.

"Or se taisent, or se taisent d'ores en avant les clers mesdisans de femmes, qui en ont parlé en blasme et⁷ en parlent en leurs livres et dictiez, et tous leurs complices!⁸ Et baissent les yeux de honte de ce que tant en ont mesdit,⁹ considerant verité qui contredit a leurs ditz, voiant ceste noble dame Carmentis, laquelle par la haultece de son entendement les a apris comme leur maistresse a l'escole—ce ne peuent ilz nier—la leccion de laquele savoir se tiennent tant haultaines et honnourez, c'est assavoir les nobles lettres du latin.

"Mais que diront les [fol. 58v a] nobles et les chevaliers dont tant y a, et c'est chose contre droit, qui mesdient si generaument de toutes femmes? Reffraingnent leur bouche d'ores en avant, avisant que l'usage des armes porter, fa[i]re¹⁰ batailles, et combatre en ordenance, duquel mestier tant s'alosent et tiennent grans: leur est venu et donné d'une femme.

---

¹ de citez et de villes] de villes et de citez
² soustenues ceulx] ceulz soustenus
³ d'arbres] d'arbres portans tant de bons fruis
⁴ tant bonnes et tant couvenables] tant couvenables
⁵ toutes leurs] leurs
⁶ dis] dis adont
⁷ femmes qui en ont parlé en blasme] femmes ceulx qui en ont parlé en blasme et qui
⁸ complices] complisses et consors
⁹ mesdit] osé dire
¹⁰ fa[i]re : *farre*

many cytees and towne[s][1] are replenysshed and susteyned, and some to do other necessary werkes to lyve by.

"Isys, the same wyse in orchardes and gardynes: who may somme the grete welthe that she procured to the worlde, to gyve the manere to lyfte up plantes and trees, and so many good herbes covenable to the nourysshynge of man?

"Mynerve also, that pourveyed by her wytte to mannes nature so many dyvers necessary thynges as clothynge of wolle, whiche were before clothed with skynnes of beestes. Also she put them out of payne that they had to bere all theyr necessary thynges bytwene theyr armes from one place to another, and ordeyned and founde the manere to make cartes and charyottes for theyr socoure. And to the nobles and knyghtes, she founde the crafte and the usage to make harnoys to cover theyr bodyes for the more suretye in the warre, more fayre and stronger and more covenable than they had before, whiche was onely with the hydes of beestes."

Christine and I sayd to her: "Ha, madame! Nowe I perceyve by that that ye saye more than ever I dyde the grete unkyndnesse and unconnynge of these men that so moche evyll sayth of women. For notwithstandynge that it sholde seme that there is cause ynoughe of praysynge of them by that woman is moder to man, and al other welthes that [Nn2r] one maye se openly that generally women dothe to men, truely I se nere the ryght hepe of benefyses and of soverayne largenesse that they have receyved and receyve of them.

"Nowe lette them holde theyr peas from hensforthe, these evyll sayenge cler-kes of women that have blamed and spoken shrewdely of women in theyr bokes and dyttyes and other suche. And lette them caste down theyr eyen for shame of that they have myssesayd, consyderynge the trouthe whiche is contrary unto theyr wrytynge, seynge this noble Lady Carmentis, the whiche by the hyghnesse of her understandynge hath taught them as theyr maystresse at the scole suche a lesson by the whiche understandynge they holde them so hyghe and worshypfull; that is to knowe, the noble letters of Latyne.

"Yet what shall these nobles and knyghtes say to this thynge, so moche agaynst ryght, that saythe evyll generally of all women? Lette them refrayne theyr mouthes and from hensforth, advysynge the usage to bere armes in batayle and to fyght in ordenaunce, of the whiche crafte they prayse them and holde them grete: and all is come to them by women.

---

[1] towne[s] : *towne*

"Et generaument tous hommes qui vivent de pain, et qui vivent civilement es citez par ordre de droit, et aussi ceulx qui coultivent les gaingnages: ont ilz cause de blasmer[1] tant femmes comme plusieurs d'eulx font, pensant ces grans benefices? Certes non. Et que par femmes — c'est assavoir Minerve, Ceres, et Ysis — leur sont venus tant de biens et tant de proffis,[2] desquelz benefices ont leur vie a honneur et se[3] vivent et vivront a tousjours. [fol. 58v b]

"Sont ces choses appeser? Sans faille, dame, il me semble que la doctrine d'Aristote, qui moult a proffité a l'engin humain et dont on tient si grant compte, et a bon droit: ne de tous les autres philosophes qui oncques furent, n'est point de tel[4] profit au siecle comme ont esté et sont le savoir des dictes dames."[5]

| *Chapitre 39* | Ci dit de la pucelle Arenie qui trouva l'art de taindre les laines, et de faire les draps ouvrez que on dit de haulte lice; et aussi trouva l'art de cultiver le lin, de le filer, et faire toyles[6] |
|---|---|

"Non mie seulement[7] par ycelles dames a Dieu volu pourveoir au monde de plusieurs choses couvenables et neccessaires, mais semblablement par maintes autres si comme par une pucelle de la terre d'Asie qui fut nommee Areine, fille de Ydomete [fol. 59r a] Tholophone, laquelle de merveilleuse soubtiveté et engin estoit. Et tant se soubtiva que elle fu la premiere qui trouva l'art de taindre laines en diverses couleurs, et a tissir ouvrages en draps comme[8] font paintres, en la maniere que nous dirions ces draps de haulte lice; et en tout fait de tisserie fu de merveilleuse soubtiveté. Et fut celle dont la fable dit que elle estriva a Pallas, qui demut yraigne.[9]

"Aultre science plus neccessaire trouva ceste femme, car ce fu celle qui trouva premierement[10] la maniere du lin et chanvre cultiver, ordener, rouir, teiller, cerancer, et filer a la conoille, et faire toille:[11] laquelle chose me semble estre[12] assez

---

[1] blasmer] blasmer et debouter
[2] venus tant de biens et tant de proffis] venus tant de prouffis
[3] se] s'en
[4] tel] pareil
[5] le savoir des dictes dames] et sont les oevres faictes par le savoir des dictes dames. Et elle a moy dist, "Cestes ne furent pas seules, ains en y ot maintes autres dont d'aucunes te diray . . ."
[6] le lin, de le filer, et faire toyles] le lin et faire toiles
[7] seulement] voirement sanz plus
[8] comme] si comme
[9] demut yraigne] la mua en yraigne
[10] trouva premierement] premierement trouva
[11] toille] toiles
[12] estre] a esté

"And generally al men that lyveth by brede, and that lyveth in cytees and townes by the ordre of ryght, and also those that tylleth the lande: have they soo moche cause to blame women as many of theym dothe, thynkynge upon these benefeytes and goodnesses whiche they have done for them? Forsothe, naye. And that by these women—that is to understande [Mynerve],[1] [Nn2v] Ceres, and Isys—there ben come to them so many dyvers welthes and profytes, of the whiche benefyses they have theyr lyfe worshypfully; and so they lyve and shall lyve alway.

"These thynges ben wel appeased without fayle, madame. But yet it semeth me that the doctryne of Arystotle, whiche was of ryght grete profyte to mannes wytte and wherof one holdeth of grete counte, and of ryght—none of all that other phylosophres that ever were, there is not of so grete profyte to the worlde as have ben and ben by the doctryne of these foresayd ladyes."

## Chapter 39     Of the mayden Arenye that founde the crafte to shere sheepe, to dresse the wolles, and to make clothe

"Not onely by these ladyes God hadde lust to pourvey to the worlde many dyvers thynges and necessaryes, but also in the same wyse by many dyvers others so as by a mayde of the lande of Assye that was named Arenye, doughter of Ydmuete Cholophone, the whiche was of mervayllous and subtell wytte. So moche she laboured her wyttes that she founde fyrst the crafte to dye wolle into dyvers coloures, and to make werkes in clothe as paynters dothe, in the manere that we sholde calle the clothes of hyghe lyst; and in this crafte she was mervayllous subtyll. And it was she wherof the fable speketh and saythe that she stryved with [Nn3r] Pallas whiche became a flee.

"This woman founde another scyence more necessarye, for this was she that founde fyrst the maner of flaxe and maner of werkes to make lynnen clothe, the whiche thynge semeth to be ryght necessarye to the worlde thoughe that

---

[1] [Mynerve] : *Myverne*

neccessaire au monde, quoy que l'excercite soit[1] par pluseurs hommes reproché aux femmes. Ceste Araine aussi trouva [fol. 59r b] l'art de faire roiz[2] et filez a prendre oysiaulx et les poissons, et trouva l'art de pescherie, et de prendre et decepvoir les fortes et crueles bestes sauvages par filez et roiz, et les connins et lievrs, et aussi les oysiaulx, dont par avant riens ne savoient. Si ne fist pas en ce comme il me semble ceste femme petit servise au monde qui depuis en a eu et a maint[3] proffit.

"Non obstant que aucuns aucteurs et mesmes[4] cellui poete Bocace, qui raconte ces dictes choses, ont dit que le siecle valoit mieulx quant la gent ne vivoient fors de ceneles et de glans, et ne vestoient ne mais les piaux des bestes que il n'a fait depuis que les choses a plus delicativement vivre leur ont esté enseingnees. Mais sauve la reverence du dit aucteur,[5] et de tous ceulx [fol. 59v a] qui pourroient[6] dire que prejudice soit au monde que telles choses pour laisse[7] et nourrissement du corps humain fussent trouvees, je dis que de tant que creature humaine reçoit plus de biens, de graces, et de grans dons de Dieu, tant plus est tenue de le servir mieulx.[8] Et que se elle use mal des biens que Dieu lui a premis et ottroiez et en user[9] bien et couvenablement, et que pour usage d'omme et de femme fist, que ce vient de la mauvaistié et perversité de ceulx qui mal en usent, et non pas que les choses de soy ne soient tres bonnes et licites a en user.[10] Jhesucrist lui mesmes en sa personne le monstra bien,[11] car Il usa de pain, de vin, de char, de poison, de robe de couleur de linge, et de tous si fais neccessaires, laquelle chose [fol. 59v b] n'eust point faicte se mieulx fust user de glans et de ceneles. Et grant honneur fist a la science que Ceres trouva, c'est assavoir au pain, quant Il lui plot donner a homme et femme son digne corps soubz l'espece de pain, et que ilz en usassent."

---

[1] soit] en soit
[2] roiz] rois las
[3] maint] maint ayse et maint
[4] mesmes] mesmement
[5] Mais sauve la reverence du dit aucteur] Mais sauve sa grace
[6] pourroient] vouldroyent
[7] telles choses pour laisse] tele chose pour l'aise
[8] servir mieulx] mieulx servir
[9] Dieu lui a premis et ottroiez et en user] son createur lui a promis et ottroyez a en user
[10] licites a en user] prouffitables a en avoir l'usage et a s'en ayder licitement. Et
[11] monstra bien] nous monstra

some men say that the exercyse therof be reprofe to women. This Arenye also founde fyrste to make nettes and craftes to take byrdes and fysshes, and founde the crafte of fysshynge, and to take and deceyve the stronge wylde beestes, and conyes and hares, and byrdes with nettes, whiche was not knowne before. So me semeth that this woman made no lytell servyce to the worlde, by the whiche syth men have founde grete profyte.

"Notwithstandynge that dyvers auctoures and also this Bocace, whiche telleth the foresayd thynges, have sayd that the worlde was better when the people lyved not but with hawes and acornes, and that they ware but skynnes of bestes, then it hathe ben syth, when that they were taught to use others more delycatyfe. Yet save the reverence of the sayd auctoure, and all them that shall saye that it is prejudyce to the worlde to use suche thynges and that the nourysshynge of mannes body sholde be founde and used, I saye that insomoche that ony creature receyveth more of graces and of grete gyftes of God, by soo moche is he the more beholdynge to serve Hym the better. And that yf ony creature use evyll of well that God hathe provyded for hym, and graunted hym to use them well and covenably and made them for the [Nn3v] usage of man and woman, that it cometh of the shrewdenesse and cursydnesse of them that useth it evyl and not that the thynges of Hym sholde not be evyl but good to use. Jhesu Cryst Hymselfe in His owne persone shewed it wel for He used brede and wyne, flesshe and fysshe, robe of coloure, of lynnen, and of all other thynges necessary, whiche had not be done yf it had ben better to use to eate acornes and hawes. And also He honoured moche the scyence that Ceres founde, that is to knowe of brede, when it pleased Hym to gyve to man and woman His owne body in fourme of brede, and that they sholde use it."

*Chapitre 40*   **Ci dit de Pamphile, qui trouva l'art de traire la soye des vers, et la taindre,[1] et faire draps de soye**

"De sciences trouvees par femmes bonnes et proffitables[2] entre les autres ne fait mie a oublier celle qui[3] trouva la noble Pamphile qui fut du païs de Grece. Ceste dame fut de tres soubtil engin en divers ouvrages, et tant se delicta a investiguer et encerchier choses estranges que elle fut la premiere qui trouva toute l'art de la soye. Car si comme elle fut moult soubtive[4] et ymaginative, elle avisa [fol. 60r a] les vers qui font la soye naturelment sus les branches des a[r]bres.[5] Si prist les bocetes que les vers avoient fait,[6] que elle vit moult belles. Et prist les filles de plusieurs a assembler ensemble, et a denvider, puis essaia[7] se belle taincture en diverses couleurs prendroit cellui fille.[8] Et quant elle ot tout ce esprouve[9] et veu que belle chose estoit, elle se prist a faire et a tissir les draps de soye. Pour laquel chose de la science de ceste femme est venu grant beauté et proffit au monde, moulteplié en toutes terres. Car Dieu en est honnoures et servis en plusieurs paremens, et en sont faictes les nobles robes et paremens des prelas au divin office, et ainsi des empereurs, et des roys, et princes. Et mesmement au peuple d'aucune terre qui n'usent[10] d'autres [fol. 60r b] vestemens par ce que ilz n'ont nulles laines, et ont foison vers."

*Chapitre 41*   **Ci dit de Thamar, qui fu souveraine maistresse en l'art de painterie, et d'une autre semblablement qui fu nommee Yrane, et de [Marcia][11] la Rommaine**

"Que veulx tu que je te die? Se nature de femme est abille a trouver et[12] a apprendre les sciences speculatives, et aussi les ars manueles, semblablement est[13] tres propre et tres soubtive a les executer et mettre en[14] oeuvre tres soubtivement quant aprises les a. Si qu'il est escript d'une femme qui eut nom Thamar, qui fut de si

---

[1] la taindre] de la taindre
[2] bonnes et proffitables] bonnes, couvenables, et prouffitables
[3] qui] que
[4] soubtive] speculative
[5] a[r]bres : *abres*] arbres ou pays ou elle estoit
[6] les vers avoient fait] ces vers avoient faites
[7] a assembler ensemble, et a denvider, puis essaia] ensemble a assembler puis esprouva
[8] fille] fil
[9] esprouve et] essayé
[10] n'usent] n'use
[11] [Marcia] : *Mantoa*
[12] a trouver et] et prompte
[13] les ars manueles semblablement est] a les trouver, et semblablement les ars manuelles? Je te promet que aussi est elle
[14] en] a

*Chapter 40*     **Of Pamphyle that founde the crafte to drawe sylke of the wormes**

"Of scyences good and profytable founde by women, amonge others we ought not to forgete the noble Pamphyle of the countre of Grece. This lady was of ryght subtyll wytte in dyvers werkes, and so moche delyted to serche straunge thynges that she was the fyrst that founde the crafte of sylke. For as she was ryght subtyll and ymagynatyfe, she advysed her of these wormes that maketh sylke naturally upon the braunches of trees. So she toke the bothomes that these wormes had made, and she sawe that they were ryght fayre. And then she toke many thredes and put theym togyder and twyned them, and then she assayed if this [Nn4r] threde wolde take ony fayre coloure. And when she had proved all this, and sawe that it was ryght a fayre thynge, she toke it to make and to weve into clothes of sylke. For the whiche thynge of the connynge of this woman there is come grete beaute and profyte to the worlde, multyplyed in all co[u]ntres;[1] for God is wor-shypped and served in dyvers arayes therof, and the noble robes and raymentes of prelates in devyne offyces ben made therof, and also of emperours, kynges, and prynces. And the same wyse the people of some landes useth none other clothynge, for that they have no wolles and they have ynowe of sylke wormes."

*Chapter 41*     **Of Thamar that was a soverayne maystresse in the crafte of payntynge, and of another named Irayne**

"What woldest thou I sholde say? Yf nature of woman be able to fynde and to lerne the speculatyfe scyences and also these hande craftes, the same wyse it is empropryed to execute them and put them in werke ryght subtylly when they have lerned them. So as it is wryten of a woman that was named Thamar,

---

[1] co[u]ntres : *conntres*

grant subtiveté en l'art et science de painterie que elle en estoit a son vivant la souveraine que on sceust. Ceste, ce dit Bocace, fut fille de Nycon, peintre, et fut ou temps de la nonentiesme Olimpe. Olimpe estoit un[1] jour d'une solempnité, ainsi appelle, en [fol. 60v a] laquelle on faisoit divers jeux, et cellui qui gaingnoit, on lui ottroioit ce qu'il demandoit se c'estoit[2] chose raisonnable. Laquelle feste et jeux se faisoient en l'onneur du dieu Jupiter, et estoit cellebree de .vi. ans en .vi. ans, .iiii. ans frans entre deux. Et ordenna ceste feste premierement Hercules, et du premier commencement que elle fut instituee faisoient leur date ainsi que font les crestiens de l'incarnacion de Jhesucrist.

"Ceste Thamar toutes oeuvres[3] de femmes laissees par subtiveté d'engin suivi l'art de son pere. Dont ou temps que regnoit Archelaon sus le Macedonoirs[4] elle eut singuliere louenge, en tant que ceulx de la contree de Ephese qui aouroient la deesse Dyane firent par grant cure paind[re][5] a ceste Thamar en un table[t][6] l'ymage de leur deesse, lequel [fol. 60v b] ilz garderent tres long temps après[7] en grant digneté comme chose faicte par grant soubtiveté et solempnelment peinte[8] et ne monstroient cel ymage fors a la feste et solempnité de la deesse, laquelle paintture comme elle durast par tres grant aage porta si tres grant tesmoing de la soubtiveté de celle femme que jusques au jourd'ui est faicte memoire[9] de son engin.

"En ceste science de peinterie fu autressi si souverainement apprist[10] une autre femme et mesmement de Grece, de laquelle[11] fu nommee Yrane, que elle passa tous ceulx du monde en son temps. Ceste fut disciple d'un peintre appellé Cracin, qui estoit souveraine ouvrier. Mais celle fu tant soubtille et tant aprist de la science que elle passa et exceda son maistre si merveilleusement,[12] laquelle chose tourna a la gent de lors [fol. 61r a] a si grant mervieille que pour memoire d'elle firent faire son ymage qui estoit comme une pucelle qui peingnoit, et l'asseirent par honneur entre les ymages des souverains ouvriers de certains ouvrages qui avoient esté devant elle. Car tel coustume les anciens avoient[13] que ilz honnouroient tant ceulz et celles[14] qui passoient les autres en aucune excellence fust de

---

[1] un : *une*
[2] se c'estoit] qui fust
[3] oeuvres] communes oeuvres
[4] Macedonoirs] Macedonnois
[5] paind[re] : *painder*
[6] table[t] : *tablel*
[7] tres long temps aprés] aprés tres lonc temps
[8] grant soubtiveté et solempnelment peinte] souveraine excellence et soubtiveté
[9] memoire] mencion
[10] apprist] apprise
[11] et mesmement de Grece, de laquelle] mesmement de Grece, laquelle
[12] si merveilleusement] merveilleusement
[13] les anciens avoient] avoient les ancians
[14] ceulz et celles] ceulx

whiche was of so grete subtylte in the crafte and scyence of payntynge, that in those dayes whyle she lyved, there was none suche as she was in connynge. This woman [Nn4v] as Bocace sayth was doughter to Nyton, peyntre, and was in that tyme of Olympe. *Olympe* was a grete solempne day so called in the whiche there were made dyvers playes. And he that gate it sholde be graunted unto hym that he asked, yf it were a reasonable thynge. The whiche feest and playes was done in the honoure of Jupyter, and it was halowed from .vi. yere unto .vi. yere, .iiii. yere free bytwene bothe. And Hercules ordeyned fyrst this feest; and of the fyrst begynnynge that it was ordeyned, they made theyr date so as dothe the Crysten men of the incarnacyon of Jhesu Cryst.

"This Thamar lefte all women's werkes and folowed the crafte of her fader by ryght grete subtelte of wytte. In the tyme when Archylans reygned upon the Macedonyes, she had synguler praysynge insomoche that they of the countre of Ephese, that there worshypped the goddesse Dyane, made by grete charge that this Thamar sholde paynte the ymage of theyr goddesse, whiche they kepte longe tyme after in grete dygnyte as a thynge made by grete subtylte and solempnely paynted. And they shewed never this ymage but at the feest and solempnyte of the goddesse, the whiche payntynge as it endured by ryght grete age bare so grete wytnesse of the subtylte of this woman that unto this day there is memory of her wytte.

"In this scyence of payntynge there was also a woman of Grece soveraynly lerned, whiche was named Irane, that she passed al those that were in her tyme. This woman was a [Oo1r] dyscyple of a payntoure called Cracyne, the whiche was a soverayne werkeman. Yet she was subtyll and so moche lerned in the scyence that she passed and exceded her mayster so mervayllously that for the remembraunce of her they lete make an ymage whiche was as a mayden that paynted. And they lyfte it for honoure amonge the other ymages of soverayne werkemen of certayne workes that had ben before her. For suche custome had these auncyent men that they worshypped bothe men and women that passe other in

savoir, ou de force, ou de beaulté, ou d'autre grace, que pour faire¹ leur memoire perpetuelle au monde ilz faisoient mettre leurs ymages en haulx et honnourables lieux.

"Marcia la Rommaine, qui fu aussi² vierge de moult grant vertu en noble vie et en meurs, comment fut elle³ autressi de noble engin en l'art de painterie. Ceste par si grant art en ouvra et si magistraument que elle en passoit tous [fol. 61r b] hommes et mesmement Gays et Spolin, qui estoient reputez les souverains peintres du monde en leur temps. Celle⁴ surmonta et attaingni le comble de tout quanque on puet savoir d'ycelle science selon que⁵ disoient les maistres. Ceste Marcia, afin que memoire de sa science demourast aprés elle, entre ses notables oeuvres fist une table par grant art ou elle peingny sa figure en se regardant en un mirouer si proprement que tout homme qui la veoit la jugoit estre vive, laquelle table fut puis long temps tres souverainement gardee et monstree aux ouvriers comme un tresor de solempnité."

Lors dis a elle: "Dame, par ceste exemple⁶ peut estre aperceu qu'ancienement moult plus estoient⁷ honnourez les sages que ores ne sont, et en plus grant pris tenues les sciences.⁸ [fol. 61v a] Mais apropos de ce que vous dites de femmes expertes en la science de peinterie, je congnois aujourd'uy une femme que on appelle Anataise qui tant est experte et apprise a faire vigneteures d'enlumineure en livres et champaignes d'ystoires, qu'il n'est mencion d'ouvrier en la ville de Paris ou sont les souverains du monde qui point l'en passa,⁹ ne qui aussi doulcetement face floreteure et menu ouvrage que elle fait, ne de qui on ait plus chier la besoingne, tant¹⁰ soit le livre riche ou chier, que on a d'elle qui finer en puet. Et ce sçay je par experience, car pour moy mesmes a ouvré aucunes choses qui sont tenues singuliers entre les vignetes des aultres grans ouvriers."

*Response*: "De ce te croy je bien, belle fille.¹¹ Assez de femmes soubtilles en diverses choses¹² trouveroit on par le monde qui cerchier le¹³ [fol. 61v b] vouldroit. Et encore ad ce propos te diray d'une femme rommaine."

---

¹ de savoir, ou de force, ou de beaulté, ou d'autre grace, que pour faire] de
² fu aussi] aussi fu
³ comment fut elle] comment
⁴ Celle] A tout dire, elle
⁵ que] ce que
⁶ ceste exemple] ces exemples
⁷ plus estoient] estoient plus
⁸ tenues les sciences] les sciences tenues
⁹ passa] passe
¹⁰ tant] tout
¹¹ ce te croy je bien, belle fille] ceste croys je bien, chere fille
¹² soubtilles en diverses choses] soubtilles
¹³ cerchier le] cercher les

excellence, whyder it were of understandynge, or of strengthe, or of beaute, or of ony other grace or vertue, that for to make theyr perpetuall remembraunce they made to set theyr ymages in hyghe and worshypfull places.

"Marcya the Romayne, that was also a vyrgyne, was of ryght grete vertue in noble lyvynge and in good condycyons; she was also of noble wytte in the crafte of payntynge. This woman wrought by so grete crafte and so maysterly that she passed all men, and the same wyse Gaye and Spolyn that were called the moost soverayne payntoures of the worlde in theyr tyme: she passed them and attayned the worshyp of all that myght be knowne of that scyence after that that the may-stres sayd. This Marcya, to that entente that the remembraunce of that scyence sholde shewe after her, amonge her noble werkes she made a table by grete crafte where she paynted her fygure beholdynge her in a myroure so properly that every man that sawe it juged it to be on lyve, the whiche table ryght longe syth was [Oo1v] soveraynely kepte, and shewed to werkemen as a treasoure of solempnyte."

Then I sayd to her, "Madame, by this ensample one may perceyve that in the olde tyme these wyse people were more worshypped than they be nowe, and the scyences holdeth in moche more pryce. Yet to the purpose of that that ye saye of women experte in the scyence of payntynge, I knowe at this day a woman that men calleth Anastase that is so moche experte and lerned to make vynyettes of enlumynynge in bokes and chasynge hystoryes, that there is mencyon made of ony werkeman in the towne of Parys yet there ben suche in that towne that ben called the soveraynest werkemen of the worlde but that she passeth them, ne that so swetely maketh flourysshynges as she dothe. And this I knowe by experyence, for she hathe wrought for myselfe dyvers thynges whiche ben holden syngulers by themselfe amonge the vynyettes of other werkemen."

*Responce*: "Of that I byleve thee well, fayre doughter, for thou mayst fynde women ynowe whiche ben wel experte in dyvers thynges who that wolde serche aboute in the worlde. And yet to the same purpose, I shall telle thee of a woman of Rome."

## *Chapitre 42*     Ci dit de Sempronie de Romme

"Ceste Sempronie, qui fut de Romme, fut femme de moult grant beaulté. Mais non obstant que la fourme de son corps et de son viaire passa en son temps si comme toutes femmes en beaulté, encore plus passa et exceda l'excellence de la soubtilleté de son engin, lequel elle eut si tres prompt[1] que il n'estoit chose tant fust soubtille, fust en parole ou en oeuvre, que tantost ne retenist si entierment que elle ne[2] failloit point, si faisoit tout quanque elle vouloit et rapportoit[3] tout quanque elle oioit dire, ja si grant enarracion ne fust. Ceste ne savoit pas tant seulement[4] lettres latines, mais les greques entierement, et les escrisoit[5] si tres engenieusement que grant amiracion estoit a[6] veoir.

"*Item*, de parolle, de [fol. 62r a] façonde et de maniere si belle, si avenante et tant propice que par[7] ses paroles et manieres elle savoit atraire toute personne ad ce que elle vouloit, si triste ne just que elle ne provoucast[8] a solas et a joye. Et se a yre vouloit, ou a plourer, ou[9] a tristece, semblablement y sceust esmouvoir tout homme. Ou a hardiece, ou a aucun fait de force, ou d'aultre chose emprendre pouoit esmouvoir[10] se elle vouloit tous ceulx qui parler l'avoient.[11] Et avec ce, tant estoit sa maniere de parler et le maintien de son corps plein de courtoisie et de doulceur, que on ne se pouoit saouler de la regarder et oir. Elle chantoit tres melodieusement, et par grant art jouoit de tous instrumens[12] souverainement, et a tous jeux vaincoit. Et a brief dire, a toutes choses faire qu'engin humain peust comprendre, elle estoit tres abille et engenieuse."

---

[1] eut si tres prompt] ot si tres grant

[2] ne] n'y

[3] et rapportoit] de l'abilleté de son corps et repetoit

[4] tant seulement] seulement

[5] escrisoit] escripsoit

[6] a] du

[7] par] pour

[8] vouloi si triste ne just que elle ne provoucast] vouloit, car se a gieu vouloit esmouvoir ja ne fust personne si triste qu'elle ne esmeust et provocast

[9] a yre vouloit, ou a plourer, ou] vouloit a yre, ou a plourer, et

[10] pouoit esmouvoir] pouoir condescendre

[11] l'avoient] l'ouoient

[12] instrumens] instrumens de bouche

*Chapter 42*     **Here it speketh of Semproyne**

"Semproyne of Rome was a woman of grete beaute, yet notwithstandynge that the shap of her body and of her vysage passed in her tyme all other women in beaute, yet she passed and exceded [Oo2r] in excellence of subtylte of her wytte, the whiche she had so redy that there was nothynge soo subtyll in worde nor in werke but anone she wolde have it so hooly that she wolde not fayle, but as her lyste she wolde reporte it all that she had herde saye, thoughe it were ryght a grete narracyon. This lady knewe not onely the Latyne letters but the Grekysshe also entyerly, and wrote them so wyttely, that it was grete mervayle to se.

"Also of speche, and faconde, and of fayre manere so comely and so gentyll that by her wordes and maners she coude drawe ony persone to that she wolde, yf she wolde or lyst to provoke them to solace or joye. To wepe or to sorowe, in the same wyse, she coude move every man therto, other to hardynes, or to ony dede of strengthe, or to lerne ony other thynge she coude styre them therto and she had spoken with them. And with that, so moche she was of maner of speche and of countenaunce, and ful of courtoysye and of swetnesse, that one sholde never be satysfyed to beholde her and here her. She songe so melodyously, and by grete crafte played in all instrumentes soveraynly, and she coude all maner of playes. And to saye shortely, she was ryght able and wytty to do al maner of thynges that mannes wytte myght comprehende."

*Chapitre 43*   **Demande Christine a Raison se en naturel sens de femme a prudence, et response que Dame Raison[1] lui fait** [fol. 62r b]

Je, Christine, encore dis a elle: "Dame, vrayement je voy bien que c'est voir que Dieux, Il en soit louez, a donné a entendement de femme asses comprehensive de toutes choses entendibles concepvoir, et cognoistre, et retenir. Mais pour ce que on voit asses de gens qui ont l'engin moult soubtil, et pront a sentir et entendre[2] tout ce que on leur veult monstrer, et sont si soubtilz en sentement et retentive[3] qu'il n'est science qui ne leur soit aperte tant que par frequenter estude[4] acquierent tres grant clergie. Et toutevoies, a maint[5] en y a mesmement des plus reputez grans clers et pleins de science voit on avoir assez[6] petite prudence en meurs et en governement mondain, dont j'ay grant merveille, car n'est point de doubte que les sciences introduictes[7] et aprenent les meurs. Si faroie[8] voulentiers de vous, dame, se il vous plaisoit, se[9] entendement [fol. 62v a] de femme—qui asses est, comme il me semble par voz preuves et ce que je voy, comprehensif[10] et retentif es choses soubtilles, tant en sciences comme aultres[11]—est autressi prompt et abille es choses que prudence enseingne? C'este assavoir, avoir[12] avis sur ce qui est le meilleur a faire, et a ce qui doit estre laissié souvenance des choses passees, par quoy on soit plus expert par l'exemple que on a veu sage[13] ou gouvernement des choses presentes, et que on ait[14] pourveance sur celles avenir.[15] Ces choses comme il me semble enseingne prudence."

*Response*: "Tu dis voir, fille. Mais ycelle prudence dont tu parles, saches que elle[16] vient par Nature a homme et a femme[17] aux uns plus, aux autres moins, et ne la donne mie science du tout, combien que elle la perface moult en ceulz qui naturelment sont prudens car tu peux savoir [fol. 62v b] que .ii. forces en semble

---

[1]   et response que Dame Raison] et la responce que Raison
[2]   et pront a sentir et entendre] en sentement et en entendre
[3]   soubtilz en sentement et retentive] ingenieux et prompts a concevoir toutes choses
[4]   estude] l'estude
[5]   a maint] mains
[6]   on avoir assez] on aucunefoiz assez
[7]   introduictes] introduisent
[8]   faroie] saroie
[9]   se] se en
[10]   comprehensif] comprenent
[11]   comme aultres] comme en aultres choses
[12]   assavoir, avoir] assavoir qu'elles ayent avis
[13]   on soit plus expert par l'exemple que on a veu sage] plus soient expertes par l'exemple que ont veu sages
[14]   que on ait] qu'elles ayent
[15]   avenir] a avenir
[16]   que elle] qu'elles
[17]   a femme] femme

*Chapter 43* 	Here Christine asketh of Reason yf naturall prudence be in woman

I, Christine, yet sayd to her: "Madame, truely I se well that it is true that God, worshypped be He, [Oo2v] hath gyven understandynge to woman comprehensyfe in all thynges to understande, knowe, and to holde. Yet for that that one seeth people ynowe that have ryght subtyll wytte, and redy to fele and to understande all that one wolde showe them, and ben so subtyl in felynge and retentyfe that there is no scyence but that it be open ynoughe to them whiche by hauntynge of the scole geteth ryght grete clargye. And neverthelesse, there ben many also that be of grete reputacyon amonge clarkes and full of scyence that have but lytell wysdome in maners and in worldely governaunce, wherof I have grete mervayle for it is no doubte that the introduccyon of scyence techeth the good condycyons and vertues. So I wolde knowe ryght fayne of you my lady, yf it pleased you, if the understandynge of woman—whiche is ynoughe, as me semeth, by your proves, and that I se it by takynge and retentyfe in subtyll thynges and scyences as others ben—but I wolde wyte yf theyr understandynge be prompte and abyle in thynges that prudence techeth? That is to knowe, to have advyse upon that whiche is best to do, and of that that ought to be leest remembraunce of thynges passed, by the whiche one maye be the more experte by the ensample that one have wyse syght in governaunce of present thynges, and that one have pourveyance upon thynges to come. These thynges as me semeth techeth prudence."

*Answere*: "Thou sayst trewe, doughter. But this prudence of whiche thou spekest, knowe that it cometh by Nature to man and woman to some more, to [Oo3r] some lesse, and not to al lyke, howe be it that she dothe so moche tha naturally they ben prudent, for thou mayst knowe that two strengthes togyder

sont plus poissans et plus resistances que n'est chascune force a par soy. Et pour ce dis je[1] que personne qui par nature ait[2] prudence, que on appelle sens naturelle, et avec ce science acquise, a celle personne affiert los de grant excellence. Mais tel a l'un, si comme toy mesmes as dit, qui n'a pas l'aultre: car l'un est don de Dieu,[3] et l'autre est acquis par long estude. Si sont bons tous deux.

"Mais aucunes[4] plus tost esliroient sens naturel sans science acquise[5] a pou de sens naturel, et toutevoyes sur cest proposicion peuent estre fondees maintes opinons, desquelles peuent sourdre assez de questions. Car on pourroit dire que cellui bien fait plus a eslire qui plus est valable ou prouffit et en l'utilité[6] publique et commune. Et il est ainsi que les sciences savoir et singuliere personne profite plus [fol. 63r a] a tous par la demonstrance que il en fait aux autres,[7] que ne feroit tout de sence naturel que il pourroit avoir. Car cellui sens naturel ne puet durer que la vie durant de la personne qui l'a, et quant elle muert, son sens muert avec[8] lui. Mais les sciences acquises durent a perpetuité a ceulx qui les ont, c'est assavoir en los, et proffitent a maintes gens en tant que il[9] les aprenent aux aultres et en font livres pour ceulx a venir, si ne meurt pas leur science avecques eulx. Si que je te puis monstrer par exemple d'Aristote et des autres, par lesquelx les sciences furent baillees au monde que plus profite au siecle le savoir acquis d'yceux que ne fait toute la prudence sans science acquise de tous les hommes passez et qui sont. Non obstant que par la prudence de maint [fol. 63r b] pluseurs royaumes et e[m]pires[10] ont esté bien gouvernez et adreciez, mais toutes ycelles choses sont fallibles et s'en vont avec les hommes; et science[11] tousjours dure.

"Mais ycestes questions te lairay insolues et a determiner aux autres, car elles n'affierent au propos du bastissement de nostre cité, et retourneray a la demande que tu m'as faicte, c'est asavoir se en femme a naturele prudence. De laquel chose je te respons que si, et ce peux tu des ja congnoistre par ce que devant te est dit. Si comme tu peux veoir generaument ou gouvernement d'elles es offices qui a faire leur sont establies, et y prens garde se bon te semble: tu trouveras que de leur maisnage gouvernez et pourvoir a toutes choses selon leur poissance, sont communement toutes en[12] la plus grant partie tres curieuses, soingneuses, et [fol. 63v

---

[1] dis je] disoie
[2] ait] a
[3] Dieu] Dieu par naturelle influence
[4] aucunes] aucuns
[5] acquise] acquise que grant science acquise
[6] en l'utilité] utilité
[7] aux autres] a tous
[8] avec] avecques
[9] il] ilz
[10] e[m]pires : *enpires*
[11] et s'en vont avec les hommes, et science] et s'en vont avec le temps, et la science
[12] en] ou

ben more and more resystynge than is every strengthe by hymselfe. And therfore I saye to thee that every persone that by Nature hathe prudence, that is called naturall wytte, and with that connynge gotten to that persone bryngeth hym to praysynge of grete excellence. Yet suche hathe one, as thou thyselfe hathe sayd, that another hath not. For that one is the gyfte of God, that other is goten by longe studyenge, yet they ben bothe good.

"But some sooner shall chose naturall wytte without scyence goten than goten with scyence, and nevertheles upon this preposycyon there may many opposycyons be founde, of the whiche maye sprynge questyons ynowe. For one myght say that he dothe well to chose the more whiche is moost avaylable or profyte in the comune nede. And it is so that to knowe scyences it profyteth a synguler persone and more to all persones by the shewynge that he dothe to others, that all sholde not do of naturall wytte that he sholde have. For this naturall wytte maye not endure but durynge the lyfe of the persone that hathe it, and when he dyeth, his wette dyeth with hym. But the scyence that is goten endureth perpetually forever to theym that hathe it for to knowe in praysynge. And it profyteth unto many people in soo moche that they do teche it unto others, and maketh bookes unto theym that ben to come, [Oo3v] so theyr scyence dyeth not with them. So as I may shewe thee by ensample of Arystotle and of others, by the whiche the scyences were brought to the worlde that profyteth more to the worlde the connynge goten of them than dothe all the prudence without scyence goten of all the men passed or those that ben. Notwithstandynge that by prudence many dyvers royalmes and empyres hathe ben well governed and dressed, yet al these thynges ben faylynge and gothe with these men; and scyence endureth ever.

"But yet this questyon I shall leve unassoylled and to determyne to others, for it draweth not to the purpose of the strengthynge of our cyte. And I shall tourne agayne to the questyon that thou hast made to me; that is to knowe, yf there be natural prudence in woman. Of the whiche thynge I answere thee soo that thou mayst knowe by that that is sayd to thee before, so as thou mayst se generally by the governaunce of them in offyces that are put to them to do. And yf thou take hede it shall seme thee good: thou shalte fynde that to governe theyr housholde and to pourvaye for it in all thynges after theyr puyssaunce, they ben comunely and for the moost partye ryght curyous, quycke, and dylygent insomoche that

a] diligentes, et tant que aucuneffois on[1] anuye a aucuns de leurs negligens maris de ce que il leur semble que trop les timonnent et sollicitent de faire ce que a eulx apertient a pourveoir, et dient que elles veulent estre maistresses et plus saiges que eulx. Et ainsi revertissent en mal ce que maintes femmes[2] leur dient en bonne entencion.

"Et de ces prudentes femmes parle *L'Epistre Salemon*, duquel la sustance selon nostre propos veult dire ce qui s'ensuit."

## *Chapitre 44*     *L'Espitre Salemon* ou *Livre des Proverbes*

"Qui trouvera femme forte, c'est a dire prudente, son mary n'ara pas faulte de tous biens. Elle est renommee par tout païs, et son mary s'i fie, car elle lui rent tout bien et toute prosperité en tout temps. Elle quiert et pourchace laines, c'est a entendre ouvrage pour embesoingner ses maingnés en aucunes oeuvres proffitables, garnist [fol. 63v b] son hostel, et elle mesmes met les mains a la besoingne. Elle est comme la nef du marchand qui aporte tous biens et pourvoit du[3] pain. Elle donne ses dons a ceulz qui le valent, et ceulx sont ses privez, et toute habondance de viandes sourdent mesmes a ses servantes. Elle considere la value du manoir ains que elle l'achate, et par l'ouvrage de son sens elle a planté la vigne dont l'ostel est pourveu. Elle avironne[4] ses reins de force en la constance de solicitude, et ses bras sont endurcis en continuele bonne oeuvre: elle sent que son embesoingnement est bon, et pour ce le continue.[5] Et pour tant la lumiere de son labour ne sera ja estaincte, quelque temps tenebreux qu'il face, elle s'embesoingne mesmes des[6] fortes choses, et avec ce ne desprise pas les femmenins ouvrages ains elle mesmes y oeuvre.[7] Elle estent ses [fol. 64r a] mains[8] aux pouvrez et souffraicteux en les secourant. Sa maison par sa pourveance est gardee de froidure et de neges, et ceulx que elle a a gouverner sont vestus de doubles robes. Elle fait pour soy robe de soye et de pourpre d'onneur et de renommee, et son mary est honnouré quant il est assis des premiers avec les anciens de la terre. Elle fait toilles et linges deliez que elle vent. Et sa vesteure est force et honneur, et pour ce joye lui sera perpetuel. Sa bouche dit tousjours paroles de sapience, et la loye de debonnaireté est en sa langue. Elle considere provisions de son hostel,[9] ne point ne mengue son pain oiseuse. Les meurs de ses enfans monstrent que elle

---

[1] on] en
[2] mal ce que maintes femmes] malice que maintes
[3] du] de
[4] avironne] a avironné
[5] elle sent que son embesoingnement est bon, et pour ce le continue] *omits*
[6] des] es
[7] oeuvre] met les dois
[8] mains] dois
[9] provisions de son hostel] les provisions de son hostel par les angles

theyr neglygent housbandes thynketh that it is grete anoyaunce to them that they busy them so moche to do that that perteyneth to them to pourvaye, and then they saye that they wolde be maystresses and more wyse than they. And thus they wolde tourne it into evyl that that many women say [Oo4v] to them in good entente.

"And of these wyse women speketh the *Epystle of Salamon*, of whiche the substaunce after our purpose wyll say that it foloweth so."

## Chapter 44     The Epystle of Salamon in the *Boke of Proverbes*

"Who shall fynde a stronge woman, that is to say wyse? Her housbande shall not faute of all good. She is praysed of all the countre, and her housbande trusteth her wel, for she yeldeth hym al welthe and prosperyte in all tymes. She seketh and pourchaseth wolles, that is to understande werke to kepe her meyny in profytable werkes to garnysshe her housbande, and she herselfe put her handes to the busynesse. And she is as a shyp of a marchaunte that bereth all manere of goodes and pour[v]ayeth[1] for brede. She gyveth her gyftes to them that ben worthy, and those ben her counsayllours, and all haboundaunce of meetes and drynkes spryngeth also to her servauntes. She consydereth the value of a maner or she bye it, and by the werke of her wytte she hath planted vynes with the whiche her housholde is pourvayed. She gyrdeth her raynes with strengthe and constaunce of busynesse, and her armes ben in contynuall good werke: she seeth that her busynesse is good, and therfore she contynueth it. And for so moche that the lyght of her laboure shall never be quenched, what darke tyme that cometh, she busyeth herselfe in stronge thynges, and with that she dyspraayseth not women's workes but she [Oo4v] herselfe worketh it. She stretcheth her handes to the poore and feble in theyr socoure. Her house by her pourveyaunce is kepte from al maner of coldnes of snowe, and those that she hath to governe ben clothed in double robes. She maketh for herselfe robes of sylke of purple, of worshyp and of renowne, and her housbande is worshypped when he is set with the fyrst auncyent men of the erthe. She maketh cloth lynnen and wollen that she selleth. And her clothynge is strengthe and worshyp, and for that joye perpetuall shal be to her. Her mouthe speketh alway wordes of wysedome, and the lawe of buxomnesse is in her tongue. She consydereth the provysyons of her house, and she eteth not her brede ydell. The condycyons of her chyldren sheweth that she is theyr moder, and the werke

---

[1] pour[v]ayeth : *pournayeth*

est leur mere, et les oeuvres de eulx preschent sa beneurté. Le net aournement de son mary lui [fol. 64r b] rent louenge. Elle est maistresse de ses filles en toutes choses: quoy que elles soient grandes, elle desprise fausse gloire et vaine beauté. Telle femme craindra Nostre Seigneur, sera louee. Et il lui rendra fruit selon ses oeuvres, qui la louent en toutes places."

### *Chapitre 45*     Ci dit de Gaye Cirile

"Au propose qui dit *L'Epistre Salemon* de femme prudent, bien peut estre ramenteue la noble royne Gaye Cirile. Ceste dame fu de Romme ou de Touscane, et mariee au roy des Rommains nommé Tarquin. Elle fut de moult grant prudence en fait de gouvernement, et moult vertueuse. Et avec le grant sens naturel, loiaulté, et bonté que elle avoit, sur toutes femmes fu renommee d'estre tres grant mainagiere et de notable pourveance. Et tout fust elle royne et bien se peust passer de [fol. 64v a] ouvrer de ses mains, tant avoit celle dame le cuer a tousjours proffiter en aucune chose et n'estre nul temps oiseuse que tousjours labouroit en aucune oeuvre, et semblablement faisoit labourer les dames et pucelles d'environ elle et qui la servoient. Elle trouva la maniere de sortir laines, et faire fins draps et de pluseurs sortes, et en ce s'occupoit, qui estoit pour le temps tres honnourable chose, par quoy celle noble dame en fu par tout[1] louee, honnouree, prisé, et renommee. Par quoy, pour la reverence[2] et memoire d'elle, les Rommains qui puis crurent encore en moult plus grant poissance (que ou temps d'elle n'estoient) ordennerent et maintindrent tousjours la[3] coustume que aux nopces de leurs filles, quant l'espousee entroit premierement en la maison de l'espoux, on lui demandoit comment [fol. 64v b] elle seroit nommee? Et elle respondoit 'Gaye,' et ce donnoit a entendre que elle vouloit ycelle dame ensuivre en fais et en oeuvres selon sa poissance."

### *Chapitre 46*     Ci dit de l'avis[4] de la royne Dido

"Prudence, si que toy mesmes cy devant as dit,[5] est de avoir avis et regart sur les choses que on veult emprendre comment ilz pourront estre terminees. Et que femmes soient en tel regart avisees mesmes en grans choses te donray encore exemple d'aucunes poissans dames, et premierement de Dydo. Ycelle Dydo, qui premierement fut nommee Elixa, demonstra bien le savoir de sa prudence par ses

---

[1] tout] tout le monde
[2] et renommee. Par quoy, pour la reverence] par quoy pour la renommee
[3] la] tel
[4] l'avis] de la prudence et advis
[5] cy devant as dit] as dit cy devant

of them sheweth her goodnesse. The clene rayment of her housbande yeldeth her praysynges. She is maystresse of her doughters in al thynges, thoughe they be grete. She dysprayseth false praysynges and vayne beaute. Suche a woman shall drede Our Lorde and shall be praysed. And she shall yelde her fruyte after her werke, whiche prayseth her in all places."

## Chapter 45    Here it speketh of Gay Cyryle

"To the purpose that the *Epystle of Salamon* sayth of a wyse woman maye well be remembred the noble Quene Gay Cyryle. This lady was of Rome, or of Constaunce, and maryed to a kynge of the Romaynes. She was of prudence in the dede of governaunce, and ryght vertuous. [Oo5r] And with the grete naturall wyt, trouthe, and bounte that she had, above all women she was praysed to be ryght a grete vyander and of notable pourveyaunce. And thoughe she were a quene and myght well leve to werke with her handes, yet she had the herte alwaye to profyte in some thynge and noo tyme to be ydle but alway laboured in some werke. And the same wyse, she made the ladyes and damoyselles aboute her to laboure, and in especyall those that served her. She founde the maner to sorte wolles, and to make fyne clothe and of dyvers sortes, and in that she occupyed her, whiche is for the tyme a ryght honourable thynge, by whiche this noble lady in all places was praysed and worshypped. By whiche, for the reverence and memory of her, the Romaynes whiche after encreased in ryght grete puyssaunce (whiche in her tyme were not) ordeyned and maynteyned the custome that to the weddynge of [theyr]¹ doughters, when the spouse sholde entre fyrst into the house of her housbande, one asked howe she sholde be named, and she answered: 'Gaye.' And that gave to understande that she wolde folowe this same lady in dedes and in werkes after her puyssaunce."

## Chapter 46    Here it speketh of the advyse of Dydo, quene of Cartage

"Prudence, so as thyselfe hast sayd before, is to have advyse and a beholdynge upon thynges that one wyll take on hande howe that they sholde be determyned. And that women sholde be in suche [Oo6r] respecte advysed in grete matters, I shall gyve thee yet ensample of some puyssaunt ladyes, and fyrst of Dydo. This

¹ [theyr] : *her*

oeuvres, si que je te conteray.[1] Elle fonda et edifia en la terre d'Auffrique une cité appellee Carthage, de laquelle elle fu dame et royne. Et la maniere du fonder, d'acquere[2] la terre, et de la posseder [fol. 65r a] demonstra sa grant constance, noblece, et vertu, sans lesquelles grace avoir ne puet estre en personne droicte prudence.

"La venue de ceste dame fu de ceulx de Fenice qui des derrenieres parties d'Egipte vindrent en la terre de Sirie, et la ediffierent et fonderent pluseurs nobles villes et citez. Entre lesquelz gens ot un roy appellé Agenor, duquel descendi par lignage le pere de ceste Dido, qui fu nommé Beel et fut roy de Fenice, et subjugua le royaume de Chipre. Cestui roy avoit[3] un seul filz nommé Pymalion, et ceste pucelle Dido sans plus d'enfans. Quant il vint a mort, il encharga moult a ses barons que loyaulté et amour portassent a ses deux enfans, et que ainsi le feroient leur fist promettre. Quant le roy fu mort, ilz couronnerent Pymalion son filz et marierent Elixe, qui moult estoit [fol. 65r b] belle pucelle, et[4] un duc du païs le plus grant aprés le roy qui avoit nom Acerbe Cice, ou Ciceus. Et estoit cellui Cyceon grant prestre du temple de Hercules, selon leur loy, et a merveilles riche. Si s'entre amoient moult lui et sa femme, et bonne vie menoient.[5]

"Mais Pymalion le roy estoit de mauvaises meurs, cruel, et la plus couvoiteuse personne que veoir on peust: ne tant ne savoit avoir que plus[6] ne couvoistast. Elixe sa su[er],[7] qui bien congnoissoit sa grant couvoitise, et savoit bien que son mary avoit grant tresor et que grant renom estoit de sa richece, lui conseilla et avisa que il se gardast du roy et meist son avoir en lieu secret, afin que le roy ne lui ostast. Ce conseil creut Cyceus, mais ne se garda pas bien sa personne des agays du roy si que elle lui avoit dit: si le fist un jour occire le roy[8] afin que il eust ses grans [fol. 65v a] tresors. De laquel mort tel dueil ot Elixe que a pou de dueil ne moru,[9] et fut par long temps en plours et[10] gemissemens, regraitant piteusement son ami et son seigneur, en maudisant son cruel frere qui fait mourir l'avoit.

"Mais le felon roy, qui trouva fraudé de son opinion[11]—s'estoit par ce qu'il avoit pou ou neant trouvé de l'avoir de Cyceus—portoit grant rancune a sa suer, car il pensoit que elle eust l'avoir mucié. Et celle, qui vit bien que elle estoit en grant peril de sa vie, fut amonnestee par sa mesmes prudence de laissier son

---

[1] conteray] compteray
[2] d'acquere] et d'acquerre
[3] avoit] ot
[4] belle pucelle, et] a
[5] menoient] ensemble menoient
[6] plus] il
[7] su[er] : *sure*
[8] un jour occire le roy] le dit roy un jour occire
[9] ne moru] mouru
[10] et] et en
[11] trouva fraudé de son opinion] de son oppinion trouvé fraudé

Dydo was fyrst named Elyxa; the connynge of her prudence shewed well by her werkes, as I shall tell thee. She founded and edyfyed a cyte in the lande of Auffryke named Cartage, of the whiche she was lady and quene. And the maner of the foundynge to gete the lande and to possede it shewed in her grete constaunce, noblesse, and vertue, without whiche to have by grace veray prudence maye not be in ony persone.

"The comynge of this lady was of them of Fenyce, whiche of the last partyes of Egypte came into the lande of Syrye. And there they founded and buylded dyvers noble townes and cytees, amonge the whiche people there was a kynge called Agenor, of the whiche descended by lygnage the fader of this Lady Dydo, whiche was named Beel and was kynge of Fenyce; and he put the royalme of Cypre under his subjeccyon. This kynge had one sone named Pygynalyon, and this mayden Dydo without mo chyldren. And when he came to the dethe, he charged gretely his barons that they sholde bere to these .ii. chyldren love and trouthe, and so to do they made promyse to hym. When the kynge was deed, they crowned Pygynalyon his sone and wedded Elyxe, whiche was ryght a fayre mayde, to a duke of the countre whiche was grettest after the kynge and was called Acerbe Cyte, or Cytens. And this Cyteon was the grete preest of the temple of Hercules, after theyr lawe, and was a mervayllous ryche man. And so he and his wyfe loved moche togyder and ledde a good lyfe.

"But this Kynge Pygynalyon was of shrewde condycyons, cruell, and the moost coveytous persone that one myght se, for he coude not have so moche but he wolde coveyte more. Elyxe his syster, whiche knewe well his grete coveytyse, and also she knewe well that her housbande had grete treasoure and there was grete spekynge of this rychesse, she counsaylled and advysed hym that he sholde kepe hym from the kynge, and sholde put his goodes in some secrete place to that entente that the kynge sholde not take it awaye. Cycyens byleved well this counsayle, yet he kepte not well his persone from the awaytes of the kynge, as she had tolde hym. So the kynge made hym to be slayne on a daye to the entente that he myght have his grete treasoures, of the whiche dethe Elyxe had so grete sorowe that she was nere hande deed, and was longe tyme in wepynge and wayllynge, sorowynge pyteously her husbande and her lorde, cursynge her cruell brother that made hym to dye.

"But the false kynge that founde a wyle, of his opynyon—whiche was for that that he had founde lytell or nought of the goodes of Cytens—and bare grete rancoure to his syster, for he thought that she had hydden the goodes. And she, whiche sawe well that she was in grete peryll of her lyfe, was warned by her

propre paÿs et de s'en aler. Ceste chose deliberee, elle prist en soy par vertueux
courage avis de ce que elle feroit, et se arma de force et de constance pour mestre
a effait ce qu'entreprendre vouloit. Si savoit bien celle dame que le roy n'estoit[1]
amés de tous les barons, ne du peuple [fol. 65v b] pour les grans cruaultez et extorcions que il faisoit, si t[i]ra[2] a soy aucuns des princes, et des citoyens, et aussi de
ceulx du peuple. Et aprés ce que leur ot fait jurer que secrete la tendroient, elle
pour moult belles parolles leur prist a declairier son entencion, tant que ilz furent
d'accord de eulx en aler avecques elle, et lui jurerent estre bons et feaulx. Si fist
la dame au plus tost que elle pot aprester son navire tout secretement, et par nuit
s'en parti a tout ses grans tresors et foison gens avecques elle, et enchargia moult
aux maroniers de fort esploitier d'aler.

"Plus grant malice fist ceste dame, car elle savoit bien que son frere, si tost
que il saroit son allee, envoieroit appres. Et pour ce fist emplir secretement grosses
males, et bahus,[3] et grans fardiaulx de choses de nulle value, pesantes comme se
ce[4] fust [fol. 66r a] son tresor, afin que en baillant ycelles malles et ces fardiaulx a
ceulx que son frere envoieroit aprés, ilz la laissassent aler et n'empeschassent son
erre. Laquelle chose avint: car n'orent pas moult longuement erré quant foison
gent de par le roy vindrent fuiant aprés elle pour l'arrester. Mais la dame bien et
saigement parla a eulx, et dist que elle aloit en un sien pellerinage, si ne la voul-
sisent empechier. Mais quant la dame vid que riens ne lui valoit celle excusance,
elle dist que elle savoit bien qu'il[5] n'avoit que faire d'elle mais au fort s'il vouloit
avoir son tresor, que voulentiers lui[6] envoieroit. Et ceulx qui savoient bien que le
roy ne tendoit a autre chose, distrent que hardiement le leur baillast car par ce
mettroient peine de conter[7] le roy et de l'apaisier vers elle. Et lors la dame, a triste
chiere [fol. 66r b] comme se envis le faist, leur fist livrer et chargier sur leurs nefs
toutes les dictes malles et bahus. Et ceulx qui bien cuidirent avoir esploitié, et que
joyeuses[8] nouvelles portassent au roy, s'en partirent a tant.

"Et la royne, sans de ce faire nul semblant, fait penser de son erre au plus tost
que elle pot. Et ainsi tant errerent, que jour que nuit, que ilz arriverent en l'isle de
Chypre. La un pou se reffreschirent, puis tantost monta la dame sur son naivere[9]
quant fait ot aux dieux ses oblacions. Et en amena avecques elle le prestre de Jovis

---

[1] n'estoit] n'estoit mie
[2] t[i]ra : *tera*
[3] males et] et
[4] choses de nulle value, pesantes comme se ce] choses pesans de nulle vale comme se
[5] excusance, elle dist que elle savoit bien qu'il] excusacion dit que bien savoit que le
roy son frere
[6] lui] le lui
[7] conter] contempter
[8] joyeuses] bonnes
[9] naivere] navire

prudence to leve her owne countre and to go thens. This thynge remembred, she toke advyse in herselfe by vertuous [Oo6v] courage of that she sholde do, and armed her with strengthe and constaunce to put in effecte that she wolde take on hande. So this lady knewe well that the kynge was not welbyloved of his lordes, nor of his people for the grete crueltyes and extorcyons that he dyde. So she toke to her certayne lordes, and cytesyns, and also of the comune people. And after that that she had made them swere that they sholde holde it in counsayle suche thynges as she wolde devyse to them, she by ryght fayre language began to declare her entente, so moche that they accorded to go with her, and therto they made theyr othe to be trewe and faythfull. So this lady, as soone as she myght, made redy her navye all secretly. And by nyght she departed with al her grete treasours and foyson of people with her, and she charged gretly her maryners to employ them to go.

"More gretter malyce dyde this lady for she knewe well that her broder, as soone as he knewe of her goynge wolde sende people after her. And secretly she made fylle grete males and grete fardelles of thynges of noo valewe. But they were hevy as it had ben grete treasoure, to that entente that in delyverynge these foresayd males and fardelles to them that her broder wolde sende after, it sholde let her passe and not to hurte her goynge. Whiche thynge came all to the poynte for they were not longe gone but grete foyson of people came from the kynge sewynge after her to have arested her. But the lady wel and wysely spake to them, and sayd that she wente in her pylgrymage so they letted her not. But when this [Pp1r] lady sawe that this excusacyon wolde not advayle, she knewe wel that he wolde nothynge with her but to have her treasoure. And she sayd that she wolde sende it to hym with a good wyll and [to] those[1] that knewe wel that they wolde do theyr payne to contente the kynges appetyte, and to apease the kynge. And then the lady, with a sorowfull chere as thoughe she toke sorowe for it, made to be delyvered all these males and bagges to them. And those that trowed verely that they had done well theyr devoyre, and that they sholde brynge joyfull tydynges to the kynge, departed from her.

"And the quene, without makynge semblaunt of that, thought on her goynge as soone as she myght. And they wente so longe, by day and by nyght, that they aryved in the Ile of Cypre. And there they refresshed them a lytell whyle, and anone after she toke her shyppes when she had done her oblacyons unto the goddes. And she brought with her the preest of Jovys and his wyfe and all his

---

[1] [to] those : *those*

avec sa femme, et toute sa famille; et il avoit deviné avant[1] que il vendroit une dame des parties de Phenice, pour laquelle il lairoit son paÿs et s'en yroit avec[2] elle. Ainsi s'en alerent et laisserent derriere eulx la terre de Crete, et a destre la terre de Secille. Et [fol. 66v a] longuement nagerent coste la terre de Mesulie tant que ilz arriverent en Auff[ri]que,[3] et la descendirent.

"Et tantost vindrent des gens du païs pour veoir le navire et quel gent y avoit. Et quant la dame virent et que gens de paix estoient, foison vivres leur aporterent.[4] Et la dame parla a eulx moult amiablement, et dist que pour le bien que elle avoit ouy dire de celle contree, estoit venue[5] pour y demourer, se il leur plaisoit; et ilz respondirent que bien le vouloyent. Et la dame, qui fist semblant que moult grant habitacle ne vouloit faire sur estrange terre, leur requist a vendre sus la marine tant de terre seulement comme un cuir de bueuf pourroit enclore pour y faire edefier aucune herberge pour elle et pour sa gent; laquelle chose lui fut [fol. 66v b] ottroyee et les couvenances et marchié fait et juré entre eulx. La dame qui adonc demonstra son savoir et grant prudence fist prendre un cuir de bueuf et le fist tranchier par les plus deliees conroies que faire se pouoit, et lier ensemble toute en une ceinture, puis les fist estendre sus la terre tout environ la marine, qui contenoient[6] a merveilles grant païs. De laquel chose les vendeurs furent moult esbahiis, et moult esmerveilliez de la cautelle[7] de ceste femme, et non pour [t]ant[8] couvint que son marchié lui tenissent.[9]

"Et ainsi celle dame ot acquise terre en Auffrique, et en la dicte pour prise fu t[r]ouvee[10] la teste d'un cheval; par laquelle teste, et par le cry et vol[11] des oysiaulx, ilz entendirent selon leurs devinemens qu'en la cité qui la seroit fondé aroit gens guerrieurs [fol. 67r a] et moult preux aux armes. Si envoya tantost celle dame par tout querre ouvriers, et desplia[12] son tresor une cité fist edifier a merveilles belle, grande, et forte que elle nomma *Carthage*, et la tour et le donjon elle appella *Birse*, qui est a dire cuer de buef.

---

[1] avec sa femme, et toute sa famille; et il avoit deviné avant] Jovis et sa meisgnee, lequel avoit par avant deviné
[2] avec] avecques
[3] Auff[ri]que : *Auffaque*
[4] foison vivres leur aporterent] ilz leur apporterent foison vivres
[5] de celle contree, estoit venue] d'icelle contree estoient venus
[6] tout environ la marine, qui contenoient] environ la marine qui contenoit
[7] moult esbahiis, et moult esmerveilliez de la cautelle] moult esbahis et esmerveilliez de la cautelle et sens
[8] [t]ant : *quant*
[9] son marchié lui tenissent] lui tenissent son marchié
[10] t[r]ouvee : *touvee*
[11] le cry et vol] le vol et cry
[12] desplia] desploya

housholde. And he had dyvyned before that there sholde come a lady of the partyes of Phenyce, for the whiche he sholde leve his countre and sholde go with
her. Thus they wente and lefte behynde them the lande of Grece and the lande
of Cecyll in the ryght hande, and they sayled longe by the lande of Mesulye so
moche that they aryved in Aufryke and there toke the lande.

"And anone came the people of the countre to se the manere and what people they were. And when they sawe the lady and her people, they brought plentye
of vytayles. And the lady spake to them ryght frendly, and sayd that for the grete
welthe that she had herde say of that [Pp1v] countre, she was come thyder to dwell
there, yf it pleased them; and they answered that they wolde well. And the lady
that made semblaunt that she wolde make no grete dwellynge upon a straunge
lande requyred them to selle to her upon the see coste so moche lande onely as
the hyde of an oxe wolde enclose, there to make dwellynge places for her and
her people; the whiche thynge was graunted to her, and the covenauntes and the
pryce sworne bytwene them. The lady then (whiche shewed her wyt and grete
prudence) made to take an hyde of an oxe and made to cutte it by the smallest
thonges that myght be made, and knytte them togyder all on lengthe, and after
made to stretche it upon the grounde all aboute the see coste, whiche conteyned
a mervayllous grete countre. Of the whiche thynge the sellers were mervayllous
sore abasshed, and mervaylled moche of the cauteyles of this woman, and not for
that yet they must holde theyr pryce.

"And thus this lady gate this lande in Auffryke, and in the sayd fortakynge there was smyten off the heed of an horse, by the whiche heed and by the
crye and the flyght of byrdes they understode after theyr dyvynynge that in that
cyte that sholde be founded, there sholde be in tyme to come men of warre and
wyse in armes. Then this lady sente anone all aboute to seke werkemen, and
opened her treasoure, and made to buylde a cyte mervayllous grete, fayre, and
stronge whiche she named *Cartage*, and the towre of the dongeon she called
*Byrse*, whiche is to say the hyde of an oxe.

"Et ainsi comme[1] elle commençoit ja a edefier sa cité, elle ouy nouvelles de son frere, qui fort la menaçoit, elle et[2] tous ceulx qui l'avoient acompagnee,[3] pour cause que elle l'avoit moquié et gabé du tresor. Mais elle respondi aux messages que le tresor estoit bon et bel que baillié avoit pour porter a son frere, mais que par aventure[4] ceulx qui l'avoient porté le pristrent et mistrent en lieu fausses choses; ou que il pouoit bien estre que pour la vengence de la mort de son mary, les dieux n'avoient voulu que cellui [fol. 67r b] qui fait mourir l'avoit joist de son avoir, et pour ce l'avoient ainsi transmué.[5]

"Mais quant a la menace, elle pensoit a l'aide des dieux bien se deffendroit de son frere. Et adonc fist appeller tous ceulx que elle avoit amenez, et leur dist que ne vouloit mie[6] que avec elle remansissent malgré leur[7] corage, ne que par elle leur venist[8] aucun encombrier; par quoy se retourner s'en vouloient, tous ou aucuns d'eulx, que[9] leur restitueroit leurs labours et les envoieroit.[10] Et ilz respondirent, tous d'une voix, qu'ilz vivroient et mourroient avec[11] elle sans partir jour de leurs vies.

"Si s'en partirent les messages, et la dame tant comme elle pot esploicta de parfaire sa cité. Et quant parfaicte fu, elle establi lois et ordenances au peuple pour vivre selon droit et justice. Et tant [fol. 67v a] se gouverna notablement et par grant prudence qu'en toutes terres en aloient les nouvelles, et ne parloit on se d'elle non tellement que pour la grant vertu qui fu venue[12] en elle tant pour la hardie[13] et belle entreprise que fait avoit comme pour son tres prudent gouvernement. Lui tresmuerent son nom et l'appellerent *Dido*, qui vaut au tant a dire en latin comme *virago*,[14] qui est a dire celle qui a vertu et force d'omme. Et ainsi vesqui glorieusement un grant temps, et tousjours eust fait se Fortune ne lui eust neu. Mais comme elle soit souvent envieuse de ceulx qui sont en prosperité, lui desteempa dur buvrage a la perfin,[15] si comme cy aprés en temps et en lieu te diray."

---

[1]  ainsi comme] si comme
[2]  elle et] et
[3]  l'avoient acompagnee] accompaignee l'avoient
[4]  par aventure] il pouoit estre que
[5]  le pristrent . . . transmué] l'avoient robé et mis faulses choses en lieu; ou, par aventure, que pour le pechié que le roy avoit commis de son mari faire occire, les dieux n'avoient pas voulu que il jouysist de son trésor, si l'avoient tresmué
[6]  que ne vouloit mie] que mie ne vouloit
[7]  malgré leur] contre leur bon gré et
[8]  leur venist] peussent avoir
[9]  ou aucuns d'eulx, que] ou aucun d'eulx qu'elle
[10]  envoieroit] en envoyeroit
[11]  avec] avecques
[12]  venue] veue
[13]  hardie] hardiece
[14]  en latin comme virago] comme virago en latin
[15]  dur buvrage a la perfin] a la parfin trop dur buvrage

"And so as she began to buylde her cyte, she herde tydynges of her broder, [Pp2r] whiche manaced her gretely and all that were in her company for bycause she had mocked hym of the treasoure. But she answered to the messangers that the treasoure was good and fayre that she toke to bere to her broder, but that by adventure those that brought it toke it awaye and put instede of that some false thynges; or that it myght well be for the vengeaunce of the dethe of her housbande the goddes had no wyl that he that slewe hym sholde rejoyce his goodes, and therfore they have chaunged it.

"But as for the manasynge, she thought by the helpe of her goddes she sholde defende her from her broder. And then she made to call all those that she had brought thyder with her, and sayd to them that she wolde not that they sholde abyde with her agaynst [theyr] courage,[1] ne that by her sholde come encombraunce to them. By the whiche yf they wolde tourne home agayne, all or some of them, that she wolde restore them for theyr laboure and sende them forthe. And they answered, all with one voyce, that they wolde lyve and dye with her without partynge all the dayes of theyr lyves.

"Then departed the messangers, and the lady as moche as she myght busyed her to perfourme her cyte. And when it was al made, she ordeyned lawes to the people for to lyve after ryght and justyce. And thus she governed so notably and by gret prudence that in al countres wente her renowne. And every man spake of her not onely for the grete vertue that was in her, but as moche for hardynesse of the fayre entrepryse that she had made and for the grete prudent governaunce. They chaunged her name and called her [Pp2v] *Dydo*, whiche is as moche to say in Latyne as *virago*, that is to saye she that hath vertue and strengthe of man. And thus she lyved gloryously a grete whyle—and longer had done, if Fortune had ben favourable to her, but as she often tymes [is][2] envyous to them that ben in prosperyte, dystempered to her an harde draught of drynke at the last so as hereafter in tyme and place I shall tell thee."

---

[1] [theyr] courage : *her*
[2] tymes [is] : *tymes*

## *Chapitre 47*    De[1] Opis, royne de Crete

"Opis ou Ops, qui puis fu appellee deesse et mere des dieux, fu es tres ancians
aages reputee prudente pour ce que selon [fol. 67v b] que[2] dient les ancienes histoires
moult prudemment et constament se sceut contenir entre les prosperités et adversitez qui lui avindrent en son temps. Ceste dame fut fille de Urane, qui fu homme
tres poissant en Grece, et de Vesta sa femme. Moult rude et pou savant estoit
encore le siecle; adonc elle ot a espoux Saturnus le roy de Crete, qui son frere estoit.
Si ot en avision cellui roy de Crete que sa femme devoit enfanter un filz masle
qui l'occiroit, et pour ce pour[3] [o]bvier[4] a celle destinee, ordenna que tous les filz
masles que la royne auroit fussent occis. Mais pour ce que la dame fist tant par son
savoir que elle, par cautelles, bien sceut trouver respita[5] ses troys filz de mort: c'est
asavoir Jupiter, Neptunus, et Pluto. Fut puis moult honnouree et sa prudence louee.
Et pour son savoir et pour l'auctorité de ses enfans, acquist en son [fol. 68r a] temps
si grant voix et honneur au monde que la fole gent l'appellerent 'deesse' et 'mere
des dieux,' car ses filz furent des leur vies[6] reputez dieux pour ce que ilz estoient
en aucunes choses plus savans que les autres hommes, qui tous estoient bestiaulx.
Si fust a ceste dame constituez temples et sacrefices,[7] laquelle opinion comme folz
tindrent par long temps. Et mesmement a Romme ou temps de la prosperité des
Rommains duroit celle folie, et avoient celle deesse en grant reverence."[8]

## *Chapitre 48*    De Lavine, fille du roy Latin

"Lavine, qui fu royne des Latins, eut[9] aussi renommee de prudence. Ceste noble
dame estoit descendue d'ycellui Saturnus, roy de Crete dont parlé avons, et fu
fille du roy Latin, et puis [mariee a Eneas. Et ains que][10] mariee fust, Turnus, le
roy des Turiliens, la covoitoit a avoir. Mais son pere, qui avoit eu [fol. 68r b] respons
des dieux que elle devoit estre donnee a un duc de Troye, retardoit tousjours le
mariage, non obstant que sa femme l'empressast.[11] Et quant Eneas fu arivé en

---

[1] De] Ci dit de
[2] que] ce que
[3] pour ce pour] pour ce affin de
[4] [o]bvier : *abvier*
[5] par cautelles bien sceut trouver respita] par sage cautelle respita
[6] leur vies] en leurs vies
[7] temples et sacrefices] temple et sacrefices
[8] reverence] renommee
[9] Latins eut] Laurentins ot
[10] [mariee a Eneas. Et ains que] : *skips to next* mariee] mariee a Eneas. Et ains que
[11] sa femme l'empressast] la royne, sa femme, moult l'en pressast

*Chapter 47*     Here it speketh of Opis

"Opys or Ops that syth was called goddesse and moder of goddes was of the auncyent people had in reputacyon as ryght a wyse woman for that after the sayenge of the olde hystoryes ryght prudently and constauntly she coude holde her contente amonge the prosperytees and adversytees that happened to her in her tyme. This lady was doughter of Urane that was ryght a puyssaunt man in Grece, and of Vesta his wyfe, whiche was ryght rude and lytell knowynge of the worlde. And this Lady Opys or Ops was wedded to Saturnus, the kynge of Crete, whiche was her broder. So this kynge had a vysyon that his wyfe sholde be delyvered of a man chylde that sholde slee hym, and for to voyde this foresayd destenye he ordeyned that all the men chyldren that the quene sholde have sholde be slayne. Yet for all that, this lady dyde so moche by her wytte whiche founde suche cauteyles that she respyted her thre sones from the dethe: that is to knowe Jupyter, [Pp3r] Neptunus, and Pluto. And she was gretely worshypped syth, and her wysedome praysed. And for her understandynge and for the auctoryte of her chyldren, she gate in her tyme so grete voyce and worshyp in the worlde that the lewde people of the countre called her goddesse and moder of goddes, for her sones in theyr lyvynge was counted for goddes for that they were in some thynges more knowynge then other men, that were all as bestes. So there were ordeyned and sacryfyed temples, the whiche opynyon the foles kepte longe tyme. And the same wyse at Rome in the tyme of the prosperyte of the Romaynes was this folye and then had this goddesse in grete reverence."

*Chapter 48*     Of Lavyne, doughter of the Kynge Latyn

"Lavyne, whiche was quene of the Latynes, had also praysynge of prudence. This noble lady was descended of this Saturnus, kynge of Crete, of whome we have spoken, and was doughter of the Kynge Latyn. And after Turnus, the kynge of Turylyens, coveyted to have her to wyfe. But her fader whiche had answere of the goddes that she sholde be gyven to a lorde of Troye, whiche taryed the maryage longe tyme, notwithstandynge that his wyfe laboured the contrary. And when

Ytalie, il fist demander congié ad ce[1] roy Latin de descendre en sa terre; mais il ne
lui donna pas seulement ce congié, ains lui ottroya tantost Lavine sa fille en mariage. Et pour celle cause, Turnus esmut guerre contre Eneas, en laquelle ot faicte
grant occision et lui mesmes y fut occis. Et Eneas ot la victoire, et espousa Lavine
qui ot puis un filz de lui, duquel demoura enceinte quant Eneas trespassa. Mais
quant vint a l'enfanter, pour la grant paour que elle avoit que un filz que Eneas
avoit eu d'une autre femme, que on nommoit Aescaneus, ne faist pour couvoitise
de regner mourir l'enfant que elle enfanteroit, elle ala enfanter en un bois, et mist
a l'enfant a nom [fol. 68v a] Juleus Silvius. Ceste dame ne voult oncques puis estre
mariee, et se gouverna en sa veusveté moult prudemment et maintint le royaume
par grant savoir. Son fillastre sceut tenir en si grant amour que il n'ot nul mal
vouloir contre elle, ne contre son frere; ains aprés ce que il eut edifiee pour soy[2]
la cité d'Albe, il y ala demourer. Et Lavine avec son filz gouverna tres sagement
tant que l'enfant fut parcreus, duquel enfant descendirent[3] Remus et Romulus,
qui fonderent Romme, et les haulz princes Rommains qui puis vindrent.

"Que veulx tu que plus t'en die, fille chiere? Il me semble que assez produit
ay[4] de preuves a mon entencion; c'est assavoir, de te demonstrer par vive raison
et exemple que Dieux n'a point eu ne a en reprobacion le sexe femmenin, ne que
cellui des hommes, [fol. 68v b] si que tu vois clerement. Et comme il a apparu et
apparra par la deposicion de mes autres deux seurs qui si sont. Car b[i]en[5] me
semble que des or mais doit souffire en ce que je t'ay basti es murs de la closture
de la Cité des Dames. Or[6] sont tous achevez et enduis; viengnent avant mes autres
deux seurs, et par leur aide et devis soit par toy parfait le surplus de l'ediffice."

**Explicit la premier partie du *Livre de la cité des dames***

---

[1] ad ce] a cellui
[2] eut edifiee pour soy] ot ediffiee
[3] descendirent] dessendirent puis
[4] assez produit ay] assez ay produit
[5] b[i]en : *ben*
[6] Or] Et

Eneas was aryved in Italy, he asked leve of the [Pp3v] Kynge Latyne to descende upon his lande; but he gave hym not onely that leve, but he graunted hym his doughter in maryage. And for this cause, Turnus moved warre agaynst Eneas, in the whiche was grete slaughter and Kynge Turnus was slayne hymselfe. And Eneas had the vyctory, and wedded Lavyne that had syth a sone by hym, of whome she [w]as[1] grete when Eneas dyed. But when it came that she sholde be delyvered, for the grete drede that she had that a sone that Eneas had of another woman, whiche chylde was named Astanyus, that for covetyse of reygnyge sholde not slee the chylde that she was delyvered of, she wente and was delyvered in a woode, and gave the chylde a name Julyus Sylvyus. This lady wolde never after be maryed, and she governed her in her wydowhode ryght prudentely and maynteyned the royalme by grete wysedome. And her sone-in-lawe had her in so grete love that he had none evyll wyll agaynst her, nor his broder; but after that that he had buylded the cyte of Alba, he wente to dwel there. And Lavyne governed the lande ryght wysely tyll the chylde was growne, of the whiche chylde came Remus and Romulus whiche founded Rome, and the hyghe Romayne prynces that came syth.

"What woldest thou that I sholde saye more, dere doughter? Me semeth that I have brought forthe proves ynowe to myne entente; that is to understande, of that I shewe by quycke reason and ensample that God hathe not had, ne hathe in [Pp4r] reprobacyon the femynyne use as these men have, so as thou seest clerely, and as it hathe appered, and yet shall appere by the dysposycyon of myne other two systers that ben here. For well me semeth that frome hensforthe it ought to suffyse in that that I have made the walles of the cloystre of the Cyte of Ladyes. Nowe ben all thynges accheved and ordeyned; nowe cometh forthe myne other two systers, and by theyr helpe and devyse lette the remenaunte of the buyldynge be perfourmed and made an ende by them."

**Here endeth the fyrste parte of the** *Boke of the Cyte of Ladyes*. [Pp6v]

---

[1] [w]as : *mas*

Here begynneth the seconde partye of the
Boke of the Cyte of Ladyes

*the whiche telleth howe and by whome the cyte was buylded
within and peopled.* [A1r]

*Chapitre 1*    Cy commence la seconde partie du *Livre de la cité des dames,*
[fol. 70r b]    **laquelle parle comment et par qui la cité fu au par dedens maisonnee, edifiee, et peuplee, ou premiere chapitre parle des .x. sebi[l]es**[1] [fol. 70v a]

Aprés les paroles de la premiere dame qui fu nommee Raison,[2] se tyra vers moy la seconde, laquelle ot nom Droicture,[3] et ainsi me dist: "Amie chiere, je ne doy pas me tirer arriere, n'estre laisant d'edifier[4] et maisonner avec ton aide ou circuit de la closture et de la muraille ja bastie par ma seur Raiso[n][5] de la Cité des Dames. Si[6] prens tes outilz, et vien avant:[7] si destrempe le mortier en ton cornet,[8] et maçonne fort a la trampe de ta plume. Car assez de quoy te livreray, et en peu d'eure par vertu divine arons edifiees les haulx palais, royaulx et nobles mansions des excellens dames de grant gloire et renommee, qui en ceste cité seront hebergés et demoureront a perpetuité, et a tousjours mais."

Donc[9] je, Christine, [fol. 70v b] oyant la parole de la dame honnouree, dis en ceste maniere: "Tres excellent dame, vees me cy preste. Or commandez, car mon desir est d'obeir."

Et celle a moy dit ainsi: "Regarde, amie, les belles pierres plus que nulles precieuses et reluisans[10] que je t'ay aquerrees et rendues prestes pour alouer en ce maçonnage. Ay je donc esté oyseuse tendis que toy avec Raison bastissiez?[11] Or les arenge[12] selon ma ligne que tu vois cy, par l'ordennance que je te diray.

"Entre les dames de souveraine digneté [s]ont[13] bien a mettre en reng de haultece[14] les tres remplies de sapience sages sebilles, lesquelles si que mettent les plus autentiques aucteurs en leurs institucions furent .x. par nombre, quoy que aucuns n'en mettent que .ix.

---

[1] du *Livre de la cité des dames,* laquelle parle comment et par qui la cité fu au par dedens maisonnee, edifiee, et peuplee, ou premiere chapitre parle des .x. sebibes] de ce livre laquelle parle comment la Cité des Dames fu au par dedens maisonnee, ediffiee, et peuplee

[2] fu nommee Raison] Raison estoit nommee

[3] laquelle ot nom Droicture] qui Droiture avoit a nom

[4] n'estre laisant d'edifier] d'edifier

[5] Raiso[n] : *Raiso*

[6] Si] Or

[7] vien avant] viens avec moy

[8] en ton cornet] ou cornet

[9] Donc] Adont

[10] pierres plus que nulles precieuses et reluisans] reluisans pierres plus precieuses que autres nulles

[11] bastissiez] fort bastissoies

[12] arenge] arrenges

[13] [s]ont : *font*

[14] bien a mettre en reng de haultece] de haultece

*Chapter 1*     And the fyrst chapytre speketh of the [.x.]¹ sybylles

After the wordes of the fyrst lady that was named Reason, the seconde lady drewe her towarde me, the whiche was named Ryghtwysnesse, and thus sayd to me:

"Dere frende, I ought [not]² to drawe me abacke, nor to be slowe to buylde and to make the stone worke with thy helpe in cyrcuyte of the cloystre of the walle, nowe made by my syster Reason, of the Cyte of Ladyes. Nowe take thy toles, and come before and tempre thy morter in every corner, and buylde on fast with the foote of thy penne. For I shall delyver ynoughe wherof, and by the vertue of God we shall have good buyldynge and hyghe palayces, royal and noble mansyons of these excellente ladyes of grete worshyp and renowne [who]³ shal be lodged in this cyte, and shal abyde perpetually fro hensforth."

Then I, Christine, herynge the worde of this worshypfull lady, sayd in this manere: "Ryght excellente lady, se me here all redy. Nowe commaunde, for my desyre is to obeye."

And she sayd to me thus: "Frende, beholde these fayre stones, more fayrer than ony precyous stones and shynynge, whiche I have sought for thee and ordeyned them redy to lodge them in the masonry. Semeth thee that I have ben ydle whyle my syster Reason and you have ben busy? Or set them arowe after my lyne that thou seest here, by the ordynaunce that I shall tell thee.

"Amonge the ladyes of soverayne dygnyte maye well be put in the rowe of hyghnesse the hyghly fulfylled of sapyence, the wyse sybelles, the whiche as olde [A1v] antentyke auctours put in theyr wrytynges were. x. by nombre, thoughe that some put but .ix.

---

¹ [.x.] sybylles : *.v. sybylles*
² ought [not] to : *ought to*
³ [who] : *che*

"O, amie chiere, prens cy garde: quel plus grant [fol. 71r a] honneur en fait de revelacions[1] fist oncques Dieux a prophete quel qu'il fust tant l'amast qu'il donna et ottroya a ces tres nobles dames dont je te parle? Ne mist il en elles Saint Esperit de prophecie tant et si avant que il ne sembloit mie de ce que elles disoient[2] que ce fust prenosticacion du temps ad venir, ains sembloit que ce fussent si comme croniques de choses passees et ja avenues, tant estoient clers, entendibles,[3] et plains leurs diz escrips? Et mesmes de l'avenement Jhesucrist, qui de moult long temps vint aprés, plus clerement et plus avant en parlerent[4] que ne firent si qu'il est trouvé tous les prophetes. Cestes[5] dames userent toute leur vie en virginité et polucion despriserent, et[6] furent toutes nommees *sebilles*. Et n'est mie a entendre que ce fust leur propre nom, ains est [fol. 71r b] a dire *sebille* ainsi comme[7] 'savant la pensee de Dieu,' et furent ainsi appellees pour ce que elles prophetiserent choses si merveilleuses[8] que il couvenoit que ce qu'elles disoient leur venist de la pure pensee de Dieu: si est nom d'[o]ffice,[9] et non pas propre. Cestes furent nees en diverses contrees du monde, et non [m]ie[10] tout en un temps. Et toutes prophetiserent grant foison choses a avenir, et par especial de Jhesucrist et de son avenement si que dit est tres clerement,[11] et toutevoyes furent elles toutes payenes et non mie de la loy des Juifs, qui lors estoit la loy de Dieu.[12]

"La premiere fut nee[13] de la terre de Perse, et pour ce est nommee Persia.

"La seconde fut de Libé, si fut nommee Libica.

"La tierce de Delphe ou temple d'Appolin engendree,[14] pour ce ot nom Delphica. Et ceste predit a[15] long temps devant la [fol. 71v a] destruccion de Troye, et d'elle mist Ovide en son livre plusieurs vers.

"La quarte fut d'Ytalie, et fut nommee Cymeria.

"La quinte fut nee en Babilonie, et fut nommee Erophile. Ceste respondi a ceulx de Grece qui lui en demandoient: que Troye et Ylion le fort chastel par eulx

---

1 revelacions] revelacion
2 elles disoient] elle disoit
3 clers, entendibles] clers et entendibles
4 plus clerement et plus avant en parlerent] en parlerent plus clerement et plus avant
5 Cestes] Ycestes
6 polucion despriserent et] despriserent polucion si
7 comme] que
8 prophetiserent choses si merveilleuses] prophetisierent si merveilleuses choses
9 d'[o]ffice: *deffice*] office
10 [m]ie: *nie*
11 si que dit est tres clerement] tres clerement si que dit est
12 qui lors estoit la loy de Dieu] *omitted*
13 fut nee] fu
14 ou temple d'Appolin engendree] engendree ou temple d'Appolin
15 predit a] predit

"O my dere frende, take hede here: what more worshyp in dede of revelacyons dyde God ever to a prophete that He loved more than He gave and graunted to these ryght noble ladyes, of whome I speke to thee? Dyde not He sende into them the Holy Spyryte of prophecy so moche that it semed not onely of that that they sayd that it sholde be a pronostycacyon of tyme to come, but it semed as it were of cronycles of thynges passed and came, so moche that they were clerely understandynge in theyr thynges wryten? And also of the comynge of Our Lorde Jhesu Cryst, whiche came ryght longe tyme after, they spake more clerely as it is founde than dyde al the prophetes. These ladyes used al theyr lyves in maydenhode and dyspraysed pollucyon, and all were named *sybelles*. And it is not to understande that it was theyr propre names, but *sybelle* is to say as 'knowynge the thought of God.' And so they were called for that that they prophecyed mervayllous thynges, that it was convenyent that that they sayd sholde come to them of the pure thought of God; so it is a name of offyce, and no propre name. These ladyes were borne in dyvers countres of the worlde, and not all in one tyme. And all they prophecyed grete foyson of thynges to come, and in especyall of Our Lorde Jhesu Cryst and of His comynge soo as it is sayd ryght clerely, thoughe that they were al paynymes and not of the lawe of Jewes, whiche [A2r] that tyme was the lawe of God.

"The fyrst was borne in the lande of Perse, and for that she was named Persya.

"The seconde was of Lybye, and was called Lybyca.

"The thyrde of Delphe engendred in the temple of Appolyn, and was named Delphyca. And this lady preched the destruccyon of Troye longe tyme before, and Ovyde put many verses of her in his boke.

"The fourthe was of Ytalye, and was called Symerya.

"The fyfte was of Babylon, and was called Erophyle. This lady answered to them of Grece of thynges that they demaunde her: that Troye and Ylyon the stronge castell sholde perysshe by them, and that Omere sholde wryte lesyngly.

periroit, et que Omer en escriproit mençongeusement. Ainsi fu ceste appellee Eritel[1] pour ce qu'en celle ysle demora, et la furent ses livres trouvez.

"La .vi.ᵉ fu de l'isle de Samos, et fut nommee Samia.

"La .vii.ᵉ fu appellee Cumana, et fu d'Itale nee en la cité de Cumins, en la terre de Champagne.

"La .viii.ᵉ fu nommee Helespontine, et fu nee en Hespont ou champ de Troye, et flourissoit ou temple[2] du noble aucteur Solin et de Tyrr.

"La .ix.ᵉ fu de Frige, pour ce fut nommee Frigica. Cest[e][3] moult parla du decheement de plusieurs seingneuries, [fol. 71v b] et moult[4] aussi parla de l'advenement du faulx propheto[5] Antechrist.

"La .x.ᵉ fu dicte Tyburtine, par autre nom nommee Albunia, de laquelle les dictiez sont moult honnourez, pour ce que elle escript tres clerement de Jhesucrist.

"Et non obstant que ce[s][6] sebilles fussent venus et nees des payens, toutes reprouverent de loy d'iceulx et blasmerent a aourer pluseurs dieux, disant que il n'en estoit fors que un, et que les ydoles estoient vaines."

*Chapitre 2*      **Ci dit de Sebile Eritee**

"Il est assavoir que entre toutes[7] les sebiles, Erithee ot la plus grant prerogative de sapience, car de ceste fu tant grande la vertu par don singulier et especial de Dieu que elle escripst[8] et prophetisa plusieurs choses a avenir tant clerement que ce semble mieulx estre euvangille que prophecie. Et a la requeste des [fol. 72r a] Grieux tant clerement en dictiez mist leurs labours,[9] les batailles, et la destruccion de Troye, que ce n'estoit point plus clere chose après le fait que devant. Semblablement descripst et composa en pou de parolles et vraies l'empire et seingneurie des Rommains et leur[10] diverses aventures par avant long temps que il fust avenu, et tellement que ce semble mieulx estre une brieve memoire des choses passees que choses predictes du temps avenir.[11]

---

[1] Ainsi fu ceste appellee Eritel] Ceste fu nommee Erithee

[2] temple] temps

[3] Cest[e] : *Cest*

[4] moult] moult au vif

[5] propheto] prophete

[6] ce[s] : *ce*

[7] que entre toutes] qu'entre

[8] escripst] descript

[9] tant clerement en dictiez mist leurs labours] escript tant clerement en dictiez leurs labours

[10] l'empire et seingneurie des Rommains et leur] l'empire de Romme et la seignourie des Rommains et leurs

[11] predictes du temps avenir] a avenir

Also she was called Erytell for that she dwelled in that ile, and there were her bookes founde.

"The .vi. was of the Ile of Samos, and was called Samya.

"The .vii. was called Cunyana and was borne of Ytallye in Cumynys, in the lande of Champayne.

"The .viii. was named Elespontyne and was borne Hesponte, in the felde of Troy, and floured in the temple of the noble auctores Solyn and Tyry.

"The .ix. was of Frygya, therfore she was named Frygica. This lady spake moche of the fallynge of dyvers lordshyps, and she spake moche of the comynge of the false prophete Antecryst.

"The .x. was called Tyburtine, and by another name Albuyna, of whom the wrytynges are moche praysed for that that she wrote clerely of Jhesu Cryst.

"And notwithstandynge that these sybylles were borne of paynymes all, they reproved theyr lawe [A2v] and blamed them that they worshypped dyvers goddes, saynge that there is but one God, and that all theyr ydolles were but vayne."

## Chapter 2        Here it speketh of Sybyll Erytee

"Amonge the other sybelles, Eryte had the gretest prerogatyve of wysdome, for of her the vertue was so grete by a synguler and a specyall gyfte of God that she wrote and prophecyed dyvers thynges to come so clerely that it semed better to be a gospell than prophecye. And at the request of the Grekes, she put theyr laboures clerely in wrytynges, theyr bataylles and the destruccyon of Troy, that it was never clerer after it was done than it was before. The same wyse she descryved and put togyder in fewe wordes and true the empyre and the lordshyp of the Romaynes and theyr dyvers adventures longe tyme before that it was come, and soo it semed better to be a shorte remembraunce of thynges passed than of thynges of tyme to come.

"And a more greter dede she dyde, and a more mervayle, for she prophecyed and opened playnely the secretenesse of the thought of God, that was never

"Et plus grant fait dist, et plus merveillable, car elle predist et manifesta plainement le secret de la pensee[1] de Dieu, qui n'estoit point revelé par les prophetes fors par figures et paroles obscures et couvertes: c'est assavoir, du Saint Esperit, le hault mistere de l'incarnacion du filz de Dieu en la Vierge. Et en son livre avoit escript, 'Jhesus, [fol. 72r b] ceytos cenyos sother,' c'estoit[2] a dire en latin, 'Jhesucrist, Filz de Dieu, Sauveur,' la vie et les oeuvres de lui, la traison, la prise, les moqueries,[3] la mort, la resurreccion, la victoire, et l'assencion,[4] la venue du Saint Esperit aux apostres, l'advenement de Lui au jour du jugemement.

"Et tellement que elle avoir[5] dit et composé en brief les misteres de la foy crestiene et non mie avoir predit les fais a avenir. Ceste dist du jour du jugement:[6] 'A cellui tremblable jour, terre en signe de jugemement suera sang. Du ciel venra le Roy, qui jugera tout le siecle, si le verront bons et mauvais. Toute ame reprendra son corps, et chascun ara loyer selon sa dessert. Lors faudront richesses et les faulx ymages. Le feu ardra terre et mer, et toute chose perira fors les sains de Dieu amez. La n'ara riens mucié: tout sera appert, [fol. 72v a] et toute riens morra.[7] Lors ara plours et tristece, gens estreindront leurs dens par destrece. Soleil, lune, et estoilles perdront leur clarté. Mons et valees seront faictes onnies; mer, terre, et toutes choses de ça jus seront ramenees a esgalité. La trompe du ciel appellera humaine espece pour venir[8] au jugement, lors sera grant la freeur chascun plurera[9] sa folie. Adonc[10] sera fait terre neufve: roys, princes, et toutes gens seront devant le Juge, qui donnera a chascun sa desserte. Feu de souffre partira du ciel qui chierra en enfer.'

"Et ycestes choses sont contenues en .xxvii. vers que ceste [s]ibille[11] fist, pour lesquelx merites ce dit Bocace, et tous autres sages aucteurs qui d'elle ont escript le tiennent est a croire que elle fu tres amee de Dieu, et que elle soit a honnourer plus que autre femme [fol. 72v b] aprés les saintes crestienes de paradis. Ceste avec v[ir]ginité[12] que elle garda toute sa vie est a pressumer que elle estoit eslevé en

---

[1] pensee] puissance
[2] ceytos cenyos sother, c'estoit] ceytos ceny yos sother, c'est
[3] moqueries] moqueries et
[4] l'assencion] l'assompcion
[5] avoir] semble avoir
[6] jugement] jugement ces paroles
[7] Le feu ardra terre et mer, et toute chose perira fors les sains de Dieu amez. La n'ara riens mucié: tout sera appert, et toute riens morra] Le feu sera appert et toute riens vivant mourra
[8] humaine espece pour venir] l'umaine espece a venir
[9] la freeur chascun plurera] la fureur chacun plourera
[10] Adonc] Et adont
[11] [s]ibille : *fibille*
[12] v[ir]ginité : *vn ginite*

opened by the prophetes but by fygures and derke wordes and coverte; that is to knowe, the Holy Ghost, the mystery of the Incarnacyon of the Sone of God in the mayden Mary. And in her boke there was wryten *Jhesus, Ceytos, Cenyos, Sothor*, whiche was to say in Englysshe: 'Jhesu Cryst, Sone of God and Savyoure.' And there was also the lyfe and the werkes of Hym: the treason and [A3r] the takynge, and al the scornynges and His dethe; the Resurreccyon, the vyctory, and the Assencyon; the comynge of the Holy Ghost to the apostles, the comynge at the Day of Jugement.

"And the same wyse that she had sayd and compounded shortely the mys-tery of the Crysten faythe, and not onele, she tolde the dedes to come: that is to say, the Day of J[u]gement,[1] the tremblynge day the erthe shall swete blode. The Kynge shal come fro heven that shall juge all the worlde, and that bothe good and evyll shal se. Every soule shall take agayne his body, and every soule shal have praysynge after his deserte. There rychesse shall fayle, and the false ymages also. The fyre shal brenne bothe see and lande, and al thynge shal perysshe excepte the sayntes loved of God. There shall be no thynge hydde: all shall be open, and all thynges shall dye. There shal be wepynge, and sorowful people shal strayne theyr tethe for dystres. The sone, the mone, the sterres shal lose theyr clerenesse. Hylles and valays shal be made even; the see and the lande and all thynges shall be brought in egalnes. The trompe of heven shall call mankynde to come to the Jugement; then there shall be grete drede, and every man shal wepe for his folye. Then shal the erthe be made newe: kynges and prynces shal come before the Juge, whiche shall gyve every man after his deserte. Fyre of brymstone shall departe frome heven, whiche shall fall into helle.

"And all these thynges ben conteyned in .xxvii. verses that this sybylle made, for the whiche merytes as Bocace sayth, and other wyse auctoures whiche [A3v] that wryteth of her holdeth that she was ryght welbyloved with God, and that she ought to be honoured more than ony other woman after the holy sayntes of paradyse. This woman kepte her in vyrgynyte all the dayes of her lyfe, and so it is to presume that she was brought up in all clennesse. For in an herte evyll tatches

---

[1] J[u]gement : *Jngement*

toute purté, car en cuer tachié et ordoyé de vices ne puest avoir tant de lumiere[1] et cognoiscence des choses a avenir."

## *Chapitre 3*       De Sebile[2] Almethea

"Sebille Almethea fut nee comme dit est de la terre de Campaingne, qui siet vers Romme. Ceste autresi eut[3] tres especial grace d'esperit de prophecie et fut nee, si comme dient aucunes histoires, des le temps de la destruccion de Troye et vesqui jusques au temps de Tarquin l'Orgueilleux; aucuns l'appel[e]rent[4] Deiphile. Ceste dame, non obstant que elle vesquist merveilleusement grant aage, si fut elle vierge toute sa vie. Et pour la grant sapience de ceste cy aucuns poetes faingnirent que elle [fol. 73r a] fu amee de Phebus, que[5] appelloient dieu de sapience, et que par le don de cellui[6] Phebus elle acquist si grant savoir et vesqui longuement, qui est a entendre que pour sa virginité et pour elle[7] fut amee de Dieu, soleil de sapience qui l'enlumina de clarté de prophecie, par le quel elle a predit et escript plusieurs choses a avenir.

"Oultre ce est escript que elle, estant au rivage de Baioul empres le lac d'enfer, eut une noble et merveilleuse response et revelacion divine, qui est escripte et gardee en son nom, et est en vers rimez. Et tout soit la chose moult anciene, toutevoies d[on]ne[8] elle encore admiracion de la grandeur et excellence de celle femme a qui bien la considere et regarde. Aucunes fictions dient que elle mena Eneas en [fol. 73r b] enfer et la[9] ramena.

"Ceste vint a Romme et aporta .ix. livres, lesquelx presenta a vendre au roy Tarquin. Mais comme il reffusast a en donner le pris que elle en demandoit,[10] elle en ardi trois en sa presence. Et comme l'autre jour elle lui demandast des autres .vi. livres qui estoient demourez[11] ycellui mesmes pris que elle avoit demandé des .ix., et affermast que se on ne lui donnoit ce pris que elle demandoit, tantost ardoit trois d'yceulx livres, et au jour ensuivant les autres troys; le roy Tarquin lui donna le pris que elle avoit premierement demandé. Si furent ces[12] livres bien

---

[1] tant de lumiere] tant grant lumiere
[2] De Sebile] Cy dit de Sebille
[3] autresi eut] ot semblablement
[4] appel[e]rent : *appelrent*
[5] que] que ilz
[6] de cellui] d'icellui
[7] sa virginité et pour elle] sa virginité et purté elle
[8] d[on]ne : *dune*
[9] la] le
[10] en demandoit] demandoit
[11] estoient demourez] demourez estoient
[12] ces] les

or fouled with vyces it maye not be that moche lyght of knowynge of thynges to come myght have his beynge."

### *Chapter 3*      Of the Sybyll Almethea

"Almethea the sybylle was borne, as it is sayd, in the lande of Champayne whiche is nyghe Rome. This lady had also ryght especyall grace of the spyryte of prophecy. And she was borne, as some auctours say, in the tyme of the destruccyon of Troye and lyved unto the tyme of Tarquyne the Proude; and some called her Deiphyle. This lady, notwithstandynge that she lyved a mervayllous grete age, she was a vyrgyne all her lyfe. And for the grete wysdome of her, some poetes fayned that [she][1] was loved of Phebus whiche they called god of wysdome, and that by the gyfte of this Phebus she gate so moche of understandynge and lyved longe, whiche is to understande that for her maydenhode and for that she was loved of God the sone of sapyence, whiche enlumyned her with the clerenesse of prophecye by the whiche she hath sayd before and wryten many dyvers thynges to come.

"Over this it is wryten that she, beynge at the ryvage of Bayoule nyghe the lake of helle, had a noble and [A4r] a mervayllous answere and revelacyon devyne, whiche is wryten and kepte in her name, and is in ver[s]e[2] rymed. And thoughe it be ryght an auncyent thynge, it is yet a grete mervayle of the gretenesse and the excellence of this to whom it is well consydered and beholden. Some faynynges say that she ledde Eneas to helle and brought hym agayne.

"This woman came to Rome and brought with her .ix. bokes, the whiche she presented to sell to Tarquyne the kynge. But as he wolde refuse to take them of the pryce that she asked, she brente .iii. of theym in his presence. And that other day she asked for the other .vi. bokes that were lefte the same pryce as she asked for the hole .ix., and sware that yf one wolde not gyve the same pryce that she asked, anone she wolde brenne .iii. of them, and the day after; the Kynge Tarquyne gave her the same pryce that she asked fyrst. So these bokes were well

---

[1] that [she] was : *that was*

[2] ver[s]e : *vere*

gardez et fu trouvé que ilz declaroient entierement les fais qui aux Rommains estoient a avenir. Et les grans cas qui puis leur [fol. 73v a] avindrent, trouvoient[1] tous preditz es dis livres, lesquelx es tresors des empereurs furent tres singulierement gardez si comme pour conseil recouircer[2] a eulx comme a response divine.

"Or prens cy garde, doulce amie,[3] comment Dieu donna si grant grace a une seule femme que elle eut sens de conseillier et aviser non mie seulement un empereur a son vivant, mais si comme tous ceulx qui le monde durant estoient a avenir a Romme, et tous les fais de l'empire. Si me dy, je t'en pry, ou fu oncques homme qui ce feist? Et tu, comme fole, n'a guaires te tenoies[4] mal content d'estre du sexe de telx creatures, pensant que Dieux l'eust si comme en reprobacion. De ceste sebile parla en vers Virgile en son livre. Elle fina ses jours en Siche, et le tombel d'elle fu par long temps monstré." [fol. 73v b]

*Chapitre 4*   **De plusieurs dames prophetes**

"Mes[5] ne furent mie seulement ycestes dis[6] dames au monde par don[7] de Dieu prophetizantes, ains tres grant foison en a esté voire en toutes les loys qui ont esté tenues. Car se tu quiers en la loy des Juifs, asses en trouveras, si comme Delborra qui fu femme prophete ou temps des juges de Israeil, par laquel Delbora et par son sens fu delivré le peuple de Dieu de la servitude du roy de Canaan,[8] qui .xx. ans les avoit tenues[9] serfs.

"La benoite[10] Helizabeth, cousin[11] de Nostre Dame, ne fut elle pas prophete[12] quant elle dist a la benoit[13] Vierge qui l'estoit alee veoir: 'Dont vient ce que la mere de Dieu soit venue a moy?' Toutevoyes ne savoit elle pas que elle eust conceu du Saint Esperit se ce n'estoit par esperit de prophesie. [fol. 74r a] Aussi Anne, la bonne dame hebrieue qui alumoit les lampes du temple, n'ot elle esperit de prophecie[14] ainsi que ot Symeon le prophete, auquel Nostre Dame presenta

---

[1] trouvoient] trouverent
[2] recouircer] recourir
[3] amie] amie et vois
[4] n'a guaires te tenoies] te tenoies n'a gaires
[5] Mes] Mais
[6] dis] dix
[7] don] don singulier
[8] roy de Canaan] roy Canam
[9] avoit tenues] avoient tenus
[10] La benoite] Item, la benoite
[11] cousin] cousine
[12] pas prophete] prophete
[13] benoit] glorieuse
[14] prophecie. Aussi Anne, la bonne dame hebrieue qui alumoit les lampes du temple, n'ot elle esperit de prophecie] *R skips from* prophecie *to next occurrence*

ke[p]te,[1] and it was founde that they declared clerely the actes that sholde come unto the Romaynes. And the grete case that syth hath happened they founde wryten in the sayd bokes, the whiche syngulerly be kepte in the treasourye of the emperours as for to receyve counsayle of them as it were an answere devyne.

"Nowe take hede here, swete frende, howe God gave so grete grace to a wom[a]n[2] that she had wytte to counsayle and advyse not onely one emperour in his lyfe, but to all them that were to come to Rome, and all the dedes of the empyre durynge the worlde. So tell me, I thee pray, where was there ever a man that sholde do that? And thou as a fole not longe ago heldest thee evyll contente to [A4v] be of the kynde of suche creatures, thynkynge that God wolde have had it in repro[ba]cyon.[3] Of this sybylle speketh Vyrgyll in his boke all in verses. She ended her dayes and her tombe was shewed longe after."

*Chapter 4*        Of dy[v]ers[4] ladyes prophetes

"These foresayd ladyes were not onely by the gyfte of God prophetysynge to the worlde, but there hath ben grete foyson of others in al lawes that hath ben holden. For yf thou loke in the lawe of Jewes, thou shalte fynde ynowe, as Delborra, whiche was a woman prophete in the tyme of juges of Israell, by the whiche Delborra the people of God were delyvered out of the bondage of the kynge of Canaan, whiche had holden them in servytude .xx. yeres.

"The blessyd Elysabeth, cosyne to Our Lady: was not she a prophete when she sayd to the Blessyd Mayden that came to vysyte her, 'Whens cometh this that the moder of God is come to me?' Yet she knewe [not][5] that she was conceyved of the Holy Ghost but it was by the spyryte of prophecye.

"Also, my frende, the good Lady Anne, Hebrewe, that lyghted the lampes in the temple: had not she the spyryte of prophecy as Symeon had, the prophete to

---

[1] ke[p]te : *kekte*
[2] wom[a]n : *women*
[3] repro[ba]cyon : *reprocyon*
[4] dy[v]ers : *dyders*
[5] knewe [not] : *knewe*

Jhesucrist le Jour de la Chandeleur a l'autel du temple? Et le saint prophete sceut que ce estoit le Sauveur du monde, et entre ses bras le prist.[1] Mais la bonne dame Anne, qui aloit par le temple faisant son office, aussi tost que elle vid la Vierge tenant son enfant entrer ou temple, elle cogneut en esperit que c'estoit le Sauveur: si s'agenoilla et l'aoura et a haulte voix dist que c'estoit celle[2] qui estoit venu pour sauver le monde.

"Asses de femmes prophetes trouveras en la loy des Juifs, se tu y estudies[3] en celle des crestiens comme [fol. 74r b] infinies comme les sainctes.[4] Mais passons oultre cestes yci, pour ce que on pourroit dire que Dieux les eust par especial don previlegiees, et alons oultre encore parlant des payemmes.

La royne Sabba, de laquelle la Saincte Escripture mesmement fait mencion, que quant elle qui estoit de souverain entendement ouÿ parler de la sapience de Salemon, dont la renommee couroit par tout le monde, elle le desira a veoir. Et pour ce des parties[5] d'Orient du cornet de la dereniere partie du monde, se mut et laissa[6] son païs et chevaucha par la terre d'Ethiope et de Egipte, par les rivages de la Rouge Mer, et par les grans desers d'Arabe; et a tout moult noble compagnie de princes, de seigneurs, de chevaliers, et de nobles [fol. 74v a] dames a moult grant estat, et tresors de plusieurs choses precieuses, vint et ariva en la cité de Jheruselm pour veoir et viseter le sage[7] Salemon, et pour savoir se voir[8] estoit ce que on disoit de lui par tout le monde.

"Si le[9] receut Salemon a moult grant honneur, comme raison estoit. Et fut avec lui grant piece, et esprouva sa sapience en maintes choses. Plusieurs demandes et questions lui fist et maintes demandes lui proposa obscures et couvertes,[10] auxquelles il respondi selon que elle demandoit si grandement que elle dist que non pas par engin humain Salemon avoit si grant sagece, mais par especial don de Dieu. Ceste dame lui donna plusieurs choses precieuses, entre lesquelles furent plaintes[11] de petiz arbres qui rendent liqueur [fol. 74v b] et portent le basme, lesquieulx le roy Salemon fist planter empres un lac appellé Allephater,

---

[1] le prist] le prist lors qui'il dit, 'nunc dimittis'
[2] celle] cellui
[3] Asses de femmes prophetes trouveras en la loy des Juifs, se tu y estudies] Assez d'autres femmes prophetes trouveras, se tu y prens garde, en la loy des Juifs
[4] comme les sainctes] si comme les saintes plusieurs
[5] des parties] se mut des parties
[6] se mut et laissa] et laissa
[7] le sage] le sage roy
[8] savoir se voir] esprouver et veoir se voir
[9] le] la
[10] demandes lui proposa obscures et couvertes] devinailles obscures et couvertes lui proposa
[11] plaintes] plantez

whom Our Lady presented Jhesu Cryst on Candelmasse Day upon the awter of the temple? And the holy prophete knewe that it was the Savyour of the worlde, and toke hym bytwene his armes; yet the good Lady Anne whiche wente aboute in the temple doynge her offyce, anone as she sawe the Holy Vyrgyne holdynge her Sone entre into that temple, she knewe in spyryte that it was the Savyour of the worlde. [A5r] She kneled downe and worshypped Hym, and sayd with an hyghe voyce that it was He that was come to save all the worlde.

"Thou shalte fynde women prophetes ynowe in the lawe of Jewes and thou loke after them, and in the Crysten lawe as infynyte as the sayntes. But nowe passe we over these here, for that that one myght saye that God had pryvyleged them by his specyall gyfte, and let us passe over spekynge yet of paynymes.

"The quene of Saba, of whome Holy Scrypture maketh mencyon that when she that was of soverayne understandynge herde speke of the wysdome of Salamon, of whom the fame ran by al the worlde, she desyred to se hym. And for that that she came out of a corner of the Oryent, one of the last partyes of the worlde, she lefte her countre and rode by the londe of Othyope and of Egypte by the passages of the Reed See, and by the grete desertes of Arabe; and with a noble company of pryntes, lordes and knyghtes, and of many noble ladyes with grete estate, and treasoure of many precyous thynges, and aryved in the cyte of Jherusalem to se and vysyte the wyse Salamon, and to knowe yf it were true that folke sayd of hym in all the worlde.

"So Salamon receyved her with grete worshyp, as it was reason. And she was with hym a grete whyle, and proved his wysdome in many thynges. Many demaundes and questyons she made to hym whiche were ryght derke and coverte, the whiche he answered after that she asked so gretely that she sayd that he myght not have so grete wysdome by mannes wytte, but [A5v] by the specyall gyfte of God. This lady gave hym many dyvers precyous thynges, amonge the whiche there were plantes of lytell trees that yelded lycoure and bare bawme, the whiche Kynge Salamon made plante nyghe a water called Allephater, and

et commanda que la fussent coultivez et labourez soingneusement. Et pareillement lui donna le roy plusieurs joyaulx precieux.

"De la sapience de ceste dame[1] et de sa prophecie parlent aucunes escriptures
qui dient que si que elle estoit en Jherusalem, et que Salemon la menoit pour veoir
la noblece du temple que il avoit fait edifier, elle vid une longue ais plate qui estoit
couchee en travers d'un fangas et d'une boe et en faisoit on planche a[2] traverser
celle fondriere. Adonc la dame s'aresta en regardant la planche, et l'aoura et dist:
'Ceste planche qui ores est tenue en grant vilté et mise soubz les piez, sera encore
honouree[3] sur tous les fuz du monde, et aournee de [fol. 75r a] pierres precieuses
es tresors des princes. Et dessus le fust de ceste planche mourra cellui par qui
sera anientie la loy des Juifs.' Cest parole en[4] tindrent mie a truffe les Juifs, ains
l'osterent de la et l'enterrerent en lieu ou ilz cuidierent que jamais ne fust trouvee.
Mais ce que Dieux veult garder est bien sauvé:[5] car si bien ne la scevrent[6] Juifs
mucier que elle ne fust trouvee ou temps de la passion de Nostre Seigneur Jhesucrist. Et de celle planche veult on dire que fut faicte la croix sur laquelle Nostre
Sauveur souffri mort et passion, si fut lors avoirie la prophecie d'ycelle dame."

## Chapitre 5     Encore de Nicostrate, et de Cassandra, et de la royne Basine

"Ycelle Nicostrate, dont cy devant a esté parlé, autressi fut femme prophete, car
aussi tost que elle eut passé le fleuve du Tybre, et elle avec [fol. 75r b] son filz
Evander, duquel les histoires font assez mencion, fu montee [sur le mont][7] Palentin, elle prophetisa que sur ce mont seroit edefiee une cité la plus renommee
qui jamais fust au monde, et qui seroit le chief et souveraine de toute seigneuries
mondaines. Et a la fin[8] que elle fust la premiere qui pierre y asseist, elle y edifia
un fort chastel si que dit est devant, et la fu puis Romme assise et edefiee.

"*Item*, Cassandra, la noble vierge troyenne, fille Priant le roy de Troye et
suer du preux Hector, qui tant fust grant clergece que elle savoit toutes les ars,
ne fu elle autressi[9] femme prophete? Car comme celle pucelle, oncques ne voulsist prendre homme a baron tant fust grant prince, eust[10] en esperit ce qui estoit

---

[1]  dame] femme
[2]  a] au
[3]  sera encore honouree] sera tel temps vendra honoree
[4]  Cest parole en] Ceste parole ne
[5]  sauvé] gardez
[6]  scevrent] sorent
[7]  [sur le mont] : *su le*
[8]  a la fin] affin
[9]  autressi] semblablement
[10]  eust] et sceust

commaunded that they sholde be laboured and kepte wysely. And also she gave hym many precyous jewelles.

"Of the wysdome of this lady and of her prophecy speketh many dyvers scryptures that sayth that as she was in Jherusalem, and that Salamon ledde her for to se the noblesse of the temple that he had made to buylde, she sawe a longe borde that was couched attravers of a myre and made as a planke to passe over the depnesse. Then the body rested in beholdynge the planke, and worshypped it and sayd, 'This planke whiche is nowe holden in grete foulenesse and put under the feete, shall be yet worshypped above all the trees of the worlde, and garnys-shed with precyous stones and treasoure of prynces. And upon this same planke He shall dye that shall brynge the Jewes lawe to nought.' They helde this worde but for a scorne or a jape, but put hym away and hydde hym in the erthe in a place whereas they trowed that it sholde never be founde. But that that God wyll have kepte is well saved: for as well as they coude hyde it, yet it was founde at the last in the tyme of the Passyon of Our Lorde Jhesu Cryst and of this planke was the crosse on the whiche Our Savyoure suffred His Passyon, and then was the prophecye made true of this lady." [A6r]

## Chapter 5    Of Nycostrate, and of others

"This Nycostrate, of whom mencyon was made before, was also a woman proph-ete. For as sone as she had passed the flode of Tybre, and she with her sone Evander where hystoryes ynowe maketh mencyon was upon the Mounte Pal-lentyne, she prophecyed that upon that hyll sholde be buylded a cyte the most named that ever was in the worlde and sholde be the chefe and soverayne of al lordshyppes worldly. And to the conclusyon that she wolde be the fyrst that sholde laye a stone, she buylded there a stronge castell so as it is sayd before, and there is Rome buylded syth and edyfyed.

"Also Cassandra the noble mayde of Troye, doughter to Kynge Pryamus of Troye and syster to the worshypfull Hector: she was so grete a clarke that she knewe all the craftes and was also a prophete, for this mayde wolde never take man thoughe it had ben a grete prince, and she had in spyryte that that was to

avenir,[1] tousjours estoit en tristece. Et quant elle veoit[2] la grant prosperité de
Troye plus flourie[3] et estre en [fol. 75v a] magnificence, des avant que la guerre
commençast que Troyens orent puis aux Grieux, tant plus celle ploroit, crioit, et
faisoit grant duel, regardant la noblece et richece de la cité, ses beaulx freres si
renommez, le noble Hector qui tant avoit de pris; elle ne se pouoit taire du grant
mal qui leur[4] estoit a avenir.

   "Et quant elle vid la guerre encommencier, adonc enforça[5] son duel: si ne
finoit de crier et braire et timonner son pere et ses freres pour Dieu que ilz feissent paix aux Grieux, ou sans[6] faille par celle guerre seroient destruis. Mais
de toutes ces paroles faisoient conté,[7] ne point ne l'en creoient. Et toutesvoyes
comme celle qui moult plaingnoit (et a bon droit) celle grant perte et ce dommage, ne s'en pouoit taire, par quoy maintes fois en fu [fol. 75v b] batue de son pere
et de ses freres, qui disoient que fole estoit. Mais pour tant ne s'en teut mie ne
pour mourir, ne s'en souffrist de sans cesser leur dite;[8] par quoy couvint se paix
vouldrent avoir qu'en une chambre longtaine de gens l'enfermassent pour oster
sa noise de leurs oreilles. Mais mieulx leur vaulsist l'avoir creue, car ce[9] leur avint
que predit leur avoit: si l'en crurent a la fin,[10] mais ce fut trop tart pour eulx. Et
ainsi souvent avient que fole ne croit jusques qu'il prent.[11]

   "*Item*, ne fut ce pas autresi merveilleuse prenosticacion que fist la royne
Basine, qui ot esté femme du roy de Thoringe et puis fut femme a Childerich,
le quart roy de France, si que les croniques le racontent? Car dit l'ystoire que la
nuyt des nopces d'elle et du dit roy Childerich, [fol. 76r a] elle lui dist que il se
tenist celle nuyt chastement, et il verroit merveilleuse avisi[o]n.[12] Si lui dist tantost
après[13] que il se levast et alast a l'uis de la chambre et nottast ce que il verroit. Le
roy y ala, et lui sembla que il veist grans bestes que on nomme unicornes, liepars,
et lyons qui aloient et venoit par le palais. Si s'en retourna tous espoventez et
demanda a la royne que ce signifioit. Et elle lui respondi que au mattin lui[14] diroit,
et que il n'eust nulle paour ains retournast de rechief, et il si fist. Si lui sembla

----

   [1]  estoit avenir] estoit a avenir aux Troyens
   [2]  veoit] savoit
   [3]  flourie] flourir
   [4]  leur] lui
   [5]  enforça] enforcy
   [6]  ou sans] ou que sanz
   [7]  conté] compte
   [8]  ne s'en souffrist de sans cesser leur dite] ne s'en teust ne souffrist de leur dire
sanz cesser
   [9]  l'avoir creue, car ce] avoir creue car tout ce
   [10]  si l'en crurent a la fin] si s'en repentirent a la parfin
   [11]  Et ainsi souvent avient que fole ne croit jusques qu'il prent] *omitted*
   [12]  avisi[o]n : *avisin*
   [13]  tantost aprés] tantost
   [14]  lui] le lui

come. She was ever full of sorowe and hevynesse. And when she sawe the grete prosperyte of Troy so gretely flourysshed in magnyfycence before that the warre began bytwene the Troyans and the Grekes, she made moche sorowe and wepte sore, beholdynge the noblesse and rychesse of the cyte, her fayre and worshypfull bretherne, and specyally the noble Hector that was so worshypfull a man: she myght not holde her peas for the grete sorowe that was to come.

"And when she sawe the warre begyn, than began her sorowe. So she seased not to crye and wayle, and counsayled her fader [A6v] and her bretherne to make peas with the Grekes, or elles without fayle with the warre they sholde be destroyed. But they toke no charge of all her wordes, nor byleved her. And alway as she that gretely playned, and of good ryght, this grete losse and damage myght not be styll, by the whiche often tymes she was beten of her fader and of her bretherne that sayd she was a fole. But for al that, she wolde not holde her in peas to dye therfore, ne spared not to speke without seasynge; for the whiche, to make her holde her peas, they made her to be shytte in a chambre to put awaye her noyse from theyr eeres. Yet it had ben better that they had byleved her, for it happened to them as she had tolde them before. So they byleved at the ende, and then it was too late for them. And so it happeneth ofte tymes that a fole wyl never byleve a thyng tyll he have it.

"Also was it not a mervayllous pronostycacyon that the Quene Basyne made, that had ben the wyfe of the kynge of Thorynge and syth was wyfe to Chylderyke, the .iiii. kynge of Fraunce, so as the cronycles conteyneth it? For the hystory sath that the nyght of the weddynge of her and of the Kynge Chylderyke, she sayd to hym that he sholde holde hym chast that nyght, and he sholde se a mervaylous vysyon. And then she sayd to hym anone after that he sholde ryse and go to the dore of the chambre and not[e][1] well that that he sholde se. The ky[n]ge[2] wente thyder, and it semed hym that he sawe grete bestes that men call unycornes, leopardes, and lyons that wente and came by the palays. So he retourned agayne all [B1r] aferde and demaunded the quene what that sholde sygnyfye? And she answered hym that she wolde tell hym in the mornynge, and that he sholde have no drede, but to go thyder agayne. And soo he dyde, and it semed hym

---

[1] not[e] : *not*
[2] ky[n]ge : *kyuge*

que il veist grans ours et grans loups qui se voulsissent courir sus l'un a l'autre. La royne lui renvoia la tierce fois, et il lui sembla que il veist chiens et petites bestes, qui s'entre despeçoient toutes. [fol. 76r b] Et comme le roy fust moult espoventés et esmerveilliez de ceste chose, la royne lui dist que l'avision des bestes que il avoit veues signifioit diverses generacions de princes qui en France devoient regner qui de eulx descendroient, lesquelx[1] leurs meurs et leurs fais se retrairoient a la nature de diverses[2] des bestes qu'il avoit veues.

"Si pues[3] clerement veoir, belle amie, comment Nostre Seigneur a manifesté et manifeste souvent au monde se[s][4] secrez par femme."[5]

## Chapitre 6    De Anthonie, qui devint empereris

"Ce ne fut pas petit secret que Dieux revela par femme[6] a Justinien, qui puis fu empereur de Constantinoble, si que racontent les hystoires.[7] Cellui Justinien en estoit[8] garde des tresors et des coffres de l'Empereur Justin. Avint un jour que, comme [fol. 76v a] cellui Justinien se fust alez esbatre sur les champs, et avoit mené avec[9] lui pour le soulacier une femme que il amoit, laquelle avoit nom Anthoine; quant l'eure de midi fut venue, volenté de reposer vint[10] a Justinien, si se couscha soubz un arbre pour dormir et mist sa teste ou giron de s'amie. Et si comme il se fut endormis, adonc Anthoine vid venir un grant aigle voulant par dessus eulx, qui se penoit d'estendre ses elles pour garder le visage de Justinien de l'ardeur du soleil.

"Celle, qui fu sage, entendi la segnefiance. Et quant[11] il fu esveillié, elle l'araisonna par belles paroles, et lui dist: 'Beau doulz ami, je vous ay moult amé et aime, si comme vous qui estes tout maistre de mon corps, et de m'amour pouez savoir. Si n'est [fol. 76v b] mie raison que amant bien amé de s'amie lui doie riens reffuser, et pour ce vous vueil requerir en guerdon de mon pucellage et de m'amour que un don, lequel, tout soit il tres grant a moy et a vous semblera estre tres petit, vous me vueilliez ottroyer.'[12] Justinien respondi a s'amie que elle

---

[1] lesquelx] des quieulx
[2] nature de diverses] nature et diversité
[3] pues] pouez
[4] se[s] : *se*
[5] femme] femmes
[6] femme] vision de femme
[7] si que racontent les hystoires] *omitted*
[8] en estoit] estoit
[9] avec] avecques
[10] vint] prist
[11] Et quant] quant
[12] a vous semblera estre tres petit, vous me vueilliez ottroyer] semblera a vous estre tres petit me vueillez ottroyer

that he sa[w]e[1] grete beres and wolves that wolde renne one upon another. The
quene sente hym agayne the thyrde tyme, and hym semed that he sawe dogges
and lytell beestes, eche of theym dyspysynge other. And as the kynge was moche
adradde of this thynge, the quene tolde hym the advysyon of the beestes that he
had sene, whiche sygnyfyed dyvers generacyons of prynces that sholde reygne
in Fraunce that sholde come of theym, the whiche theyr condycyons and theyr
dedes sholde drawe after the nature of those beestes that he had sene. Soo thou
mayste clerely se, fayre love, howe Our Lorde hathe made open often tymes His
secretes to the worlde by women."

## Chapter 6        Here it speketh of Anthonye that became empresse

"That was noo lytell secrete that God shewed by revelacyon of a woman to
Justynyan whiche was syth emperoure of Constantynoble, as the hystoryes telleth. This Justynyan was keper of the treasours and coffers of the Emperoure
Justyne. It happened in a day that as this Justynyan was gone to dysporte hym
in the feldes and [B1v] had brought with hym to be his comforte a woman that
he loved moche, whiche was called Anthony, and when the houre of nyght was
come and that this Justynyan had luste to slepe, and layde his heed in his lover's
lappe; and when he was on slepe, then Anthony sawe a grete egle come flyenge
over them whiche payned hym to come downe to kepe the vysage of Justynyan
fro the brennynge of the sone with his wynges.

"This woman, whiche was wyse, understode the sygnyfyaunce. And when
he was awaked, she reasoned with hym by fayre wordes and sayd: 'Fayre swete
love, I have loved you moche, and love you as hym whiche is the mayster of my
body and of my love as ye knowe wel. So it is no reason that a lover wel loved
of his love ought to denye her nothynge. And for that, I wolde requyre you in
rewarde of my maydenhede and of my love but one gyfte, the whiche thoughe it
be ryght grete to me, it shal seme to you but ryght lytell, yf ye wyl graunte it me.'

---

[1] sa[w]e : *same*

requeist hardiement, et que ja ne fauldroit a chose que il ottroyer peust. Adonc dist Anthoine: 'Ains le don[1] que vous requier est que quant vous serez empereur, que vous n'aiez en despris vostre povre amie Anthoine, ains soit compaigne de vostre honneur et de vostre empire par loial mariage; et ainsi tres[2] maintenant promettre le me vueilliez.' Quant Justinien ot ainsi ouÿ parler la damoiselle, arrire s'en commença,[3] cuidant que ce eust [fol. 77r a] elle dit par truffe. Et comme cellui qui tenoit que ce fust chose impossible que avenir peust,[4] lui promist que sans faille a femme la prendroit quant il seroit empereur,[5] et ainsi lui juroit[6] par tous ses dieux. Et adonc[7] celle l'en mercia, et pour enseignes de ceste promesse se fist donner son annel, et elle lui redonna le sien. Et tantost elle lui prist[8] a dire, 'Justinien, je t'anonce certainement que tu seras empereur, et ce t'avendra en brief terme.' Et a tant, s'en[9] departirent.

"Si ne passa long temps aprés que ainsi comme l'Empereur Justin avoit assemblé son ost pour aler sur ceulx de Perse, une maladie le prist dont il morut. Et comme aprés les barons et princes fussent assemblez pour eslire nouvel empereur, et ilz ne puessent bien accorder,[10] avint [fol. 77r b] que par manire de despit l'un de l'autre, ilz eslirent Justinien pour estre empereur, lequel ne songia mie ainsi tantost tres viguoureusement a grant host couru sus aux Persans et gaingna la bataille, prist le roy de Perse, et grant honneur et avoir y conquesta.

"Et quant il fu retourné en son palaiz, Anthoine s'amie ne s'oublia pas ains fist tant que elle entra, par grant sobtiveté, la ou il se sëoit en son trosne avec ses princes. Et la, agenoillee devant lui, commença sa raison, et dist que elle estoit une pucelle qui lui estoit venue[11] demander droit et raison d'un varlet qui l'avoit fiancee, et lui avoit donné son annel et pris le sien. L'empereur, qui mais ne pensoit a elle, lui respondi que s'il l'avoit fiancee que raison estoit que il la prist et que s'elle pouoit prouver ce que [fol. 77v a] disoit que tantost lui en feroit droit et

---

[1] Ains le don] Le don

[2] tres] des

[3] arrire s'en commença] il s'en commença a rire

[4] Et comme cellui qui tenoit que ce fust chose impossible que avenir peust] comme cellui qui tenoit que impossible fust qu'il peust avenir qu'il fust empereur

[5] seroit empereur] empereur seroit

[6] juroit] jura

[7] Et adonc] Et

[8] prist] print

[9] s'en] se

[10] bien accorder] accorder

[11] estoit venue] venoit

Justynyan answered to his love that she sholde requyre hym hardely, and that she sholde fayle of nothynge that he myght graunte her. Then sayd Anthony, 'My love, the gyfte that I requyre of you is this: that when ye shal be emperour, that ye have not in dyspraysyng your poore love Anthony, but that she may accompanye her with your worshyp and with your empyre by true maryage: and so to promyse me right anone.' When Justynyan had herde the damoysell thus speke, he began to laughe, trowynge that she sayd it in jape. [B2r] And as he that helde it as a thynge impossyble to happen to hym, promysed her that without fayle he wolde take her to his wyfe when he sholde be emperoure, and so he sware by al his goddes. And then she thanked hym hertely, and in token of this promyse she gave hym her rynge, and he gave his to her. And anone she began to saye, 'I brynge thee tydynges certaynly that thou shalte be emperoure, and that it shall be in shorte tyme.' And then they departed.

"So it passed not longe tyme after that as the Emperour Justyne had assembled his hoost to go upon them of Perce, a sykenesse toke hym thrughe the whiche he dyed. And as after the prynces and barons were assembled to chose a newe emperoure and they myght not wel accorde, it happened that in maner of dyspyte of another they chose Justynyan to be emperour, the whiche slewthed not but as soone as he myght ryght vygorously with a grete hoost ranne upon these Percyens, and wanne that batayle, and toke the kynge of Perce, and conquered there grete good and worshyp.

"And when he was retourned home into his palays, Anthony his love forgate hym not but dyde that she myght to entre by grete subtylte there where he sate in his trone with his prynces. And she kneled before hym and began her reason, and sayd that she was a mayde that was come to hym to aske ryght and reason of a man that had betrouthed her, and had gyven her his rynge and taken hers. The emperoure, whiche yet thought not on her, answered her and sayd if that man had betrouthed her, reason wolde that [B2v] he toke her; and yf she myght prove that she sayd, that she sholde have ryght and that he sholde take her. And

le contraindroit a la prendre.[1] Et adonc[2] Anthoine tira l'anel de son doit et lui
tendi, disant: 'Noble empereur, je le puis prouver par cest annel: regarde se tu le
cognoistras?' Adonc vid bien l'empereur que il s'estoit pris par ses parolles; et non
pour tant, lui voult garder sa promesse, et tantost la fist mener en ses chambres et
parer de nobles parement, et la prist a femme."

## Chapitre 7     Dit Christine a Dame Droicture

"Dame, par ce que j'entens et voy manifestement le grant droit des femmes, contre ce de quoy sont tant accusees, me fait mieulx cognoistre que oncques mais
le grant tort de leurs accuseurs. Et encore ne me puis je traire[3] d'une coustume
qui cuert assez communement [fol. 77v b] entre les hommes, et mesmement entre
aucunes femmes. La commune coustume[4] est telle: que quant les femmes sont
enceintes et elles enfantent fille,[5] les maris s'en troublent; pluseurs y a et[6] mur-
murent pour ce que leur femme n'a[7] filz enfanté. Et leurs nices femmes, qui
doivent[8] avo[i]r[9] souveraine joye de ce que Dieux a sauveté les a delivrees et l'en[10]
mercier de bon cuer,[11] semblablement s'en troublent pour ce que elles voient que
leurs maris en sont troublés. Et dont vient ce, dame, que ainsi s'en marrissent?
Leur sont doncques filles de plus grant prejudice que les filz, ou se de moins
d'amour sont a leurs parens, et plus non chalantes de eulx que les masles ne sont?"

*Response*: "Amie chiere, pour ce que tu me [fol. 78r a] demandes la cause dont
ce vient, je te respons certeinement que ce vient de tres grant simplece et ignorance a ceulz qui s'en troublent, non obstant que la cause principale que les muet
est pour le coustange[12] qu'ilz ressoingnent de leur avoir que il leur couvient des
bourser et mettre hors quant elles sont en aage de marier.[13] Et aussi aucuns le font

---

[1] l'avoit fiancee que raison estoit que il la prist et que s'elle pouoit prouver ce que
disoit que tantost lui en feroit droit et le contraindroit a la prendre] se il estoit ainsi que
aucun l'eust fiancee, que raison estoit que cellui la prensist et que voulentiers lui en feroit
droit mais qu'elle le prouvast

[2] Et adonc] Adont

[3] traire] taire

[4] La commune coustume] qui

[5] fille] filles

[6] et : *et et*

[7] femme n'a] femmes n'ont

[8] doivent] deussent

[9] avo[i]r: *avorr*

[10] l'en] le

[11] cuer] cuer et

[12] coustange] coustement

[13] de leur avoir que il leur couvient des bourser et mettre hors quant elles sont en aage
de marier] de ce que marier les couvient si fault que ilz y mettent de leur avoir

then Anthony drewe the rynge from her fynger and shewed it to hym, and sayd: 'Noble emperoure, I maye prove it by this rynge: beholde it, yf thou knowe it?' Then the emperoure sawe well that he was taken by his wordes; yet not for that, he thought to kepe his promyse, and anone he made her to be ledde into his chambre to araye her in noble garmentes and toke her to wyfe."

## Chapter 7     Here Christine speketh to Ryghtwysnes

"Madame, by that that I understande and se openly, the grete ryght of women agaynst that of whiche they be so moche accused maketh me to knowe better frome henseforthe the wronge of theyr accusers. And yet I maye not holde me styll of a comune custome that renneth amonge these men, and in the same wyse amonge some women, that the comune custome is this: that when these women be with chylde and be delyvered of a mayde chylde, the husbandes ben wrothe with it often tymes and chydeth for that his wyfe was not delyvered of a sone. And theyr nyce wyves, whiche ought to have soverayne joye of that that God hath saufely delyvered them, and thanke Hym with good herte, they troubled themselfe also for that theyr housbandes ben troubled with it. And madame, frome [B3r] whens cometh that that they be wrothe? Be the doughters of more prejudyce than the sones, or be they of lesse love to theyr fader and moder, and lesse charge to them than be the sones?"

*Answere*: "Dere frende, for that that thou demaundest me the cause whens it cometh, I answere thee certaynly that that cometh of ryght grete symplenesse and ygnoraunce to them that troubleth them so. Notwithstandynge that, the pryncypal cause that moveth them therto is for the cost of theyr goodes that they must unpurse and laye out when they be in the age of maryage. And also some

pour ce que ilz redoubtent les perilz, que par mauvais conseil en simple[1] aage elles puissent estre deceues. Mais toutes ces causes au regart de raison sont nulles.

"Car quant est a la doubte que elles facent folie, il n'y a que de les sagement introduire quant elles sont petites, et que la mere leur donne bon exemple par soy mesmes [fol. 78r b] en honnesteté et doctrine; car se la mere estoit de fole vie, petit exemplaire seroit a la fille. Et que elle soit gardee de mauvaise compagnie et court tenue a enfans en joeunece est le[2] preparatoire de bonnes meurs a toute leur vie.

"*Item*, quant a la coustange, je croye que[3] les parens regardoient bien ce que les filz leur coustent[4] tant en faire aprendre science ou mestier comme en tenir estat, et mesmement en despenses superflues[5]—en foles compagnies, et en maintes nycettes—je croy que ilz ne trouveront gaires plus d'avantages es filz ne que es filles. Et le courroux et soussi qui[6] donnent plusieurs y a souventes fois a peres et a meres des brigues et noises[7] que ilz font ou de suivre vie dissolue, et tant[8] au grief et coust de leurs parens, [fol. 78v a] je croy que ce montera veu[9] au soussi qu'ilz ont de leurs filles.

"Et pour ce que tu demandes se plus treuvent d'amour es filz que es filles,[10] regardes quans filz tu trouveras qui nourrissent pere et mere en leur vieillece, douclement et humblement, si que faire doivent; je croy que clers les trouveras semez non obstant qu'il en ait esté et soit maint, mais c'est a tart.[11] Ançois quant pere et mere auroit[12] de leurs filz comme de leur dieu et ilz sont ja grans devenus, se ilz sont riches et leur pere pouvre, il[13] le despriseront et en seront tanez et honteux quant le verront.[14] Et se le pere est riche, ilz desireront sa mort pour avoir le sien.[15] Tous ne sont pas telz,[16] mais maint en y a. Et [s]'ilz[17] sont mariez, Dieux scet la grant couvoitise qu'ilz ont de tousjours traire [fol. 78v b] de pere ou de mere

---

[1]  simple] simple et jeune

[2]  a enfans en joeunece est le] et en crainte, car discipline tenue a enfans et aux jeunes leur est

[3]  que] que se

[4]  coustent] font

[5]  superflues] superflues soient de grant estat, ou moyen, ou de petit

[6]  qui] que

[7]  noises] riottes

[8]  tant] tout

[9]  croy que ce montera veu] pense que ce peut bien monter

[10]  Et pour ce . . . filles] *omitted*

[11]  je croy que clers les trouveras semez non obstant qu'il en ait esté et soit maint, mais c'est] je tiens que ilz sont cler semez, non obstant qu'il en soit et ait esté maint, mais ce avient

[12]  auroit] ont fait

[13]  se ilz sont riches et leur pere pouvre, il] *R revises text; see notes*

[14]  le verront] ilz le voient

[15]  *R adds passage here; see notes*

[16]  Tous ne sont pas telz] Je ne vueil mie dire que tous soient tieulx

[17]  [s]'ilz : *filz*

dothe it for that they doubte the perylles that they maye be deceyved by evyll counsayle in symples. But al these causes in regarde be of no reason.

"For as touchynge the doubte that they do foly, there ben but fewe but they enfourme theyr chyldren when they ben yonge and lytell and that the moder gyveth them good ensamples bytwene themselfe in honeste and techynge; for yf the moder were of a foly lyfe, it sholde be lytell ensample to the doughter. And that she be kepte from evyll company and holden shorte in tyme of youthe, it is the prerogatyve to good condycyons all her lyfe.

"*Item*, as to the cost, I trowe yf the fader and moder beholde well that that the sone cost them as to make them to lerne scyences or crafte as to holde them in estate, and also in superfluous despenses—in lewde companyes, and in many nycetees—I trowe they sholde fynde but lytel advauntage in sones more than in doughters. And the wrathe and sorowe that they [B3v] cause often tymes theyr faders and moders to have as in folowynge of dyssolute lyfe, and so moche grefe and cost to theyr faders and moders, I trowe it sholde passe the sorowe that they have for theyr doughters.

"Beholde how many sones thou shalte fynde that have nourysshed swetely and mekely theyr faders and moders in theyr age, so as they ought to do: I trowe thou shalte fynde them but thynne sowne. And thoughe the fader and moder make as moche of theyr sones as theyr goodes, when they be wexen myghty and ryche and theyr fader poore, they wyll dyspyse hym and they wyll be wrothe and shamefull when they se hym. And yf theyr fader be ryche, they wyll desyre his dethe to have his good. All be not suche, but there be many of them. And whan the sones be maryed, God knoweth the grete coveytyse that they have alway to

et[1] pou[2] leur chaudroit se ilz[3] mouroient de fain mais que ilz eussent tout.[4] Ou
se leur mere demeure vesve,[5] la ou ilz la deussent reconforter et estre le baston et
port de sa[6] vieillece, ilz lui menront noise et riote avoir le sien, et tousjours traire
d'elle; et s'elle ne leur baille assez a leur gré, ne se feront ja conscience les anemis
de lui mouvoir plait.[7] De telz filz est il assez, et de telz filles ce puet bien estre;
mais se tu bien y prens garde, je croy que plus d'enfans pervers aux peres et aux
meres[8] trouveras filz que filles.

"Et poson encore[9] que tous fussent bons, si voit on communement les filles
tenir plus grant compagnie a peres et a meres que les filz et plus les visetent, con-
fortent, et gardent en leur[10] maladies et vieillece. [fol. 79r a] La cause si est: pour ce
que les filx vont plus a val[11] le monde, et ça et la, et les filles sont plus coyes, si s'en
tiennent plus pres. Ainsi que de toy mesmes le peux veoir: car non obstant que tes
freres fussent tres naturelx et de grant amour,[12] ilz sont alez par le monde, et tu
seule es demouree pour compagnie a ta bonne mere, qui lui est souverain reconfort en sa vieillece. Et pour ce, en conclusion, te dis que trop folz sont[13] ceulx qui
se troublent[14] et marissent quant filles leur naissent. Et pour ce que sur[15] ce propos
m'as mise, dire te vueil d'aucunes femmes dont entre les autres les escriptures
parlent qui moult furent naturelles[16] a leurs parens."

---

[1] de pere ou de mere et] du pere et de la mere tant que
[2] pou : *pour*
[3] se ilz] se les las de vielles gens
[4] *R adds* Ha, quel nourriture!
[5] leur mere demeure vesve] leurs meres demeurent vesves
[6] port de sa] le port de leur
[7] ilz lui menront . . . plait] *omitted; see notes for revised text*
[8] aux peres et aux meres] *omitted*
[9] poson encore] poson
[10] leur] leurs
[11] a val] avau
[12] amour] amour et bons
[13] folz sont] sont folz
[14] troublent] courroucent
[15] sur] sus
[16] furent naturelles] sont naturelles et de grant amour

drawe from the fader and moder, and they wolde not recke thoughe they sholde dye for hongre so that they myght have al. And whereas the moder abydeth wedowe, and whereas they ought to comforte her, and to be staffe and berer up of her age, they wyll crye on her tyll they have drawne from her that that she hath. And yf she wyl not gyve them ynoughe after theyr entente, they wyl have no conscyence to move plee ayenst her. Of suche sones there be ynowe, and some doughters haply also. Yet if thou take good hede, I trowe thou shalte fynde sones more shrewysshe to the fader and moder than doughters.

"And yet I put case that all were good, it is comunely sayd the [B4r] doughters holde better company to the faders and moders than the sones, and more vysyteth, comforteth and kepeth them in theyr sykenes and ege. The cause is this: for that that the sones travaylleth more up and downe in the worlde, here and there, and the doughters be more coye and holde theym more nyghe, so as thou mayste se thyselfe. For notwithstandynge that thy bretherne were ryght naturall and of grete love, they be gone into the worlde, and thou alone arte abydynge to kepe company with thy good moder, the whiche is a soverayne comforte in her age. And for that I saye to thee, in conclusyon, that they be more foles that troubleth theym and be wroth when they have borne doughters. And for that that upon this purpose thou hast put me, I wyl tell thee of some women of whome amonge other the hystoryes wryteth, whiche were ryght kynde unto theyr fader and moder."

*Chapitre 8*     **Commence a parler de filles qui amerent pere et mere,[1] et premierement de Dripetrue** [fol. 79r b]

"De grant amour a son pere fu Dripetrue, royne de Leodocie. Celle fut fille du grant roy Mitridates, et tant l'ama que en toutes ses batailles le suivoit. Elle estoit moult laide, car elle avoit double renc dedens, qui estoit chose moult defourmé. Mais de tant grant amour estoit a son pere que oncques ne le laissa, ne en prosperité, ne en mal fortune. Et tout fut elle royne et dame de grant royaume, par quoy bien peust estre aise et a repos en son païs, elle fu par tout participant des peines et travaulx que son pere ot,[2] en mainte armee ou il fu. Et quant il fu[3] vaincu du grant Pompee, oncque elle ne le laissa ains le servoit par grant cure et diligence."

*Chapitre 9*     **De[4] Ysiphile**

"Ysiphie se mist en peril de mort pour sauver son pere, qui avoit nom [fol. 79v a] Thoant et estoit roy des Levidiniens. Et comme son païs se rebellast contre lui, et a grant fureur venist[5] au palais pour occire le roy. Ysiphile tantost le muça[6] en un de ses escrins; et puis sailli dehors pour appaisier le peuple, mais ce ne lui valu[7] riens. Et comme ilz queissent le roy par tout et ne le puissent trouver, ilz appointerent les glaives contre Ysiphile et moult la[8] menasserent de mort se elle ne leur enseignoit, et avec ce lui promettoient que se par elle pouoient savoir ou il estoit,[9] qu'a royne la couronneroient et a elle obeiroient. Mais elle, qui plus couvoitoit[10] la vie de son pere que estre royne, ne point n'estoit flechie pour paour de mort, leur respondoit de tres hardi courage et sans signe de nulle paour,[11] que [fol. 79v b] sans faille il s'en estoit fuis grant piece avoit. Et a la parfin par ce que ilz ne le porent trouver, et que elle tant asseurement leur affermoit que fuis s'en estoit, l'en creurent et la couronnerent a royne, et une piece paisiblement regna sur eulx. Et celle[12]

---

   [1] Commence a parler de filles qui amerent pere et mere] Ci commence a parler des filles qui amerent leurs parens
    [2] ot] ot eu
    [3] fu] ot esté
    [4] De] Ci dit de
    [5] venist] courussent
    [6] occire le roy. Ysiphile tantost le muça] le occire. Sa fille Ysyphyle le muça tantost
    [7] valu] valt
    [8] la] le
    [9] par elle pouoient savoir ou il estoit] se elle leur enseignoit
   [10] elle, qui plus couvoitoit] la bonne et naturelle fille, qui mieulx amoit
   [11] et sans signe de nulle paour] *omitted*
   [12] Et celle] Mais elle

*Chapter 8* **Here it begynneth to speke of doughte[r]s**[1] **that loved fader and moder, and fyrst of Drypetrue**

"Of grete love to her fader was Drypetrue, quene of Laodocye. She was doughter to the grete Kynge Mytrydaces, and she loved hym soo moche that she folowed hym in all bataylles. She was of a straunge shappe in some thynges, for she had a double rewe of tethe, whiche was a grete deformyte. But she was of so grete love to her fader that she lefte hym never, nother in prosperyte, ne in evyll fortune. [B4v] And thoughe she were a quene and lady of a grete lande, by the whiche she myght well be at rest and ease in her countre, she was in every place partycypante of all the paynes and travayles that her fader had in many dyvers armyes there as he was. And when he was overcomen of the grete Pompee, she lefte hym never but served hym by grete charge and dylygence."

*Chapter 9* **Of Isyphyle**

"Isyphyle put her in peryll of dethe to save her fader, whiche was named Thoant and was kynge of Levydynyens. And as his countre rebelled ayenst hym and with a grete woodnesse came to the palays to sle the kynge, Isyphyle anone hydde hym in one of her coffres; and after she lepte out to appease the people, but it avayled her nothynge. And as they sought the kynge all aboute and myght not fynde hym, they put the poyntes of theyr glayves ayenst Isyphyle and gretely manaced her of dethe yf she wolde not tell them of her fader. And with that, they promysed her if they myght knowe by her where he was, they wolde crowne her quene and they wolde obaye to her. But she, whiche coveyted more the lyfe of her fader then to be quene, ne was not aferde for drede of dethe, answered them with an hardy courage and without sygne of ony drede, that without fayle he was fledde a grete whyle before. And at the last, for [C1r] that they myght not fynde hym and that she so surely affermed them that he was fledde, they byleved her and crowned her quene; and a whyle she reygned peasybly upon them. And she

---

[1] doughte[r]s : *doughtes*

qui une piece de temps ot son pere gardee secretement, de paour qu'a la parfin par quelque envieux peust estre accusé, le mist hors par nuyt et l'en envoya par mer a seureté a tout grant avoir. Mais comme ceste chose fust a la perfin revelee aux desloiaux citoiens, ilz chacierent leur royne Ysiphile, et occise l'eussent se sa grant bonté gardee ne l'en eust."[1]

## *Chapitre 10* De la vierge Claudine

"Comme[2] grant signe d'amour monstra la vierge Claudine a [fol. 80r a] son pere, lors que par les biens fais de lui et par les grans victoires que il avoit eues en maintes batailles, lui, retourné victorieux, fu receu a Romme en la souveraine honneur que ilz appelloient *triomphe*, qui estoit une honneur moult grant en laquelle recevoient les princes quant ilz retournoient vainquers d'aucun grant fait. Ainsi ycellui[3] pere de Claudine, qui un des princes estoit de Romme[4] moult vaillant, estant en cellui[5] honneur de triomphe, fu assailli de fait par un autre des seigneures de Romme qui le haioit. Mais quant Claudine sa fille, qui estoit sacree a la deesse Vesta (si que nous dirions[6] religieuse d'aucune abbay) et estoit avecques les dames de son ordre qui estoient alees a la procession [fol. 80r b] a l'encontre d'ycellui prince, si que la coustume estoit, ouÿ la noise et sceut que son pere estoit assailli de ses anemis. Adonc la grant amour que la fille avoit au pere lui fist oublier tout le simple et coy maintien que vierge religieuse sceult avoir communement, et aussi lui fist mettre arriere toute crainte et toute paour en tel maniere, que tantost elle sailli jus du char ou elle avoit ses compaingnes estoit ala fuiant par la presse et hardiement se ficha entre les espees[7] que elle veoit sur son pere, et de fait ala prendre a la gorge cellui que elle vid plus pres, et de son pouoir prist fort a deffendre son pere; la fu grande la presse, qui tantost la meslee departi. Mais comme les vaillans Rommains eussent de coustume de faire moult grant [fol. 80v a] compte de toute personne qui faisoit aucun fait digne d'admiracion, priserent moult ceste vierge et lui donnerent grant louenge de ce que elle eust[8] fait."

---

[1] Ysiphile, et occise l'eussent se sa grant bonté gardee ne l'en eust] Deiphile et occise l'eussent, mais ce qu'elle estoit tant bonne mut a pitié les aucuns d'eulx

[2] Comme] O comme

[3] ycellui] cellui

[4] estoit de Romme] de Romme estoit

[5] cellui] ycel

[6] nous dirions] dirions maintenant

[7] espees] glaives et espees

[8] eust] ot

that a lytel whyle had kepte her fader secretely, for drede at the last that by some envyous persone he might be accused, put hym out by nyght, and sente hym by see to another place with grete goodes. But as this thynge was at the last opened to the untrue cytezyns, they chaced theyr Quene Isyphyle out of the royalme, and wolde have slayne her yf her grete goodnesse had not kepte her."

*Chapter 10*     Of the mayde Claudyne[1]

"As a sygne of grete love shewed the mayden Claudyne to her fader then when, by the good dedes of hym and by the grete vyctoryes that he had had in many batayles, retourned hym and vyctoryously was receyved at Rome in the soverayne worshyp that they called the *tryumphe*, whiche was a ryght grete worshyp in the whiche they receyved princes when they retourned overcomers of ony grete dedes. Soo this same fader of Claudyne, whiche was one of the prynces of Rome ryght worshypfull, beynge in this honoure of tryumphe, was assayled by another of the lordes of Rome that hated hym. But when Claudyne his doughter, whiche was sacred to the goddes [V]esta[2] [C1v] (as we say here, a relygyous of some abbay) and was with the ladyes of her ordre, that were gone to the processyon agaynst this foresayd prynce so as the custome was, herde the noyse and knewe that her fader was assayled of his enemyes. Then the grete love that the doughter had to the fader made her forgete al the symple behavynge that a relygyous woman sholde have comonly, also she put backe all drede and fere in suche manere that anone she lepte forthe and wente flyenge thrughe the prece, and boldely wente amonge the swerdes that she sawe upon her fader, and toke hym by the throte that she sawe nexte hym, and to her power toke strongly upon her to defende her fader; there the prece was so grete that anone the medlynge was departed. Then, as the worshypfull Romaynes had of custome to set moche by every parsone that dyde ony worshypful acte of mervayle, praysed gretely this mayden and gave her grete laude of that she had done."

---

[1]  C[l]audyne : *Caudyne*
[2]  [V]esta : *Besta*

### *Chapitre 11*      D'une[1] femme qui alaitoit sa mere en la prison

"Grant amour semblablement ot a sa mere une femme [de] Romme,[2] dont les hystoires parlent. Il avint que la dicte mere, pour certain crisme dont elle fu attaincte,
fu condempnee a prison perpetuelle et que on ne lui donneroit qu'eue ne que
menger, par quoy en telle maniere finast sa vie.[3] Sa fille, contraincte de grant
amour filiale, dolente de ceste condempnacion, requist de grace especiale a ceulx
qui la prison gardoient que sa mere peust par chascun jour viseter tant comme elle
seroit en vie a celle fin que amonnester de pacience la [fol. 80v b] peust. Et a brief
dire, tant esploicta[4] et tant en pria que les gardes des prisons en orent pitié, et lui
ottroierent que tous les jours visetast[5] sa mere, mais ançois que devers elle la meis-
sent moult bien la cerchoient que elle ne lui portast aucune chose a vivre.

"Et comme ceste visitacion eust ja duré par tant de jours que impossible
sembla aux joliers que la femme prisonnier peust naturelment tant vivre sans
mengier,[6] et toutevoies n'estoit pas mort et considéré que autre ne la visitoit que
sa fille, laquelle tres diligement[7] cerchoient ains que devers sa mere enstrast,
s'esmerveillierent[8] moult forment que ce pouoit estre. Et de fait un jour espierent
la mere et la fille ensemble, et adonc virent que la lasse fille, qui assez [fol. 81r a] de
nouvel avoit eu enfant, donnoit a tete[9] a sa mere tant que tout lui avoit la mere tiré
le lait de ses mamelles. Et ainsi rendoit la fille a sa mere en sa vieillece ce que elle
avoit pris d'elle en son enfance. Ceste diligence continuele[10] et ceste grant amour
de fille a mere mut a grant pitié les joliers, et le fait raporté aux juges; meus de
humaine compassion, delivrerent la mere et renderent a sa fille.

"Encore a propos d'amour de fille a pere peut on dire de la tres bonne et sage
Grisilidis qui puis fut marquise de Saluce, de laquelle te raconteray[11] cy aprés la
grant vertu, fermetté, et constance. O, comme[12] grant amour par loiale nature en
elle avivee lui faisoit tant estre[13] soingneuse de servir si humblement [fol. 81r b] et
tant obeissemment son povre pere Janicole, malade et vieil, que elle en sa purté et

---

   [1] D'une] Ci dit d'une
   [2] femme [de] Romme : *femme Romme*
   [3] a prison perpetuelle et que on ne lui donneroit qu'eue ne que menger, par quoy en
telle maniere finast sa vie] fu condampnee a mourir en prison et que on ne lui donnast
que boire ne que menger
   [4] esploicta] en ploura
   [5] visetast] peust visiter
   [6] mengier] mourir
   [7] tres diligement] songneusement
   [8] s'esmerveillierent] se merveillerent
   [9] a tete] la tette
   [10] diligence continuele] continuelle diligence
   [11] raconteray] racompteray
   [12] comme] comment
   [13] tant estre] estre tant

*Chapter 11*     Here it speketh of a woman that gave her moder sowke in the pryson

"Grete love also had a woman of Rome to her moder, of whome the hystoryes speketh. It happened that the sayd moder for a certayne cryme that she was attaynted of was condempned to perpetuall pryson, and that none sholde gyve her neyther mete nor drynke, by the whiche in this maner she sholde fynysshe her lyfe. The doughter, constrayned [C2r] of grete love, beynge sory for this condempnacyon, requyred them that kepte the pryson of a specyal grace that she myght vysyte her moder every daye whyle she was on lyve, to that entente that she myght counsayle her of pacyence. And shortely to saye, so moche she employed and prayed that the kepers of the pryson had pyte on her and graunted her that she sholde vysyte her moder every daye but or she sholde go to her, that she bare with her no vytayle.

"And when this vysytacyon had endured by so many dayes that it was impossyble to the jayloures that the woman prysoner myght lyve so longe naturally without mete, and yet was not dede, and consydered that none other vysyted her but her doughter whiche they serched ryght dylygently or she sholde go in to her moder, they mervaylled ryght strongely what that myght be. And on a day they spyed the moder and the doughter togyder, the whiche was lately delyvered of a chylde. And then they sawe her gyve the tete to her moder, so moche tyl she had al, and thus the moder drewe mylke of the pappes of her doughter. And thus the doughter yelded to the moder in her age that that she had taken of her in her youthe. This contynuell dylygence and grete love of the doughter to the moder moved the jaylours to grete pyte, and they reported it to the juges; then, of manly compassyon they delyvered the moder to the doughter.

"Also to the purpose of love of the doughter to the fader, one may say of the good and wyse Grysylde whiche syth was marquyse of Saluce, [C2v] of whome I shall telle hereafter the grete vertue, stablenesse, and constaunce. O, howe true love hath Nature gyven unto her to be so busy to serve her fader Janycle, so humbly

virginité et en fleur de joeunece nourrisoit et gouvernoit tant diligentment par le labour et mestier de ses mains, gaingnant[1] a grant cure et sollisitude la povre vie de eux deux. O, tant sont de bonne heure nees filles de telle bonté et de si grant amour a peres et a meres! Car non obstant que elles facent ce que elles doivent, toutevoies y acquierent grant merite a l'ame, et grant los au monde leur en doit estre donné, et semblablement au filz.

"Que veulx tu que je t'en die plus? Sans cesser exemples te pourroie dire de cas semblables, mais a tant te souffise." [fol. 81v a]

## *Chapitre 12*  Ci dit Droicture que elle achieve la[2] maisonnage de la cité, et qu'il est temps que peuplee soit

"Des or me semble, tres chiere[3] amie, que bien est avancié nostre edifice, et la Cité des Dames, hault maisonnee tout au long de ces larges rues, et les palais royaulx fort edifiez, et ces dongions et tours deffensables haulz levez et droiz si que ja de loings[4] les puet on veoir. Si est bien temps de cy[5] en avant que a peuplier commencions ceste noble cité, afin que elle ne soit vague ne vuide, ains habitee toute de dames de grant excellence, car autre gent ne[6] voulons.

"O, tant seront eureuses les citoienes de nostre edefice car n'aront besoing d'avoir crainte ne doubte d'estre deslogees de leur possession par estranges ostes, car tel est la proprieté de nostre ouvrage que estre deboutees n'en pourront [fol. 81v b] les possidentes.[7] Et or est un nouvel royaume de Femmenie encommencié, mais trop plus est digne que cellui de jadis car ne couvendra aux dames yci hebergees aler hors de leur terre pour concepvoir ne enfanter nouvelles heritieres pour maintenir leur possession par divers aages, de ligne en ligne, car assez souffira pour tousjours mais de celles que ores y mettrons. Car telle en est la destinee: que jamais ne mourront, et sans cesser demoureront ou mesmes aage, beaulté, et frescheur, soient joeunes ou vieilles, que nous les y mettrons.[8]

"Et quant nous l'arons peuplee de nobles citoienes, venra aprés Dame Justice, ma serour, qui y amenra[9] la royne sur [fol. 82r a] toutes excellente, acompagnie[10]

---

[1] gaingnant] gaignoit
[2] achieve la] a achevé le
[3] tres chiere] chere
[4] si que ja de loings] que de loings ja
[5] temps de cy] des or
[6] autre gent ne] autres gens n'y
[7] nostre ouvrage que estre deboutees n'en pourront les possidentes] ouvrage que les possessarresses n'en pourront estre deboutees
[8] Car telle . . . mettrons] *omitted*
[9] y amenra] amenra
[10] acompagnie] accompaignee

and obeysauntely, in his sykenesse and in his age, that she in her clennesse and vyrgynyte and in the floure of her youthe nourysshed and governed so dylygentely by the laboure and the crafte of her handes, getynge with grete charge and busynesse the poore lyfe of theym bothe! O, in a good houre were those doughters borne of suche bounte, and so grete love to theyr fader and moder! For notwithstandynge that that they do that they ought to do, yet they gete grete meryte to the soule, and grete praysynge is gyven them of the worlde and in the same wyse to the sones that ben of that condycyon.

"What woldest thou that I sholde say more? I coude tell thee ensamples ynowe of lyke case, but ynoughe suffyseth."

## Chapter 12     Here Ryghtwysnesse sayth that she hathe accheved the stone werke of the cyte, and it is tyme to people it

"Nowe me semeth, ryght dere frende, that our buyldynge is well lyfte up of our Cyte of Ladyes, and the hyghe masonry al alonge the large stretes and the royall palayces, stronge buyldynges of dongeons and defensable towres, lyfted ryght hyghe that it maye be sene afarre. Soo it is tyme [C3r] fro hensforthe that we begynne to people this noble cyte to the entente that she be not waste nor voyde, but enhabyted of ladyes of grete excellence; for we wyll none other people.

"O, howe fortunate shall the cytezynes of our cyte be, for they shall have no nede to have drede nor doubte to be dyslodged of theyr possessyon by straungers, for this is the propryete of our werke, that the owners shall not nede to be put out. And nowe there is a newe femenyne royalme bygon, but it is moche more worthyer than that other was for it shall [not] nede[1] that the ladyes lodged here goo out of theyr lande for to conceyve, ne brynge forthe newe heyres to maynteyne theyr possessyon by dyvers ages fro lygne to lygne, for it shall suffyse ynoughe forever of them that we shall put in it nowe. For this is the destyne of them: that they shall never dye, and without fayle they shall abyde in the same age, beaute, and fresshnesse, be they yonge or olde, that we shall put therin.

"And when we have peopled it with noble cytezynes Dame Justy[c]e,[2] my syster, shall come after that shall brynge thyder the Quene above all other women

---

[1] shall [not] nede : *shall nede*
[2] Justy[c]e : *Justyne*

de princeces de tres grant digneté, lesquelles habiteront es plus haultes places et es souverains dongions. Si est bien raison que quant la Royne y venra, que elle treuve[1] sa cité garnie et peuplee de nobles dames, qui a honneur la reçoivent comme leur souveraine Dame Empereris de tout leur sexe. Mais quelz citoiennes y mettrons nous? Seront ce femmes dissolues, ou diffammees? Certes non, ains seront toutes preudefemmes de grant auctorité,[2] car plus bel peuple ne plus grant parement ne puet estre en cité que bonnes preudefemmes. Or sus, chiere amie, or te met en besoingne et passe avant si les alons querre."

## Chapitre 13    Demande Christine a Dame Droicture se c'est voir ce que les livres et les hommes [fol. 82r b] dient, que la vie de mariage soit si dure a porter pour l'occasion des femmes et aler[3] grant tort; et y respont Droicture, et commence a parler de la grant amour de femmes a leurs maris

Adonc en alant querre les dictes dames par l'ordenance de Dame Droicture, disoie en alant cestes paroles: "Dame, sans faille[4] vous et Raison m'avez soluez et concluses si bien et si bel[5] toutes mes questions et demandes que repliquer plus ne[6] saroie, et me tiens pour tres bien infourrmee de ce que je queroie. Et assez par vous deux ay apris comment toutes choses faisables et scibles, tant en forces[7] de corps comme en sapience d'entendement, et de toutes vertus sont possibles et aisees a estre excecutees [fol. 82v a] par femmes. Mais encore vous prie que dire me vueilliez et certifier se c'est vraye chose ce que ces hommes dient, et tant de aucteurs le tesmoingnent, dont je suis en trop grant pensee: que la vie de l'ordre de mariage soit aux hommes pleine et avironnee de si grant tempeste par la coulpe et impetuosité des femmes et de leur rancuneuse moleste, comme il est escript en mains livres, et assez de gens le tesmoingnent? Et que[8] elles si pou aiment leurs maris et leur compaignie que riens tant ne leur anuye? Par quoy pour obvier a[9] ces inconveniens plusieurs ont conseillié aux sages que ilz ne se marient, certifians que pou[10] d'elles soient loialles a leur partie.

---

[1] treuve] treuve ja
[2] de grant auctorité] de grant beauté et de grant auctorité
[3] aler] a leur
[4] sans faille] vrayment
[5] si bien et si bel] *omitted*
[6] ne] n'y
[7] forces] force
[8] Et que] que
[9] obvier a] obvier et eschever
[10] pou] nulles ou pou

moost excellent, accompanyed with pryncesses of grete dygnyte, whiche shall enhabyte the moost hyghe places and hyghe dongeons. For it is good reason that when the Quene shal come thyder, that she fynde the cyte garnysshed and peopled of noble ladyes that sholde receyve her with grete worshyp as theyr soverayne lady and empresse of all theyr kynde. Yet what cytezyns shall we put there? Shall they be unstable [C3v] women, or defamed? Certaynly nay, but they shal be al worshypfull women and of grete auctoryte, for more fayre people ne more grete aray may not be in a cyte than good women and worshypfull. Nowe ryse, leefe frende: nowe put thee in busynes, and go before and lette us seke them."

*Chapter 13*   **Here Christine asketh of Dame Ryghtwysnesse yf that be true that these bokes and these men sayth, that the lyfe of maryage is harde to bere for the occasyon of women and to theyr grete wronge; and Ryghtwysnesse answereth, and begynneth to speke of the grete love of women to theyr husbandes**

Then in goynge to seke the foresayd ladyes by the ordynaunce of Dame Ryghtwysnesse, in goynge I sayd these wordes: "Madame, without fayle ye and Reason have assoyled and concluded soo wel and so fayre my questyons and dema[u]ndes[1] that I cannot replye no more, and I holde me ryght well enfourmed of that that I sought. And by you two I have lerned ynoughe howe al thynges able ought to be done and lerned, as moche in strengthe of bodyes as in wysdome of understandynge, and yf al vertues be possyble to be executed by women. But yet I pray you that ye wolde telle and certyfye me yf it be true that these men say and so many auctours bereth wytnesse, thrughe the whiche I am in ryght a grete thought: that the lyfe [C4r] of the ordre of maryage be to men hevy, and envyronned of so grete tempest by the blame and importunyte of women and of theyr ravenous grefe, as it is wryten in many bokes and people ynowe wytnesseth it. And that they love theyr husbandes and theyr company so lytell that nothynge noyeth them so moche, by the whiche to voyde suche inconvenyences many have counsayled the wyse men that they mary not, certefyenge that fewe of them be true in theyr partye.

---

[1] dema[u]ndes : *demanndes*

"Et mesmement Valere a [fol. 82v b] Rufin en escript, et Theofrastus en son livre dit que nul sage ne doit prendre femme, car trop a en femme de cures, pou d'amour, et moult de[1] gengleries. Et que se l'omme le fait pour estre mieux servi et gardé en ses maladies, que trop mieulx et plus loyaument le servira et gardera un loyal serviteur, et ne lui coustera pas tant; et que se la femme est malade, le mari est alangouré et ne s'osera bougier d'empres elle. Et assez de telz choses dit, qui trop longues a reciter seroient.[2] Donc je die, chiere dame, que se cestes choses sont vraies, tant sont ces deffaux vaillans que toutes autres graces et vertus que avoir porroient en sont anienties et du tout[3] estaintes." [fol. 83r a]

*Response*: "Certes, amie, si que toy mesmes autre fois as[4] dit a ce propos, bien a son aise menie par ces qui plaide sans partie;[5] et te promet que les livres qui ce dient, ne firent pas les femmes. Mais je croy[6] que qui des debas de mariage vouldroit faire veritable nouvel livre et que on se infourmast de la pure verité du fait,[7] on trouveroit autres nouvelles. Helas,[8] chiere amie, quantes [f]emmes[9] est il, et tu mesmes le sces, qui usent leur lasse vie en[10] lian de mariage, par durté de leurs maris, en plus grant penitence que se elles fussent esclaves entre les Sarrazins? Ha, Dieux,[11] quantes dures bateures sans cause et sans raison? Quantes laidenges, quantes villenies, injures, servitudes, et oultrages y [fol. 83r b] sueffrent maintes bonnes preudefemmes, qui toutes ne[12] crient pas harou? Et de telles qui muerent de fain et de meseise a tout plein foier d'enfans, et leurs maris sont en la taverne ou en lieux dissolus;[13] et encore les pouvres femmes seront batues au retourner, et ce sera leur soupper.[14]

---

[1] moult de] foison

[2] a reciter seroient] seroient a reciter

[3] et du tout] et

[4] autre fois as] as autre fois

[5] bien a son aise menie par ces qui plaide sans partie] qui meine proces sanz partie bien a son aise plaide

[6] ne firent pas les femmes. Mais je croy] les femmes ne les firent mie mais je ne doubte pas

[7] veritable nouvel livre et que on se infourmast de la pure verité du fait] informacion pour en faire nouvel livre selon le vray

[8] Helas] Ha

[9] [f]emmes : *semmes*

[10] vie en] de vie ou

[11] Ha, Dieux] Dieux

[12] ne] n'en

[13] en la taverne ou en lieux dissolus] en lieux dissolus ou mainent les gales par la ville ou es tavernes

[14] soupper] soupper. Qu'en dis tu? Mens je en veis tu oncques nulle de tes voisines ainsi atournees?" Et je a elle: "Certes, dame, si ay fait mainte dont grant pitié avoie." "Je t'en croy [. . .]"

"And also Walere wryteth to Ruphyn, and Theophrastus in his boke sayth that noo wyse man ought to take a wyfe for there is but lytell love in a woman, but grete charge and janglynge. And yf the man do it to be the better served and kepte in his sykenes, more better and more truely a true servaunt shall kepe hym and serve hym, and shal not cost hym so moche; and yf the woman be syke, the husbande is in grete sorowe and dare not speke one worde nyghe her. And ynoughe of suche thynges he telleth whiche sholde be too longe to reherce. Wherfore I say, myne owne lady, that yf these thynges be true, these defaultes be so grete that all the grace and vertues that they may have be brought to nought and quenched."

*Answere*: "Certes, dere frende, so as thou thyselfe hath sayd somtyme to the purpose, that one may lede a processe well at his ease that pledeth without partye; and I promyse thee that the bokes that so sayth, women made them not. But I trowe that he that wolde make a newe booke that were true of the debates of maryage and that he were enfourmed of the trouthe, one sholde fynde other tydynges. [C4v] Alas, dere frende, howe many women be there, as thou knowest thyselfe, that useth theyr wery lyfe in the bande of maryage, by the hardnesse of theyr husbandes in more greter penaunce than they were esclaves amonge the Sarazynes? Ha, God, howe many harde betynges without cause and reason—howe many vylanous wronges and outragyous bondages suffreth many of these good and worshypfull women, whiche all crye not out an harowe? And suche that dye for hungre and for mysease, and theyr husbandes ben at the taverne and in other dyssolute places; and yet the poore women shall be beten at theyr comynge home—and that shal be theyr souper.

"Et a dire que les maris soient tant adoulez pour les maladies de leurs femmes: je te prie, m'amie, ou sont ilz? Et sans[1] que je plus t'en die, tu peux bien savoir que ces babuiseries dictes contre les femmes, qui que le die,[2] furent et sont choses trouvés dictes a volenté et contre verité. Car les maris sont maistres sur les femmes, et non mie les femmes leurs maistresses, si ne souffriroient jamais a leurs femmes[3] tel autorité.

"Mais je te promet [fol. 83v a] que tous les mariages ne sont mie maintenus en telz content, et domage seroit,[4] car il en est qui vivent en grant paisibleté, amour, et loiaulté ensemble par ce que les parties sont bonnes, et discretes, et raisonnables; ne[5] quoy qu'il soit des mauvais mariz, il en est de tres bons, vaillans, et sages, et que les femmes que[6] les encontrerent nasquirent quant a la gloire du monde de bonne heure pour elles.[7] Et ce pueux tu bien savoir par toy mesmes qui tel l'avoies qu'a[8] ton jugment nul autre homme de toute bonté, paisibleté, loiaulté, et bonne amour ne le passoit, duquel les regraiz de ce que mort le te tolli jamais de ton cuer ne partiroit. Et quoy que je te die, et il est voir que il soit moult de bonnes femmes moult mal menees par leurs divers [fol. 83v b] mariz, saches pour tant qu'il en est de moult diverses males, cruelz, perverseurs,[9] et sans raison—car se je disoie que toutes fussent bonnes, assez de legier porroie[10] estre prouvee menterresse—mais en[11] la mendre partie; et de celles qui sont telles[12] je ne me mesle, car telles femmes sont comme chose hors de sa nature.

"Mais a dire des bonnes, pour ce que cellui Theoffrastus dont tu as parlé dit que aussi loyaulment et autant[13] soingneusement sera un homme gardé en sa maladie ou essoine par son servant que par sa femme: ha, quantes bonnes femmes sont autant soingneuses de leurs mariz servir sains et malades, par loial amour, que se[14] fussent leurs dieux? Je croy que on ne trouveroit point de tel serviteur.

---

[1] Et sans] Sans

[2] babuiseries dictes contre les femmes, qui que le die] babuises dites et escriptes contre les femmes

[3] les maris sont maistres sur les femmes, et non mie les femmes leurs maistresses, si ne souffriroient jamais a leurs femmes] les hommes sont maistres sur leur femmes et non mie les femmes sur leur maris maistresses, si ne leur souffreroient jamais

[4] et domage seroit] *omitted*

[5] bonnes, et discretes, et raisonnables; ne] bonnes, discretes, et raisonnables; et

[6] que] qui

[7] quant a la gloire du monde de bonne heure pour elles] de bonne heure quant a la gloire du monde de ce que Dieux les y adreça. Et ce

[8] qu'a] qu'a fin souhaid ne sceusses mieulx demander et qui a

[9] males, cruelz, perverseurs] *omitted*

[10] assez de legier porroie] pourroie assez de leger

[11] en] c'est en

[12] qui sont telles] qui teles sont

[13] et autant] autant

[14] se] ce

"And to say that these husbandes ben ony thynge sorowful for the sykenesse of theyr wyves: I praye thee, my love, where be they? And without that that I say more to thee, thou mayst knowe well that these sclaundres sayd agaynst women, whoso saythe it, they were and be thynges founde and sayd of vyolence and ayenste trouthe. For the husbandes ben maysters over the women, and not the women theyr maystresses; so they wolde never suffre suche auctorite of theyr wyves.

"But I promyse thee that all maryages be not maynteyned in suche contentes. It were grete damage, for there ben some that lyveth in peasyblenesse, love, and trouthe togyder by that that the partyes be good and dyscrete and reasonable; thoughe it be not of evyll husbandes, there ben ryght good, worshypfull, and wyse, and that the women that meteth with them lyveth as to the glory of the worlde [C5r] in ryght a good houre for them. And that thou mayst well knowe by thyselfe that and thou haddest suche one that in thy jugement none other man passed hym in al bounte, peasyblenes, trouthe, and good love, of the whiche the sorowes of that that dethe toke hym away from thee shall never parte from thyne herte. And thoughe that I say to thee and it is trouthe that there ben many good women ryght evyll ledde by theyr dyvers housbandes, knowe it for trouthe that there be many dyvers women shrewde, cruell, and cursed and without reason (for yf I sholde say that all were good, lyghtly I myght be proved a lyer) but in the lesse partye; and of that partye whiche be [not] good¹ I medle me not, for suche evyll women ben as thynges out of theyr nature.

"But for to speke of those that ben good, for that that this Theofrastus of whome thou hast spoken sayth that also truely and as busely shall a man be kepte in his sykenesse or in his nede by his servaunt as by his wyfe—A! howe many good women ben there so busy to serve theyr husbondes, hole or syke, by true love as and they were theyr goddes? I trowe that one shal not fynde but fewe

---

¹ be [not] good : *be good*

Et pour ce [fol. 84r a] que entrees[1] sommes en ceste matiere, je t'en donray mains exemple[2] de grant amour et loiauté de femmes portee a leurs maris. Et or sommes Dieux mercis retournees a nostre cité a tout belle compagnie de nobles preudefemmes que nous y hebergerons. Et voy cy ceste noble royne Hipsitrate, femme jadis du riche roy Mitridates: pour ce que moult est d'ancien temps, et sa valeur de grant digneté, premiere y hebergerons ou noble[3] palais qui lui est apresté."

*Chapitre 14*    [Dit de la royne Ypsitrate][4]

"Comment pourroit estre nulle creature de plus grant amour a aultre que fut la tres belle, bon[n]e,[5] loyale Hypsitrare a son mary? Et bien lui monstra. Ceste fu femme du grant roy Mitridates qui seigneurisoit les contres de .xxiiii. [fol. 84r b] languages. Et ja soit que cestui roy fust sur tous poissant, les Rommains lui menerent moult dure guerre. Mais en tout le temps que il vaca longuement et par grans cures es bata[i]lles,[6] ou que il alast oncques sa bonne femme ne le laissa. Et combien que cestui roy selon la maniere barbarine eust plusieurs concubines, toutevoies ceste noble dame fu tousjours en parfaicte amour embrasee en tel maniere que nulle part ne souffrist que il alast sans elle, ou souvent estoit avec[7] lui es grans batailles en peril de perdre son royaume en aventure de mort contre les Rommains, mais alast en region estrange ou en longtain païs passoit la mer ou desers et forefs[8] perilleux, oncquezs n'ala en lieu que elle [fol. 84v a] ne fust tousjours sa tres loiale compagne sans point departir. Car elle l'amoit de si parfaicte amour que elle pensoit que nul homme ne pourroit si nettement[9] ne si bien servir son seigneur comme elle feroit. Et contre ce que le philosophe Theofrastus dit touchant ceste matiere, ceste dame, pour ce que elle savoit que souventes fois roys et princes ont de[10] faulx serviteurs, dont s'ensuit faulx service, elle comme loiale amente a celle fin que a son seigneur les choses neccessaires et couvenables[11] peust tousjours administrer: ja soit ce que elle y souffrist grant peine, le voult tousjours suivir.

---

[1] que entrees] qu'entree
[2] exemple] exemples
[3] noble] lieu et noble
[4] [Ypistrate] : omitted
[5] bon[n]e : *bone*
[6] bata[i]lles : *batalles*
[7] avec] avecques
[8] passoit la mer ou desers et forefs] passast la mer ou desers
[9] si nettement] si nettement, si loyaument
[10] de: *des*] de
[11] neccessaires et couvenables] couvenables et neccessaires

suche servauntes. And for that that we be entred into this matter, I shal gyve thee many ensamples of grete love and trouthe of women borne to theyr housbandes. And nowe we be, thanked be God, retourned to our cyte with a noble company of worshypfull women that we shall lodge there. And se here this noble lady and Quene Hypsytrace, wyfe sometyme of the ryche Kynge Mytrydaces. [C5v] For that that she is of olde tyme, and her valure of grete dygnyte, we shall lodge her fyrst in the noble palays that is arayed for her."

## *Chapter 14*    Here it speketh of the Quene Hypsytrace

"Howe myght there be ony creature of gretter love to another than was the ryght fayre, good, and true Hypsytrace to her husbande? And it shewed wel. She was wyfe of the grete Kynge Mytrydaces, whiche governed the countres of .xxiiii. languages. And thoughe it so were that this kynge was myghty and puyssaunt, the Romaynes moved ryght harde warre agaynst hym. But in all the tyme that he laboured by grete charges in the batáylles, where that ever he wente his good wyfe lefte hym not. And thoughe that this kynge after the maner of barbaryne had dyvers concubynes, neverthelesse this noble lady was alway embraced in parfyte love in suche maner that in no wyse she suffred not that he sholde go without her, where she was ofte tymes in batáylles with hym in peryl to lose his royalme and in adventure of his lyfe ayenst the Romaynes. But when he sholde go into a straunge regyon or into a ferre countre, or passe the see, or destres and peryllous forestes, he wente never but she was alway his ryght true felawe without departynge. [C6r] For she loved hym of so parfyte love that she thought that no man sholde serve her lorde so clenly, ne so well as she sholde. And agaynst that that the phylosophre Theofrastus sayth touchynge this matter, this lady for that that she knewe that often tymes kynges and prynces have false servauntes, wherof foloweth false servyce, she as a true lover to that entente that she myght mynystre al necessaryes and convenable thynges to her lorde: thoughe it so be that she suffred grete payne, she wolde alway folowe hym.

"Et pour tant qu'a tel fait l'abit de femme n'estoit pas couvenable ne expedient que un[e][1] femme au costé d'un si grant roy et [fol. 84v b] si noble combatant en bataille, fust veue[2] afin que homme semblast estre, couppa ses cheveux blons[3] comme or qui au parement des femmes est chose moult avenant.[4] Mais avec ce n'espargna pas[5] la belle frecheur de son visage, ains prist le heaume, sobz lequel fu souvent soillee, pleine de sueur et de poudre. Et son beau corps et souëf vesti d'armes et de haubergion chaucee de fer; et les aneaulx precieux et les riches aournemens ostez, et en lieu de eulx tenir es mains haches,[6] dures lances, ars, et saiettes, ceindre espee en lieu de riches conroies. Et en telle maniere se gouvernoit celle noble royne[7] par force de grant et loiale amour que la tendreté de son beau corps joeune, delié,[8] et souëf nourry, estoit convertie [fol. 85r a] si comme en un tres fort et vigoureux chevalier armé.

"O, ce dit Bocace, qui ceste histoire raconte, que est ce que amours ne face faire, quant celle qui avoit acoustumé a vivre tant dilicativement, couchier souëf et toutes choses avoir a son aise, et maintenant demenee par sa france voulenté comme se fust homme dur et fort, par montaingnes et par valees, nuit et jour, gesant es desers et es forests, souventes fois sus[9] la terre, en paour des anemis, avironnee de toutes pars de bestes et de serpens? Mais tout ce lui estoit doulz pour tousjours estre coste son mary, pour le conforter, conseiller, et servir en tous[10] ses affaires.

"Et encore aprés, quant elle eut par longue espace endurer[11] souffert [fol. 85r b] maint durs[12] travaulx, avint que son mary fu desconfit moult crueusement par Pompee, prince de l'oste des Rommains, si que il fu contraint de fuir. Mais comme il fust de tous les siens delaissié et demourast seul, ne le delaissa pas sa bonne femme, ains courant aprés par montaignes et valees, par forestz et lieux obscures, le suivoit ades.[13] Et lui, qui de tous ses amis estoit relenqui,[14] ne plus n'avoit esperance, estoit reconforté par sa bonne femme, qui doulcement

---

[1] un[e] : *un*
[2] en bataille, fust veue] fust veue en bataille
[3] blons] loncs et blons
[4] avena[n]t : *avenat*
[5] pas] mie
[6] es mains haches] haches es mains, et
[7] royne] dame
[8] joeune, delié] jeune et delié
[9] sus] sur
[10] tous] toutes
[11] espace endurer] enduree
[12] durs] dur
[13] valees, par forestz et lieux obscures le suivoit ades] par valees et lieux obscurs et sauvages ades le suivoit
[14] relenqui] delaissié et relenqui

"And for so moche that to suche a dede the habyte of a woman is not convenable, nor it is not expedyent that a woman so nyghe a grete kynge and soo noble a fyghter in batayle sholde be sene, to that entente that a man sholde seme, [made]¹ to smyte off her yelowe heres as golde whiche to the apparellynge of a woman is a thynge ryght well semynge. But with that she spared not the fayre fresshnesse of her vysage but ware her helme, under the whiche she was ofte tymes soylled, and full of swetynge and duste. And her fayre body and softe used the harneys and habergyon, hosed with yron; and the precyous rynges and the ryche ornamentes put a parte, instede of whiche she bare in her handes axes, harde speres, bowes and arowes, stretchynge a swerde. And in this maner, this noble quene governed her by strengthe of grete love and true, and thus she chaunged the tendernes of her fayre body and yonge whiche was wonte to be cherysshed softely and delycately, and she lyved after the manere of a stronge armed knyght. [C6v]

"O, sayth Bocaca that wryteth this story, what is that that love causeth not one to do, when she that had it of custome to lyve so delycately, to lye softe and to have al thynges at her ease and nowe demeaned, by her free wyll, as it were an harde man and a stronge, lyenge day and nyght in the mountaynes and valays, in the desertes and in forestes, often tymes upon the bare erthe, for drede of enemyes, in every syde of her wylde beestes and serpentes? But all this was swete to her to be alwaye nyghe her husbande, for to comforte hym, counsayle hym, and serve hym in all his nedes.

"And yet after, when she had suffred to endure longe tyme many harde travayles, it happened that her husbande was dyscomfyted ryght cruelly by Pompee, prynce of the hoost of the Romaynes, so that he was constrayned to fle. Yet when he was forsaken of al his owne people and lefte alone, his good wyfe lefte hym never but rennynge after folowed hym, by hylles and valays, by forestes and by many strayte passages. And he whiche was forsaken of all his frendes, and had noo maner of hope, yet was he comforted by his good wyfe, whiche counsaylled

---

¹ [made] to : *to*

l'amonnestoit d'avoir esperance de meilleur fortune. Et tant que[1] lui et elle estoient en plus grant desolacion, et plus celle mettoit peine de lui donner soulas et de
l'esjouïr par les doulceurs[2] de ses paroles, afin qu'il entroubliast sa melancolie par
gracieux jeux et solacieux[3] que elle savoit trouver. [fol. 85v a] Pour lesquelles choses, et par[4] la grant doulceur d'elle,[5] tant lui donnoit de consalacion ceste dame,
que en quelconques misere ou souffraicte que il fust, tant eust de tribulacion, elle
lui faisoit si houblier que souvent il disoit que il n'estoit point exille,[6] ains lui sembloit que il estoit[7] tres delicieusement en son palais avecques[8] sa loiale espouse."

*Chapitre 15*      [De l'empereris Triare][9]

"Asses pareille et semblable a la sus dicte royne en cas et en loial amour vers
son mary fut la noble empereris Triare, femme de Lucien Urilien,[10] empereur
des Rommains. Elle[11] l'amoit de si grant amour que elle le suivoit par tout, et
en toutes batailles, armee comme un chevalier estoit, hardiement coste lui et se
combatoit viguoreusement. [fol. 85v b] Donc il avint ou temps que cellui empereur ot guerre a Vaspazien pour cause de la seigneurie de l'empire, que comme il
alast contre une cité des Volques, et par nuit feist tant que il entrast dedens,[12] il
trouva les gens endormis, auxquelx il couru sus cruelment. Mais celle noble dame
Triare, qui par toute la nuit avoit suivi son mary, n'en estoit mie adonc loings,
ains desirant que il eust la victoire, elle toute armee, l'espee ceinte, se combatoit
fierement en la route coste son mary—maintenant ça, maintenant la—par les
tenebres de la nuit, n'avoit point de paour ne de orreur, ains tant s'i porta vigore-
usement que de celle bataille elle eut de tous le pris et merveilles y fist. [fol. 86r a]
Si demonstra bien, ce dit Boucace, la grant amour que elle avoit a son mary en
approvant le liam de mariage que autres veulent tant reprover."[13]

---

[1] tant que] quant
[2] les doulceurs] la doulceur
[3] gracieux jeux et solacieux] gracieux et solacieux gieux
[4] par] pour
[5] d'elle] d'elles
[6] exille] homme exillé
[7] estoit] fust
[8] avecques] avec
[9] [Triare] : *omitted*
[10] Urilien] Utilien
[11] Elle] Celle
[12] dedens] dedens ou
[13] reprover] reprocher

hym swetely to have hope of better fortune. And the more that he and she were in grete trybulacyon, the more she payned herselfe to do hym solace and to rejoyse hym by the swetnesse of her, to the entente to appease his malancoly by goodly playes that she coude fynde. By the whiche thynges, and by the grete swetenesse of her, so moche she comforted hym that in every [D1r] mysery that he suffred in all his trybulacyons, she made hym so to forgete it that he sayd often tymes that he was not in exyle but hym semed that he was ryght delycyously in his palays with his true spouse."

## Chapter 15    Of the Empresse Tryayre

"Right lyke to the foresayd quene in case and in true love towarde her husbande was the noble Empresse Tryayre, wyfe of Lucyan Urylyan, emperoure of the Romaynes. She loved hym of so grete love that she folowed hym in every place and in all batoylles, armed lyke a knyght, alway ryght nyghe hym and fought ryght strongly. Wherof it happened on a tyme that this emperoure had warre with Vaspasyan bycause of the lordeshyp of the empyre, and whan he sholde go ayenst a cyte of Volques, and sholde do by nyght that he sholde entre into the towne, he founde the people a slepe and he wente upon them cruelly. But this noble Lady Tryayre, whiche all the nyght had folowed her husbande and was not ferre fro hym, but alway desyrynge that he myght have the vyctory of the batayle, alwaye in harnays, the swerde gyrde aboute her, fyghtynge ryght fyersely in the rowte nyghe her husbande—nowe here, nowe there—by the darkenesse of the nyght havynge no drede nor fere, but that she bare her so worshypfully that she had the pryce of the batayle above al others, [D1v] and dyde many mervayles. So it shewed wel, as Bocace sayth, the grete love that she had to her husbande in provynge the bande of maryage that other wolde so moche reprove."

*Chapitre 16*     [Encore de la royne Archemise]¹

"Des dames qui ont amé de grant amour leurs maris et qui de fait l'ont monstré
puis encore dire de celle² noble dame Archemise, royne de Care que comme elle
eust pareillement que dessus est dit³ suivi en mainte bataille le roy Mansole et
il venist a mort elle oultree⁴ de si grant douleur que creature puet porter se elle
avoit bien demonstré en sa vie que elle l'amoit n'en fist mie moins a la fin. Car
en faisant toutes les solempnitez qui a l'usage de lors se peussent faire a roy fist
ardoir a grant obseque et compagnie⁵ [fol. 86r b] de princes et de barons le corps
duquel elle mesmes en cueilli la cendre en faisant la lexive de ses larmes et la
mist en un vaissel d'or. Si lui sembla que ce n'estoit pas raison que les cendres de
celui⁶ que tant avoit amé eussent autre sepulcure que le cuer et le corps ou estoit
la rasine de celle grant amour. Et pour ce elle but les dictes cendres par succession de temps meslees avecques⁷ buvrage petit a petit jusques elle ot toute⁸ pris.

"Mais non obstant ce⁹ en remembrance de lui volt faire un tel sepulcre qu'a
tousjours en fust memoire. Et pour ce faire n'espargna nul avoir si fist querre
certains ouvriers qui savoient pourpenser et faire ouvrages merveilleux en edefi-
ces: c'est assavoir Scope, Briaxe, Thimothe, et Leothare, qui estoient [fol. 86v a]
ouvriers de grant excellence et a ceulx dist la royne comment elle vouloit que
un sepulchre fust fait au roy Mansole son seigneur le plus solempnel que roy ne
prince qui¹⁰ ou monde fust eust, car elle vouloit que¹¹ par l'euvre merveilleuse le
nom de son mary durast tousjours.¹² Et ceulx dirent que bien le feroient. Si leur
fist la royne querre pierre de marbre asses, et de jaspe de diverses couleurs, et tout
quanque ilz demanderent.

"La fin de l'ouvrage fu telle¹³ que les dictes ouvriers devant la cité de Eli-
carnase, qui est la maistre cité de Care, esleverent un grant estre de pierre de
marbre en taille moult noblement. Et fu de quarre figure: et en chascune querre
ot .lxiiii. piez, et de hault .c. et .xl. piez. Et plus grant merveilles fu, car tout ce
tres grant edifice fu [fol. 86v b] assis sus .xxx. grosses colompnes de marbre; et

---

¹ [Archemise] : *omitted*
² de celle] d'icelle
³ que dessus est dit] que comme dessus dit
⁴ oultree] atainte et oultree
⁵ compagnie] a grant compaignie
⁶ ce[l]lui : *celui*
⁷ avecques] avec
⁸ toute] tout
⁹ ce] ceste chose voult
¹⁰ qui] que
¹¹ vouloit que] desiroit car
¹² tousjours] a tousjours
¹³ telle] tel

*Chapter 16*     Of the Quene Archemyse

"Of ladyes that have loved theyr husbandes of grete love and shewed it in dede, I may say yet of the noble Lady Archemyse, quene of Carye, that as it is sayd before, folowed the Kynge Mansole her husbande in many grete batayles tyll he came to the dethe. And she, outraged with so grete sorowe as moche as ony creature myght bere—yf she shewed it well in his lyfe that she loved hym wel, she dyde no lesse in the ende. For in makynge all the solempnytes that was in the usage there as moche as myght be made for a kynge, with grete company of prynces and of barons made brenne the body of her housbande, wherof she herselfe gadred the asshes, quenchynge them with her teeres, and put them in a vessell of golde. So she semed that it was no reason that the asshes of hym that she had loved so moche sholde have other sepulture than the herte and the body where the rote of this grete love was, and therfore she dranke the foresayd asshes by successyon of tyme medled with her drynke, by lytel and lytel, tyl she had [D2r] taken all.

"Yet notwithstandynge that, for the remembraunce of hym she wolde let make suche a sepulture whiche sholde be alway for hym a perpetuall memory, and to make it she spared no treasoure. So she made to seke certayne werkemen that coude devyse and make mervayllous werkes in buyldynge, that is to knowe Scope, Bryaxe, Thymothe, and Leothayre, whiche were werkemen of grete excellence. And the quene sayd to them that she wolde have a sepulture made for the Kynge Mansole her lorde the moost solempne that kynge or prynce myght have in the worlde, for she wolde that by the mervayllous werke the name of her husbande sholde endure alwaye. And they sayd that they wolde do it ryght well. So the quene made them to seke stones of marble ynowe, and of jasper of dyvers colours, and all that ever they wolde aske.

"The ende of the werke was suche that the foresayd werkemen before the cyte of Elycarnase, whiche is the mayster cyte of Carye, lyfted up a grete werke of marble stone wrought by entayle ryght nobly. And it was made square: and in every squarenesse it was of .lxiiii. fote, and on hyght an .c. and xl. fote. And yet it was more mervaylous, for al this grete buyldynge was sette upon .xxx.

chascun des .iiii. ouvriers en tailla par estrif l'un de l'autre l'une des quarreures de l'edifice, dont l'oeuvre fut tant merveilleuse que elle ne donna pas tant seulement remembrance d'ycellui[1] pour qui avoit esté faicte, mais donna admiracion de la soubtiveté des ouvriers. Le quint ouvrier vint a celle [oe]uvre[2] perfaire, qui ot nom Ytraire, et cellui fist la haultece de l'eguille du dit sepulchre, laquelle il leva par dessus ce que les autres avoient fait par .xl. degrez. Et aprés vint le .vi.ᵉ ouvrier, nommé Pichis, lequel tailla un chariot de marbre et le mist en la haultece de l'edifice. Ceste oeuvre fu tant merveilleuse que elle fut reputee l'une des .vii. merveilles du monde. Et pour [fol. 87r a] ce que elle fut faicte pour le roy Mansole, l'oeuvre en prist son nom et fu appellé *mansole*. Et pour ce que cellui fut le plus solempnel sepulchre qui oncques fut fait pour roy ne pour prince,[3] tous les aultres sepulcres des roys et des princes[4] ont puis esté appellés *mansoles*. Et ainsi apparut en fait et en signe la loyale amour que Archemise eut a son loyal espoux, laquelle amour dura tant comme elle vesqui."

## *Chapitre 17*     Cy dit de Argine, fille du roy Adrastus

"O, la tres grant amour esprouvee que ot Argine, fille de Adrastus, le roy d'Arges, envers Polinices son mary! Qui est cellui qui jamais ose[5] dire que pou d'amour ait en femme[6] a son mary se il considere ceste dame? Cellui Polinices, qui mary estoit d'Argine, contendoit a son frere Ethiocles pour cause de la seigneurie [fol. 87r b] du royaume de Thebes, qui lui apertenoit par certaines couvenances que entre eulx avoient. Mais comme Ethiocles se voulsist du tout attribuer le royaume, Polinices son frere lui mut guerre, auquel aide ala son seigneur le roy Adrastus a toute sa poissance. Mais si mal tourna la Fortune[7] contre Polinices que lui et son frere s'entre occirent en la bataille, et ne demoura de tout l'ost en vie fors le dit roy Adrastus sur[8] .iii.ᶜ de gent.

"Mais quant Argine sceut que son mary estoit mort en la bataille, elle se parti et avec elle toutes les dames de la cité d'Arges et laissa son siege royal. Et de ce que elle fist, dit Bocace en ceste maniere: la noble dame Argine ouÿ dire que le corps de Polinices son espoux gisoit[9] non enseveli entre les corps et charongnes du [fol. 87v a] peuple commun qui la estoit occis. Tantost elle, pleine de

---

[1] d'ycellui] de cellui
[2] [oe]uvre : *eouvre*
[3] ne pour prince] ne prince
[4] princes] princes ce dit Bocace
[5] jamais ose] ose
[6] en femme] femme
[7] Fortune : *Fourtune*
[8] sur] lui
[9] gisoit] gisoit mort

grete pyllers of marble. And eche of the .iiii. werkemen wrought by stryfe one with another, wherof the werke was so mervaylous that it gave not onely remembraunce of hym that it was made for, but it was mervayle of the subtylnesse of the werkemen. [D2v] The [fyfte] [1] werkeman to perfourme this werke, that was called Itrayre, made the hyghnesse of the sepulture to be lyfted up by .lx. degrees. And after came the syxte werkeman, named Pychys, the whiche wrought a charyote of marble and set it in the hyghnesse of the buyldynge. This werke was soo mervaylous that it was called one of the .vii. mervayles of the worlde. And insomoche that it was made for the Kynge Mansolee, the werke toke his name and was called *mansolee*. And for that that it was the moost solempne sepulture that ever was made for kynge or for prynce, all other sepultures of kynges and prynces have ben called syth *mansolees*. And thus appered wel in dede and in sygne that the true love dured all the whyle she lyved."

### *Chapter 17*    Of Argyne, doughter of the Kynge Adrastus

"O, the grete love proved that Argyne had, doughter to Adrastus, kynge of Arge, towarde her housbande Polymyte! O, what is he that dare saye that there is but lytel love in a woman towarde her husbande yf he consyder well this lady? This Polymyte that was the husbande of Argyne stryved with his broder Ethyocles for bycause of the lordeshyp of the royalme of Thebes, whiche pertey[n]ed [2] to hym by certayne covenauntes that were made bytwene them. But as Ethyocles wolde [D3r] not in no maner wyse graunt hym the royalme, Polymyte his broder moved warre agaynst hym, to the helpe of whome Kynge Adrastus came with al his power. Yet Fortune tourned shrewdely ayenste Polymyte, whiche slewe his broder and his broder hym in batayle and the hoost bode not longe on lyve, but onely the Kynge Adrastus, and slewe the thyrde parte of his people.

"But when Argyne knewe that her husbande was deed in batayle, she departed and all her ladyes with her out of the cyte of Arge and forsoke her royal see. And of that that she dyde, Bacace saythe in this manere: the noble Lady Argyne herde say that the body of Polymyte her husbande laye unburyed amonge the bodyes and caraynes of the comune people that there were slayne, anone she

---

[1] [fyfte] : *fyrst*
[2] pertey[n]ed : *perteyned*

doleur, laissa l'abit et aournement royal, et la molece et doulceur de demourer en ses chambres parees, et avec ce surmonta et vainqui par grant desir et ardeur d'amour la foiblece et tendrece femmenine. Et tant ala par ses journees que elle vint ou lieu ou avoit esté la bataille, ou quel chemin ne l'avoit point espoventee les embusches des agaitans anemis, ne rendue lassa la longueur de la voye.[1] Et elle venue ou champ ne l'espoventa point les bestes crueues, ne le[s][2] grans oisiaulx suivans les corps mors, ne les mauvais esperis lesquelx comme plusieurs fols oppinent volent en tour les corps des hommes.

"Et qui est chose plus [fol. 87v b] merveilleuse, ce dit Bocace, ne doubta point le edit et commandement du roy Creonce, qui avoit comandé et fait crier sur peine capitale que nul ne visetast ne ensevelist yceulx corps,[3] qui qu'ilz fussent. Mais n'estoit pas alee celle part pour obeir a cellui commandement, ains si tost que elle y fu arivé, qui fu environ l'anuiter, ne[4] laissa pas aussi pour la pueur qui moult grant yssoit des charoingnes que elle, menee par moult ardent et triste courage, ne prensist a patoier les corps, puis les uns, puis les autres, en cerchant cellui qui elle amoit, puis ça, puis la. Et ainsi ne cessa jusques ad ce que, a la lumiere d'un petit brandon que elle tenoit congneut son tres amé mary, et ainsi trouva ce [fol. 88r a] que elle queroit.

"O, ce dit Bocace, merveilleuse amour et tres ardent desir et affeccion de femme! Car comme la face de son mary, par l'enroilleure des armes moitié mengié et toute emplie de pulenteur,[5] toute ensanglantee, pouldreuseur chargee[6] d'ordure, tout palle et noirci[7] qui ja estoit comme descongnoissable, ne pot estre mucié a celle femme tant ardemment l'amoit. Ne la pugnaisie du corps ne l'ordure du viaire n'ont peu empescher, que elle ne le baisast ne[8] embraçast estroictement. Ne le edit et commandement du roy Creonce ne la pot retraire que elle ne criast a haulte voix, 'Lasse, lasse! J'ay trouvé cellui que j'amoye!' et que elle ne plourast par grant habondance. Car comme elle eust quis par plusieurs baisiers de bouche se en [fol. 88r b] lui estoit plus l'ame, et eust lavé de ses larmes les membres ja tous puans, et souvent par grans cris, et pleurs,[9] et gemissemens l'eust appellé. Finablement, comme elle veist que l'ame estoit partie, fist alumer un feu, si comme estoit la maniere de lors d'ensevelir les roys et les nobles;[10] afin[11] que elle lui feist le

---

[1] lassa la longueur de la voye] lasse la longueur de la voye ne la chaleur du temps
[2] le[s] : *le*
[3] yceulx corps] les corps
[4] ne] adont ne
[5] pulenteur] puanteur
[6] chargee] chargiee et tachee
[7] tout palle et noirci] toute palle et noircie
[8] ne] et
[9] cris, et pleurs] cris, pleurs
[10] Finablement . . . nobles] *omitted*
[11] afin] Adont affin

full of sorowe lefte the habyte and the ornamentes, the noblesse and swetnesse of her courte, to dwelle in her chambres worshypfully arayed, and with that by grete desyre, the brennynge of love, surmounted and overcame the feblenesse and womanly tendrenesse. And so moche she wente by her journeys tyll that she came to that place where the batayle had ben, on the whiche waye she had no fere of the busshmentes nor of the waytynge of her enemyes, ne was never wery of longnesse of the way. And she came into the felde, dredynge not the cruell bestes ne the grete byrdes sewynge the deed bodyes, ne the wycked spyrytes whiche after the lykenesse of dyvers fowles flyeth aboute deed bodyes.

"And whiche is a thynge more mervaylous, [D3v] as Bocace sayth, she doubted not the precepte nor the commaundement of Kynge Creonce, whiche had commaunded and made crye upon the payne of losynge of theyr heedes that none sholde vysyte nor bury those bodyes, whose soo ever they were. For she was not come thyder for to obey to that commaundement, but as sone as she was aryved, whiche was aboute the nyght, she lefte not for no stynkynge that came out of the caraynes, but wente with a grete brennynge and a sorowfull courage and underset the bodyes—nowe one, nowe another—sekynge for hym that she loved so moche—nowe here, nowe there. And thus she seased not tyll that, with the lyght of a lytell bronde of fyre that she helde in her hande, she knewe her ryght entyerly beloved husbande, and so she founde that she sought.

"O, sayd Bocace, the mervaylous love, the brennynge desyre and the affeccyon of women! For as the face of her husbande, for the rustynesse of his harnoys halfe eten, all full of stynkynge, all forbledde, full of dust charged with foulenesse, all pale and blacke whiche was as at that tyme unable to be knowen myght [not] be[1] hydde from this woman, so brennyngly she loved hym. Thus the stynkynge of the body and the foulenesse of the vysage myght not let her, but that she kyssed hym and embraced hym straytely bytwene her armes. Notwithstandynge the precepte and commaundement of Kynge Creonce, she spared not but that she cryed with an hyghe voyce: 'Alas, alas! I have founde hym that I loved so moche!' And then she wepte [D4r] with grete plente of teeres. For as she knewe by often tymes kyssynge his mouthe that there was no lyfe in hym, and had wasshed hym with her teeres, al stynkynge, and often tymes by grete cryes, wepynges, and waylynges called upon hym; fynably as she sawe that the soule was departed fro the body, made to lyght up a grete fyre so as it was the maner there of buryenge of kynges and of grete states, to that entente that she wolde

---

[1] myght [not] be : *myght be*

derrenier et piteux office, le mist ou feu a grans cris, duquel elle recueilli la cendre chierement en un vaissel d'or.

"Et quant elle ot tout ce fait, comme celle qui vouloit espouser[1] son corps a mort pour vengier son mary, fist tant et y mist tel peine a l'aide des aultres dames, dont grant quantité y avoit, que les murs de la cité de Thebes[2] furent perciez, et gangnerent la ville, et tout mirent a mort."

## *Chapitre 18*      Dit de[3] la noble Dame Agrippine [fol. 88v a]

"Bien doit estre mise entre les nobles dames de grant amour a leurs maris la noble[4] Egripine, fille de Marc Egrippe et de Julie, fille de l'empereur Othovien, seigneur [d]e[5] tout le monde. Et comme ceste noble dame fust donnee en mariage a Germaince—tres noble prince, bien moriginé, sage, et cultiveur du bien publique de Romme—Thybere, l'empereur de mauvaises meurs qui lors estoit[6] prist telle[7] envie du bien que il oyoit dire de Germanice, mary de la dicte Agripine, et de ce que chascun l'amoit, que il le fist agattier et occire, de laquelle mort sa bonne femme ot tel dueil que elle volsist semblablement estee occise. Et de ce faisoit bien semblant car ne se traisoit[8] mie de dire grans villenies a Tybere, par quoy il la fist batre et tormenter cruelment, et tenir en [fol. 88v b] chartre.

"Mais comme celle, qui pour la douleur de son mary que elle ne pouoit oublier,[9] mieulx amast la mort que la vie, proposa de jamais plus ne boire, ne mengier. Mais ce propos venu a la congno[i]scence[10] du tirant Tybere; pour plus longuement la tourmenter, la voult contraindre par tourmens[11] que elle mengiast, mais riens n'y valu.[12] Si lui voult a force faire gitter de la viande en l'estomach, mais elle lui monstra que il avoit bien poissance de faire gent occire, mais de les garder de mort[13] non se ilz vouloient car elle fina ainsi ses jours."

---

[1] espouser] exposer
[2] de Thebes] *omitted*
[3] Dit de] De
[4] noble] la bonne et loyale Agripine
[5] [d]e : *le*
[6] lors estoit] qui adonc regnoit
[7] telle] tel
[8] traisoit] taisoit
[9] que elle ne pouoit oublier] que oublier ne pouoit
[10] congno[i]scence : *congnonscence*
[11] plus longuement la tourmenter la voult contraindre par tourmens] pour la tourmenter plus longuement la volt par tourmens contraindre
[12] valu] val
[13] occire, mais de les garder de mort] mourir mais de les en garder

do the last and pyteous offyce put hym in the fyre with many sorowfull cryes, of whome she gadred the asshes ryght derely in a vessel of golde.

"And when she had done al this, as she that wolde adventure her body to the dethe for to venge her husbande, dyde so moche and put to suche payne with the helpe of other ladyes, wherof there was grete quantyte, that the walles of the cyte of Thebes were overthrowen, and gate the towne and put all to dethe."

## *Chapter 18*    Of the noble Lady Egryppyne

"Well ought to be put amonge these noble ladyes of grete love to theyr housbandes the noble Lady Egryppyne, doughter of Marke Egryppyne and of Julye, doughter of the Emperour Octavyan, lorde of all the worlde. And as this noble lady was gyven in maryage to Bermanyce, the ryght noble prynce—well manered, wyse, and an encreaser and multeplyer of the comune profyte of [D4v] Rome—Tybere the Emperour, whiche was of evyll condycyons, toke suche envye of the welthe that he herde of Bermanyce, husbande of the sayd Lady Egryppyne, and of that that every man loved hym, that he lete make watche upon hym and slewe hym. Of whose d[e]the[1] his good wyfe had suche sorowe that she wolde in lykewyse be slayne, and that semed ryght wel for she withdrewe not to say grete vylanyes to Tybere, for the whiche he made her to be beten and tourmented cruelly, and put her in pryson.

"But as she, that the sorowe of her housbande myght not forgete, loved better the dethe than the lyfe, purposed never to ete nor drynke. But this purpose came to the tyraunt Tybere to tourment her longer and wolde constrayne her by tourmentes that she sholde ete, but it avayled not. So he wolde by strengthe make to caste the mete into the stomake. But she shewed well to hym that he hadde puyssaunce to make folke to be slayne, but not to kepe them from dethe yf they wolde, for thus she ended her dayes."

---

[1] d[e]the : *dothe*

*Chapitre 19*      **Dit Christine, et puis Droicture respond, donnant exemple et**[1] **de la noble Dame Julie, fille de Julius Cesar et femme du Prince Pompee**[2]

Tandis que Dame Droicture[3] me disoit ces choses, je lui repliquay [fol. 89r a] en tel maniere: "Dame, certes moult me semble estre grant honneur au sexe femmenin de tant de tres excellens dames ouïr raconter, et entre les autres vertus d'elles, moult doit estre agreable a toute gent que si grant amour puist estre ou[4] cuer de femme ou loyain[5] de mariage. Or se voisent couschier[6] et se taisent Matheolus et tous les aultres gengleurs, qui envieusement et mençongeusement[7] en ont parlé contre les femmes.

"Mais, dame, encore me souvient que le philosophe Philostratus,[8] dont j'ay parlé cy dessus, dit que les femmes heent leurs maris quant ilz sont vieux, et aussi que elles n'aiment pas hommes de science ne clers, car il dit que les cures que il couvient avoir es dongiers des femmes et l'estude de[9] livres sont ensemble contraires."

*Response*: "O chiere amie, tais toy! [fol. 89r b] J'ai t'ay tantost trouvé exemples contraires a leurs[10] dis, par quoy les tendrons a non voir disans.[11]

"Julie fu en son temps la plus noble des dames rommaines, fille de Julius Cesar qui puis fu empereur et de Cornille sa femme, descendus de Eneas, venu[12] de Troye. Ceste dame fu femme de Pompee le grant conquereur, lequel, ce dit Bocace, en vainquant les roys, en les deposant et refaisant des autres, en subjuguant les nacions et destruisant les larrons de mer ayant[13] la f[a]veur[14] de Romme et des roys de tout le monde, en acquerant les seigneuries non pas tant seulement des terres mais aussi de la mer et des eaues par merveilleuses victoires, en souverain honneur estoit ja envieillis et debrises. Mais non pour tant, [fol. 89v a] la

---

[1]  respond donnant exemple et ] lui respont donnant exemples et dit
[2]  du Prince Pompee] de Pompee
[3]  Droicture] Raison
[4]  ou] en
[5]  loyain] lien
[6]  couschier] dormir
[7]  mençongeusement] par tant de menteries
[8]  Philostratus] Theofrastus
[9]  de] des
[10]  leurs] leur
[11]  tendrons a non voir disans] rendrons non voir disant
[12]  Eneas, venu] Enee et venus
[13]  de mer ayant] ayant
[14]  f[a]veur : *feveur*

*Chapter 19*     Here Christine speketh and Ryghtwysnes answereth, gyvynge ensamples of the noble Lady Julye, doughter of Julyus Cesar, wyfe of the Prynce Pompee

When that my Lady Ryghtwysnes sayd to me these wordes, I replyed her in suche maner: "Madame, truely it semeth [E1r] me to be grete honoure to the kynde of women to here tell of so many excellent ladyes. And amonge other vertues of them ought to be ryght agreable to al people that so grete love may be in the herte of a woman in the bonde of maryage. Nowe let them slepe and holde theyr peas, this Matheolus and all other janglers that envyously and lyengly have spoken agaynst women.

"But, madame, yet me thynketh that the phylosophre Phylostratus, of whome I have spoken here above, sayth that these women hateth theyr husbandes when they be olde, and also that they love not these connynge men that be clerkes, for he sayth that the charges that one ought to have in daungers of women and the studyenge of bokes ben contrary togyder."

*Answere*: "O dere frende, holde thy peas! I have anone founde thee ensamples contrary to theyr sayenge, by the whiche we shal holde them as no sayenges true.

"Julye was in her tyme the moost noblest of the ladyes of Rome, doughter of Julyus Cesar whiche was syth emperoure of Rome and of Cor[n]ylle[1] his wyfe, comynge downe fro Eneas of Troye; this lady was wyfe of Pompee, the grete conqueroure. The whiche as Bocace sayth—in overcomynge the kynges, in puttynge downe in makynge agayne of other, in puttynge under subjeccyon dyvers nacyons, in destroyenge theves of the see, havynge the favoure of Rome, of all the kynges in the worlde, in gettynge the lordshyppes not onely of the landes but also of the see and caves by mervayllous vyctoryes [E1v] in soverayne worshyp—was than waxen olde and sore brused. But not for that, the noble Lady

---

[1] Cor[n]ylle : *Coruylle*

noble Dame Julie sa femme, qui moult joeune encores[1] estoit, l'amoit de si tres perfaicte[2] et grant amour que elle en fina sa vie par estrange[3] aventure.

"Car il avint un jour que Pompee ot devocion de donner louenge aux dieux des nobles victoires que il avoit eues et voult sacrefier selon la coustume de lors. Et comme la beste sacrefiee fust sur l'autel, et Pompee par devocion la tenist d'un coste, sa robe fut toillé du sang ysant de la plaie de la beste, par quoy Pompee[4] se despoilla et envoia par un de ses serviteurs en son hostel la robe que vestu avoit, pour querre[5] une autre nette et fresche. Si avint par male fortune que cellui qui portoit la robe[6] encontra Julie, la femme de Pompee, laquelle quant elle vit la robe de son [fol. 89v b] seigneur si toillé de sang, adonc pour ce que elle savoit bien que aucunes fois avenoit a Romme[7] que a ceulx qui estoient les meilleurs on couroit sus par envie, et a la fois les occioit on, fu surprise soubdeinement par le signe que elle vid de certaine creance que ains[i][8] fust avenu de son mary par quelconque fortune. Par quoy telle douleur soubdaine lui prist au cuer, comme celle qui plus ne vouloit vivre que elle, estant gros[9] d'enfant, cheut pasmee, palle et destraintee et les[10] yeulx tournez en la teste, ne si tost n'y pot estre remede mis ne celle paour ostee que elle ne rendist l'esperit, laquelle mort par raison dot[11] estre grant dueil au mary. Mais ne fu mie seulement prejudiciable a lui, ne aux Rommains, [fol. 90r a] ains le fu aussi a tant[12] le monde du temps de lors: car se elle et son enfant eussent vescu, la grant gu[e]rre[13] ne eust jamais esté qui puis fu entre Julius Cesar et Pompee, laquelle guerre fut en toutes terres prejudiciable."

## *Chapitre 20*     De la noble Dame Tierce Emuliene

"Ne hay pas son mary pour estre vieil autressi la belle et bonne Tierce Emuliene, femme du prince Scipion le premier Affrican. Ceste dame estoit de moult grant prudence et tres vertueuse. Et comme son mary fust ja envieilliz, et elle encore

---

[1]   moult joeune encores] ancore moult jeune
[2]   perfaicte] parfaicte, loyale
[3]   estrange] diverse
[4]   Pompee] il
[5]   par un de ses serviteurs en son hostel la robe que vestu avoit pour querre] et envoya la robe que vestue avoit par un de ses serviteurs en son hostel pour querir
[6]   la robe] la dicte robe
[7]   avenoit a Romme] a Romme
[8]   ains[i] : *ainst*
[9]   gros] grosse
[10]   et les] les
[11]   mort par raison dot] mort dot par raison
[12]   tant] tout
[13]   gu[e]rre : *gurre*

Julye his wyfe, whiche was but yonge as yet, loved hym of soo grete love that she ended her lyfe by a straunge adventure.

"For as it happened in a day that Pompee had devocyon, to gyve praysynge to goddes that he had goten by noble vyctoryes and wolde do sacrefyse after the custome of that countre, and as the beest sacryfyed was upon the awter and Pompe as by devocyon helde hym by that one syde, his robe was soylled with the blode yssuynge oute of the wounde of the beest. Wherfore Pompe dyde off his robe and sente it home by one of his servauntes, and for to brynge another clene and fresshe. So it happened by an evyll fortune that he that bare the robe mette with Julye, the wyfe of Pompe. The whiche, when she sawe the robe of her lorde so soyled with blode, then for that that she knewe wel that dyvers tymes it happened in Rome, that to them that were the best, one wolde renne upon hym for envye and sle hym, wherwith she was supprysed sodaynly by the sygne that she sawe of certayne bylevynge that it had happened soo to her husbande by some fortune. By whiche suche sodayne sorowe toke her at the herte that as she that wolde no longer lyve she, beynge grete with chylde, fell flatte to the erthe, pale and styffe, and the eyen tourned in her heed, that there myght noo remedy be had soo sone to put her oute of that drede but that she yelded up the spyryte, whiche dethe by reason ought to be grete sorowe to the husbande. But it [E2r] was not onely prejudycyable to hym, nor to the Romaynes, but it was also to all the worlde of that tyme. For yf she and her sone had lyved, the grete werre had never ben that was syth bytwene Julyus Cesar and Pompe, the whiche warre was prejudycyable to all the londes of the worlde."

## Chapter 20    Of the noble Lady Tyerce Emulyene

"The fayre and good Tyerce Emulyene, wyfe of Prynce Scypyon the fyrste Affrycan, hated not her husbande also thoughe he were olde. This lady was of grete prudence and ryght vertuous, and as her husbande was olde, and she yet fayre and

belle et joeune, non obstant, ce se couchoit avec une serve[1] qui estoit chamberiere d'elle, et par tant de fois y ench[e]ut[2] que la vaillant dame s'en aperçut. Elle,[3]
non obstant que le cuer lui en doulist,[4] usa de la vertu de son grant savoir [fol. 90r
b] et non mie de passion de jalousie. Car le dissimula si sagement[5] que oncques
son mary ne autre n'en ouÿ parler, car ne le voult mie dire a lui,[6] pour ce que il
lui sembla que honte seroit de reprendre un si grant homme comme il estoit, et
d'en faire mension a aultre[7] encore pis, car ce seroit en reprimant et amenuisant
la loenge de tant sage homme, et contre l'onneur de sa personne, qui tant avoit
conquis de royaumes et d'empires. Si ne l'en laissa oncques la bonne dame a servir
loiaulment, amer, et honnourer. Et q[u]ant[8] il fu mort, elle franchi la femme et la
maria a un homme franc"

Et je, Christine, respondis adonc: "Certes, dame, ad ce propos que vous dites,
me souvient avoir veu femmes semblables, [fol. 90v a] lesquelles[9] pour chose que
elles sceussent bien que petite loiauté leur portoient leurs maris, ne les en laisoient[10]
a amer, et faire bonne chiere, et relevoient, et confortoient les femmes de qui ilz
avoient des enfans. Et mesmes l'ay ainsi ouÿ dire d'une dame de Bretaingne qui n'a
gaires vivoit et estoit contesse de Coemen,[11] qui estoit en fleur de joeunece et belle
sur toutes dames. Et par sa tres grant constance et bonté, ainsi le faisoit."

## *Chapitre 21*     Ci dit de Xancippe, femme du philosophe Socrates

"Xancippe, la tres noble dame, femme[12] de grant savoir et bonté, si ot a espoux[13] le
tres grant philosophe Socrates. Et non obstant que il fust[14] ja envieillis, et que il eust
plus grant cure de cerchier et reverchier les livres que de pourchacier a sa femme
choses [fol. 90v b] souëfves et curieuses, la vaillant dame ne le laissa pas pour ce a
amer, ains extimoit estre tant grant chose l'excellence de son savoir et de la[15] grant
vertu de lui et de sa constance que elle l'avoit en souveraine amour et reverence.

---

[1]  avec une serve] avecques une sienne serve
[2]  ench[e]ut : *enchut*
[3]  Elle] Mais elle
[4]  le cuer lui en doulist] moult lui en feist mal
[5]  le dissimula si sagement] si sagement le dissimula
[6]  car ne le voult mie dire a lui] car a lui ne le voult pas dire
[7]  aultre] autre vauldroit
[8]  q[u]ant : *qant*
[9]  le[s]quelles] : *lequelles*
[10]  laisoient] laissoient pour tant
[11]  contesse de Coemen] vicontesse de Coitmen
[12]  femme] dame fu
[13]  a espoux] ot espousé
[14]  que il fust] fust
[15]  de la] la

yonge; that notwithstandynge, he laye with a bonde woman whiche was her servaunt, and so often it fell that this worshypfull lady perceyved it. She, notwithstandynge that her herte was sorowfull, used the vertue of her grete understandynge and not onely of the passyon of jalousye, for she dyssymyled so wysely that
her husbande, ne none other herde her never speke of it; for she wolde not telle
it to hym for that that he sholde seme that it were shame to hym that she sholde
reprove so wyse and so grete a man as he was; and to make mencyon therof to ony
other, for that sholde be a maner of repreffe and losynge of the praysynge [of]¹
so wyse a man and ayenst the honoure of his persone, whiche had conquered so
many royalmes and empyres. Soo she never lefte hym, this good lady, to serve
hym truely, to love hym, and worshyp hym. [E2v] And when he was deed, she
made the mayden fre and wedded her to a free man."

And I, Christine, answered: "Then truely, madame, to this purpose that ye
saye, I have sene often tymes women in lyke case, whiche for ony thynge that
they knewe, wolde not saye, thoughe they knewe well that theyr husbandes had
them but in lytell love. And yet they loved them and made them good chere, and
releved them, and comforted them of whome they had chyldren before. And also
I have herde say of a lady of Brytayne that lyved but late and was countesse of
Coemen, whiche was in the floure of her youthe, fayre above all the ladyes. And
by her grete goodnesse and constaunce, she dyde the same."

## *Chapter 21*      Of Vancyppe, wyfe of the phylosopre Socrates

"Vancyppe, the ryght noble lady, a woman of grete connynge and bounte, so
she had to husbande the grete phylosophre Socrates. And notwithstandynge
that he was in grete age, and that he had grete charge to serche and tourne the
bokes [than]² to pourchace for his wyfe softe thynges and curyous, the worshypful woman lefte never to love hym, but trowed that it was so grete a thynge the
excellent understandynge and the grete vertue of hym, and of his constaunce,
that she had [E3r] hym in soverayne love and reverence.

---

¹ [of] so : *so*
² bokes [than] to : *bokes to*

"Et quant ceste vaillant dame sceut que son mary estoit condempnés a mort par ceulx d'Athenes, pour ce que il les blasmoit[1] d'aourer les ydoles, et disoit que il n'estoit que un seul Dieu que aourer et servir on devoit, ceste noble dame ne pot avoir de ceste chose pascience, ains s'en fuy, toute eschevellee, pleine de dueil, plourant et batant au palais ou son mary estoit, que elle trouva entre les faulx juges, qui ja lui avoient livré le buvrage venimeux pour abregier sa vie. Et comme elle [fol. 91r a] arrivast sur le point que Socrates vouloit mettre la[2] hanap a la bouche pour le venim boire,[3] elle aff[ui][4] celle part et par grant yre lui arracha le hanap des mains, et tout versa par terre. Mais S[o]crates l'en reprist[5] et l'amonnesta de pacience et la reconforta. Et comme celle ne peust mettre empeschement en sa mort, fort se doulousoit[6] en disant: 'Ha! quel domage et quel grant perte, faire mourir un si juste homme a tort et a pechié!' Et Socrates tous dis la reconfortoit, et lui dit[7] que mieulx valoit que il mourust a tort que a cause; et ainsi fina, mais ne fina mie le dueil ou cuer de celle qui l'amoit toute sa vie."[8]

## *Chapitre 22*    Ci dit de[9] Pompaye Pauline, femme de Seneque

"Seneque, le tres sage philosophe, non obstant que il fust ja tout envieilliz[10] et que toute s'entente estoit [fol. 91r b] a l'estude, ne demoura pas pour ce que il ne fust tres amé de sa femme belle et joeune, qui nommee estoit Pompeye Pauline. Toute la cuer de celle noble dame estoit de le servir et garder sa paix, comme celle qui tres loyaument et chierement l'amoit. Et quant elle sceut que le tyrant Empereur Noyron a qui il avoit esté maistre l'avoit condempné a mourir, par estre seigniez en un baing, celle comme forsennee devint de douleur, et comme celle qui avec son mary bien mourir[11] voulist, ala crier moult de vilennies au tirant Noyron afin que il estendist sa cruaulté sur elle autressi.[12] Mais comme toute ce riens ne lui vaulsist, tant se dolosa de la mort de son espoux que gaires aprés ne vesqui."

---

[1] blasmoit] reprenoit
[2] la] le
[3] le venim boire] boire le venim
[4] aff[ui] : *affin*
[5] Mais S[o]crates l'en reprist : *Sacrates*] De laquelle chose Socrates la reprist
[6] fort se doulousoit] s'en doulousoit forment
[7] et lui dit] en disant
[8] le dueil ou cuer de celle qui l'amoit toute sa vie] toute sa vie le dueil ou cuer de celle qui l'amoit
[9] Ci dit de] De
[10] tout envieilliz] enviellis
[11] bien mourir] mourir
[12] sur elle autressi] semblablement sur elle

"And when this woman knewe that her husbande was condempned to the dethe by them of Athenes for that that he blamed them that they worshypped the ydolles, and sayd that there was not but one God that ought to be worshypped and served, this noble lady myght not have pacyence of this thynge but fledde, her heere hangynge aboute her chekes, full of sorowe, wepynge, and betynge at the palays gate where her housbande was. And there she founde hym amonge the false juges, whiche hadde taken to hym a venymous drynke to shorten his lyfe. And when it came to the poynte that Socrates wolde put the cuppe to his mouthe to drynke the venyme, she wente to hym with a grete wrathe and raced the cuppe out of his hande, and threwe it all togyder on the erthe. But Socrates repreved her and counsayled her to have pacyence, and comforted her. And when she myght not let hym in no wyse fro that dethe, she sorowed strongly and sayd: 'Ha, what harme and what losse is it to make so juste a man to dye wrongefully and synfully!' And Socrates alway comforted her, and sayd to her that it was better that he sholde dye wrongfully, then ryghtfully, and so he passed. But the sorowe ended not in the herte of her that loved hym so moche all her lyfe." [E3v]

## *Chapter 22*      Of Pompe Paulyne, wyfe of Seneke

"The ryght wyse phylosophre Seneke, notwithstandynge that he was ryght olde and al his entent was in studyeng, it fayled not but that he was well byloved of his wyfe fayre and yonge, whiche was named Pompee Paulyne. All the charge that this noble lady had was to serve hym and kepe hym in peas, as she that ryght truly and derely loved hym. And when she knewe that the tyraunt Emperour Nero, to whom he had ben mayster, had condempned hym to dye, to be drowned in a bayne fatte, then as she that became out of herselfe [with][1] sorowe, and as she that wolde fayne dye with her husbande, wente cryenge many vylanyes to the tyraunt Nero to the entente that he sholde stretche his cruelte upon her also, but all that avayled her not. So moche she sorowed the dethe of her housbande that she lyved not longe after."

---

[1] herselfe [with] : *herselfe*

Et je, Christine, dis adonc [fol. 91v a] a la dame qui parloit: "Certes, dame honnouree, voz paroles m'ont ramenteu et trait a memoire maintes autres femmes belles et jeunes[1] tres parfaictement amantes leurs maris, non obstant que moult fussent lai[t][2] et vieulx. Et mesmes en mon temps l'ay assez veu que ama tres parfaictement son seigneur, et loyale amour lui porta tant qu'il vesqui. La noble[3] fille d'un des grans barons de Bretaingne qui fut donnee par mariage au tres vaillant connestable de France messire Bertran de Claquin, laquelle[4] non obstant fust il tres lait de corps et vieil, celle noble[5] dame estant en la fleur de sa jounece, qui plus regarda au grant pris de ses vertus que a la façon de son corps,[6] l'ama de tres grant amour, tant que toute sa vie a plainte et doulousee [fol. 91v b] la mort de lui. Et d'asses d'autres semblables[7] pourroie dire, que je laisse pour briefté."

*Response*: "De ce te croy je moult bien. Et encore te diray des dames amantes leurs maris."

*Chapitre 23*    Ci dit de[8] la noble Sulpice

"Sulpice fut femme de Lentulius Crussolien, no[b]le[9] homme de Romme, que elle ama de si grant amour comme il ypparu. Car comme cellui fust condempnes par les juges de Romme pour certaines choses dont il fu encoulpés a estre envoiez miserablement en exil, et que la pouvrement usast sa vie, la bonne[10] Dame Sulpice, non obstant que elle fust a Romme de moult grant richece, et peust demourer aise en delices et a repos, mieulx ama[11] suivre son mary en sa pouvreté et exil que demourer en habondance de richeces sans lui. Si renonça [fol. 91r a] a tous ses heritages, a ses avoirs, et a son païs, et fist tant que a quelque peine se embla[12] de sa mere et de ses parens, qui pour celle cause moult curieusement la gardoient. Et en habit mescogneu fist tant que elle[13] ala a son mary.

Dit Christine: "Certes, dame, il me souvient par ce que vous dictes d'aucunes femmes que j'ay veu en mon temps auques en cas pareil. Car de telles ay cogneues

---

[1] jeunes : *jueunes*
[2] lai[t] : *laiz*
[3] noble] noble dame
[4] laquelle] lequel
[5] noble] vaillant
[6] son corps] la personne
[7] toute sa vie a plainte et doulousee la mort de lui. Et d'asses d'autres semblables] a toute sa vie plainte la mort de lui. Et ainsi d'assez d'autres en cas pareil
[8] Ci dit de] De
[9] no[b]le : *nole*
[10] bonne Dame Sulpice] tres bonne Sulpice
[11] aise en delices et a repos mieulx ama] aise et en delices a repos ama mieulx
[12] se embla] que elle s'embla
[13] fist tant que elle] *omitted*

And I, Christine, sayd then to the lady that spake to me: "Certes, madame, your wordes hathe remembred me and drawne to mynde many other women fayre and yonge ryght perfytely lovynge theyr husbandes, notwithstandynge that they were ryght feble and olde. And in my tyme I have sene ynowe that have loved theyr husbandes perfytely and hath borne them true love all the whyle they lyved, and namely the noble doughter of one of the grete barons of Brytayne that was gyven by maryage to the ryght worshypfull constable of Fraunce Syr Bertram Claquyn, the whiche, notwithstandynge that he was ryght lewde of shap of his body and olde, this noble lady, beynge in the [E4r] floure of her youthe, whiche toke hede more to the grete pryce of his vertue then to the facyon of his body, loved hym of ryght grete love, so moche that all her lyfe she had plente of sorowe for his dethe. And ynowe of other lyke I myght telle, whiche that I lette passe for short[n]esse[1] of tyme."

*Answere*: "Of that I leve thee ryght well. And yet I shall tell thee of mo ladyes lovynge theyr husbandes."

## Chapter 23     Of the noble Sulpyce

"Sulpyce was wyfe of Lentylyus Consulyennole, a man of Rome, whome she loved of so grete love as it appered, for when he sholde be condempned by the juges of Rome for certayne thynges of whiche he was blamed to be sente wretchedly into exyle, and there to use his lyfe poorely, the good Lady Sulpyce, notwithstondynge that she was in Rome of ryght grete rychesse and myght abyde in ease and reste, loved better to folowe her husbande in his poverte and exyle than abyde in haboundaunce of rychesse without hym. So she renounced all her herytage, goodes, and countre, and dyde so moche that she stale away fro her moder and cosynes, whiche kepte her for the same cause that she sholde not go away. And in an unknowne wede dyde so moche that she wente to her housbande."

Christine sayd, "Certes, madame, it semeth me by that that ye say of some women that I have sene in my tyme in lyke case, for of suche I have knowne of

---

[1] short[n]esse : *shortuesse*

de qui leurs maris demouroient[1] meseaulx, et que il couvenoit que ilz fussent separez du siecle et mis en maladies.[2] Mais leurs bonnes femmes oncques pour ce ne les laissierent,[14] et mieulx amoient aler avecques eulx pour les servir en leurs maladies,[3] et leur tenir la loyal foy promise [fol. 92r b] en mariage que demourer sans leurs maris bien aises en leurs maisons. Et cuide[4] aujourd'uy congnoistre telle qui est joeune et bonne et belle, de laquelle le mari est souspeçonné de[5] tel maladie. Mais comme ses parens la timonnent souvent, et la pressier[6] de laissier sa compagnie et s'en aler demourer avecques eulx, elle leur respont que jour de sa vie ne le laira. Et que se il[7] le font esprouver et il est trouvé attaint de la dicte maladie, par quoy il couviegne que il laisse le siecle, que sans faille elle yra avec lui. Et pour celle cause ses parens le laissent a faire esprouver.

"*Item*, autres femmes je cognois, et les laisse a nommer pour ce que par aventure leur[8] en desplairoit, qui ont maris si pervers et de si desordennee vie [fol. 92v a] que les parens des femmes vouldroient que mors fussent,[9] et mettent toute peine pour[10] retraire ycelles femmes avecques eulx et hors de leurs mauvaiz mariz. Mais elles aiment mieulx estre bien batues, maupeues, et estre en[11] grant pouvreté et subgeccion avecques leurs maris que les laissier, et dient a leurs amis, 'Vous le m'avez donné; avec lui morray et vivray.'[12] Et ce sont choses que on voit tous les jours, mais chascun ne considere pas."[13]

## Chapitre 24    Ci dit de pluseurs dames ensemble qui respiterent leurs mariz de mort

"De plusieurs femmes ensemble, pareillement que les subdites,[14] de grant amour a leurs maris te vueil encore[15] raconter.

---

[1] demouroient] devenoient

[2] maladies] maladerie

[3] leurs maladies] leur maladie

[4] cuide] si cuide

[5] souspeçonné de] moult souspeçonné d'avoir

[6] pressier] pressent

[7] il] ilz

[8] leur] il leur

[9] mors fussent] ilz fussent mors

[10] pour] de

[11] et estre en] en

[12] avec lui morray et vivray] avecques lui vivray et mourray

[13] on voit tous les jours, mais chascun ne considere pas] chacun jour on voit mais chacun n'y vise

[14] pareillement que les subdites] pareillement ensemble que les susdictes

[15] encore] ancores

whom the husbandes [E4v] have become lyppers and that it were convenyent that they were departed fro the worlde and put in syke houses. But theyr good wyves, evermore for that that they wolde not leve them, loved better to goo with them for to serve them in theyr sykenesse and to holde them the true faythe and promyse in maryage than to byde without theyr housbandes well at ease in theyr houses. And I trowe I knowe one that is yonge, fayre, and good of whome the housbande is had in suspeccyon of suche sykenesse. But as her frendes hath warned her, and preched to her to leve his company and to dwell with them, she answered that the dayes of her lyfe she wolde not leve hym. And yf they make it to be proved that he is ataynte of the sayd maladye, by whiche it is convenyent that he forsake the worlde, that without fayle she wolde go with hym. And for that cause her frendes have lefte it to make a proffe therof.

"Also other women I knowe, that I leve to be named for that that by adventure I sholde dysplease them, whiche that have housbandes so cursed and of so an unordynate lyfe that the fader and the moder of the woman wolde that they were deed, and dothe all that they may for to withdrawe the women to them from theyr shrewde husbandes. But they love better to be beten with many paynes, and to be in grete poverte and subjeccyon with theyr husbandes then for to leve them. And they saye to theyr frendes, 'Ye have gyven me to hym; with hym shall I lyve and dye.' And these thynges be sene all daye, but all people consydereth it not." [E5r]

*Chapter 24*     **Here it speketh of dyvers ladyes that respyted theyr husbandes fro the dethe**

"Of many women also in the same wyse as those before sayd, of grete love to theyr husbandes I wyll tell you yet.

"Il avint aprés ce que Jason ot esté en Colcos pour querre[1] la toison [fol. 92v b] d'or, que aucuns des chevaliers que il mena avec[2] lui, qui estoient d'une contree de Grece que on nommoit Menudie, laissierent leur propre païs et cité et s'en alerent demourer en une autre cité de Grece que on nommoit Lacedemonie. Si y furent grandement receus et honnourez, tant pour leur anciene noblece comme pour leurs richesces. La se marierent a des nobles filles de la cité. Et tant enrichierent yceulx, et monterent en honneurs, que ilz se esleverent en si grant orgueil que conspiracion vouldrent faire contre les souverains de la cité, et eulx attribuer la seingneurie; si fu sceu[3] leur machinacion, par quoy tous furent mis en prison et condampnes a mort.

"De cestes[4] chose furent leurs femmes a moult grant douleur, et [fol. 93r a] ensemble se assemblerent comme pour faire leur dueil. Si se vont la conseillier entre elles se aucune voye pourroient trouver comment leurs maris peussent delivrer, en[5] la fin fu le fait[6] de leur conclusion tel: que toutes ensemble, par nuit, se vestirent[7] de mauvais[8] robes, et affublerent[9] leurs tetes de maintiaux comme se elles le feissent pour non estre cogneues. Et en cel estat alerent a[10] la prison, et tant prierent en plourant avecques dons[11] aux gardes des prisons que ilz leur soffrirent aler veoir leurs maris. [Quant les dames furent la, elles vestirent leurs maris][12] de leurs robes, et pristrent les robes que ilz vestues[13] avoient, et puis les mirent hors; et les gardes cuiderent que ce fussent les femmes qui s'en retournassent. Quant vint au jour que mourir devoient, les bourreaulx les menerent au tourment. [fol. 93r b] Et quant il fu veu que c'estoient[14] femmes, chascun ot admiracion de leur sage cautelle. Si en furent loees, et les citoiens orent pitié de leurs filles. Si n'en moru nulle, et ainsi ces vaillans femmes delivrerent de mort leurs maris."

---

    [1] querre] conquerre
    [2] avec] avecques
    [3] sceu] descouverte
    [4] cestes] ceste
    [5] en] a
    [6] fait] effect
    [7] vestirent] vestiroient
    [8] mauvais] mauvaises
    [9] affublerent] affubleroient
    [10] a] en
    [11] avecques dons] avec promesses et dons
    [12] Quant les dames furent la, elles vestirent leurs maris : *omitted*] Quant les dames furent la, elles vestirent leurs maris
    [13] vestues] vestus
    [14] c'estoient] s'estoient

"It happened after that that Jason had ben in Coltos to gete the golden fleece, that some of his knyghtes that he brought with hym, whiche were of a countre of Grece that is called Menudye, lefte theyr owne countre and cyte and wente to dwelle in another cyte of Grece that is called Lacedemonye. Soo they were there gretely receyved and honoured, as moche for theyr auncyent noblesse as for theyr rychesse. And there they maryed the moost noblest maydens of the cyte, and so moche they waxed ryche and mounted in worshyp that they lyfted up themselfe in so grete pryde that they wolde make a conspyracyon ayenst the soveraynes of the cyte. And so they dyde to have the lordeshyp; so theyr ymagynacyon was knowen, wherfore all were put in pryson and condempned to the dethe.

"Of this thynge theyr wyves were in greate sorowes, and they assembled them togyder as for to make theyr sorowes. So it was counsayled amonge them yf ony way myght be founde howe they myght delyver theyr husbandes, and in the ende this was theyr conclusyon: that in a nyght they sholde araye them in lewde gownes, and they sholde cover theyr heedes [E5v] with mantelles as thoughe they wolde not be knowne. And in suche a wyse they wente to the pryson, and soo moche they prayed with wepynge and gyftes to the kepers of the pryson that they wolde suffre them to go se theyr husbandes. And when they were with theyr husbandes, they gave them theyr lewde gownes and toke those gownes that they were clothed in, and syth put them out of the pryson; and the kepers trowed that it were the women that had tourned agayne. And when it came to the daye that they sholde dye, the kepers brought them to the tourment. And when it was sene that they were women, eche of them had grete mervayle of theyr wyse cauteyle. Soo they were gretely praysed, and the cytezynes had pyte of theyr doughters, so there dyed none. And so these worshypful women delyvered theyr husbandes fro the dethe."

*Chapitre 25*      **Dit Christine a Dame [Droicture]¹ contre ceulx qui**
**dient que femmes ne scevent riens celer, et la response**
**que elle lui fait est de Porcia, fille de Catho**

"Dame, je cognois certainement maintenant et autre fois l'ay aperceu que grant
est l'amour et la foy que maintes ont et ont eu a leurs maris. Et² pour ce je me
donne merveille d'un language qui cuert communement³ entre les hommes, et
mesmement Maistre Jehan de Meun trop fort l'afferme en son *Romant de la Rose*,
et autres aucteurs aussi le font, que homme ne die a sa femme chose qu'il vueille
celer, et que [fol. 93v a] femmes ne scevent⁴ taire."

*Response*: "Amie chiere, tu dois savoir que toutes femmes ne sont mie sages,
et semblablement ne sont les hommes. Par quoy se un homme a aucun savoir, il
doit bien voirement aviser quel sens sa femme a et quel bonté ains que il lui die
gaires chose qu'il vueille celler, car peril y puet avoir. Mais quant un homme sent
que il a une femme bonne, sage, et discrete, il n'est ou monde chose plus fiable,
ne qui tant le puist⁵ reconforter.

"Et que femmes fussent si pou secretes comme yceulx veulent dire, et
encore ad ce propos de femmes amans leurs maris, n'ot mie celle oppinion jadis
a Romme le noble homme Brutus, mari de Porcia. Celle noble Dame Porcia fut
fille de Chato le Mendre, qui nepveu estoit au grant Chato. Son dit [fol. 93v b]
mary Brutus,⁶ qui la senti tres sage, secrete, et chaste, lui dist l'entencion que il
avoit lui et Cassien (qui estoit un autre noble homme de Romme) de occire Julius
Cesar au conseil. Laquelle chose la sage dame, avisant le grant mal qui en venroit,
de toute sa poissance lui desconseilla, et du meschief de ceste chose⁷ toute la nuit
dormir ne pot.

"Le matin venu, quant Brutus yssoit de sa chambre pour aler perfornir son
emprise, la dame qui moult voulentiers l'en destournast prist le rasouer du barbier si comme pour tranchier ses ongles et le laissa cheoir, puis fist maniere de
le reprendre et tout de gré en la main le se ficha,⁸ par quoy ses femes qui navré
la virent durement s'escrierent si fort⁹ que Brutus retourna. [fol. 94r a] Et quant
blecié la vit, il la blasma et dist que ce n'estoit mie son office de ouvrer de rasouer,
mais au barbier. Et elle lui respondi que elle ne l'avoit pas fait si folement comme

¹ [Droicture] : *Raison*
² ont et ont eu a leurs maris. Et] femmes ont eu et ont a leurs maris
³ communement] assez communement
⁴ scevent] se scevent
⁵ puist] peust
⁶ mary Brutus] mari
⁷ desconseilla et du meschief de ceste chose] desconseilla et desloua, et du soucy de
ceste chose fu a si grant meschef que
⁸ en la main le se ficha] le se ficha en la main
⁹ durement s'escrierent si fort] si fort s'escrierent

*Chapter 25*     Here Christine speketh to Dame Ryghtwysnes ayenste
them that sayth that women cannot kepe noo counsayle;
and the answere that she maketh of Porcya

"Madame, I knowe certaynely nowe and also I have perceyved that grete is the
love and the trouthe that many have had and hath to theyr husbandes. And
therfore I have grete mervayle of a language that renneth comunely amonge
these men, and also Mayster Johan de Meun affermeth [E6r] it so strongly in his
*Romaunce of the Rose* and other auctours also dothe it, that what a man saythe to
his wyfe, it maye not be kepte pryve and that women cannot holde theyr peas."

*Answere*: "Dere frende, thou oughtest to knowe that all women be not wyse,
and the same it is of men, by the whiche yf a man have ony wytte, he ought well
to advyse hym what wytte his wyfe hathe and what goodnesse or he saye ony
thynge that he wolde have kepte close, for therof myght come foly. But when a
man knoweth that he hath a good wyfe, wyse and dyscrete, there is nothynge
more trusty in the worlde, nor that so moche may comforte a man, for dyscrecyon
and secretenesse are to be commended in ony persone.

"And yet to the purpose of women lovynge theyr husbandes, there was
late a man in Rome ryght notable named Brutus, whiche was maryed to a
gentylwoma[n]¹ named Porcya. This noble Porcya was doughter of Chaton
the Lesse, whiche was nevewe to Grete Chaton. Her foresayd housbande Brutus [who] felte² that his wyfe was ryght wyse, secrete, and chaste tolde her his
entente that he and Cassyen, another noble man of Rome, were in purpose to
sle Julyus Cesar at the Counsayle. The whiche thynge, the wyse lady advysynge
the grete evyl that myght come of it, with al her puyssaunce counsayled hym the
contrary and warned hym of the myschyefe that myght falle therof, and myght
not slepe all the nyght.

"Then the morowe comen when that the foresayd Brutus wente oute of
his [E6v] chambre to goo to perfourme his entrepryse; the lady, whiche wolde
full fayne tourne his purpose, toke a rasoure frome the barboure as thoughe she
wolde have pared her nayles and lete the rasoure falle, and after made as thoughe
she wolde have taken it up. And anone she smote herselfe in the hande, wherfore
her women that sawe her so wounded cryed so pyteously and so strongely that
Brutus tourned agayne. And when he sawe her hurte, he blamed her and sayd
that it was not her offyce to werke with a rasoure, but of the barboure. And she

---

¹ gentylwoma[n] : *gentylwoman*
² Brutus [who] felte : *Brutus felte*

il pensoit. Car ce avoit elle fait tout de gré pour essaier comment elle se occiroit, se de l'entreprise[1] que il avoit faicte venoit mal pour lui. Mais cellui ne s'en laissa oncques et ala, et occist tantost aprés entre lui et Cassien Julius Cesar.

"Mais ilz en furent exillez et en fu puis occis Brutus, non obstant que il s'en fust fuis hors de Romme. Mais quant Porcia sa bonne femme sceut sa mort, sa douleur fu si grande[2] que elle renonça a joye et vie. Et pour ce que on l[u]i[3] tolli costeaulx et toutes [fol. 94r b] choses[4] dont occire se peust, car on veoit bien ce que faire vouloit. Elle ala au feu et prist charbons ardens et les avala, et ainsi se ardi et estaingni. Et par ceste[5] voye qui fu la plus estrange dont oncques autre morust fina la noble Porcia."

## *Chapitre 26*    A ce mesmes propos, dit de la noble dame Curia

"Encore te diray ad ce propos contre ceulx qui dient que femmes riens ne scevent celer,[6] et tousjours continuant la matiere de la grant amour que maintes femmes ont[7] a leurs maris: Curia la noble Rommaine fu[8] de merveilleuse foy, constance, sagece, et amour[9] envers Quintus Lucrecius son mary. Car comme son dit mary et aussi d'autres semblablement fussent condempnez a mort pour certain crime que on leur mettoit sus, et il leur [fol. 94v a] venist a congnoiscence que on les queroit pour estre justiciez, tant de bien leur avint que ilz orent espase de eulx en fuir. Mais pour la grant paour que avoient d'estre trouvez, ilz s'aloient cacher[es][10] cauvernes de[11] bestes sauvages, et encore pas bien abiter n'y osoient. Mais Lucrecius, par le sens et bon conseil de sa femme, oncques ne se parti de sa chambre. Et quant ceulx qui le queroient vindrent la, elle le tenoit entre ses bras en son lit. Mais si sagement le cachoit[12] que oncques ne l'aperceurent, et entre les murs de sa chambre si bien le cacha que oncques maisgne ne personne ne le sceut. Et par si grant cautelle et sagece le savoit celer[13] que elle, vestue de pouvres draps,

---

[1] se de l'entreprise] se l'emprise
[2] sa douleur fu si grande] tant fu grande sa douleur
[3] l[u]i : *li*
[4] toutes choses] toute chose
[5] ceste] celle
[6] ne scevent celer] celer ne scevent
[7] femmes ont] ont
[8] fu : *feu*
[9] amour] bonne amour
[10] cacher[es] : *cacher*] cachant es
[11] de] des
[12] cachoit] cachoit et muçoit
[13] cacha que oncques maisgne ne personne ne le sceut. Et par si grant cautelle et sagece le savoit celer] sceut celer et mucier que oncques mesgnee que elle eust ne personne ne le sceut, et par si grant cautelle savoit couvrir le fait

answered hym that she had not done it soo folyly as he thought for that that she
had done was a purpose to assaye howe she myght sle herselfe yf the entrepryse
that he had made sholde tourne hym to evyll. But for all that he wolde not leve,
but wente anone and bytwene hym and Cassyen they slewe Julyus Cesar.

"And anone after they were exyled, and Brutus was slayne, notwithstandynge
that he was fled out of Rome. But when Porcya his good wyfe knewe that he was
deed, her sorowe was so grete that she forsoke the joye of her lyfe. And for that
that men toke awaye from her her knyves and all thynges that she myght sle her
with, for folkes sawe wel what she wolde do. She wente to the fyre and toke brennynge coles, and brente her, and dyed. And by this waye ended this noble Lady
Porcya, whiche was the moost straungest dethe that ever ony dyed on." [F1r]

*Chapter 26*     **And yet of the same matter: and speketh of the noble
                 Lady Curya**

"And yet I shall tell thee to that purpose ayenst them that saye that women cannot kepe no counsayle, and alwaye contynuynge the matter of the grete love
that many women have to theyr husbandes: Curya the noble Romayne was of
mervayllous fayth, constaunce, wysdome, and love towarde Quyntus Lucrecyus
her husbande. For when her sayd husbande and other in lykewyse sholde be condempned to the dethe for a certayne cryme that was put upon them, and it sholde
come to his knowledge that one sought them to be justyfyed, it happened hym
so well that they had space to flee. But for the fere that they had to be founde,
they wente to hyde them in caves of wylde beestes, and yet they durst not abyde
there. But Lucrecyus, by the good counsayle of his wyfe, parted never out of his
chambre. And when they that sought them came there, she helde hym bytwene
her armes in her bedde. And she hyd hym soo wysely that they never perceyved
hym, and after had hym so wysely bytwene the walles of her chambre that never
none of her meynye perceyved it ne knewe it. And she coude so well kepe his
counsayle by grete cautele and wysdome that she clothed her in poore clothes,

eschevelee et esplouree, batant ses [fol. 94v b] paumes, fuioit et traçoit par les rues, par les temples[1] et par moustiers comme se fole fust, et par tout demandoit et encerçoit se personne savoit que son mary estoit devenu, ne ou il estoit fuis? Car ou qu'il fust, aler voulsist avec[2] lui pour estre compagne de son exil, et de ses miseres. Et par celle voye si sagement savoit faindre que jamais homme ne l'apperceust, et ainsi le sauva. Et avec ce son mary,[3] plein de paour, reconfortoit. Et a brief parler tant fist et tant pourchaça que elle de mort et de exil le sauva."

## *Chapitre 27*     Encore ad ce propos[4]

"Et pour ce que nous sommes en propos[5] de dire exemples contre ceulx qui dient que femmes ne scevent riens celer, certes infinis dire t'en porroye. Mais souffise toy seulement d'un que je te diray encore.

"Ou [fol. 95r a] temps que Noiron le tyrant empereur regnoit a Romme, furent aucuns hommes qui considererent que pour les tres grans maulx et cruaultes que le dit Noiron faisoit, que grant bien et grant prouffit seroit de lui tollir la vie. Si firent conspiracion contre lui et deliberent de le tuer. Yceulx hommes repairoient tous chieux[6] une femme en qui tant se fioient que point ne laissierent a dire le fait de leur conspiracion devant elle. Et comme il avenist un soir que ilz avoient deliberé de mettre l'endemain a effait leur entreprise, souppoient chieux la dicte femme. Et pas asses sagement ne se gardoient[7] de parler, par quoy par mesaventure furent oÿs de tel,[8] qui pour flater et avoir la grace de l'empereur lui ala tantost dire ce qu'il [fol. 95r b] avoit ouÿ. Par quoy ne s'en furent pas plus tost partis dechieux la dicte femme les hommes qui la conspiracion avoient faicte que vindrent a l'uis de la femme les sergens de l'empereur. Mais pour ce que pas les hommes n'y trouverent, la femme menerent devant l'empereur,[9] lequel moult lui enquist de ceste chose. Mais comme oncques ne[10] peust tant faire par beaulx dons donner ne[11] promettre, ne par force de tourmens ou il ne l'espargna mie, que il

---

[1] les temples] temples
[2] avec] avecques
[3] mary] mari, qui estoit
[4] ce propos] ce mesmes propos
[5] en propos] entrez
[6] tous chieux] cheus
[7] gardoient] garderent
[8] de tel] et escoutez de personne
[9] *skips to next* empereur] l'empereur, lesquieulx pour ce que pas ne trouverent les hommes menerent la femme devant l'empereur
[10] ne] il ne
[11] donner ne] offrir et

her heere hangynge aboute her chekes, al forwepte, betynge her handes togyder, wente aboute by the stretes and by the [F1v] temples, and asked all aboute
after her husbande and serched yf ony persone knewe where her husbande was
become, or to what place he was fled: 'For my desyre is to be felawe with hym in
his exyle, and in his myseryes.' And by this way so wysely she coude fayne that
never man perceyved it, and so she saved hym. And with that she comforted her
housbande, full of sorowe. And shortely to saye, so moche she dyde and so moche
she purchaced for hym that she delyvered hym not onely from his exyle, but from
his dethe also."

## Chapter 27     Yet of the same purpose

"And for that we be in purpose to telle ensamples ayenst them that say that
women cannot kepe noo counsayle, truely I myght tell thee of ynowe of them
without nombre. But let it suffyse thee of one that I shall tell thee yet.

"In the tyme that Nero the tyraunt and emperour reygned in Rome, there
were certayne men that consydered that, for the ryght grete myscheves and crueltes that the sayd Nero dyde, that it sholde be grete welthe and profyte to take away
the lyfe fro hym. So they made conspyracyon ayenst hym and were advysed to sle
hym. These same men repayred al to the house of one woman in the whiche they
trusted so moche that they spared not [to][1] saye the dede of theyr conspyracyon
before her. And as it happened in an evenynge tyde that [F2r] they were advysed
to put to effecte in the mournynge theyr entrepryse, they souped with the sayd
woman. And they kepte them not wysely fro spekynge, by the whiche by mysadventure there were some that herde them, whiche for to flatter and to have grace
of the emperoure wente and tolde hym what they herde them say. By the whiche
they were not so soone departed from the sayd woman but that the sergeauntes of
the emperoure came to the woman's house. But bycause that they founde not the
men there that conspyred thus the dethe of the emperour, they toke the woman
and ledde her before the emperoure, whiche enquyred gretely of this matter. But
he coude never doo so moche by gyvynge of grete gyftes, nor by promyse, nor
by force of tourmentes of whiche he spared none, that he myght knowe of this

---

[1] not [to] saye : *not saye*

peust traire de ceste femme qui ces hommes estoient, ne mesmement que elle en
sceust riens, fu esprouvee constan[t]e[1] et secrete merveilleusement."

## *Chapitre 28*   Preuves contre ce que aucuns dient que homme est vil qui croit au conseil de sa femme, ne y ajouste foy: demande Christine, et Droicture lui respont

"Dame, par les raisons que j'entens de vous et par ce que je voy tant de sens et de
bien estre en femme, je me merveil[2] de ce que plusieurs dient que yceulx hommes
sont vilz et folz qui croient ne adjoustent foy au conseil de leurs femmes."

*Response*: "Je t'ay ja dit devant que toutes femmes ne sont mie sages. Mais
ceulx qui les ont bonnes et sages font que folz quant ne[3] les croient, si que tu
pueux veoir par ce que cy devant t'ay dit. Car se Brutus eust creu Porcia sa femme
de non occire Julius Cesar, lui[4] mesmes ne eust pas esté occis, ne le mal ne feust
avenu qui en avint. Et pour ce qu'en ce propos sommes entrez, te diray de plusieurs a qui semblablement en est mal avenu par non les croire. Et aussi te diray
aprés de plusieurs [fol. 95v b] a qui bien est venu[5] par les croire.

"Se Julius Cesar dont nous avons parlé eust creu sa tres sage et bonne
femme—laquelle, par plusieurs signes que elle avoit veu apparans qui signifioi-
ent la mort de son mary, et l'orrible songe que la nuit devant en avoit fait, par quoy
en tout quanque elle avoit peu elle avoit[6] destourné que il n'alast celle journee au
conseil—il ne[7] fust pas alez et n'eust mie esté occis.

"*Item*, semblablement Pompee qui avoit eu espousee Julie fille du dit Julius
Cesar si que devant t'ay dit, et aprés celle en avoit espousee une autre moult noble
dame nommee Cornelia, laquelle au propos dessus dit tant l'ama que oncques
pour malle fortune qui lui avenist ne le voult laissier. Et mesmement [fol. 96r a]
quant il fu contrainte de s'en fuir par mer aprés la bataille ou il ot esté desconfit
par Julius Cesar, la bonne dame estoit avec[8] lui et en tous perilz l'acompaignoit.
Et quant il arriva ou royaume d'Egipte et que Ptholomee, le roy du lieu, fist
semblant par traison que il avoit joye de sa venue et envoia au devant de lui ses
gens en semblant de le recevoir a joye—et ce estoit pour le occire. Lesquelz
gens lui distrent que il entrast en leur nef,[9] et que il laissast ses gens afin que

---

[1] constan[t]e : *constance*
[2] merveil] merveille
[3] ne] ilz ne
[4] lui] il
[5] plusieurs a qui bien est venu] aprés de ceulx a qui il est bien venu
[6] elle avoit] avoit
[7] ne] n'y
[8] avec] avecques
[9] distrent que il entrast en leur nef] dirent que il entrast en leurs nefs

woman what men they were, ne that she knewe ony thynge of suche matters. And thus this woman was mervayllously proved bothe secrete and constaunte."

## Chapter 28     Proves ayenst them that say that a man is but lewde that byleveth the counsayle of his wyfe, or taketh ony hede therto

"Madame, by these reasons that I understande of you, and by that I se so moche wyt and welthe to be in a woman, I mervayle of that that dyvers men saye that these men ben lewde fooles that byleve and gyveth credence to the counsayle of theyr wyves." [F2v]

*Answere*: "I have sayd to thee before that all women be not wyse. But those that have wyves good and wyse dothe grete foly when they byleve them not, so as thou mayste se by that that I have sayd to thee before. For yf Brutus had byleved Porcya his wyfe as for sleynge of Julyus Cesar, he hadde not be slayne hymselfe, ne the evyll had not happened that felle. And for that that we be entred into this purpose, I shall tell thee of dyvers to whome it hath happened evyll in the same wyse that they byleved not theyr wyves. And also I shall tell thee after of dyvers to whome it hathe well happened that they byleved theyr wyves.

"Yf Julyus Cesar, of whome we have spoken, had byleved the ryght wyse and good woman whiche by many tokens that she had sene apperynge that betokened the dethe of her husbande, and the horryble dreme that she had the nyght before, by the whiche she counsayled hym to tourne his purpose, that he sholde not come at the Counsayle that daye—yf he had not come there, he had not ben slayne.

"Also in the same wyse Pompe that had wedded Julye the doughter of Julyus Cesar, as I have sayd before, and after her he wedded another noble lady named Cornelya, whiche to the purpose abovesayd loved hym so moche that for none evyll fortune that happened hym wolde not leve hym. And also when he was constrayned to fle by the see after the batayle in whiche he was dyscomfyted by Julyus Cesar, the good lady was alway with hym, and bare hym company in al his perylles. [F3r] And when he aryved in the kyngdome of Egypte, and that Tholomee the kynge of that countre made semblaunte by treason that he had joye of his comynge, sente his people before hym as thoughe they sholde receyve hym with joy—and that was for to sle hym—the whiche people sayd to hym that he sholde entre into theyr shyppes, and that he sholde leve his people to that entente that

plus legierement le peussent mettre a port pour leur vaissel qui estoit plus legier. Mais[1] il y voulsist entrer, sa sage et bonne femme Cornille lui desconseilloit qu'il n'y alast nullement, et qu'il ne se separast[2] point des siens. Et quant elle vit que il ne l'en vouloit croire, elle a qui ce de cuer[3] n'en [fol. 96r b] disoit nul bien se voult lancier en la nef avec lui, mais ce[4] ne voult il souffrir et la couvint tenir si comme a force. Dont des lors lui commença son dueil[5] qui puis ne lui failli toute sa vie: car ne l'ot pas moult esloingnié q[ue][6] elle qui n'avoit le regart ailleurs,[7] le vit murdrir aux traitteurs dedens leur nef, par[8] lequel dueil en mer se fust gitte, se a force n'en eust esté gardee.

"*Item*, pareillement en mesavint au preux Hector de Troye, car comme la nuit devant qu'il fu occis Andromacha sa femme[9] eust eu en avision trop merveilleuse que se Hector aloit en bataille l'endemain, que il y mourroit sans faille. Par quoy la dame, effraié de ceste chose qui ne fust mie songié[10] mais vraye prophicie, le pria a jointes mains, agenoillee devant lui, en lui aportant [fol. 96v a] entre ses bras ses deux beaulx enfans, que il se voulsist a cellui jour deporter d'aler en la bataille. Mais comme il deprisast du tout ces[11] parolles, pensant que a tousjours mais ce lui sembloit lui deust avoir esté un reproche[12] que pour le conseil et paroles d'un[e][13] femme laissast a aler[14] en la bataille. Ne pour priere de pere ne de mere, a qui elle l'en faist[15] requerir, ne s'en voult deporter. Par quoy il[16] en avint ainsi que dit avoit: car occis y fu par Achilles, dont mieux lui vaulsist l'avoir creue.

"De infinis cas te porroie dire[17] d'ommes a qui il est mesavenu[18] en plusieurs manieres par non daignie croire le conseil de leurs[19] bonnes et sages femmes. Mais se mal en vient a ceulx qui le desprisent, ne doivent mie estre plains."

---

[1] Mais] Mais comme
[2] separast] departist
[3] ce de cuer] le cuer
[4] lancier en la nef avec lui, mais ce] lancier a toutes fins en la nef avecques lui mais il
[5] son dueil] le dueil a la vaillant dame
[6] q[ue] : *qz*
[7] le regart ailleurs] ailleurs son regart et qui aux yeulx le suivoit
[8] par] pour
[9] Andromacha sa femme] sa femme Andromacha
[10] songié] songe
[11] ces] ses
[12] deust avoir esté un reproche] sembloit lui eust tourné a reprouche
[13] d'un[e] : *d'un*
[14] a aler] d'aler
[15] a qui elle l'en faist] par qui elle l'en fist
[16] Par quoy il] si
[17] te porroie dire] dire te pourroye
[18] mesavenu] malvenu
[19] daignie croire le conseil de leurs] daigner croire le conseil de leur

they myght brynge theyr vesselles to the porte more lyghtely. But when he wolde have entred into theyr shyppes, his good and wyse wyfe Cornylle counsayled hym the contrary that he sholde not go into ony, nor to put his people away from hym. And when she sawe that he wolde not byleve her nor do by her counsayle, she wolde have gone into the shyp with hym, but he wolde not suffre her and made her to be holden with strengthe. Then began her sorowe that never fayled after all the dayes of her lyfe: for he was not ferre from her but she had alwaye her beholdynge after hym, and there she sawe the traytours murther hym within the shyp, for the whiche she wolde have drowned herselfe in the see, yf she had not ben kepte with strengthe.

"Also as it happened myschevously to Ector of Troye for as the nyght before that he was slayne, A[n]dromatha[1] his wyfe had a ryght mervaylous vysyon that yf Ector wente to the batayle in the morowe, that he sholde dye without fayle; by the whiche this lady, affrayed of this thynge whiche was no dreme but a mervaylous prophecy, prayed hym with joyned handes upon [F3v] her knees before hym, beryng bytwene her armes his two fayre sones, that as that day he sholde not come at the batayle. But he dyspysed her wordes, thynkynge that evermore it semed hym that it sholde be reproffe to hym that for the counsayle and wordes of a woman he sholde leve to go to the batayle. Nother for prayer of fader nor moder, to whom she hadde prayed to requyre hym, wolde he not leve, wherby it happened hym as it is sayd before for he was slayne by Achylles. Therfore it had ben better that he had byleved her.

"Of case infynyte I myght tell thee of men to whom it happened full evyl by dyvers maners that they dysdeyned not to byleve the counsayle of theyr good and wyse wyves. But yf ony evyll come to them that dyspyseth theyr counsayles, those women ought not to be blamed."

---

[1] A[n]dromatha : *Adromatha*

## *Chapitre 29* Des hommes a qui bien est ensuivi de croire leurs femmes donne exemple d'aucuns [fol. 96v b]

"De ceulx a qui il est bien avenu[1] de croire le conseil de leurs femmes te diray d'aucuns, et te souffise pour preuve. Car de tant dire en pourroie que proces seroit sans finer, et vaille ce que ja devant ay dit de maintes qui pueent servir ad ce propos.[2]

"L'Empereur Justinien, dont cy devant ay parlé, avoit un sien baron que il tenoit a compaignon et l'amoit comme soy mesmes, et avoit cellui a nom Belisere, qui moult vaillant chevalier estoit. Si l'avoit fait l'empereur maistre et gouverneur de sa chevalerie, et le faisoit seoir a sa table, servir comme soy mesmes.[3] Et a tout dire tant lui monstroit signes d'amour que les barons en orent tres grant envie, et tant que ilz dirent a l'empereur que il[4] tendoit a le faire mourir et a se revestir [fol. 97r a] de l'empire. Ceste chose crut l'empereur trop legierement, et pour trouver voye couvertement comment le peust faire mourir, lui commanda que il alast combastre contre une gent que on appelloit les Vouendres, dont nul[5] ne pouoit venir a chief pour leur grant force. Quant Belisere entendi ce commandement, il vit bien et cognut que ja l'empereur[6] ne lui enchargast ceste chose se il n'estoit forment decheut de grace et[7] benivolence. Si en fu si durement dolent que plus ne peust, et s'en ala en son hostel.

"Quant sa femme que[8] Anthoine on nommoit, et suer de l'empereis estoit, vit son mari gitté sur le lit pale, pensif,[9] et les yeulx pleins de larmes, elle qui grant pitié en eut lui enquist tant qu'a toute peine lui dist sa[10] cause de son dueil. Et quant la sage dame l'ot entendu, [fol. 97r b] adonc elle fist semblast d'estre tres joyeulx[11] et le reconforta, et dist: 'Sire, n'aves vous autre chose? De ce ne vous desconfortez.'[12] Et est assavoir que ou temps de lors, la foy de Jhesucrist estoit encore[13] assez nouvelle; et pour ce la bonne dame, qui crestiene estoit, prist a dire: 'Aiez fiance en Jhesucrist le crucefié, et de ce vendrez vous a l'aide de lui bien a chief. Et se

---

[1] avenu] pris

[2] ce que ja devant ay dit de maintes qui pueent servir ad ce propos] a ce propos ce que j'ay devant dit de maintes sages et bonnes dames

[3] servir comme soy mesmes] et servir comme lui proprement

[4] il] Belisere

[5] nul] il

[6] ja l'empereur] l'empereur ja

[7] et] et de sa

[8] que] qui

[9] pale, pensif] palle et pensif

[10] sa] la

[11] joyeulx] joyeuse

[12] Sire, n'aves vous autre chose? De ce ne vous desconfortez] Comment! N'avez vous autre chose? De ce ne vous desconfortez nullement

[13] encore] ancores

*Chapter 29*    Here it speketh of them that there is good comynge of it
that byleveth that counsayle of theyr wyves, and gyveth
ensample of dyvers ladyes

"Of them to whome it hathe fortuned well by the bylevynge of the counsayle
of theyr wyves, I shall tell thee of some and let it suffyse thee for a proffe. Soo
moche I myght say that the processe sholde be without ende, and lette that avayle
thee whiche is sayd before of many that maye serve to the same purpose.

"The Emperoure Justynyan, of whome it is sayd before, had a baron with
hym [F4r] that he helde hym as a felawe and loved hym as hymselfe, and was
called Bellyfere, whiche was ryght a worthy knyght. So the emperoure had made
hym mayster and governoure of his chevalry, and made hym to syt at his table,
served as hymselfe. And to say also, he shewed hym many sygnes of love that
the barons had grete envye therof, in soo moche that they sayd to the emperour
that he entended to slee hym, and to take the empyre upon hym. The emperour
byleved this thynge too sone, and to fynde the way covertly howe that he myght
make hym to dye, then he commaunded that he sholde go fyght ayenst a people
that was called the Voendres, whereas no man myght have the better for the grete
strengthe that they were of. When Bellyfere understode this commaundement,
and knewe well that the emperour charged hym not with this thynge but yf he
had be fallen out of his grace and benyvolence, so he was so mervaylously sorowfull that he myght not be more, and wente home to his house.

"When his wyfe, whiche was called Antonye and was syster to the empresse,
sawe her husbande lye upon his bedde pale and pensyfe, and the eyes full of
teeres, she that had grete pyte of hym demaunded hym so moche that with grete
payne he tolde her the cause of his sorowe. And when the lady understode it, then
she made semblaunt to be ryght joyous, and comforted hym and sayd: 'Syr, have
ye none other thynge that dyscomforteth you but this?' And yt is to understande
that [F4v] the faythe of Jhesu Cryst was as yet but ryght newe; and therfor the
good lady, whiche was a Crysten woman, began to saye: 'Have ye trust in Jhesu
Cryste that was crucyfyed, and ye shall have that hygher hande of your enemyes

envieux[1] vous beent a nuyre, vous ferez tant par vostre vaillance que vous les rendrez menteurs de ce que ilz dient.[2] Si me croiez et ne desprisiez mes paroles, si soit toute vostre esperance en Dieu le vif. Et je vous promet que vous vaincrez.

"'Et gardez bien que ne monstez nul semblant d'avoir de ceste chose aucune desplaisance et que nul[3] ne vous voy triste, mais tres joyeux comme cellui qui moult en est content. Et je vous diray que nous ferons [fol. 97v a] assemblez vostre host le plus hastivement que vous pourez, et gardez que nul ne sache quel part vous voulez aler. Et autressi faictes que aiez du naviere assez, et puis partes vostre host en deux partiez, et le plus tost et le plus secretement que vous pourez, a tout une partie de vostre host entrez en Aufrique, et tantost courez sus a voz anemis; et je raray l'autre partie de voz gens avec moy, et par mer arriverons de l'autre part au port. Et t[a]ndis[4] que ilz attendront a vous donner la bataille, nous entrerons de l'autre part es villes et es citez, et mettrons tout a mort et a feu et a flamme,[5] et tous les destruirons.'

"Ce conseil de sa femme crut Belisaire, si fist que sages.[6] Car ne plus, ne moins que elle avoit dit il ordenna de son[7] [fol. 97v b] erre, dont si bien lui prist que il vainqui et subjugua ses anemis, et prist[8] le roy des Vandres, et ot par le bon conseil et par le sens[9] et vaillance de sa femme si noble victoire que l'empereur l'ama mieulx que oncques mais.[10]

"*Item*, le roy Alixandre n'ot pas en despris les paroles[11] de la royne sa femme, qui ot esté fille de Daire le roy de Perse. Lors que le dit Alixandre senti que il avoit esté empoisonnez par ses serviteurs[12] et de la grant doleur que il sentoit, se voloit aler getter en une riviere pour plus tost finer sa vie. Et la dame qui l'encontra, quoy que elle eut grant doleur, le prist a reconforter et lui dist que il retournast, et se couchast en son lit; et la parlast a ses barons, et feist ses ordennances comme a tel prince[13] que il estoit apertenoit, car trop seroit [fol. 98r a] grant

---

[1] envieux] les envieux
[2] vous ferez tant par vostre vaillance que vous les rendrez menteurs de ce que ilz dient] par leurs faulses parolles vous les rendres par voz bien fais menteurs et decheus de leur fraude. Si me croyez
[3] aucune desplaisance et que nul] ceste chose nulle pesance et que on
[4] t[a]ndis : *tendis*
[5] a flamme] flame
[6] sages] sage
[7] de son] son
[8] et prist] prist
[9] conseil et par le sens] conseil, sens
[10] *R see annotations for second Belisere example*
[11] les paroles] le conseil et paroles
[12] serviteurs] desloyaulx serviteurs
[13] comme a tel prince] si comme a tel empereur

with the helpe of Hym. And thoughe the envyous wolde noye you, ye shall do soo moche by your worthynesse that ye shall yelde them lyers of that that they saye. So byleve me well and dyspyse not my wordes, and lette all your hope be in God. And I promyse you that ye shall overcome them.

"'And be well ware that ye shewe noo maner semblaunt to have ony dyspleasaunce of this thynge and that no man se you sory, but ryght joyfull as he that is well contente. And ye shal assemble your hoost in the hastyest wyse that ye maye, and beware also that no man knowe at what porte ye wyll aryve. And also loke that ye have shyppes ynowe, and then parte your hoost into two partes as soone as ye maye, secretly with one partye entrynge into Auffryke, and anone renne upon your enemyes. And I shall have that other partye of youre people with me, and we shal aryve by the see at an haven. And I tell you that they shall abyde to gyve you batayle; and we shall entre into that other parte in townes and cytees, and we shall put theym all to the dethe, and brenne and destroy all that they fynde.'

"Bellyfere byleved well this counsayle of his wyfe, soo he dyde as a wyse man, for more ne for lesse that she had sayd, he ordeyned hym on his waye, of the whiche it came so well to passe that he overcame [G1r] his enemyes and put them under subjeccyon, and toke the kynge of Voendres. And so he had this noble v[i]ctory[1] by the counsayle and wytte of his worshypfull wyfe, and then the emperour loved hym better than ever he dyde before.

"Also Kynge Alexander had not in despyte the wordes of the quene his wyfe that was doughter of Dayre, kynge of Perse. When the sayd Alexander felte that he was empoysoned by his servauntes, and of the grete sorowe that he felte, he wolde go cast hymselfe in a ryvere to ende his lyfe the sooner. And the good lady that wente ayenst hym, thoughe she had ryght grete sorowe, toke hym and comforted hym and sayd to hym that he sholde tourne agayne and sholde laye hym in his bedde, and she wolde speke to his barons and wolde make his ordynaunce as was perteynynge to suche a prynce, for it sholde be a grete losynge of his worshyp

---

[1] v[i]ctory : *voctory*

amenrissement de son honneur se aprés lui on pouoit dire que impacience l'eust convancu.[1] Si crut sa femme, et par son conseil fist ses ordennances."

### *Chapitre 30*     Ci dit du grant bien qui est venu au monde et vient tous les jours par[2] cause de femmes, dit Christine

"Dame, je voy infinis biens au monde venus par femmes, et toutevoies ces hommes dient qu'il n'est [mal][3] qui par elles ne viengne."

*Response*: "Belle amie, tu pueux veoir par ce que ja pieça t'est dit, que le contraire de ce que ilz en dient est vray car il n'est homme qui sommer peust les tres grans[4] biens qui par femmes sont avenus, et chascun jour avient. Je[5] le t'ay prouvé par les nobles dames qui les sciences et ars donnerent au monde. Mais se il ne te souffist ce que dit t'ay des biens [fol. 98r b] temporeux qui par elles sont venus, je te diray des esperituelx. O, comment est jamais hommes si ingrat que il oublie que par femme la porte de paradis lui est ouverte? C'est par la Vierge Marie. Quel plus grant bien puet il demander et que Dieux est fait homme, si que devant t'a esté dit? Et qui veult oublier les grans biens que font les meres a leurs filz, et femmes a tous hommes? Et a[6] tout le moins, je leur pry que les biens qui touchent dont[7] esperituelx, ilz ne veullent pas oublier. Et regardons en l'ancienne loy des Juifs: se tu veulx regarder l'istoire de Moise,[8] a qui Dieu donna la loy escripte des Juifs, tu trouveras que par femme cellui saint prophete par qui puis tant de grans biens vindrent fu respité de mort, si que je te diray.

"Qu temps que les Juifs estoient en la servitude [fol. 98v a] des roys d'Egipte, il estoit prophesié que un homme naistroit des Hebrieux qui tueroit[9] le peuple d'Israel de la servitude d'yceulx. Sy avint que quant Moyse, le noble duc, fu nez, sa mere, qui nourrir ne l'osoit, fu contrainte de le mettre en un petit escrin et l'envoier contre val la riviere. Si avint si comme[10] Dieux voult, qui sauve ce qui lui plaist, que Thermich la fille du roy pharaon s'esbatoit sus[11] le rivage a l'eure que l'escrinet floutoit sur l'eauue, par quoy tantost le fist prendre pour savoir qu'il avoit ens. Et quant elle vid que un enfant estoit, et si tres bel que plus bel

---

[1]  convancu] convaincus
[2]  Ci dit du . . . par] Du . . . pour
[3]  [mal] : *omitted*] mal
[4]  tres grans] grans
[5]  Je] Ja
[6]  Et a] a
[7]  dont] dons
[8]  de Moyse] des Juifs
[9]  tueroit] tireroit
[10]  comme] que
[11]  sus] sur

yf one myght say after that ympacyence had overcome hym. So he byleved his wyfe, and by her counsayle made his ordynaunces."

### Chapter 30     Here it speketh of the grete welthe that is come to the worlde and every daye cometh by the cause of women

"Madame, I se infynyte welthes come to the worlde by women. And alwaye these men say that there is none but it cometh by them."

*Answere*: "Fayre frende, thou mayst se by that that [G1v] I have sayd to thee longe ago that the contrary that they saye is true, for there is no man that may some the grete welthe that is come to the worlde by women and every daye cometh. I have proved to thee by the noble ladyes that hathe brought to the worlde scyences and craftes; but yf it suffyse thee not that I have sayd to thee of temporall welthes that ben come by them, I shal tell thee of the spyrytualles. O, howe is every man so unkynde that he forgeteth that by women the gate of paradyse was opened to us—that is, by the Vyrgyne Mary? What gretter welthe may one desyre and that God is made man, as I have sayd to thee before? And who may forgete the grete welthes that the moders do to the chyldren, and women to all men and to all the worlde? I praye them that they wolde not forgete the welthes that toucheth of whens they be spyrytuall. And let us beholde in the olde lawe of Jewes: yf thou wylte beholde the hystory of Moyses, to whome God gave the lawe of the Jewes wryten, thou shalte fynde that by a woman that same holy prophete by whome came so many grete welthes was respyted frome dethe, as I shall telle thee.

"In the tyme that the Jewes were in the thraldome of the kynge of Egypte, there sholde a man be borne of the Ebrues that sholde defende the chyldren of Israell from the bondage of them. So it happened when that Moyses, that noble duke, was borne of his moder, whiche durste not nourysshe hym, was constrayned to put hym in a lytell basket and put hym into the ryvere. So it [G2r] happened as God wolde that he sholde be saved, that Chermyche the doughter of Kynge Pharao sported her upon the ryvere that tyme that the basket floted upon the water, by the whiche anone she made to take it up for to save that she hadde goten. And when she sawe that it was a chylde, and soo fayre that noo fayrer

ne peust[1] estre veu, elle eut a merveilles grant joye. Si le fist nourrir, et dist que
il estoit sien. Et pour ce que, par miracle, il ne vouloit alaictier femme qui fust
d'estrange loy, elle le fist alaitier et nourrir par une femme [fol. 98v b] hebrieue.
Cellui Moyse, de Dieu esleu quant il fu grant, fu cellui a qui Dieu[2] donna la loy
et qui tira les Juifs hors des mains des Egipciens, et passa la Mer Rouge, et fu duc
et conduiseur des enfans d'Israel. Et ainsi vint si[3] grant bien aux Juifs a cause de
la femme qui le sauva."

*Chapitre 31*      **Ci dit de[4] Judic, la noble dame veusve**

"Judic, la noble dame veusve, sauva le peuple d'Israel de estre periz ou temps que
le second Nabugodonozor avoit envoié Holophenez, duc de sa chevalerie, sur les
Juifs aprés ce qu'il ot conquis la terre d'Egipte. Et comme le dit Holophernes eust
a moult grant poissance assigiez les Juifs en la cité, et ja les avoit si mal menez que
mais ne se pouoient tenir, et les conduis de l'iaue leur avoit toleus et tous vivres
leur estoient comme au fallir, ne mais n'avoient[5] [fol. 99r a] Juifs esperance de eulx
pouoir tenir, et estoient[6] si comme ou[7] point d'estre pris de cellui qui moult les
menaçoit, dont ilz estoit[8] a grant douleur. Et ades estoient en oroisons priant
Dieu qu'il voulsist avoir pitié de son peuple, et les voulsist deffendre des mains de
leurs anemis. Dieu ouÿ leurs oroysons, et si comme il voult sauver l'umain lignage
par femme, voult Dieux yceulx autressi secourir et sauver par femme.

"En celle cité estoit adonc Judich, la noble preudefemme qui encore joeune
femme estoit et moult belle mais[9] trop plus chaste, et meilleure estoit. Celle ot
moult grant pitié du peuple qui en tel desolacion estoit, et prioit Dieu jour et
nuyt[10] que secourir les voulsist. Et si comme Dieu l'inspira, en qui avoit fiance,
elle s'avisa[11] de [fol. 99r b] grant hardement. Et une nuyt, se recomandant a Nostre
Seigneur, se parti de la cité entre lui et sa servant,[12] et ala tant que elle vint en
[h]ost[13] de Olophernes. Et quant ceulx qui faisoient le gait de l'ost aperceurent sa

---

[1] peust] pot
[2] Dieu] Nostre Seigneur
[3] si] ce
[4] Ci dit de] De
[5] ne mais n'avoient] ne n'avoient mais
[6] estoient] estoient Juifs
[7] ou] au
[8] estoit] estoient
[9] mais] mais ancore
[10] qui en tel desolacion estoit, et prioit Dieu jour et nuyt] qu'elle veoit en si grant
desolacion si prioit jour et nuit Nostre Seigneur
[11] s'avisa] se va aviser
[12] lui et sa servant] elle et sa servante
[13] [h]ost : *vost*

myght be sene, she had a mervaylous grete joy. So she made it to be nourysshed, and sayd that it was her chylde. And for that that by myracle he wolde not souke no woman of a straunge lawe, she made it to souke and to be nourysshed by a woman of the Ebrues. This Moyses, chosen of God when he was of age, it was he to whome God gave the lawe and that drewe the chyldren of Israell out of the hondes of the Egypcyens and passed the Reede See, and was duke and conduytoure of the chyldren of Israel. And thus came so grete welthe to the Jewes by the cause of this woman that saved hym."

### Chapter 31  Of Judyth, that noble lady

"The noble lady and wydowe Judyth saved the people of Israell frome perysshynge in the tyme that the seconde Nabugodonosor had sente Holophernes, duke of his chevalry, upon the Jewes after that he had conquered the lande of Egypte. And as the sayd Holophernes with a grete puyssaunce hadde besyeged the Jewes in a cyte, and also he fared soo fowle with theym that [G2v] they myght not abyde it longe, and had taken away the conduytes of water from them, and al theyr vytaylles began to fayle them, nowe the Jewes had no hope to have power ayenst hym, and they were as upon the poynte to be taken of hym that manaced them gretely, wherfore they were in grete sorowe. And then they wente to theyr prayers, besechynge Almyghty God that He wolde have pyte of His people and to defende them from theyr enemyes. God herde theyr prayers, and as He wolde save all mankynde by a woman, He wolde save them and socoure them by a woman.

"In that cyte was Judyth than, the wyse woman whiche was yet but yonge and ryght fayre, but yet more chaste, and that was better. She had moche pyte of the people that were in suche desolacyon, and prayed God nyght and daye that He wolde socoure them. And so as God enspyred her in whome she had grete trust, she advysed her of grete herdynesse. And in a nyght she commended her to God, and departed out of the cyte she and her servaunt, and wente so moche

grant beaulté a la lumiere de la lune,[1] ilz la menerent tantost a Olophernes, qui moult la receut[2] a grant joy pour ce que belle estoit, et coste lui la fist sëoir, et moult prisa son favoir et beaulté. [3] Et en la regardant estoit fort embrasé d'elle, et par grant desir la couvoitoit.

"Mais celle, qui ailleurs pensoit, prioit tousjours Dieu en son courage qu'il lui pleust lui estre en aide de perfurnir ce que faire vouloit. Celle par belles paroles avoit tousjours pour mené Holophernes tant que elle veist son point, quant vint a la .iii.ᵉ nuytee. Holophernes avoit donné a souper a ses barons et avoit moult bien beu, si fu eshaufé de vin et de viande, et ne voult plus attendre de coushier [fol. 99v a] avec la femme hebrieue, si la manda et elle vint devers[4] lui. Il lui dist sa voulenté et celle point ne l'en escondist. Mais elle lui dist que elle lui prioit que pour plus grant honnesteté il feist vuidier son pavillon de toute gent. Et qu'il ce[5] couchast le premier, et que elle vendroit a lui sans faille environ midnuyt, quant chascun dormiroit. Ainsi[6] cellui l'acorda.

"Et la bonne dame se mist en oroison, priant tousjours Dieu que a son cuer femmenin et paoureux donnast hardement et force de delivrer son peuple du fel tirant. Quant Judich pensa que Holophernes fust endormi, elle vint tout coiement entre elle et sa mechine, et escoutoit[7] a l'uis du pavilon, et entent que cellui dormoit treffort. Adonc dist la dame: 'Alons hardiement, car Dieux est avec nous.' Si entra dedens, et sans paour prist l'espee qu'elle vit au chevet et la trait [fol. 99v b] nue, puis la hauce de toute sa force, et trenche a H[o]lophernes[8] la teste sans que de nul fust ouÿe, si met le chief en son giron.

"Et le plus tost que elle pot, s'en vait vers la cité tant que sans encombre vint[9] aux portes, si hucha: 'Venez, venez ouvrir, car Dieu est avec nous!' Et quant elle fu dedens entré, nul ne scet la joye qui fut faicte de celle aventure. Et le matin pendirent la teste a une perche sus[10] les murs, et tous se armerent et hardiement coururent sus a leurs anemis, qui encore[11] estoient en leurs liz, car de eulx jamais ne se gardassent.[12] Et quant ilz furent au pavillon de leur duc pour le faire lever hastivement,[13] et mort le trouverent, oncques gens ne furent plus esperdus. Si les

---

[1] sa grant beaulté a la lumiere de la lune] a la lumiere de la lune sa grant beauté
[2] qui moult la receut] qui
[3] favoir et beaulté] savoir, beauté, et maintien
[4] devers] vers
[5] ce] se
[6] Ainsi] Et ainsi
[7] escoutoit] escoute
[8] H[o]lophernes : *Helophernes*
[9] vint] s'en vint
[10] sus] sur
[11] encore] ancores
[12] de eulx jamais ne se gardassent] jamais de ceulx ne se gaitassent
[13] pour le faire lever hastivement] ou ilz esoient fuys pour le resveiller et faire hastivement lever

tyll that she came to the hoost of Holophernes. And when they that made the watche of the hoost perceyved her grete beaute by the lyght of the mone, they ledde her anone to Holophernes, whiche receyved her with grete joye for that she was so fayre, and made her to sytte by hym, and praysed moche her wytte and her beaute. And in the beholdynge of her he was gretely embraced with love, and by grete desyre he coveted her.

"But she that thought [G3r] otherwyse prayed God alway in her thought that He wolde her helpe to perfourme that she wolde do. And she ledde Holophernes alway forthe with fayre wordes tyll that she sawe her tyme, when it was come to the thyrde parte of the nyght. Holophernes had gyven a souper to his barons and had well dronken and was well chaufed with wyne and mete, and myght abyde no lenger fro bedde, and sente for this good Lady Judyth that she sholde come before hym. And then he tolde her his wyll, and that tyme she sayd nothynge contrary to his entente. But she sayd that she wol pray hym that for the more honeste he wolde make voyde his pavylyon of all people. And that he sholde goo fyrst to bedde, and that she wolde come to hym without fayle aboute mydnyght, when all men slepte. And thus he accorded.

"And the good lady put her to her p[r]ayers,[1] alway prayenge God that He wolde gyve hardynes to her womanly herte and ferefull to delyver His people fro the felle tyraunt. When Judyth thought that Holophernes was on slepe, she came stylly and her mayden with her, and herkened at the dore of the pavylyon and understode that he slepte strongely. Then sayd the lady: 'Go we hardely, for God is with us.' So she entred in, and without drede toke the swerde that she sawe at his beddes hede and drewe hym out naked, and lyfte hym up with all her strengthe, and smote off the heed of Holophernes without herynge of ony body, and put the heed in her lappe.

"And as soone as she myght, she dressed her towarde the cyte so moche that without ony lettynge came to the gate, and cryed: [G3v] 'Come, come and open, for God is with us!' And when she was entred in, no man knewe the way that was made of this adventure. And on the morowe she hanged the heed upon a perche above the walles, and all the people of the cyte armed them and manfully ranne upon theyr enemyes, the whiche were yet in theyr beddes, for they toke no hede of them of the cyte. And when they came into the pavylyon of theyr duke to make hym aryse hastely, and there they founde hym deed, and al his people began to sparcle. So they slewe and toke all that they myght fynde. And thus

---

[1] p[r]ayers : *payers*

occirent tous et pristrent les Juifs.[1] Et ainsi fu delivré le peuple de Dieu des mains de Holophernes par Judic [fol. 100r a] la preudefemme, qui a tousjour en la Saincte Escripture en sera louee."

### *Chapitre 32*      Ci dit de la royne Hester[2]

"Par la noble et sage[3] royne Hester voult autresi D[i]eu[4] delivrer son peuple de sa[5] servitude du roy Assuere. Cellui roy Assuere estoit de moult grant poissance sur tous rois possedoit[6] moult de royaumes; payen estoit, et tenoit les Juifs en servage.

"Et comme ycellui[7] feist querir par tous royaumes les plus nobles pucelles, les plus belles, les[8] mieulx enseingnees pour choisir une qui mieulx lui plairoit pour estre sa femme, entre les autres lui fu amenee la noble, sage, bonne, belle,[9] et de Dieu amee la pucelle Hester, qui estoit hebrieue, laquelle lui pleut sur toutes et l'espousa. Et tant l'ama cellui de grant amour que ne lui reffusast chose qu'elle requeist.

"Avint une[10] temps aprés que un faulx flateur, qui nommez Naman [fol. 100r b] estoit, cellui[11] enorta tant le roy contre les Juifs que il fist tant que il[12] commanda que, par tout ou ilz seroient trouvez, fussent pris. Et[13] de ceste chose ne savoit riens la royne Hester; car se elle le sceust, lui pesast[14] malement que son peuple fust ainsi mal menez. Toutevoiez un sien oncle nommé Mardocius, qui estoit comme chief des Juifs, lui fist savoir, et que elle y remediast tost car le jour estoit brief dedens lequel on devoit excecuter la sentence du roy.

"De ceste chose fu moult dol[e]nte[15] la royne, si se vesti et para le plus noblement que elle pot, et ala avecques ses femmes[16] comme pour soy esbatre en un jardin ou elle savoit que le roy estoit aux fenestres. Et quant vint au tourner vers la

---

[1] tous et pristrent les Juifs] tous les Juifs et prirent
[2] Hester] Hester qui sauva le peuple
[3] noble et sage] noble sage
[4] D[i]eu : *Deu*
[5] sa] la
[6] rois possedoit] roys et possedoit
[7] ycellui] cellui
[8] les] et
[9] bonne, belle] bonne et belle
[10] une] un
[11] nommez Naman estoit, cellui] nommé estoit Naman
[12] que il fist tant que] *omitted*
[13] pris. Et] pris et occis
[14] lui pesast] moult lui en pesast
[15] dol[e]nte : *dolonte*
[16] avecques ses femmes] ses femmes avecques elle

was the people of God delyvered fro the handes of Holophernes by Judyth the worshypfull lady, whiche shall evermore be praysed gretely in Holy Scrypture."

*Chapter 32*     Of the worshypfull Quene Hester

"Bi the noble and wyse lady Quene Hester, God wolde also delyver his people from the bondage of Kynge Assuere. This Kynge Assuere was of greate puyssaunce above al other kynges in those dayes and posseded many royalmes; and he was a paynyme, and helde the Jewes in servage.

"And as the kynge made to seke in al royalmes the moost noble maydens, the moost fayre, the best taught for to chose one amonge them al that myght please hym best to be his wyfe. And amonge all others was brought before hym the noble, good, wyse, and fayre, and loved of God, the mayden Hester that [G4r] was an Ebrue, whiche pleased hym moost above all others. And so he wedded her, and so moche he loved her of grete love that he wolde not denaye her of nothynge that she wolde requyre hym of.

"It happened on a tyme after that a false flatterer whiche was named Naman, and he exhorted the kynge ayenst the Jewes. That he dyde so moche that he commaunded all aboute where that ever the Jewes were founde, that they sholde[1] be taken. And the quene knewe nothynge of this; for yf she had knowne it, it wolde have greved her evyll that the people sholde be so evyll entreated. Nevertheles, an uncle of hers named Mardocheus whiche was as chyefe of the Jewes made her to knowe it, and prayed her that she wolde remedy it as soone as she myght, for the daye was shorte within the whiche that the sentence of the kynge sholde be executed.

"Of this the Quene Hester was ryght sory, soo she clothed and arayed her in the moost noblest wyse that she myght and wente with her woman as to dysporte her in a gardyne where she knewe well that the kynge was at the wyndowes. And

---

[1] sholde : *shoulde*

chambre du roy comme se elle ne[1] pensast point, et elle veist le roy aux fenestres, tantost celle se laissa cheoir a geneulx et toute[2] estendue sur sa [fol. 100v a] face le salua. Et le roy a qui moult pleut son humilité, et qui a grant plaisance regarda la grant beauté dont elle resplendissoit, l'appella et lui dist que elle demandast quelconques chose que elle vouldroit, et elle l'aroit. Et la dame lui dist[3] que autre chose ne vouloit fors que il alast disner en ses chambres, et que il menast avec lui Naman; et il lui ottroya.[4]

"Et comme par trois jours suiventment il y disnast et tant eust[5] agreable la chiere, l'onneur, la bonté, la[6] beauté de celle dame que il ne la laissast en paix que elle lui demandast aucun grant don.[7] Celle se gitta a ses piez et en plourant lui prist a dire que elle lui prioit que il eust pitié de son peuple, et que il ne la voulsist mie tant aviler, puis qui en[8] si hault honneur l'avoit mise que son lignage et ceulx de sa nacion fussent si villainement destruis. [fol. 100v b]

"Adonc le roy, tout ayrez, respondi: 'Dame, qui est ce[9] qui l'ose faire?'

"Elle respondi: 'Sire, ce fait faire Naman, vostre provost, qui yci est.'

"A te dire en brief,[10] le roy rappella sa sentence, et fu Naman qui tout ce avoit basti pendu.[11] Et Mardocius oncle[12] de la royne mis en son lieu, les Juifs franchis et fais les plus previlegiez de tous autres peuples, et les plus honnourez. Et ainsi semblablement que de Judich volt Dieux a ceste fois sauver son peuple par feme. Et ne cuides pas que cestes deux femmes[13] soient seules en la Saincte Escripture par qui Dieux volt sauver par diverses fois son peuple, car asses en y ot d'autres que je laisse pour briefté, si comme Delborra dont j'ay cy dessus parlé, qui delivra aussi le peuple de servitude."[14]

---

[1]  ne] n'y

[2]  geneulx et toute] genoulx toute

[3]  lui dist] respondi

[4]  avec lui Naman; et il lui ottroya] avecques lui Naman et il luy ottroya voulentiers

[5]  il y et tant eust] y disnast et eust

[6]  la] et

[7]  il ne la laissast en paix que elle lui demandast aucun grant don] ades la pressoit de lui faire aucune requeste

[8]  qui en] qu'en

[9]  ce] cil si hardis

[10]  en brief] la chose en brief

[11]  et fu Naman qui tout ce avoit basti pendu] Naman, qui par envie avoit tout ce basti, fu prins et pendu par ses desmerites

[12]  oncle] l'oncle

[13]  femmes] dames

[14]  servitude] servitude et semblablement le firent d'autres

when at the tournynge towarde the chambre of the kynge as thoughe she thought not on hym, and she sawe the kynge at the wyndowes, anone she fell downe on her knees and saluted hym. And the kynge, to whome it pleased her humylyte, and whiche had grete pleasure to beholde her grete beaute of the whiche she had ynoughe, called her and sayd to her that she sholde demaunde what thynge she wolde and she sholde have it. [G4v] And the quene sayd to hym that she wolde none other thynge but that he sholde come and dyne with her in her chambre, and that he sholde brynge with hym Naman; and the kynge graunted her.

"And when thre dayes were past, the kynge came and dyned with her, and he had soo agreable chere that pleased hym well. And then he behelde her countenaunce, her worshyp, her bounte, and beaute, and wolde not leve her in peas but that [s]he[1] sholde aske some maner grete gyfte. Then she fell downe at his feete and in wepynge she began to say that she wolde pray hym that he wolde have pyte on the people of the Jewes, and that he wolde not put them to so grete myschyefe syth that he had put her in so grete worshyp. For it was grete pyte to se her lygnage and them of her nacyon so vylanously to be destroyed.

"And then the kynge all wrothe answered her and sayd: 'Myne owne lady, what is he that durste do it?'

"She answered, 'Syr, Naman your provost maketh it to be done, whiche is here present.'

"And to say it shortely, the kynge called agayne his sentence, and Naman was hanged whiche had caused all that to be done. And Mardocheus, uncle to the quene, was put in his place, the Jewes fraunchysed and made moost privyleged of ony other people and moost had in worshyppe. And soo in the same wyse that God wolde by Judyth, He dyde by this noble Quene Hester that His people were saved. And byleve it not that these two ladyes were alone in the Holy Scrypture by whom God wolde save His people dyvers tymes, [G5r] for there ben ynowe of others whiche I leve for shortnes of tyme, as of Delborra of whom I have spoken above whiche delyvered the people fro bondage."

---

[1] [s]he : *he*

## *Chapitre [33]*[1]   Des dames de Sabine[2]

"Des dames de la loy ancienne des paiens [fol. 101r a] aussi te pourroie dire de maintes qui pareillement[3] furent cause de sauver païs, et villes,[4] et citez, mais de deux exemples moult notables sans plus, pour toutes preuves d'elles me passeray.

"Quant Remus et Romulus orent fondee la cité de Romme, [et][5] Romulus ot peupliés la dicte cité et remplie de tous les chevaliers et hommes d'armes que il avoit peu finer et assembler aprés plusieurs victoires que il avoit eues, Romulus moult volentiers pourchaçast que ilz eussent des femmes afin que[6] ilz peussent avoir lignee qui a tousjours possedast la cité et seignourie, mais ne savoit pas bien comment peust faire que lui et tous ses compagnons eussent femmes et fussent mariez car les roys, et les princes, et les gens du païs moult ressongnoient avoir affinité a eux pour ce que trop leur sembloient gents voulages, fiers, et divers, [fol. 101r b] si ne leur vouloient donner leurs filles.[7]

"Et pour ce Romulus, avisé de grant cautelle, fist crier un tournoy et unes joustes par tout païs et que il pleust aux princes, et aux roys, et seigneurs, et a toute gent d'onneur de amener[8] les dames et les damoiselles pour veoir l'esbatement des chevaliers estranges. Le jour de la feste venue grant y fu l'assemblé d'un cousté et d'autre, et la furent venues grant foison dames et pucelles pour les jeux regarder. Entre les autres y ot amené le roy de Sabine une moult belle et gente fille que il avoit avec[9] toutes les dames et pucelles de la contree qui suivie l'avoient. Si furent les joustes ordonnees hors de la cité en une plaine lez une montagne, et les dames furent assises toutes de renc au dessus sur le mont. La s'efforcierent les chevaliers les uns contre les autres de faire vassellages,[10] [fol. 101v a] car les belles dames que ilz veioient leur croissoient ades cuer force et hardement de faire chevaleries.

"A te faire le compte brief, quant asses orent tournoié et que temps sembla[11] a Romulus de faire ce qu'il avoit ordené, il saisi[12] un grant cor d'olifant et tres hault

---

[1]   [33] : *xxxiiij*

[2]   Sabine] Sabine qui mirent paix entre leurs amis

[3]   dire de maintes qui pareillement] de maintes raconter qui

[4]   païs, et villes] païs, villes

[5]   Romme [et] : *Rommeur*

[6]   que ilz eussent des femmes afin que] que

[7]   moult ressongnoient avoir affinité a eux pour ce que trop leur sembloient gents voulages, fiers, et divers si ne leur vouloient donner leur filles] ne leur vouloient donner leur filles pour ce que trop leur sembloient gent volages et ressongnoient a avoir affinité a eulx, car trop estoient fiers et divers

[8]   d'onneur de amener] d'y mener

[9]   avoit avec] avoit et avec elle

[10]  vassellages] forces et vasselages

[11]  temps sembla] il sembla temps

[12]  saisi] print

*Chapter 33* **Of the ladyes of Sabyne**

"Of ladyes of auncyent lawe of paynymes also I may tell thee of many whiche in the same wyse were cause of savynge of countres, cytees, and townes, but I shall passe over excepte two ensamples ryght notable without mo, for all proveth of them.

"When Remus and Romulus had founded the cyte of Rome, and Romulus had peopled the cyte and fulfylled it of knyghtes and men of armes that he had chosen and assembled after dyvers vyctoryes that he had, Romulus wolde fayne purchace that they myght have wyves to the entente that they myght have yssue that myght posses the cyte and the lordeshyp. But he wyste not well howe he myght do that he and his felawshyp myght have wyves and that they were maryed for the kynges, and the prynces, and the people of the countre desyred not gretly to have affynyte with them for that it semed them that they were fyerse people, and dyvers, and so they wolde not gyve them theyr doughters in maryage.

"And therfore Romulus, advysed of a grete cautele, made to crye a tourney and a joustes by all the countres, and that it pleased the [G5v] kynges, and prynces, and lordes, and all other people sholde brynge ladyes and damoyselles to se the dysporte of the straunge knyghtes. The daye of the feest was come and grete was the assemble, what of one syde, what of that other, and thyder came grete foyson of ladyes and of maydens to beholde the playe. And amonge all others, the kynge of Sabyne had brought with hym a fayre mayden, whiche was his doughter, with all the ladyes and gentylwomen of that countre that folowed her. Thus were the joustes ordeyned without the cyte in a fayre playne besyde an hylle. And the ladyes were al set by rowe on hye upon the hylle. There the knyghtes enforced them one agaynst another to make dysporte, for the fayre ladyes that they sawe encreased theyr hertes in strengthe and hardynesse to make knyghtes.

"And to make the tale shorte, when they had ronne togyder ynoughe, and Romulus semed that it was tyme to do that they had ordeyned, he toke a grete

prist a corner.¹ Ce son et celle enseigne entendirent: bien tost si laisierent² le jeu, et tous coururent vers les dames. Romulus prist la fille du roy, dont ja moult estoit ferus, et tous les aultres semblablement pristrent chascun la sienne. Et a force les leverent sur leurs³ chevaulx, et a tout s'en alerent fuiant vers la cité, et leurs⁴ portes bien et bel cloirent. La fu grande la criee et le duel mené des peres et parens de dehors et des dames aussi qui a force estoient ravies. Mais leur pleur riens ne valu.⁵ [fol. 101v b] Romulus a grant feste espousa la siene, et pareillement firent les autres.

"De ceste chose s[o]urdi⁶ grant guerre car au plus tost que le roy de Sabine pot, a moult grant ost vint⁷ sur les Rommains. Mais n'estoit mie⁸ legiere chose a les desconfire, car trop⁹ estoient vaillant gent: .v. ans entiers avoit ja duré la guerre quant un jour se durent assembler en champ atour¹⁰ leur poissance d'un costé et d'autre, et moult estoit la chose taillee¹¹ que grant perte de gent et grant occision y deust avoir. Ja estoient yssus les Romains dehors¹² a moult grant host quant la royne assembla a parlement en un temple toutes les dames de la cité. Adonc celle, qui moult estoit sage et bonne et belle, leur prist ainsi a dire:

"'Dames honnourees de Sabine, mes chiers seurs et compagnes, vous savés la [fol. 102r a] ravissement qui fu fait de nous par nos mariz, pour laquel cause noz perez et parens leur mainent guerre, et noz mariz a eulx. Si ne puet de nostre part en nulle maniere terminer ceste mortel guerre ne estre maintenue qui qu'en ait la victoire, que ce ne soit a nostre prejudice. Car se noz maris sont vaincus, ce devra estre a nous qui les amons (si que raison est, et qui ja des enfans en avons) grans courroux et desolacion, et que ja noz pitiz¹³ enfans demourent orphelins. Et se il avient que noz mariz aient la victoire, et que noz peres et par[e]ns¹⁴ soient mors et destruis, certes, moult devions¹⁵ avoir grant pitié que pour nous soit tel mechief avenu. Ce qui est fait ne puet estre autrement.¹⁶ Et pour ce me semble que moult

---

¹ hault prist a corner] tres haultement corna
² entendirent: bien tost si laisierent] entendirent bien tous, si laissierent
³ leurs] leur
⁴ leurs] les
⁵ ne valu] ne leur val
⁶ s[o]urdi : *surdi*
⁷ a moult grant ost vint] vint a tout grant ost
⁸ mie] pas
⁹ trop] moult
¹⁰ atour] a toute
¹¹ taillee] disposee
¹² les Romains dehors] dehors les Rommains
¹³ desolacion, et que ja noz pitiz] desolacion que ja noz petis
¹⁴ par[e]ns : *parons*
¹⁵ devions] devrions
¹⁶ Ce qui est fait ne puet estre autrement] Et ce qui est fait est fait et ne peut autrement estre

horne of an holofaunt and began to blowe ryght hyghe. That blowynge and that token they entended well and anone lefte the playe, and all they ranne towarde the ladyes. And Romulus toke the kynges doughter, for he was gretely smyten with love, and all that others in the same wyse toke eche of them one. And anone they set them on theyr horses and fledde towarde the cyte, and they shytte the gates ryght well and surely. There was a grete crye and grete sorowe of the faders and moders that theyr doughters [G6r] were so taken awaye with strengthe. But theyr wepynge avayled them not. Romulus made a grete feest and wedded this lady, and so dyde all the others.

"Of this sprange grete warre, for as sone as the kynge of Sabyne myght he came with a grete hoost upon the Romaynes. But it was no lyght thynge to overcome them nor to dyscomfyte them, for they were ryght manly men. The warre endured bytwene them .v. yeres. And on a day when bothe hostes sholde mete togyder—and this thynge was gretely sorowed of the ladyes of the cyte that there sholde be so grete manslaughter—and when this Romulus was yssued out of the cyte with a grete hoost, the quene assembled to a parlyament al the ladyes of the cyte into a temple. And then, she whiche was ryght wyse, good, and fayre began thus to say:

"'Worshypfull ladyes of Sabyne, my ryght dere systers and felawes, ye knowe the ravysshynge that was done on us by our housbandes, for the whiche cause our faders and frendes hath moved warre to our husbandes, and our husbandes ayenst them. So we may not in our parte in no maner determyne this mortall warre,[1] nor to be mayntened who that ever wyn the vyctory, but it must be grete prejudyce to us. For yf our husbandes be overcome, it ought to be to us that love them (as reason is and that we have chyldren by them) ryght grete sorowe and desolacyon, and that our lytel chyldren sholde be orphelynes—that is to say, without faders. And yf it happen that our husbandes have the vyctory, and that our faders and frendes be deed and destroyed, [G6v] certes we ought to have grete pyte that for us there sholde suche myschyefe happen, and that that is done maye be none otherwyse. And therfore me semeth it sholde be grete welthe if that ony counsayle

---

[1] warre : *warres*

seroit grant bien se aucun conseil par nous y pouoit estre trouvé que paix fust mise
en ceste guerre. Et [fol. 102r b] s'il vous plaist[1] me suivre et faire ce que je feray, je
tiens que de ce venrons nous bien a chief.'

"Aux paroles de la dame respondirent toutes que elle commendast et elles
obeiroient.[2] Adonc la royne se eschevela et mist nus piez, et toutes les autres[3]
pareillement le firent. Et celles qui avoient enfans entre leurs bras les porterent[4]
et menerent avecques elles. Si y avoit ja foison enfans et de femmes enceintes. La
royne se mist devant, et a toute[5] celle piteuse procession s'en[6] vint ou champ de
la bataille droittement a l'eure que assembler devoient. Et entre les deux hosts
s'ala mettre tellement que assembler ne peussent fors parmi elles. Si s'agenoilla la
royne et toutes aussi firent, criant a haulte voix: 'Peres et parens, tres chiers seigneurs, mariz[7] tres amez, pour Dieu faictes paix; ou cy nous occies!'

"Quans les mariz virent la leurs femmes et leurs enfans, n'est mie [fol. 102v
a] doubte que moult furent esbahis et bien envis corrussent parmi elles. Semblablement aux peres d'ainsi veoir leurs filles moult apitoya les cuers.[8] Par quoy
regardent les uns les auttres, et[9] la pitié des dames qui si humblement les prioient, tourna leur felonnie et maltalent[10] en amoureuse pitié comme de filz a peres,
tant que ilz furent contrains a gitter jus leurs armes d'ambe deux pars, et d'aler
embracier les uns les auttres, et de faire bonne paix.[11] Romulus mena le roy de
Sabine, son sire, en s[a][12] cité et grandement l'onnoura et toute la compagnie. Et
ainsi par le sens et vertu de celle royne et des dames furent gardez les Romains et
les Sabins d'estre destruis."

---

[1]  Et s'il vous plaist] Et se mon conseil en voulez croire et
[2]  elles obeiroient] ilz obeiroient tres voulentiers
[3]  autres] dames
[4]  entre leurs bras les porterent] les porterent entre leurs bras
[5]  a toute] toute
[6]  s'en] aprés si
[7]  parens, tres chiers seigneurs, mariz] parens tres chiers et seigneurs maris
[8]  ou cy nous occies!' Quans les mariz virent la leurs femmes et leurs enfans, n'est
mie doubte que moult furent esbahis et bien envis corrussent parmi elles. Semblablement
aux peres d'ainsi veoir leurs filles moult apitoya les cuers] Ou se non, toutes voulons ycy
mourir soubz les piez de voz chevaulx.' Les maris qui la virent plourans leur femmes et
leur enfans moult furent esmerveillez et bien enviz n'est pas doubte courussent parmy
eulx. Semblablement apitoya et atendri moult les cuers aux peres d'ainsi veoir leur filles
[9]  et] pour
[10]  felonnie et maltalent] felonnie
[11]  faire bonne paix] faire paix
[12]  s[a] : *son*

myght be founde by us that peas were set in this warre. And yf it please you to
folowe me, and do as I shall do, I trowe we shal come wel to our entente.'

"And all the ladyes answered to the wordes of the quene and sayd that she
sholde commaunde, and they wolde obey. And then the quene wente with her
heere aboute her chekes and bare-foote, and all the others dyde in the same
wyse. And those that had chyldren bare them bytwene theyr armes, and ledde
them with them: and there was grete foyson of chyldren and of women with
chylde. The quene put herselfe before in this pyteous processyon, and so they
came to the felde ryght there as the batayle sholde be the same houre that they
began to assemble. And she wente to put herselfe bytwene bothe hoostes, with all
the company of ladyes and gentylwomen, so that they myght not assemble. For
the quene and al the other ladyes kneled bytwene them, cryenge with an hyghe
voyce: 'Faders and frendes, ryght dere lordes, entyerly byloved housbandes, for
goddes sake make peas! Or elles sle us here, and let us no longer lyve.'

"When the housbandes sawe theyr wyves and theyr chyldren bytwene theyr
armes, it is no doubte that they were gretely abasshed and dysmayde. And the
same wyse to the faders to se theyr doughters: it fylled theyr hertes ful of pyte.
[H1r] By whiche they loked one upon another, and behelde the pyte of the ladyes
whiche prayed them so mekely, the whiche caused bothe partyes to tourne all
theyr wrathe and malyce into amourous pyte as of the sones to the fader, so
moche that they were constrayned to cast off theyr harneys on bothe partyes and
to embrace eche other, and to make a fynall peas. Romulus ledde the kynge of
Sabyne, his fader, into the cyte and gretely worshypped hym and all the company. And thus by the w[i]sdome[1] and vertue of this quene and of the other
ladyes were the Romaynes and Sabynes saved that they be not destroyed."

---

[1] w[i]sdome : *wosdome*

## *Chapitre 34*     De Veturie[1]

"Veture fu une noble dame de Romme, mere d'un tres grant homme romain appellé Marcien, homme plain de grant vertu et conseil soubtilz et prompt, preux, [fol. 102v b] et hardi. Ce noble chevalier, filz de Veturie, fu envoyé par les Rommains a tout grant host contre les Coriens, desquelx il ot la victoire et prist la forteresse des Voulques; pour laquelle victoire que il ot sur les Coriens, fut appellé Coriolus. De ceste chose fut tant honnouré cestui que il ot aucques tout le gouvernement de Romme. Mais comme ce soit chose moult dongereuse que de gouverner un peuple au gré de chascun, a la parfin les Rommains, ayrez contre lui, le condempnerent a exil et fu bannis hors de Romme. Mais de ce se sceut[2] il bien vengier, car il s'en ala devers les Coriens[3] que il avoit par devant[4] desconfis, et les fist rebeller contre les Rommains. Et ilz le firent leur chevetaine, et a tres grant poissance vindrent sur la cité de Romme, et moult grant dommage faisoient par tout ou ilz aloient.

"Ceste chose moult redoubterent les Rommains. [fol. 103r a] Et pour le perilz ou ilz se virent, envoierent vers lui leurs messages pour traictier de paix. Mais Marcien ne les daingna ouïr. De rechief y envoierent, mais riens n'y valu,[5] et tousjours cellui les domagioit. Si y envoierent les prestres et les evesques[6] tous revestus, le suppliant moult humblement, mais riens n'y firent tant que les Romains, qui ne savoient que faire, envoierent les dames[7] de la cité vers la noble dame Veturie, mere de Marcien, lui supplier que elle se voulsist travaillier de pacifier son filz vers eulx.

"Adoncques la bonne dame Veturie se partie de la cité, avec[8] elle toutes les nobles dames, et a celle procession s'en ala devers son filz. Lequel, comme bon et humain, si tost que il sçot sa venue, descendi de son cheval et lui ala a l'encontre et si humblement la receut que filz doit faire mere. Et adonc, comme celle le voulsist prier de la paix, [fol. 103r b] il respondi que il apartenoit a mere de commander a filz, et non mie supplier. Et ainsi celle noble dame le ramena a Romme. Et par elle furent les Rommains a celle foiz gardez d'estre destruis, et elle seule y fist ce que les haulx legaz de Romme n'avoient peu faire."

---

[1] De Veturie] De la noble dame Veturie qui apaisa son filz, qui vouloit destruire Romme
[2] sceut] sot
[3] les Coriens] ceulx
[4] devant] avant
[5] valu] val
[6] les prestres et les evesques] les evesques et les prestres
[7] les dames] les nobles dames
[8] avec] avecques

## *Chapter 34*     Of Vetury, the noble lady of Rome

"Vetury was a noble lady of Rome, moder of the ryght worshypful Romayne named Marcyan, a man of vertue and counsayle, subtyll and redy, wyse and hardy. This worshypful knyght, sone of Vetury, was sente by the Romaynes with a grete hoost ayenst the Coryens, of whome he had the vyctory and toke the fortresse of Volques; for the whiche vyctory that he had upon the Coryens, he was named Coryolus. Of this thynge this man was so gretely worshypped that he had all the governaunce of Rome. But as that was a thynge ryght daungerous to governe the people every man after his entente, [H1v] at the last the Romaynes were wrothe ayenst hym, and condempned hym to be exyled and was banysshed out of Rome. But of that he coude ryght well revenge hym, for he wente towarde the Coryens that he had dyscomfyted before and made them to rebelle ayenst the Romaynes. And they made hym theyr capytayne, and with a grete puyssaunce came upon the cyte of Rome and dyde them moche harme wheresoever they wente.

"The Romayns doubted this matter gretely, and for the peryll whiche they sawe themselfe in they sente messages to them to treate for the peas. But Marcyen dysdeyned not to here them; and as often as they sente, it avayled them not, but evermore dyde them moche harme. So they sente to hym the bysshoppes and the preestes all revested in vestymentes, praynge hym ryght humbly for the peas, but it avayled not. And then the Romayns wyst not what to do, but they sente ladyes of the cyte to the noble Lady Veturye, moder of Marcyen, to praye her that she wolde take the payne to treate for the peas unto her sone.

"Then this good Lady Vetury departed out of the cyte, and with her the noblest ladyes of the towne, and in this processyon she wente to her sone. The whiche sone, as a good knyght, as soone as he knewe the comynge of his moder descended from his hors, and wente on fote to mete her, and receyved her ryght humbly as a sone ought to do his moder. And then as she began to praye hym for the peas, he answered that it perteyned to the moder to commaunde [H2r] the so[n]e,[1] and not to praye. And thus this noble lady ledde hym agayne to Rome. And by her were the Romaynes as that tyme kepte from dystruccyon, and thus she dyde alone that all the hyghe legates of Rome myght not do."

---

[1] so[n]e : *soue*

*Chapitre 35*     Ci dit de la royne de France Clotilde[1]

"Des grans biens qui sont venus par femme a regarder a l'esperitualité, si que devant t'avoie dit: Crotilde, fille du roy de Bourgoingne et femme du fort Cladouvie roy de France, ne fut elle pas celle par qui la foy de Jhesucrist fut premierement mise et espandue es rois et es princes de France? Quel plus grant bien pourroit estre faist que celle y fist? Car comme elle fut enluminee de la foy, et bonne crestienne[2] et saincte dame, elle ne finoioit de t[im]onner[3] et prier son seigneur que il voulsist recevoir la saincte foy, et estre baptizié. Mais [fol. 103v a] comme il ne s'i voulsist acorder, tousjours[4] celle dame ne cessoit de prier Dieu en larmes, en jeunes et en pleurs[5] que il voulsist enluminer le cuer du roy. Et tant en pria que a la parfin Nostre Sire[6] ot pitié de son affliction, et inspira le roy en tel maniere: que comme il fust une fois alé en bataille contre le roy des Almans, et la desconfiture venist[7] sur lui, adonc le roy Cloudovees si que Dieux le voult inspirer leva les yeulx vers le ciel, et par grant affeccion deist: 'Dieu tout poissant que la royne ma femme croit et l'aoure,[8] vueilles moy aidier en ceste bataille, et je te promet que je recevray ta saincte foy.'

"Il n'ot pas plus tost dit le mot que le fait de la bataille se tourna pour lui et ot plaine victoire. Si rendi graces a Dieu et lui retourne a grant consolacion[9] de lui et de la royne fu ba[p]tiziez,[10] [fol. 103v b] et aussi tous ses[11] barons, et puis tout le peuple. Et de telle heure fu et tant y estendi[12] sa grace par les prieres de celle bonne dame et saincte royne[13] que oncques puis ne deffailli la foy en France. Ne oncques, Dieu mercis, n'y ot roy heretique ce qu'il n'a mie esté d'autres roys et de plusieurs empereurs, laquelle chose est grant louenge a eulx, et pour ce sont appellez tres crestiens.

"Se tous te vouloie dire les grans biens qui par femme sont venus, trop grant escripture y couvendroit. Mais encore sur le fait qui touche l'esperitualité, quans sains martirs[14] furent reconfortez, hebergiez, et repeus par femmeletes,[15] veusves,

---

[1] Clotilde] Crotilde, par laquelle son mari le roy Clodovee fu convertis a la foy
[2] crestienne] crestienne qu'elle estoit
[3] timonner : *tonnonner*
[4] comme il ne s'i voulsist acorder, tousjours] accorder ne s'i vouloit par quoy
[5] en larmes, en jeunes et en pleurs] en grans larmes en jeunes et devocions
[6] Sire] Seigneur
[7] desconfiture venist] la perte et desconfiture de la bataille tournast
[8] l'aoure] aoure
[9] consolacion] joye et consolacion
[10] ba[p]tiziez : *batiziez*
[11] ses] les
[12] estendi] estendi Dieu
[13] royne] royne Crotilde
[14] martirs] martirs si que je diray cy aprés
[15] femmeletes : *femmemeletes*

*Chapter 35*     Of the Quene of Fraunce Crotylde

"Of grete welthes that be come by women to beholde the spyrytualte as I have sayd to thee before Crotylde, doughter of the kynge of Burgoyne, wyfe of the stronge Clodonne, kynge of Fraunce: was it not she by whom the faythe of Jhesu Cryst was fyrst brought and spredde to the kynges and prynces of Fraunce? Where myght there be a better thynge done than that was that she dyde? For as she was made lyght with the fayth of Our Lorde and she was a good lady and an holy, she never seased to comune with her husbande and pray hym that he wolde receyve the faythe and be baptysed. But he wolde not accorde to her. Alway this lady seased not to pray unto God, in wepynge and fastynge, that He wolde enlumyne the herte of the kynge insomoche that at the last Our Lorde had pyte of her afflyccyon, and enspyred the kynge in suche manere: that as he was ones gone to do a batayl ayenst the kynge of Almaunce, and the dyscomfyture of the batayle came upon hym, and then the Kynge Clodon, soo as God wolde enspyre hym, lyfted up his eyen [H2v] towarde heven and by grete affeccyon sayd these wordes: 'Almyghty God, whiche that the quene my wyfe byleveth and worshyppeth, let Thyne infynyte grace shyne on me this daye to helpe me in this batayle, and I promyse Thee that I shall receyve Thyne holy faythe.'

"He had no soner sayd these wordes but that the dede of the batayle tourned to hym and had the playne vyctory. Then he yelded thankynges to Our Lorde and retourned home with grete comforte and joye, and receyved baptyme with the quene and all his barons, and after al the people. And from that houre unto this day Our Lorde hathe stretched his grace soo plenteously on us that the faythe fayled never syth in Fraunce, and all by the prayers of this good lady and holy quene. Ne there was never kynge heretyke worshypped by God as there hathe ben of dyvers other kynges and emperoures, the whiche thynge is gretely to be praysed in them, and therfore they be called very Crysten people.

"If I wolde tell thee all the grete welthes that cometh by women, the wrytynge sholde be to grete. But yet upon the acte that toucheth the spyrytualte, howe many holy martyrs have there ben comforted, harboured, and refresshed

bonnes preudefemmes? Se tu le lis,[1] tu trouveras que il plaisoit a Dieu que tous ou la plus grant partie en leurs adversitez et martire fussent reconfortez par femmes. Que dis je? Les martirs voire autressi [fol. 104r a] les apostres, saint Pol, et les aultres, et mesmement Jhesucrist peus et reconfortez par les femmes.

"Et les François qui ont eu si grant devocion le[2] corps de monseigneur saint Denis — et a bonne cause, qui aporta premier la foy en France — n'ont ilz ce benoit corps, et ceulx de ces[3] benoys compaignons saint Rustic[4] et saint Eleuthere, a cause d'un[e][5] femme? Car le tirant qui les avoit faiz decoller ordenna que les corps fussent gittez en Saine. Et ceulz qui ce devoient faire les mirent en un sac pour les y porter. Ilz se hebergierent chieux une bonne dame vesve, qui nommé estoit Catule, laquelle les enyvra et puis osta les sains corp, et mist ou sac porciaulx mors;[6] et enterra les benois martirs au plus honnourablement que elle pot en sa maison, et mist en escript dessus afin que le temps avenir fust sceu. Et long temps aprés, [fol. 104r b] autressi[7] par une femme, fut en ce lieu premierement faicte[8] chappelle en l'onneur de eulx: ce fu par ma dame saincte Genevieve, jusques a ce que le bon roy de France Daugobert y fonda l'eglise qui ores y est."

## Chapitre 36    Ci dit contre[9] ceulx qui dient qu'il n'est pas bon que femmes aprennent lettres

Aprés ces choses dictes je, Christine, dis ainsi: "Dame, je voy bien que mains grans biens sont venus par femmes, et se aucuns maulz sont ensuivis par aucuns mauvaises, toutevoyes me semble il que trop plus sont grans les biens qui par les bonnes[10] avienent et sont avenus, et mesmement par les sages et par les lettreez apprises es sciences, dont cy dessus est faicte mension. Par quoy je me merveil trop fort de l'oppinion d'aucuns hommes qui dient que ilz ne voudroient point que leurs filles ou femmes [fol. 104v a] ou parentes apprensissent science,[11] et que leurs meurs en empireroient."

*Response*: "Par ce pueux tu bien veoir que toutes oppinions d'ommes ne sont pas fondees sur raison, et que yceux ont tort. Car il ne doit mie estre presumé

---

[1] le lis] lis leur legendes
[2] le] au
[3] ces] ses
[4] saint Rustic] saint Rustin
[5] d'un[e] : *d'un*
[6] ou sac porciaulx mors] pourciaulz mors ou sac
[7] autressi] pareillement
[8] en ce lieu premierement faicte] ou dit lieu faite premierement
[9] Ci dit contre] Contre
[10] bonnes] bons
[11] science] sciences

by women, wyves, and wydowes? If thou wylte rede, thou shalte fynde that it pleased God that all for the moost parte, in theyr adversytees and martyrdomes were comforted by women, not onely the martyres but also the appostles, Saynt Poule, and other; and in the same wyse, Jhesu Cryst was refresshed [H3r] and comforted by women.

"And the Frensshemen that have in soo grete devocyon the body of Saynt Denys—a good cause why, for he brought fyrst the faythe into Fraunce: have not they that blessyd body, and the bodyes also of his blessyd felawes Saynt Rustyke and Saynt Ele[u]there¹ thrughe the helpe of a woman? For the tyraunt that made them to be heeded ordeyned that the bodyes sholde be cast into the ryver of Sayne. And they that sholde have done it put the bodyes in a sacke to bere it thyder. And they were harboured with a good woman, a wedowe whiche was named Catule, the whiche opened the sacke and toke out the holy bodyes, and put into the sacke deed hogges, and buryed these holy martyres as worshypfully as she coude in her owne house and set wrytynge over them, to the entente that in tyme to come they sholde be knowne. And longe tyme after, also by a woman, there was made fyrst a chapell in the honoure of them: that was by my lady Saynt Gevenyene, tyll unto that tyme that the good Kynge of Fraunce Dangobert founded the chyrche that is nowe there."

*Chapter 36*    Here it speketh ayenst them that say that is not good that women sholde lerne letters

After these thynges before sayd I, Christine, sayd thus: "Madame, I se well that many grete welthes cometh by women. And yf ony evyll have folowed by ony [H3v] evyll women, nevertheles it semeth me that there ben many mo welthes come by good women, and in the same wyse by wyse women and by them that have lerned scyences, of whom there is mencyon made before. By the whiche I mervayle gretely of the opynyon of some men that saye that they wolde not in no wyse that theyr doughters, or wyves, or kynneswomen sholde lerne scyences, and that it sholde apayre theyr condycyons."

*Answere*: "Thou mayst se well by that that al the opynyons of men be not founded upon reason, and that they have wronge. For it ought not to be

---

¹ Ele[u]there : *Elenthere*

que de savoir les sciences moralez et qui apprennent vertu[1] les meurs en doient empirer, ains n'est point de doubte que ilz en anoblissent et amendent. Comment est il a penser[2] que qui suit bo[n]ne[3] leccon de[4] doctrine en doye empirer? Ceste chose n'est a dire, ne soustenir. Je ne di pas[5] que bon fust que homme ne femme estudiast es sciences de sors[6] et deffendues, car pour neant ne les a pas l'Eglise Saincte ostees de commun usage. Mais que les femmes empirent de savoir le bien n'est[7] pas a croire.

"N'estoit pas de celle oppinion Quintus Ortencius, qui estoit a Romme grant rethoricien [fol. 104v b] et souveraine dicteur. Cellui ot une fille nommee Hortence que il moult ama pour la subtilletté de son engin, et lui fist apprendre lettres et estudier en la dicte science de retthorique. Dont elle tant en apprist que non pas tant seulement, ce dit Bocace, a Hortencius son pere par engin et bonne[8] memoire elle ressembla et en tout façonde, mais aussi de bien prononcier et de tout ordre de parleure si bien que en riens il ne la passoit. Et au propos de ce qui est dit dessus du bien qui vient par femme,[9] le bien qui par ceste femme et par son savoir avint fu, entre les autres, qui[10] ou temps que Romme estoit gouvernee par troys hommes, Hortence entreprist[11] a soustenir la cause des femmes et a demener ce que homme n'osoit entreprendre, c'estoit de certaines charges que on vouloit imposer sur elles et sur leurs[12] aournemens [fol. 105r a] ou temps de la neccessité de Romme. Et de ceste femme tant estoit belle la eloquence que non pas moins voulentiers que son pere estoit ouÿe, et gaingna sa cause.

"Pareillement a parler de plus nouveaulx temps sans querre les anciennes histoir[e]s[13] Jehan Andry, le solempnel legiste a Boulongne la Grasse n'a mie .lx. ans, n'estoit pas d'oppinion que mal fust que femmes fussent lettrees quant a sa belle et bonne fille que il tant ama, qui ot nom Nouvelle, fist apprendre lettres et si avant es lois que quant il estoit occuppez d'aucune essoine par quoy ne pouoit vaquer a lire les leccons a ses escoliers, il envoioit Nouvelle sa fille en son lieu lire aux escoles en chaiere. Et afin que la beauté d'elle n'empeschast la pensee des oyans, elle avoit une petite [fol. 105r b] cortine au devant d'elle. Et par celle

---

[1] apprennent vertu] enseignent les vertus
[2] anoblissent et amendent. Comment est il a penser] amendent et anoblissent comment est il a penser ne croire
[3] bo[n]ne : *bone*
[4] de] et de
[5] pas] mie
[6] sors] sors ne en celles qui sont
[7] n'est] ce n'est
[8] bonne] vive
[9] femme] femmes
[10] fu entre les autres, qui] fu un nottable entre les autres, c'est assavoir que
[11] troys hommes, Hortence entreprist] .ii. hommes, ceste Ortence prist
[12] leurs] leur
[13] histoir[e]s : *histoirs*

presumed that of knowynge the scyence moral and they that lerne vertue the condycyons of them ought not to be enpayred by that, but it is no doubte that they nobled therby and amended. Howe is it thought that he that lerneth a good lesson of doctryne sholde enpayre? This thynge is not to say, ne to susteyne. I say not that it is good that a man or a woman sholde study in scyences of sorcery, or of suche as ben forbydden, for it is not for nought that the chyrche hathe put them out of the comune usage. But that the women apayreth with connynge it is not well to byleve.

"Quintus Ortencyus was not of the same opynyon that was a grete rethory-cyen in Rome and a soverayne endytoure. The same man had a doughter named Hortence whome he loved moche for the subtylnesse of her wytte, and made her to lerne lettres, and to study in the foresayd scyence of rethoryke. Wherof she lerned soo moche that not onely, [H4r] as Bocace sayth she resembled her fader by wytte and good remembraunce, and in all facultes, but also of well pronoun-synge and of all ordre of spekynge so well that he passed her in nothynge. And to the purpose of that that is sayd above of welthe that cometh by women, the welthe that cometh by this woman and by her connynge was, amonge other, that in the tyme that Rome was governed by thre men, this woman Hortence toke upon her to susteyne the causes of women and to demeane that that a man durste not take on hande, that was of certayne charges that one wolde put upon them and on theyr araymentes in the tyme of necessytes of Rome. And the eloquence of this woman was so fayre that she was herde with no lesse wyll than her fader was, and gate her cause.

"In the same wyse, to speke of more newe tyme without lokynge after olde hystoryes, Johan Andry, a solempne legyster of Boloyne la Grace, was not of the same opynyon that it was evyll that women were lettered as to this fayre dough-ter and good that he loved so moche, whiche was named Nouvelle, made her to lerne letters. And she had the lawes that when he was occupyed in ony busynesse by the whiche he myght not entende to rede the lessons of his scolers, he sent Nouvelle his doughter in his place to rede to the scolers in the chayre. And to the entente that her beaute sholde not hurte the thought of them that she taughte, she had a lytell curtyne before her. And by suche manere she ful[f]ylled[1] the

---

[1] ful[f]ylled : *fullylled*

maniere suppleoit et alegoit aucuneffois les occupances de son pere, lequel[1] l'ama tant que pour mettre le nom d'elle en memoire fist une notable lecture d'un livre de lois que il nomma du nom de sa fille, la *Nouvelle*.

"Si ne sont mie plusieurs hommes qui sont sages de la sur dicte oppinion.[2] Ton pere, qui fu grant naturien et philosophe, n'oppinoit pas que femmes pis voulsissent par science aprendre. Ains de ce que encline te veoit aux lettres, si que tu sces, grant plaisir y pronoit et par la coulpe de ta mere qui par commune oppinion femmenine l'empeschoit fus retardee en ton enfance d'enteer plus en perfont es sciences. Mais si que dit le proverbe, *Ce que Nature donne, ne peut estre tollu*: si[3] ne te pot empeschier le sentir [fol. 105v a] des sciences, que tu[4] n'en aies recueilli a tout le moins des petites goutelletes, desquelles je tiens que tu cuides[5] pas pis valoir, ains le tiens[6] a grans tresoir, et sans faille tu as cause."

Et je, Christine, a tant respondis:[7] "Dame, ce que vous dictes est voir com Pater Noster."

## Chapitre 37   Dit Christine a Droicture, et responses contre ceulx qui dient que il soit[8] pou de femmes chastes, et parle de Susanne

"Ad ce que je voy, dame, les biens[9] et toutes les vertus peuent estre trouvees en femmes; et dont vient ce que ces hommes dient qu'il ne soit si pou de chastes? S'il estoit ainsi, tout seroit neant leurs autres vertus, comme chasteté soit souveraine vertu en femme. Mais par ce que ouÿ dire vous ay, il est tout autrement."[10]

*Response*: "Par ce que [fol. 105v b] ja t'ay dit voirement et ce que tu en sces est[11] assez manifeste le contraire, et encore t'en pense[12] dire, et tousjours diroye: O, de quantes vaillans dames chastes parle la Saincte Escripture, qui avant eslussent[13] la mort que fraindre[14] leur chasteté et netteté de corps et de pensee? Si comme la

---

[1]  lequel : *lequelle*
[2]  plusieurs hommes qui sont sages de la sur dicte oppinion] *R for revised passage, see annotations*
[3]  tollu: si] tollir: ne
[4]  tu] tu par inclinacion naturelle
[5]  desquelles, je tiens que tu cuides] desquelles choses je tiens que tu ni cuides
[6]  le tiens] le te repputes
[7]  a tant respondis] respondis a tant
[8]  soit] est
[9]  les biens] tous les biens
[10]  autrement] altrement que ilz ne dient
[11]  est] t'est
[12]  pense] puis
[13]  eslussent] eslisissent
[14]  fraindre] enfraindre

occupacyons of her fader, whom [H4v] he loved so moche that for to put the name of her in remembraunce made a notable letter of a boke of lawe that he called it after the name of his doughter, *Nouvelle*. So there be not many men that be wyse of the opynyon abovesayd.

"Thy fader, that was a naturall phylosophre, had not that opynyon that women sholde not lerne letters. But insomoche that he sawe [thou][1] enclyned to lernynge, as thou knowest well, he had grete pleasure of it and by the blame of thy moder, whiche by the comune opynyon of women thou were taryed in thy youthe to entre more in the depnesse of scyences. But as the proverbe saythe, *that Nature gyveth maye not be taken awaye*: so it may not hurte the felynge of connynge that thou hast gadred togyder the lytel droppes, of the whiche I trowe that thou wenest be not of lytell valure, but thou holdest theym in grete treasoure, and without fayle thou haste cause."

And I, Christine, answered: "Madame, that you say is as true as the Pater Noster."

*Chapter 37*  **Here Christine to Ryghtwysnesse, and she answereth agaynst them that saye there be but fewe women chaste and telleth of Susanne**

"Madame, to that that I se that these grete welthes and all vertues may be founde in women: and whens cometh it that these men saye that there be but fewe women chast? And yf it be so, al other [I1r] vertues sholde be as nought, insomoche that chastyte sholde be the moost soverayne vertue in a woman. But by that I have herde you say, it is all other wyse."

*Answere*: "By that that I have sayd to thee truely and that thou knowest is open ynoughe the contrary, and yet I thynke to saye and alwaye shall: O, of howe many worshypful ladyes chaste speketh Holy Scrypture, whiche rather chase the dethe than to breke theyr chastyte and clennesse of body and of thought? So as

---

[1] sawe [thou] : *sawe she*

belle et bonne Susanne, femme de Joachim, qui estoit homme de la lignee des Juifs, riche, et de grant auctorité.[25]

"Et comme une foiz ceste[1] vaillant dame Susanne s'esbatist seulete[2] en son jardin, entrerent devers elle deux vieillars faulx prestres et la requirent de pechié, et elle du tout les escondit; par quoy, quant ilz virent que priere n'y valoit, ilz la menacierent d'acuser a la justice de lui mestre[3] sus que trouvee [fol. 106r a] l'avoient avec un jouvencel.

"Et comme celle ouïst leurs menaces, car la coustume de lors estoit que femmes estoient en tel cas lapidees, elle dist adonc: 'Angoisses m'evironnent de toutes pars! Car se je ne fais ce que ces hommes me requierent, j'encourray mort corporelle. Et se je le fais, je offense devant la face de Creature.[4] Maiz non pour tant, trop mieulx m'est innocent soustenir la mort corporelle que cheoir par pechié en l'ire de mon Dieu.'

"Si s'escria adonc Susanne et les gens de l'ostel vindrent. Et a brief dire, tant firent les faulx tesmoignage[5] que Susanne fut condempnee a mort. Mais Dieux, qui tousjours pourvoit a ses amis, ouvroy la bouche du prophete Daniel, qui estoit petit enfant entre les bras de sa mere. Lequel, [fol. 106r b] quant on menoit Susanne a la justice a grant procession de gent qui aprés elle plouroient, s'escria que a grant tort estoit jugee[6] l'innocent Susanne. Si fu ramenee et les faulx prestres mieulx examinez, et trouvez par leur mesmes confession coulpables: et Susanne, innocent, fu delivré et eulx justiciez."


*Chapitre 38*      **Ci dit de Sarra**

"De la chasteté et bonté de Sarra parle la Bible environ le .xx.[e] chapitre du premiere livre. Ceste dame fu femme de Habraham, le grant patriarche. Moult de grans biens sont diz d'elle[7] en la Saincte Escripture que je laisse a te dire pour briefté. Mais de sa chasteté puet estre dit au propos que nous disions cy dessus, que assez de belles femmes sont chastes. Car elle fu de si souveraine beauté qu'en [fol. 106v a] son[8] temps, toutes femmes elle passoit tant que mains princes la couvoitierent, mais si loiale estoit que nul ne daignoit ouïr. Dont entre[9] les autres qui la couvoiterent fut le roy pharaon tant que a force la tolli a son mary. Mais

---

[1] Et comme une foiz ceste] Et comme ceste
[2] seulete] seule
[3] mestre] mettre
[4] de Creature] de mon Createur
[5] faulx tesmoignage] les faulx prestres par leur desloyal tesmoignage
[6] jugee] condampnee
[7] d'elle] de ceste dame
[8] son : *sont*
[9] ne daignoit ouïr. Dont entre] n'en daigna ouÿr. Entre

the fayre and goo[d][1] Susanne, the wyfe of Joachym that was a man of the lygnage of Jewes, ryche and of grete auctoryte.

"And as upon a tyme this good lady sported her alone in a gardyne, there
entred to her two false olde prestes and requyred her to synne with them. And
she alwaye denyed them, by whiche when they sawe that theyr prayer avayled
not, they manased her to accuse her to the justyce and to put on her that she was
founde with a yonge man.

"And when she herde theyr manases, for the custome was there that women
founde in suche case were stoned to the dethe, she sayd than, envyronned with
anguysshe in every parte: 'If I do not that these men requyre me, I shall have corporall dethe. And yf I do it, I offende before the face of my Creatoure. But not
for that, it is better to be innocent and suffre corporall dethe then fall by synne
into the wrathe of my Lorde God.'

"And then cryed Susanne and the people that were within came anone. And
to say shortly, so moche wytnesse these false preestes made that Susanne [I1v] was
condempned to the dethe. But God, whiche provyded alwaye for His frendes,
opened the mouthe of the profyte Danyel whiche was a yonge chylde bytwene
the armes of his moder. The whiche, when they ledde Susanne to the jugement
with grete multytude of people that wente wepynge after her, cryed and sayd that
the innocent Susanne was juged by grete wronge. So she was ledde home agayne,
and the false preestes, better examyned, were founde by theyr confessyon culpa-
ble: and the innocent Susanne was delyvered, and they were juged to the dethe."

## Chapter 38    Of Sarra, the wyfe of Abraham

"Of the chastyte and goodnesse of Sarra speketh the Byble aboute the .xx. chapytre of Genesis. This woman was wyfe of Abraham, the grete patryarke. Moche
good thynge is there sayd of her in Holy Scrypture, whiche that I leve to tell thee
for shortnesse. But of her chastyte may one saye to the purpose that we spake
of before, that there ben fayre women ynowe that be chaste. For she was of so
soverayne beaute that in her tyme she passed all other women, so moche that
many prynces coveted her, but she was so true that she dysdeyned not to here
theym. Wherof amonge all the others that coveyted her was the Kynge Pharao,
in soo moche that he toke her awaye by strengthe frome [I2r] her husbande. But

---

[1] goo[d] : *goo*

la grant bonté d'elle, qui encore[1] passoit la beaulté, lui empetra que Nostre Seigneur[2] l'amoit si tendrement que il la garda de toutes[3] villennie. Car il tormenta
tant pharaon et lui et sa maisnee de cuer et de cors, par griefves maladies et par
diverses visions, que oncques ne la coucha[4] et qu'il fut contraint a la rendre."

## *Chapitre 39*     Ce dit de Rebeca

"Ne fut pas moins bonne et belle de Sarra la tres loué[5] preudefemme Rebecha,
femme de Ysaac le patriarche, pere de Jacob. Ceste est louee merveilleusement
[fol. 106v b] en la Saincte Escripture de moult de choses et est escript d'elle ou
.xxiiii.ᵉ chapitre du premier livre de la Bible. Ceste estoit tant preudefemme,
et bonne et honneste, que elle estoit exemple de chastité a toutes celles qui la
veoient. Et avec ce elle se portoit a merveilles humblement envers son mary et
si simplement[6] que il sembloit que elle ne fust pas dame. Et pour ce le prodoms
Ysaac l'onnoroit et amoit a merveilles.

"Mais plus grant bien que l'amour de son mary empetra pour sa grant chasteté
et bonté ceste dame: ce fu la grace et amour de Dieu, que elle ot si grandement
que, non obstant fust elle ja envieillie et brehaigne, Dieu lui donna deux enfans a
une ventree. Ce fu Jacob et Esau, desquelz vindrent les lignees de Israel." [fol. 107r a]

## *Chapitre 40*     Ci dit de Ruth

"Assez te pourroye dire de dames bonnes et chastes, desquelles la Saincte Escripture faicte mencion que je laisse pour abregier. Ruth fu une autre noble dame de
qui lignee descendi David le prophette. Ceste fut moult chaste, et semblablement[7] en sa veusveté et de grant amour a son mary, comme il ypparu. Car pour
la grant amour que elle avoit eu a lui, elle laissa quant il fu mort son propre païs
et nascion,[8] et ala demorer et user sa vie avec les Juifs, dequel lignee avoit esté son
mary, et mesmement avec la mere de lui voult demourer. Et a brief dire, tant fut
bonne et chaste ceste noble dame que un livre fut faicte de lui et de sa vie, ou quel
ces choses sont escriptes."

---

[1]  encore] ancores
[2]  empetra que Nostre Seigneur] empetra tel grace que Nostre Seigneur
[3]  toutes] toute
[4]  coucha] toucha
[5]  loué] bonne
[6]  simplement] humblement
[7]  Ceste fut moult chaste, et semblablement] Ceste dame fu moult chaste en mariage
et autresi
[8]  nascion] sa nacion

the grete goodnesse of her, whiche yet passed her beaute, desyred of God that she loved soo tenderly that He wolde kepe her frome all maner of vylanyes. And Almyghty God, herynge her petycyon, tourmented so moche Pharao and his people, bothe of body and of herte by grevous sykenesses and dyvers vysytacyons, that he touched her never, and so was he constrayned to yelde her agayne."

## Chapter 39    Of Rebecca

"Rebecca, the wyfe of Isaac the patryarke, fader of Jacob, was not moche lesse to prayse than the fayre and good Sarra. This Rebecca is mervayllously praysed in Holy Scripture of dyvers thynges, and it is wryten of her in the .xxiiii. chapytre of the fyrste boke of the Byble that she was so good, wyse, and honest that she was ensample of chastyte unto all women that knewe her. And with that she bare her mervayllously mekely towarde her housbande, and soo symply, that she semed not that she was a lady. And therfore the good man Isaac worshypped her, and loved her mervayllously well.

"But this good woman Rebecca hadde of Almyghty God a better gyfte than the love of her housbande for her grete chastyte and goodnesse. For this noble lady that was so moche in the love and in the grace of Our Lorde Jhesu, [I2v] she had it so gretely that notwithstandynge she was olde and barayne God gave her two chyldren in one wombe, whiche was Jacob and Esau, of whome came the lygnages of Israell."

## Chapter 40    Of the noble woman Ruth

"Of good ladyes and chaste I myght tel thee of whiche Holy Scrypture maketh mencyon, whiche I leve for shortenes. Ruth was a noble lady and a good, whiche dessended of the lygnage of Davyd the prophete. She was ryght chaste and in lykewyse in her wydowhode of ryght grete love to her husbande, as it appered. For the grete love that she had to hym, when he was deed she forsoke her owne countre and nacyon and wente to dwelle and use her lyfe with the Jewes, of the whiche lygnage her husbande came, and dwelled with his owne moder. And to say shortly, this noble lady was so good and chaste that there was a boke made of her and of her lyfe, in the whiche these thynges before sayd be wryten."

*Chapitre 41*     De Penelope, femme de Ulixes

"Des dames paiennes asses de chastez et de bonnes preudefemmes treuve l'en
es escriptures. Penelope, la femme [fol. 107r b] du prince Ulixes, fu dame moult
vertueuse. Et entre les autres graces qu[e][1] elle ot, moult fu louee de la vertu de
chasteté. Et d'elle font moult grant mencion plusieurs hystoires, car ceste dame,
tant que son mary fu au siege devant Troye qui dura .x. ans, se gouverna moult
sagement. Et non obstant que moult fut requise de plusieurs roys et princes, pour
ce que tres belle estoit,[2] nul ne vouloit escouter ne ouïr parler; et[3] estoit sage, prudent, devote aux dieux, et de belle [vie].[4]

"Et mesmement aprés la destruccion de Troye, attendi son dit mary autres .x.
ans et cuidoit on que il fust periz en mer, ou il ot maintes pestillences. Et quant
il fu retourné, il la trouva assigiee d'un roy qui a force la vouloit avoir en mariage
pour sa grant chasteté et bonté. Son mary vint en guise [fol. 107v a] d'un pelerin et
enquist d'elle, si fut moult joyeux des bonnes nouvelles que dire en ouÿ.[5] Et grant
joye ot de son filz Thelemacus, que il avoit laissié petit, et le trouva ja parcreus."[6]

Et je, Christine, dis ainsi: "Dame, par ce que dire vous ay,[7] n'en laissierent
pas a estre chastes icelles dames pour tant se belles furent; car assez d'ommes
dient que a trop grant peine est trouvee belle femme chaste.

*Response*: "Ceulx qui le dient faillent a parler que moult en est, fut et sera de
belles tres chastes."

*Chapitre 42*     **Ci dit contre ceulx qui dient que a peines sont belles
femmes chastes: dit de Mariamire**

"Mariamire fu femme hebrieue,[8] fille du roy Aristobolus. Elle fut de si grant
beaulté que non pas tant seulement en ycellui temps on creoit que elle passoit
et excedoit toutes femmes [fol. 107v b] en beaulté, mais jugoit on que plus tost fut
ymage celestiel et divin que femme mortelle. Et de ceste fu peinte la figure en un
table[t][9] et envoiee au roy Anthoine d'Egipte, lequel par tres grant admiracion
de tel beauté dit et juga que elle estoit fille du dieu Jupiter, car ne creoit mie que
de homme mortel peust estre engendree. Ceste dame, non obstant son excellent

---

[1] qu[e] : *qui*
[2] pour ce que tres belle estoit] pour sa grant beauté
[3] vouloit escouter ne ouir parler; et estoit] volt ouÿr ne escouter. Elle
[4] belle [vie] : *belle*
[5] dire en ouÿ] il en ouÿ dire
[6] ja parcreus] parcreus
[7] dire vous ay] ouÿ dire vous ay
[8] hebrieue] hebree
[9] table[t] : *tablel*

## *Chapter 41*    Of Penolope, wyfe of Ulyxes

"Of chaste ladyes paynymes there be founde ynowe ryght good and worshypfull in dyvers cronycles: Penolope, the wyfe of Prynce Ulyxes, was [I3r] rygh[t][1] a vertuous lady. And amonge other vertues that she had she was gretely praysed for her chastyte, and many dyvers hystoryes maketh mencyon of her for this lady, al the whyle that her husbande was at the syege before Troye that endured .x. yeres, she governed her ryght wysely. And notwithstandynge that she was requyred of many kynges and prynces, for bycause that she was so fayre, she wolde not herken to them nor here them speke. And she was wyse and prudent, and devoute to her goddes, and of fayre and good behavynge.

"And also after the dystruccyon of Troye, she abode her sayd husbande other .x. yeres; and men supposed that he was perysshed in the see, where there were many pestylences. And when he was come home, he founde her besyeged with a kynge that wolde have had her by strengthe in maryage for her grete beaute and chastyte. Her husbande came in the guyse of a pylgryme and enquyred of her, and when he herde good tydynges of her, he was ryght joyous. And he had grete joye of his yonge sone Thelomachus, whiche he lefte with her ryght lytell, and he founde hym then parfytely growne."

And I, Christine, sayd thus: "Madame, by that that I have herde you saye, these foresayd ladyes lefte not to be chaste thoughe they were fayre; for many men say that of grete payne there be founde ony fayre women chaste."

*Answere*: "Those that so saye fayleth for there be, hathe ben, and shall be fayre women chaste." [I3v]

## *Chapter 42*    Here it speketh ayenst them that saye that it is a payne for to fynde ony fayre woman chaste

"Maryamyre was a woman of Ebrue, doughter of Kynge Arystobolus. She was of so grete beaute that not onely in that tyme men wende that she had passed and exceded all other women in beaute, but they juged her that she was rather a celestyall ymage and godly than a mortall woman. And the fygure of her was paynted in a table and sente to Kynge Anthony of Egypte, the whiche for the grete mervayle of suche beaute sayd and juged that she was doughter of Jupyter the god, for he wolde not byleve that she myght be engendred by a mortall man. This lady, notwithstandynge her excellent beaute, and that she was tempted and

---

[1] rygh[t] : *rygh*

beaulté, et que elle fut temptee et essaiee a avoir de pluseurs grans princes et roys, toutevoies par grant vertu et force de courage resista a tous, et pour tant fu plus louee et plus resplendi en renommee.

"Et encores qui plus croist son grant los est que elle estoit tres mal mariee, c'est assavoir a Herode Anthipater, roy des Juifs, qui fu homme de grant cruauté [fol. 180r a] et qui mesmement avoit fait mourir le frere d'elle. Pour laquel cause, et pour maintes durtés que il lui faisoit, elle l'eust en haine. Mais pour tant n'en laissa estre preudefemme et chaste. Et encore avec ce vint a cognoiscence a la dicte dame que il avoit ordenné que se il mouroit avant que elle, que tantost on la feist mourir afin que aultre n'eust la possession de si grant beaulté aprés lui."

## Chapitre 43     Encore de ce mesmes dit de Anthonie, femme de Druse Thibere

"Pour ce que on dit communement que c'est aussi fort chose que une belle femme se puist garder entre les jovenceaulx et les gens curiaulx desireux d'amours, sans ce que elle soit prise, que c'este de estre entre les flammes sans[1] ardoir, bien s'en sceut deffendre la belle et bonne [fol. 108r b] Anthoine, femme de Druse Thybere, frere de Noiron l'empereur. Ceste dame demoura en la fleur de souveraine beaulté et de grant jonece[2] veusve de Thybere son mary, qui fu de son frere par venim occis,[3] dont la noble dame ot moult grant doleur et proposa de jamais plus non estre[4] mariee et vivre en chasteté,[5] lequel propos elle tint tant que elle vesqui si tres entierement que nul[le][6] dame des paiens n'ot oncques plus grant loz de chasteté.

"Si fist de ceste chose tant plus a louer, ce dit Bocace, qu'en telle continence estoit demourant a court entre les jouvenceaulx bien parez et j[o]lis[7] et amoureux vivans a court oisivement.[8] Celle y usa sa vie sans not et sans blasme de quelconques legiereté. Laquel chose, ce dit l'aucteur, est digne de estre [fol. 108v a] eslevee en louenge, si comme d'une joene femme, en beauté tres excellente, qui estoit fille de Marc Anthoine qui menoit vie moult luxurieuse et lubre; mais non

---

[1] sans] sanz soy

[2] souveraine beaulté et de grant jonece] sa jeunece resplandissant de tres souveraine beauté

[3] de son frere par venim occis] occis de son frere par venim

[4] non estre] n'estre

[5] chasteté] chasteté de vesvage

[6] nul[le] : *nul*

[7] j[o]lis : *jalis*

[8] j[o]lis et amoureux vivans a court oisivement] assesmez jolis et amoureux vivans oysivement

assayed to be had of dyvers grete prynces and kynges, neverthelesse by grete vertue and strength of courage she resysted all. And for that she was the more praysed and more shynynge in renowne.

"And yet she was more to prayse insomoche that she was wedded ryght evyll, that is to knowe to Herode Anthypater, kynge of Jewes, whiche was a man of grete cruelte. And also he had made to be slayne the broder of this good lady, for the whiche cause, and many others that he dyde to her, she had hym in hate. But for al that, she lefte never to be a good woman and chaste. And yet with this it came to [I4r] the knowledge of this lady that he had ordeyned that yf he dyed before her, that she sholde be slayne anone after to the entente that none other sholde have the possessyon of so grete beaute after hym."

## Chapter 43    Also the same purpose of Anthony, wyfe of Druse Tybere, broder of the noble Emperoure Nero

"For that that one sayth comunely that it is as stronge a thynge that a fayre woman maye kepe her amonge yonge men and courtyours desyrous of love without takynge, as it is to be amonge the flambes of fyre without brennynge, well she coude defende her the fayre and good Anthonye, wyfe of Druse Thybere, broder of Nero the emperoure. This lady dwelled in the floure of her soverayne beaute and grene youthe wedowe of Druse Thybere her husbande, whiche his broder Nero had slayne with poyson, wherof this noble lady had so grete sorowe that she purposed never after to be maryed but to lyve in chastyte, the whiche purpose she helde as longe as she lyved so holy that there was never paynyme lady that had gretter praysynge of chastyte.

"So she dyde of this thynge soo moche more to be praysed, as Bocace saythe, that in this chastyte and contynuence she was abydynge amonge in the courte amonge the yonge lusty people, fresshe and joly lovers lyvynge courtely. There [I4v] she used her lyfe without spotte of ony blame or of ony maner of lyghtnesse. The whiche thynge, as the auctoure saythe, is worthy to be lyfted up in praysynge soo as of a yonge woman, ryght excellent in beaute, whiche was the doughter of Marke Anthonye that ledde his lyfe full synfully. But not for that the lewde

pour tant les laiz exemples que elle veoit, demoura saine entre les feux ardens,[1] pleine de chasteté et non pas pou de temps, mais toute sa vie perseverante jusques a la mort de vieillece.

"De telles belles et tres chastes vivans entre les mondains, et mesmement a court et entre les jouvenceaulx, asses d'exemples te trouveroie, et aujourd'uy mesmes. N'en doubtes pas en esté[2] mainte et il en est bien besoing, quoy que les mauvaises langnes[3] dient. Et de celles[4] bonnes et chastes dames menans[5] vie honneste, mesmes entre[6] les plus mondains, parle Valere de la noble dame Supplice, qui de grant beaulté estoit, et toutevoyes entre toutes les dames [fol. 108v b] de Romme elle fu reputee la plus chaste."

### Chapitre 44   Ci dit contre ceulx qui dient que femmes veulent estre efforcees, donne exemple pluseurs,[7] et premierement de Lucrece

Donc[8] je, Christine, dis ainsi: "Dame, moult bien croy ce que vous dites et suis certaine qu'assez est de belles femmes bonnes et chastes, et qui bien se scevent garder des agaiz des deceveurs. Si me anuye et me grieve de ce que mains hommes dient[9] que femmes se veulent efforcier, et que ne[10] leur desplaist mie, quoy que elles escondissent de bouche, de estre par hommes efforcees. Mais fort me seroit a croire que agreable leur fust."[11]

*Response*: "Ne[12] doubtes pas, amie chiere, que ce n'est mie plaisir aux dames chastes de cuer et de pensee[13] estre efforcees, ainsi leur est injure et douleur[14] sur toutes autres. Et que ce [fol. 109r a] soit vray l'ont demonstré plusieurs d'elles par vray exemple, si comme de Lucrece la tres noble Rommaine, souveraine en

---

[1] les laiz exemples que elle veoit, demoura saine entre les feux ardens] ne pour lait exemple qu'elle veist ne laissa qu'elle ne demourast saine entre les flames ardens

[2] esté] est

[3] langnes] *R for added text, see annotations*

[4] de celles] d'icelles

[5] menans] menant

[6] entre] demourans et frequentans

[7] Ci dit contre ceulx . . . exemple pluseurs] Contre ceulx . . . exemple de plusieurs

[8] Donc] Adont

[9] mains hommes dient] hommes dient tant

[10] ne] il ne

[11] fust] fust si grant villenie

[12] ne] n'en

[13] de cuer et de pensee] et de belle vie

[14] injure et douleur] douleur

ensamples that she sawe made her never to falle, but that she abode alway in chastyte amonge the brennynge fyres, and it was noo lytell whyle but that she was perseveraunt tyll that she dyed for age.

"Of suche that were fayre and chaste, lyvynge amonge the worldely people, and also in courte amonge the yonge lusty folkes, of ensamples I m[y]ght[1] fynde thee ynowe, and at this daye also. Nor doubte thee not but there ben many, thoughe that the evyll tongues lysteth for too saye shrewdely. And of suche good and chaste ladyes, ledynge theyr lyves amonge these worldely people, speketh Valery of this noble and worthy Lady Sulpyce, the whiche was of greate beaute, and yet she was named the moost chaste amonge all the ladyes of Rome." [15r]

## Chapter 44 — Here it speketh agaynst them that saythe that women wolde be ravysshed, and gyveth ensamples of dyvers; and fyrste it speketh of the noble and worthy Lady Lucresse, wyfe of Tarquyne Collatyn

Then I, Christine, sayd thus: "Madame, I byleve it well that ye saye. And I am sure that there ben ynowe fayre women chaste, and that can kepe them from the awayte of the deceyvours. Yet it greveth me of that that many men say that women wolde be ravysshed, and that it dyspleaseth them not thoughe they saye the contrary with theyr mouthe. But it were a grete thynge to make me byleve it that it were agreable to theym."

*Answere*: "Doubte it not, fayre frende, that it is noo pleasaunce to these chaste ladyes of herte and thought to be ravysshed, but it is to theym ryght grete sorowe above all other. And that it be true there be many of them that have shewed it by fayre ensamples, as of Lucres the ryght noble woman of Rome, soverayne in

---

[1] m[y]ght : *mght*

chasteté entre toutes les dames[1] romaines, femme d'un noble homme[2] Tarquin
Colatin. Et comme Tarquin l'Orgueilleux, filz du roy,[3] fust ferment espris de
l'amour de ceste noble Lucrece, et ne lui osast dire pour la grant chasteté dont il la
veoit, desesperé d'y avenir par dons[4] ou priere, se pourpensa de l'avoir par cautele.
Il se disoit estre moult ami du mary de elle, par quoy il avoit assez entré en son
hostel quant il lui plaisoit. Par quoy, comme une foys il y alast qu'il savoit que le
dit mary n'y[5] estoit, la noble dame le receupt[6] comme cellui qui elle tenoit estre
grant ami de son mary. Mais Tarquin, qui a autre chose pensoit, fist tant que il
entra la nuit [fol. 109r b] en la chambre de Lucrece, dont elle fu moult espoentee.

"Et a brief dire, quant il l'eut assez sermonnee par grans promesses, dons,
et offres que faire voulsist sa voulenté, et il veist que priere n'y[7] valoit, il tira son
espee et la menaça de occire se elle disoit mot, et se elle ne ce consentoit a sa
voulenté. Et celle respondi que hardiement l'occeist, et que amoit morir que ce
consentir. Tarquin, qui vid[8] que riens ne lui valoit, s'avisa d'une autre grant malice, et dist que il diroit publiquement que il l'avoit trouvee avecques un[9] de ses
sergens. Et a brief dire, de ceste chose tant l'espoventa, pensant que on trairoit[10]
aux parolles de lui, que au paraler elle souffri sa force.

"Mais ne pot Lucrece porter paciemment ce grant desplaisir. Dont quant
vint au jour, elle envois[11] [fol. 109v a] querre son mary, et son pere, et ses prochains[12]
qui estoient les plus grans de Romme. Si leur regehy a grans pleurs et a grans
gemissemens ce qui lui estoit avenu. Et[13] comme son mary et parens qui la veoient
oultré de grant douleur la reconffortassent, elle tira un coutel que elle avoit soubz
sa robe en disant, 'Se il est ainsi que je me assoille de pechié et que je monstre
mon innocence, toutevoyes je ne me delivre pas de tourment, ne de peine, ne me
mez hors. Ne d'or en avant ne vivra femme hontoyee ne vergondee par l'exemple
de Lucrece.' Et ces choses dictes, elle par grant force se ficha le coutel pointu en
la poitrine, si chut tantost en morant; voiant son mary et ses amis. Si coururent
comme touz forsennez sus [fol. 109v b] a Tarquin.

---

[1]  dames] femmes
[2]  homme] homme nommé
[3]  roy] roy Tarquin
[4]  par dons] pour don
[5]  n'y] pas n'y
[6]  receupt] receut honnourablement
[7]  n'y] riens ne lui
[8]  amoit morir que ce Tarquin, qui vid] mieulx amoit mourir que s'i consentir. Tarquin qui vit bien
[9]  un : *une*
[10]  trairoit] croiroit
[11]  envois] envoya
[12]  prochains] prochains parens
[13]  Et] Adont

chastyte amonge all the ladyes of Rome, wyfe of the noble Tarquyne Collatyn.
And as Tarquyne the Prowde, sone of the kynge, was taken with the love of this
Lady Lucres, and durst not tell it her for the grete chastyte that she was of, but
dyspayred to come therto by gyftes or prayer, so he thought to come to it by cautele.
He sayd that he was well byloved with her husbande, by the whiche he entred into
her house when it pleased hym. By the whiche, as in a tyme he wolde go thyder
when he knewe verely that her housbande was not at home and she receyved hym
ryght worshypfully, as hym whiche she thought was a ryght good frende to her
housbande. But [15v] Tarquyne, whiche thought all otherwyse, dyde so moche that
he entred at nyght into her chambre, of the whiche she was gretely aferde.

"And to say shortely, when he had spoken ynoughe by grete promyses,
gyftes, and offres that he myght do his wyll with her, and sawe that all avayled
not, he toke his swerde and manaced her to slee her yf she spake one worde, but
that she sholde consente to his wyll. And she answered that he sholde sle her
hardely, for she loved more to dye than to consente. Tarquyne, that sawe that
nothynge avayled hym, advysed hym of another grete malyce, and sayd that he
wolde tell it openly that he had founde her with one of her servauntes. And to say
shortely, she was so gretely aferde of this thynge, thynkynge that folkes wolde
soone byleve suche a thynge by the wordes of hym, she suffred his strengthe.

"But yet myght not Lucresse bere pacyentely this grete dyspleasure. Wherfore when it was daye, she sente to seke her husbande, and her fader and kynnes-
folke, whiche were the grettest of Rome. And when they were come to her, she
tolde them with grete wepynges and waylynges that whiche was done to her. And
as her housbande and kynnesfolkes sawe her in soo grete sorowe recomforted her,
she drewe a knyfe that she had under her gowne, sayenge: 'Thoughe it be so that
I clere me of this synne and I shewe myne innocence, neverthelesse I delyver me
not from tourment, nor I put me out of payne. Ne fro hensforthe there shal never
woman lyve shamed [16r] by the ensample of Lucresse.' And these thynges sayd,
by grete strengthe she fyxed the knyfe into her brest, and fell downe dyenge in
the syght of her husbande and frendes. So they ranne al as they had ben out of
themselfe upon this Tarquyne.

"Et pour celle cause fut tout Romme esmeue et chasierent le roy hors, et le filz eussent occis, se trouvez fust. Ne oncques puis roy n'ot[1] a Romme. Et a cause de cel oultrage fait a Lucrece, comme dient aucuns, vint la loy que homme mourroit pour prendre femme a force, laquelle loy est couvenable, et juste,[2] et saincte."

### *Chapitre 45*      De ce mesmes propos dit de la royne des Gausgres

"Bien au propos dessus dit fait l'istoire de la noble royne, femme de Orgiagontes, roy des Gausgres.[3] Il avint ou temps que les Rommains faisoient leurs grans conquestes sus les estranges que cellui dit roy[4] des Gausgres fu pris en une bataille, et [s]a[5] femme avec lui, par les diz Rommains. Quant ilz furent au logis, la noble royne qui moult belle estoit,[6] [fol. 110r a] simple, chaste, et bonne, pleut moult a un des conestables du dit host de Romme, qui tenoit pris le roy et elle. Si la pria moult et requist par grans offres. Mais quant il vid que priere riens ne valoit, il l'efform[7] de fait. De ceste injure ot moult grant duel la dame, et ne finoit de penser comment vengier s'en pourroit. Si attendi et dissimula tant que son point veist. Quant vit[8] que la rençon fut apportee pour delivrer son mary et elle, la dame voult que la finance fust baillee, elle presente, au sus dit conestable qui les tenoit. Auquel elle dist que elle vouloit que il pesast l'or, afin de mieulx avoir son conte, et que deceu ne fust. Et ainsi que elle vid que il entendoit a peser l'or, et qu'il n'y avoit [fol. 110r b] ains[9] de ses gens, la dame, qui fu saisie d'un coutel, le frappa en la gorge et l'occist, et en prist le chief, et sans nul encombrier le porta a son mary et lui dist le fait,[10] et comment la [vengence][11] en avoit prise."

---

[1] roy n'ot] n'ot roy
[2] est couvenable, et juste] est couvenable, juste
[3] royne, femme de Orgiagontes, roy des Gausgres] royne des Gausgres, femme de Orgiagontes, roy
[4] sus les estranges que cellui dit roy] sur les estranges terres que cellui roy
[5] [s]a : *fa*
[6] belle estoit] estoit belle
[7] ne valoit, il l'efform] n'y valoit il l'efforça
[8] vit] vint
[9] ains] nul
[10] le fait] tout le fait
[11] [vengence] : *vence*

"And for this cause all Rome was moved and chased the kynge out of the towne, and they wolde have slayne his sone yf they myght have fou[n]de[1] hym. And never syth there was no kynge in Rome bycause of this grete outrage done to Lucres. And as some say for bycause of her, there was a lawe made that yf ony man that ravysshed a woman sholde dye, the whiche lawe is convenable and juste."

*Chapter 45* **Of the same purpose, of the quene of Gausegres**

"Well to the purpose abovesayd the hystory maketh mencyon of the noble quene and wyfe of Orgyagontes, kynge of Gausegres. It happened in the tyme when the Romayns made theyr grete conquestes upon straungers that this sayd kynge was taken by the sayd Romaynes in a batayle, and his wyfe with hym. And when they were at theyr lodgynge, the noble quene whiche was ryght fayre, symple, and chaste, pleased gretely one of the constables of the sayd hoost of Rome, whiche had taken the kynge and her. So he prayed and requyred her by grete offres, but when he sawe that prayers avayled hym not, he lefte off and spake no more. Then this noble [16v] lady had grete sorowe for the wronge that this constable dyde to her, and she lefte not to thynke how she myght be revenged. So she taryed and dyssymyled tyll she sawe her tyme. And when she sawe that the raunsome was brought for to delyver her husbande and her, the lady wolde that this money sholde be payde to the sayd constable, she beynge present, to whom she sayd that she wolde that he sholde waye the golde, to the entente that he sholde have noo wronge and that he were not deceyved. And when she sawe that he entended to way the golde, and that there was no[n]e[2] of his people aboute hym, the lady toke a knyfe and smote hym in the throte and slewe hym, and smote off his hede, and without ony trouble brought it to her husbande and tolde hym howe she had done, and howe she had revenged her wronge."

---

[1] fou[n]de : *fouude*
[2] no[n]e : *noae*

*Chapitre 46*    Encore de ce mesmes, dit des Sicambres et d'autres[1] vierges

"Se je te puis donner exemple de femmes mariees, dont assez te compteroie a qui la doleur d'estre efforcees fut importable, ne t'en diroie pas moins des veusves et des vierges.

"Sisponne fu une femme de Grece. Elle fu prise et ravie des mariniers et escumeurs de m[e]r,[2] qui anemis estoient de la contree. Laquelle femme, comme elle fust de grant beaulté, fu par eulx moult requise. Et quant elle vid que eschapper ne pourroit sans estre efforcee, [fol. 110v a] elle eut celle chose en si grant orreur et desplaisance que elle amast mieulx mourir. Et pour ce se lança en la mer, et fu noyee.

"*Item*, les Sicambrins qui ores sont appellez François a grant host et multitude de gens assaillirent une foiz entre les autres la cité de Romme. Et en esperance de la destruire, avoient mené avecques eulx leurs femmes et leurs enfans. Avint que la desconfiture tourna sur ceulx de Sicambre: quant les femmes virent ce, elles se conseillerent entre elles que mieulx leur valoit mourir en deffendant leur chasteté car bien savoient que selon l'usage de guerre, toutes seroient efforcees que estre si faictement deshonnourees. Si firent environ elles forteresses de leurs[3] charettes et charioz et s'armerent contre les Rommains, et tant se [fol. 110v b] diffendirent comme elles porent et moult en occirent. Mais comme au desrain elles fussent occises aucques toutes,[4] celles qui[5] demourerent prierent au[6] joinctes mains que elles ne fussent touchees en vilennie, et que elles peussent user le demorant de leur vie en servant au temple des vierges de la deesse Vesta. Mais pour ce que il ne leur fu pas ottroyé, elles mesmes se vouldrent avant occire que estre efforcees.

"*Item*, des vierges semblablement si comme de Virgine, la noble pucelle de Romme que le faulx juge Claudien cuida avoir par cautelle et par force quant il ot veu que priere riens n'y valoit. Mais elle, non obstant fust[7] moult jeunete, ot plus chier estre occise que efforcee.

"*Item*, une cité fu prise en Lombardye par les anemis, qui [fol. 111r a] le seigneur tuerent. Les fillez du dit seigneur qui moult belles estoient, pour ce que elles se pensoient que on les vendroit efforcer, y pourvoirent d'estrange remede dont moult font a louer, car elles prisdrent char de pouscins crue et la mistrent en leurs sains si fu tost corrompue pour la chaleur. Dont il avint que quant ceulx qui

---

[1] d'autres] d'aucunes
[2] m[e]r : *mor*
[3] leurs] leur
[4] occises aucques toutes] auques toutes occises
[5] *F omits substantial amount of text, continues with Griselda's last trial (chap. 50)*
[6] prierent au] requirent a
[7] fust] fust elle

*Chapter 46*    Yet of the same: and of the ladyes of Sycambres, and other maydens

"Also, thoughe I maye gyve thee ensamples of maryed women of whome I myght tell thee ynoughe of whom the sorowe to be ravysshed was importable, I shall tell thee of wydowes and maydens.

"Sysponne was a woman of Grece, and she was taken and ravysshed with maryners and scommers of the see, whiche were enemyes to that countre. The whiche lady, as she that was of grete [K1r] beaute, was requyred by them ryght gretely. And when she sawe that she myght not escape but to be ravysshed, she had this thynge in so grete abhomynacyon and dyspleasa[u]nce[1] that she had lever to dye. And therfore she lepte into the see, and was drowned.

"Also the Sycambres (whiche nowe ben called Frensshmen) assayled on a tyme amonge other the cyte of Rome with a grete hoost and a multytude of people. And in hope that they sholde have destroyed the cyte, they brought theyr wyves with them and theyr chyldren. And it happened that the dyscomfyture tourned upon the Sycambres; when theyr wyves sawe that, they counsayled amonge them that it was better to dye in defendynge theyr chastyte, for they knewe that after the usage of warre, they sholde be ravysshed than to be deedly dyshonoured. So they made fortresses aboute them with theyr charyottes and cartes, and armed them ayenst the Romaynes. And they defended them as moche as they myght, and slewe many of them, but at the last they were slayne the moost parte of theym. And those that were lefte on lyve prayed with joyned handes that they wolde not touche them in no vylany, and that they myght use the ende of theyr lyves in servynge in the temple of maydens of the goddesse Vesta. But for that that it was not graunted to them, they wolde sle them rather than to be ravysshed.

"Also of maydens in lykewyse, so as of Vyrgyne, the noble mayde of Rome whiche the false juge Claudyen trowed to have by cautele and [Kk1v] by force and when he sawe that prayer avayled hym not. But she, notwithstandynge her grene yo[u]the,[2] had lever to dye than to be ravysshed.

"Also there was a cyte taken in Lombardy by the enemyes whiche that slewe the lorde. The doughters of the sayd lorde whiche were ryght fayre, insomoche that they thought they sholde be solde to be ravysshed, they pour[v]eyed[3] them of a straunge remedy for the whiche they were gretely to prayse, for they toke the flesshe of chekyns rawe and put it in theyr bosomes so it was anone corrupte by hete. Wherof it happened that when they that wolde ravysshe them came nyghe to

---

[1] dyspleasa[u]nce : *dyspleasannce*
[2] yo[u]the : *yonthe*
[3] pour[v]eyed : *pourneyed*

efforcer les vouloient¹ en cuidierent approchier, et ilz sentirent la pueur, tantost les laissierent² en disant, 'Dieux, que ces Lombardes puent!' Mais celle pulentise les rendi bien³ odorans."

### *Chapitre 47* Preues contre ce que on dit de l'inconstance des femmes parle Christine, et puis Droicture lui respont de l'inconstance et fragilité d'aucuns empereurs

"Dame, merveilleuse constance, fermeté, et vertu de tres grant courage⁴ [fol. 111r b] me racontez de femmes; que pourroit on plus dire des plus fors hommes qui oncques furent? Et toutevoies sur tous les vices que hommes et mesmement les livres dient estre en femmes, crient tous d'une voix sur elles qui variables sont, inconstance, muables, legieres,⁵ et de fraile corage, flechissans comme enfans, ne qu'il n'y a nul⁶ fermeté. Sont ces hommes doncques⁷ si constans que varier leur soit⁸ pou commun et fort a faire, qui tant accusent femmes d'inconstance? Certes, se ilz ne le sont, trop leur est lait et mal seant demander a autrui la vertu que ilz mesmes⁹ ne scevent avoir."

*Responce*: "Belle doulce amie, n'as tu pas tousjours ouÿ dire que le fol aperçoit trop bien la petite buschete en la face de son voisin, mais il ne se donne de garde du grant [fol. 111v a] tref qui lui pent a l'ueil? Si te monstreray grant contradicion en ce que les hommes tant dient de la variacion des femmes. Tous generaument acordent¹⁰ que femmes par nature sont moult fresles, et toutevoies ilz leur demandent trop plus grant constance que eulx mesmes ne scevent avoir. Car eulx qui se dient tant estre fors et de noble condicion ne se peuent tenir de cheoir en plusieurs tres grans deffaulx et pechiez, et scevent bien que ilz mesprennent. Et ilz

---

¹ ceulx qui efforcer les vouloient] ilz
² laissierent] laissierent aler
³ bien] tres
⁴ merveilleuse constance, fermeté, et vertu de tres grant courage] certes merveilleuse constance, force, et vertu, et fermeté
⁵ variablles sont, inconstance, muables, legieres] variables et inconstans sont muables et legieres
⁶ nul] aucune
⁷ ces hommes doncques] doncques ces hommes
⁸ soit] soit comme chose hors de tout leur usage
⁹ pou commun et fort a faire, qui tant accusent femmes d'inconstance? Certes, se ilz ne le sont, trop leur est lait et mal seant demander a autrui la vertu que ilz mesmes] ou pou commun qui tant accusent femmes de muableté et d'inconstance. Et certes, se ilz ne sont bien fermes trop leur est lait d'accuser autrui de leur mesmes vice, ou d'i demander la vertu que ilz
¹⁰ des femmes. Tous generaument acordent] et inconstance des femmes. It est ainsi que tous generaument afferment

them, and they felte the stynke, anone they lefte them, saynge: 'O goddes, howe these Lombardes stynke!' But that stynkynge made them to smell ryght swete."

*Chapter 47*  **Proves agaynst that that one speketh of the inconstaunce of women: Christine speketh, and Ryghtwysnes answereth of the inconstaunce and fragylyte of dyvers emperoures**

"Madame, ye tell me mervayllous constaunce, stablenesse, and vertue of the grete courage of women; what myght one saye more of the moost strongest men that ever were? Yet above all vyces that men and also the bokes say to be of women, cryeth all of one voyce upon them that they [Kk2r] be varyable, inconstaunte, chaungeable, lyght, and of frayle courage, bowynge as chyldren. Are these men, then, so constaunte[1] that they may not vary? And it is a grete thynge to do, that so moche accuseth women of inconstaunce? Certes, yf they do too moche, it is ryght lewde and evyl semynge to ask of another a vertue that they cannot have themselfe."

*Answere*: "Fayre swete love, haste not thou alwaye herde say that a fole perceyveth better the lytell mote in the face of his neyghboure then he beholdeth the grete beme that hangeth over his owne eye? So I shall shewe thee grete contradyccyon in that that these men saye so moche of the varyaunce of women. They accorde all generally that women by nature be ryght frayle, and yet these men desyre that women sholde be of gr[e]tter[2] constaunce then they can be themselfe. For those that so calleth themselfe to be so stronge and of so noble condycyon, yet they maye not holde them from fallynge into many ryght grete defautes

---

[1] constaunte : *constaunnte*
[2] gr[e]tter : *grtter*

cuerent tant sus aulx femmes se aucune en chiet en aucunes deffaillances dont
eulx mesmes sont cause et par leurs cauteles les y atirent a grant peine et a grant
labour. Maiz puis que tant frailles les reputent ilz deussent aucunement subporter
leur [fol. 111v b] fragilité, et ne reputer a elles petite deffaillance estre grant crisme.
Mais ne ilz ne les veulent supporter, ains leur font et dient moult de griefs assez
en est il,[1] ne ilz ne les daingnent reputer fortes et constantes quant elles endurent
leurs deurs oultrages; et ainsi a tous propos veulent avoir les hommes le droit pour
eulx, et les deux bous de la conroie. Et de ce as tu assez souffis[a]mment[2] parlé
en ton *Epistre du dieu d'amours.*

"Mais ad ce que tu me demandes[3] se les hommes sont tant fors et tant constans que ilz aient cause de blasmer autrui d'inconstance, se tu regardes depuis
les aages et temps anciens jusques a aujourd'uy,[4] par les livres et par ce que tu
en as veu en ton aage et tous les jours, [fol. 112r a] pueux veoir aux yeulx non mie
es simples hommes, ne de bas estat, mais des plus grans tu pourras congnoistre
la perfeccion de la constance. Je ne te diray mie absoluement qui est en eulx si
comme ilz dient generaument des femmes, mais qui est et a esté en partie de eulx.
Et[5] pour ce que ainsi que se es courages des hommes n'eust aucune inconstance
ne varieté ilz accusent tant les femmes de ce vice: prens cy garde, et je te donray exemple des plus poissance princes et des plus esleuz es estaz, qui est chose
impertinent plus que es autres sens aler querre es plus anciens aages.[6]

"Que fut oncques courage de femme tant fraille, tant paourex, ne si mal
ostru, [fol. 112r b] ne moins constant que fu cellui de l'Empereur Claudien? Il estoit
tant variable que tout quanque il ordennoit a une heure, il despeçoit a l'autre. Ne
quelconques fermeté n'estoit trouvee en sa parole: il s'accordoit a tous consaulz.
Il fist occire sa femme par sa folie et cruaulté, et puis au so[i]r[7] demanda pour
quoy elle ne s'aloit couschier; et a ses familiers qu'il[8] avoit fait trenchier les testes,

---

    [1] sont moult fresles . . . griefs assez en est il] *R see annotations for revised text*
    [2] souffis[a]mment : *souffisomment*
    [3] me demandes] m'as demandé
    [4] a aujourd'uy] aujourd'uy je te di que
    [5] congnoistre la perfeccion de la constance. Je ne te diray mie absoluement qui est en
eulx si comme ilz dient generaument des femmes, mais qui est et a esté en partie de eulx.
Et] veoir et congnoistre la perfeccion la force et la constance qui y est voire generaument
en la plus grant partie combien que il en soit de sage, constans, et fors et il en est bien
besoing. Et se tu veulx que je t'en donne preuves et de pieça et du temps d'ores
    [6] ce vice: prens cy garde, et je te donray exemple des plus poissance princes et des
plus esleuz es estaz, qui est chose impertinent plus que es autres sens aler querre es plus
anciens aages] cellui. Regardes es estas des plus poissans princes et des greigneurs hommes qui est chose impartient plus que es aultres que te puis je dire des imperiaulx je te
demande ou fu oncques
    [7] so[i]r : *sor*
    [8] qu'il] a qui il

and synnes, and knowe well that they mysse take. And they laboure so moche to the women that yf ony of them fall in ony defaute of whiche they are the cause and by theyr cautayles they have drawne them therto by grete payne and laboure. Yet syth they name them soo frayle, they ought in some wyse for to supporte theyr fragylyte, and not to calle a lytell faute a grete cryme. Yet they lyst not to supporte them, but maketh and saythe many greate gryefes of theym, and they denaye not to calle theym stronge and [K2v] constaunte when they endure theyr grete outrages; and thus at all purposes these men wolde have the ryght from them. And of that thou hast spoken ynoughe in thy *Pystle of the God of Love.*

"But to that thou demaundest me yf these men be so stronge and so constaunte that they have cause to blame other of theyr constaunce, if thou beholde syth the ages and auncyent tyme unto this daye, by the bokes and by that thou haste sene in thyne age and at all tymes, the[n]¹ mayst se it before thyne eyes not onely in symple men, nor of lowe estate, but of the grettest thou mayst knowe the perfeccyon of theyr constaunce. I wyll not saye absolutely that it is with them so generally as they say of women, but as it hathe ben and is in some of theym. And for that that yf there be in the courage of men no inconstaunce but accuse the women of that vyce: take hede nowe here, and I shall gyve thee ensamples of the grettest prynces and moost lyfted up in estate, whiche is a thynge not perteynynge to the same vyce more than in others without sekynge in more auncyent ages.

"Where was there ever courage of women soo frayle, nor so evyll accustomed and lesse constaunt then was the Emperour Claudyen? He was soo varyable that what so ever he ordeyned in one houre, he dyspysed it in another. And there was never stablenes founde in his worde: he accorded to all counsayle. He caused his wyfe to be slayne by his cruelte, and after at nyght he asked wherfore she came not to bedde, and commaunded his servauntes that [K3r] he had made smyte off theyr

---

¹ the[n] : *theu*

manda que ilz venissent[1] jouer avecques lui. Cestui estoit tant de chetif courage que ades il trembloit, ne de nul ne se fioit. Que t'en diroie? Toutes maleurtés de meurs et de courage furent en ce chetif empereur. Mais a quoy te dis je de cestui, fu il seul en l'empire seant plein de tel fragilité? Tybere l'empereur, de combien valu il [fol. 112v a] mieulx! Toute inconstance, toute varieté, toute lubrieté n'estoit elle en lui plus qu'il n'est trouvé de nulle femme?"

## *Chapitre 48*     Ci dit de Noiron[2]

"Et Noiron, quel fut il, puis que nous sommes entrez es faiz dez empereurs? De cestui apparut la grant variableté[3] car au commencement il fu assez bon, et mettoit peine de plaire a tous mais aprés n'ot nul frain a sa luxure, a sa rapine, ne a sa[4] cruaulté. Et pour mieulx la excerciter, souventeffoiz il s'armoit par nu[i]t,[5] et s'aloit[6] avec les gloutons ses complices es gloutonnies et lieux dissolus, jouant et foloiant par les rues, faisant tous maulx. Et pour trouver occasion de ma[l][7] faire, il boutoit ceulx qu'il encontroit; et s'ilz disoient mot, il les navroit et [fol. 112v b] occioit. Il rompoit tavernes et huis deshonnestes; il prenoit femmes a force, dont a pou fu une fois occis du mary d'une femme que efforcee avoit. Il faisoit faire bains dissolus et mengoit toute nuit. Il ordenoit une chose, et puis une[8] aultre, selon que sa f[o]lie[9] lui amonnestoit diverses choses. Toutes lecheries, toutes superfluites, toutes curiositez, tout orgueil et foles pensees[10] il excercitoit.

"Il amoit les mauvais et persecutoit les bons. Il fu consentant de la mort de son pere, et sa mere fist il puis mourir. Et quant elle fut mort, il la fist ouvrir pour veoir le lieu ou il avoit esté conceu et dist, quant il l'ot veue, que elle avoit esté belle femme. Il occist Octaviene sa femme qui [fol. 113r a] estoit bon[ne][11] dame; une autre prist que il ama moult au commencement et puis l'occist. Il fist mourir Claudiene, fille de son devancier, pour ce que elle ne le vouloit[12] prendre a mary. Il fist morir son fillastre dessoubz l'aage de .vii. ans pour ce que on le portoit jouer comme filz de duc; Seneque son maistre, le noble philosophe, fist mourir pour

---

[1] venissent] se venissent
[2] Ci dit de Noiron] Ci parle de Neron
[3] grant variableté] tres grant fragilité et variance
[4] ne a sa] et
[5] nu[i]t : *nut*
[6] s'aloit] aloit
[7] ma[l] : *ma*
[8] une] un
[9] f[o]lie : *falie*
[10] pensees] despenses
[11] bon[ne] : *bon*
[12] vouloit] volt

heedes to come and play with hym. This emperoure was of so caytyfe a courage that he trembled alwaye, nor he trusted nobody. I cannot tell thee all the
shrewdenesse of the condycyons of this lewde emperoure but that he was full of
fragylyte.

"Tybere the emperoure, what was he more wrothe? All inconstaunce, all
varyaunce, all slyppernesse was mor [i]n[1] hym than ever was founde in woman."

## *Chapter 48*    Of Nero the cruell emperoure

"And Nero, [w]hat[2] was he syth we be entred in the dedes of emperoures? Of
this Nero the grete varyablenesse appered, for at the begynnynge he was good
ynoughe, and dyde his payne to please all people. But after, he had no refrayne
of his lechery, of his ravyne, nor of his cruelte. And to exercyse it the more, often
tymes he armed hym by nyght and wente with his glotons and his felawes to
unthryfty places, playenge and japynge by the stretes, doynge all shrewdenes.
And to fynde occasyon to do shrewdely, he shouldred them that he mette; and
yf they spake ony worde, other he wolde wounde them or sle them. He brake
tavernes and dores of lewde houses. He toke women by strengthe, wherby he was
almoost slayne ones of the husbande of a woman that he had ravysshed. He lete
make bathes for lewdenesse, and ete and dranke [K3v] all the nyght, and slepte
the day. He ordeyned nowe one thynge, nowe another as his foly styred hym to
do dyvers thynges. All lechery, al superfluytes, all pryde, and al maner thoughtes
of foly was in hym.

"He haunted al evyll. He loved noughty folkes and tourmented the good.
He was consentynge to the dethe of his fader and of his moder. And when she
was deed, he made her to be opened to se the place where he was conceyved; and
when he had sene it, he sayd that she was a fayre woman when she lyved. He
slewe his wyfe Octovyene that was ryght a good woman, and toke another that
he loved moche at the begynnynge, and after slewe her. He lete sle a kynneswoman of his owne bycause she wolde not be maryed to hym. He made to sle his
lytell doughter within the age of .vii. yeres bycause one bare her to playe with a
dukes sones. He lete sle the noble phylosophre Seneke, whiche was his mayster,

---

[1] more [i]n : *mor en*
[2] [w]hat : *that*

ce que il ne ce[1] pouoit tenir d'avoir honte de ce qu'il faisoit devant lui. Il empoisonna son prevost, en faignant que il le gariroit desdens. Les nobles princes et barons anciens et de grant auctorité qui avoient grant governement il empoisona en boires et mengiers. Il fist tuer son ante, et prist ses biens. Il [fist destruire][2] tous les plus nobles de Romme [fol. 113r b] et aler en exil, et leurs enfans destruit. Il fist acoustumer a un cruel homme de Egipte et mengier char d'omme crue, afin que par cellui il feist mengier hommes tous vifs.[3]

"Que t'en diroie? On ne pourroit tout raconter les orribles[4] maulx que il fist, ne ses grans mauvaistiez. Et en comble de tout, il fist boutter le feu par toute la cité de Romme par .vi. jours et par .vi. nuys, et par celle pestillence morurent moult de gens. Et il regardoit l'embrasement de[5] la ruine de sa tour, et faisoit grant joye de beaulté[6] de la flamme, et chantoit. Il fist decoler a son mengier[7] saint Pierre et saint Pol, et moult d'autres martirs. Et en telles choses faisant, quant il ot regné l'espace de .xiiii. ans, les Rommains [fol. 113r a] qui trop en avoient souffert se rebellerent contre lui: et il se desespera, et s'occist lui mesmes."[8]

*Chapitre 49*      Ci dit de[9] l'Empereur Galba et d'autres

"T'ay je dit par grant merveille comme il te semble par aventure de la mauvaistié de cestui[10] Noyron et de ses fragilitez? Mais je te promet que l'empereur qui lui succeda, qui fu nommé Galba, ne fu gaires meilleur se autant eust vescu: sa cruauté fust desmesuree. Et avec ces[11] autres vices, estoit tant muable que il n'y avoit quelconques arrest, ne point n'estoit en un estat: maintenant cruel et sans mesure, maintenant trop mol et sans justice; negligent, envieux, et souspeçonneux, pou amant ses princes et ses chevaliers, chetif et paoureux de courage, [fol. 113v b] et couvoiteux sur toute riens. Ne regna que .vi. moys car occis fu pour abregier ses cruauté[s].[12]

---

[1]  ce] se
[2]  [fist destruire] : *fistruire*
[3]  hommes tous vifs] tous vifs
[4]  tout raconter les orribles] tous raconter les crueulx
[5]  de] et
[6]  beaulté] la beauté
[7]  mengier] disner
[8]  et s'occist lui mesmes] et lui mesmes s'occist
[9]  Ci dit de] De
[10]  cestui] cellui
[11]  ces] ses
[12]  crauté[s] : *crauté*

for that that he was alwaye ashamed when he sawe hym. He enpoysoned his provost, faynynge that he wolde hele hym agayne. He enpoysoned with metes and drynkes all the noble auncyent pryncates and barons of grete auctoryte that had grete governaunce. He made to sle his aunte and toke her goodes. He made to destroye all the nobles of Rome and put them in exyle, and destroyed theyr chyldren. He made a cruell man of Egypte to be accustomed to ete mannes flesshe rawe, to the entente that by hym he wolde make men to be eten quicke.

"What shall I say? One may not tell the horryble dedes [K4r] that he dyde, ne gathered togyder the crueltees of hym. He made fyre to be caste all aboute Rome .vi. dayes and .vi. nyghtes, and by that pestylence dyed moche of the people. He behelde the fallynge of his toure, and made grete joye and songe. He made to sle Saynt Peter and Saynt Poule, and many other martyres. And in doynge these thynges, when he had reygned the space of .xiiii. yeres, the Romaynes that had suffred too moche rebelled ayenst hym: and he fell in dyspayre, and slewe hymselfe."

*Chapter 49*    Of the Emperoure [Galba],[1] and of others

"Bi grete mervayle I have tolde thee as that it semeth by adventure of the cursednesse of Nero and of his fragylytes, but I promyse thee that the emperoure that succeded hym, whiche was named Galba, was but lytell better yf he had lyved longe, for his cruelte was out of measure. And with his other vyces, he was so varyable that there was no maner of restraynynge, ne he was never in one estate: nowe cruell and without measure, nowe too softe and without justyce; neglygent, envyous, and full of suspeccyon, lytell lovynge his pryncates and his knyghtes, caytyfe and fereful of courage, coveytous above all thynge. He reygned but .vi. monethes for he was slayne to shorten his crueltes. [K4v]

---

[1] [Galba] : omitted

"Mais Othoun¹ qui le succeda, de combien valoit² il mieulx? Pour³ ce que on dit que femmes sont curieuses, cestui estoit mignot et delicatif de son corps,⁴ de chetif courage, ne querant que ses aises,⁵ fol large, grant glouton, faint, luxurieulx, faulx traittre, et plein de maleurté, plein de desdaing.⁶ Et la fin de lui fut que il s'occist aprez ce qu'il ot regné troys mois, pour ce que ses anemis avoient eu victoire sur lui.

"Vincilien qui a cestui Othon succeda ne fut de riens meilleur mais plein de toute perversité. Ne sçay que plus⁷ t'en diroye: ne cuides pas qu'il⁸ te mente. Lis lez histoires des empereurs et les proces [fol. 114r a] de leurs vies, et tu trouveras qu'en⁹ bien petit nombre de tous¹⁰ quansque ilz furent en a esté de bons, de droitturiers, et de constance, desquelz bons fut l'Empereur Trayan et Titus.¹¹ Mais je te promet que contre ces .ii. bons,¹² tu en trouveras .x. mauvais,¹³ et pareillement je te dis des papes et des gens de Saincte Eglise qui plus doivent estre esleus.¹⁴ Mais quoy que au commencement de la crestienté fussent sains, depuis que l'Empereur Constantin ot douee l'Eglise de grans revenues et de richeces, la sainte qui y a esté¹⁵—ne fault que lire en leurs gestes et croniques, et se tu me veulx dire que ces choses fussent jadis et que a present soyent bons. Tu pueux veoir aujourd'uy¹⁶ se le monde [fol. 114r b] va en amendant, et se grant fermeté et grant constance a es faiz et es consaux, tant des princes temporeux comme des esperitueulx: il yppert assez, plus ne t'en diray.¹⁷ Si ne sçay a quoy hommes parlent d'inconstance ne varieté de femmes, ne¹⁸ comment ilz n'ont honte d'en ouvrir la bouche quant ilz regardent comment es grans faiz par eulx gouvernez, et non mie par les femmes,

---

¹ Othoun] Othon l'empereur
² valoit] valt
³ Pour] Certes, pour
⁴ mignot et delicatif de son corps] tant mignot et delicatif de son corps que oncques chose ne fu plus mole
⁵ querant que ses aises] queroit que ses ayses grant rapineur
⁶ et plein de maleurté, plein de desdaing] plain de desdaing et de toute maleurté
⁷ plus] plus riens
⁸ qu'il] que je
⁹ qu'en] que
¹⁰ tous] tout
¹¹ l'Empereur Trayan et Titus] Julius Cesar, Othovien, Trayan l'empereur, et Titus
¹² ces .ii. bons] un de ces bons
¹³ mauvais] tres mauvais
¹⁴ qui plus doivent estre esleus] qui plus que autre gent doivent estre parfais et esleus
¹⁵ sainte qui y a esté] sainteté qui y est
¹⁶ aujourd'uy] aujourd'uy en tous estas
¹⁷ diray] dy
¹⁸ ne] et

"But Othomy whiche that succeded hym was no better. For that some saye that women ben curyous, the emperoure was curyous and delycate of his body, caytyfe of courage, sekynge after nothynge but his ease folyly large: a grete gloton, faynte, lecherous, a false traytoure and full of all shrewdenesse, full of dysdayne. And the ende of hym was that he slewe hymselfe after that he had reygned thre monethes for bycause that his enemyes had the vyctory of hym in batayle.

"Vyncylyen that succeded this Othomy was noo better but full of cursed-nesse. I wote not what I shal tell thee more. And thou trowe that I lye, rede the hystoryes of emperours and the processe of theyr lyves, and thou shalte fynde that there were but fewe in nombre that were of good condycyons, ryghtfull, and constaunt, of the whiche good was the Emperour Trayane and Tytus. But I promyse thee that ayenst these two good, thou shalte fynde .x. evyll, and in the same wyse of the popes and of people of holy chyrche, whiche ought to be more chosen. But thoughe that at the begynnynge of Crysten faythe there were sayntes, syth the Emperour Constantyne gave to the chyrche grete revenues and rychesses, the holynesse that hath ben—rede theyr gestes and crownacles, and tell me yf they be of the same perfeccyon nowe. And nowe thou mayst se at this daye yf the worlde be in amendynge, and yf grete stablenesse have ben and grete constaunce in the dedes and counsayles as moche of temporall prynces as of spyrytuall, [L1r] it appereth ynoughe. I shall say to thee more: I wote not to whom men speke of inconstaunce nor of var[y]aunce[1] of women, nor howe they have no shame to open theyr mouthe when they beholde how in the grete dedes governed by them, and not by the women, with so moche inconstaunce and varyaunce as

---

[1] var[y]aunce : *varaunce*

a tant de inconstances et varietez que ce semblent fais d'enfans, et comment sont bien[1] tenus les propos et accors que ilz font en leurs plus grans conseulx.[2]

"Et te diray tout en un mont sur ses choses: nulle autre chose n'est inconstance ne varieté ne mais faire contre ce que raison enseigne. Et creature raisonnable cree a l'ymage de Dieu et qui de ce a cognoiscence, qui [fol. 114v a] plus encline a sensualité que a raison, celle est fraille; et devant que la mauvaistié est plus grande, de tant est le regart plus loings de raison, et doit estre dicte la fragilité greingneur. Et je me fais fort que lis tout au long des histoires de quanque il en est escript, quoy que philosophes et mains aucteurs ayent dit et afferme en tasche et a voulenté estre si grant fragilité es femmes,[3] que tu ne trouveras point oncques[4] avoir esté quelconques femme de si grant perversité que ont esté en grant quantité d'ommes.

"Les plus mauvaises femmes que tu trouveras en nulle escripture furent Athalis et Jesobel sa mere, roynes de Jherusalem, qui persecuterent le peuple d'Israel; Bruneheut, royne de France, et aucunes aultres. Mais avise moy la [fol. 114v b] perversité de Judas qui si durement[5] trahi son bon maistre, le doulz Jhesus,[6] a qui il estoit apostre, qui[7] tant de biens lui avoit fais? Et me prens Julien l'Apostat, Denis le Tirant,[8] tant de mauvais roys en diverses contrees, de desloyaulx empereurs, de papes hereges, et d'autres prelas sans foy, pleins de couvoitise, les antescristz qui doivent estre: et tu trouveras que hommes se ont beau taire, et que femmes doivent beneistre Dieu et louer, qui a mis le tresor de leurs ames en vaissiaulz femmenins. Si me tairay a tant de ce, et pour contredire par exemples aux diz d'iceulx qui si frailles les appellent te diray d'aucunes femmes tres fortes, desquelles les histoires sont belles a ouïr et de bon exemples."[9]

---

[1] sont bien] bien sont

[2] plus grans conseulx] consaulx

[3] Et te diray . . . fragilité es femmes] *R see annotations for revised text*

[4] oncques avoir] avoir

[5] durement] cruellement

[6] maistre, le doulz Jhesus] maistre

[7] qui] et qui

[8] lui avoit fais . . . tirant] faiz la durté et cruaulté des Juifs et du peuple d'Israel qui n'occirent pas tant seulement Jhesucrist par envie mais aussi plusieurs sains prophetes qui devant lui furent, les un sierent parmi les autres assommerent et diversement occirent. Et me prens aussi Julien l'appostat, lequel pour sa grant perversité aucuns reputent avoir esté l'un des antecrists; Denis le faulx tirant de Cecile qui tant estoit detestable que deshonneste chose est de lire sa vie; avec ce

[9] exemplles] exemple

it were the dedes of chyldren, and howe well theyr purpose and accorde abydeth that they make in theyr grete counsayles.

"And I shal tell thee all at ones upon these thynges: there is none other inconstaunce nor varyaunce but to do agaynst that that reason techeth. And a creature reasonable made after the ymage of God and that hathe knowlege, of that that enclyneth more to sensualyte than to reason, that is frayle; and the more that the shrewdenesse is grete, the ferder it is fro reason and ought to be called the gretter fragylyte. And I am certayne that rede al alonge the hystoryes of whom that ever they are wryten, thoughe phylosophers and many auctours have sayd and afferme that there is so grete fragylyte in women, that thou shalte not fynde ony woman of so grete cursednesse as there hathe ben in grete quantyte of men.

"The worste women that thou shalte fynde in Holy Scrypture was Athalys and Jesobell her moder, quenes of Jherusalem, whiche poursued the chyldren of Israell; Brunehent, quene of Fraunce, and some other. But advyse thee of the cursednesse of Judas that so myschevously betrayed his good mayster, swete Jhesus, to whom he was appostle, that had done hym so moche good. [L1v] And take hede of Julyan the apostata, Denys the tyraunt, so many of shrewde kynges in dyvers countrees, of false emperoures and popes, and other prelates without faythe, full of coveytyse, the antecrystes also. And thou shalte fynde also that men have cause to holde theyr peas, and that women have cause to thanke God and prayse Hym that hathe put the treasoure of so many good soules in the bodyes of women. So I shall saye noo more as nowe agaynst them by ensamples of the dedes of them that call these women so frayle, and I shall tell thee of dyvers women ryght stable and constaunt, of whome the hystoryes ben ryght good to here of good ensamples."

### *Chapitre 50*    Ci dit de Grisilidis,[1] marquise de Saluce, forte femme en vertu [fol. 115r a]

"Il est escript que il fut un marquis de Salucez nommé par nom Grautier[2] sans Per. Cellui estoit bel de corps et preudomme asses, mais moult estrange de meurs. Ses barons souvent l'amonnestoient et prioient que pour avoir lignee marier se voulsist. Mais comme pour long temps accorder ne si voulsist, au derrain leur dist que mais que promettre lui voulsissent que agreable aroient telle femme comme il vouldroit prendre, que il s'accorderoit a estre mariez, laquel chose lui accorderent et jurerent ses barons.

"Cellui marquis hentoit souvent deduit de chace et d'oisiaux. Si y avoit adoncques[3] pres de sa forteresse une petite ville champestre en laquelle entre les [fol. 115r b] pouvres hommes laboureurs[4] d'ycelle demouroit un tres povre homme impotent et vieil, qui avoit nom Janicola, bon homme et preudoms avoit esté toute sa vie. Cellui preudoms avoit une sienne fille de l'aage de .xviii. ans nommee Grisilidis, qui le servoit par grant diligence et le gouvernoit du labour de sa filasse. Le dit marquis, qui souvent par la passoit, avoit bien avisé les bonnes meurs et l'onnesteté d'icelle pucelle, qui asses belle de corps et de viaire estoit, dont il l'avoit moult en grace.

"Avint que le marquis, qui avoit accordé a ses barons que il prendroit femme, leur va dire que a certain jour fussent assemblez pour ces[5] noces et ordenna que toutes les dames y fussent, si fist faire grant appareil. Et au [fol. 115v a] dit jour comme tous et toutes fussent assemblez devers lui, fist toute la route monter a cheval pour aler avec lui querir l'espousee. Si s'en ala droit a la maison de Janicola, et encontra Grisilidis a tout une cruce d'eaue sur son chief, qui de la fontaine venoit. Il lui demanda ou estoit son pere. Et Grisilidis s'agenoilla et lui dist que il estoit a l'ostel.

"'Va le querre,' dist il.

"Et le bon homme venu, le marquis lui dist que il vouloit prendre sa fille par mariage. Et Janicolas lui respondi que il feist son plaisir. Si entroient les dames dedens la petite maisonnete et vesterent et parerent l'espousee moult noblement si comme a l'estat[6] du marquis apartenoit, de robes et de joyaulx que il [fol. 115v b] avoit fait aprester. Si l'en amena et l'espousa[7] en son palais. Et a faire le conte brief, ceste dame tant bien se porta vers toute personne que les nobles, et grans,

---

[1] Grisilidis] Gliselidis
[2] Grautier] Gautier
[3] adoncques] auques
[4] laboureurs] povres laboureurs
[5] ces] ses
[6] l'estat : *l'estatat*
[7] l'espousa] espousa

*Chapter 50*   Of Grysylde, marquys of Saluce: a woman of grete
vertue, and specyally in pacyence

"Wryten it is that there was a marquys of Saluce named by name Gautyre sans
Pere. He was fayre of body and a worshypfull man, but ryght straunge of condycyons. His lordes often tymes counsayled hym and prayed hym that he wolde
mary that he myght have yssue. But it was longe tyme or he wolde accorde to
them. At the last, he sayd to them that he wolde with a good wyll if it sholde
be agreable to them that he myght take suche a woman as he wolde chose to be
maryed [L2r] unto, to the whiche thynge they accorded and made theyr othe
therto.

"This marquys haunted often tymes the dysporte of huntynge and hawkynge
in the feldes, in the whiche amonge the poore men labourers of that towne there
dwelled a ryght poore man, impotent and olde that was called Janycle, and was
a good true man al his lyfe. This same good man had a doughter of the age of
.xviii. yeres named Grysylde, whiche served hym by grete dylygence and founde
hym by the laboure of her spynnynge. The sayd marquys, whiche often tymes
passed that waye, had well advysed the good condycyons and the honeste of this
mayden, whi[ch]¹ was ryght fayre of body and of vysage, whom he had ryght
gretely in his grace.

"It happened that the marquys, that was accorded with his barons that he
sholde take a wyfe, sayd to theym that they sholde assemble at a certayne day for
the weddynges. And he ordeyned that all the ladyes sholde be there, so he lete
make grete araye. And at that daye as all men and women were assembled before
hym, he made al the route to take theyr horses for to go with hym for to fetche
home his spouse. Soo they wente ryght unto the house of Janycle, and there they
mette with Grysylde with a potte of water upon her heed, whiche came fro the
welle. He demaunded of her where her fader was. And this Grysylde mekely
kneled downe and sayd unto hym that he was at home.

"'Go seke hym,' sayd he unto her.

"And when the good man was come, the marquys sayd to hym that [L2v] he
wolde take his doughter by maryage, and Janycle answered hym that he sholde
do his pleasure. So the ladyes entred into the lytell house and clothed and arayed
the spouse ryght nobly so as it perteyned to the estate of a marquys, of robes and
of jewelles that he had ordeyned for her. Soo he ledde her home and wedded
her in his palays. And to make the tale shorte, this lady bare her so wel to every

---

¹ whi[ch] : *whi*

et petiz, et tout le peuple moult l'amoit. Et tant bien s'y[1] savoit avoir avec chascun que tous s'en tenoit pour contens,[2] et son seigneur servoit, et chierissoit si que elle devoit.

"Celle annee la marquise ot une fille qui a grant joye fut receue. Mais quant elle fut en aage que elle fut sevree, le marquis fist a croire a la dame pour esprouver sa constance[3] que il desplaisoit aux barons que la lignee d'elle seigneurisist sur eulx, et pour ce vouloit que l'enfant fust occis. A ceste chose, qui dure deust estre a toute mere, respon[di][4] [fol. 116r a] Grisilidis que la fille estoit sienne, et que faire en pouoit son plaisir. Si la fist bailler a un sien escuier, lequel en faisant semblant que il la venist querre[5] pour occire la porta secretement a Boulongne la Grasse a la contesse de Panigo, qui estoit suer du marquis pour la garder et nourrir. Mais de tout ce ne faisoit quelconques semblant de tristece Grisilidis, qui cuidoit sa fille estre occise.

"Au chief d'un an aprés, la marquise fu enceincte et se delivra d'un tres bel filz, a grant joye receu.[6] Mais de rechief voult le marquis essaier sa femme comme devant,[7] et lui dist que il couvenoit que il fu occis pour contenter les barons et ses hommes. Et Grisilidis[8] [fol. 116r b] respondit que se il ne souffisoit que son filz mourust, que elle estoit preste de mourir, se il lui plaisoit. Si le bailla a l'escuier semblablement que ot fait la fille, sans que nul semblant de tristece feist, ne autre chose dire[9] fors tant que elle pria a l'escuier que quant il aroit l'enfant occis, que il le voulsist enterrer, afin que la tendre char de l'enfant ne fust pas mengee des bestes sauvages, ne des oysiaulx.

"De ceste grant durté n'apparut oncques chiere muee a Grisilidis. Maiz ne se passa mie a tant le marquis encore la voult plus essaier. Ja avoient esté .xii. ans ensemble, ou quel temps la bonne dame tant bien se estoit[10] portee que asses devoit[11] [fol. 116v a] souffrire l'espreuve de sa vertu, quant le marquis un jour[12] l'appella en sa chambre, et lui dist que il estoit mal de ses chevaliers et subgiez,[13] et en peril de perdre sa seigneurie pour elle, car trop avoient grant desdaing de tenir pour dame et maistresse la fille de Janicola. Si couvenoit, se il les vouloit

---

[1]  s'y] se

[2]  tenoit pour contens] tenoient tres pour contemps

[3]  fist a croire a la dame pour esprouver sa constance] pour esprouver la constance et pacience de Gliselidis lui fist a croire

[4]  respon[di] : *response*

[5]  querre] querir

[6]  receu] receus

[7]  sa femme comme devant] comme devant sa femme

[8]  Grisilidis] la dame

[9]  dire] dist

[10]  bien se estoit] s'estoit bien

[11]  devoit] deust

[12]  le marquis un jour] un jour le marquis

[13]  ses chevaliers et subgiez] de ses subgez et de sa gent

creature that the nobles grete and lytell, and all the people loved her. And so well she coude behave her with every persone that every man helde them contente, and she served and cherysshed her lorde so as she ought.

"This yere this lady had a doughter, whiche was taken in grete joye. But when she was in age that she was taken fro the pappes, the marquys made the lady to byleve for to prove her constaunce that she dyspleased the lordes that the lygnage of her sholde lordeshyp upon them, and[1] therfore he wolde that the chylde were slayne. To this thynge, whiche ought to be ryght harde to every moder, Grysylde answered that the doughter was his owne, and that he myght do his pleasure. So he made the chylde to be taken to a squyer of his, the whiche in makynge semblaunt that he came thyder to sle the chylde, and he bare it secretly to Boloyne la Grace to the Countesse of Payngo, whiche was syster to the marquys, to kepe and to nourysshe it. But for al this, Grysylde made never semblaunt of hevynesse that trowed her doughter to be slayne.

"Agayne in the yere after, the lady was [L3r] with chylde and was delyvered of a fayre sone; the fade[r][2] receyved it with grete joye. And yet agayne the marquys wolde assaye his wyfe as he dyde before, and sayd to her that the chylde must nedes be slayne to contente the lordes and his people. And Grysylde answered that yf it suffysed not that her chylde sholde dye, that she was redy to dye, if it myght please hym. So he toke the chylde to the squyer in the same wyse as he dyde that other. And yet she made never semblaunt of sorowe, ne sayd other worde but that she prayed the squyer that when he had slayne the chylde, that he wolde bury hym to the entente that the tender flesshe of the chylde were not eten with wylde beestes, ne with byrdes.

"Of this grete hardnesse there appered never chaungynge chere in Grysylde. But yet it was not longe after that the marquys wolde assay her agayne when they had ben togyder [.xii.][3] yeres, in the whiche tyme the good lady had borne her so well that it ought to have suffysed the provynge of her vertue, when the marquys on a daye called her into his chambre and sayd to her that he was in poynte to lose his lordshyp by his knyghtes and his squyers for her, for they had grete dysdayne to holde for theyr lady and maystres the doughter of Janycle. So it is

---

[1] and : *and and*
[2] fade[r] : *fade*
[3] [.xii.] : *.vii.*

apaisier, que elle s'en ralast schieux son pere avisé que elle en estoit[1] venue, et que il en espousast une aultre plus gentil femme.

"A ceste chose, qui moult griefve et dure lui deut estre, respondi Grisilidis: 'Monseigneur, je savoye bien tousjours et souvent le pensoie qu'entre ta noblece et magnificence et ma pouvreté ne pourroit avoir aucune proporcion;[2] ne oncques ne me reputay non pas [fol. 116v b] tant seulement digne d'estre ton espouse, mais d'estre ta mechine. Et des maintenant je suis appareillé de retourner en la maison [de][3] mon pere, ou quel lieu je useray mon[4] vieillece. Et quant est du douaire que tu as ordonné, que je doy enporter je le voy: tu sces bien que quant tu me pris a l'issue de l'ostel de mon pere tu me fis despoullier toute nue, et me revestir de robes, avec lesquelles avec toy je vins; ne oncques[5] du mien autre donte n'aportay fors que foy, meureté, amour, reverence, et povreté. Si est raison que je te restitue ton meuble. Et voy cy ta robe dont je me despoille, et si te restitue l'anel dont tu m'espousas, et te rens tous les autres aniaulx, joyaulx,[6] vestemens, et [fol. 117r a] atours, par lesquelx j'estoye aournee et enrichie en ta chambre. Toute nue de[7] la maison de mon pere je yssis, et toute nue je retourneray, sauve que se[8] me semble chose inconvenable que cestui ventre ou quel furent les enfans que tu as engendrez deust apparoir tout nue devant le peuple. Par quoy, s'il te plaist et non autrement, je te prye que pour reconpensacion de ma vierginité que je aportay en ton palais, laquelle je n'en raporte pas, que il te plaise que une seulle chemise me soit laissé, de laquelle je couvriray le ventre de ta femme, jadis marquise.' Adonc le marquis ne se pot plus tenir de plorer de compassion, et toutevoies vainqui son courage et, partant [fol. 117r b] de la chambre, ordenna que une chemise lui fust baillee.

"Adonc en la presence de tous les chevaliers et dames Grisilidis se despoilla, et deschauça, osta tous ses aournemens, et ne lui remaint que la seulle chemise. Ja estoit espendue[9] la renommé par tout que le marquis se vouloit departir de sa femme, et tous et toutes estoient venus au palais, de ceste chose moult dolens.[10] Et Grisilidis, tout nue en sa chemise, nue teste et deschaucee, fu monté a cheval et acompagnié[11] des barons, chevaliers, et dames qui tous et toutes plouroient, maudisant le marquis et regraitant la bonté de la dame. Mais oncques Grisilidis

---

[1] avisé que elle en estoit] ainsi qu'elle estoit
[2] proporcion] preposicion
[3] [de] : *omitted*
[4] mon] ma
[5] avec lesquelles avec toy je vins ne oncques] avec lesquelles je vins avec toy ne
[6] aniaulx, joyaulx] joyaulx, aniaulx
[7] de] en
[8] retourneray sauve que se] y retourneray sauve que ce
[9] espendue] respandue
[10] de ceste chose moult dolens] moult dolens de ceste chose
[11] monté a cheval et acompagnié] montée a cheval et accompagniee

convenyent, yf he wolde appease them, that she wente home agayne to her fader so as she came thens, and that he sholde wedde another more gentyllwoman, and of more hygher blode.

"To this thynge, whiche ought to be ryght grevous and harde [L3v] to her, answered Grysylde: 'My lorde, I knewe well alway and oftymes thought that bytwene thy noblesse and magnyfycence and my poverte myght be no proporcyon. Nor I thought me not onely worthy to be your spouse, nor also to be the poorest of your house. And nowe I am redy to retourne into the house of my fader, in the whiche I shall were myne age. And as to my dowre that thou hast ordeyned me to have, that I ought to have I se it well. Thou knowest well that when thou tokest me out of my fader's house, thou madest me to be dyspoyled all naked and clothed me agayne in good robes, with the whiche I came with thee. Ne never other thynge of myne owne brought I with me but fayth, maner, love, reverence, and poverte. So it is reason that I yelde to thee agayne thy movable goodes. And se here thy robe, of whiche I me despoyle. And so I yelde to thee the rynge with the whiche thou dydest wedde me, and I yelde to thee all other rynges, jewelles, clothynge, and araye by the whiche I was worshypped and enryched in thy chambre. All naked out of my fader's house I came, and all naked I shall tourne agayne, save that it me semeth a thynge unconvenable that this wombe in the whiche the chyldren were that thou haddest engendred sholde appere all naked before the people. For the whiche, yf it pleas thee and none otherwyse, I praye thee that for the recompensacyon of my vy[r]gynyte[1] that I brought into thy palays, the whiche I bere not agayne, that it maye please thee that there myght be lefte unto me a symple smocke, with the whiche [L4r] I shall cover the wombe of thy wyfe, sometyme marquyse.' And then the marquys myght not holde hym no more from wepynge for compassyon, and yet he overcame his courage and ordeyned that there was brought to her a smocke.

"Then in the presence of all the knyghtes and ladyes, Grysylde dyspoyled her and dyde off her hosen and shoes, and put off all her ornamentes, and nothynge remayned but onely the smocke. Then stretched the rumoure all aboute that the marquys wolde departe from his wyfe, and all men and women were come to the palays, sorowynge gretely of this thynge. And Grysylde, all naked save her smocke, bareheeded and bare fote, was set upon an horse and with company of lordes, knyghtes, and ladyes that all—men and women—wepte, cursynge the marquys and sorowed gretely the goodnesse of the lady. Yet Grysylde never caste

---

[1] vy[r]gynyte : *vygynyte*

larme n'en gitta, fu convoyee en la maison de son pere, lequel[1] vieillart [fol. 117v a] avoit tousjours esté de ce en doubte, pensant que son seigneur seroit quelque jour saoulé de si pouvre mariage. Adonc cellui, oyant le bruit, ala a l'encontre de sa fille, et lui aporta sa vieille cote, tout desconte,[2] qu'il avoit gardee. Si l'en revesti sans monstrer semblant d'aucune doleur. Et ainsi demoura Grisilidis avec son pere une piece de temps en tel humilité et pouvreté, et en servant son pere comme faire soloit sans que nul semblant d'aucune tristece ou d'aucune[3] regrait fut veus en lui, ains reconfortoit son pere de la tristece que il avoit[4] de veoir sa fille cheoir[5] de si grant haultece en si grant povreté.

"Quant au marquis ot assez semblé que souffisemment [fol. 117v b] avoit esprouvee sa loyal espouse, il manda a sa seur que el[le][6] venist vers lui tres noblement acompagnié de seingneurs et de dames, et amenast ses deux enfans sans faire semblant[7] que siens fussent. Et il fist entendant a ses barons et subgiez que il vouloit prendre nouvelle femme et espouser une moult noble dame que sa suer avoit en garde.[8] Si fist assembler moult belle compangnie de chevaliers et de dames[9] en son palais au jour que sa suer arriver devoit, et moult y avoit belle feste faicte apprester.

"Si manda Grisilidis et lui dist en tel maniere: 'Grisilidis, la pucelle que je doy[10] espouser sera demain yci. Et pour ce que je desire que ma suer et toute sa [fol. 118r a] noble compagnie soient noblement[11] receus; pour ce que tu cognois mes meurs, et comment[12] on doit recevoir seigneurs et dames, et sces les chambres et lieux;[13] afin que chascun soit receu selon son estat, et par especial m'espouse qui sera, je vueil que tu aies[14] la charge, et tous les offices t'obeiront. Si penses que tout soit bien ordenné.'

"Grisilidis respondi que ce feroit elle tres volentiers. Et l'endemain[15] la compagnie fut arivee: grande y fu la feste. Et Grisilidis ne laissa pas pour sa mauvaise robe que elle n'alast a lié face a l'encontre de la pucelle, nouvelle espouse

---

[1] lequel : *lequelle*

[2] desconte] desroupte *F omits text after chap. 64, resumes* qu'il avoit gardee

[3] d'aucune] d'aucun

[4] avoit] pouoit avoir

[5] cheoir] choite

[6] el[le] : *el*

[7] semblant] nul semblant

[8] dame que sa suer avoit en garde] noble pucelle que sa seur avoit en gouvernement

[9] dames] dames et de tous gentilz hommes

[10] doy] vueil

[11] noblement] grandement

[12] comment] scez comment

[13] lieux] les lieux

[14] aies] en ayes

[15] l'endemain] l'endemain que

teere out of her eyes and was convayed unto the house of her fader, the whiche good olde man had ben alway in doubte, thynkynge that his lorde sholde be full every daye of so poore a maryage. Then he, herynge the noyse, wente to mete with his doughter and brought to her her olde cote all to-torne, whiche he had kepte. So she clothed her agayne without shewynge semblaunt of ony sorowe. And thus dwelled Grysylde with her fader a whyle in suche humylyte and poverte, and in servynge her fader as she was wonte, no sorowe shewynge outwardes nor no hevy countenaunce was sene in her, but recomforted her fader of his hevynesse that he had for to [L4v] se his doughter to fall frome so grete hyghnesse into so grete poverte.

"And when the marquys semed that he had proved his true spouse ynoughe, he sente to his syster that she sholde come to hym ryght nobly accompanyed with lordes and ladyes, and sholde brynge with her his two yonge chyldren without makynge semblaunt that they were his. And he made his barons and sugectes to understande that he wolde take a newe wyfe and wedde a ryght notable lady whiche his syster had in kepynge. So he made to assemble a ryght fayre company of knyghtes and of ladyes in his palas that same daye that his syster sholde aryve, and he lete make ryght a fayre feest and a grete.

"So he sente to Grysylde and sayd to her in this manere: 'Grysylde, the mayden that I shall wedde shall be here tomorowe. And for that I desyre that my syster and her company sholde be ryght nobly receyved; for that that thou knowest my condycyon, and howe I ought to receyve lordes and ladyes, and thou knowest the chambres and places; and to the entente that every persone be well lodged after his estate, and in especyall my spouse that shall be, for I wyll that thou have all the charge, and all offycers shall obaye unto thee. So thynke theron, and se that all be well ordeyned.'

"Grysylde answered and sayd she wolde doo it with ryght a good wyl. And in the mornynge the company were aryved: grete was there the feeste. And Grysylde lefte not for her lewde coote but that she wente with [L5r] a glad chere

comme elle cuidoit, lui faire humblement la reverence s'agenoilla devant elle,[1] disant: 'Bien viegnes, [fol. 118r b] ma dame,' et aussi[2] au filz et a tous et toutes de la compagnie, chascun selon lui receut joyeusement. Et combien que elle fut en abit d'une tres povre femme, si sembloit il[3] a son maintien que elle estoit femme de tres grant honneur et de merveilleuse prudence, tant que les estranges s'esmerveillierent comment tel façonde et tel honneur pouoit estre soubz si pouvre abit. Grisilidis avoit fait si bien[4] ordenner toutes choses que riens n'y avoit fait mal a point. Mais tant voulentiers se tiroit pres de[5] la pucelle et vers le filz que partir ne s'en pouoit.[6]

"Le marquis avoit fait aprestes[7] toutes choses comme pour espouser la pucelle. Et quant vint a l'eure de chanter la [fol. 118v a] messe, adonc vint le marquis et present tous, appella Grisilidis et lui dist comme par ramposne devant tous:[8] 'Que te semble, Grisilidis, de ma nouvelle espouse? N'est elle belle et honneste?'

"Et celle respondi[9] hautement: 'Certainement, monseigneur, plus belle ne plus honneste ne pourroit estre trouvee. Mais d'une chose par bonne foy je te vueil prier et amonester, c'est que tu ne la vueilles pas molester ne aguillonner des aguillons dont tu as l'autre si fort esprouvee. Car ceste est plus joeune et plus delisieusement[10] nourrie, si ne pourroit pas souffrir par aventure comme l'autre a fait.'

"Adonc le marquis, oyant les paroles de Grisilidis, cons[id]erant[11] sa grant fermeté, force, [fol. 118v b] et constance, et[12] grant admiracion de sa vertu, petié[13] lui prist de ce que tant et si longuement lui avoit donné et donnoit a souffrir, sans aucune desserte d'elle. Si prist adonc en presence de tous ainsi a dire:

"'Grisilidis, il doit asses souffire l'espreuve de ta constance et de ta vray foy, loyauté, et grant amour, obeissance, humilité[14] bien esprovee que tu as ver[s][15] moy.

---

[1] humblement la reverence s'agenoilla devant elle] la reverence humblement

[2] 'Bien viegnes, ma dame,' et aussi] disant: 'Ma dame, vous soiez la bien venue,' et ainsi

[3] il] il bien

[4] fait si bien] si bien fait

[5] n'y avoit fait mal a point. Mais tant voulentiers se tiroit pres de] n'y avoit mal a point. Mais se tiroit voulentiers vers

[6] pouoit] pouoit et regardoit ententivement leur beauté que elle moult louoit

[7] aprestes] apprester

[8] comme par ramposne devant tous] devant tous

[9] respondi] respont

[10] delisieusement] souëf

[11] cons[id]erant : *conserant*

[12] et] ot

[13] vertu, petié] vertu et pitié

[14] obeissance, humilité] obeissance et humilité

[15] ver[s] : *ver*

to mete the mayden and newe spouse as she trowed, and makynge reverence humbly kneled before her, sayenge: 'Welcome, my lady,' and also to the sone, and to all men and women of the company, and thus receyved them eche after theyr estate ryght joyously. And thoughe so be that she was in the habyte of a poore woman, it semed by her behavoure that she was a woman of ryght grete worshyp and of mervayllous prudence, so moche that the straungers mervaylled them howe suche fayre speche and suche worshypfull myght be under so poore an habyte. Grysylde had made so well to be ordeyned al thynges that there was nothynge amysse at the poynte, but with so good a wyll drewe her nyghe this mayden and the sone that she coude not departe from them.

"The marquys had made redy all thynges as for to wedde the yonge mayden. And when it came to the houre to synge the masse, then came the marquys and before all he called Grysylde, and sayd to her: 'Howe semeth thee, Grysylde, of my newe spouse? Is she not fayre and goodly?'

"And she answered full goodly: 'Certaynly, my lorde, there maye not be founde a goodlyer ne a fayrer. But of one thynge I wyll pray thee in good fayth and counsayle thee, that is that thou make her not sory, ne prycke her not with the nedles of whiche thou hast proved that other. For this is more yonge and more delycyously nourysshed, so paradventure she shall not not suffred as that other hathe done.'

"Then the marquys, herynge the wordes of Grysylde, [L5v] consyderynge her grete stablenesse, strengthe, and constaunce had grete mervayle of her vertue, and pyte toke hym that he had gyven her to suffre, without sayenge the contrary. Soo he began to saye thus in the presence of all the people:

"'Grysylde, it ought ynoughe to suffyse the provynge of thy constaunce, of thy veray faythe, trouthe and grete love, hobeysaunce and mekenesse well proved

Et croiez qu'il n'y a homme soubz le cieulx[1] qui par tant d'espreuves ait congneue l'amour de mariage comme j'ay fait en toy.' Et lors le marquis s'approcha d'elle, qui tenoit le chief enclin de honte pour sa grant louenge qu'il disoit d'elle.[2] Si l'embracha [fol. 119r a] estroictement et baisa en disant: 'Tu seule es mon espouse: autre noz oncques[3] ne jamais n'aray. Ceste pucelle que tu pensoies qui deust estre mon espouse est ta fille et la moye, et cestui enfant est ton filz. Si sachent tous ceulx qui cy sont que ce[4] que j'ay fait a esté pour esprouver ma loial espouse, et non pas condempner. Et mes enfans ay fait nourrir a Boulongne la Grasse avec[5] ma seur, et non pas occire: et veez les cy.'[6] Adonc la marquise, oyant les paroles de son seigneur, fu de joye comme pasmee. Et quant elle revint a soy, les enfans prist entre ses bras,[7] et n'est pas doubte que son cuer avoit merveilleuse joye. Et tous[8] ploroient de joye et de petié.

"La fu ottorisee Grisilidis [fol. 119r b] plus que oncques mais. Si fu revestue, et paree moult richement; si fu la feste[9] grant et moult joyeuse, ou tous tenoient grans paroles[10] de la louenge de celle dame. Et vesquirent ensemble[11] .xx. ans en joye et paix. Et le marquis fist Janicola, pere d'elle, dont il n'avoit fait compte le temps passé,[12] venir au palais, et le tint en grant honneur. Ses enfans maria haultement, et apre[s][13] sa fin son filz le succeda par bon vouloir des barons."

*Chapitre 51*      Ci dit de Florence de Romme

"De[14] Grisilidis, marquise de Saluce, ot vertueuse force et constance, assez l'en retray la noble Flerence, empereris de Romme, qui par merveilleuse patience porta grant adversité, si que il est escript d'elle es *Miracles de Nostre Dame*. Ceste dame estoit de souverayne beaulté, [fol. 119v a] mais encore plus chaste et vertueuse.

---

    [1] ver moy. Et croiez qu'il n'y a hommesoubz le cieulx] vers moy. Et croy que il n'a homme soubz les cieulx
    [2] qui tenoit le chief enclin de honte pour sa grant louenge qu'il disoit d'elle] *omitted*
    [3] noz oncques] ne vueil
    [4] ce] tout ce
    [5] avec] avecques
    [6] cy] ycy
    [7] ses bras] ses bras et de joyeuses larmes tous les arrosoit
    [8] tous] tous et toutes qui ce veoyent
    [9] si fu la feste] et la feste fu
    [10] grans paroles] grant parolle
    [11] ensemble] depuis ensemble
    [12] fait compte le temps passé] les temps passé fait compte
    [13] apre[s] : *apre*
    [14] De] Se

towarde me. And byleve it that there is noo man under heven that by so many proves hathe knowne the love of maryage as I have done in thee.' And then the marquys wente nere her, whiche helde downe her heed for shame for the grete praysynge that he sayd to her. So he embraced her straytely in his armes, and kyssed her in sayenge: 'Thou arte myne only spouse: other weddynges shal I never have. This mayde that thou thynkest that sholde be my spouse is thy doughter and myne, and that other is thy sone and myne. So knowe they all that be here that that I have done hathe ben to prove my true spouse, and not to condempne her. And I have made my chyldren to be nourysshed at Boloyne la Grace with my syster, and not slayne them: now se them here.' Then this lady, herynge the wordes of her lorde the marquys, fell downe flatte for joy. And when she came to herselfe, she toke the chyldren in her armes, and it was no doubte but her herte had mervayllous joye. And all the people wepte for joye and pyte.

"There was she greued more than ever she was before. So she was clothed agayne [L6r] and arayed ryght rychely; so the feest was grete and ryght joyous, where every man had grete wordes of the praysynge of this lady. And they lyved togyder .xx. yeres in grete joye and peas. And the marquys made Janycle her fader, of whome he made no grete compte before, to come to the palays, and there helde hym in grete worshyp. He maryed his chyldren hyghly, and after hym his sone succeded by the good wyll of the lordes, and of the comunes also."

## Chapter 51      Of Florence of Rome

"Of Grysylde, marquyse of Saluce that had ynoughe of vertuous strengthe and constaunce I have sayd to thee. Nowe I shall telle thee of the noble Florence, empresse of Rome, whiche by mervaylous pacyence suffred grete adversyte soo as it is wryten of her in the *Myracles of Our Lady*. This lady was of soverayne beaute, but she was more chaste and vertuous.

"Avint que l'empereur son mary deuvt aler a[1] une longue guerre en voiage assez loings. Si laissa garde de son païs et de sa femme un frere que il avoit; lequel, tempté de l'Anemi aprés la departie de l'empereur, couvoita folement sa seroinge.[2] Et a brief parler, tant la tint court que elle s'accordast a sa volenté que, de paour que aprés les prieres il voulist user de force, le fist[3] emprisonner en une tour, et la fut jusques a la venue de l'empereur. Quant vint que nouvelles furent aportees que le dit empereur s'en retournoit, la dame qui jamais ne cuidast que a son tort il[4] se plaingnist d'elle, le fist mettre hors pour garder pais a fin que il alast a [fol. 119v b] l'encontre de son frere, auquel, a lui arrivé, dist de la dame tous les maulx que dire se peut, de la pire qui soit. Par quoy[5] l'empereur, qui l'en crut, envoya ses gens et ordenna que avant qu'il arrivast, sans faire de ce nul mencion, que elle fut occise. Car veoir ne la vouloit, ne trouver vive. Mais elle, moult esmerveillé de ces nouvelles, pria tant a ceulx qui a ce faire estoient commis que vive l'en laisserent aler en abit mescongneu.

"Si ala tant celle[6] noble dame, que par estrange aventure qui lui avint elle fu commise a garder l'enfant d'un grant prince. Si avint que le frere d'icellui prince[7] fu espris de l'amour d'elle en tant que [fol. 120r a] aprés ce qu'il l'eut assez requise, par despit que accorder elle[8] ne le vouloit, il occist le petit enfant coste elle si que elle dormoit afin de la faire destruire. Toutes ces asversitez qui ne furent pas petitez porta ceste[9] noble empereris tres paciemment, et par tres fort et constant courage. Et quant elle deust estre menee au lieu pour estre destruitte, comme celle que on cuidoit que l'enfant eust occis, tel pitié prist[10] au seigneur et a la dame pour la belle vie et grans vertuz que[11] ilz avoient veus en elle, que cuer n'orent de la faire mourir, ains l'envoyerent en exil.

"Ou quel lieu comme elle fust en tres grant pouvreté, et tres paciente, et devote vers Dieu et sa [fol. 120r b] doulce Mere, une fois s'en dormi aprés ses

---

[1] l'empereur son mary deuvt aler a] avint que son mari dot aler en

[2] seroinge] serourge Flourence

[3] le fist] le fist la dame emprisonner

[4] il : *ile*

[5] il se plaingnist d'elle, le fist mettre hors pour garder pais a fin que il alast a l'encontre de son frere, auquel, a lui arrivé, dist de la dame tous les maulx que dire se peut, de la pire qui soit. Par quoy] il mesdisist d'elle, le fist mettre dehors affin que l'empereur ne sceust la faulseté de son frere, et que il lui alast a l'encontre. Mais quant il fu arrivé devers l'empereur dit de la dame tous les maulx que dire se pourroit de la pire qui soit, et que pour sa mauvaistié faire plus a son loisir l'avoit tenu en prison

[6] celle] ceste

[7] d'icellui prince] de cellui

[8] que accorder elle] de ce que accorder

[9] ceste] celle

[10] prist] prist d'elle

[11] que] qui

"It happened that the emperoure her husbande ought to go to a grete warre ryght a grete waye thens. So he lefte to kepe his countre and his wyfe a broder that he had; the whiche, tempted with the Enemy after the departynge of the emperoure, coveyted folyly his brother's wyfe. And to speke shortely, he helde her so shorte that she sholde accorde to his wyl, that for drede that after the prayers he wolde use her by force, he put her in pryson in a stronge toure, and there she was tyll the comynge of [L6v] the emperoure. When it came that the tydynges were brought that the sayd emperoure was come agayne, he made the lady to be taken out of pryson, she not wenynge that he wolde complayne on her wrong-fully. And he dyde it to the entente that she sholde kepe the countre whyle he wolde go ayenst his broder, at the arry[vy]nge¹ of whome he toke all the evyll of this good lady and the worste that myght be sayd, by the whiche the emperoure that byleved hym sent his people and ordeyned that or he sholde aryve, without makynge ony mencyon of it, that she sholde be slayne: for he wolde not se her, ne fynde her on lyve. But she, mervayllynge moche of these tydynges, prayed so moche to them that were commytted to do this thynge that they sholde let her go in an habyte unknowne. So they graunted her her desyre.

"Then this noble lady wente, and by a straunge adventure that happened her, she was commytted to kepe a chylde of a grete prynce. So it fortuned that the broder of that prynce was taken with the love of her in soo moche that after that he had requyred her ynoughe, for despyte that she wolde not accorde to hym, he slewe the yonge chylde by her as she slepte to the entente to make her to be destroyed. All these adversytees, whiche were not lytell, suffred this noble lady the empresse ryght pacyently and by ryght stronge and constant courage. And when she sholde be ledde to the place where she sholde be put to the dethe, as she that some supposed had slayne the chylde, suche pyte came to the lorde [Mm1r] and to the lady for the fayre lyfe and the grete vertues that they had sene in her that theyr hertes coude not suffre her to dye, but they put her in exyle.

"In the whiche place as she was in grete poverte, and was ryght pacyent and devoute towarde God and His swete moder, she slepte on a tyme after her prayers

---

¹ arry[vy]nge : *arrynge*

oroisons faictes[1] en un vergier. La eust[2] en avision de la Vierge que elle cuillist une certaine herbe qui estoit soubz sa teste; et de ce gaingneroit sa vie, en garissant de toutes maladies. Et comme un[3] temps aprés par la dicte herbe la dame eust ja gariz tant de malades que par tout en estoit renommee, avint que[4] le frere du prince qui avoit occise le dit enfant fu malade du grant mal trop orriblement, par quoy fu envoié querre ceste femme pour le guarir. Et comme elle fust venue en sa presence, elle lui dist que il pouoit bien veoir que Dieu le batoit de ses verges, et que il recogneust son pechié [fol. 120v a] publiquement, et il seroit gueris; car autrement garir ne le pourroit. Et adonc cellui, meu de grant contriction, confessa son orrible mauvaistié, et comment il mesmes avoit occis l'enfant dont il avoit encoulpee la bonne dame qui en garde l'avoit. De ceste chose fut moult ayrez le prince et vouloit a toutes fins faire justice de son frere. Mais la noble dame tant l'empria que elle l'apaisa vers lui, et le guari. Et ainsi lui rendi bien pour mal selon le commandement de Dieu.

"Avint semblablement ne demoura pas moult que le frere de l'empereur, par qui Fleurence avoit esté exillee, cheut en si orrible maladie de meselerie[5] que il estoit comme tous pourris. Et comme la voix fut ja par [fol. 120v b] tout le monde comment une femme estoit qui garissoit toutes maladies, fu envoyee querre de part l'empereur sans qu'il eust cognoiscence qui elle estoit, car pieça cuidoit sa femme mort. Et si que elle fu venue devant luy, elle lui dist que il couvenoit que il se confessast publiquement, autrement elle ne le pourroit garir. Mais comme il le reffusast longuement, au desrain regehy toute la mauvaistié que il avoit faicte et bastie sans cause et sans raison[6] a l'empereris, pour lequel pechié bien savoit que Dieux le punissoit. Ceste chose de l'empereur ouÿe, lui comme enragiez de ce que ainsi cuidoit avoir fait mourir sa loyal espouse, que tant amoit, vouloit[7] occire son frere. Mais la bonne [fol. 121r a] dame se manifesta, et pacifia l'empereur vers son frere. Et ainsi recouvra Fleurence par le merite de sa pacience son estat et sa felicité, a grant joye de l'empereur et de toutes gens."

---

    [1] faictes] dites
    [2] eust] ot
    [3] un : *une*
    [4] avint que] avint si que Dieux le volt que
    [5] maladie de meselerie] meselerie
    [6] il avoit faicte et bastie sans cause et sans raison] sanz cause et sanz raison avoit faicte et bastie
    [7] vouloit] vouloit faire

made to God in a fayre grene place. Then she had a vysyon of the blessyd Vyr-gyne Mary that she sholde gader a certayne herbe that was under her heed, and with that herbe she sholde gete her lyvynge in helynge all maner of sykenesses. And on a tyme after by the sayd herbe the lady had heled so many syke folkes, of whom the renowne sprange all aboute, it fortuned that the broder of the prynce that had slayne the chylde abovesayd was syke of a grete sykenesse ryght hor-rybly, for whom men were sente to fetche this woman to hele hym. And when she was come into his presence, she sayd to hym that he myght well se that God bete hym with His roddes, and that he sholde confesse his synne openly, and he sholde be hole; for otherwyse she myght not hele hym. And then he, moved with grete contrycyon, confessed his horryble wyckednesse and howe he hymselfe had slayne the chylde, thrughe whiche the good lady was blamed that kepte hym. The prynce was passynge wrothe with this, and wolde at all tymes do justyce on his broder but the noble lady prayed hym so moche that she appeased hym to hym, and then she heled hym anone. And thus this good lady yelded good for evyll, after the [M1v] commaundement of God.

"It happened in the same wyse and it taryed not longe after but that the broder of the emperour, by the whiche Florence was exyled, felle in soo horryble sykenesse of the lyppre that he was all stynkynge. And as the voyce wente in all the worlde howe there was a woman that wolde hele al maner of sykenesse, anone men were sente out to seke her by the commaundement of the emperoure without ony knowlege what she was, for he demed his wyfe to be deed longe before. And when she was come before hym, she sayd to hym that it was conve-nyent that he sholde confesse hym openly, for otherwyse he myght not be heled. But as he refused it longe tyme, at the laste he opened all his wyckednesse that he had done to the empresse, for the whiche he wyst well that God punysshed hym. This thynge herde of the emperour, beynge passynge wrothe of that that he trowed that he had made his true spouse to dye that he loved so moche, wolde have slayne his broder. But the good lady opened herselfe to the emperoure, and made the peas bytwene hym and his broder. And thus Florence recovered by the meryte of her pacyence her estate and felycyte, with grete joye of the emperoure and of all people." [M2r]

### Chapitre 52    De la femme Barnabo le Genevoys

"Encore a propos de femmes constans et fortes[1] puet bien estre [remenee][2]
l'istoire que Bocace raconte en son *Livre des Cent Nouvelles* comment une fois
avint a Paris, comme[3] plusieurs marchans lombars et ytaliens se trouverent
ensemble a un souper, ou[4] quel comme ilz parlassent de maintes choses, cheurent a parler de leurs femmes tant qu'entre les autres un Janevois qui avoit nom
Barnabo prist moult a louer sa femme de beauté, de sens, de chasteté sur toute
riens et de toutes vertus. Si y ot [fol. 121r b] un oultrageux en la compaingnie
nommé Ambroise, qui va dire que il estoit bien fol de tant louer sa femme, par
especial de chasteté, et qu'il n'en estoit nul[5] tant fu fort que qui bien la presseroit
par dons, par promesses, et belles paroles que on n'en finast bien. De ceste chose
commença grant estrif entre eulx deux, et a tant vint que ilz gaigierent la somme
de .v.[m] flourins: Barnabo mettoit que l'autre ne couscheroit mie avec sa femme
pour tout sa poissance, et Ambroise gagoit que si feroit, et si bonnee enseigne[6] lui
en apporteroit que il lui souffiroit. Grant peinne mirent les autres de deffaire ce
debat, mais riens n'y valu.

"Ambroise s'en parti au plus tost que il pot, et a Genes s'en ala. Lui venu
celle part, moult enquist de la vie et [fol. 121v a] de l'ordennance de la femme de
Barnabo. Mais a brief dire, tant en ouÿ recorder de grans biens que il perdi toute
l'esperance de jamais y avenir, dont moult se trouva hebahy et repentant de sa
folie, et s'avise de grant malice car moult lui doloit le cuer de ainsi perdre .v.[m]
flourins. Si fist tant que il parla a une vieille pouvre femme qui repairoit a l'ostel
de celle dame, et tant lui donna et promist que en une huche ou il se mist fu
portez en la chambre de la dicte dame; a qui la vieille avoit fait entendant que en
celle huche avoit de moult bonnes choses qui lui avoient esté baillees en garde, et
que les larons l'avoient volu desrober, et pour ce lui prioit qu'en sa chambre lui [fol.
121v b] vousist un petit[7] de temps garder tant que ceulx a qui les choses estoient
fussent revenues, laquel chose la dame lui avoit volentiers accordee. Ambroise,
qui en la huche estoit, tant agaita la dame par nuit que il la vit toute nue, et avec
ce prist une boursete et une conroye,[8] faicte a l'eguille, que elle avoit faicte moult
bien ouvré. Puis s'en rentra en sa huche si coyement que la dame, qui dormoit et

---

[1] fortes] sages
[2] remenee : *rementenee*
[3] comme] que
[4] ou] au
[5] nul] nulle
[6] et si bonnee enseigne] et que si bonnes enseignes
[7] petit] pou
[8] conroye] çainture

*Chapter 52*     Of the wyfe of Barnabo the Genevoys

"To the purpose yet of women that be constaunte maye well be brought to remembraunce the hystory that Bocace telleth in his *Boke of Cent Nouvelles* howe it happened on a tyme in Parys, as many marchauntes Lombardes and Italyens were togyder at a souper in whiche as they spake of many thynges, they fell to speke of theyr wyves, so moche that amonge others a Janevoys that was called Barnabo began gretely to prayse his wyfe of beaute, of wytte, of chastyte above all thynges, and of al vertues. So there was another outragyous felawe in the company named Ambrose whiche sayd that he was a foole to prayse his wyfe so moche and specyally of chastyte, and that there was none so stronge but that one sholde overcome her by gyftes, by promyse and fayre wordes, and so to come to his entente. Of this thynge began a grete stryfe bytwene them twayne, and it came so ferre forthe that they layde in wager the some of .v. thousande floryns. Barnabo sayd that that other sholde not lye with his wyfe, for al that he coude do; and Ambrose layde that he sholde, and that he wolde brynge so good a token that it sholde suffyse. The other marchauntes dyde as moche as they coude to seas the debate, but it avayled not.

"Ambrose departed thens as soone as he myght and wente to Gene. And when he came there, he enquyred gretely of the lyfe of the wyfe of Barnabo. But to saye shortely, soo moche he herde recorde of her grete goodnesse that he lost al [M2v] his hope that he sholde never come to his entente, wherof he founde hymselfe gretely abasshed and repentaunt of his foly. And he advysed hym of a grete malyce, for it greved his herte ryght sore to lose so .v. thousande floryns. Soo he dyde so moche that he spake to an olde poore woman that repayred ofte tymes to the house of the good woman, and gave and promysed her so moche that he was put in a grete cofre, and was borne into the chambre of the sayd good woman, to whom the olde poore woman had made to understande that there was moche good gere in the cofre whiche was taken her to kepe, and theves laboured to robbe her. And therfore she prayed her that it myght abyde a lytell whyle in her chambre to be kepte tyll they came home that ought it, to the whiche thynge the good woman consented with a good wyll. Ambrose, whiche was in the cofre, made suche awayte upon the lady by nyght that he sawe her all naked, and with that wente prevyly out of the cofre and toke a gyrdell and a purse made with the nedle that she had wrought by good crafte, and after entred into the cofre agayne soo prevyly that the lady that slepte and with her a lytel doughter that she had,

une petite fille[1] que elle avoit avec lui, riens n'en sentirent. Et quant ainsi y ot esté trois jours, la vieille revint querre sa huche.

"Ambroise, qui grant joye avoit et bien lui sembla avoir bien esploitiez,[2] raporta au mary tout devant la belle compaignie que sans faille il avoit [fol. 122r a] couchié tout a son aise avec sa femme. Et tout premierement lui dit l'enseigne de la chambre, et des painteurs qui y estoient. Aprés lui monstra la bourse et la çeinture que il bien congnoissoit, et dist que elle lui avoit donnee. Et en sur que tant[3] il ot dit la façon du corps tout nue de la dame, il dist que elle avoit un sain comme un petit porel[4] soubz la mamelle senestre.

"Le mary crut fermement par les enseingnes les paroles d'Ambroise, dont s'il fu dolent, nul nee[5] demant. Et toutevoies lui paia tous contens les .v.ᵐ florins, et au plus tost que il pot s'en ala a Genes. Et[6] avant que il y arrivast, manda expressement a un sien facteur qui gouvernoit [fol. 122r b] son fait,[7] en qui il se fioit de toutes choses, la maniere comme il vouloit que il occist sa femme.[8] Lequel, veu la comandement, fist la dame[9] monter a cheval, et lui fist a croire que au devant de son mary la vouloit mener. Et la dame, qui l'en crut, a grant joye avec lui ala.[10] Mais comme ilz fussent arrivez en un bois, lui dist comment il couvenoit que il l'occeist par le commandement de son mary. Et a brief dire, tant fist celle dame qui bonne et belle estoit, et tant le sceut preschier, que cellui la[11] laissa aler par si que elle lui promist que hors du païs s'en yroit.[12]

"Celle qui fu esschappee ala en un[e] ville,[13] et fist tant a une bonne femme que elle lui acheta robes d'ommes: si couppa[14] ses cheveux, et en guise d'un jovencel se mist. Et tant [fol. 122v a] ala que elle se mist avec un[15] riche homme de Cateloingne, que on nommoit Signir Ferant, qui estoit la descendu de sa nef[16] pour se refreschir. Si le servi tant bien que a mervailles se tenoit pour content,[17]

---

[1] fille] fillette

[2] sembla avoir bien esploitiez] sembloit avoir exploitié

[3] tant] tout quant

[4] porel] porel vermeil

[5] nee] ne le

[6] Et] Mais

[7] fait] faict et

[8] la maniere comme il vouloit que il occist sa femme] que il vouloit comment qu'il fust qu'il occisist sa femme et la maniere comment il l'occiroit

[9] la dame] ycelle

[10] a grant joye avec lui ala] voulentiers et a grant joye avecques lui ala

[11] sceut preschier que cellui la] sçot prescher que cellui l'en

[12] païs s'en yroit] pays yroit

[13] un[e] : *un*] une villette

[14] couppa] rongna

[15] se mist avec un: *une*] print a servir un

[16] la descendu de sa nef] de sa nef descendu a un port

[17] se tenoit pour content] s'en tenoit pour contempt

felte nothynge of it. And when he had ben there .iii. dayes, the olde poore woman came agayne to fetche her cofre.

"Ambrose, that had grete joye and wende that he had well employed his entente, wente to Parys agayne and reported to her husbande before all the company that he had lyne with his wyfe at his ease. And fyrste he tolde [M3r] hym the token of the chambre, and of the payntynge that was in it. After he shewed hym the purse and the gyrdell that he knewe well, and sayd that she had gyven it to hym, and tolde hym all the facyon of her body, and that he sawe her all naked. And he tolde hym also that she had a lytell spotte as it were a warte under the lyfte pappe.

"Then the husbande byleved stably by the tokens the wordes of Ambrose, of whiche yf he were sory no man mervayle. And then he payed hym and contented hym of this v. thousande floryns, and as soone as he myght he wente to Gene. And before that he sholde aryve, he sente expressely to his factoure that governed all his doynges there, in whome he trusted above all thynges, the maner howe he wolde that he sholde sle this woman his wyfe; the whiche, the commaundement sene, made the good woman to mounte on horsebacke and made her to byleve that he wolde brynge her to her husbande. And the good woman, whiche byleved hym well, wente with hym with grete joye. But when they were come into a wode, he tolde her that he must nedes sle her by the commaundement of his mayster her housbande. And to make the tale shorte, this woman dyde so moche whiche was so good and so fayre, and so moche she coude preche that he lete her go so that she sholde promyse hym that she sholde go out of the countre.

"She that was thus escaped wente unto a towne and dyde so moche to a good woman that she bought her clothynge for a man; so she cutte off her heere, and [M3v] she arayed her in the lykenesse of a yonge man, and she dyde so moche that she put herselfe with a ryche man of Cateloyne named Syguyr Ferant that was come downe from his shyp to refresshe hym. So she served hym so well that he

ne oncques n'avoit trouvé ce disoit si bon serviteur; et se faisoit celle dame appeller Sagurat d'Afinoli. Cellui Signir Ferant qui fu rentré en sa nef, Sagurat avec[1] lui, ala tant par mer que il vint en Alixandrie, et la acheta faucons moult beaulx, et chevaulx. Et a tout ala devers [le][2] soubdain de Babiloine, a qui avoit grant amistié. Et comme il y fust ja demouré un temps, et le soubdain avisat Sagurat qui servoit tant diligenment son maistre, et qui tant lui sembloyt [fol. 122v b] bel et gracieux lui plut a merveille,[3] tant qu'il pria a Signir Ferant que il lui voulsist donner, et il le feroit grant maistre. Et cellui, quoy que il le feist envis, lui ottroia. A brief dire, tant et si bien servi Sagurat le soubdain que il ne se fioit qu'en lui, et estoit si grant maistre entour lui que il le gouvernoit comme tout.

"Avint qu'en une ville du soubdain devoit avoir une tres grant foire, ou marchans venoient de toutes pars. Le soubdain ordenna a Sagurat que il alast en celle ville pour garder la foire, et se prendre garde de son droit. Et comme il avenist si que Dieux voult que a celle foire fust venus, avecques[4] autres Ytaliens qui avoient porté joyaulx, icellui [fol. 123r a] faulx Ambroise dessus dit, qui moult estoit enrichis de [l]'avoir[5] de Barnabo. Sagurat qui estoit en la ville lieutenant du soubdain estoit de tous moult honnourez, et pour ce que il estoit grant seigneur et grant maistre, les marchans lui aportoient tous les jours joyeulx[6] a vendre tant que entre les autres vint vers lui cellui Ambroise. Et si comme ot[7] ouvert un petit escrinet plein de joyaulx devant Sagurat afin que il les veist, en celle[8] escrinet avoit la petite boursete et la ceinture dessus dicte. Par quoy aussi tost que Sagurat la vit, il la recognut et la prist en sa main et fort la regarda, en s'esmerveillant comment la pouoient estre venues.[9] Et Embroise, qui en piece ne pensast l'aventure, se prist fort a soubz rire.

"Et [fol. 123r b] Sagurat, qui le vit rire, lui dist: 'Amis, je croi que vous ries de ce que je me suis amusé a regarder[10] chose femmenine. Mais elle est moult belle.'

"Ambroise lui respondi, 'Monseigneur, elle est bien en vostre commandement. Mais je me rioye pour ce que il me souvenoit de la maniere comment je l'eus.'[11]

"'Se Dieux te doint joye,' ce dist[12] Sagurat, 'di moy comment tu l'eus?'[13]

---

[1]  avec] avecques
[2]  [le] : *la*
[3]  merveille] merveilles
[4]  voult que a celle foire fust venus, avecques] le volt que la feust venus avec
[5]  [l]'avoir : *bavoir*
[6]  tous les jours joyeulx] tous joyaulx estranges
[7]  ot] il ot
[8]  celle] cellui
[9]  venues] venue
[10]  de ce que je me suis amusé a regarder] pour ce que je me suis amusee a ceste boursette, qui est
[11]  souvenoit de la maniere comment je l'eus] souvient de la maniere comment je l'oz
[12]  ce dist] dist
[13]  l'eus] l'oz

helde hym contente mervayllously, for he founde never so good a servaunt; and this same woman called herse[lf]e[1] Sagurat d'Affynoly. This Saguyr Ferant that wente agayne into the shyp, and Sagurat d'Affynoly with hym, wente so moche by see tyll he came into Alexandre, and there he bought faucons ryght fayre and good, horses also. And after that he wente towarde the sowdan of Babylone, with whom he had good frendeshyp. And when he had byden there a whyle, and the sowdan advysed well this Sagurat d'Affynoly, the whiche served so dylygently his mayster, and the whiche semed to hym so fayre and gracyous that he pleased hym mervayllously, so moche that he prayed this Saguyr Ferant that he wolde gyve hym to hym, and he wolde make hym a grete mayster. And he graunted hym, ayenst his wyl. And to saye shortely, soo well this Sagurat d'Affynoly served the sowdan that he trusted no man so moche as he dyde hym, and was so grete mayster aboute hym that he governed all.

"It happened that in a towne of the sowdan's sholde be a grete fayre where marchauntes came of all partyes. The sowdan ordeyned Sagurat that he sholde go into that towne to kepe the fayre, and to take hede of his ryght. And as it happened as God wolde [M4r] that to that fayre was come with other Italyens that brought many jewelles this false Ambrose abovesayd, whiche was gretely enryched with the goodes of Barnabo. Sagurat that was lyeutenaunt of the towne of the sowdan's was gretely worshypped of all people, and for he was a grete lorde and a grete mayster, the marchauntes brought to hym everyday jewelles to selle. So amonge others there came to hym that same Ambrose, and as he had opened a lytell cofre full of jewelles before Sagurat to the entente that he sholde se them and in this cofre was the purse and the gyrdell before sayd; by the whiche as soone as Sagurat sawe it, he knewe it well, and toke it in his hande and behelde it, strongely mervayllynge gretely howe they myght come thyder. And Ambrose, that but lytell thought of that adventure, began to laughe ryght faste.

"And Sagurat, that sawe hym laughe, sayd to hym, 'Frende, I suppose that thou laughest of that that I muse to beholde this woman's thynge. And forsothe, it is ryght fayre.'

"And Ambrose answered hym, 'My lorde, it is at your commaundement. But I laughe for that that I bethynke me of the manere howe I had it.'

"'So God gyve me joye,' sayd Sagurant, 'I praye thee, tell me howe thou haddest it?'

---

[1] herse[lf]e : *herseife*

"'Par ma foy,' dist Ambroise, 'Je l'oz d'une belle dame[1] qui la me donna, avec laquel je couchay une nuit. Et avec ce je gaignay .v.^m florins pour une gaigure que je fis au fol mary d'elle qui a nom Barnabo qui osa mettre a moy que je ne[2] coucheroie mie, et le maleureux homme en occist sa femme. Mais il avoit mieulx desservi punicion que elle,[3] car homme doit savoir que tout femme [fol. 123v a] est fraille et de legier vaincue: si n'y doit avoir tel fiance.'

"Adonc cognut la dame la cause de l'yre de son mary, que elle n'avoit oncques mais sceue. Mais comme tres prudent et ferme que elle estoit, sagement le voult dissimuler jusques en temps et en lieu. Si fist semblant d'avoir de ceste chose moult grant solaz, et lui dist que il estoit un tres bonne compaignon et que a lui vouloit[4] avoir singuliere amistié, et que il vouloit que il demourast ou païs et marchandast fort pour eulx deux, et que il lui bailleroit assez de quon entre mains.[5] De ce ot moult grant joye Ambroise, et de fait Sagurat lui fist ballier un hostel. Et pour le mieulx decepvoir,[6] lui mist [fol. 123v b] argent entre mains, et lui monstroit si grant signe d'amour que il estoit tous les jours avec[7] lui, et la truffe lui fist conter devant le soubdan pour[8] le faire rire.

"A dire brief[9] comment la chose fust terminee, tant fist et tant pourchaça Sagurat que il fist tant a Genevois qui estoient en icellui[10] païs aprés ce que il ot sceu de l'estat de Barnabo qui estoit cheoit en pouvreté, tant pour la grant fiance que il avoit ballié comme pour le courroux que il avoit eu, que le dit Barnabo se transporta en ycellui[11] païs par le mandement du soubdain. Et quant il fut venu devant le dit soubdan, tantost Sagurat envoya querre Ambroyse. Mais il [fol. 124r a] avoit ançois bien infourmé le soubdan que Ambroise mentoit de la vantance que il faisoit d[e][12] la dame et lui avoit prié que ou cas que la verité lui en vendroit a congnoiscence, que il voulsist punir justement selon le cas le dit Ambroise. Laquel chose,[13] quant Ambroise et Barnabo[14] furent devant le soubdan, Sagurat prist a dire en tel maniere:

"'Ambroise, il plaist a nostre sire le soubdan, qui cy est, que tu contes la truffe tout au long comment tu gaingnas a Barnabo qui cy est les .v.^m florins, dont tu le

---

[1]  dame] femme
[2]  ne] n'y
[3]  que elle] d'elle
[4]  vouloit] il vouloit
[5]  de quon entre mains] d'argent entre mains pour eulx .ii.
[6]  mieulx decepvoir] decevoir mieulx
[7]  avec] avecques
[8]  pour] si comme pour
[9]  brief] en brief
[10]  icellui] cellui
[11]  ycellui] cellui
[12]  d[e] : *da*
[13]  laquel] laquelle chose le souldan lui avoit accordee
[14]  Ambroise et Barnabo] Bernabo et Ambroise

"'By my faythe,' sayd Ambrose, 'I shall tell you howe I gate it: I had it of a fayre gentylwoman that gave it me, with whome I laye all a hole nyght. And moreover, besyde that I gate fyve thousande floryns of good golde for a wager that I dyde make [M4v] with the folysshe husbande of her that is named Barnabo, whiche durst so lewdely laye it with me that I sholde not lye with his wyfe. And nowe the unhappy man hath slayne her also, but he hathe better deserved to be punysshed than she for a man may well knowe that every woman is frayle and lyght to overcome, soo there is no man that ought to have affyaunce in a woman.'

"Then knewe Sagurat the cause of the wrathe of her housbande that she knewe never before. But as a ryght prudent and stable, wysely she dyssymyled unto the tyme that it come to the poynte; so she made semblaunt to have ryght grete solace of this thynge, and she sayd to hym that he was ryght a good felawe and that he wolde have hym ryght specyally in frendeshyp, and that he wolde that he sholde abyde and bye marchaundyse for them bothe, and that he wolde take hym ynoughe wherof in his handes. Of that Ambrose hadde grete joye, and forthwith Sagurat made to delyver hym an house. And for to deceyve hym the better, she toke hym money in his handes and shewed hym so grete sygne of love that he was alwaye with hym, and she made hym to tell that jape before the sowdan to make hym to laughe.

"And to saye shortely howe the thynge was determyned, so moche Sagurat dyde and pourchased that she dyde so moche to the Jenevoys that were in that countre after that that she knewe the estate of Barnabo that was fallen in poverte, what for the grete fynaunce that he had payed and for [N1r] the grete sorowe that he toke, therfore that Barnabo sholde come over into that countre by the commaundement of the sowdan. And to make the tale shorte, when he was come into that countre, he came before the sowdan; and anone Sagurat made seke after Ambrose. But or he came, he had wel enfourmed the sowdan howe Ambrose lyed in makynge his avaunte that he made of this woman. And she prayed hym also that in case that the trouthe were come to knowlege that he wolde punysshe justely the sayd Ambrose; the whiche thynge, when Ambrose and Barnabo were come before the sowdan, Sagurat began to saye in this maner:

"'Ambrose, it pleaseth to our lorde that is here that thou tell the jape all alonge howe thou dydest gete of Barnabo that here is .v. thousande floryns,

as conté par quel[1] maniere tu couchas avec sa femme.' Adonc Ambroise changia couleur comme cellui a qui verité souffroit a peine vaincre si desloial fraulde car trop lui fu la [fol. 124r b] chose soubdaine, de laquelle garde ne se donnoit.

"Toutevoies il reprist un pou sa maniere et respondi: 'Monseigneur, il ne puet ja chaloir que je le die. Barnabo le scet assez; j'ay honte[2] de sa honte.' Et adonc Barnabo, plein de douleur et de honte, supplia que il n'en ouïst jamais parler, et que il en fust laissié aler. Mais Sagurat respondi comme en soubriant que il ne s'en yroit mie, et que il couvenoit que il oulst lache.[3]

"Adonc Ambroise, qui vit que il en estoit contraint, commença a dire[4] tout a voix tremblant la chose comme[5] il l'avoit donné a entendre a Barnabo, et comme il leur avoit contee.[6] Et quant il ot finé sa raison, Sagurat demanda a Barnabo se c'estoit voir ce que[7] Ambroise avoit dit. Et il repondi [fol. 124v a] que oil, sans faille.

"'Et comment,' ce dit Sagurat, 'estes vous bien certain que cest homme cy couschat avec vostre femme, pour tant que il vous dit[8] aucunes enseignes? Estes vous si beste que vous ne doivez savoir que par asses de voies frauduleusement il pouoit savoir la façon du corps d'elle sans y avoir couschié? Et l'avez pour celle cause fait morir? Vous estes digne de mort, car vous n'aviez mie preuve souffisant.' Adonc ot Barnabo grant paour.

"Et lors Sagurat, qui plus ne voult taire ce qu'il[9] lui sembla temps de dire, dist a Ambroise: 'Faulx traittre desloial, dis la verité, dis la verité sans te faire tourmenter car de ce que tu dis mens par ta fausse gorge. Et[10] la femme dont tu te [fol. 124v b] vantes n'est pas morte, ains est asses prochain de cy[11] pour contredire tes desloiaulx mençonges—car oncques ne la touchas.'[12]

---

[1] qui cy est les .v.<sup>m</sup> florins, dont tu le as conté par quel] que vois cy les .v.<sup>m</sup> flourins, dont tu lui as compté et par quelle
[2] honte] grant honte
[3] oulst lache] il ouyst la chose
[4] a dire] a dire et a compter
[5] comme] ainsi comme
[6] contee] compté
[7] ce que] que
[8] que il vous dit] se il vous rapporta
[9] taire ce qu'il] tarder ce qui
[10] te faire tourmenter car de ce que tu dis mens par ta fausse gorge. Et] ce que pour la dire tu te faces tourmenter, car dire la te couvient. Et c'est chose certaine que de ce que tu as dit mens par ta faulse gorge et vueil que tu saches que
[11] de cy] de toy
[12] touchas] touchas et c'est chose certaine

wherof thou haste tolde hym by what maner thou dyde lye with his wyfe.' And then Ambrose chaunged coloure as he to whom the trouthe myght unethes suffre to cover soo an untrue fraude, for it was to hym a sodayne thynge, of the whiche he toke no hede.

"Then he toke to hym a lytell maner and answered, 'My lorde, it is no force thoughe I tell it not. Barnabo knoweth well ynoughe; I have shame of his shame.' And then Barnabo, full of sorowe and of shame, prayed that he myght never here of it more, and that he wolde lette hym leve. But Sagurat answered as in laughynge that he sholde not go, and that it was convenyent that he lete hym tell it.

"Then Ambrose, whiche sawe that he was constrayned, [N1v] began to say all with a tremblynge voyce that he had made Barnabo to understande, and all as he had tolde them. And when he had ended his reason, Sagurat asked of Barnabo yf it were true that Ambrose had sayd? And he answered and sayd, 'Ye, without fayle.'

"'And howe,' sayd Sagurat, 'be ye well certayne that this man here laye with your wyfe, for that that he tolde to you certayne tokens? Be you suche a beest that you cannot knowe that by wayes ynowe fraudelently he myght knowe the facyon of her body, without lyenge with her? And ye have, for this cause, made your wyfe to dye! Ye are worthy to dye yourselfe, for ye have no suffycyent profe.' Then Barnabo had grete drede.

"And then Sagurat, that wolde no longer be styll, and that her semed tyme to speke, sayd to Ambrose: 'False traytoure! Saye the trouthe without makynge thee to be tourmented; and the woman of whom thou avauntest thee is not yet deed, but she is not ferre hens to say the contrary to thy false lesynges for thou touched her never.'

"La estoit grande l'assemblee, tant de[1] barons du soubdan comme de tres grant foison le[2] Lumbars, qui a merveilles escouttoient ceste[3] chose. Et a le faire brief, a tant fu mener[4] Ambroise que devant le soubdan et present tous confessa tout[5] la fraude comment il avoit ouvré pour couvoitise de gaingnier[6] les .v.ᵐ florins. Quant Barnabo ouÿ ceste chose, a pou que il ne vint comme tout forsonnez[7] de ce que il cuidoit sa femme estre occise.

"Mais la bonne dame vint a lui, et lui dist, 'Que donroyes tu, Barnabo, que[8] te rendroit ta femme vive, entiere, et chaste?'

"Barnabo [fol. 125r a] dist que il donroit[9] tout quanque finer pourroit.

"Adonc lui dist celle, 'Comment, Barnabo, frere et ami, ne la congnois tu mie?' Et comme cellui fust tant esbahy qu'il ne savoit qu'il faisoit, elle desboutonna[10] sa poittrine et lui dist: 'Regarde, Barnabo, je suis ta chiere[11] compagne que tu, sans cause, avoyes condempné a mort.' Adonc s'entre embracierent par merveilleuse joye.

"Et le soubdan et tous furent moult esmerveilliez de ceste chose, et moult grandement louerent la vertu de ceste dame, et grans dons lui furent donnez. Et tout l'avoir de Ambroise fu sien, que le soubdain fist mourir a grant doleur. Et ainsi s'en retournerent en leur païs."

*Chapitre 53*  **Aprés ce que Droicture a conté des dames constantes, Christine lui demande** [fol. 125r b] **se c'est voir ce que plusieurs hommes dient que si pou en soit de loiales en la vie amoureuse, et puis respont Droicture**[12]

Quant toutes ces choses m'ot Dame Droicture raconté, et assez d'autres que je laisse pour briefté: si comme de Loonce qui fu femme grecque, laquelle ne voult oncqu[e]s[13] pour tourment que on lui feist accuser deux hommes, dont elle estoit

---

[1] de] des
[2] le] de
[3] ceste] celle
[4] mener] menez
[5] tout] toute
[6] pour couvoitise de gaingnier] par couvoitise de gaigner
[7] vint comme tout forsonnez] devint comme tous forcenez
[8] que] qui
[9] donroit] donneroit
[10] desboutonna] se desboutonna
[11] chiere] loyal
[12] se c'est voir ce que plusieurs hommes dient que si pou en soit de loiales en la vie amoureuse, et puis respont Droicture] pour quoy c'est que tant de vaillans femmes qui ont esté n'ont contredit aux livres et aux hommes qui mesdisoient d'elles et les responces que Droiture fait
[13] oncqu[e]s : *oncqus*

"There was a grete assemble, what of lordes of the sowdan's as of grete foy-son of Lombardes whiche mervayllously herkened this thynge. And to saye it shortely, this Ambrose was so ledde that he confessed before the sowdan and all the people all the fraude and howe he had wrought by coveytyse to gete those .v. thousande floryns. When Barnabo herde this almost he was out of hymselfe, for that he wyste none other but that his wyfe was slayne.

"But the good woman [N2r] came to hym and sayd, 'What woldest thou gyve hym that wolde yelde thee thy wyfe agayne alyve, hole, and chaste?'

"Barnabo answered and sayd that he wolde gyve all that ever he coude make in the worlde.

"And then she sayd unto hym, 'Barnabo, broder and frende, howe is that thou knowest not her?' And as he was abasshed that he wyst not what he dyde, she unbotened her brest and sayd to hym, 'I am thy dere felawe that thou haste condempned to the dethe without cause.' And then they embraced eche other in mervayllous grete joy.

"And the sowdan and all the people was gretely admervayled of this thynge, and ryght gretely praysed the grete vertue of this woman, and they gave her grete gyftes. And all the goodes that was perteynynge to Ambrose was gyven to her, and he was put unto the dethe ryght myschevously. And ryght so Barnabo and the good woman his wyfe tourned home agayne into theyr countree, and there they lyved togyder longe tyme after in prosperyte and joye."

*Chapter 53*   Here it sheweth howe after that that Ryghtwysnesse had tolde of these constaunce, my Lady Christine asked her yf it be true that dyvers men saye that there ben but fewe women true in theyr amourouse lyfe; and therto answered Ryghtwysnes [N2v]

When my Lady Ryghtwysenesse had tolde me all these thynges and ynoughe of others whiche I leve for shortnesse, so as of Loonce that was a woman of Grece, the whiche wolde never for tourmentes that ony man wolde do to her accuse two

accointe, ains copa sa longue a ses dens devant le juge pour lui oster l'esperance
que elle lui deist par force de tourmens; et d'assez d'autres dames que[1] dist, qui
tant furent de constant courage que elles mieux amerent[2] boire venim et morir
que flechir contre droicture et verité.

Je lui respondi adonc:[3] "Dame, asses m'avez demonstré grant [fol. 125v a] constance en courage de femme[4] et toutes autres vertus, que[5] vraiement plus grant
ne se pourroit dire de nul homme. Si me merveil trop comment tant de vaillans dames qui ont esté et de si sages et de si lettrees, et qui le bel stile ont eu de
dicter et faire[6] beaulx livres, ont peu souffrir[7] si longuement sans contredire tant
d'oreurs estre tesmoignés contre elles par divers hommes quant elles bien savoient
que a grant tort estoit."

*Response*: "Amie chiere, ceste question est assez legiere a souldre. Tu le
pueux[8] veoir par ce que devant t'ay dit que des[9] dames dont je t'ay conté les grans
vertus cy dessus en diverses oeuvres differenciees l'une de l'autre leur entendement occupoient,[10] [fol. 125v b] et non mie toutes en une mesmes chose. Ceste oeuvre a bastir estoit a toy reservee, et non mie a elles. Et aux gens de bon entendement, estoient asses les femmes loués sans autre escript.[11] Et quant a la longueur
du temps passé sans estre contredit,[12] toutes choses viennent bien a point et asses
a heure au regart du long siecle, comme[13] souffri si longuement Dieux estre les
hereges[14] au monde contre sa saincte loy, qui encore durassent, qui ne les eust

---

[1] pour lui oster l'esperance que elle lui deist par force de tourmens; et d'assez d'autres
dames que] affin qu'il n'eust esperance que par force de tourment lui feist dire; et d'assez
d'autres dames aussi me

[2] mieux amerent] amerent mieulx

[3] Je lui respondi adonc] Et je lui dis aprés ces choses

[4] femme] femmes

[5] que] et tant que

[6] faire : *fraire*

[7] peu souffrir] souffert

[8] le pueux] peus

[9] t'ay dit que des] t'est dit comment les

[10] conté les grans vertus cy dessus en diverses oeuvres differenciees l'une de l'autre
leur entendement occupoient] raconté cy dessus les grans vertus occuppoient les diverses
oeuvres differenciees l'une de l'autre leur entendement

[11] Et aux gens de bon entendement, estoient asses les femmes loués sans autre escript]
car par leurs oeuvres estoient assez les femmes louees aux gens de bon entendement et de
consideracion vraye sanz ce que autre escript elles en feissent

[12] contredit] contrediz leurs accuseurs et mesdisans, je te di que

[13] comme] car comment

[14] hereges] heresies

men with the whiche she was aquaynted, but cutte off her tonge with her tethe before the juge to put hym out of hope that she sholde tell hym by strengthe of tourmentes; and ynowe of other ladyes and gentylwomen, whiche were of constaunte courage that they had lever to drynke poyson and dye than to bowe ayenst ryght and trouthe.

And then I sayd to her, "Madame, ye have shewed me ynoughe grete constaunce in the courage of women and all other vertues, that truely there maye no more be sayd of no man. Soo I mervayle me gretely howe so many worshypfull ladyes that have ben so wyse and so well lettred, and that have goten the fayre style of endytynge and to make fayre bokes, hath suffred so longe without sayenge the contrary so many errours to be wytnessed ayenst them by dyvers men when that they knewe well that it was of grete wronge."

*Answere*: "My dere frende, this questyon is lyght ynoughe to assoyle. Thou mayst se by that that is sayd before that the grete vertues of these ladyes of whome I have tolde thee here above in dyvers werkes dyfferenced one frome another, ententyfely occupyed, and not all in one selfe thynge. This werke was reserved to thee to make, [N3r] and not to them. An[d][1] to people of good understandynge, the women were praysed ynoughe without other wrytynge. And as to the longnesse of tyme passed without gaynesaynge, all thynges cometh well to poynte and ynoughe to the beholdynge of the longe worlde. How longe suffreth God heresyes to be in the worlde ayenst the holy lawe, whiche yet endureth, that He

---

[1] An[d] : *an*

debatus.[1] Ainsi est il de maintes autres choses qui longuement sont souffertes sans contredit et puis sont[2] redarguees."

De rechief je, Christine, dis a elle: "Dame, moult bien dites. Mais je me rens certaine que maintes murmures naistront entre les mesdisans de ceste present [fol. 126r a] oeuvre, qui diront que s'il est[3] voir que aucunes femmes aient esté ou soient bonnes, toutevoies ne le sont elles pas toutes."[4]

*Response*: "Quel merveille que toutes ne le soient nottes, que de la compagnie de Jhesucrist ou n'estoient que .xii., si en y ot il un tres mavais? Et les hommes oseroient dire que toutes deussent estre bonnes: et eulx, que devroient ilz estre? Je tiens quant tous seront perfais, que les femmes les ensuivront."[5]

Je, Christine, respondis: "Dame, or laissons aler ycestes questions; mais un pou yssant hors des termes dont avons parlé jusques cy,[6] moult voulentiers vous feisse[7] aucunes demandes ad ce mesmes propos mais que je sceusse[8] que annuier ne vous en deust, pour [fol. 126r b] ce que la matiere, quoy que elle[9] soit fondee sur loy de Nature, ne vient mie du tout par[10] l'attrempement de raison."

Et elle[11] a moy respondi "Amie chiere, dis ce que tu vouldras,[12] car le disciple qui[13] demande au maistre ne doit estre repris se il ne quiert ce que savoir desire."[14]

"Dame, il cueurt au monde une loy naturelle des homme aux femmes, et des femmes aux hommes: non mie loy faicte par establissement de gens, mais par inclinacion charnelle par laquelle ilz s'entre aiment de tres grant et enforcee amour par une fois[15] plaisance, et si ne scevent a quel cause, ne pour quoy tel

---

[1] encore durassent, qui ne les eust debatus] a si grant peine en furent estirpees et ancore durassent qui ne les eust contredictes et convaincues

[2] sans contredit et puis sont] qui puis sont debatues et

[3] qui diront que s'il est] car ilz diront que supposé que il soit

[4] toutevoies ne le sont elles pas toutes] que toutevoyes ne le sont elles mie toutes, ne meismes la plus grant partie

[5] Response... les ensuivront] *R adds more text, new chapter division* (II.53+II.54) — *see annotations*

[6] Je, Christine, respondis: "Dame, or laissons aler ycestes questions; mais un pou yssant hors des termes dont avons parlé jusques cy] *chapter II.54 begins*: En procedant oultre je Christine dis de rechef ainsi: "Dame, or passons oultre ycestes questions et yssant un petit hors des termez continuez jusques ycy

[7] feisse] feroie

[8] ad ce mesmes propos mais que je sceusse] se je savoie

[9] matiere, quoy que elle] matiere sur quoy je parleroie quoy que la chose

[10] ne vient mie du tout par] yst aucunement hors de

[11] elle] celle

[12] Amie chiere, dis ce que tu vouldras] Amie, dis ce que il te plaira

[13] qui] qui pour apprendre

[14] ne quiert ce que savoir desire] enquiert de toutes choses

[15] fois] fole

hathe not destroyed them? So it is of many other thynges that ben suffred longe without gaynesayenge, and syth they be reproved at the last."

Then I, Christine, sayd to her: "Madame, ye say passynge well. But I yelde me certayne that many noyses groweth amonge the evyll sayers of this present werke whiche wyll saye that yf it be true that some women have ben and ben good, yet they be not so al."

*Answere*: "What mervayle thoughe they be not all noted, that of the company of Jhesu Cryst there were but .xii., yet was one ryght evyll? And these men durst saye that all women sholde be good: what sholde they be? Than I suppose when all men be parfyte, that the women shall folowe them."

I, Christine, answered: "Madame, nowe let us leve thyse questyons; but a lytel yssuynge out of termes wherof we have spoken tyll nowe, ryght gladly I wolde make you some demaundes to the same purpose yf that I knewe that it sholde not noy you, for that that the mater, thoughe it be founded upon the lawe of kynde, it cometh not all by the attemperynge of reason."

And she answered unto me: "Dere frende, say what thou wylte, for the dyscyple that asketh of the mayster [N3v] ought not to be reproved thoughe he aske that he desyreth to knowe."

"Madame, there renneth in the worlde a naturall lawe of men to women, and women to men: not the lawe made by the stablynge of people, but by carnal enclynacyon by the whiche they love eche other of ryght grete and stronge love by one pleasaunt tyme, and so they knowe not to what cause ne wherfore suche love

amour l'un de l'autre se fiche en eulx.[1] Et en ycelle amour, qui est assez commune et que on [fol. 126v a] appelle la vie amoureuse, dient communement les hommes que femmes, quoy que elles promettent, y sont moult pou arrestees en un lieu de[2] pou d'amour et a merveilles fausses et fainctes, et que tout ce leur vient de la legiereté de leur courage. Et entre les autres aucteurs qui de ce les accuse,[3] Ovide en son *Livre de l'art d'amours* leur donne moult grant charge; et dit cellui Ovide, et semblablement les autres quant assez ont blasmees sur celle chose[4] les femmes, que ce que ilz mettent en leurs livres tant de[5] meurs decevables d'elles comme de leurs mauvaistiez que il[6] le font pour le bien publique et commun, afin de aviser les hommes de leur[7] cauteles pour mieux les eschevez, si comme du serpent mucié soubz [fol. 126v b] l'erb. Si vous plaist, chiere dame, de ceste chose m'apprendre[8] le vray?"

*Response*: "Amie chere, quant est ad ce qu'ilz dient que si decevables soyent, ne sçay a quoy plus t'en diroye, car toy mesmes as assez souffisemment traictié la matiere tant contre cellui Ovide comme contre autres en ton *Epistre du dieu d'amours* et es *Epistres sur le Romans de la Rose*.

"Mais sur le point que tu m'as touchié, que ilz dient que pour le bien commun le firent, je te monstreray que pour ce ne fusse[9] mie. Et voy cy la raison: autre chose n'est le bien[10] commun ou publique en une cité, ou païs, ou communité de peuple fors un proffit et bien general, ou quel chascun—tant femmes, comme hommes—a part.[11] Mais la chose qui seroit faicte [127r a] en cuidant proffiter aux uns, et non aux autres, seroit appellé bien privé ou propre et non mie publique. Et encore moins le seroit le bien que on touldroit aulx uns, pour donner aulx autres: et tel chose doit estre appellee non mie seulement bien privé ou propre,[12] mais droit extorcion, faicte a autr[ui][13] en faveur de partie. Si puez veoir et apparcevoir clerement que favourablement le firent et ou prejudice d'une partie[14] et a son grief pour soustenir l'autre. Car ilz ne parlent point aux femmes en les avisant que ilz[15] se gardent des agaiz des hommes. Et toutevoies est ce chose

---

[1] se fiche en eulx] en eulx se fiche
[2] de] et de
[3] accuse] accusent
[4] celle chose] celles choses
[5] de] des
[6] il] ilz
[7] leur] leurs
[8] de ceste chose m'apprendre] m'apprendre de ceste chose
[9] fusse] fust ce
[10] le bien] bien
[11] a part] particippent ou ont part
[12] privé ou propre] propre ou privé
[13] autr[ui] : *autron*
[14] Si puez . . . d'une partie] *omitted*
[15] les avisant que ilz] en elles avisant que elles

one of another is fyxed in them. And in this love, that is comune ynoughe and
it is called the amourous lyfe, that men say comunely that women, thoughe they
promyse, there be but fewe abydynge in one place, and of lytell love ryght subtyll
and faynte, and all that cometh of the lyghtnesse of theyr courage. And amonge
all other auctours that accuseth them of that, Ovyde in his *Boke of the Crafte of
Love* gyveth them ryght grete charge. And this Ovyde sayth, and others in the
same wyse when they have blamed ynoughe the women upon that thynge that
they put in theyr bokes as well of the descyvable condycyons of them as of theyr
wyckednesse that they doo it for the comune welthe, to the entente to advyse the
men of theyr cauteyles the better to eschewe them, so as of the serpent whiche is
hydde under an herbe. So please it you, myne owne lady, to teche me the trouth
of this thynge?"

*Answere*: "My dere frende, as to that that they say that women be desceyv-
able, I wote not what I shall say to thee more, for thyselfe hath treated suffycyently ynoughe of this matter, as well ayenst this Ovyde as ayenst others in thyne
*Epystle of the God of Love*, and in the *Epystles upon* [N4r] *the Romaunce of the Rose*.

"But upon the poynte that thou hast touched to me, that they saye that they
doo yet for the comune welthe, I shall shewe thee that it was nothynge for that
cause. And se here the reason: the comune profyte in a cyte, or a countre, or in
comunalte of people is none other thynge but one profyte; and the generall welthe is of the whiche eche one hath his parte. But the thynge that sholde be done
in profyte some, and not to some, sholde be called the pryvate welthe or propre
and not the comune. And yet that shall do the lesse good that is taken away from
one, and gyven to another; and this thynge ought to be called not pryvate welthe
or propre, but ryght grete extorcyon, made to another in favoure of the partye. So
thou mayst se and perceyve clerely that they do it favourably and in prejudyce of
one parte to his gryefe to sustayne that other. For they spake not to the women
in advysynge them that they kepe them from the awaytes of men. And yet it is

certaine que tres souvent et menu ilz deçoivent les femmes par leurs cauteles et faulx semblans. Et n'est mie doubte que les femmes sont aussi bien ou [fol. 127r b] nombre[1] de creature humaine que sont les hommes.[2] Donquez je conclus que ce pour le bien commun le feissent, c'est assavoir des .ii. parties, ilz eussent aussi bien parlé aux femmes que ilz se gardassent[3] des hommes, comme ilz ont fait aux hommes que ilz se gaittent[4] des femmes.

"Mais a laissier aler ceste question[5] et ensuivant l'autre, c'est assavoir que femmes ne soient mie de si pou d'amour la ou leur cuer s'applique, et que plus y soient[6] arrestees que ilz ne dient, me souffira de le te prouver par exemples[7] de celles qui jusques a la mort y ont persev[e]ré.[8] Et premierement te diray de la noble Dido, royne de Cartage, dont cy dessus de sa grant valoir a esté parlé, quoy que toy mesmes autre fois en ayes touchié."[9]

*Chapitre 54*[10]   Ci dit de[11] Dido, royne de Cartage, a propos d'amour ferme en femme [fol. 127v a]

"Si comme cy dessus est dit, Dido, royne de Cartage, estant en sa cité a joye et a pais, regnant glorieusement, vint par Fortune Eneas fuitis[12] de Troie aprés la destruccion d'ycelle, duc et chevetaine de grant foison Troyens degeté par diverses tempestes, ses nefs cassoes, ses vivres faillis, a grant perte des siens; souffraitteux de repos, diseteux de pecune, las de errer par mer, besoingneux de heberge arriva au port de Cartage. Et comme[13] pour doubte de mesprendre, il ne se voulsist en hardir de descendre sans licence de la royne; envoya devers elle savoir se il lui plairoit. Mais[14] la noble dame, pleine d'onneur et de vaillance, qui

---

[1] nombre] nombre du peuple de Dieu
[2] les hommes] les hommes et non mie une autre espece ne de semblable generacion par quoy elles doyent estre forcloses des enseignemens moraulx
[3] ilz se gardassent] elles se gardassent des agais
[4] gaittent] gardassent
[5] ceste question] ycestes questions
[6] soient] sont
[7] exemples] exemple par deduisant en tesmoing partie
[8] persev[e]ré : *persevre*
[9] de sa grant valoir a esté parlé, quoy que toy mesmes autre fois en ayes touchié] a esté parlé de sa grant valeur quoy que toy mesmes en tes dictiez autre fois en ayes parlé
[10] *R* chap. 55
[11] Ci dit de] De
[12] fuitis] fuitif
[13] comme] adont
[14] il ne se voulsist en hardir de descendre sans licence de la royne; envoya devers elle savoir se il lui plairoit. Mais] se a terre descendist sanz licence, il envoya devers la royne savoir se il lui plairoit que port prensist

a thynge ryght certayne often tymes that they desceyve women by theyr cauteylous and false semblaunt. And it is noo doubte that the women be as well in the
nombre of the creatures erthely as be the men. Then I conclude that they sholde
do for the comune welthe, that is to understande of .ii. partes, they sholde have
spoken as well to the women that they sholde beware of the men, as they have
done to the men to beware of the women.

"But for to leve to goo to questyon and in folowynge that other, that is to
understande that women be not of so lytell love there as theyr hartes is sette, and
[N4v] that they be more stabler than they say, it shall suffyse to prove it by ensample of them that have perceyvered unto the dethe. And fyrst I shal tell thee of
the noble Dydo, quene of Cartage, of whome it is spoken here above of her grete
valoure, as thyselfe hathe touched other tymes."

| Chapter 54 | Here it speketh of Dydo, quene of Cartage, to the purpose that love is stable in a woman |
|---|---|

"So as it is sayd above, Dydo, quene of Cartage, beynge in her cyte in joy and
peas, reygnynge gloryously, come by Fortune Eneas, fledde frome Troye after
the destruccyon of [it].[1] The duke and capytayne of many Troyans cast by dyvers
tempestes, theyr shyppes broken, theyr vytayles fayled, and grete losse of people,
desyrous of rest, wery of rovynge by the see, busy to gete lodgynge, aryved at the
porte of Cartage. And as for doubte of mystakynge, he wolde not be so hardy to
take londe without lycence of that of the quene, but sente to her to knowe whyder it pleased her or no. But the noble lady, full of worshyp and of worthynes,

---

[1] of [it] : *destruccyon of the duke*

bien savoit que les Troyens estoient plus [fol. 127v b] que nacion du monde pour le temps en grant reputacion, et que cellui duc Eneas estoit de la lignee royale de Troye, ne donna pas seulement la congié que il descendist,[1] ains elle mesmes a tres noble compagnie de barons, et de dames, et pucelles[2] lui vint a l'encontre jusques a la marine, et a tres grant honneur receut lui et toute sa compagnie le mena en sa cité, et tres grandement l'onnoura, festoya, et aisa.

"Que t'en feroye long compte? Tant fu la Eneas a[3] sejour, aisé, et a repos que mais lui souvint[4] petit de tous les tourmens que eus avoit. Et a tant vint la frequentacion que amours, qui soubtilment scet cuers surprendre,[5] les fist enamourer l'un de l'autre. Mays selon ce [fol. 128r a] que l'experience le[6] monstra, moult fu plus grande l'amour de Dido vers Eneas que celle de lui vers elle. Car non obstant que il lui eust sa foy ballee que jamais autre femme que elle ne prendroit, et que a tousjours mais sien seroit, il s'en[7] parti aprés ce que elle l'eut tout reffait et enrichi d'avoir et d'aise, ses nefs reffreschies et ordennez,[8] plein de tresor et de biens, comme celle qui n'avoit mie[9] espargné l'avoir la ou le cuer estoit tout mis.[10] S'en ala sans congié prendre, de nuit, en recellee traicteusement sans le sceu d'elle: et ainsi paya son hoste. Laquelle departie fu si grant doleur a la lasse Dido, qui trop amoit, que elle voult renoncier a joye et vie. Et de fait, aprés ce que elle eut fait as[s]es[11] de regrais, se gitta en un grant feu [fol. 128r b] que fait alumé avoit; et autres dient que elle se occist de la mesme espee de Eneas. Et ainsi piteusement fina la noble royne Dydo, qui tant avoit esté honnouree[12] que elle passoit en renommee toutes les femmes de son temps."

---

[1] la congié que il descendist] le congié de dessendre
[2] de barons, et de dames et pucelles] de barons, de dames, et de pucelles
[3] a] la a
[4] souvint] souvenoit
[5] surprendre] soubtraire
[6] le] se
[7] s'en] se
[8] reffreschies et ordennez] refrechies, refaites, et ordenees
[9] n'avoit mie] n'avoit
[10] tout mis] mis
[11] as[s]es : *ases*
[12] avoit esté honnouree] honoree avoit esté

whiche knewe well that the Troyans were of more reputacyon for that tyme then was ony nacyon of the worlde, and that this Duke Eneas was of the noble blode royall of Troye, she gave hym not onely lycence that he sholde take the lande, but she herselfe with a noble company of lordes, and ladyes, and gentylwomen came agaynst hym unto the see syde, and [N5r] receyved hym and all his company with grete worshyp. She ledde hym into her cyte and gretely worshypped hym, feested hym, and eased hym.

"Why sholde I make the tale longe? So longe Eneas was there at sojourne, ease, and reste that he thought but lytell of all the tourmentes that he had before. And so moche was theyr hauntynge that love, whiche subtylly can sette hartes on fyre, made that one to love that other. But after that that experyence shewed, she loved moche better Eneas than he dyde her. For notwithstandynge that he had gyven to her his faythe that he sholde never take other woman, but that he sholde be hers evermore, he departed after that that she had refresshed hym with good and ease, his shyppes garnysshed full of treasoure and goodes as she that had not spared her goodes there as the herte was holly sette; wente away without takynge leve, by nyght, ryght traytourously without knowynge of her—and thus he payed his hostesse. The whiche departynge was to her so grete sorowe of hym that she loved so moche, that she wolde forsake all joye and her lyfe also. And indede, after that she had wepte and wayled ynoughe, she cast herselfe in a grete fyre that she lete make, and so she brente herselfe; and others say that she slewe herselfe with the swerde of Eneas. And thus pyteously ended the noble Quene Dydo, the whiche had ben so gretly worshypped that she passed in renowne all other women in her tyme." [N5v]

*Chapitre 55*     De Medee amoreuse[1]

"Mede, fille du roy de Colcos qui tant avoit de savoir, ama de trop grant et trop ferme[2] amour Jason. Cellui Jason fu[3] un chevalier de Grece moult preux aux armes. Il ouÿ parler qu'en l'isle de Colcos, qui estoit ou païs dont le pere de Medee estoit roy, avoit un mouton[4] semblast comme impossible a conquerre; toutevoies, estoit prophetisié que par un chevalier devoit estre conquise. Jason qui ceste chose entendi, lui comme desireux d'accroistre de mieulx en mieulx sa renommee, se [fol. 128v a] parti de Grece a grant compagnie en entencion de s'esprouver en ycelle[5] conqueste. Et comme il fust arrivez ou dit païs de Colcos, le roy de la terre lui dist que impossible estoit[6] que par armes, ne par proece d'omme fust conquise la toison d'or; car c'estoit chose faee, et que plusieurs chevaliers qui essaiez si y estoient periz y avoient esté,[7] si ne voulsist pas perdre la vie en tel maniere. Brief et court, Jason dist que puis qu'en s'entrepris l'avoit, ne le lairoit pour mourir.

"Medee, la fille du roy, qui vid Jason de tel beaulté et de si grant renommee, et de lignee royal[8] que il lui sembla que bon mariage seroit pour elle. Et que mieulx ne pourroit emploier s'amour, le voult garder de mort, car trop grant pitié lui prist que tel chevalier [fol. 128v b] deust ainsi perir. Si parla a lui longuement et a loisir. Et a brief dire, elle lui ballia charmes et enchantemens, comme celle qui tous les savoit, et lui aprist toute la maniere comment et par quel voyes il conquerroit la toison d'or, par si que Jason lui promist la prendre a femme sans jamais avoir aultre, et l'amer loyaulment.[9] Mais de ceste promesse lui menti Jason, car aprés ce qu'il fu du tout avenu a son entente, il la laissa pour une autre. Dont elle qui plus tost se laissast detraire que lui avoir fait ce tour fu comme desesperee, ne oncques puis bien ne joye son cuer n'ot."

---

[1] amoreuse] amante
[2] grant et trop ferme] grant
[3] fu] estoit
[4] mouton] mouton d'or merveilleux gardé par divers enchantemens, et que non obstant que la toyson d'icellui mouton
[5] en ycelle] a celle
[6] estoit] seroit
[7] periz y avoient esté] y avoient esté perilz
[8] beaulté et de si grant renommee, et de lignee royal] beauté de lignee royal et de si grant renommee
[9] avoir aultre, et l'amer loyaulment] autre avoir, et que loyale foy et amour a tousjours lui porteroit

## *Chapter 55*    Of Medea the true lover

"Medea, doughter of the kynge of Colcos whiche had so moche understandynge, loved of too grete love and stable Jason. This Jason was a knyght of Grece ryght manly in armes. He herde tell that in the Ile of Colcos, whiche was in the countre of whiche the fader of Medea was kynge, there was a shepe that semed as impossyble to conquere; and yet it was prophecyed that by a knyght it sholde be conquered. Jason, whiche understode this thynge, as ryght desyrous to encreas his renowne from good to better, departed from Grece with a grete company to the entente to prove hym in this conquest. And as he was aryved in the foresayd countre of Colcos, the kynge of the londe sayd to hym that it was impossyble that by the prowesse of armes of man the golden fleece myght be goten, for it was a thynge made by enchauntement; and that as many knyghtes as assayed it were perysshed, so he wolde not that he sholde lese his lyfe in suche manere. And Jason sayd shortely that syth he had taken the enterpryse in hande, he wolde not leve to dye therfore.

"Medea, the doughter of the kynge, whiche sawe Jason of suche beaute and of so grete renowne, and of the lygnage of a kynge, semed that he were a good maryage for her. And that he myght the better employe his love to her, she thought to kepe hym from the dethe, for grete pyte toke her that suche a knyght sholde perysshe so. So she spake to hym longe and at laysoure. And to say shortely, [N6r] she toke hym charmes and enchauntementes, as she that coude all, and taught hym all the maner howe and by what waye he sholde conquere the golden fleece, so that Jason sholde promyse her to take her to wyfe without havynge other, and to love her truely. But of this promyse lyed Jason, for after that that he was come to his entente, he lefte her for another. Wherof as sone as he had lefte her, she fell in suche dyspayre that there was never after joy in her herte."

## *Chapitre 56*     De Tysbe la pucelle[1]

"Ovide reconte en son *Livre de Methamorphoseos*[2] qu'en la cité de Babiloine eut deux riches citoiens et nobles [fol. 129r a] hommes si prochains voisins que les parois des palaiz ou ilz demouroient s'entre joingnoient. Ces deux[3] avoient deux enfans sur tous autres beaux et avenans: l'un un filz qui avoit nom Piramus, et l'autre une fille qui nommee estoit Tysbe. Ces deux enfans, qui encore estoient sans malice comme de l'aage de .vii. ans, s'entre amoient des ja si parfaictement que durer ne pouoient l'un sans l'autre. Et tart leur estoit tous les jours de lever au matin ou de avoir pris leur reffeccion sur leurs peres, pour aler jouer avec les autres enfans de leur aage, affin[4] que ilz s'entre trouvassent. Et tousjours a tous leurz jeux les veist[5] on ces deux ensemble. Et ainsi dura si longuement que ja furent grandelez.

"Et au feur que leur aage croissoit, [fol. 129r b] multeplioit la flamme de leur amour[6] et tant que pour la grant frequentacion qui fu d'aucunes aperceue d'entre eulx[7] nasqui souspeccion, par quoy raporté fu a la mere de Tysbe. Laquelle, ayree de ceste chose, prist sa fille et[8] l'enferma en ses chambres, et dist que bien la garderoit[9] de la hentice de Pyramus. De ceste prison furent tant dolens les deux amans,[10] que moult piteux estoient leurs pleurs et plains,[11] et trop leur estoit la doleur dure de ce que veoir ne s'entre pouoyent. Longuement dura celle distresce, laquelle point n'appetissoit, ne leur amour n'alentissoit[12] pour tant s'ilz ne s'entre veoient, ains tousjours avivoit au fueur de leur aage,[13] tant que ja furent venus comme en l'aage si comme de[14] .xv. ans.

"Avint [fol. 129v a] un jour, si que Fortune le voult, que Tysbe qui ailleurs ne pensoit, regardant toute esplouree[15] en sa chambre la paroit qui estoit moyenne entre les deux palais, en disant piteusement: 'Ha, paroit de pierre dure, qui fais la

---

[1]  De Tysbe la pucelle] De Thisbe

[2]  *Methamorphoseos*] *Methamorphoseos* si que tu le scez

[3]  Ces deux] yceulx

[4]  au matin ou de avoir pris leur reffeccion sur leurs peres, pour aler jouer avec les autres enfans de leur aage, affin] matin ou de prendre leur reffeccion en leurs maisons affin que ilz alassent jouer avec les autres enfans, et

[5]  le veist] veist

[6]  amour] amour en leur courage

[7]  qui fu d'aucunes aperceue d'entre eulx] d'entre eulz qui fu d'aucuns apperceue

[8]  Laquelle, ayree de ceste chose, prist sa fille et] qui

[9]  dist que bien la garderoit] dist yreement que bien garderoit sa fille

[10]  amans] enfans

[11]  pleurs et plains] plains et pleurs

[12]  ne leur amour n'alentissoit] ne n'amendrissoit leur amour

[13]  aage] ans

[14]  si comme de] de

[15]  esplouree] esplouree seule

## Chapter 56     Of Tysbe the mayden

"Ovyde telleth in his *Booke of Methamorphoseos* that in the cyte of Babylone were .ii. noble and ryche cytezynes, ryght nyghe neyghboures, that the walles of theyr houses that they dwelled in joyned togyder. These .ii. men had .ii. chyldren fayre above all others: that one a sone that was named Pyramys, and that other a doughter whiche was named Tysbe. These .ii. chyldren, whiche yet were without malyce as of the age of .vii. yeres, loved so parfytely togyder that they myght not abyde one frome another. And it was theyr guyse alwaye that every day to ryse in the mornynge togyder to take theyr refeccyon of theyr faders for to go to play with other chyldren of theyr age, to the entente that they myght be alway togyder. And at al theyr playes one myght se them togyder, and thus endure tyll they were waxen grete.

"And as they grewe in age, so encreased the flambes of theyr love so moche that by theyr hauntynge they were perceyved. And so some had suspeccyon, by [N6v] the whiche it was reported to the moder of Tysbe. The whiche toke suche wrathe of this thynge that she shytte her faste in her chambres, and sayd that she wolde kepe her well ynoughe fro the hauntynge of Pyramys. Of this pryson were ryght sorowfull these two lovers, that theyr wepynges and complayntes were ryght pyteous. And so was this sorowe to them ryght harde for that none of theym myght se other. This dystresse endured passynge longe, the whiche made not lesse theyr love, ne made them nothynge the slower for so moche as they sawe not eche other; but alway encreased the hete of theyr age, so moche that they were come to the age of .xv. yeres.

"It happened on a daye, so as Fortune wolde, that Thysbe that thought alwaye in her love all wepynge in her chambre, beholdynge the walle that was bytwene the .ii. houses, in saynge pyteously, 'O, thou walle of harde stone whiche

decevrance d'entre[1] mon ami et moy! S'il avoit en toy aucune pitié, tu fendroies afin que je peusse veoir cellui que j'ay tant desiré.'[2] Et si comme elle disoit ces paroles, elle vit d'aventure en un coingnet la paroit crevacee,[3] par ou la lueur de l'autre part apercevoit. Adonc elle fouy a la creveure et a tout le mordent de sa ceinture, car autre outil n'avoit creut aucunement le pertuis tant que le mordant ficha tout oultre, afin que Pyramus le peust apercevoir. Laquelle chose avint, et comme par [fol. 129v b] celle enseingne les deux amans moult souvent s'assemblassent a parler ensemble ou[4] dit pertuis, ou leurs piteux complains faisoient.

"A la parfin, contrains par trop grant amour, pristrent complot de eulx embler par nuit de leurs parens, et de eulx entre trouver[5] sus une fontaine soubz un meurier blanc ou en leur enfans aler jouer souloient. Et comme Tysbe qui plus amoit fut la premiere venue a la fontaine, attendant son ami, elle espoventee d'un lion que elle ouÿ venir[6] pour boire a la fontaine, s'en foy[7] cacher en un buisson la pres, et en alant laissa cheoir un blanc cueuvrechief,[8] lequel le lion trouva et vomi sus[9] l'entraille des bestes que devourees avoit. Piramus vint ains que Tysbe s'osast bougier[10] du buisson. Et pour ce que il trouva [fol. 130r a] le cueuvrechief de Tysbe, qu'il aperceut a la lune[11] chargee des entrailles, cuida fermement que s'amie fust devouree. Si eut si grant doleur que il mesmes s'occeist de s'espee. Et si comme il mouroit, Tisbe vint qui en ce point le trouva. Et par l'enseingne du cueuvrechief que elle lui vit tenir embracié, elle sceut la cause de celle mal aventure, dont elle eut telle[12] doleur que plus vivre ne voult. Et quant elle vid que l'esperit de son ami estoit hors, aprés moult piteux regraiz que elle fist, s'occist de la mesmes espee."

## Chapitre 57   Ci dit de Hero

"Hero la noble jouvencelle n'ama pas moins Lehander que fist Tysbe Piramus. Car comme cellui Lehander, pour garder l'onneur d'elle, amast mieulx se exposer a grant peril [fol. 130r b] afin que leur amour fust celle[13] que ce que baudement et

---

[1] d'entre] de
[2] j'ay tant desiré] je tant desire
[3] crevacee] crevee
[4] ou] au
[5] par nuit de leurs parens, et de eulx entre trouver] de leurs parens par nuit en recellee, et de eulx entre trouver dehors la cité
[6] que elle ouÿ venir] ouÿ venir bruyant
[7] foy] fuy
[8] cueuvrechief] cueuvrechef que elle avoit
[9] sus] dessus
[10] bougier] bouger
[11] a la lune] a la lumiere de la lune
[12] telle] tel
[13] celle] celee

makest the departynge bytwene my love and me! Yf there were ony pyte in thee, thou woldest cleve in sondre to the entente that I myght se hym that I have desyred so moche.' And as she sayd these wordes, she sawe by adventure in a corner the walle cleved, by the whiche she perceyved the lyght of that other parte. And then she dygged in the clefte with the pendant of her gyrdell, for other toole had she none. The hole encreased so moche that she put thrughe the pendant, to the entente that Pyramys sholde perceyve it. The whiche thynge happened, as by this token these .ii. lovers often tymes assembled [O1r] to speke togyder in the foresayd hole, where they made theyr pyteous complayntes.

"And at the last, constrayned by grete love, they toke counsayle that they wolde stele awaye by nyght fro theyr faders and moders, and that eche of them sholde fynde other at a welle under a whyte mulbery tre, where they were wonte to play in theyr youthe. And as Tysbe whiche loved more was the fyrst come to the welle, abydynge her love, she beynge aferde of a lyon that she herde comynge to drynke at the well, she fled to hyde her in a busshe there by. And in goynge, she lete fall a whyte coverchefe, the whiche the lyon founde and caste upon it the entrayles of beestes that he had devoured. Pyramys came or that Tysbe durste come out of the busshe. And for that he founde the coverchefe of Tysbe, whiche he perceyved by the mone lyght charged with the entraylles, trowed verely that his love was devoured. So he had so grete sorowe that he slewe hymselfe with his swerde. And as he was in dyenge, Tysbe came whiche founde hym in that poynt. And by the token of the coverchefe that she sawe hym have in his hande, she knewe the cause of that evyll adventure, wherof she had suche sorowe that she wolde lyve no longer. And when she sawe that the spyryte of her love was out of his body, after many grete lamentacyons that she made, she slewe herselfe with the same swerde."

*Chapter 57*    **Of the good woman Hero** [O1v]

"The noble yonge woman Hero loved not moche lesse the Hander than dyde Tysbe Pyramys. For as this Hander, to kepe the worshyp of her, loved better to put hym in grete peryll than she sholde be blamed for hym. To the entente that

a la veue des gens alast vers elle avoit pris une telle maniere de veoir sa dame que souvent et menu: il se levoit par nuyt de son lit affin que personne ne le sceust, et tout seul s'en aloit a un bras de mer assez large, que on nommoit Herles. Et tout a nou le passoit tant que il venoit a un chastel que on nommoit[1] Habidon, qui seoit sus la rive de l'autre part, ou quel Hero demouroit, qui l'entendoit[2] a une fennestre, et es longues nuis obscuers d'iver[3] elle tenoit un brandon de feu a une fennestre afin que elle lui donnast adrece d'aler droit celle part.

"Par plusieurs annees continuerent les deux amans ceste vie[4] tant que Fortune ot envie de leur vie solacieuse [fol. 130v a] et destourner les voult,[5] car comme il avenist une fois ou dit temps d'iver que par orage de temps la mer fust moult tempestueuse, grosse, enflee, et perilleuse, laquelle tempeste durast par tant de jours sans cesser que moult fust la longue attente de veoir l'un l'autre anuyeulx[6] aux deux amans et moult fort se complaingnoient du vent et du temps qui tant duroit. A la parfin Lehander, qui[7] grant desir trop chaçoit, par[8] ce que il vid une nuyt le brandon a la fenestre que Hero tenoit, lui sembla que elle par ce signe l'appellast,[9] et que a grant recreandise lui devroit tourner en quelque peril que il se mist que il n'y alast pour.[10] Et la lasse, qui de ce se doubtoit et que[11] voulentiers lui deffendist que il n'y alast pour se mettre [fol. 130v b] en tel peril se elle le peust,[12] tenoit le brandon a l'aventure pour lui donner adrece ou cas que il s'i seroit.[13] Si avint tellement la male aventure[14] que Lehander qui se fu mis a nou ne pot estriver contre les flos de la mer qui loins le porta, tant[15] que noyer le couvint. La povre Hero, qui[16] le cuer disoit ce que avenu estoit, ne cessoit de plourer. Et quant l[e][17] cler jour apparu, comme celle qui point ne dormoit,[18] se mist de rechief a la

---

[1] nommoit] appelloit

[2] l'entendoit] l'attendoit

[3] obscuers d'iver] de yver obscures

[4] vie] voye

[5] voult] en volt

[6] la longue attente de veoir l'un l'autre anuyeulx] anuyeuse la longue attente de veoir l'un l'autre

[7] qui] que

[8] par] pour

[9] elle par ce signe l'appellast] par ce signe elle l'appelloit

[10] que il n'y alast pour] se il n'y aloit helas et

[11] qui de ce se doubtoit et que] qui se doubtoit et qui

[12] le peust] peust

[13] si seroit] s'i seroit mis

[14] aventure] fortune

[15] loins le porta, tant] le porterent si loings

[16] qui] a qui

[17] l[e] : *la*

[18] dormoit] dormoit ne repposoit

theyr love myght endure the longer, without espyenge of ony people, he toke suche a maner to se his lady often tymes: he rose by nyght from his bedde to the entente that no man sholde knowe it, and wente alone to an arme of the see ryght large, whiche was called Herles and passed over swymmynge tyll he came to a castell named Habydon that stode upon the ryvere in that other syde where that Hero dwelled, whiche abode at a wyndowe, and in the longe nyghtes of wynter helde out a bronde of fyre at the wyndowe to the entente that he sholde come the ryght way thyder.

"These .ii. lovers contynued this lyfe many yeres tyll Fortune had envye of theyr solacyous lyfe and thought to trouble theym. For as it happened on a tyme of wynter, that by the woodnesse of the see the ryvere was full of tempest and passynge depe and peryllous, the whiche tempest durynge so longe without seasynge that they thought it ryght longe the one to se that other, whiche was ryght noyous to the .ii. lovers and gretely they complayned them of the wynde and of the tempest that endured so longe. At the last the Hander, whome grete desyre chased, by that that he sawe in a nyght the bronde at the wyndowe that Hero helde, it semed hym that she called hym, [O2r] and he thought grete cowardyse that he put hym not in peryll and that he wente not, for drede of whiche he doubted hym. And she wolde fayne defende hym that he sholde not go to put hym in suche peryll, yf she myght; notwithstandynge, she helde out the bronde at adventure to teche hym the ryght way, yf he wolde nedes do it. So thus happened the unhappy adventure that the Hander put hymselfe in the ryvere and myght not stryve agaynst the flode of the water, whiche bare hym soo ferre that he must nedes drowne. The good Hero, to whom her herte gave as it happened, seased never wepynge. And when the clere day appered, as she that slepte not, wente agayne to the wyndowe where she had ben all the nyght, and she sawe the

fenestre ou toute nuit avoit esté. Et si comme elle vid le corps[1] de son ami floter par dessus la marine, elle qui plus aprés ne voult vivre, se gita en la mer,[2] et tant fist que elle l'alla embrasier, et ainsi[3] fu perie."

## *Chapitre 58*     Ci dit de[4] Sismonde, fille du prince de Salerne

"Bocace raconte ou *Livre* [fol. 131r a] *des Cent Novelles* que un prince de Salerne nommé Tancre fu lequel avoit une tres belle fille moult gent, et avenant, et courtoise qui estoit nommee Sismonde. Il amoit celle fille de si grant amour que a trop grant peine se voult accorder par le timonement de ses barons de marier au compte de Champaigne. Mais comme elle ne demourast gaires en mariage, le dit conte mort; le pere la reprist de rechief vers lui, deliberant de jamais ne la marier. La dame, qui moult estoit norrie souefment, et qui estoit belle et en fleur de jounesce, et qui sceut la voulenté de son pere de non jamais la marier, va aviser entre les serviteurs de son pere un escuier, lequel sur tous les autres—quoy que grant foison de chevaliers et de gentilz hommes [fol. 131r b] y eust—lui sembla belle et bon digne d'estre amez et tant que elle delibera pour passer sa joiennece plus joieusement de prendre sa plaisance en. Et par longue piece ains que ceste chose descouvrist, regarda par chascun jour si que elle se seoit a la table de son pere les manieres, les contenances et condicions d'icellui, qui nommez Guiscart estoit, tant que de jour en jour lui sembloit estre plus parfait entre toutes choses. Par quoy, un jour le manda vers elle, et en tel maniere lui dist:[5]

"'Guiscart, beaulx amis, la feance que j'ay en vostre bonté, et beauté, et predomie[6] m'amonneste a me descouvrir a vous d'aucunes choses qui me touchent moult secretes, lesquelle[s][7] je ne diroie a nul autre. Mes je vueil, ainçois que les[8] vous dye, avoir vostre [fol. 131v a] serment que jamais par vous ne sera revelé.'[9]

"Guiscart respondi: 'Ma dame, ne vous fault doubter[10] que ja par moy ne sera sceu[11] chose que me disiez, et de ce par ma loyaulté vous asseure.'

---

[1] le corps] le corps mort
[2] elle qui plus aprés lui ne voult vivre, se gita en la mer] Adont comme celle qui plus aprés lui ne vouloit vivre se geta en mer
[3] ainsi] ainsi par trop amer
[4] Ci dit de] De
[5] nommé Tancre . . . lui dist] *R see annotations for revised passage*
[6] bonté, et beauté, et predomie] bonté, loyauté, et prodommie me meut et
[7] lesquelle[s] : *lesquelle*
[8] les] le
[9] revelé] revellé ne sceu
[10] doubter] ja doubter
[11] sceu] revellé

body of her love flete upon the water nyghe the brynke. She, that wolde not lyve no longe after, caste her into the see and dyde so moche that she toke her love in her armes, and so dyed, and thus she was perysshed."

## Chapter 58    Of Sysmonde, doughter of the prynce of Salerne

"Bocace telleth in the *Boke of Cent Nouvelles* that a prynce of Salerne named Tancre[1] had a fayre doughter ryght gentyll and courtoys whiche was named Sysmonde. He loved this doughter of soo grete love that with grete payne he wolde accorde unto the styrynge of his lordes to marye her to the erle of Champayne. But as she [O2v] that sholde not abyde longe in maryage, this erle dyed and the fader toke her home agayne to hym, thynkynge never to marye her agayne. The lady, whiche was nourysshed tenderly and was ryght fayre and in the floure of her youthe, and whiche that knewe the wyll of her fader that she sholde [not] be[2] maryed agayne, wente and advysed her amonge all the servauntes of her fader of a squyer, the whiche above al the others — thoughe there were grete foyson of knyghtes and gentyll men — he semed to her fayre, and good, and worthy to be loved, and so moche that she thought to passe her youthe more joyously to take her pleasaunce. And longe tyme or she wolde dyscover this thynge, she behelde every day when she sate at her fader's table the maner, countenaunce, and condycyons of the squyer, whiche was named Guyscart, so moche that from day to day he semed to her more parfyte amonge all thynges, by the whiche she called hym on a day before her and sayd to hym in this manere:

"'Guyscart, fayre frende, the trust that I have in your bounte, beaute, and wysdome counsayleth me to dyscover to you of dyvers thynges that toucheth me ryght secrete, the whiche I wolde not tell to none other body. But I wolde, or that I tell it you, to have your trouthe that shal never be opened by yo[u].'[3]

"Guyscart answered, 'Madame, you nede not to doubte that there shall be nothynge knowne by me that ye tell me. And for that I assure you by my trouthe.'

---

[1] Tancre : *Cancre* here and elsewhere
[2] sholde [not] be : *sholde be*
[3] yo[u] : *yon*

"Adonc lui dist Sismonde: 'Guiscart, saches¹ que ma plaisance est en un gentil homme que j'aime et vueil aimer. Et pour ce que je ne puis pas bien parler a lui, ne² par qui lui mander mes vouloirs, je vueil que tu soies moyen de nos amours. Or regart se grant fiance ay en toy sur tous autres,³ quant je vueil mon honneur mettre en tes mains.'⁴

"Adonc cellui se mist a geneulx et dist: 'Ma dame, je sçay bien qu'en vous a tant de sens et de bonté⁵ que ne vouldriez faire chose descouvenable. Si vous mercy tres humblement dont en moy avez fiance plus que nul autre. Or commandez [fol. 131v b] voz bons plaisirs a moy, vostre serviteur, et je y obeiray a mon pouoir et serviray cellui maiz que je sache qui il est, qui tant est eureulx qu'il a l'amour de dame de si haulte value que vous estes. Car certes, il n'a pas failli a noble amour.'⁶

"Quant Sismonde, qui l'avoit voulu esprouver, l'ot ouÿ si sagement parler, adonc le prist par la main et lui dist: 'Amis Guiscart, saches que tu es cellui que j'ay choisi pour seul ami et en qui prendre vueil toute ma plaisance. Car il me semble que la noblece de ton courage, et les bons meurs dont tu es plein, te rendent digne d'avoir haulte amour.'

"De ceste chose ot moult grant joye le jouvencel, et moult humblement⁷ l'en mercia. Et a brief dire, longue piece continuerent leurs amours sans ce que novelle aucune en fust sentue.⁸ Mais Fortune, envieuse [fol. 132r a] de leur soulaz, ne voult plus souffrir⁹ en joye les deux amans, ains tourna leurs¹⁰ deduis en moult amere tristece par¹¹ merveilleuse aventure.

"Il avint a un des jours d'esté que Sismonde s'esbatoit en un jardin avec ses damoiselles. A celle heure son pere, qui n'avoit autre bien que¹² quant il la veoit,

---

¹ saches] je vueil que tu saches
² ne] ne n'ay
³ grant fiance ay en toy sur tous autres] j'ay fiance en toy plus que en nul autre
⁴ mains] mains et baillie
⁵ bonté] vaillance
⁶ humblement . . . a noble amour] humblement de ce que en moy plus qu'en nul autre avez tel fiance que descouvrir me voulez le secret de vostre pensee. Si me pouez commander, tres chiere dame, tous voz bons plaisirs sanz nulle doubtance comme a cellui qui cuer et corps offre a obeir a tous voz bons commandemens de toute ma puissance. Et avec ce je m'offre a estre tres humble serviteur a cellui qui tant est eureux qui a l'amour de dame de si digne vale comme vous estes car vrayement il n'a mie failli a haulte et tres noble amour
⁷ moult humblement] humblement
⁸ sentue] sentie
⁹ souffrir] souffrir vivre
¹⁰ leurs] leur
¹¹ par] et par
¹² autre bien que] bien fors

"And then sayd Sysmonde to hym, 'Guyscarte, knowe [O3r] it for trouthe that my pleasaunce is in a gentylman that I love and wyl love. And for that that I may not well speke to hym, nor by whome to sende hym my wyll, I wolde that ye were meane of our loves. Nowe beholde yf I have grete truste in you above all others, when I wyll put myne honoure in your handes.'

"And there he set hym on his knees and sayd, 'Madame, I knowe wel that ye have suche wytte and goodnesse that ye wolde not do the thynge unconvenable. Soo I thanke you ryght mekely that ye trust in me more than in another. Nowe commaunde your good pleasure to me, your servaunt. And I shall obey to my power and serve hym yf I knewe whiche he were that were so happy to have the love of a lady of so grete worthynesse as ye are. For certes, he hath not fayled of a noble love.'

"When Sysmonde, that had wyll to prove hym, had herde hym speke so wysely, then she toke hym by the hande and sayd, 'Frende Guyscart, knowe it that thou arte he that I have chosen for myne onely love, and in whom I wyll take all my pleasaunce. For me semeth that the noblesse of thy courage, and the good maners of whiche thou arte full, yeldeth thee worthy to have an hyghe love.'

"The yonge man had grete joye of this thynge, and thanked [her][1] ryght humbly. And shortely to say, longe tyme contynued theyr love without that that ony tydynges was felte therof. But Fortune, envyous of theyr solace, wolde no longer suffre these .ii. lovers in joy, but tourned theyr dysporte into grete and bytter [O3v] sorowe by mervaylous adventure.

"It fortuned in a somer's day that Sysmonde dysported her in a gardyne with her maydens. At that houre her fader, that had none other welthe but when he

---

[1] thanked [her] : *thanked*

ala tout seul en la[1] d'elle pour deviser et s'esbatre. Mais comme il trovast les fenestres closes et les courtines du lit tirés, et que ame n'y estoit, cuida que elle dormist.[2] Si ne la voult mie esveillier, ains se coucha en un couchete,[3] et la moult fort s'en dormi. Sismonde, quant assez lui sembla avoir demouré ou jardin, s'en vint en sa chambre sus son lit se coucha comme pour dormir. Toutes ses femmes fuist vuidier et clore l'uis sur elle, sans [fol. 132r b] ce que son pere fust d'elle ne d'autre aperceu. Quant elle se vit toute seule, se leva de son lit et ala querre[4] Guiscart, qui en un[e][5] de ses garde robes estoit enclos, et le mena en sa chambre.[6] Et si comme ilz devisoient entre eulx deux entre les courtines comme ceulz qui tous seulz se cuidoient estre,[7] le prince s'esvilla et entendi que un homme av[e]c[8] sa fille estoit.[9] De ceste chose ot si grant doleur que a peines la consideracion que sa fille deshonnoureroit le pot garder que seure ne lui courust;[10] toutevoies se souffri et bien entendi que il estoit, et[11] fist tant que il sailli de la chambre sans ce que ilz se[12] sentissent. Quant les deux amans orent asses ensemble esté, Guiscart se parti.

"Mais le prince, qui l'eut fait agaitier, tantost le fist prendre et emprisonner; [fol. 132v a] puis vint devers sa fille, et seul a seul en sa chambre, a yeux plains de larmes et a tristece,[13] lui prist a dire en tel maniere:

"'Sismonde, je cuidoie avoir en toy fille sur toutes femmes belle, chaste, et sage. Mais de tant suis je plus convaincus d'ire comme envis[14] le contraire cuidasse. Car se a mes yeux veu ne l'eusse, riens ne fust qui a croire me fist que d'amour d'omme se ton mari ne fust peusses estre surprise. Mais comme de ce[15] je soye certaine, la tristece en sera le tourment de ma vieillece et de ce pou de temps que j'ay a vivre. Et ce qui plus engrige[16] mon yre, c'este que je te cuidoye estre de

---

[1] la] la chambre
[2] dormist] se dormist a remontee
[3] en un couchete] sur une couche
[4] ala querre] querir ala
[5] un : _une_
[6] le mena en sa chambre] en sa chambre le mena
[7] tous seulz se cuidoient estre] se cuidoient tous seulz
[8] av[e]c : _auc_
[9] un homme avec sa fille estoit] homme estoit avec sa fille
[10] a peines la consideracion que sa fille deshonnoureroit le pot garder que seure ne lui courust] a peine s'en pot garder la consideracion qu'il deshonoreroit sa fille que il ne lui courust sus
[11] que il estoit et] qui estoit cellui
[12] se] le
[13] a tristece] a triste visage
[14] envis] plus envis
[15] ce] ce qui en est
[16] engrige] ancore engrige

sawe her, wente alone into her chambre to dysporte hym with her. But when he
founde the wyndowes shytte and the curteynes of the bedde drawne, and that
there was nobody there, trowed that she had ben aslepe; so he wolde not awake
her but layde hym on a lytell couche, and there he slepte strongly. When Sysmonde thought that she had ben longe ynoughe in the gardyne, she wente to her
chambre and layde her on her bedde as for to slepe. All her women were voyded
and shytte the dore upon her, not perceyvynge that her fader or ony other was
there. And when she sawe herselfe alone, she rose from her bedde and wente to
seke Guyscart, whiche was in one of he[r]¹ wardrobes, and brought hym into her
chambre. And so as they devysed bytwene them two within the curteyns, as they
that trowed that they were alone, the prynce awoke and understode that there
was a man with his doughter. He had so grete sorowe of that thynge that of payne
the consyderacyon that he sholde dyshonoure his doughter myght not kepe hym
but that he had departed them; neverthelesse, he suffred and understode wel who
it was, and dyde so moche that he lepte out of the chambre, they not knowynge of
hym. And when these two lovers had ben ynoughe togyder, Guyscarte departed.

"But the prynce that had made watche upon hym, anone he made hym to be
taken [O4r] and prysoned hym; and after wente to his doughter, and they beynge
alone in the chambre, the eyes full of teeres and with grete sorowe, began to saye
to her:

"'Sygysmonde, I trowed to have in thee a doughter above all women fayre,
chaste, and wyse. But of so moche am I the more overcome to say as thoughe
I had trowed the contrary. For yf I had not sene it with myne eyes, there was
nothynge that sholde have made me byleve that thou had be supprysed with the
love of ony man but it had ben thyne housbande. But as of that I am certayne,
the sorowe therof shall be the tourment of myne age and of that lytell tyme
that I have to lyve. And that whiche engrudgeth moost my wrathe is that that I

---

¹ he[r] : *he*

plus noble courage que femme nee. Et je voye bien[1] le contraire, par ce que tu te[2] prise a un des mendres de mon hostel. Car [fol. 132v b] se tel chose vouloies faire, trop de plus nobles trouvasses a ma court sans te prendre[3] a Guiscart auquel bien cuide rendre[4] la doleur que j'ay par sa cause. Car je vueil que tu saches que mourir le feray; et semblement de toy feist,[5] se je peusse deffaire de mon cuer l'amour que j'ay en[6] toy trop plus grande que oncques pere n'ot a fille,[7] qui le me destourne.'

"Quant Sismonde entendi ceste chose et que son pere condempnoit a mort cellui que elle tant amoit, tant fu dolent que mourir voulsist en l'eure.[8] Toutevoies par tres affermé courage et constante chiere, sans gitter larme, quoy que elle se disposast de non plus vivre, ainsi respondi:[9]

"Pere, puis que ainsi est que Fortune vous a consenti savoir ce que je tant voloye celé,[10] [fol. 133r a] je n'ay mestier de vous faire aucune requeste, excepté se je cuidoie empetrer de vous romission et vie a cellui que vous menaciez de mort:[11] je vous supplieroye que la mien[ne][12] prenissiez, pour laissier la sienne. Car quant est que je vous demande pardon ou cas que ferez de lui ce que vous dictez, je ne quier, car je ne vueil plus vivre. Car[13] de tant vous fais je certaine: que par sa mort, vous m'occirez.[14]

"Mais de ceste chose qui vous muet a si grant yre contre nous, n'avez cause que de vous prendre[15] a vostre mesme coulpe? Car vous qui estes de char, ne penssiez vous avoir engendree fille de char, et non pas de pier[r]e[16] ou de fer? Et souvenir vous devoit, tout soiez vous envieilli, quelle et comment grant[17] est la moleste

---

[1]  voye bien] voy

[2]  te] t'es

[3]  prendre] estre prise

[4]  rendre] vendre cher

[5]  feist] feisse

[6]  l'amour que j'ay en] la fole amour que j'ay a

[7]  oncques pere n'ot a fille] pere n'ot oncques fille

[8]  ceste chose et que son pere condempnoit a mort cellui que elle tant amoit, tant fu dolent que mourir voulsist] son pere avoit congnoissance de la chose que tant celer voulsist se elle ot douleur, nul ne le demand. Mais ancore sur tout le comble de sa pesance lui destraignoit le cuer de ce que il menaçoit de mort cellui que elle tant amoit; si voulsist bien

[9]  ainsi respondi] respondi ainsi

[10]  vous a consenti savoir ce que je tant voloye celé] a voulu consentir que vous saches ce que tant vouloie secret

[11]  menaciez de mort] tant menaciez de mort par me offrir en lieu

[12]  mien[ne] : *mien*

[13]  Car] Et

[14]  vous m'occirez] mettres vous a fin ma vie

[15]  que de vous prendre] de vous prendre que

[16]  pier[r]e : *piere*

[17]  grant] grande

trowed thee to be of more noble courage then ony woman borne. And I se well the contrary, by that that thou hast taken thee to one of the leest of myne house-holde. For yf thou wolde have done suche a thynge, thou myghtest have founde some of more noblesse and worshyp in my courte then when thou toke Guyscart, to whome I trowe to yelde the sorowe that I have by his cause, for I wolde that thou knowe it that I shall make hym to dye; and the same wolde I do by thee, yf I myght destroy fro myne herte the love that I have in thee more gretter than ever fader had to his doughter, whiche tourneth me fro it.'

"When Sysmonde understode this thynge, and that her fader condempned hym to deth that she loved so moche, she was so sorowfull that she wolde fayne dye that houre. Yet by ryght stable courage and constaunte chere, without [O4v] castynge ony teeres out of her eyes thoughe she was dysposed to lyve no longer, she answered thus:

"'Fader, syth that it is so that Fortune hathe made that to be knowne whiche that I wolde so fayne have covered, I have noo nede to make noo request of you, excepte yf I wyste to aske of you remyssyon and lyfe to hym that ye manace of dethe: I wolde beseche you to take myne, and leve his. For in that that I aske you pardon, and ye wolde do to hym as ye saye, I wolde not aske it, for I wyll noo lon-ger lyve. For of so moche I make you certayne: that by his dethe, ye shall sle me.

"'But of this thynge that moveth you to so grete wrathe ayenst us, have ye not cause to take it unto your owne blame? For ye that be of flesshe, have not ye engendred a doughter of flesshe, and not of stone nor of yron? And ye ought to thynke, thoughe ye be olde, what and howe grete is the hevynesse of youthe,

de joeunesce, vivant en d[e]lices[1] et a aise,[2] et les aguillons [fol. 133r b] fors a passer
qui y sont. Et puis que je vi que vous aviez deliberé de non jamais[3] me marier, et
me sentant joeune et stimulee de ma joliveté, m'en amouray de cestui—et non
mie sans cause, ne sans grant deliberacion consenti et accorday a mon cuer ce
qu'il vouloit, ains ançois[4] bien avisay le[s][5] meurs de lui, perfait en toutes vertus
plus qu'en[6] nul aultre de vostre court: et ce pouez vous savoir vous mesmes[7] qui
l'avez nourry. Et qu'est autre chose noblece[8] fors vertus? Car du sanc et de la char
que n'est que fiens[9] ne vient elle mie. Si n'avez cause de dire que prise me soye
au moins noble de vostre gent. Et n'avez mie[10] achoison de si grant yre vers nous,
consideree vostre coulpe que vous dites.[11]

"'Mais au fort se si grant punicion de ce meffait voulez prendre, sur lui [fol.
133v a] n'apartient elle mie[12] estre prise, ains sera a tort et a pechié. Mais a moy
mieulx affiert[13] qui de ce amonnestay lui, qui n'y pensoit: et que deust il doncques
avoir fait? Certes, trop eust eu le cuer vilain de reffuser dame de tel parage. Si
devez supploier le[14] meffait sur lui, et non pas sur moy?'

"Le marquis a tant se parti[15] de Sis[m]onde,[16] mais non pas pour ce appaisé
vers Guiscart, ains l'endemain le fist occire et commanda que le cuer du ventre
lui fust arrachié. Lequel cuer le pere mist en une tres belle et riche[17] coupe d'or,
et par un sien secret message l'envoia a sa fille, et lui manda que il lui envoioit ce
present pour lui faire joye de la riens que il[18] plus amoit, ainsi que elle lui avoit[19]
fait joieux de la riens que il plus tenoit chiere.

---

[1] d[e]lices : *dilices*
[2] a aise] ayses
[3] non jamais] jamais ne
[4] ançois] tout avant
[5] le[s] : *le*
[6] qu'en] que
[7] vous savoir vous mesmes] savoir vous mesmes
[8] autre chose noblece] doncques noblece autre chose
[9] que n'est que fiens] *omitted*
[10] gent. Et n'avez mie] court. Et n'avez
[11] nous consideree vostre coulpe que vous dites] nous que vous dites consideree
vostre coulpe
[12] meffait voulez prendre, sur lui n'apartient elle mie] voulez prendre pour tant
n'affiert elle mie sur sa personne
[13] a moy mieulx affiert] sur moy affiert mieulx
[14] supploier le] suppleer ce
[15] a tant se parti] se parti a tant
[16] Sis[m]onde : *Sisononde*
[17] tres belle et riche] *omitted*
[18] il] elle
[19] lui avoit] l'avoit

lyvynge in delyces and at ease, and the pryckynges whiche are to passe. And syth that I sawe that ye thought never mary me agayne, and felynge me yonge and prycked with lustynesse, I fell to love this same gentylman—and not without a cause, ne without grete delyberacyon I consented and accorded to myne herte that he desyred. Yet or that, I advysed well the condycyons of hym, parfyte in all vertues more than ony other of your courte; and that ye may knowe yourselfe whiche have nourysshed hym. And what other thynge is noblesse, but vertues? For it cometh not of flesshe and blode, whiche is but donge. So ye have [P1r] not cause to saye that I have taken me to the leest noble of your courte. And thus ye have no cause of wrathe towarde us, your owne blame consydered.

"'But at all yf ye wyll take so grete punysshment of hym for that trespace, it perteyneth not to be taken but it sholde be taken of wronge and of synne. But it is more ryght that I have it, whiche styred hym therto, whiche thought that he ought to have it. For certes, it sholde have ben too moche in the herte of a vylayne to have refused a lady of suche parentage. Ought ye, then, to employe this trespace all upon hym, and not upon me?'

"Then the prynce departed from Sysmonde. But yet he was not appeased towarde Guyscart, but in the mornynge made hym to be slayne and commaunded that the herte sholde be taken out of the body, the whiche herte the fader put in a ryght ryche cuppe of golde, and by a secre[t][1] messagere sent it unto his doughter; and he sholde say that he sent her that presente, and to enjoy of that thynge that she loved moost.

---

[1] secre[t] : *secre*

"Le message venu [fol. 133v b] devant Sismonde fait son present, et dist ce que enchargié lui estoit. Elle prist la coulpe[1] et l'ouvry, et tantost congnut l'aventure.[2] Mais quoy que elle eust doleur inextimable, de riens ne fu desmeue de son haultaine corage qui la fist respondre, sans muer chiere, en disant:[3]

"'Mon ami, dites au marquis que aucune[4] chose l'aperçoy je sage ce est: que a si noble cuer a baillé tel sepulchre qui lui apartient,[5] car autre que d'or ne[6] de pierres precieuses ne doit il avoir.'

"Puis se baissa sur la coupe, et baisa le cuer, en disant piteusement: 'Ha, tres doulz cuer, heberge de tous mes plaisirs! Maudite soit le cruaulté de cellui qui a mes yeulx ores[7] te fait veoir; assez m'estoies present es yeux de la pensee. Or as tu passé le cours de ta noble vye [fol. 134r a] par divers fortune, mais[8] de ton anemi as tel sepulchre que ta valeur a meritee. Si apartient bien pour donnier office que[9] tu soies lavé et baigné des larmes de celle que tant amoyes, et tu n'y fauldras mie; et avec ce, ne sera pas ton ame sans la sienne car ce n'est pas raison ains te feray[10] en brief terme compagnie. Mais malgré Fortune qui tant t'a esté contraire t'est venu en tant bien[11] a point que mon cruel pere t'a a moy envoyé, afin que plus soies[12] honnouree, et que je parle a toy ains que je meure et que mon ame voye[13] la tienne, dont je desire la compagnie, car je sçay bien que ton esperit desire[14] le mien.'

"Telz paroles et asses d'autres disoit Sismonde tant piteuses que personne ne l'ouÿst qui fondre[15] ne deust. Et si fondomment plouroit qu'il sembloit que [fol. 134r b] deux fontaines eust au chief qui sans cesser decourussent en celle coupe[16] sans mener noise ne crie mais a basse voix en baisant le cuer. Les dames et les damoiselles qui entour elle estoient moult avoient grant merveil[le][17] de ceste chose, car

---

[1] coulpe] coupe

[2] congnut l'aventure] apperceut ce qui estoit fait

[3] en disant] disant

[4] aucune] en aucune

[5] a baillé tel sepulchre qui lui apartient] au baillié sepulcre tel qu'il lui appartenoit

[6] ne] et

[7] yeulx ores] yeulx

[8] passé le cours de ta noble vye par divers fortune, mais] par diverse fortune passé le cours de ta noble vie mais mal a gré de la faulse fortune tu as receu mesmes

[9] pour donnier office que] si appartient bien, mon doulx cuer, que pour derrenier office

[10] te feray] lui fera

[11] malgré Fortune qui tant t'a esté contraire t'est venu en tant bien] ancore en despit d'icelle desloyale Fortune qui tant t'a nuit t'est ancores en tant bien venu

[12] soies] tu soies

[13] meure et que mon ame voye] parte de ce monde et que mon ame voise avec

[14] desire] demande et desire

[15] fondre] fondre en larmes

[16] decourussent en celle coupe] en celle couppe descourussent

[17] merveil[le] : *merveil*

"The messagere came before Sysmonde, and made his present, and sayd that he was charged therwith. And she toke the cuppe and opened it, and anone she knewe the adventure. But thoughe she had sorowe inestymable, she was not dysmayed of her hyghe courage, but made her answere to hym in this wyse without chaungynge her chere, sayenge:

"'My frende, say to the prynce that one thynge perceyve I well, that is this: that to so noble a herte he hathe gyven suche a sepulture that perteyneth to hym, for other than golde and [P1v] precyous stones ought he not have.'

"Than she stouped over the cuppe and kyssed the herte, in sayenge pyteously, 'Ha, ryght swete herte, herboure of all my pleasure! Cursed be the cruelte of that [one who] maketh[1] me to see thee in this plyte! Ye were alwaye present in myne herte, and the veray eyen of my thought. Now hast thou passed the course of thy noble lyfe by dyverse fortunes, but yet thou hast suche a sepulture of thyne enemye as thy worthynesse hath deserved. So it pertayneth well that I do myn offyce that thou be wasshed and bayned with the teeres of her that thou loved so moche, and thou shalte not fayle therof; and with that, thy soule shal not be longe without myne, for that is no reason but that I shall make thee companye in short tyme. Yet maulgre Fortune that hath be to thee so contrarye, there is come to thee so moche of wele nowe that my cruell fader hath sent thee to me, to th'entent that thou be more worshypped, and that I speke to thee or that I dye and that my soule maye se thyn, of whom I desyre the companye above all thynge, for I knowe well that thy spyryte desyreth myne.'

"Suche wordes and others ynowe sayd Sysmonde so pyteous that ony persone that harde it ought to have grete pyte of it. And so depely she wepte that it semed that she had .ii. welles in her hede that ran without ceasynge into the cup without makynge noyse or crye but with a lowe voyce, kyssynge alwaye the herte. The ladys and gentylwomen that were about her had grete mervayle of this thynge, for they

---

[1] [one who] maketh : *maketh*

ne savoient riens de l'aventure, ne quelle estoit[1] la cause de ce tres grant dueil. Si plouroient toutes pour la pitié[2] et se penoient de la reconforter, mais riens n'y valoit, et en vain lui demandoient ses plus privees la cause de son dueil.

"Et celle, vaincue[3] de merveilleuse doleur, quant asses ot plouré dist: 'O tres amé cuer, tout mon office ay fait vers toy. Plus ne reste a faire fors d'envoier mon ame faire compagnie a la tienne.' Et dites ces paroles,[4] elle se leva et ala ouvrir un[e][5] armoire, et prist une buirete ou elle avoit mis herbes [fol. 134v a] venimeuses dissouldre[6] en eaue pour trouver prestes quant le cas seroit avenu. Si versa celle eaue en la coupe ou le cuer estoit, et sans quelconques paour tout[e][7] la but. Et sur son lit se coucha[8] attendant la mort, tenant tousjours la coupe[9] tres estroictement.

"Quant les damoiselles virent son corps transmuer par signes de mort, dolentes a merveilles mandirent le pere qui un pou s'estoit[10] alé esbatre, et arriva a l'eure que ja le venim s'espandoit par les vaines. Et lui, plein de doleur du cas avenu, repentant[11] de ce que fait avoit, prist a parler a elle par doulces paroles, en la cuidant reconforter, moult grant dueil menant.[12]

"Et sa fille, si que elle pot,[13] lui re[s]pondi:[14] 'Tancre, reserve tes larmes aultre part, car ilz n'ont cy[15] mestier, ne je ne les desire mie.[16] Tu ressembles la guiere[17] [fol. 134v b] qui occist l'omme, et puis le pleure. Ne te vaulsist il pas mieux que ta lasse fi[l]le[18] vesquist a sa plaisance, secretement amant un bon homme que veoir par ta cruaulté sa[19] dure mort, a ta grant douleur? Laquelle mort fera la chose qui secrete estoit apparoir manifeste.' Et a tant plus ne pot parler, le cuer lui creva, tenant la

---

[1] estoit] pouoit estre
[2] la pitié] la pitié de leur maistresse
[3] vaincue] qui fu vaincue
[4] dites ces paroles] ces paroles dictes
[5] un[e] : *un*
[6] herbes venimeuses dissouldre] dissouldre herbes venimeuses
[7] tout[e] : *tout*
[8] se coucha] se getta
[9] coupe] couppe entre ses bras
[10] mandirent le pere qui un pou s'estoit] manderent le pere qui un pou se estoit pour oublier sa merencolie
[11] repentant] et repentant
[12] en la cuidant reconforter, moult grant dueil menant] en menant moult grant dueil et reconforter la cuidoit
[13] pot] pot parler
[14] re[s]pondi : *repondi*
[15] ilz n'ont cy] cy n'ont elles
[16] desire mie] desire ne vueil
[17] la guiere] un serpent
[18] fil[l]e : *fisle*
[19] sa] si

knewe nothynge of the adventure, [P2r] ne what was the cause of that grete sorowe. So they wept all for pytye and payned them to recomforte her, but it avayled not, and in vayne they asked her moost pryve women the cause of her sorowe.

"And she, overcome with mervayllous sorowe, whan she had wepte ynough sayd: 'O ryght welbyloved herte, I have done al myne offyce that longed to thee. Nowe there resteth nought to doo but to sende my soule to make companye with thyne.' And with these wordes she lyfte her up and opened an almarye, and toke out a boxe where she had put venymous herbes to dyssolve in water to have it redy whan the cause happed. So she cast the water into the cuppe where the herte was, and without ony maner drede dranke it all, and layde her done upon her bed aby-dynge the dethe, holdynge the cup alwaye ryght stratly.

"Whan the women sawe her body chaunge by sygnes of dethe, sorowynge mervayllously, cursed the fader whiche was gone a lytell whyle to dysporte hym. And than he came at the houre that the venym bygan to stretche aboute in the vaynes. And he, ful of sorowe of the case that was happed, repentynge hym of that he had done, bygan to speke to her by swete wordes, trowyng to have recom-forted her, makynge grete sorowe.

"And his doughter answered hym, 'Tancre, reserve thy teeres tyl another tyme, for here is no nede of them and I desyre them not. Thou resemblest the mad man that slewe a man, and after wepte for it. Had it not be better that thou haddest let thy dou[gh]ter[1] lyve at plesaunce, secretly lovyng a man, than to se her hard deth by thy cruelte, [P2v] to thy grete sorowe? The whiche dethe shall make that thynge that was secrete to appere openly.' And then she myght speke no more for her herte brake, holdynge the cuppe ryght straytely in her handes.

---

[1] dou[gh]ter : *dozter*, using z for *yough*

coulpe. Et le las de pere aprés elle[1] mourut de dueil. Et ainsi fina Sismonde, fille du prince de Salerne."

## *Chapitre 59*       Ci dit d'Elisabeth et d'autres amantes

"De rechief conte Bocace ou dit[2] *Livre des Cent Nouvelles* que en la cité de Messino en Ytalie ot une jovencelle jeune fille[3] nommee Lizabeth, laquelle trois freres que elle avoit, par leur escharceté, retardoient de la marier. Et comme yceulx eussent un leur facteur et gouverneur de toutes leurs [fol. 135r a] besoingnes moult belle et avenant jeunes homs, qui[4] leur pere avoit nourry tres[5] son enfance, avint que par la continuele frequentacion[6] de ycellui et d'Elizabeth que ilz s'en amorerent l'un de l'autre. Et celle amour continuerent un temps assez joieusement. Mais a la perfin comme les freres s'en aperceussent comme ceulx qui a grant injure le tindrent, mais grant noise n'en voudrent[7] faire pour non deshonnourer leur seur, delibererent de l'occire. Et de fait, un jour menerent cellui joeunes homs qui Lorens avoit a nom[8] avecques eulx en un leur manoir, et quant la furent venus en leur jardin, l'occistrent[9] et entre arbres l'enterrent. Et eulx, retournez a la Mesinee, firent a croire[10] que Laurens avoient envoyé loing en leurs besoingnes.

"Lizabeth, qui amoit Laurens[11] de grant amour, [fol. 135r b] n'estoit pas aise de ce que elle avoit perdue la presence de son ami. Et le cuer lui en disoit mal tant que une fois, comme contraintte de trop grant amour, ne se pot tenir de demander a l'un[12] de ses freres ou estoit alé Laurens, qui tant demouroit?[13] Par quoy le frere lui respondi, par grant fierté: 'A toy qu'en apartient[14] du savoir? Se plus tu parles de lui, mal pour toy.' Adonc aperçut Helizabeth certainement que ses freres avoient aperçu la chose. Si crut tout certainement[15] que Laurens avoient occis, par quoy merveilleux dueil menoit quant seulete se trouvoit et par nuit, sans prendre nul repos, plouroit parfondement en regraitant cellui que elle amoit

---

[1] la coulpe. Et le las pere aprés elle] la couppe et le las viellart de pere
[2] ou dit] ou
[3] jovencelle jeune fille] jeune fille
[4] belle et avenant jeunes homs, qui] bel et avenant jones homs estoit, lequel
[5] tres] des
[6] que par la continuele frequentacion] par la continuelle frequentacion ensemble
[7] mais grant noise n'en voudrent] non obstant que grant noise n'en voulsissent
[8] a nom] nom
[9] en leur jardin, l'occistrent] ilz l'occirent en leur jardin et
[10] a la Mesinee, firent a croire] a Messine firent a croire a leurs gens
[11] Laurens] le jouvencel
[12] l'un] un
[13] ou estoit alé Laurens, qui tant demouroit] ou ilz avoyent envoyé Laurens
[14] qu'en apartient] qu'appartient
[15] certainement] fermement

And anone after her the fader dyed for sorowe. And thus ended Sysmonde, the doughter of the prynce of Salerne."

### Chapter 59     Of Lyzabeth, and of other lovers

"Also Bocace telleth in the sayd *Booke of Cent Nouvelles* that in the cyte of Messyne in Italy there was a yonge woman named Lyzabeth, the whiche .iii. bretherne of hers by theyr coveytousnes taryed her of maryenge. And they had a factoure and a governoure of all theyr busynesses ryght fayre and a goodly yonge man, whiche that theyr fader had nourysshed all his youthe.

"It happened by the contynuell frequentacyon that they had bytwene them they loved eche other, and this love contynued a whyle ryght joyously. But at the last, as these bretherne perceyved, as they that wolde not make grete noyse for dyshonourynge of theyr syster, were advysed to sle hym. And indede they ledde this yonge man, whiche was named Laurence, with them unto a manere of theves. And when they were come thyder, they had hym into a gardyne and slewe hym, and buryed hym amonge the trees. And they came home agayne to theyr [P3r] house, made them to byleve that they had sente this Laurence ferre into another countre in theyr message. Lyzabeth, whiche loved Laurence of so grete love, was nothynge at hertes ease bycause she had lost the presence of her love. And her herte gave her straungely of this matter, so moche that in a tyme constrayned of ryght love, myght not suffre noo longer but that she asked of one other bretherne where that Laurence was, and why he taryed so longe? By the whiche her broder answered her ryght fyersly and sayd, 'What perteyneth it to thee to knowe?' And then Lyzabeth perceyved certaynly that they had slayne Laurence, for the whiche she made mervaylous sorowe when she was alone. And she wepte all the nyght ryght depely, without takynge ony maner of rest in

tant que malade devint, ou quel mal requist a ses freres que un petit la laissassent aler esbatre en leur heritage de hors [fol. 135v a] la cité.[1]

"Et comme ilz lui eussent ottroyé, et celle a qui le cuer le [disoit][2] toute l'aventure, se trouvast seule ou jardin ou Laurens gisoit mort. En regardant par tout, vit ou estoit le corps la en terre de nouvel soulevé,[3] adonc a tout un pic que elle avoit ap[po]rté[4] fouÿ la terre et fist tant que le corps trouva. Adonc le corps embraçant[5] par grant destrece fist dueil oultre mesure. Mais pour ce que bien savoit que la ne pouoit mie estre longuement de paour que aperceue fust, le corps recouvry de la terre et prist la teste de son ami que ses freres avoient trenchiee, et lia en un cueuvrechief,[6] et l'enterra dedens un de ses[7] grans poz ou l'en plante violiers, et dessus planta de trop belles plante[8] d'une herbe belle et souëf flaurant[9] que on nomme baselic, et a tout ce pot s'en retourna [fol. 135v b] en la cité.

"Mais tant avoit chier ce pot, que d'une fenestre a l'air ou mis l'avoit partir ne ne se pouoit, ne d'autre eaue ne l'arrousoit fors de ses larmes et jour et nuit. Ne par briefs jours ne dura mie[10] ceste chose si que hommes dient que de legier femmes houblient, ains sembloit que son marissement[11] creust de jour en jour. Si fu ja le baselic bel et grant pour la gresse de la terre. Et a brief dire, tant mena celle vie sur ce pot que il avint que aucuns voisins aperceurent comment, sans cesser, celle plouroit a celle fenestre sur ce pot,[12] et aux freres le dirent qui l'espierent et virent la merveille de son dueil. Si furent moult hebahis que ce pouoit estre, et par nuit lui amblerent son pot,[13] dont l'andemain lui sourdi novel anui quant ne [fol. 136r a] le trouva et pour toute grace requeroit que rendu lui fust, et qu'elle leur quittoit

---

[1] de hors la cité] hors de la cité
[2] [disoit] : *blank space*] disoit
[3] ou estoit le corps la en terre de nouvel soulevé] la terre soubzlevee de nouvel la ou le corps estoit
[4] ap[po]rte : *aprte*
[5] le corps embraçant] le embrassant
[6] et lia en un cueuvrechief] et quant assez l'ot baysee, la mist en un beau cueuvrechef
[7] ses] ces
[8] plante] plantes
[9] flaurant] flairant
[10] d'une fenestre a l'air ou mis l'avoit partir ne ne se pouoit, ne d'autre eaue ne l'arrousoit fors de ses larmes et jour et nuit. Ne par briefs jours ne dura mie] ne se partoit d'une fenestre jour ne nuit la ou mis l'avoit et ne l'arrosoit d'autre eaue ne mais de ses larmes, et ne dura pas par briefs jours
[11] de legier femmes houblient, ains sembloit que son marissement] femmes oublient de leger ains sembloit que son dueil
[12] sans cesser, celle plouroit a celle fenestre sur ce pot] cesser celle sur ce pot plouroit a la fenestre
[13] amblerent son pot] emblerent

complaynynge hym that she loved so moche. And therwith she became ryght syke, for the whiche sykenesse she requyred her bretherne that they wolde let her go to dysporte her at theyr maner without the cyte a lytel whyle.

"And when they had graunted her, she wente thyder. And she, to whome her herte gave all this adventure, wente alone into the gardyne where this Laurence lay deed. And lokynge all aboute, she sawe where the body was buryed by the raysynge of the newe erthe. And then she dygged the erthe with a pycoys that she founde there so moche tyll she founde the body; then, embrasynge the body by grete dystresse, made sorowe out of measure. But for so moche that she knewe that she myght not be longe there for fere she sholde be perceyved, toke the body out of the erthe [P3v] and toke the heed of her love that her bretherne had smyten off, and knytted it in a coverchefe and buryed it in one of her grete pottes, wheron they use to set herbes and plantes, and an herbe above it swetely smellynge that is called *basylycon*. And with this potte, she tourned home to her house agayne.

"But she had this potte in so grete cherete that she coude not parte from it but put it in one of her chambre wyndowes in the ayre, and she watered it with none other water but with the teeres of her eyen, nyght and daye. And this thynge endured no lytell whyle, as some of these men saye women forgeteth lyghtly, but it semed that her sorowe encreased from day to daye. And thus was the basy-lycon waxen fayre and grete for the fatnesse of the erthe. And to tell shortely, so moche she ledde this lyfe upon the potte, that it happened that some of her neyghboures perceyved howe she wepte without seasynge at this wyndowe upon the potte, and tolde to her bretherne the mervayle of her sorowe. So they were gretely abasshed what it myght be and by nyght stale awaye the potte, wherof in the mornynge there began to sprynge a newe noyaunce when she founde not her potte. And for all grace she requyred that she myght have her potte agayne,

mais que elle le reust sa part de tous autres biens. Et piteusement disoit en soy[1]
complaingnant:

"'Helas, dequel heure m'enfanta ma mere avec se[2] crueulx freres? Qui tant
heent ma mesuré plaisance que un povre pot de baselic, qui riens ne leur cos-
toit, ne m'ont pas voulu laissier, ne rendre ne le me vuelent et si leur demande
pour tout mariage[3] et pour tout douaire. Helas, envis grant chose me donroient.'[4]
Ainsi la lasse ne cessoit[5] son dueil, tant que au lit s'a gista et tres[6] malade fu. En
laquelle maladie, quoy que on lui offryst ou presentast, elle pour toutes joyes[7] ne
requeroit que son pot: et en ce la morut piteusement. Et ne croy mie que ceste
chose soit mençonge car par dela firent de la complainte de ceste [fol. 136r b] et de
son pot une chançon, que encore ilz chantent.

"Que t'en diroy plus? Je te tendroye longuement se je vouloie de[8] histoires de
femmes en telle fole amour surprises qui trop ont amé de grant amour.[9] D'une
autre raconte Bocace a qui son mary fist mengier le cuer de son ami, qui oncques
puis ne menga; autressi le fist la Dame de Faiel, qui ama le chastelain de Coussi,
la chastelain de Vergy par[10] trop amer. Si fist Yseult qui trop ama Tristan; Dya-
nire, que Hercules amoit, se occist quant il fu mort. Si n'est mie doubte que
moult est grant l'amour d'une constant femme ou elle se assiet, quoy que il soit
des legieres femmes.

"Mais ces piteux exemples et assez d'autres que dire te pourroie, ne doivent
mie estre cause d'esmouvoir les courages des femmes [fol. 136v a] de eulx fichier
en celle mer perilleuse[11] et dampnable de fole amour. Car tousjours en est la fin
en[12] leur grant prejudice et grief en corps, en biens, ou[13] en honneur, et a l'ame,
qui plus est. Si feront que sages, celles qui par bon sens le saront eschuier[14] et
non donner audience a ceulx qui sans sesser se travaillent d'elles decepvoir en
t[e]ll[15] cas."

---

[1] soy] se

[2] se] si

[3] pour tout mariage et] *omitted*

[4] donroient] donnassent

[5] cessoit] finoit

[6] tres] moult

[7] ou presentast, elle pour toutes joyes] elle pour toute joye

[8] diroy plus? Je te tendroye longuement se je vouloie de] diroie? Tousjours te pourroie raconter des

[9] amour] amour sanz varier

[10] de Vergy par] du Vergi mourut par

[11] perilleuse] tres perilleuse

[12] en] a

[13] ou] et

[14] le saront eschuier] la saront eschever

[15] t[e]ll : *tol*

and she wolde quyte it them thoughe she sholde gyve her parte of all her other goodes, and sayd pyteously in complaynynge:

"'Alas, in what houre brought my moder me forthe into this worlde with my cruel bretherne? The whiche hateth my symple pleasaunce, [P4r] that they wyll not leve me a lytell poore potte of basylycon whiche cost them nought, nor yelde it me agayne. And I aske them nothynge elles for my maryage and for my dowry. Alas, it is not grete that I desyre of them.' And thus she lete it passe, but her sorowe never seased, so moche that she layde her on a bed and was sore syke; in the whiche sykenesse, whatsoever one offred her she set not by it, ne by no joye in the worlde but onely her potte. And thus she dyed pyteously. And I thynke not that this thynge is a lesynge, for there they made a songe of the complaynte of this gen[t]ylwoman[1] and of her pot, whiche they synge yet.

"What shall I tell thee more? I sholde holde thee too longe yf I tolde thee the hystoryes of women in suche maner of love taken, whiche have loved of ryght grete love. Of another also telleth Bocace of whome the housbande made to eate the herte of her love, whiche never ete after. The same dyde the Lady of Fayllee, whiche loved the Chastelayne of Coussy by too grete a love. Also Isoude, Trystram; Tyamere, whiche loved Hercules so moche that she slewe herselfe when he was deed. So it is no doubte that there is ryght grete love in a constaunte woman where she setteth her herte, thoughe it be so that there be some women lyght.

"But these pyteous ensamples, and ynowe of others that I myght tell thee, ought not to be the cause to move the courage of women to put them in this peryllous see and dampnable of lewde love. For alway the ende therof is to them grete prejudyce in grefe of body and goodes, [P4v] or dyshonoure in the soule, whiche is most. So they shall do as wyse women, whiche by good wyt can eschewe and not to gyve audyence to them whiche without seasynge travaylleth them to deceyve theym in suche case."

---

[1] gen[t]ylwoman : *gencylwoman*

*Chapitre 60*      Ci dit de Juno, et de pluseurs dames renommees[1]

"Or t'ay raconté[2] de grant foison dames desquelles les histoir[e]s[3] font mencion, mais comme de toutes dire seroit infini proces, laquel chose entrepris n'ay. Et[4] me souffit sans plus que je produise en tesmoingnage aucunes pour[5] contredit ad ce que tu m'as proposé que aucuns hommes dient. Te vueil en conclusion dire d'aucuns[6] qui ont [fol. 136v b] esté au monde moult renommez par divers accidens plus que par grans vertus.

"Juno, fille de Saturnus et de Opis selon les dictiez des poetes et l'erreur des payens, fut tres renommee sur toutes autres femmes de celle[7] loy plus pour sa bonne fortune que pour autre excellence. Elle fut suer[8] Jupiter et mariee a lui, que on clamoit souverain dieu, et pour la grant richece et fortune propice en quoy elle vesqui et habonda avec son mary fut reputee deesse d'avoir. Et les Saniens creoient que pour son estature[9] que ilz avoient aprés sa mort que ilz en estoient mieulx fortunez et lui attribuoient[10] aussi les confors des drois de mariage, ot[11] a son aide recouvroient les femmes en oroisons. Et de toutes pars furent[12] temples [fol. 137r a] d'elle, autelx, prestres, jeux, et sacrefices. Et ainsi fu longuement honnouree des Grieux et de ceulx de Cartage; et avec ce fu aprés portee a Romme et mise ou capitole en la celle de Jupiter coste son mary, et la fu des Rommains qui estoient seigneurs du monde honnouree de plusieurs et diverses serimonies par long temps.

"*Item*, Eur[o]pa[13] qui fu fille de Agenor, roy[14] de Phenice, fu autressi moult renommee pour ce que Jupiter qui l'ama nomma la tierce partie du monde de son nom et est assavoir que des noms de plusieurs femmes ont esté diverses terre[s],[15] citez, et villes nommees, si comme Angleterre d'une femme qui fu nommee Angle, et ainsi[16] autres.

---

[1] *F reverses chap. 60, 61*

[2] raconté] dit

[3] histoir[e]s : *histoirs*

[4] seroit infini proces, laquel chose entrepris n'ay. Et] entrepris n'aye et seroit infini proces

[5] aucunes pour] pour

[6] en conclusion dire d'aucuns] dire en conclusion d'aucunes

[7] de celle] d'icelle

[8] suer] seur de

[9] estature] ymage

[10] attribuoient] attribuerent

[11] ot] et

[12] furent] firent

[13] Item Eur[o]pa : *itemc Euerpa*

[14] Agenor, roy] Agenor

[15] terre[s] : *terre*

[16] ainsi] aussi

## *Chapter 60*       Of Juno, and of other dyvers ladyes of renowne

"Nowe I have tolde thee of grete foyson of ladyes of the whiche the hystoryes maketh mencyon, but for to saye of all the processe sholde be infynyte, the whiche I have not taken in honde; and it suffyseth me without more that I brynge forth some in wytnessynge to saye the contrary to that that thou hast purposed that dyvers men say. I wyl tell thee, in conclusyon, of some that hathe ben in the worlde gretely praysed by dyvers accydentes more than by grete vertues.

"Juno, doughter of Saturnus and of Opys after the sayenges of poetes and the erroure of paynymes was gretely praysed above all other women of that lawe more for her good fortune than for ony other excellence. She was syster of Jupyter and maryed unto hym, whome they called soverayne god, and for the grete rychesse and fortune in whiche she lyved and habounded with her housbande was reputed as goddesse of rychesse. And those madde people byleved that for her stature that she had after her dethe that they were the better fortuned. And they graunted to her also the comforte of the ryghtes of maryage, and by her helpe [P5r] the women recovered in praynge to her. And they made temples of her all aboute: awters, preestes, playes, and sacrefyses. And thus was she longe worshypped of the Grekes, and of them of Cartage. And with that she was brought to Rome after and put in the capytole in the celle of Jupyter, her housbande. And there she was worshypped of Romaynes, that were lordes of the worlde, with many dyvers cerymonyes by longe tyme.

"Also Europe that was doughter of Agenor, kynge of Phenyce, was also gretely praysed for that that Jupyter, whiche loved her, named the thyrde parte of the worlde after her name. And it is to knowe that of the names of dyvers women hathe ben dyvers landes, cytees, and townes named, so as Englonde of a woman that was called Angle, and so of others.

"Jocaste[1] fu royne de Thebes renommee pour sa tres grant infortune, car par mesaventure elle [fol. 137r b] ot espousé son filz aprés ce que il[2] ot occis son propre pere,[3] dont elle et lui riens ne savoient. Et vit que il se despera quant il sceut l'aventure, et puis vid entre occire deux filz que elle en avoit eu.

"*Item*, Meduse ou Gargon fu renommee pour sa tres grant beauté. Elle estoit fille du tres riche roy Porce, duquel le royaume tres habondant estoit enclos de mer. Ceste Meduse, si que dient les anciennes histoires, estoit de si merveilleuse beauté que non pas seulement passoit les autres femmes, mais qui est[4] tres merveilleuse chose et sus nature. Elle avoit le regart tant plaisant avec l'autre beauté du corps et du viaire, et de ses[5] blons cheveux comme fil d'or, longs et crespes, que elle attraioient toute mortelle creature que elle regardoit si a soy que [fol. 137v a] elle rendoit les gens inmouvables.[6] Et pour ce faigny la [f]able[7] que de pierre devenoient.

"Helaine, femme de Menelaus roy de Lacedemoine, fille de Tindarus roy de Ceballe et de Leida sa femme, fu moult renommee pour sa grant beaulté. Et pour ce que il en avint pour cause de[8] ravissement que Paaris fist d'elle, qui fut la choison par quoy Troye fu destruicte, de ceste (quoy que il soit dit de la beauté des autres) afferment les histoires que elle fut la plus belle femme qui oncques

---

[1] Jocaste] Item, Yocaste
[2] il : *ilz*
[3] son propre pere] son pere
[4] est] estoit
[5] de ses] des
[6] inmouvables] comme inmouvables
[7] [f]able : *table*
[8] pour cause de] du

"Jocasta, quene of Thebes, was praysed for her grete infortune for by mysadventure she had wedded her owne sone after that that [he][1] had slayne his owne fader, wherof none of theym bothe knewe. And she sawe that he dyspayred when he knewe the adventure, and after sawe hym slayne bytwene two sones that she had.

"Also Meduse, or [G]argon,[2] was praysed for her grete beaute. She was doughter of the ryche Kynge Porce, of whome the royalme was ryght haboundauntly closed with the see. This Meduse, as the auncyent hystoryes sayth, was of soo mervayllous beaute that not onely she passed all other women but that is a mervayllous thynge and above nature. She had her countenaunce so [P5v] pleasaunt with her beaute of body, and of vysage, and of her yelowe heeres as longe thredes of golde and cryspe, that she drewe every mortall creature that she behelde to her so that she was unmovable to all people. And therfore the fable fayneth that she became a stone.

"Helayne, wyfe of Menela[u]s,[3] kynge of Lacedemoyne, doughter of Tyndarus, kynge of Ceballe and of Leyda his wyfe, was gretely renowmed for her grete beaute. And for that that it happened for bycause of the ravysshynge that Parys made of her, whiche was the cause by the whiche Troye was destroyed, of this quene (thoughe it be sayd of the beaute of others) the hystoryes affermeth that

---

[1] [he] : *she*
[2] [G]argon : *Bargon*
[3] Menela[u]s : *Menelans*

nasquist de mere. Et pour ce distrent les pouetes que elle estoit engendree du dieu Jupiter.

"*Item*, Polixenne, qui fut la mainsnee fille du roy Priant, fut aussi la plus belle pucelle de quoy il soit mencion en nulle histoire. Et avec ce fut [fol. 137v b] de tres ferme et constant courage, comme elle[1] le demonstra en recevant la mort sans changer visage ne chiere quant elle fu decollé[2] sus la tumbe Achilles[3] lors que elle dist que plus lui venoit a gré mourir que estre mené en servage. D'autres asses te pourroy dire, que je laisse pour briefté."

*Chapitre 61*    Dit[4] Christine et Droicture lui respont contre ceulx qui dient que femmes attraient les hommes par leurs jolivetez

Je, Christine, dis ainsi: "Dame, vrayement au propos devant dit, la perilleuse vie amoureuse ad ce que je voy voirement[5] fait moult a eschiver aux femmes qui ont aucun savoir comme elle leur soit tres prejudiciable.[6] Mais grant blasme est donné a celles qui se delittent en estre jolies de leurs atours et [fol. 138r a] vestemens,[7] et dist on que pour attraire les hommes a leur amour le font."

*Response*: "Amie chiere, je ne excuseray mie[8] celles qui trop curieuses et cointes de leurs abillemens sont, car sans faille ce est vice et non mie petit, ne nulle cointerie hors l'estat qui appertient a chascune porter[9] n'est sans blasme. Par quoy,[10] non mie pour excuser le mal, mais afin que nul ne se charge de donner plus grant blasme ne autre qu'il n'y affiert a de telles que on voit jolies, je te dis certainement que il ne vient mie a toutes pour cause d'amours qui leur face faire, ains vient a plusieurs tant hommes comme femmes par droicte condicion et inclinacion naturelle, que ilz se delittent en jolivetez, et[11] en biaulx habiz et [fol. 138r b] riches, en[12] netteté, et en chose proffitables.[13] Et se il leur vient de Nature, fort leur seroit a l'eschiver, combien que le plus vertueux[14] seroit.

---

[1] comme elle] si comme bien
[2] elle fu decollé] on la decola
[3] Achilles] de Achilles
[4] Dit] Cy dit
[5] voy voirement] voy
[6] tres prejudiciable] prejudiciable
[7] de leurs atours et vestemens] en leur vestemens et atours
[8] je ne excuseray mie] il ne m'appartient a excuser
[9] porter] a porter
[10] Par quoy] Mais neant moins
[11] et] ou
[12] en] ou
[13] chose proffitables] choses pontificales
[14] leur vient de Nature, fort leur seroit a l'eschiver, combien que le plus vertueux] se il est ainsi que de Nature leur viengne, fort leur seroit a l'eschever combien que grant vertu

she was the fayrest woman that ever was borne of moder. And therfore these poetes saye that she was engendred of Jupyter, the grete god.

"Also Polexene, that was the meke doughter of Kynge Pryamus, was also as fayre a mayde as is made mencyon in ony hystore. And with that, she was ryght stable and constaunte of courage, as she shewed in receyvynge the deth without vysage or chere when she was heeded upon the tombe of Achylles, then she sayd that it was more agreable to her to dye than to be ledde in servage. Of others ynowe I myght tell thee, whiche that I leve for shortenesse."

*Chapter 61*  **Here speketh Christine, and Ryghtwysnesse answereth ayenst them that [say that]**[1] **women drawe men to them by theyr gaynesse** [P6r]

I, Christine, sayd thus: "Madame, truely to the purpose abovesayd, the peryllous lyfe of foly love, to that that I se, truely it ought to be eschewed of women that have ony understandynge, in soo moche that it is to them so prejudyable. But there is grete blame gyven to them that delyte them to be gay in theyr araye and clothynge, and some saye that they do it for to drawe these men to theyr love."

*Answere*: "Dere love, I shall not excuse them that be curyous and quaynte of theyr aray, for without fayle that [is][2] vyce and not lytell, ne no quayntenesse out of estate that perteyneth to every persone to bere is not without blame. By the whiche not to excuse the evyll, but to the entente that none charge them to gyve greter blame ne other that it affermeth not of suche women that one seeth fresshe and gaye, I say to thee certaynely that it cometh not to all women bycause of love that they do so. But it cometh to many, as well men as women, by ryght good condycyon and naturall inclynacyon that they delyte theym in fresshenesse, and in fayre habytes and ryche, in clennesse, and in profytable thynges. And yf it come to them by kynde, it were herde to them to eschewe it, howe be it that it sholde be the more vertuous.

---

[1] that [say that] : *them that*
[2] that [is] vyce : *that vyce*

"N'est il pas escript de l'apostre saint Barthelmeu,[1] qui fu gentil homme, que non obstant que Jhesucrist[2] preschast pouvreté et simplece en toutes choses, toutevoies le benoit apostre toute sa vie vesti de drap de soye, frangé dessoubz[3] et ourlé de pierres precieuses? Et par Nature lui venoit d'estre richement vestu, qui est communement chose curieuse et pompeuse, et toutevoyes ne pecha il pas. Et aucuns veulent dire[4] que pour celle cause souffry Nostre Seigneur qu'en son martir il y laissast la pel et fut escorchiez. Et ces choses je te dis pour monstrer que nul ne doit jugier de [fol. 138v a] conscience d'autruy pour habit ne pour vestemens,[5] car a seul Dieu apartient jugier des creatures. Et te diray sur ce aucuns exemples."

*Chapitre 62*     De Claudine, femme rommaine

"Bocace raconte et pareillement le dit Valere que Claudine, qui fu noble dame de Romme, moult se delictoit en beaulx vestemens et delicatifs.[6] Et pour ce que en ce estoit[7] aucunement plus delicative que les autres dames de Romme, aucuns presumerent mal contre elle et contre sa chasteté au prejudice de sa renommee. Si avint en l'anne .xv.ᵉ de la bataille seconde de Auffrique que l'ymage de Pissimunde,[8] mere des dieux selon leur oppinion, dot estre apportee de[9] Romme. La furent assemblees toutes les nobles dammes de [fol. 138v b] Romme pour aler a l'encontre, et fut mis l'ymage ou[10] une nef sus le Tibre, mais le mariniers ne pouoient de toute leur force arriver a port. Adonc Claudine, qui bien savoit que elle estoit mescreue a tort pour[11] sa joliveté, s'agenoilla devant l'ymage et fist sa priere tout hault, en disant a la deesse que, ainsi vrayement que elle savoit que sa chasteté estoit entiere et neant corrompue, lui voulsist donner grace que elle seule peust tirer la nef a port.[12] Et adonc confiant a[13] sa purté, prist sa ceinture et fist lier

----

[1]  saint Barthelmeu] Berthelemi
[2]  Jhesucrist] Nostre Seigneur
[3]  toute sa vie vesti de drap de soye, frangé dessoubz] fu toute sa vie vestu de drap de soie frangé
[4]  Et aucuns veulent dire] en ce et veulent dire aucuns
[5]  pour vestemens] vestemens
[6]  delicatifs] curieux et en joliz atours
[7]  estoit] elle estoit
[8]  que l'ymage de Pissimunde] Pisismunde
[9]  de] a
[10]  ou] en
[11]  pour] pour cause de
[12]  la nef a port] la nef
[13]  confiant a] se confiant en

"It is not wryten of the appostle Saynt Barthylmewe, the whiche was a ryght grete gentyllman, that notwithstandynge that Our Savyoure Cryste Jhesu preched and teched strongly of poverte and symplenesse in all maner of thynges, yet the blessyd [P6v] apostle all his lyfe ware clothes of sylke, frenged aboute with golde and precyous stones. And it cometh to hym of kynde to be rychely arayed, the whiche is comunely a curyous thynge and full of pryde, and yet he synned not; and some wyll say that for that cause, Our Lorde suffred that for his martyr-dome he lefte his skynne and was slayne. And these thynges that I tell thee for to showe that no man ought to juge another of conscyence for his habyte, ne for his araye, for it perteyneth onely to God to be juge of all creatures. And upon that, I shall tell thee some ensamples."

## Chapter 62    Of Claudyne, a woman of Rome

"Also Bocace and Valere telleth that Claudyne, whiche was a noble lady of Rome, delyted gretely in fayre clothynges and delycate. And for that that she was mo[re]¹ delycatyfe than the other ladyes of Rome, some presumed shrewdely ayenst her and ayenst her chastyte, to the prejudyce of her good name. So it happened in the .xv. yere of the seconde batayle of Aufryke that the ymage of Pyssemonde moder of the goddes after opynyon had ben borne fro Rome. There were assembled all the noble ladyes of Rome to go mete with the ymage, whiche was put in a shyp upon Tybre. But the maryners myght not aryve at the porte for all theyr strength. Then Claudyne, whiche knewe well that she was mysbyleved [Q1r] of wronge for her fresshnesse, she kneled before the ymage and made her prayer all on hyghe in sayenge to the goddesse, that as truely as that she knewe that her chastyte was hole and not corrupte, that she wolde gyve her grace that she alone myght drawe the shyp to the haven. And then, trustynge to her clennesse, toke her gyrdell and bounde it to the sterne of the shyp, and a[f]ter² drewe the shyp to the ryvayle

---

¹ mo[re] : *mo=*
² a[f]ter : *after*

au bot de la nef, et puis la tira a rive aussi legierement comme[1] se tous les mariniers du monde y eussent esté, ad[o]nc[2] chascun fut esmervelliez.

"Ceste exemple ne t'ay pas dit [fol. 139r a] pour chose que je cuide que celle
ymage, que ilz comme folz et mescreans appelloient deesse, eust poissance de
exsaucier la priere de Claudine. Mais l'ay dit pour monstrer que celle qui tant
estoit jolie ne laissoit pas pour tant a estre chaste. Et par ce le demonstra que elle
ot fiance que la verité de sa chasteté lui fust secourable, laquel chose lui ayda et
non autre deesse."

*Chapitre 63*     **Comment ne dit pas estre mesjugie sur aucunes femmes
pour tant se en biaulx habiz se delittent**[3]

"Et que femmes poson que elles voulsissent estre amees se penassent pour
celle cause d'estre jolies, baudes, mignotes, et curieuses, je te prouveray que celle
achoison ne les fait pas plus tost ne mieulx amer de hommes sages et de value,[4]
et que plus tost et mieulx sont [fol. 139r b] amees[5] de ceulx qui aiment honneur les
vertueuses femmes, et honnestes, et simples, que les plus jolies poson que mains[6]
fussent belles. Si me pourroit doncques estre respondu, puis que femmes attraient
les hommes par leur vertu et honnesté,[7] mieulx vaudroit que moins bonnes fussent; mais celle raison[8] riens ne vauldroit. Car les bonnes et proffitables choses
ne doivent pas estre laissees a cultiver et a acroistre pour tant se le[9] folz mal en
usent, et chacun doit faire son devoir en bien faisant quoy que avenir doye. Et
qu'il soit ainsi que maintes soient amees pour leurs vertus et honnesté je t'en
donray exemple, premierement de plusieurs sainctes de paradis te pourroie dire[10]
qui furent couvoitees d'ommes pour leur honnesteté.

"*Item*, Lucrece, de [fol. 139v a] laquelle cy dessus t'ay parlé qui fu efforcee, la
grant honnesteté d'elle fu cause de en amourer Tarquin plus que ne[11] sa beaulté.

---

   [1] comme] que
   [2] ad[o]nc : *adnc*] Dont
   [3] Comment ne dit pas estre mesjugie sur aucunes femmes pour tant se en biaulx
habiz se delittent] Dit Droiture que plusieurs femmes sont amees pour leurs vertus plus
que autres pour leurs jolivetez
   [4] value] vale
   [5] sont amees] amees sont
   [6] les vertueuses femmes, et honnestes, et simples, que les plus jolies poson que
mains] les vertueuses, honnestes, et simples que les plus cointes poson que moins
   [7] honnesté] honnesteté puis que c'est mal que ilz soient attrais
   [8] celle raison] cest argument
   [9] le] les
   [10] de plusieurs sainctes de paradis te pourroie dire] te pourroie dire de plusieurs
saintes de paradis
   [11] ne] ne fu

as lyghtly as thoughe all the maryners of the worlde had ben there. And then everybody mervaylled therof.

"I have not tolde thee this ensample for the thynge that I wene that the ymage, that they as foles and myscreauntes call a goddesse, that had myght to lyfte up the prayer of Claudyne. But I have tolde it thee for to shewe thee that she that was so gaye lefte not for so moche to be chaste. And by that she shewed that she had that the trouthe of her chastyte was socourable to her, the whiche helped her and not the goddesse."

*Chapter 63*    **Howe they lye not upon some women for so moche thoughe they delyte them in fayre clothynge and araye**

"And those women that wolde be byloved payne them for the cause to be gaye, nyce, and curyous: I shall prove thee that encheson maketh them not the sooner ne the better to be loved of wyse men and of worshyp, and more sooner and better ben these [Q1v] vertuous women, honest, and symple, loved of them that love worshyp than the moost jolyest and fayrest. So one myght answere me thus, syth that women drawe these men to theym by theyr vertue and honeste, it were better that there were fewer good women; but the reason sholde be nought worth. For the good and profytable thynges ought not to be lefte to be tolde and to encrease for that thoughe the foles abuse them. And every man ought to do his devoyre as wel doynge thoughe it fortune the contrary. And that it is soo that many women ben loved for theyr vertues and honeste I shall shewe thee ensamples, fyrst of dyvers sayntes of paradyse I myght tell thee that were coveyted of men for theyr honeste.

"Lucresse of whom I spake here above, whiche was ravysshed: the grete honeste of her was cause that Tarquyne loved her more than her beaute. For as her

Car comme le mary d'elle fust une fois a un soupper la ou estoit cellui Tarquin qui puis l'efforça et d'autres plusieurs chevaliers, pristrent a parler de leurs femmes, et chascun disoit que la sienne estoit la meilleur. Mais pour savoir la verité et esprouver laquelle de leurs femmes estoit digne de plus grant louenge, monterent a cheval et alerent en leurs maisons, et celles que ilz trouverent occuppees en plus honnestes[1] office et eouvre furent les plus reputees.[2] Dont il avint que Lucrece en toutes les autres[3] fut trouvee la plus honnestement occuppé comme tres sage et tres preudefemme, [fol. 139v b] vestue d'un[e][4] simple robe parmi son hostel entre ses femmes ouvrant de laine et parlant de vertueuses choses. La fut venue[5] le dit Tarquin, filz du roy, avec le mary d'elle qui regardant sa tres grant honnesteté, son simple[6] maintien, et sa maniere coye fu tant enamorez d'elle que il se mist a faire la folie que il fist puis."

## Chapitre 64 . Ci dit de la royne Blanche, mere de saint Louys, et d'autres bonnes amees[7] pour leurs vertus

"Semblablement fu amee pour son tres grant savoir, prudence, vertu,[8] et bonté la tres noble royne Blanche de France,[9] mere de saint Louis, du conte de Champaigeie, non obstant eust elle ja passé la fleur de sa joeunesce. Mais ycellui noble conte, escoutant la royne[10] parlant a lui [fol. 140r a] par si sages paroles lors que il avoit entrepris guerre contre le dit saint Loys — et la bonne[11] dame l'en reprenoit[12] en disant que ce ne deust il mie faire consideré les biens que son filz lui avoit fais — le conte la regardoit par grant entente, se esmerveillant du grant bien et vertu d'elle. Par quoy il fu si fort surpris de s'amour[13] que il ne savoit que faire, ne dire, ne lui osast[14] pour mourir car bien savoit qu'en elle avoit tant de bien et de vertu[15] que jamais ne s'i accorderoit. Si en souffry depuis celle heure moult de maux par fol desir qui le contraignoit; toutevoies, lui respondi adoncque elle ne

---

[1] honnestes] honneste
[2] reputees] reputees et les plus honorees
[3] autres] autres femmes
[4] d'un[e] : *d'un*
[5] venue] venu
[6] simple] simple et bel
[7] bonnes amees] bonnes et sages amees
[8] vertu] vertus
[9] royne Blanche de France] royne de France Blanche
[10] royne] sage et bonne royne
[11] bonne] vaillant
[12] reprenoit] reprenoit sagement
[13] s'amour] l'amour
[14] dire, ne lui osast] lui osast dire
[15] de bien et de vertu] de bonté

housbande was ones at a soupere there as this Tarquyne was whiche ravysshed
her after, and dyvers other knyghtes with theym, they began to speke of theyr
wyves and every man sayd that his was best. But to knowe the trouthe and to
prove whiche of theyr wyves was moost worthy to be praysed, every man wente
to horsebacke and wente to theyr houses, and tho[s]e[1] that they founde occupyed
in the moost honest offyces and the werke were the more of reputacyon. Wherof
it fortuned that Lucresse amonge all the other was founde the moost honestly
occupyed as ryght a wyse and a good woman, clothed [Q2r] in a symple gowne
amonge her maydens and her women, werkynge in wulles and spekynge of vertuous thynges. And thyder came the sayd Tarquyne sone of the kynge with her
housba[n]de,[2] whiche beholdynge her grete honeste, her symple countenaunce
and her styll manere was so amerous of her that it caused hym to do the folye that
he dyde after."

## Chapter 64     Of Quene Blaunche, moder of Saynt Lewes, and of other good women loved for theyr vertues

"The same wyse was loved for her grete understandynge, wysdome, vertue, and
bounte the ryght noble Quene Blaunche, moder of Saynt Lewes, of the erle of
Champayne, notwithstandynge she had passed the floure of her youthe. But this
noble erle, herynge the quene speke to hym with so wyse wordes when he had
begon to warre agaynst the sayd[3] Saynt Lewes—and the good lady spake to hym
of it, sayenge that he ought not to do so consyderynge the welthes that her sone
had done to hym—the erle behelde her by grete entent, mervaylynge hym of the
grete goodnesse and vertue of her, by the whiche he was so strongely undertaken
with her love that he wyst not what to say nor do, ne durst never warre ayenst
hym after. For he knewe wel that there was so moche welthe in her, and of vertue
also, that he coude never do otherwyse but accorde with hym and her. So he suffred fro that houre for the [Q2v] many troubles by lewde desyres that constrayned
hym, yet she answered hym by the same. And then when she doubted not that

---

[1] tho[s]e : *thoughe*
[2] housba[n]de : *housbade*
[3] sayd : *sayd sayd*

se doubtast que jamais guerre ne feroit au roy ains vouloit estre tout sien, [fol. 140r b] et que elle fust certaine que cuer, et corps, et quanque il avoit estoit tout soubsmis a son commandement.[1] Si l'ama toute sa vie depuis celle heure et ne laissa pour pou d'esperance que il eust d'avenir a s'amour. Si[2] faisoit ses complaintes a amours en dictiez, en louant moult grandement sa dame,[3] lesquelx moult beaulx dictiez que il fist furent mis en chant moult delitables, et en sa sale a Prouvins et aussi a Troyes les fist escripre; et encore en plusieurs lieux apparent.[4] Et ainsi te pourroye dire d'assez d'autres."

Et je, Christine, respondis a tant:[5] "Certainement, dame, a vostre propos cas[6] aucques parelz ay veu[7] par experience car je congnois des femmes moult vertueuses que par ce que elles moult confessé en [fol. 140v a] eulx[8] complaingnant a moy de la desplaisance que elles y prenoient plus ont esté requises depuis[9] le temps que leur plus grant beaulté et jounece a esté passee que elles n'estoient en leur grant[10] fleur. Dont elles disoient, 'Helas,[11] que veult ce dire? Voyent ces hommes en moy aucune contenance fole, par quoy ilz aient couleur et cause de penser que je fusse d'accord de faire si grant folie?' Et j'ape[r]çoy[12] maintenant manifestement par ce que vous dites que le grant bien d'elles[13] estoit cause de les faire amer, et est bien contre l'oppinion de plusieurs gens qui dient que une preudefemme qui veult estre chaste ne sera ja celle[14] ne veult couvoitié ne requise."

---

[1] a son commandement] au commandement d'elle

[2] si] et

[3] dictiez en louant moult grandement sa dame] ses dictiez en louant moult gracieusement dame

[4] en chant moult delitables, et en sa sale a Prouvins et aussi a Troyes les fist escripre; et encore en plusieurs lieux apparent] en chants moult delitables et les fist escripre en sa sale a Prouvins et aussi a Troys, et ancores y apperent

[5] a tant] adont

[6] cas] car

[7] veu] veus

[8] des femmes moult vertueuses que par ce que elles moult confessé en eulx] de femmes vertueuses et sages, lesquelles, par ce que elles m'ont confessé en elles

[9] plus ont esté requises depuis] ont esté plus requises puis

[10] grant] plus grant

[11] 'Helas, . . .'] 'Dieux! Et que . . .'

[12] Et j'ape[r]çoy : *japecoy*] Mais j'apperçoy

[13] d'elles] d'elle

[14] celle] se elle

he sholde never make warre to the kynge but wolde be all his, and that she was in certayne that herte and body and all that ever he had was submytted to her commaundement, soo she loved hym all his lyfe after. And he lefte not for a lytell wanhope that he myght come to her love. So he made his lovely complayntes in dyttyes, praysynge gretely his lady, the whiche goodly dyttyes that he made, he put them to a musycyen to set them into songe ryght delectably. And in his halle at Provynce and also at Troyes he made wryte them and yet they appere in many places. And thus myght I tell thee of many other."

And I, Christine, answered: "Madame, to your purpose in lyke case I have sene by experyence, for I knowe many vertuous women that by that they have confessed them to me, in complaynynge them to me of the pleasaunce that they toke there they have ben more requyred syth the tyme that theyr grete beaute and youthe hath ben past than they were in theyr grete floure, wherof they sayd: 'Alas, what wyll ye that I say to these men—seynge in me ony countenaunce of foly, by the whiche they have coloure and cause to thynke that he was of accorde to do so grete foly?' And I perceyve nowe openly by that that ye saye that the grete welthe of them hathe ben cause to make them to love. And it is well contrary to the opy[n]yon[1] of dyvers folke that say [Q3r] that a good woman that wolde be chaste shall never be that woman that lyst to be coveyted nor requyred."

---

[1] opy[n]yon : *opyuyon*

*Chapitre 65*      **Dit Christine et Droicture lui respont contre ceulx qui dient que femmes par nature sont escharces** [fol. 140v b]

"Je ne vous sçay plus que repliquer, chiere dame: toutes mes questions sont solues, et m'est bien avis que assez avez prouvé[1] faulx les mesdiz que tant d'ommes dient sur femmes, et mesmement qu'entre les vices femmenins leur soit avarice chose naturelle. Mais ce ne m'appert mie par ce que vous dites."[2]

*Response*: "Amie chiere, je te dy certainement que avarice n'est point plus naturelle es femmes que[3] es hommes; et se moins y est, ce scet Dieux. Et ce pueux tu veoir par ce que trop plus de maulx se font au monde et encuerent par la grant avarice de divers hommes, que par la petite[4] des femmes. Mais si que devant t'ay[5] dit, trop bien congnoit le fol [fol. 141r a] le petit meffait de son voisin, mais son grant crime[6] il ne apperçoit. Et par ce que on voit aucunes fois[7] que femmes se delittent en amasser toilles, filez, telz chosetes,[8] on les repute averes. Mais je te promet que grant foison en y a[9] que s'elles avoient de quoy, elles ne seroient pas escharces ne averes en honneurs faire mais qu'en puet. Mais pouvre homme, s'il est eschars,[10] on les tient communement si estroictes[11] d'argent que ce pou que elles ont, elles[12] gardent pour ce que bien scevent que ne leur est pas legier avoir de l'autre. Et si y a[13] aucunes gens qui les reputent escharces, pour ce que aucunes[14] ont mariz folz, larges gasteurs de biens et gormans. Et les pouvres femmes qui scevent bien [fol. 141r b] que le mainage de l'ostel a dicité de ce que folement est despendu, et que elles et leurs las d'enfans le pourront comparer chier, ne s'en[15] peuent tenir d'en parler a leurs mariz et de les amonester de mendre

---

[1] prouvé] prouvé estre
[2] mesmement qu'entre les vices femmenins leur soit avarice chose naturelle. Mais ce ne m'appert mie par ce que vous dites] mesmement n'appiert pas ce que ilz tesmoignent tant communement que entre les vices femenins avarice leur soit chose si naturelle
[3] que] ne que
[4] la petite] celle
[5] t'ay] t'est
[6] crime: *craime*] crisme
[7] aucunes fois] communement
[8] toilles, filez, telz chosetes] toiles, et filez, et telz chosettes qui sont propices a mesnage
[9] que grant foison en y a] qu'il est assez de femmes et a grant foison
[10] eschars] escharces ne averes en honneurs faires et donner largement ou bien seroit employé. Mais qu'en peut mais povre personne se elle est escharce
[11] si estroictes] si a destroit
[12] ont, elles] elles peuent avoir, le gardent
[13] ne leur est pas legier avoir de l'autre. Et si y a] a grant peine en peuent recouvrer. Et si est
[14] aucunes] les aucunes d'elles
[15] chier, ne s'en] ne se

## Chapter 65     Christine asketh, and Ryghtwysnes answereth ayenst them that saye that women by nature ben scarse

"Replye you I can no more, myne owne lady, for my questyons ben well assoyled, and it semeth me that ye have ynoughe proved false the evyll sayenges that so many men saye upon women. And also amonge other vyces of women, they saye that avaryce is a naturall thynge in them, but it appereth not so to me by that that ye saye."

*Answere*: "Dere doughter, I tell thee certaynly that avaryce is no more naturall in women than in men; and yf there be lesse, God knoweth it. And that thou mayst se by that that by the covetysenesse of dyvers men there is moche more harme done to the worlde than by the lytell covetysenesse of women. But as I have sayd to thee before, that the fole knoweth better the lytell trespace in his neyghboure than he dothe the grete cryme of hymselfe. And by that that one sethe often tymes that women delyte them in lovynge to spynne and carde, suche thynges men call covetyse. But I promyse thee that there ben grete foyson of them that yf they had wherof, they wolde not be scarse ne covetouse as of that that sholde be [Q3v] to theyr worshyp. But poore men holde comunely theyr wyves so strayte that they must nedes kepe that they have, for they wote well it were no lyght thynge to have more. And so there ben some people that calleth women scarse, for that they have maryed full large wastours of theyr goodes. And the poore women that knewe well that theyr housbandes have spended lewdely that that sholde fynde theyr housholde, and that they and theyr chyldren dare not compare chere, and maye not holde them to speke to theyr housbandes

despense. Si n'est mie tel choses¹ avarice ne escharceté ains est signe de tres grant prudence.² Et tel debat voit on souvent es mariages par ce que aux hommes ne plait pas tel amonnestement, et par ce donnent blasme aux femmes de ce de quoy louer les deussent. Mais qu'il soit vray que cellui vice d'avarice ne soit pas si en elles comme aucuns veulent dire, il appert aux aumosnes que tres voulentiers elles font, et Dieux scet quans prisonniers, mesmes en terre de Sarazins, quans diseteus et quans besoingneux, gentilx hommes, et [fol. 141v a] aultres ont esté et sont tous les jours aval le monde reconfortez³ et secourus par les femmes et par leur avoir.⁴

"Ne furent pas escharces les dames de Romme quant ou temps que la cité estoit moult grevee de guerre,⁵ par quoy tout le commun tresor de la ville estoit despendu en⁶ gens d'armes, dont a grant doleur⁷ estoient les Rommains de trouver voye d'avoir argent pour mettre sus une grant armee que a force⁸ leur estoit neccessaire. Mais les dames par leur franche liberalité, et mesmement les veusves, s'assemblerent et tous leurs joyaulx et ce que elles avoient sans riens espargner, porterent aux princes de Romme et franchement leur baillerent. De laquel chose moult [fol. 141v b] furent les dames louees, et depuis leur furent rendus leurs joyaulx, et a bon droit car cause avoient esté de⁹ racouvrement de Romme."

*Chapitre 66*     **Ci dit de la riche dame liberale nommee Buise**

"De liberalité de femme autressi est escript es *Fais de Rommains* de la vaillant riche preudefemme Buise ou Pauline, qui estoit en la terre de Puille ou temps que Hammibal grevoit tant les Rommains par feu, par fer, que aucques toute Ytalie despouilla d'ommes et de biens. Avint que de la grant desconfiture de Canes, dont Hamibal ot si noble victoire, plusieurs Rommains s'en fuirent qui eschapperent de la bataille, navrez et bleciez. Mais celle vaillant dame Buse recevoit tous ceulx que elle pouoit avoir tant que jusques [fol. 142r a] au nombre de .x.ᵐ en recueilli en ses maisons, car moult estoit de grant richece. Si les fist garir a ses despens, et tous secouru de s[on]¹⁰ avoir, tant que par l'aide et reconfort que elle leur fist, s'en porent retourner a Romme et remettre sus leur armee, de laquel

¹ choses] chose
² prudence] prudence. Voire, j'entens de celles qui le font discretement
³ reconfortez] de confortez
⁴ *R see annotations for added passage*
⁵ guerre] guerres
⁶ en] es
⁷ doleur] douleur et souci
⁸ force] faire
⁹ de] du
¹⁰ s[on] : *sa*

and to counsayle them of lesse despence. So suche thynges is no coveytyse ne scarsenesse, but it is a sygne of ryght grete prudence. And suche debates one may se often tymes in maryages by that that suche counsayllynge pleaseth not to the men, and by that they gyve blame to the women of that they ought to prayse them of. But that it be true of that this vyce of avaryce be not in them, so as some wyll say, it appereth to almesse that with ryght good wyll they do dayly. And God knoweth it howe many prysoners in the londe of the Sarazyns, howe many nedy gentylmen and others have ben and ben all dayes lowe in the worlde comforted and socoured by women and by theyr goodes.

"The ladyes of Rome were not scarse when in the tyme that the cyte was gretely greved with warre, by the whiche all the comune treasoure of the towne was wasted and spended on men of armes. Wherof it was grete sorowe to the Romaynes to fynde the way to have sylver to put forth an armye, whiche [Q4r] was of force ryght necessary for them. But the ladyes by theyr owne fre wyll and also the wydowes assembled them, and brought all theyr jewelles and al that they had, without sparynge ony thynge to the prynces of Rome, and freely toke it them. Of the whiche thynge the ladyes were gretely praysed, and afterwardes all theyr jewelles and goodes were yelded to them agayne, and of good ryght: for they were the cause of the recoverynge of Rome."

*Chapter 66*     **Of the ryche lady and lyberall named Buyse**

"Of the lyberalyte of women, also it is wryten in the *Dedes of the Romaynes* of the worshypfull ryche woman Buyse or Paulyne, whiche was in the londe of Puylle in the tyme that Hanyball greved so moche the Romaynes by fyre and yren that he despoyled almost all Italy of men and of goodes. It happened that of the grete dyscomfyture of Canes, wherof Hanyball had so noble a vyctorye, many Romaynes fledde that scaped from the batayle, wounded and hurte. But this worshypfull Lady Buyse receyved all them that she myght have anone to the nombre of .x. thousande, and gadered them into her houses, for she was of grete rychesse. Soo she made them to be heled at her cost and charge and socoured them all with her goodes, soo moche that [Q4v] by the helpe and comforte that she dyde to them they myght tourne agayne to Rome and set up theyr armes agayne, of the whiche

chose elle fut moult grandement louee. Si ne doubtes pas, amie chiere, que de infinies largeces, courtoisies, et liberalitez de femmes te pourroye dire.

"Et mesmement sans aler plus loins querre histoires, combien que d'asses d'aultres largeces de dames de ton temps se pourroit dire? Ne fusse[11] pas grant liberalité que la noble dame de la Riviere nommee Margarite, qui encores est en vie? Et femme fu jadis [fol. 142r b] de Messire Burel, seign[eur][12] la Riviere, premier chamberlan du sage roy Charles. Celle dame, comme elle ait tousjours esté sage, vaillant, et bien morigniee, avint une fois entre les autres que elle, estant a une moult belle feste ou[13] avoit moult grant foison de nobles dames et de chevaliers, et de gentilz[14] hommes en grans paremens; adonc celle noble dame qui belle estoit et joeune,[15] comme elle regardast la noble chevalerie que la estoit, avisa que point n'y estoit entre les autres un moult notable chevalier et de grant renommee pour vivant[16] que on nommoit Messire Emenion de Pommiers. Celle dame[17] ne laissa pas pour tant se cellui Emonion[18] estoit moult viaulx a avoir memoire [fol. 142v a] de lui pour cause de sa bonté et vaillance, ains lui[19] sembla que plus bel parement ne puet estre en une assemblee que hommes notables et de renommee, tout soient envieillis.[20] Si va demander moult[21] ou estoit cellui Messire Emenion,[22] que il n'estoit a l'essemblee? Si[23] lui fut dit que il estoit en prison ou chastellet de Paris pour .v.ᶜ frans en quoy il estoit[24] obligiez a cause des voyages que souvent il faisoit en armes.

"'Ha!' dist la noble dame. 'Quel grant honte ad ce royaume, souffrir une seule heure un tel homme estre en prisonne pour debte!' Adonc celle prist le chapel d'or que elle avoit sur sa teste, moult riche[25] et bel, et sur ses blons cheveux mist en lieu une chappel de pervanche. Si le bailla a certains messages et dist: 'Alez et baillez

---

[11] fusse] fu ce

[12] seig[neur] : *seig*] de

[13] estant a une moult belle feste ou] estoit en une moult belle feste que faisoit a Paris, le duc d'Angiou, qui puis fu roy de Cecile, en laquelle feste

[14] de gentilz] gentilz

[15] celle noble dame qui belle estoit et joeune] dame qui belle et jeune estoit

[16] vivant] lors vivant

[17] Celle dame] Elle

[18] Emonion] Messire Emenion de Pommiers

[19] pour cause de sa bonté et vaillance, ains lui] ains la bonté et vaillance dont il estoit en fist avoir souvenance a la dame, a qui bien sembla

[20] envieillis] ilz vieulx

[21] demander moult] moult demander

[22] Messire Emenion] chevalier

[23] Si] Il

[24] estoit] s'estoit

[25] sa teste, moult riche] son chef, riche

thynge she was ryght gretely praysed. So doubte ye not, dere frende, that of infynyte women large, curtoys, and lyberall I myght tell thee ynoughe.

"And also without sekynge more ferther the hystoryes as well of other largesse of ladyes I myght tell thee ynoughe. Ne was not the lyberalyte grete of the noble lady de la Ryvere named Margarete whiche is yet on lyve, and was somtyme wyfe of the Lorde Burell, lorde de la Ryvere and fyrste chambrelayne of the wyse Kynge Charles? This lady, as she that was alwaye wyse, worshypfull, and well manered, it happened in a tyme amonge others that she beynge at a grete feest where there was grete foyson of noble ladyes, and of knyghtes, and of gentylmen in grete apparayle; then this noble lady whiche was fayre and yonge, as she behel[d]e[1] the noble chevalry that was there, thought that there was [not there][2] amonge others ryght a notable knyght and of grete worshyp in his lyvynge that was called Syr Emenyon de Pomyners. This lady lefte not, for so moche that he was a goodly man to have remembraunce of hym bycause of his worthynesse and bounte, her thought that more fayrer araye myght not be in a company than notable men and of good fame, thoughe that they were olde. So she asked gretely where this Syr Emenyon was, that he was not at that assemble? So it was tolde her that he [R1r] was in pryson in the castell of Parys for fyve hondred frankes in whiche he was bounde for a vyage that he dyde in armes, as he dyde ofte tymes.

"'Ha,' sayd the noble lady, 'what shame is this to the realme, to suffre suche a man to be an houre in pryson for dette?' And than she toke the chapellet of golde that she had upon her hede, ryght ryche and fayre, and put upon her instede of that a chapellet of pervencle. And so she toke it to a certayne messagere and sayd, 'Go and put this chapellet in plegge for that he oweth, and that he be delyvered

---

[1] behel[d]e : *beheloe*
[2] [not there] : *no chere*

ce chappel en gaige [fol. 142v b] de ce qu'il doit, et que tantost il soit[1] delivré et viengne cy.' Laquel chose fu faicte, dont grant chose[2] elle fut louee."

## *Chapitre 67*      Ci dit des princeces et dames de France

Encore moy, Christine, dis ainsi: "Dame, puis que vous avez rementue ceste dame qui est a mon temps, et qu'entree estes au propos[3] des dames de France ou qui y sont demourantes, je vous prie qu'il vous plaise a me dire d'elles ce qu'il vous en semble et s'il vous est avis que bon soit que il en y ait de hebergiees[4] en nostre cité: car pour quoy doivent elles estre houbliees, ne que les estranges?"

   *Response*: "Certainement, Christine, je te respons que moult en y voy[5] de tres vertueuses, et bien me plaist que elles soient de noz citoienes. Et tout premierement n'y[6] sera pas reffusee la noble royne [fol. 143r a] de France Ysabel de Baviere, a present par grace de Dieu regnant, en laquelle n'a raim de cruaulté, extorcion, ne quelconques mal vice, mais toute bonne amour et benignieté vers ses subgiez.

   "Ne fait aussi tres grandement a louer la belle, joeune, bonne, et sage duchece de Berry, femme du duc Jehan, jadis filz du roy Jehan de France et frere du sage roy Charles? Laquelle noble duchece tant chastement et tant bien et sagement se porte en la fleur de sa[7] grant joeunece que tout le monde la loue et la renomme de moult grant vertu.

   "Que te diroye de la duchece d'Orlians, femme de Lois,[8] filz de Charles le Sage, roy de France, jadis fille du duc de Millan? Dequelle plus prudente dame se porroit dire, [fol. 143r b] forte et constante de courage, de grant amour a son seigneur,[9] avisee en gouvernement, juste envers tous, de maintien sage et en toutes choses tres vertueuse, et c'est chose notoire.

   "En la duchece de Bourgoigne, femme du duc Jehan, filz de Phillippe, jadiz filz du roy Jehan de France, qui y a[10] il a redire? N'est elle tres vertueuse, loiale a son seigneur, benigne en cuer et en maintien, bonne en meurs, et sans quelconque[11] vice?

---

   [1] il soit] soit
   [2] grant chose] grandement
   [3] au propos] ou proces
   [4] hebergiees : *hebebergiees*
   [5] voy] a
   [6] n'y] ne
   [7] sa] si
   [8] de Loïs] du duc Loÿs
   [9] de courage, de grant amour a son seigneur] en courage de grant amour a son seigneur, de bonne doctrine a ses enfans
   [10] y a] a
   [11] quelquonque] quelconques

ano[n]e[1] and come heder.' The whiche thynge was done, of the whiche she was gretely praysed."

## Chapter 67        Of pryncesses and of ladyes of Fraunce

And I, Christine, sayd thus: "Madame, sythe that ye have remembred this lady that is in my tyme and are entred to the same [purpose][2] of ladyes of Fraunce abydynge in that countre, I pray you that it please you to saye somwhat of them that ye seme ought to be sayd, and yf ye thynke that it be good that they maye be harboured in our cyte: for wherefore ought they to be forgotten, as thoughe they were straungers?"

*Answere*: "Christine, I answere thee certaynely that I se many of them ryght vertuous, and it pleaseth me wel that they be of our cytezeynes. And fyrst of all shall not be refused there the noble Quene of Fraunce Isabell de Bavere, nowe by the [R1v] grace of God reygnynge, in whom there was never founde no cruelte nor extorcyon, ne none evyl vyce, but alway in good love and benygnyte to her subjectes.

"Ne ought not gretely to be praysed the fayre, yonge, good, and wyse duchesse of Berry, wyfe of Duke Johan, late sone of Kynge Johan of Fraunce and broder of the wyse Kynge Charles? The whiche noble duchesse bare herselfe so wysely and chaste in the floure of her youthe that all the worlde praysed her of grete vertue.

"What sholde I say to thee of the duchesse of Orlyaunce, wyfe of Lewes, sone of Charles the Wyse, kynge of Fraunce, late doughter of the duke of Myllayne? Of whiche prudent lady ye myght tell the stronge and constaunte courage of grete love to her lorde, advysed in governaunce, just to every man, and wyse of her behavoure.

"What is there to saye of the duchesse of Burgoyne, wyfe of Duke Johan, sone of Phylyp, late sone of Kynge Johan of Fraunce? Was she not ryght vertuous, true to her lorde, benygne in herte and in her countenaunce, good in condycyons, and without ony vyce?

---

[1] ano[n]e : *anoue*
[2] [purpose] : *pourse*

"La contesse de Clermont, fille du sus dit duc¹ de Berry de sa premiere femme, et mariee au conte de Clermont,² filz du duc de Bourbon attendant la duchie: n'est elle toute telle que a estre apartient a toute haute princece? De grant amour a son seigneur, bien³ moriginee, en toutes [fol. 143v a] choses belle et sage, et⁴ a son bel maintien et port honnourable apperent ses vertus.

"Et celle entre les autres que singulierement tu aimes, tant pour⁵ ses vertus comme pour ce que en recevant benefices d'elle a toy estendues, par charité et bonne amour, tu y es tenue: c'este la noble duchece de Houlande et contesse de Hainault, fille du susdit duc fu Philippe de Bourgoigne⁶ et seur de cellui qui a present est. Ne doit celle⁷ dame estre mise entre les plus parfaictes? Loyale en courage, tres prudent⁸ en gouvernement, charitable et devote souverainement envers Dieu et a brief dire, toute bonne.

"La duchece de Bourbon, ne doit elle estre ramenteue entre les⁹ princeces renommee, comme tres honnouree et [fol. 143v b] digne de los en toutes choses?

"Que t'en diroye? Long temps emploier m'y¹⁰ couvendroit a de toutes dire les grans bontez!

"La bonne et belle¹¹ noble preudefemme contese de saint Pol, fille du duc de Bar, cousine germaine du roy de France, bien doit venir en place entre les bonnes.¹²

"Autressi celle que tu aimes, Anne, fille jadis du conte de la Marche et suer de cellui de present, qui est mariee au frere de la royne de France, Lois de Baviere, n'empire pas la compagnie de celles qui ont grace et sont dignes de louenge, car vers Dieu et vers le monde sont acceptees ses bonnes vertus.

"D'autres contesses, baronnesses, dames, damoiselles, bourgoises, et de tous estaz y a tant de bonnes et [fol. 144r a] de belles¹³ (malgré les mesdisans) que Dieux en soit louez qui les y maintiengne, et les deffaillans¹⁴ veulle amender. Et de ceste chose ne doubtes du contraire, car pour certain¹⁵ le t'afferme, quoy que maintes hommes¹⁶ comme mesdisans et envieux disent le contraire."

---

¹ duc] Jehan duc
² de Clermont] Jehan de Clermont
³ seigneur, bien] seigneur et bien
⁴ belle et sage, et] belle, sage, et bonne, et a tout dire a
⁵ pour] pour le bien de
⁶ Philippe de Bourgoigne] Phelippe duc de Bourgongne
⁷ celle] ceste
⁸ prudent] prudent et sage
⁹ les] mes
¹⁰ m'y] me
¹¹ bonne et belle] bonne, belle
¹² bonnes] places
¹³ de bonnes et de belles] de bonnes et belles
¹⁴ maintiengne, et les deffaillans] maintiengne. Et celles qui sont deffaillans
¹⁵ certain] voir
¹⁶ hommes] gens

"The countesse of Cleremount, doughter of the duke of Berry abovesayd of his fyrst wyfe, and maryed to the erle of Cleremount, sone of the duke of Burbon abydynge the duchy: is not the tale of her suche that perteyneth to be to every hygh pryncesse of the gret love of her lorde, wel manered, in all thynges wyse? And her vertues appered lyke to her countenaunce and honourable porte.

"And this is she that thou lovest syngulerly amonge others, as moche for her vertues as for the grete [R2r] benefeytes of her stretched unto thee, by charyte and good love thou arte beholdynge therto: the duchesse of Holande and countesse of Heynaulte, doughter of the abovesayd Phylyp, and syster of hym that is nowe. Ought not that lady to be put amonge the good ladyes, true in courage, ryght-wyse in governaunce, charytable, and soveraynely devoute to Godwarde? And to say shortly, all good.

"The duchesse of Burgon, ought she not to be remembred amonge the praysed ladyes and ryght worshypfull, worthy to be praysed in al thynges?

"What sholde I say? I must occupye longe tyme to tell all theyr grete bountees!

"The good lady and fayre, and ryght a noble woman, countesse of Saynt Poule, doughter of the duke of Bar, cosyn germayne of the kynge of Fraunce, wel ought to come in place amonge others.

"Also she that thou lovest well, Anne, doughter somtyme of the erle of Marche and syster to hym that now[e][1] is, whiche is maryed to the broder of the quene of Fraunce, Lewes de Bavyere, empeyreth not the company of them that have grace and be worthy of praysynge, for to God and the worlde her vertues ben accepted.

"Of other countesses and baronnesses, ladyes and gentylwomen, burgeyses, wyves, and of al estates there ben ynowe bothe good and fayre, maulgre the evyll sayers, that God be worshypped whiche maynteyne them and amende them that do amysse. And of this thyng doubte not the contrary, for I afferme that for cer-tayne, thoughe that many men as evyl sayers and envyous say the contrary."

---

[1] now[e] : *nowt*

Et je, Christine a tant respondis: "Certes, dame,[1] ceste novelle ouïr de vous m'est souveraine joye."

Et elle a moy respont: "Amie chiere, or ay assez souffisemment comme il me semble fait mon office en la Cité des Dames, bastir[2] de beaulx palais et de belles maisions. La[3] t'ay peuplee de nobles dames tant et a si grans routes de tous estaz que ja toute est[4] remplie. Or viengne ma suer Justice, qui perface le surplus,[5] et a tant te souffise."

## *Chapitre [68]*[6]   **Parle Christine aux princeces et a toutes femmes** [fol. 144r b]

Tres redoubtees et excellens princeces, honnourees de France et de tout païs, toutes[7] dames, damoiselles, et generaument toutes femmes qui amastes, aimez, et amerez vertu et bonnes meurs, tant celles qui sont trespasses, comme les presentes et celles avenir: esleesciez vous toutes et menez joye en nostre nouvelle cité qui ja, Dieux mercis,[8] est toute ou la plus grant partie bastie et maisonnee, et pres que peuplee. Rendez graces a Dieu, qui jusques cy[9] m'a conduicte a grant labour et estude, desireuse que heberge honnourable pour demoure perpetuelle tant que le monde durera, vous fust[10] par moy en la closture d'une cité establie. Suis jusques cy venue,[11] esperant [fol. 144v a] de aler oultre a la conclusion de mon oeuvre par l'aide et le reconfort de Dame Justice, qui selon sa promesse me sera aidable, sans delaissier, jusques elle soit close et toute parfaicte. Or priez pour moy, mes tres redoubtees.

**Explicit la seconde partie du *Livre de la cité des dames***

---

¹  dame] dames
²  bastir] l'ay bastie
³  de belles maisions. La] de maintes belles heberges et mansions. Le
⁴  toute est] est toute
⁵  perface le surplus] le surplus perface
⁶  [68] : *lxix*
⁷  toutes] et toutes
⁸  qui ja Dieux mercis] que ja Dieu merci
⁹  qui jusques cy] qui
¹⁰  fust] soit
¹¹  jusques cy venue] venue jusques cy

And I, Christine, answered: "Than certes, madame, this I sayd of you [R2v] is to me a soverayne joye."

And she answered me: "Dere frende, nowe I have suffycyently done myne offyce in the Cyte of Ladyes as in makynge the fayre palays and fayre mansyons. And I have peopled it with nobles, grete rowtes of all estates, whiche is nowe fulfylled. Nowe come my syster Justyce whiche shal perfourme the surplus, and so thou shalte be suffysed."

## Chapter 68     Christine speketh to all pryncesses, ladyes, and to all women

Moost doubted, execellente, and worshypfull pryncesse[s][1] of Fraunce and of every countree; all ladyes, gentyllwomen, and generally al women whiche loveth, loved, and shal love vertue and good condycyons, as moche those that ben passed, as those ben nowe, and those that are to come: be ye glad and make joye in our newe cyte, whiche thanked be God is al buylded for the moost parte, and nere hande peopled. Yelde ye thankes to God, whiche hytherto hath conduyted me with grete laboure and studye, and wolde that a worshypfull lodgynge for a perpetuall dwellynge as longe as the worlde shall last were made by me in the cloystre of a cyte stablysshed. To whiche I am come hytherto, hopynge to go forthe to the conclusyon of my worke by the helpe and comforte of Dame Justyce, whiche after her promyse shall be to me helpe, without beynge wery, tyll it be closed and al parfytely made. Nowe pray for me, my moost doubted ladyes.

**Here endeth the seconde parte of this boke.**

---

[1] pryncesse[s] : *pryncesse*

# Here begynneth the thyrde partye of the Boke of the Cyte of Ladyes

*whiche telleth howe and by whome the hyghe bataylementes of the towres were made and perfourmed, and what noble ladyes were chosen to enhabyte the hyghe palays and the hyghe dongeons.* [R4r]

*Chapitre 1*     Cy comence la tierce partie du *Livre de la cité des dames*,
laquelle parle comment et par qui les haulx combles
des tours furent parfais, et quelles nobles dames furent
eslites pour demourer es grans palais et es haulx donions.
L[e]¹ premier chapitre parle comment Justice amena la
Royne du Ciel pour habiter et seigneurir² en la Cité des
Dames

A tant se tira vers moy Dame Justice a sa haulte maniere, et dist ainsi: "Christine,
a droit voir dire, bien me semble que selonc ta possibilité a l'aide de mes sueurs, si
que tu l'as sceu mettre en oeuvre, bien et bel as oeuvré ou batissement de la Cité
des Dames. Et de[s]ormais³ [fol. 146r b] est temps que je me entremettre du seur-
plus si que je te promis, c'est assavoir d'y admener et logier la Royne tres excellent,
benoitree⁴ entre les femmes, avec sa noble⁵ compagnie si que la cité puist estre
d[o]minee⁶ et seigneurie par elle, et habitee de grant multitude de nobles dames⁷
de sa court et de sa maignee: car ja voy les palais et les haultes menssions prestes
et parees, et toutes⁸ les rues couvertes pour recepvoir elle et sa tres honnouree et
excellente route et assemblé.

"Or viengnent doncques princepces, dames, et toutes femmes au devant
recepvoir a grant honneur et reverence celle qui est non pas seulement leur royne,
mais qui a dominacion⁹ et seigneurie sur toutes puissance crees après un seul
Filz [fol. 146v a] que elle porta et con[c]eut¹⁰ du Saint Esperit, et qui¹¹ est Filz de
Dieu le Pere. Mais c'est bien raison que ceste tres hault et excellent¹² souveraine
princepce soit suppliee par l'assemblé de toutes femmes, qui de son humilité luy
plaise habite[r]¹³ ça embas entre elles en leur cité et congregacion, sans l'avoir en
desdaing n'en¹⁴ despris pour le regart de sa haultesce en envers¹⁵ leur petitesce.
Mais ne fault point avoir de doubte que son humilité, qui toutes autres passe, et sa
benignité, plus qu'engelique, ne luy souffrera faire reffus de demourer et habiter

---

¹ L[e] : *la*
² habiter et seigneurir] abiter
³ de[s]ormais : *de formais*
⁴ benoitree] beneuree
⁵ noble] tres noble
⁶ d[o]minee : *deminee*
⁷ nobles dames] dames nobles
⁸ parees et toutes] parees toutes
⁹ a dominacion] administracion
¹⁰ con[c]eut : *coneut*
¹¹ et qui] qui
¹² hault et excellent] haulte, excellent
¹³ habite[r] : *habite*
¹⁴ n'en] ne
¹⁵ en envers] envers

*Chapter 1*      The fyrst chapytre telleth howe Justyce ledde the Quene of Heven to enhabyte and lordeshyp in the Cyte of Ladyes

And then my Lady Justyce drewe her towarde me in her hyghe manere, and sayd thus: "Christine, to saye the ryght way, it semeth me well that after thy pos-sybylyte with the helpe of my systers, so that thou hast knowne to put in werke, thou hast wrought well and fayre in the buyldynge of the Cyte of Ladyes. And frome henseforthe it is tyme that I entremete me of the surpluse so as I have pro-mysed thee; that is to knowe, to brynge thyder and lodge the moost excellent and blessyd Quene amonge all women with her noble company, so that the cyte maye be lordeshypped and governed by her and enhabyted with a grete multytude of noble ladyes of her courte and of her meyny for I se the palays and the hyghe mansyons redy and arayed, and al the stretes covered to receyve her and her ryght honourable and excellente rowte and assemble.

"Nowe come on then ye pryncesses, ladyes, and all women before to receyve this Lady with grete worshyppe and reverence, whiche is not onely your Quene, but she whiche hathe domynacyon and lordeshyp above al puysaunce after here onely Sone, that she bare and conceyved of the Holy Ghost, and whiche is the Sone of [R4v] God the Fader. But it is good reason that this moost hyghe and excellent Pryncesse be mekely prayed by the assemble of all ladyes and women, that it please her of her grete mekenesse to dwelle here alowe amonge them in theyr cyte and congregacyon, without havynge them in dysdayne for the regarde of her hyghnesse towarde theyr lytelnesse. But it nedeth not to doubte that her mekenesse, whiche passeth all others, and her benygnyte, more than aungelyke, ne wyll not suffre her to make refuge to dwelle and enhabyte in the Cyte of

en la Cité des Dames, voire par dessus toutes ou palais que ma sueur Droicture lui
a ja appareillé, qui tout est faicte de gloire et de louenge. Or viengnent doncques
avecques moy, toute[s]¹ femmes, et lui disons ainsi:

"Nous te saluons [fol. 146v b] Royne des cieulx du salu que l'ange t'aporta,
lequel tu as agreable sur tous salus, te disant *Ave Maria.* Suppl[i]e² humblement a
toy tout le devot sexe des femmes qu'en horreur ne te soit habiter³ entre elles par
grace et par pitié comme leur deffenderresse, prote[c]taresse,⁴ et garde contre tous
assaulx d'annemis et du monde, et que de la fontaine de vertus qui de toy flue elles
puissent boire et estre raffridiees si que⁵ pechié et tout vice leur soit abominable.

"Or viens doncques a nous, Royne celleste, temple de Dieu, celle et cloistre
du Saint Esperit, abitacle de la Trinité, joye des anges, estoille et radresce des
desvoyez, esperans des vrais creans. O dame, qui est cellui tant oultragieux qui
jamays ose pensser, [fol. 147r a] ne gitter hors de sa bouche que le sexe femmenin
soit vil, consideree ta dignité? Car se tout le demourant des femmes estoit mauvais, si passe et surmonte la lueur de ta bonté a plus grant comble que autre mauvaistié ne pourroit estre. Et quant Dieux voulst en cestuy sexe eslire son espouse,
pour l'onneur de toy, dame tres excellente, tous hommes doivent eulx garder⁶ non
pas seulement de blasmer femmes, mes⁷ les avoir en grant reverence."

La response de la Vierge est telle: "Justice, la tres amee de mon Filz, tres
voulentieres je habiteray et demoureray entre mes suers et amies, les femmes:⁸
car Raison, Droicture, toy, et aussi Nature m'y encline. Elles me servent, louent,
et honneurent sans cesser, si suis et seray a tousjours chief du sexe femmenin [fol.
147r b] car ceste chose fu des oncques en la penssee de Dieu le Pere preparlee, et
ordennee ou conseil de la Trinité."

Adonc respondi Justice, avecques toutes femmes:⁹ "Dame, graces et louenges
te soyent donnees par infinis siecles! Sauves nous, dame, et pour nous prie ton
Filz, qui riens ne te reffuse."

---

¹ avecques moy, toute[s] : *toute*]  avec moy, toutes
² Suppl[i]e : *Supple*
³ habiter] d'abiter
⁴ protectaresse : *protestaresse*
⁵ raffridiees si que] si rassadiees que
⁶ pour l'onneur de toy, dame tres excellente, tous hommes doivent eulx garder] dame
tres excellente pour l'onneur de toy tous hommes se doivent garder
⁷ mes] maiz aussi
⁸ femmes] femmes et avecques elles
⁹ avecques toutes femmes] avec toutes femmes, genoulx flechis et les chiefs enclins

Ladyes above all other women in the palays that my syster Rygh[t]wysnesse[1] hath ordeyned for her, whiche is all made of glorye and of praysynge. Nowe come on then al women with me, and say we thus here:

"We salute thee with the same salutacyon that the aungell brought to thee, the whiche thou hast most agreable above al other salutacyons, saynge to thee: *Ave Maria*! All the devoute kynde of women beseche thee, mekely, that thou abhorre not to dwelle amonge them by grace and pyte as theyr defenderesse, and protectryce, and keper ayenst all the assaultes of the enemyes and of the worlde, and that they may drynke of the well of vertues that floweth fro thee and to be refresshed so that synne and all vyce be to them abhomynable.

"Nowe then come on Our Hevenly Quene, Temple of God, Selle and Cloystre of the Holy Ghost, Habytacle of the Trynyte, Joye of Aungelles, Sterre and Redresse of them that ben out of the ryght way, Hope of al true bylevynge people! O blessyd Lady, what is he so outragyous that ever dare thynke or put out of his [R5r] mouthe that the femenyne kynde is foule, consydered thy dygnyte? For thoughe all the doynges of women were evyll, so passeth and surmounteth the lyght of thy goodnesse all the evyll that may be. And when God wolde chose His spouse in this kynde, for thyne honoure, ryght excellent Lady, all men ought to be ware not onely to blame women, but to have them in grete reverence."

The answere of the blessyd Quene is thus: "Justyce, the ryght welbyloved of my Sone, with ryght good wyll I shall dwell and abyde amonge my systers and frendes, the women; for Reason, Ryghtwysnesse, and thyselfe wolde that I dyde so, and Nature enclyneth me therto, for they serve me, prayse me, and worshyp me without seasynge. So I am and shall be evermore the heede of the kynde of women, for this thynge was ever in the thought of God the Fader preparate, and ordeyned in the counsayle of the Trynyte."

Then answered Justyce, with all the women: "Lady, thankynges and praysynges be gyven to thee by the infynyte worldes! Nowe, Lady, save us and pray for us to thy Sone, whiche nothynge thee refuseth."

---

[1] Rygh[t]wysnesse : *Ryghwysnesse*

## *Chapitre 2*    Des suers Nostre Dame et de la Magdalaine

"Or est logee avec[1] nous l'empereris non pareille, vueillent ou no[n][2] les mesdisans jangleours. Sy doivent bien estre mises avec ses[3] benoites sueurs et Marie
Magdalaine, qui compaignie luy firent sans delaissier a la Passion de son Filz,
coste la croix. O, grant foy de femmes! Et grant amour qui oncques le Filz de
Dieu, qui de tous ses apostres avoit esté abandonné et relinqui, ne le laissierent
mort ne vif. Et [fol. 147v a] paru bien que Dieux ne reprouvoit mie tant amour de
femme si que [se][4] ce fust chose fraille, comme aucuns veullent[5] dire, quant ou
cuer de la benoite Magdalaine et des autres dames mist estincelle de sy fervant
amour, comme [il][6] y paru, et que il tant approuva."

## *Chapitre 3*    De sainte Katerine

"Pour faire compaignie a la Vierge, royne du ciel et princepce[7] de la Cité des
Dames, nous fault logier avecques[8] elle les benoites vierges et saintes dames,
en demonstrant comment Dieu a approuvré le sexe femmenin, par ce que semblablement que aux hommes, a donné a femmes en tendreces et de jeune aage
constance force[9] de souffrir pour sa sainte loy horribles martires, et [fol. 147v b] qui
couronnees sont en gloire. Desquelles les belles vies sont de bon exemple a ouÿr[10]
a toute femme, sur toute autre sagesce, et pour ce ycestes seront les supellatives
de nostre cité.
    "Et premierement comme tres excellente la benoite Katerine, qui fu fille du
roy Coste d'Alixandrie. Ceste beneuree pucelle estoit demouree heritiere de son
pere en l'aage de dix huit ans, et noblement gouvernoit elle et son heritage; crestienne estoit et toute donnee a Dieu, reffusant tous autres mariages. Advint qu'en
la cité d'Alixandrie fu venu l'Empereur Maxance, lequel a un jour d'une grant
sollempnité de leurs dieux avoit fait apprester grant appareil pour faire sollempnel
sacrefice. Katerine, [fol. 148r a] estant en son palais, ouÿ[11] la noise des bestes que on

---

[1] avec] avecques
[2] no[n] : *nom*
[3] ses] elle les
[4] [se] ce : *ce ce*] se ce
[5] aucuns veullent dire] aucuns font et que ilz veulent dire
[6] [il] : *yl*
[7] Vierge, royne du ciel et princepce] benoite Royne du ciel, empereris et princesse
[8] avecques] avec
[9] en tendreces et de jeune aage constance force] femmes tendres et de jeune aage
constance et force
[10] de bon exemple a ouÿr] a ouÿr de bon exemple
[11] estant en son palais, ouÿ] estoit en son palais, si ouÿ

*Chapter 2*          Of the systers of Our Lady, and of Mary Magdaleyne

"Nowe the Empresse is lodged with us, whether the evyll sayenge janglers wyl or no. And nowe ought the blessyd systers to [be][1] put in, and Saynt Mary Magdaleyne with them, whiche made her [R5v] company without levynge her in the tyme of the Passyon of her Sone, ryght nyghe the crosse. O, the grete faythe of women and grete love whiche never lefte the Sone of God, quycke nor deed, whan He was abandonned and forsaken of His apostles. And it appered well that God reproved not the love of women as it were a frayle thynge, as some men wyll say, when He put so grete love in the herte of the blessyd Mary Magdaleyne and of other ladyes as it appered, and that it proved so moche."

*Chapter 3*          Of Saynt Katheryne, the holy vyrgyne

"To make company with the Vyrgyne, Quene of Heven and Pryncesse of the Cyte of Ladyes, we must lodge with her the blessyd vyrgynes and holy ladyes in shewynge howe God hath proved the kynde of wome[n][2] by that that the same wyse that He [hath][3] gyven unto men, He hath gyven unto women for to understande in theyr yonge and tendre age for to be constaunte and stronge in sufferynge horryble martyrdomes for the holy lawe, the whiche ben crowned in glorye. Of whome the fayre lyves ben of good ensample to here to every[4] woman above all other[5] wysdome, and therfore they shall be the superlatyve degre of our cyte.

"And fyrst as a ryght excellent the blessyd Katheryn, whiche was doughter of Kynge Costes of Alexandre: this blessyd vyrgyn was lefte to be heyre of her fader in the age of .xviii. yeres, and notably she [R6r] governed her and her herytage. She was a Crysten woman and all gyven to God, refusynge all other maryages. It happened that into the cyte of Alexandre was come the Emperour Maxencyus, the whiche on a day of grete solempnyte of his goddes had made to aray grete appareyle to make solempne sacryfyse. Katheryne, beynge in her palays, herde

---

[1] [be] put : *put*
[2] wome[n] : *womeu*
[3] He [hath] gyven : *He gyven*
[4] every : *every every*
[5] other : *othher*

appareilloit pour sacrefier, et grant retentissement d'instrumens. Et comme elle
eust envoyé savoir que ce estoit, et lui fu[1] rapporté que l'empereur estoit ja au temple pour faire sacrefice, tantost y ala et l'empereur prist a corrigier de celle erreur
par moult saiges parolles; et comme grant clergiesce que elle estoit, et aprise es
sciences,[2] prist a prouver par raisons phillosophiques que il n'est que un seul Dieu,
Creature[3] de toutes choses, et que celluy doit estre aouré et non autre.

"Quant l'empereur ouÿ ceste pucelle qui tant estoit noble et de grant auctorité
ainsi parler, et qui tant estoit belle, fu[4] tous esmerveillez et ne luy s[ç]ot[5] que dire,
mais moult entendoit [fol. 148r b] a la regarder. Sy envoya par tout querre les plus
sages philosophes que on sceut par la terre de Egipte, qui de philosophie adonc
moult estoit renommee, tant que vers luy furent assemblez bien cinquante, qui se
tindrent mal contens quant ilz sceurent la cause pour quoy mandez estoient, et
distrent que pou de scens[6] l'avoit meu de les travailler de sy longtaines terres pour
disputer a une pucelle. A brief dire, quant le jour de sa[7] disputaison fut venus, la
benoite Katerine les pourmena tellement par arguemens que tous furent convaincus, ne souldre ne savoient ses questions, de laquel chose l'empereur forcenoit sur
eulx. Mais tout ce ne valoit riens, car par grace divine aux saintes parolles de la
vierge tous se convertirent et [fol. 148v a] confesserent de[8] nom de Jhesucrist, pour
lequel despit l'empereur les fist tous ardre.[9] Et la sainte vierge les reconfortoit en
leur martire et les asseuroit d'estre receuz en la gloire perpetuelle,[10] et Dieu prioit
qu'Il les tenist en vraye foy. Et ainsi furent yceulx par elle mis ou nombre des benois martirs. Et tel miracle monstra Dieu en eulx que oncques le feu ne corrompi
leurs corps, ne leurs vestemens, ains demourerent aprés le feu tous entiers sans
perdre poil, et de telz chieres que il sembloit que tous fussent en vie.

"Le tirant Maxance, qui moult couvoitoit la vierge[11] Katerine pour sa beauté,
la prist moult a blandir affin que il la tournast a sa voulenté. Mais quant il vit
que riens ne luy valloit, il se tourna aux menaces et puis aux tourmens, et la fist
[fol. 148v b] batre moult durement, et puis mettre en chartre sans estre de nul visitee par .xii. jours, et la cuidoit faire deffaillir de fain. Mais les anges de Nostre

---

[1] fu] feust
[2] et comme grant clergiesce que elle estoit, et aprise es sciences] comme grant
clergece et apprise es sciences que elle estoit
[3] Creature] Createur
[4] estoit noble et de grant auctorié ainsi parler, et qui tant estoit belle, fu] estoit belle,
noble, et de grant auctorité ainsi parler il fu
[5] s[ç]ot : *soot*
[6] distrent que pou de scens] dirent que pou de sens
[7] sa] la
[8] de] le
[9] tous ardre] ardoir
[10] les asseuroit d'estre receuz en la gloire perpetuelle] asseuroit d'estre receus en la
gloire pardurable
[11] vierge] benoite

the noyse of beestes that were arayed to do sacryfyse, and grete noyse of instrumentes. And as she had sente to knowe what it was, and it was reported to her
that the emperour was in the temple to do sacrefyse, anone she wente and began
to correcte the emperoure of that erroure by many wyse wordes, and as she was a
grete clerke and had lerned scyences, began to prove by good reasons of phylosophye that there was but one God, maker of all thynges, and that He ought to be
worshypped and none other.

"When the emperour herde this mayden whiche was so noble and of so grete
auctoryte thus speke, and whiche that [she]¹ was so fayre, was all admervaylled,
and wyste not what to say but entended to beholde her. So he sente al aboute to
seke phylosophres in all the londe of Egypte; so there came before hym .l. phylosophres, whiche helde them ryght evyll contente when they knewe the cause
wherfore they were brought thyder, and sayd that lytell wytte had moved them
to travayle frome so farre contrees for to dyspute with a mayden. And to telle
shortely, when the day of theyr dysputacyon was come, the blessyd Katheryne
ledde theym forthe so with argumentes [R6v] that they were all overcome and
coude not assoyle her questyons, for the whiche the emperoure was passynge
wrothe with them. But all that advayled nothynge, for by the grace of God and
by the holy wordes of the vyrgyne they were all converted and confessed the
name of Jhesu Cryst, for the whiche despyte the emperoure made them all to be
brente. And the holy mayden conforted them in theyr martyrdome and assured
them to be receyved in perpetuall glory, and prayed God that He wolde kepe
them in the veray faythe. And so by her they were put in the nombre of the
blessyd martyrs. And suche a myracle God shewed in them that the fyre never
hurte theyr bodyes ne theyr clothes, but that they bode al hole after the fyre was
done without losynge of ony heere off theyr heedes, but it semed that all were
on lyve.

"The tyraunte Maxencyus, whiche gretely coveyted the holy vyrgyne Katheryne for her beaute, began to flatter her that she sholde tourne to his wyll. But
when he sawe that it advayled nothynge, he tourned hym to his manasynges
and then to tourmente[s]² and made her to be beten cruelly, and after to put
her in pryson without vysytynge of ony persone the space of .xii. dayes without
mete or drynke, trowynge to have made her dye for hongre. But the aungelles of

---

¹ that [she] was : *that was*
² tourmente[s] : *tourmented*

Seigneur estoient avec elle qui la reconfortoient. Et quant aprés les .xii. jours elle fu menee devant l'empereur, et il la vit plus fresche et plus saine que devant, cuida que visitee eust esté. Si commenda estre tourmentez les gardes de la chartre. Mais Katerine, qui pitié en ot,[1] afferma que n'avoit eu confort fors du ciel. L'empereur ne savoit qu[e]lz[2] tourmens pour la tourmenter plus durs faire. Et par le conseil de son prevost, fist faire[3] roues plaines de rasouoirs qui tournoient l'un contre l'autre, et quanque estoit ou milieu estoit detrenchié. Entre ses roues fist mettre toute nue Kateryne [fol. 149r a] qui tousjours, les mains joignoit, a aourer Dieu; adonc deffendirent[4] les anges, qui par si grant force despecierent les roues que les tourmenteurs furent occis.

"Quant la femme [de][5] l'empereur sçot les merveilles que Dieux faisoit pour Katerine, elle fu convertie et blasma l'empereur de ce que il faisoit, ala visiter la sainte vierge en la chartre, et luy pria[6] que Dieu priast pour elle, pour lequel despit[7] l'empereur fist tourmenter sa femme et luy traire les mamelles. Et la vierge luy dist:[8] 'Ne doubtes point les tourmens, tres noble royne, car aujourd'uy seras receue en la joye sans fin.' Le tirant fist decoller sa femme, et grant multitude de gens qui convertis se estoient.

"L'empereur requist Katerine que elle fust sa femme, et quant [fol. 149r b] il vit que elle estoit reffusente a toutes ses peticions, ala donner[9] sa sentence que elle fust decollee. Et elle fist son oroison, priant pour tous ceulx qui aroient remembrance de sa passion, et pour tous ceulx qui son nom appelleroient en leurs tribulacions. Et la voix du ciel vint[10] qui dist que sa priere estoit essauxiee. Sy parfist son martire, et de son corps decouroit l[a]it[11] en lieu de sanc. Et les anges prisoient[12] son sainte corps et le porterent ou Mont de Sinay, qui est .xx. journees loings de la, et l'ensevelirent, ou quel tombel a Dieux fait[13] moult de miracles, que je laisse pour briefté. Et d'icelle[14] tombe decourt oeile qui garist de moult de maladies. Et l'Empereur Maxance D[i]eux[15] pugnist[16] horriblement."

---

[1] pitié en ot] en ot pitié

[2] qu[e]lz : *quilz*

[3] Et par le conseil de son prevost, fist faire] Si fist par le conseil de son prevost faire

[4] a aourer Dieu; adonc deffendirent] aouroit Dieu; adont descendirent

[5] [de] : *ou*] de

[6] pria] requist

[7] lequel despit] laquelle chose

[8] dist] disoit

[9] ala donner] a la parfin donna

[10] du ciel vint] vint du ciel

[11] l[a]it : *leit*

[12] prisoient] prirent

[13] a Dieux fait] Dieux a fait

[14] d'icelle] de celle

[15] D[i]eux : *Deux*

[16] pugnist] puni

Our Lorde were with her, whiche comforted her. And after the .xii. dayes she was brought before the emperoure, and he sawe her more fresshe and hole than she was before, and trowed that she had ben vysyted. So he commaunded the [S1r] kepers of the pryson to be tourmented, but Katheryne, whiche had pyte on them, affermed that she had no comforte save onely from heven. The emperoure wyst not what harde tourmentes he myght make to tourment her. And by the counsayle of his provoste, he lete make wheles full of rasoures whiche tourned one ayenst another, and whatsomever was in the myddes was cutte off. And bytwene these wheles he made put Saynt Katheryne all naked, whiche alwaye worshypped God with joyned handes. Then the aungelles of God came and defended her, whiche brake the wheles with so grete strengthe that all the tourmentoures were slayne with them.

"And when the emperoure's wyfe understode these mervaylles that God made for Saynt Katheryne, she was converted and blamed the emperoure of that that he dyde. And then she wente and vysyted the holy vyrgyne in the pryson, and prayed her that she wolde pray to God for her, for the whiche despyte the emperoure made to tourmente his wyfe and to drawe off her pappes. And the vyrgyne sayd to her: 'Doubte ye not the tourmentes, noble quene, for this daye thou shalte be receyved in the joye without ende.' And then the emperoure made his wyfe to be heeded, and a grete multytude of people that were converted.

"The emperoure requyred Katheryn that she wolde be his wyfe. And when he sawe that she was refusynge to all his petycyons, wente and gave his sentence that she sholde be heeded. And she [S1v] made her prayer, praynge for all them that had remembraunce of her passyon, and for theym that called her name in theyr trybulacyons, that God myght be theyr helpe and socoure. A voyce came fro heven whiche sayd that her prayer was herde. Soo she made an ende of her martyrdome, and instede of blode there ranne mylke out of her body. And the aungelles toke her holy body and bare it to the Mounte Synay, whiche is .xx. dayes journey fro thens. And there they buryed her, at the whiche tombe God hath done many myracles, whiche I let passe for shortenesse. And of the same tombe there renneth oyle whiche heleth many syke men. And God anone after punysshed the emperoure ryght horrybly."

## Chapitre 4    De sainte Marguerite

"N'oublierons pas aussi [fol. 149v a] la benoite vierge sainte Marguerite, dont la legende est assez sceue: comment elle, nee de Antioche de nobles parens, fu introduite en la foy jeunete pucelle par sa nourice, de laquelle tres humblement elle aloit par chascun jour garder les berbis. Donc il avint que Olibrius qui estoit seneschal de l'empereur la vit en passant et la couvoita, sy l'envoya querre. Et[1] pour ce que elle ne se voult consentir a sa voulenté, et que elle regehy que elle estoit crestienne, il la fist durement tourmenter, batre, et enchartrer; en laquelle chartre, pour ce que elle se sentoit temptee,[2] elle requist Dieu pour[3] veoir peust visiblement celluy qui tant de mal luy pourchassoit. Et adonc vint un serpent orrible qui durement l'espoventa [fol. 149v b] et la transglouti, mais elle, faisant le signe de la croix, creva le serpent et aprés vit a un quignet[4] de la chartre une figure noire comme d'un[5] homme Ethiopien.[6] Et adonc Marguerite l'ala hardiement regardre[7] et le couscha soubz elle, le pié lui[8] mist sus la gorge, et il crioit a haulte voix, 'Mercis!' La chartre reamplie de clarté; fu confortee Marguerite des anges.[9]

"Si fu de rechief tourmenté[10] devant le juge; lequel, quant il vit que ses admonicions riens ne luy vouloient, le fist[11] plus que devant tourmenter. Mais l'ange de Dieu vint derompre les tourmens et s'en sailli la vierge toute saine, et grant foison de peuple fu converti. Et quant le faux tirant vit ce, il ordena que elle fust [fol. 150r a] decollee. Mais elle fist premierement son oroyson, et pria pour tous ceulx qui remembreroyent sa passion, et qui la requerroyent en leurs tribulacions, pour les femmes enceintes et enffantans.[12] Et l'ange de Dieu vint qui luy dist que sa petission estoit exaucee, et que elle alast ou nom de Dieu recepvoir sa palme de victoire. Et adonc estandi le col, dec[o]llee[13] fu, et les anges son ame emporterent.

"Celluy faulx Olibrius semblablement fist tourmenter et decoller la sainte vierge nommee Regine, jeunette de l'aage de .xv. ans, pour ce que elle ne se voult acorder a lui et converti moult de gens par sa predicacion."

---

[1] Et] Et a brief dire
[2] elle se sentoit temptee] temptee se sentoit
[3] pour] que
[4] quignet] cornet
[5] un : *une*
[6] homme Ethiopien] Ethiopien
[7] regardre] requerre
[8] lui : *lui luy*
[9] confortee Marguerite des anges] reconfortee des anges Marguerite
[10] tourmenté] ramenee
[11] vouloient le fist] valoient la fist
[12] enffantans] pour leurs enfans
[13] dec[o]ller : *deceller*

## *Chapter 4*   Of Saynt Margarete

"We shall not forgete also the blessyd vyrgyne Saynt Margarete, of whome the legende is knowne full well: howe she was borne in Antyoche of noble kyn-[d]rede,[1] introducte in the faythe when she was yonge of her nouryse, of whome ryght humbly she wente every daye to kepe the shepe. Wherof it happened that Olybryus, whiche was stewarde with the emperoure, sawe her in goynge by and coveyted her. So he sente to fetche her; and for that that she wolde not consente to his wyll, [S2r] and that she tolde hym that she was a Crysten woman, he made her to be strongly tourmented, beten, and prysoned. In the whiche pryson, for that that she felte her tempted, she requyred that she myght se hym vysybly that soo moche evyll pourchased her. And then came an horryble serpente whiche gretely made her aferde and swalowed her. But she made the sygne of the crosse, and anone the serpente brake. And after she sawe at the corner of the pryson a blacke fygure as of a man of Ethyope. And then Margarete wente boldely and conjured hym, and he couched under her feete. And she sette her feete upon his throte, and he cryed with an hygh voyce, 'Mercy!' The pryson fulfylled with clerenesse; Margarete was comforted of the aungelles.

"And then she was tourmented agayne before the juge; the whiche, when he sawe that all his ammonycyons advayled hym not, made her to be tourmented more than she was before. But the aungelles of God came and brake all the tour-mentes, and the vyrgyne lepte awaye from it all hole; and there was grete foyson of people converted. And when the false tyraunte sawe that, he ordeyned that she was heeded. But she made her oryson fyrste, and prayed unto Almyghty God for all theym that remembred her passyon, and all they that prayed unto her in theyr trybulacyens, and for women grete with chylde, that Almyghty God wolde grau[n]te[2] unto them theyr petycyon. And the aungell of God came and tolde her that her prayers [S2v] were herde, and that she sholde go in the name of God to receyve the palme of the vyctory. And then she stretched forthe her necke and was heeded, and the aungelles bare her soule to heven.

"This false Olybryus also made to tourmente the holy vyrgyne named Regyne, whiche was ryght yonge of the age of .xv. yeres, for that that she wolde not accorde to hym. And she converted moche people with her holy prechynge."

---

[1] kyn[d]rede : *kynrede*
[2] grau[n]te : *grauute*

*Chapitre 5*        De[1] sainte Luce

"La benoite sainte Luce, vierge qui fu nee de Romme, ne doit pas [fol. 150r b] estre
oubliee en nostre letanie, laquelle fu ravie[2] du roy Aceya de Barbarie. Et quant
il fu en son païs et il luy cuida faire force, adonc celle par la vertu divine le commença tellement a preschier que il se merveilla de son scens, et la laissa,[3] et dist
que ce estoit une deesse; et la tint en grant honneur et reverence en son palais, et
moult reverentment[4] luy fist establir sa demeure a elle et a sa maisinee, et ordena
que nul homme n'y repairast pour l'empeschier. Et celle sans cesser estoit en jen-
nues et oroysons,[5] et menoit sainte vie, priant Dieu pour son hoste que Il le voulsist enluminer. Et il se consseilloit a elle de tous ses affaires, et bien lui prenoit de
quanque elle lui conseilloit. Quant il aloit en guerre, il luy prioit que elle priast
[fol. 150v a] son Dieu pour luy; et elle le beneissoit, et il s'en retournoit vainqueur,
par quoy il la vouloit aourer comme deesse, et lui faire ediffier temples. Mais elle
disoit[6] que de ce se gardast bien, et que il n'estoit que un seul Dieu,[7] et que elle
estoit une simple pecharresse.

"Et ainsi fu l'espace de vint ans, perseverent en sainte vie, si luy fu revelé
de Nostre Seigneur qu'elle s'en retournast a Romme, et que l'acompliroit par
martire le terme de sa vie. Et elle le dist au roy, lequel de ce fu[8] moult dollent
et luy respondi:

"'Las, se tu te pa[r]s[9] de moy, mes annemis m'asauldront et perdray ma bonne
fortune quant je ne t'array.'

"Et elle luy dist, 'Roy, vien avec[10] moy et laisse ce reigne terrien. Car Dieu
t'a esleu a posseder plus noble raigne, et qui [est][11] sans fin.' Et celluy [fol. 150v b]
tantost laissa tout et s'en ala avec la sainte vierge, non pas comme seigneur, mais
comme sergeant.

"Et quant a Rome furent arivez, et elle se fu magnifestee crestienne, elle fu
prise[12] et menee au martire. De laquel chose le roy Auceya fu moult dollent, et

---

[1] De] Ci dit de
[2] laquelle fu ravie] Ceste vierge fu ravie et prise
[3] par la vertu divine le commença tellement a preschier que il se merveilla de son
scens, et la laissa] le commença a prescher tant que par la vertu divine il fu tout hors de
son mauvais propos et moult s'esmerveilla de son sens
[4] reverentment] honorablement
[5] oroysons] en oroisons
[6] disoit] lui disoit
[7] Dieu] Dieu que on devoit aourer
[8] de ce fu] fu de ce
[9] pa[r]s : *pas*
[10] vien avec] viens avecques
[11] qui [est] : *qui*] qui est
[12] elle fu prise] prise fu

*Chapter 5*        Of the holy vyrgyne Saynt Luce

"The b[l]essyd[1] Saynt Luce whiche was borne in Rome ought not to be forgeten in our letanye, the whiche was ravysshed of the Kynge Aceya of Barbary. And when he was in his countre, he trowed to have defouled her; then she, by the vertue of God, began so to preche unto hym that he mervaylled of her wytte and lefte her and sayd that she was a goddesse, and helde her in grete worshyp and reverence in his palays. And ryght reverently he establysshed her dwellynge for her and her meyny, and ordeyned that no man sholde repayre thyder to hurte her or trouble her. And she without seasynge was in fastynges and in orysons, and ledde ryght an holy lyfe, prayenge for her hoost that it myght please God to enlumyne hym with the lyght of His holy faythe. And her hoost asked counsayle of her in all his doynges, and he toke it wel [S3r] whatsoever she counsayled hym. When he wente to the werre, he prayed her that she wolde praye to her God for hym; and she blessyd hym, and he came agayne as overcomer of his enemyes. Wherfore he wolde worshyp her as a goddesse, and wolde have made to buylde a temple for her. But she sayd that he sholde beware therof, and that there was not but one God, and that she was a symple synner.

"And thus she was by the space of .xx. yeres perseverynge in holy lyfe, so she had it by revelacyon of Our Lorde that she sholde retourne to Rome, and there she sholde accomplysshe the terme of her lyfe by martyrdome. And she tolde it to the kynge, whiche was ryght full of sorowe for it, and answered her and sayd: 'Alas, yf thou parte frome me, myne enemyes wyll assayle me. And I shall lose my good fortune when I shall not have thee!'

"And she sayd to hym, 'Thou, kynge, come with me and leve thyne erthely royalme. For thou arte chosen to posses a more noble kyngdome, whiche is without ende.' And he anone lefte all that he had, and wente with the holy vyrgyne not as a lorde, but as a servaunte.

"And when they were come to Rome, and she was knowne that she was a Crysten woman, she was taken and brought to her martyrdome. Of the whiche thynge the Kynge Aceya was ryght sorowful, and ranne aboute, and wolde have

---

[1] b[l]essyd : *biessyd*

acouru celle part, et voulentiers l'eust revenchee se la vierge ne l'eust deffendu.[1] Si plouroit tendrement, et crioit que mauvaise gent estoient de faire mal a la vierge de Dieu.

"Et quant vint que on dot couper la teste a la benoite vierge,[2] le roy ala mettre son chief coste le sien, criant: 'Je suis crestien et offre mon chief a Jhesucrist, Dieu le vif, que adoure Luce.' Et ainsi furent tous deux enssemble decollés et couronnés en gloire, et douze autres avecques eulx convertis [fol. 151r a] par la benoite Luce, dont la feste de tous ensemble est cellebree en la septiesme kalandes de juillet."

*Chapitre 6*        De sainte Martine[3]

"La benoite Martine, vierge, n'estant mie oublier.[4] Ceste beneuree fu nee de Romme de moult nobles parens et moult belle.[5] L'empereur la voulst contraindre que elle fust sa femme, et elle respondi: 'Je suis crestien, offerte a Dieu le vif, qui se delitte en corps chaste et en cuer net, et a celluy je sacrefie et m'y recommene.' Pour despit de ces parolles, l'empereur[6] la fist mener au temple pour la contraindre d'aourer les ydolles. Et la celle s'agenoilla, vers le ciel les yeux leves, les mains jointes fist a Dieu son oroison. Et tantost les ydolles tresbuchierent et froissierent.[7] Le temple rompi et furent [fol. 151r b] les prestres des ydolles occis, et le diable qui estoit en l'ydolle[8] crioit et confessoit Martine estre serve de Dieu.

"Le tirant empereur, pour revenchier ses dieux, la fist livrer[9] a cruel martire, ou quel Dieu s'aparoit a elle et la reconfortoit.[10] Et elle pria pour ceulx qui la tourmentoyent tant que ilz furent convertis par ses merites, et grant foison pueple, de laquel l'empereur fu[11] plus ostiné que devant, et la fist de plus en plus tourmenter de divers cruelz tourmens. Mais ceulx qui la tourmentoient s'escrierent que ilz veoyent Dieu et ses sains devant elle et demanderent mercis: convertis furent. Et si comme elle estoit en oroison priant[12] pour eulx, une lumi[e]re[13] avironna yceulx,

---

[1] revenchee se la vierge ne l'eust deffendu] couru sus a ceulx qui la tourmentoient, mais elle lui deffendoit que bien s'en gardast. Si plouroit
[2] la benoite vierge] la sainte vierge de Dieu
[3] De sainte Martine] De la benoite Martine, vierge
[4] n'estant mie oublier] ne fait mie a oublier
[5] moult belle] tres belle estoit
[6] Pour despit de ces parolles, l'empereur] L'empereur, pour despit de ces paroles
[7] tresbuchierent et froissierent] froissierent et trebucherent
[8] l'ydolle] la maistre ydole
[9] revenchier ses dieux, la fist livrer] pour revencher ses dieux fist livrer Martine
[10] s'aparoit a elle et la reconfortoit] se apparut a elle et la reconforta
[11] laquel l'empereur fu : *laquel fu l'empereur fu*] laquelle chose l'empereur fu
[12] priant] priant Dieu
[13] lumi[e]re : *lumire*

revenged her after his power yf the holy vyrgyne had not bydden hym the contrary. Soo he wepte tenderly, and cryed that they were cursed people to do so moche [S3v] evyll to the holy vyrgyne of God.

"And when it came that one sholde smyte off the heede of that blessyd vyrgyne, the kynge wente to put his heed by hers, cryenge, 'I am a Crysten man, and I offre myne heed to Jhesu Cryst, God and Maker of all thynge, whom that holy Luce worshyppeth!' And soo they were bothe heeded togyder and crowned in glory, and .xii. other with theym that were converted by the holy vyrgyne Saynt Luce, wherof the feest of them is halowed togyder in the .vii. kalenders of Jule."

## Chapter 6     Of the blessyd vyrgyne Saynt Martyne

"The blessyd vyrgyne Martyne maye not be forgoten. This blessyd mayde was borne in Rome of ryght noble kyn[d]red.[1] The emperoure wolde constrayne her to be his wyfe bycause of her beaute, and she answered: 'I am a Crysten woman offred to God alyve, whiche delyteth Hym in chaste bodyes and in clene herte, and to Hym I do sacrefyse and commende me.' And for despyte of these wordes, the emperoure made her to be ledde to the temple to constrayne her to worshyp the ydolles. And she kneled downe, and her eyen towarde heven lyftynge up her joyned handes, made her orysons to God; and anone the ydolles fell downe, all to-torne. The temple brake, and the prestes of the temple of ydolles were slayne, and the devyll that was in the ydoll cryed and confessed [S4r] that the holy vyrgyne Martyne was the veray servaunt of God.

"The tyraunte emperoure, for to revenge his goddes, made her to be cruelly tourmented, in the whiche God appered to her and comforted her. And she prayed for them that tourmented her so moche that they were converted by her merytes and grete foyson of people also, of the whiche thynge the emperoure was worse dysposed than before, and made her to be tourmented more and more of dyvers tourmentynges and cruel. But those that tourmented her thought verely that they sawe God and His sayntes before her, and they asked mercy of her and were converted. And soo as she was in oryson prayenge for them, a lyght came

---

[1] kyn[d]red : *kynred*

et une voix fu ouÿ du ciel [fol. 151v a] qui dist, 'Je vous espargne pour l'amour de ma tres amee Martine.'

"Et adonc[1] leur cria le prevost, pour ce que convertis estoient: 'O folz, vous estes deceuz par celle enchanterresse Martine!'

"Et yceulx respondirent, sans nulle paour: 'Mais tu es deceu par le deable qui habite en toy, car tu ne congnois Celluy qui te fist.'

"Et l'empereur, forcené, les commanda estre pendus, et derompre[2] la char de eulx; et eulx, recevant martire joyeusement, louoyent Dieu.[3]

"De rechief l'empereur fist despoullier Martine toute nue et la char d'elle estoit blanche comme lis, qui faisoit esbahir les veans pour sa grant biauté. Et quant l'empereur qui la couvoitoit l'ot longue piece admonnestee, et vit que obeir n'y vouloit, il la fist toute [fol. 151v b] detrenchier. Et de ses playes yssoit lait pour sanc, et odeur grande rendoit. Encore forcené[4] sur elle, la fist estendre et atachier a pieux, et luy derompre tout[5] le corps tant que ceulx qui la martiroient estoyent tous lassiez. Et Dieu la gardoit que elle si tost ne mourust afin que les tourmenteurs[6] eussent cause de eulx convertir, lesquelz commencerent a crier, 'Empereur, nous n'en ferons plus, car les anges nous batent de chaiennes!' Et nouvaulx bouriaulx vindrent pour la tourmenter, et tantost furent mors. Et l'empereur, confus, ne savoit que faire. Il la fist estendre et flamer de graisse ardant. Et celle tousjours gloriffioit Dieu, et de sa bouche yssoit tres grant odeur.

"Et quant les tirans l'orent tant [fol. 152r a] tourmentee que recreuz furent, ilz la gitterent en une chartre obscure. Et Emenion, le cousin de l'empereur, ala gaitier en la chartre et vit Martine avironnee d'anges, assise en un trosne moult bien paree et[7] moult grant clarté et a cha[n]s[8] melodieux. Et elle tenoit une table d'or, en laquelle avoit escript:

"'Sire, doulx Jhesucrist, tant sont louees tes oeuvres en tes benois sains.' Celluy Emenion, moult esmerveillez de ceste chose, l'ala dire a l'empereur qui respondi que il estoit deceu par les enchantemens d'elle. L'endemain la fist le tirant mettre hors, et chascun s'esmerveilloit de ce que toute garie estoit, dont moult en y ot de convertis.

"Il la fist de rechief mener [fol. 152r b] au temple pour la contraindre a sacrefier aux faulx dieux. Adonc le diable qui estoit en l'ydolle commença a braire: 'Las,

---

[1] Et adonc] Adont
[2] derompre] a desrompre
[3] eulx, recevant martire joyeusement, louoyent Dieu] ilz receurent martire joyeusement louant Dieu
[4] forcené] plus forcené
[5] tout : *toute*
[6] les tourmenteurs] les tourmenteurs et le peuple
[7] et] a
[8] cha[n]s : *champs*

rounde aboute them, and a voyce was herde from heven that sayd: 'I spare you for the love of my ryght welbyloved Martyne.'

"And then the provost cryed to them for that they were converted, and sayd: 'O fooles, ye are deceyved by this enchauntresse Martyne!'

"And they answered without drede: 'Nay, thou arte deceyved by the dyvyll that dwelleth within thee, for thou knowest not Hym that made thee.'

"And the emperour, wrothe out of measure, commaunded them to be hanged and theyr flesshe to be al to-torne; and they, receyvynge martrydome, joyfully praysed God.

"And the emperour agayne made Martyne to be dispoyled al naked, and her flesshe whyte as a lylye, that made them abasshed for her grete beaute. And when the emperour whiche coveyted her had longe tyme counsayled her, [S4v] and sawe that she wolde not obaye, made her to be cutte al aboute. And out of her woundes there came mylke for blode, and yelded grete swetnesse. And yet he, woode on her, made to stretche her abrode and raced her with hokes, and brake all the body so moche that they that tourmented her were al wery. And God kepte her that she sholde not dye so soone to the entente that the tourmentoures myght have cause to be converted, the whiche began to crye, 'Emperoure, we wyll do no more, for the aungelles beteth us with chaynes!' And then there came newe tormentoures to tourment her, and anone they were deed. And the emperour, confused, wyste not what to doo but made her to be stretched to brenne her with brennynge grees. And alwaye she gloryfyed Our Lorde, and there came out of her mouthe ryght grete swetnesse.

"And when the tyrauntes had tourmented her so moche that they were ashamed, they cast her in a derke pryson. And Emenyon, the cosyn of the emperoure, wente to loke into the pryson: and he sawe Martyne envyronned with aungelles, set in a trone ryght well arayed, and there was grete clerenesse with many dyvers songes ryght melodyous. And she helde a table of golde, in the whiche there was wryten: 'My Lorde Swete Jhesu Cryst, so moche b[e][1] Thy werkes praysed in Thy blessyd sayntes.' Emenyon, gretely admervayled of this thynge, wente to tell it to the emperoure, whiche answered that he was deceyved by her enchauntementes. In the mornynge, [T1r] the tyraunt made her to be taken out of pryson, and everybody mervaylled of that that she was all hole, thrughe whiche many was converted.

"At the last, he made her to be ledde to the tymple to constrayne her to do sacrefyse to the false goddes. Then the devyll began to braye and sayd: 'Alas, alas

---

[1] b[e] : *by*

las, je suis confondus!' Et la vierge luy couvenda[1] que il s'en yssist et se monstrast en sa laidure, et tantost vint un grant tonnoire avecques fouldre qui chay du ciel, et tresbucha l'isdole et les prestres ardi. Adonc, forcena l'empereur plus sur[2] elle et la fist estendre, et toute luy arrachier la char de son corps[3] a pignes de fer; et celle tousjours adouroit Dieu.

"Et quant il vit que elle ne mouroit pas,[4] il la fist baillier aux bestes sauvages pour devourer. Et un grant lion, qui n'avoit mengié de trois jours, vint vers elle et l'enclina, et coste elle se coucha comme se fust un petite[5] chien et [fol. 152v a] luy lechoit les playes. Et celle beneissoit Nostre Seigneur, en disant: 'Dieux, Tu soiez benis,[6] qui par ta vertu amoderes la cruauté des bestes felonnes.'[7] Le tirant, aÿré de ceste chose, commenda que le lion fust remis en sa fosse. Et le lion se adreça par grant ire et fist un sault, et occist Emenion, le cousin de l'empereur. De laquel chose il fu moult dolent, et la commenda estre gittee[8] en un grant feu; et elle dedens estant[9] a joyeuse chiere, Dieux envoya un[10] grant vent qui espandi le feu d'entour[11] elle et ardi ceulx qui la tourmentoyent.

"L'empereur commanda que sa cheveleure, qui longue et belle estoit, lui fist oster,[12] disant que les[13] enchantemens estoitent en ses cheveux. Et la vierge luy dist: 'Tu ostes la cheveleure qui est l'aournement de femme, si que dist l'apostre, et Dieu t'ostera t[on][14] raigne, te [fol. 152v b] persecutera, et tu attendras la mort a tres grant douleur.' Il la commenda estre[15] enclose en un temp[l]e[16] ou estoient ses dieux, et clouÿ et seella luy meesmes la porte de son seel. Au chief de trois jours, revint et trouva ses dieux tresbuschiez et la vierge jouant avec[17] les anges, saine et entiere. L'empereur luy demanda que elle avoit fait de ses dieux? Et elle dist:[18] 'La

---

[1] confondus!' Et la vierge luy couvenda] convaincus!' Et la vierge lui commanda
[2] plus sur] sur
[3] toute luy arrachier la char de son corps] lui esracher toute la char
[4] ne mouroit pas] ne mouroit
[5] petite] petit
[6] benis] louez
[7] des bestes felonnes] des felonnesses bestes
[8] estre gittee] a gitter
[9] elle dedens estant] si que elle estoit dedens
[10] un : *ung*
[11] espandi le feu d'entour] espardi le feu d'environ
[12] fist oster] fust ostee
[13] les] ses
[14] t[on] : *ta*
[15] commenda estre] commanda a estre
[16] temp[l]e : *temphe*
[17] avec] avecques
[18] dist] respondi

I am confounded!' And the holy vyrgyne commaunded hym to come out, and that he sholde shewe hym in his owne lewde lykenesse. And anone there came a grete thondre with lyghtnynge that came from heven and brake the ydoll and brente the preestes. And then the emperoure was woode with her and made her to be stretched abrode, and raced all the flesshe of her body with combes of yron; and she alway worshypped God.

"And when he sawe that she dyed not, he made her to be put to wylde beestes to be devoured. And a grete lyon, that had not eten in thre dayes, came to her and bowed hym to her, and laye downe by her as it were a lytell dog, and lycked her woundes. And she thanked Our Lorde in saynge, 'Blessyd be Thou, Almyghty God, that by Thy vertue hast modered the cruelte of wycked bestes.' The tyraunte, wrothe with this thynge, commaunded that the lyon sholde be put agayne into his cave. And the lyon dressed hym by grete wrathe and made a lepe and slewe Emenyon, the emperoure's cosyn, of the whiche thynge he was ryght sorowfull and commaunded her to be cast into the fyre. And she beynge within with a joyful chere, God sente a grete wynde that put away the [T1v] fyre aboute her and brente them that tourmented her.

"The emperoure commaunded that the heere of her heed sholde be cutte awaye, whiche was ryght fayre and longe, sayenge that the enchauntementes was in her heeres. And the vyrgyne sayd to hym, 'Thou takest awaye the heeres whiche is an ornamente of woman, as the apostle sayth, and God shall put thee out of thy reygne and poursue thee. And thou shalte byde the dethe with grete sorowe and payne.'

"Then he made her to be enclosed in a temple where his goddes were, and nayled the dore, and sealed it with his owne sygnete. And when thre dayes were past, he came agayne and founde his goddes all overthrowne, and the holy vyrgyne playenge with aungelles, hole and sounde. The emperoure asked her what she had done with his goddes? And she sayd: 'The vertue of Jhesu Cryste hathe overthrowne them and confounded them.'

vertu Jhesucrist les a tresbuchiez et confondus.'¹ Adonc commenda² que on luy
coupast la gorge. Lors fu ouÿe une voix qui dist: 'Martine, vierge, pour ce que tu
t'es combatue pour Mon nom, entre avec les sains et³ Mon raigne, et t'esjouÿs en
pardurableté avec Moy.' Et ainsi fina la benoite Martine.

"Et adonc vindrent l'evesque de Romme a tout le clergie et ensevelirent le
corps en l'eglise [fol. 153r a] honnourablement. Et ce meesmes jour, l'Empereur
Alixandre⁴ fu feru de tel douleur que il mengoit sa char, et se mordoit
angoisseusement."⁵

## *Chapitre 7*     D'une autre saint Luce⁶

"Une autre sainte Luce, vierge, fu de la cité de Siracuse. Et⁷ si comme elle prioit
au sepulcre de sainte Agate pour sa mere qui estoit malade, elle vit en advison
sainte Agate ou mislieu des anges, aournee de pierres precieuses, qui luy dist:
'Luce, ma suer vierge devote,⁸ a quoy requiers tu de moy ce que toy mesmes puez
donner a ta mere? Je t'anonce que si que la cité de Cachonais est surhaulciee par
moy, aussi sera par toy honnouree⁹ celle de Siracuxe, car tu as a Jhesucrist appareillé joyaulx delictables en ta purté.' Luce se leva, [fol. 153r b] sa mere garie. Elle
donna quanque elle avoit pour Dieu, puis fina sa vie par martire.

"Et entre les autres martires que elle ot, le juge la menaça de faire mener
en la place de¹⁰ folles femmes et la¹¹ en despit de son espoux seroit viollee. Et elle
respondi: 'L'ame ne sera ja soulliee se la penssee ne s'y consent; car se tu me faiz
corrompre a force, ma chasteté en sera doublee, et ma victoire.' Et ainsi comme¹²
on la vouloit mener en la dicte place, elle fu si pesente que pour chevaulx¹³ ne pour
diverses bestes que ilz atachassent¹⁴ ne pot estre remuee. Et lui misdrent cordes es

---

¹ tresbuchiez et confondus] confondus
² commenda] commanda
³ et] en
⁴ l'Empereur Alixandre] cellui empereur qui Alixandre avoit nom
⁵ et se mordoit angoisseusement] *omitted*
⁶ D'une autre saint Luce] Ci dit d'une autre saint Luce et d'autres vierges martires
⁷ Et] Celle
⁸ devote] devote a Dieu
⁹ toy honnouree] toy
¹⁰ de] des
¹¹ la] que la
¹² ainsi comme] si comme
¹³ chevaulx] thoriaulx
¹⁴ atachassent] y atachassent

"And then he commaunded that one sholde cutte her throte. Then there was herde a voyce, that sayd: 'Martyne, vyrgyne, for that that thou hast fought for My name, thou shalte entre into My kyngdome amonge My sayntes. And thou shalte enjoye with Me everlastyngly.' And thus ended the blessyd Martyne.

"And then came the bysshoppe of Rome with all his clargye and buryed the body honourably in the chyrche. And the same day, the Emperoure Alexander was smyten with suche a sorowe that he ete his owne flesshe, and gnewe hymselfe to the dethe."

## Chapter 7    Of Saynt Luce of Syracuse [T2r]

"Another vyrgyne Saynt Luce there was in the cyte of Syracuse. And so as she prayed at the sepulture of Saynt Agace for her moder, whiche was syke, she sawe Saynt Agace in a vysyon in the myddes of aungelles, arayed in precyous stones, whiche sayd to her: 'Luce, my syster devoute vyrgyne, wherfore requyrest thou of me that thou mayst gyve to thy moder thyselfe? I tell thee for certayne that so as the cyte of Cathonyas is lyfted up by me, so shall the cyte of Syracuse be worshypped by thee. For thou hast arayed to Jhesu Cryst delectable jewelles in thy clennesse.' Luce rose up, and her moder was hole. And she gave al that she had for Goddes sake, and after ended her lyfe by martyrdome.

"And amonge other martyrdomes that she had, the juge manaced her to make her to be ledde to the place where the lewde women used theyr lyfe, and there she sholde be defouled in the despyte of her spouse. And she answered, 'The soule shal never be defouled without consente of the mynde. For yf thou make me to be corrupted by force, my chastyte and my vyctory shall be doubled therby.' And so as they wolde lede her to the place abovesayd, she was so hevy that for no horse nor other bestes that sholde drawe her thyder myght not be removed. And they put cordes on her fete to drawe her forthe, but she was so

pies pour luy[1] traisner, mais elle estoit si[2] ferme comme une m[o]ntaigne.[3] Et a son trespassement, elle prophetisa ce qui estoit a avenir a l'empereur.[4]

"*Item*, digne [fol. 153v a] de grant reverence est la glorieuse vierge sainte Benoite, nee de Romme. Ceste[5] avoit avec elle douze vierges convertis par sa predication. Elle desira acroistre[6] par preschier la religion crestienne, si se parti elle et sa compaignie et traverserent ses benoites vierges maintes[7] sans avoir nulle paour, car Dieux estoit avecquez elles. Et par la voulenté de Nostre Seigneur, furent sep[a]rees[8] d'ensemble et s'espandirent en diverses contrees adfin que chascune peust prouffiter. Et comme la vierge sainte Benoite eust plusieurs païs convertis et la foy de Jhesucrist, elle fina sa vie par palme de martire, et pareillement[9] le firent ses saintes compagnes.

"*Item*, ne fu pas de mendre parfection [fol. 153v b] sainte Fauste, vierge de l'aage de .xiiii. ans, laquelle pour ce que elle ne vouloit sacrefier aux ydolles, l'Empereur Maximien la fist sier d'une scie de fer. Mais comme les scieurs ne finassent de scier depuis l'eure de tierce jusques a l'eure de nonne, et ne la peussent entamer, lui dirent: 'Par quelle vertu nous as tu tenuz par tes enchantemens sy longuement cy sans riens faire?' Et Fauste les commença a preschier de Jhesucrist et de sa loy, et les converti. L'empereur, de ce moult indigne, la fist tourmenter de divers tourmens. Et entre les autres luy fist clouer le chief de mille cloux si comme le heaume d'une[10] chevalier, et celle prioit pour ceulx qui la persecutoyent.

"Et le prevost [fol. 154r a] fu converti par ce que il vit les cieux ouvers[11] de Dieu seant avec ses anges. Et quant Fauste fu mise en la chaudiere d'iaue boullant, le dit prevost s'escria, 'Sainte serve de Dieu, ne t'en va pas sans moy!' et sailli dedens la chaudiere. Quant les deux autres que elle avoit convertis virent ce, ilz saillierent aussi en[12] la chaudiere dont l'eaue boulloit a tres grant onde. Et Fauste les touchoit, et ilz ne sentoyent nul mal. Et elle disoit, 'Je suis ou mislieu si comme la vigne portant fruit, si comme Nostre Sire dist: *La ou .ii. ou .iii. sont assemblez en nom de moy,*[13] *Je suis ou mislieu de eulx.*' Et adonc fu ouÿe une voix du ciel[14] qui dist:

---

[1] misdrent cordes es pies pour luy] mirent cordes aux piez pour elle

[2] si] aussi

[3] m[o]ntaigne : *mantaigne*

[4] l'empereur] l'empire

[5] Ceste] Celle

[6] par sa predication. Elle desira acroistre] a sa predicacion. Elle desira pouoir accroistre

[7] ses benoites vierges maintes] ces benoites vierges maintes terres

[8] sep[a]rees : *sepurees*

[9] pareillement] semblablement

[10] d'une] d'un

[11] ouvers : *ou ouvers*

[12] en] dedens

[13] Nostre Sire dist: *La ou .ii. ou .iii. sont assemblez en nom de moy* . . .] Nostre Seigneur dit: *La ou plusieurs sont assemblez en mon nom* . . .

[14] une voix du ciel] une voix

stable as it had ben an hylle. And at her passynge, she prophesyed that that was to come to the emperoure.

"Also the gloryous vyrgyne Saynt Benet [T2v] borne in Rome is worthy of grete reverence. She had with her .xii. vyrgynes converted by her predycacyon. She desyred to encrease by prechynge the Crysten relygyon so she departed, and her company, and preched and converted moche people without havynge ony drede, for God was with them. And by the wyll of God, they were departed in sondre and stretched them in dyvers countrees to that entente that every of theym myght profyte. And as this holy vyrgyne had converted dyvers countres and encreased the faythe of Our Lorde, she ended her lyfe by the palme of martyrdome, and on the same wyse dyde her holy felawes.

"And Saynt Fauste was not of lesse perfeccyon of the age of .xiiii. yeres, whiche for that that she wolde not do sacrefyse to the ydolles, the Emperoure Maxymyon made her to be sawed with a sawe of yron. But as the sawyers seased not sawynge fro the houre of tyerce anone to the houre of noone, and they myght not entame her. And they sayd to her: 'By what vertue hast thou holden us by thyne enchauntementes soo longe here without doynge ony thynge?' And the holy vyrgyne Fauste began to preche to them of Jhesu Cryst and of His lawe, and so converted them. The emperoure had grete indyngnacyon hereof and made her to be tourmented with dyvers tourmentes, and amonge others he made to nayle her heed with a thousande nayles lyke to the helme of a knyght; and she prayed for them that dyde her persecucyon.

"And [T3r] the provost was converted by that that he sawe the hevens open and God syttynge with His aungelles. And when Saynt Fauste was in the cawdron of water boylynge, the sayd provost began to crye: 'Thou holy servaunt of God, ne go thou not without me!' and lepte into the cawdron. And when the other twayne that [s]he[1] had converted sawe that, they lepte into the cawdron also, of whiche the water boyled ryght fervently. And the holy Fauste touched theym, and they felte no maner of evyll. And she sayd, 'I am in the myddes as it were a vyne berynge fruyte, as Our Lorde sayth: *where there ben two or thre assembled in My name, I am in the myddes of them.*' And then there was herde a voyce

---

[1] [s]he : *he*

'Venés, ames beneurees, le Pere vous demande.' [fol. 154r b] Et yceulx, ouÿans[1] ceste chose, rendirent les esperis joyeusement."

## *Chapitre 8*    De sainte Justine[2]

"Justine, vierge sainte[3] nee d'Anthioche, jeunete et de souveraine beauté, surmonta[4] le diable qui c'estoit[5] vanté a l'invocacion d'un [n]igromencien[6] que il feroit tant qu'elle feroit la voulenté d'un homme qui fort estoit espris de s'amour, et ne la laissoit en paix. Mais pour ce que par prieres ne promesses[7] riens n'y faisoit, il se cuida aidier de l'annemi, mais riens n'y valut,[8] car la glorieuse Justine en enchaça[9] l'annemi par plusieurs fois, qui se mettoit en fourmes diverses[10] pour la tempter. Mais il fu vaincu d'elle, et s'en ala confus. Et au derrain elle fina sa vie par martire, et converti[11] [fol. 154v a] le dit nigromencien qui avoit nom Ciprien et estoit homme de moult mauvaise vie, mais il fu par elle mis[12] en bonne. Et autres plusieurs furent convertis par les signes que Nostre Seigneur demonstra en elle.[13]

"*Item*, la benoite vierge Eulalie, nee d'Espaigne, de l'aage de douze ans s'embla de ses parens qui la tenoyent enclose pour ce que elle ne finoit de parler de Jhesucrist. Sy s'en fouy par nuyt, et ala gitter les ydolles des temples a terre, et crier aux juges qui persecutoyent les martirs qu'ilz estoient deceuz, et que en celle foy vouloit mourir. Si fu mise ou nombre des chevaliers de Jhesucrist et ot plusieurs tourmens, et maintes gens furent convertis par les signes que Nostre Seigneur demonstroit en elle.

"*Item*, une autre sainte [fol. 154v b] vierge qui nommee estoit[14] Martre fu durement tourmentee pour la foy de Dieu, et entre ses tourmens ot les mamelles arrachiees. Et aprés si comme elle estoit en la chartre ou n'en l'avoit mise,[15] Dieu

---

[1] ouÿans] oÿant
[2] De sainte Justine] Ci dit de sainte Justine et d'autres vierges
[3] vierge sainte] sainte vierge
[4] surmonta : *sourmonta*
[5] c'estoit] se estoit
[6] [n]igromencien : *igromencien*
[7] promesses] par promesses
[8] valut] val
[9] en enchaça] enchaça
[10] fourmes diverses] diverses fourmes
[11] confus. Et au derrain elle fina sa vie par martire, et converti] confus. Elle converti par sa predicacion cellui qui la couvoitoit follement, et aussi converty
[12] mis] muez
[13] en elle] en elle. Et a la fin, elle se parti du siecle par martire
[14] nommee estoit] on nommoit
[15] ou n'en l'avoit mise] *omitted*

from heven that sayd: 'Come to Me, My blessyd vyrgyne; the Fader hath asked for you.' And they that herde this thynge yelded up the ghost ryght joyously."

## *Chapter 8*      Of Saynt Justyne

"The holy vyrgyne Justyne borne in Anthyoche, yonge and of soverayne beaute, overcame the devyll whiche was called up by the callynge of a nygromancere that he sholde do so moche that she sholde consente to the wyll of a man that was gretely taken with her love, and lefte her not in peas. But for that that by prayers nor by promyses he coude doo nothynge, he trowed [T3v] that the devyll sholde helpe hym. But it advayled hym not, for the gloryous Justyne chased the enemy dyvers tymes, whiche that put hym in dyvers fourmes to tempte her. But he was overcome of her and wente his waye, confused. And at the last she ended her lyfe by martyrdome and converted the sayd nygromancere, that was called Cypryen, and had ben a man of ryght a shrewde lyfe, but by her he was put in a good lyfe; and dyvers others were converted by the sygnes that God shewed in her.

"Also the blessyd vyrgyne Eulalye, borne in Spayne, of the age of .xii. yeres stale awaye from her fader and moder that helde her in close for that that she never stynted to speke of Our Lorde Jhesu Cryst. So she fledde by nyght and wente and cast downe the ydolles of the temples to the erthe, and cryed to the juges that dyde so moche persecucyon to the martyres that they were deceyved, and that in that faythe she wolde dye. So she was put in the nombre of the knyghtes of Jhesu Cryste and had many grete tourmentes. And there was moche people converted by the myracles that God shewed to her.

"Also of another holy vyrgyne that was called Matre whiche was ryght sore tourmented for the fayth of Jhesu Cryste, and amonge her tourmentes she had her pappes raced frome her body. And after, so as she was in the pryson, God

luy envoya son ange qui luy restabli sa santé, dont le prevost fu[1] durement hebahis. Mais ne laissa pour tant que durement[2] ne la feist tourmenter de divers tourmens, et au derrain rendi l'esperit a Dieu et gist son corps pres la cité[3] de Rains.

"*Item*, la vierge[4] sainte Foy souffri martire en son enffance et ot moult de
tourmens. Et Nostre Seigneur la couronna a la fin a la veue du monde par son
ange, qui couronne de pierres precieuses luy aporta. Et moult de signes monstra
Dieux [fol. 155r a] en elle, par quoy plusieurs furent convertis.

"La benoite[5] vierge Marcienne vit que on faisoit honneur a un faulx ymage
d'une ydolle: elle prist celle ydolle et la gitta a terre, et la rompi, pour laquelle
cause elle fu tant batue que laissee fu comme morte et enchartree[6] en une place,
ou quel lieu un faulx menistre la cuida par nuit efforcier.[7] Mais par grace divine
vint entre celluy et elle un gros mur que il n'y pot aler, qui[8] fu l'endemain veue de
tout le peuple, par quoy maintes gens furent convertis. Ceste ot plusieurs grans
tourmens, mais tousjours preshoit le nom de Jhesucrist et au derrain pria a Dieu
que a soy[9] la voulsist prendre, sy fina ou tourment.

"Sainte Eufanie[10] autresi moult souffri pour le nom de Dieu.[11] [fol. 155r b] Elle
fu moult de lignee noble[12] et tres belle de corps. Le prevost Priscus l'amonnestoit
que elle adourast les ydolles, et renonçast a Jhesucrist. Et elle, par tres grans
arguemens, luy respondoit tant que souldre n'y savoit, dont si grant yre ot d'estre
surmonté[13] d'une femme que il la fist batre et tourmenter[14] de tres griefs et divers
tourmens. Mais tout fu son corps froissié par moult de [peines],[15] le sens d'elle
ades croissoit et rendoit parolles plaines du Saint Esperit. Et sy que elle estoit
tourmenter, l'ange de Dieu deffendi[16] qui despeça le tourment, et tourmenta les
tourmenteurs, et celle a visaige joyeux s'en yssi toute saine. Le faulx prevost fist
embracer une fournoise, dont la flame s'estendoit par .xl. coudes de hault, et

---

[1] fu] fu l'endemain
[2] durement] griefment
[3] pres la cité] pres de la cité
[4] la vierge] la glorieuse vierge
[5] La benoite] Item, la benoite
[6] enchartree] fu enchartree
[7] par nuit efforcier] par nuit aler efforcier
[8] un gros mur que il n'y pot aler, qui] une si haulte paroit que il n'y pot aler. Laquelle paroit
[9] a Dieu que a soy] Dieu que ainsi
[10] Eufanie] Enfante
[11] Dieu] Jhesu
[12] de lignee noble] noble de lignee
[13] surmonté] vaincus
[14] batre et tourmenter] tourmenter
[15] [peines] : *paiens*] peines
[16] tourmenter, l'ange de Dieu deffendi] ou tourment l'ange de Dieu descendi

sente unto her His aungell whiche that establysshed her helthe, wherof the provost was gretely abasshed. But he lefte not for that, but that he made her to [T4r] be gretely tourmented of dyvers paynes. And at the laste she yelded up the spyryte to God, and her holy body lyeth nygh¹ the cyte of Raynes.

"Also the blessyd vyrgyne Saynt Faythe suffred martyrdome in her youthe and had many tourmentes. And Our Lorde crowned her and sente her a crowne of precyous stones by an aungell, and God shewed for her many mervaylles, by the whiche many people were converted.

"Also the holy and blessyd vyrgyne Marcyenne, when one dyde worshyp to a false ymage of an ydoll, she toke the ydoll and threwe hym to the grounde and brake hym, for the whiche cause she was so moche beten that they lefte her for deed and prysoned in a place, in the whiche place a false mynystre trowed to have ravysshed her by nyght. But by grace devyne there came a grete walle bytwene her and hym that he myght not goo frome thens, the whiche was sene on the morowe of all the people, by the whiche there was moche people converted. This holy and blessyd vyrgyne hadde many dyvers tourmentes, but alwaye she preched of the name of Jhesu Cryste. And at the laste she prayed to God that He wolde take her unto Hym, and thus she ended her lyfe in her grete tourmente.

"Also the blessyd vyrgyne Saynt Eufenye also suffred moche for the name of God. She was of good kynred and of noble shap of body. The provost Prysens counsaylled her that she sholde worshyp the ydolles, and forsake Jhesu Cryste. And she by ryght [T4v] grete argumentes answered hym, so moche that he coude not assoyle her questyons, wherof he had so grete wrathe that he was overcome of a woman and made her to be tourmented with ryght grevous and harde tourmentes. But thoughe the body of her were sore brused, her wytte alway encreased and yelded good wordes full of the Holy Ghost. And when she was tourmented, the aungel of God defended her and brake the tourment, and tourmented the tourmentoures; and she with a gladde vysage wente out all hole. The false provost made to hete a fournoys, of whiche the flame stretched out by .xl. cubytes

¹ nygh : *nyght*

dedens la fist [fol. 155v a] gitter; et[1] chantoit dedens louenges a Dieu moult melodieusement, si hault que tous l'ouoyent. Et quant le feu fu tout consommé, elle
s'en yssy sauve et saine.[2] Le juge, plus aïré, fist aporter tenailles ardens pour luy
errachier les membres. Mais ceulx qui devoient ce faire furent sy espoventes que
nul n'y[3] osa touchier, et furent les tourmens derompus. Sy fist le faulx tirant
admener quatre lions et deux[4] bestes sauvages, mais ceulx la vindrent adourer.
Mais[5] la benoite vierge, desireuse d'aler a son Dieu, Luy pria que Il la voulsist
prendre. Et adonc elle fina, sans[6] que nulle beste la touchast."[7]

*Chapitre 9*     De la vierge[8] Theodosine, et de sainte Barbre, et de
                 sainte Dorothee

"La constance du martire de la benoite Theodosine [fol. 155v b] fait a nostre propos
bien a rementevoir. Tres noble estoit ceste vierge, et de grant biauté de l'aage de
.xviii. ans. Celle par merveilleuse scens disputoit au juge qui la menaçoit de martire se elle ne renonçoit a Jhesucrist. Et comme elle respondist parolles divines, il
la fist p[e]ndre[9] par les cheveulx et bastre durement. Et celle luy disoit: 'Certes,
chetif est celluy[10] qui veult seigneurir autruy, et ne se scet seigneurir luy meismes.
Las a celluy qui a grant cure d'estre reampli de viandes, et n'a nul soing des famil-
lieux. Mal pour celluy qui voulst estre chauffé, et ne revest ne chaufe les mal
vestus.[11] Las a celluy qui veult reposer, et les autres travaille.[12] Mal pour celluy [fol.
156r a] qui dit toutes choses estre sciennes, et il les a receues de Dieu. Las a celluy
qui veult que un[13] luy face bien, et il fait tous maulx.' Parolles dignes disoit tousjours la vierge en son tourment.

---

[1] et] elle
[2] sauve et saine] saine et sauve
[3] n'y] ne
[4] deux] .ii. autres fieres
[5] vindrent adourer. Mais] venoient aourer. Et adont
[6] Dieu, Luy pria que Il la voulsist prendre. Et adonc elle fina, sans] Dieu, pria que Il
la voulsist prendre, et adont elle fina sans ce
[7] F *wants remaining chapters, ends here*
[8] De la vierge] Ci dit de la vierge
[9] p[e]ndre : *pondre*
[10] chetif est celluy] cellui est chetif
[11] chauffé, et ne revest ne chaufe les mal vestus] eschauffé et ne eschauffe, ne revest
les mourans de froit
[12] les autres travaille] treveille les autres
[13] un] on

of hyght, and made her to be cast in it. And she sange within it, praysynge God ryght melodyously, soo hyghe that all people praysed her; and when the fyre was all consumed, she came out saufe and hole. The juge, wrother than he was, made to brynge brennynge pynsons to drawe out her membres. But those that sholde have done it were so aferde that none durst touche her, and all the tourmentes were all to-broken. So the false tyraunte made to brynge foure lyons and other .ii. wylde beestes, but they worshypped her. And the blessyd vyrgyne, desyrous to go to her God, prayed Hym that He wolde take her to Hym. And then she ended, without touchynge of ony of the wylde beestes."

## Chapter 9     Of the vyrgyne Theodosyne, Saynt Barbara, and Saynt Dorothe [T5r]

"The constaunce of the martyrdome of the blessyd Theodosyne cometh to our purpose well to be remembred. This vyrgyne was ryght noble and of grete beaute of the age of .xviii. yeres. She by mervayllous wytte dysputed with the juge whiche manaced her to tourment her yf she forsoke not Jhesu Cryst. And as she answered by godly wordes, he made her to be taken by the heere and beten ryght sore. And she sayd to hym: 'Certes, he is a caytyfe that wolde lordeshyp another and cannot governe hymselfe. Alas to hym that hath grete charge to be fulfylled with metes and drynkes, and hath no thought of the hongre. Evyl for hym that wolde be warmed, and wyll not clothe ne warme those that ben evyll clothed. Wo be to hym that wolde have rest, and travaylleth others. Evyll be it to hym that saythe all thynges ben his, and he hathe receyved them of God. Wo be to hym that wolde that one sholde do well, and he dothe al evyll.' Suche worthy wordes sayd alwaye that holy vyrgyne in her tourmente.

"Mais pour ce que elle avoit passion cuer de honte de ce que ses membres
vergongueux apparoient,[1] Dieux envoya une blanche nue qui la couvri toute. Et
Urban de plus en plus la menaçoit, auquel elle dist: 'Tu ne m'osteras nul des mes[2]
du disner qui m'est appareillé.' Et le tirant la menaça de corompre sa virginité,
auquel respondi:[3] 'Tu menaces en vain corrupcion en moy, car Dieux habite es
cuers honnestes.' Le prevost, plus enragié, la fist gitter en la mer, une pesant pierre
au col. [fol. 156r b] Et elle [fu][4] soustenue des anges, et ramenee chantant a terre,
et portoit la vierge entre ses mains[5] la pierre qui plus pisoit[6] que elle. Le tirant
fist laissier aler sur elle deux liepars, mais yceulx faillans[7] entour elle luy faisoient
feste. Au derrain le tirant, qui n'en savoit comment faire, la fist decoller, et de son
corps departi l'ame visiblement en guyse d'une blanche coulombe resplandissant.
Et celle mesmes nuit s'aparut[8] a ses parens, plus clere que le soleil, a tout couronne
precieuse, acompaignee de vierges, tenant une croix d'or, et leur dist: 'Vees quelle
est la gloire que vous me vouliez oster.' Et ceulx se converterent.

"*Item*, ou temps Maximien l'empereur flouri en vertus[9] la benoite Barbre,
vierge de noble lignee [fol. 156v a] et souverainement belle. Son pere, pour cause
de sa biauté, l'avoit enclose en une tour. Celle ot inspiracion de la foy crestienne,[10]
et pour ce que par autre ne pouoit estre baptisee, elle meesmes prist de l'iaue et
se baptisa ou nom du Pere, du Filz,[11] et du Saint Esperit. Son pere la voult marier
tres haultement, et elle reffusa tous mariages.[12] Et a la parfin, regehy que elle
estoit crestienne et avoit a Dieu vouee[13] sa virginité, le pere pour celle cause la
voulst occire; et elle s'en fouy et luy eschappa.[14] Et comme le pere la poursuivist
pour mettre a mort, au derrain la trouva par l'enseignement d'un[15] pastour, qui
tantost secha luy et ses bestes.

---

[1] cuer de honte de ce que ses membres vergongueux apparoient] en son cuer de honte
que ses membres apparoient tous nuds au peuple

[2] mes] mets

[3] respondi] elle respondi

[4] [fu] : *omitted*] fu

[5] mains] bras

[6] p[e]soit : *pisoit*

[7] faillans] sailloient

[8] s'aparut] apparut

[9] vertus] vertu

[10] crestienne] de Dieu

[11] du Filz] et du Filz

[12] mariages] mariages par lonc temps

[13] regehy que elle estoit crestienne et avoit a Dieu vouee] elle regehi que crestianne
estoit et avoit vouee a Dieu sa virginité

[14] et luy eschappa] et eschappa

[15] d'un : *d'une*

"But for that she had sorowe in her herte of the shame of that that her sham-fast membres appered openly, God sente her a whyte cloude that covered her al. And Urban the juge manaced her more and more, to whome she sayd: 'Thou shewest none of my meeses of my dyner that is ordeyned for me.' And the tyraunt manaced her that he wolde corrupte her vyrgynyte, to whom she answered: 'Thou manacest [T5v] in vayne to be corrupcyon in me, for God enhabyteth in the clene hertes.' The provost, more wode than he was, made her to be cast in the see, an hevy stone aboute her necke. And she borne up with aungelles and brought agayne to the londe syngynge and bare the stone bytwene her handes, whiche wayed moche more than herselfe. The tyraunte made to lette go upon her .ii. leoperdes, but they lepte aboute her, makynge her grete chere. At the last, the tyraunt that knewe not howe to do made to smyte off her heed, and the soule departed fro her body vysybly in the shappe of a whyte dowve, shynynge bryght. And the same nyght she appered to her fader and moder, more clerer than the sone, crowned with precyous stones, accompanyed with many vyrgynes, holdynge a crosse of golde in her hande, and sayd to them: 'Se here what is the joy that ye wolde have put awaye from me.' And by that they were converted.

"Also in the tyme of Maxymyan the emperoure floured in vertues the blessyd vyrgyne Saynt Barbara of noble lygnage and soveraynely fayre. Her fader, for bycause of her beaute, had shytte her in a toure. And she had inspyracyon of the Crysten faythe, and for that that she myght not be baptysed of none other, she herselfe toke water and baptysed her in the name of the Fader, and Sone, and the Holy Ghost. Her fader wolde have maryed her ryght hyghly, and she refused all maryages; and at the laste, she tolde that she was Crystened and hadde vowed her vyrgynyte unto God. The fader wolde [T6r] have slayne her for that cause; and she fledde and escaped. And as her fader poursued her to put her to the dethe, at the laste he founde her by the techynge of a shepeherde, whiche serched anone bothe hym and his beestes.

"Le pere la mena au prevost, lequel pour ce que elle desobehy a tous ses com-mandemens, la fist [fol. 156v b] martirier de plusieurs griefs[1] tourmens, et pendre par les piez contre mont. Et elle luy disoit, 'Chetif, ne vois tu pas que tourmens ne me font point de mal?' Et luy, forsené, luy fist errachier les mamelles, et en tel[2] estat la fist mener par la cité; et elle tousjours gloriffioit Dieu. Mais pour ce que elle avoit honte que son corps vierge fust[3] veu nue, Nostre Sire envoya son ange qui la sana de toutes ses playes, et luy couvry le corps d'un vestement blanc. Et quant elle ot assez esté[4] pourmenee, on la ramena devant le prevost, qui se forcena quant il la vit toute saine et sa face resplandissant.[5]

"Sy la fist de rechief tourmenter tant que il la commenda, quant plus ne sçot [fol. 157r a] pourpensser de tourmens, que en la tast[6] de devant luy et que on lui trenchaste la teste. Et elle fist son oroison et pria Dieu que elle fust ou l'aide[7] de tou[s][8] ceulx qui le requerroyent en remembrance d'elle, et qui recorderoyent sa passion. Et quant elle ot finé, une voix fut ouÿe, disant: 'Viens, tres amee fille. Te reposer au raigne de mon Pere[9] et reçoy ta couronne; et ce que tu as requis te sera ottroya.'[10] Et si comme elle fu montee en la montaigne ou elle fu decollee, son felon pere l'y[11] coupa luy mesmes le chief. Et si comme il descendoit de la montaigne, le feu du ciel le fouldroya et mist en cendre.

"*Item*, la benoite vierge Dorothee pareillement souffry plusieurs martires en Capadoce. Et pour ce que elle ne vouloyt prendre [fol. 157r b] nul homme a mary et pour ce avé que tant[12] parloit de son espoux Jhesucrist, le maistre des escolles qui estoit nommé Theophilus luy dist par moquerie quant on la menoit decoller que au moins quant elle seroit devers son espoux, que elle luy envoyast des roses et des pommes du vergier de son mary. Et elle dist que si feroit elle. Donc il advint que si tost que elle ot parfait son martire, un tres bel petit enfant comme de l'aage de .iiii. ans vint a Theophillus, et apportoit un petit paneret plein de souveraine-ment belles roses et pommes a merveilles bien flairans et belles, et dist que la vierge [Dorothee][13] les luy envoyoit. Adonc fu celluy esmerveillez car il estoit yver

---

[1]  griefs] tres grans tourmens
[2]  tel] cel
[3]  fust] estoit
[4]  assez esté] esté assez
[5]  resplandissant] clere comme estoille
[6]  il la commenda, quant plus ne scot pourpensser de tourmens, que en la tast] tant que les tourmenteurs estoient lassez sur elle, et au derrain dist par grant yre que on l'otast
[7]  elle fust ou l'aide] Il feust en ayde
[8]  tou[s] : *toux*
[9]  au raigne de mon Pere] ou regne de ton Pere
[10]  ottroya] ottroyé
[11]  l'y] lui
[12]  mary et pour ce avé que tant] mari et tant
[13]  [Dorothee] : *Thorodee*

"And the fader ledde her to the provost, the whiche for that that she dysobeyed al his commaundementes, made her to be martyred with many a grevous tourmente, and hanged her by the feete. And she sayd to hym: 'Cay- tyfe, ne seest thou not that the tourmentes dothe me no harme?' And he, ryght wrothe, made her pappes to be drawne frome her body, and in that estate made her to be ledde thrughe the cyte; and she alwaye gloryfyed God. But for that that she hadde shame that her vyrgynall body was sene all naked, Our Lorde sente her His aungell and heled all her woundes, and covered her body with a whyte clothe. And when she had ben ledde forth ynoughe, one ledde her agayne before the provost, whiche was wode when he sawe her all hole, and her face shynynge bryght.

"Soo he made her agayne to be tourmented soo moche that he commaunded when he coude thynke of no mo tourmentes that her heed sholde be smyten off. And she made her orysons and prayed God that He myght be in the helpe of all them that requyred her in remembraunce and recorded her passyon. And when she hadde all ended her oryson and prayer, there was a voyce herde from heven, whiche sayd unto her in this wyse: 'Come unto Me, my ryght dere welbyloved [T6v] dough- ter, to rest thee in the kyngdome of My Fader and receyve thy crowne; and that that thou hast requyred shall be graunted to thee.' And so as she was gone up upon the hylle where she sholde be heeded, her cruell fader smote off her heed hymselfe. And as he came downe the hylle, the fyre of heven brent hym al to poudre.

"Also the blessyd vyrgyne Saynt Dorothe the same wyse suffred dyvers mar- tyrdomes in Capadoce. And for that that she wolde not take no man to hous- bande and spake so moche of her spouse Jhesu Cryst, the mayster of the scoles whiche was named Theophylus sayd to her in mockery when one ledde her to be heeded, that at the leest when she sholde be with her spouse, that she wolde sende to hym of the roses and apples of the gardyne of her housbande. And she sayd that she wolde, wherof it happened that as soone as she had made an ende of her martyrdome, ryght a fayre yonge chylde as of the age of .iiii. yeres come to Theophylus and brought with hym a lytell panyer full of soveraynly fayre roses and apples, mervayllously well-smellynge and fayre, and sayd that the vyrgyne Dorothe sente them to hym. Then was he gretely admervaylled, for it was wryten

ou mois de fevrier. Sy se converti, et puis fu [fol. 157v a] martirié pour le nom de Jhesucrist.

"Se de toutes les saintes vierges qui sont ou ciel par costance de martire te vouloie raconter, longue histoire y couvendroit — si comme sainte Cecille, saint Agnes, sainte Agathe, et infinies autres — et se plus en veulx avoir, ne t'estuet que regarder ou *Mirouoir Historial*: la asses en trouveras.

"Sy te diray encore de sainte Christine et pour ce que elle est [t]a¹ marraine et moult est vierge de grant dignité, plus a plain te² diray la vie, qui moult est devote et belle."³

## *Chapitre 10*      Ci dit de⁴ la vie sainte Christine, vierge

"La benoite vierge sainte Christine⁵ fu de la cité de Tir, fille de Urban, maistre de la chevallerie. Celle, pour sa grant biauté, estoit tenue enclose de son pere en une tour, et [fol. 157v b] avoit avec elle douze pucelles. Et y avoit⁶ fait faire son pere un moult bel oratoire de ydolles pres de la chambre de Christine adfin que elle les adourast. Mais elle, qui estoit⁷ sy enffant comme de l'aage de .xii. ans estoit ja inspiree de la foy de Jhesucrist, ne des ydoles ne faisoit compte; dont ses pucelles s'esmerveilloyent, et souvent l'admonnestoyent de faire oblacion. Et celle, quant elle avoit pris l'ensence si comme pour sacrefier aux ydolles, elle s'agenoilloit devers Orient a une fenestre et regardoit vers le ciel et encençoit a Dieu inmortel. Et la plus grant part de la nuit estoit a celle fenestre, et regardant les estoilles, gemissoit et reclamoit⁸ Dieu devottement, et luy prioit [fol. 158r a] qu'en aide luy fust contre ses adversaires.

"Les pucelles, qui bien appercevoyent que son cuer avoit en Jhesucrist, souventeffois s'agenoilloient, mains jointes devant elle, luy priant que elle ne voulsist mettre s'entente⁹ en Dieu estrange, ains voulsist celebrer aux dieux de ses parens; et que se il estoit sceu, elle et toutes en seroient destruites. Christine respondoit que elles estoient deceues par le diable qui les admonnestoit de aourer tant de dieux, et que il n'en estoit que Un.

---

¹ [t]a : *la*

² te] t'en

³ devote et belle] belle et devote

⁴ Ci dit de la vie] Ci dit de

⁵ Christine] Christine, vierge

⁶ y avoit] avoit

⁷ estoit] ancore estoit

⁸ regardant les estoilles, gemissoit et reclamoit] regardoit les estoilles et gemissoit reclamant

⁹ elle ne voulsist mettre s'entente] mettre s'entente ne voulsist

in the moneth of February. So he was converted, and after was martyred for the name of Jhesu Cryst.

"So of all other sayntes vyrgynes that ben in heven by constaunce of martyrdome yf I wolde tell thee, the hystory sholde be ryght longe: so as Saynt Cecyle, Saynt Agnes, Saynt Agace, and infynyte [U1r] others. And yf thou wylte have mo, go and beholde in the *Hystoryal Myroure*, and there thou shalte fynde ynoughe. And I shall tell thee yet of Saynt Crystyne for that that she is thy godmoder and is a vyrgyne of grete dygnyte, I shall tell the lyfe of her more playne, whiche is devoute and fayre."

## Chapter 10     The lyfe of Saynt Christine, vyrgyne and martyre

"The blessid vyrgyne Saynt Christine was of the cyte of Syre, doughter of Urban, mayster of the chevalrye. This lady, for her beaute, was kepte in close by the commaundement of her fader in a toure, and she had with her seven maydens. And there her fader lete make a fayre oratory of ydolles nyghe to the chambre of Christyne to the entente that she sholde worshyp them, but she that was so yonge as of the age of .xii. yeres was enspyred of the fayth of Jhesu Cryst and made no force of the ydolles; wherof the maydens mervaylled, and often tymes they called on her to do oblacyon. And when she had taken ensence so as to make sacrefyse to the ydolles, she kneled towarde the Eest at a wyndowe and loked towarde heven, and encensed the immortall God. And the moost parte of the nyght she was at that wyndowe, beholdynge the sterres. And she, waylynge, besought God ryght devoutely and prayed Hym that He wolde be [U1v] her helpe agaynst all her adversaryes.

"The maydens, whiche perceyved well that her herte was all in Jhesu Cryste, kneled before her often tymes with joyned handes, prayenge that she sholde not put her entente in a straunge God, but that she wolde worshyp the goddes of her fader and moder; and yf that she were knowne, al they sholde be destroyed. Saynt Christine answered that they were deceyved by the devyll whiche styred them to worshyp so many goddes, and that there was but One.

"Au derrain, comme son pere sceust que sa fille ne voulsist adourer les ydolles, trop en fu dolent et moult l'en reprist. Et elle dist que elle offreroit voulentiers a Dieu du ciel. Et celluy cuida que elle [fol. 158r b] voulsist dire a Jupiter et fu joyeulx, et la voult baisier. Mais elle s'ecria: 'Ne touches a ma bouche! Car je vueil offrir offerande nette a Dieu celestre.' De ce fu encores[1] content le pere. Et elle s'en entra en sa chambre et la clouy; a[2] genolz se mist et offry sainte oroison a Dieu en plourant. Et l'ange de Nostre Seigneur descendi, qui la reconforta et luy apporta pain blanc et viande de quoy elle menga car de trois jours n'avoit gousté de viande. Aprés ce, comme Christine veist par sa fenestre plusieurs povres crestiennes mendians au pié de sa tour, et elle n'eust que leur[3] donner, elle alla querre les ydolles de son pere qui estoient d'or et d'argent, et les froissa toutes et donna les pieces aux povres.

"Et [fol. 158v a] quant son pere sçot ceste chose, il la bati tres cruellement. Et elle disoit plainement que il estoit deceu d'aourer telz[4] faulx ymaiges, et que il n'estoit que un Dieu en Trinité, lequelle confessoit, ne autre dieu pour mourir[5] n'aoureroit. Dont luy, enragié sur elle, la fist lier de chaines et mener batant par les places, et puis mettre en chartre. Et luy meesmes voulst estre juge de ceste[6] cause, sy la fist l'endemain admener devant luy et la menaça de tous tourmens se elle ne adouroit les ydolles. Et aprés ce qu'il vit bien que pour priere ne pour menaces[7] ne la tourneroit, il la fist toute nue estandre par bras et par jambes, et tant batre que .xii. hommes se recrurent dessus. Et tousjours luy demandoit le pere se elle s'aviseroit [fol. 158v b] et luy dist: 'Fille, pitié naturelle destraint durement mon couraige de ainsi tourmenter toy, qui es ma char. Mais la reverence et foy[8] que j'ay a mes dieux me contraint ad ce faire, pour ce que tu les despices.'

"Et la sainte vierge luy respondi: 'Tirant, que je ne doy appeller pere ains annemi de ma beneurté, tourmentes hardiement la char que tu as engendree, car ce puez tu bien faire. Mais a l'esperit cree de mon Pere qui est ou ciel, n'as tu pouoir de touchier[9] par nulle temptacion, car Jhesucrist mon Sauveur le garde.'

"Le cruel pere, plus forcené, fist apporter une roue qui il avoit fait faire, et fist celle doulce enffancelle estre lié dedens, et mettre feu dessoubz, et puis fist gitter huille boullant [fol. 159r a] a grant planté sur son corps. Et celle roue tournoit

---

[1] encores] ancore
[2] a] puis a
[3] leur] eulx
[4] telz] ces
[5] un Dieu en Trinité, lequelle confessoit, ne autre dieu pour mourir] un seul Dieu en Trinité, et que cellui aourer on devoit, lequel elle confessoit: ne pour mourir autre
[6] ceste] celle
[7] menaces] menaces ja
[8] reverence et foy] reverence
[9] de touchier] d'atoucher

"At the last, as her fader knewe that his doughter wolde not worshyp the ydolles, he was ryght sorowfull and reproved her. And she sayd that with a good wyll she wolde offre to God of heven. And he trowed that she mente Jupyter and was ryght glad and wolde have kyssed her. But she cryed and sayd, 'Foule not my mouthe! For I wyll offre myne offrynge clene to God of heven and of erthe.' And of that her fader was contente. And she wente into her chambre and shytte fast the dore, and set her on her knees and offred her holy oryson to God in wepynge. And the holy aungell of Our Lorde came downe and comforted her and brought her whyte brede and mete wherof she ete, for in .iii. dayes she had no maner of mete nor drynke. After that Saynt Christine sawe at the wy[n]dowes[1] many poore Crysten men beggynge at the fote of her toure, and she hadde nothynge to gyve them. And she wente to seke the idolles of her fader whiche were of golde and sylver, and she brake them all and gave the peces to the poore men. [U2r]

"And when her fader knewe that thynge, he bete her ryght cruelly. And she tolde hym playnly that he was deceyved to worshyp suche false ymages, and that there was but one God in Trynyte, the whiche she confessed, and other god wolde she not worshyp to dye therfore. Wherfore he was woode with her and made her to be bounde with chaynes and ledde her, betynge her in dyvers places and after put her in pryson, and he sayd that he wolde be juge hymselfe of that cause. Soo he made her to be brought before hym on the morowe and manaced her with all tourmentes yf she wolde not worshyp the ydolles. And after that that he sawe well that she wolde not tourne her entente for prayer ne for manaces, made her to be stryped all naked, bothe armes and legges, and beten so moche that .xii. men were wery of it. And she asked her fader alwaye yf he advysed her not. And he sayd to her: 'Doughter, naturall pyte constrayneth sore my courage to tourmente thee so, whiche arte my flesshe. But the reverence and the faythe that I have to my goddes constrayneth me to do it for that that thou dyspysest theym.'

"And the holy vyrgyne answered hym: 'Tyraunt, whiche I ought not to calle fader but enemye of myne holynesse, tourmente the flesshe hardely that thou haste engendred, and spare it not. For as for that, thou mayst wel doo at thy pleasure; but as for the spyryte, the whiche was made of my Fader the whiche is in heven, thou hast no power in no wyse to touche it [U2v] by no temptacyon, for Jhesu Cryst my Savyoure kepeth hym.'

"The cruell fader, more woode then he was, made to brynge a whele that he had let make, and made this holy swete yonge mayden to be bounde to it and to put fyre under, and after made to cast boylynge oyle grete plentye upon her body.

---

[1] wy[n]dowes : *wyudowes*

sur elle, qui tout la froissoit. Mais Dieu le Souveraine Pere[1] ot pitié de sa servant, sy envoya son ange qui tout derompi les tourmens, estaigny le feu, et delivra la vierge[2] saine et entiere, et occist plus de mil personnes qui la regardoient sans pitié. Et les anges de Dieu l'avironnerent et conforterent.[3]

"Et son pere luy demanda: 'Dis moy, qui t'a enseigné ses[4] malefices?'

"Elle[5] repondi: 'Tirant sans pitié, ne t'ay je bien dit que mon Pere Jhesucrist m'a apris ceste pacience et toute droicture en la foy de Dieu le vif? Et pour ce despite je tous tes tourmens, et vaincray en la vertu de Dieu tous les assaus du diable.'

"Et celluy, vaincu et confus, la [fol. 159r b] fist gitter en une tres orrible et obscure chartre. Et si comme elle estoit la, pensant aux tres grans misteres de Dieu, trois anges vindrent a elle a tout grant lumiere, et luy apporterent a mengier, et la conforterent. Et elle rendoit graces a Dieu.[6]

"Urban ne savoit que faire d'elle et ne finoit de pourpensser quelz[7] de tourmens faire luy pourroit. A la parfin comme tout annuyé d'elle,[8] pour en estre delivré, luy fist mettre une grosse pierre au col et gitter[9] en la mer. Mais ainsi comme un luy[10] tresbuchoit, les anges la recurent[11] et elle s'en aloit sur l'iaue avec les anges.[12] Adonc pria Christine a Jhesucrist, levant les yeux au ciel, qu'il luy pleust qu'en celle eaue receust le saint sacrement de baptesme, que elle tant desiroit[13] a avoir. Et adonc [fol. 159v a] descendi Jhesucrist en propre personne a grant compaignie d'anges, et la baptisa et nomma de son som, Christine; et la couronna et mist[14] une estoille replandissant sur son chief, et la mist a terre. Et celle nuit, Urban fu tourmenté du diable et mourut. La benoite Christine, que Dieux vouloit recevoir par martire, laquelle chose elle desiroit, fu ramenté par les felons en la chartre.

"Et le nouvel juge nommé Dyon, qui savoit ce qui estoit fait d'elle, la fist venir devant luy et la couvoita pour sa biauté. Mais quant il vit que belles parolles

---

[1] Souveraine Pere] Pere de misericorde
[2] tout derompi les tourmens, estaigny le feu, et delivra la vierge] derompi tous les tourmens et estaigni le feu, et la vierge delivra
[3] mil personnes qui la regardoient sans pitié. Et les anges de Dieu l'avironnerent et conforterent] mille tirans felons qui la regardoient sanz pitié, blasphemant le nom de Dieu
[4] ses] ces
[5] Elle] Et elle
[6] conforterent. Et elle rendoit graces a Dieu] reconforterent
[7] quelz] quieulx manieres
[8] annuyé d'elle] ennuyez
[9] gitter] la giter
[10] un luy] on l'y
[11] recurent] prirent
[12] avec les anges] avecques eulx
[13] tant desiroit] desiroit moult
[14] mist] lui mist

And the whele tourned upon her and all to brake her. But God the Soverayne Fader had pyte on His servaunt, sente His aungell whiche brake the whele all to peces and slewe the tourmentoures, staunched the fyre and delyvered the vyrgyne hole and sounde, and slewe more than a thousande persones that behelde her without pyte. And the aungelles of God came aboute her and comforted her.

"And her fader asked her: 'Tell me, who hath taught thee all th[y][1] cursednesse?'

"And she answered, 'Tyraunt without pyte, have not I tolde thee well that my Fader Jhesu Cryste hathe taught me this pacyence, and all the ryght way in the fayth of God alyve? And therfore despyse I all thy tourmentes, and I shall overcome in the vertue of God all the assaultes of the devyll.'

"And he, overcome and confused, made to cast her in ryght an horryble and a derke pryson. And so as she was there, thynkynge on the grete mysteryes of Our Lorde, there came to her .iii. aungelles with a grete lyght, and brought her mete and comforted her. And she yelded thankynges to God.

"Urban wyst not what to do with her, and lefte not to thynke before what tourmentes he myght do to her. At the last as all anoyed [U3r] with her, for to be delyvered of her, made to put a grete stone aboute her necke and throwe her into the see. But anone as they threwe her into the see, the aungelles receyved her, and she wente upon the water with the aungelles. And then Christine prayed Our Lorde Jhesu Cryst, lyftynge up her eyen to heven, that it myght please hym that she myght receyve the holy sacrament of baptyme in that same water whiche she had desyred so moche to have. And then Our Lorde Jhesu Cryst dessended in propre persone with a grete multytude of aungelles, and baptysed her, and made her after His name, Christine, and crowned her and [set a][2] shynynge sterre upon her heed, and sette her on the londe. And that same nyght, Urban was tourmented with the devyll and dyed myschevously, and in the mornynge after she was founde prayenge in her fader's halle in a corner. And thus this blessyd Christine, whiche God wolde receyve by ma[r]tyrdome[3] whiche she desyred ryght moche, was ledde agayne by the tourmentoures into the pryson.

"And the newe juge named Zyon, whiche knewe well what was done to her, made her to come before hym and coveyted her for her beaute. But when he

---

[1] th[y] : *the*

[2] and [set a] shynynge : *and shynynge*

[3] ma[r]tyrdome : *matyrdome*

riens n'y¹ valloient, il la fist de rechief tourmenter et fist emplir une grant chaudiere d'oille et poiz a grant feu dessoubz.² Et .iiii. hommes la tournoyent dedens a
grans crocs [fol. 159v b] de fer, et la sainte vierge chantoit a Dieu melodieusement,
et mouquoit les tourmenteurs et menaçoit des paines d'enffer. Et quant le felon
juge, aÿré, vit que ce riens ne luy valloit, il la fist prendre en la place devant tous
par les cheveulx que elle avoit longs et blons comme or.³ Environ elle acoururent
les femmes qui plouroient⁴ par grant pitié de tel tendre enffant⁵ ainsi tourmenter,
et crioient au felon tirant,⁶ disant: 'Cruel desloyal! Comment puet cuer d'omme
tel cruauté avoir contre pucelle tant belle et si tendre? Tu es plus felon que nulle
beste sauvage!'⁷ Et toutes luy vouloient courir sus.

"Adonc le juge luy dist:⁸ 'Christine, amie, ne te sueffres plus tourmenter [fol.
160r a] mais viens avec moy: si alons aourer le souverain dieu qui tant t'a soustenue.' Celluy entendoit de Jupiter que ilz tenoient souverain dieu, mais elle entendoit tout autrement; si luy dist, 'Tu as moult bien dit.'

"Si l'ottroy et⁹ la fist despendre et la mena au temple, et grant peuple les
suivy. Quant il l'ot menee devant les ydolles, cuidant que elle les deust adourer,
elle s'agenoilla, regardant ou ciel et fist a Dieu son oroison, puiz se leva et se
tourna vers l'idolle: 'Je te dis,¹⁰ maling esperit qui es en cel ydolle, ou nom de
Jhesucrist que tu ysses hors!' Et tantost le maling esperit sailli hors¹¹ et fist grant
et espoventable tumulte, par quoy [fol. 160r b] tous furent si espoventez que tous
cheurent a terre.

"Et le juge quant il fu relevez dist: 'Christine, tu as esmeu nostre dieu tout
puissant; mais pour ce que il a pitié de toy, il est yssu hors si¹² que il veist sa creature.'

"Et celle fu courroucee en la parolle, et le reprist durement de ce que il estoit
tant aveuglé que il ne congnoissoit la vertu divine. Si pria Dieu que l'idolle cheist
et devenist pouldre, laquel chose fu faicte. Et par les parolles et signes de la
vierge, plus de trois mille hommes et femmes furent convertis.

---

¹ n'y] ne lui
² dessoubz] dessoubz, et la fist giter dedens, le chief dessoubz
³ prendre en la place devant tous par les cheveulx que elle avoit longs et blons comme
or] pendre par les cheveulx que elle avoit loncs et blons comme or en la place devant tous
⁴ plouroient] plourant
⁵ tel tendre enffant] veoir une tele tendre enfancellette
⁶ et crioient au felon tirant] si cryoyent au juge
⁷ Cruel desloyal! Comment puet cuer d'omme tel cruauté avoir contre pucelle tant
belle et si tendre? Tu es plus felon que nulle beste sauvage] Cruel felon, plus que beste
sauvage! Comment peut avoir conceu en cuer d'omme tant de cruaulté contre pucelle tant
belle et si tendre?
⁸ Adonc le juge luy dist] Adont ot le juge paour, et lui dist
⁹ et] il
¹⁰ 'Je te dis . . . '] et dist: 'Je te commande . . . '
¹¹ le maling esperit sailli hors] le deable vint dehors
¹² hors si] hors ad ce

sawe that all his fayre wordes advayled hym not, he made her to be tourmented agayne, and made to fylle a grete cawdron full of oyle and pytche and a grete fyre undernethe it. And foure men tourmented her in the cawdron with grete hokes of yron. And the holy vyrgyne songe to God ryght melodyously, and mocked the tourmentoures [U3v] and manaced them with the paynes of helle. And when the cruell juge sawe that nothynge advayled hym, he made to hange her in the place before all people by the heere of her heed, whiche was longe and shynynge lyke golde. And the women came rennynge aboute her, whiche wepte for pyte to se so yonge a mayden tourmented and cryed to the tyraunt, sayenge: 'Thou untrewe and cruel man! Howe myght the herte of a man have suche cruelte agaynst a mayden so fayre and so tendre? Thou arte worse than ony wylde beest!' And all wolde have ronne upon hym.

"Then the juge sayd to her, 'Christine, frende, thou shalte suffre no more tourmente. But come with me, and let us worshyp the soverayne god that hath susteyned thee so moche.' He thought of Jupyter, whiche they helde for theyr soverayne god, but she thought all otherwyse. Then she sayd to hym, 'Thou hast ryght well sayd, and I graunt thee.'

"And then he made her to be unhanged and ledde her to the temple, and grete foyson of people folowed them. When he had brought her before the ydolles, trowynge that she wolde have worshypped them, she kneled downe, beholdynge towarde heven, and made her oryson to God. And then she rose up and tourned her towarde the ydoll, and sayd: 'I saye to thee, thou wycked spyryte whiche arte in this ydoll, in the name of Jhesu Cryst that thou come out.' And anone the wycked spyryte lepte out and made a grete and a ferefull noyse, by the whiche all were so ferde that they fell downe to the erthe. [U4r]

"And the juge, when he was releved, sayd: 'Christine, thou haste moved our god almyghty: but for that that he hath pyte on thee, he is come out that he myght se his creature.'

"And she was wrothe with that worde, and reproved hym strongly that he was soo blynde that he knewe not Goddes vertue. So she prayed God that the ydoll sholde falle downe al to poudre, the whiche thynge was done. And by the wordes and sygnes of the holy mayde, there were converted what of men and women mo than .iii. thousande.

"Et le juge, espoventé, dist: 'Se le roy savoit ce qui est fait contre nostre dieu par les demonstrances de ceste Christine, il me destruyroit mauvaisement.' Et maintenant celluy, plain d'angoisse, se forcena[1] et [fol. 160v a] mouru.

"Le tiers juge vint aprés, nommé Julien, et fist prendre Christine et se vanta que il luy[2] feroit adourer les ydolles. Mais pour tout sa[3] force que il y peust mettre, il ne la pot faire remouvoir du lieu ou elle estoit.[4] Si fist faire un tres grant[5] feu autour d'elle, et en ce feu demoura par trois jours. Et la dedens estoient ouÿes melodies doulces,[6] et furent les tourmenteurs espoventez par merveilleux signes que ilz virent, lesquelles choses rapportees a Julien cuida forcener. Et quant le feu fu consommé, elle s'en sailli toute saine.

"Le juge fist admener les serpens et fist gitter sur elle deux aspis, qui sont serpens qui mordent et enveniment merveilleusement, et deux grosses couleuvres. Mais ses[7] serpens se laissierent cheoir a ses piez, les testes [fol. 160v b] enclines vers elle,[8] sans luy mal faire. Et deux autres orribles serpens nommez guievres furent laissiez aler, et ilz se pendirent a ses mamelles et la lechoyent. Et Christine regardoit au[9] ciel et disoit: 'Je te rens graces, Sire Dieux Jhesucrist, qui m'as tant daigner[10] essaucier par tes saintes vertus que les serpens orribles congnoissent en moy ta dignité.'

"Et Julien, obstiné, voyant ces merveilles, escria a celluy qui estoit garde des serpens: 'N'es tu pas aussi enchanté de Christine, par quoy tu n'as pouoir desmouvoir contre elle les serpens?'[11]

"Adonc celluy qui doubta l[e] juge[12] les cuida esmouvoir contre[13] elle, et ilz luy coururent sure[14] et l'occirent. Et si comme chacun doubtoit ses serpens, nul n'osoit aler pres de Christine. Et elle[15] leur commanda [fol. 161r a] de par Dieu que ilz ralassent en leur lieu sans meffaire a creature, et ilz sy firent. Elle resuscita le mort, qui tantost se gitta a ses piez et tantost fu[16] converti.

---

[1] se forcena] forsena
[2] luy] la
[3] tout sa] toute la
[4] estoit] es estoit
[5] tres grant] grant
[6] melodies doulces] doulces melodies
[7] ses] ces
[8] enclines vers elle] enclines
[9] au] ou
[10] daigner] daigné
[11] contre elle les serpens] les contre elle
[12] l[e] : *la juge*
[13] esmouvoir contre] harer sur
[14] sure] sus
[15] ses serpens, nul n'osoit aler pres de Christine. Et elle] ces serpens et que nul n'osoit approcher, elle
[16] tantost fu] fu

"And the juge, ryght sore aferde, sayd: 'If the kynge knewe that that is done agaynst our god by the shewynge of this Christine, he wolde destroye me myschevously.' And then the juge, full of anguysshe, waxed woode and dyed.

"The thyrde juge came after, named Julyan, and made to take Christine and made his avaunt that he wolde make her to worshyp the ydolles. But for al his myght that he coude do, he myght not make her remeve out of the place where she was. So he lete make a grete fyre aboute her, and she bode in that fyre .iii. dayes and .iii. nyghtes. And there were herde many dyvers swete melodyes, and the tourmentoures were aferde by the mervayllous sygnes that they sawe; the whiche thynges, reported to Julyan, he wende to have waxen wode. And when the fyre was consumed, she came out al hole.

"The juge made serpentes to be brought forth, and made to cast upon her .ii. aspes and .ii. grete colubres, whiche bote and venymed mervayllously. But these serpentes fell downe at her fete that [U4v] the hedes enclyned towarde her, without doynge her ony herme. And then there were other .ii. horryb[l]e[1] serpentes let lowce upon her, and they hanged them at her pappes and lycked her. And Christine loked towarde heven and sayd: 'I yelde Thee thankynges, my Lorde God Jhesu Cryst, whiche hast made me so worshypfully to be enhaunced by the holy vertues that these horryble serpentes knoweth Thy dygnyte in me.'

"And this obstynate Julyan, seynge these mervaylles, cryed to hym that was keper of the serpentes: 'Arte not thou enchaunted of Christine also, by the whiche thou haste no power to move the serpentes agaynst her?'

"Then he, whiche doubted the juge, trowed to have moved the serpentes ayenst her, and they ranne upon hym and slewe hym. And so moche everybody doubted the serpentes that none durste come nyghe Christine. And she commaunded them by the vertue of God that they sholde go agayne into theyr owne place, without doynge ony harme to ony creature; and so they dyde.

"Then she raysed agayne the deed man to his lyfe, whiche anone cast hym at her feete and was converted.

---

[1] horryb[l]e : *horrybie*

"Et le juge,[1] aveuglé du diable sy que il n'appercevoit les merveilleux signes,[2] dist a Christine: 'Tu as assez demonstré tes ars magiques.'

"Et elle luy dist:[3] 'Hors du sens! Se tes yeux voissent les vertus de Dieu, tu les creusses.'

"Et adonc celluy, forcenant, luy fist arrachier les mamelles, et tantost en yssy lait en lieu de sanc. Et pour ce que elle sans cesser nommoit le nom de Jhesus, il luy fist coupper la langue; mais mieulx que devant et plus cler parloit ades des choses d[i]vines, benoissoit[4] Dieu en le regraciant des benefices que Il luy donnoit, et commença a faire son oroison et [fol. 161r b] Il luy pleust a parfaire la couronne de son martire et la recevoir vers lui. Et adonc[5] une voix du ciel fu ouÿe, disant: 'Christine, pure et nette, les cieulx te sont ouvers, et le raigne sans fin t'est appareillé. Et toute la compaignie des sains benoist Dieu pour toy, car tu as des ton enffance soustenu le nom de ton Crist.' Et elle gloriffioit Dieu, les yeulx vers le ciel. La voix de rechief fu ouÿe qui dist:[6] 'Vien, Christine, ma tres amee et tres elicte fille, et reçoy la palme et couronne pardurable, et le gardon de ta passionnable vie en la confession de mon nom.' Et le faulx Julien, qui ceste voix ot ouÿe, blasma les bourriaulx et leur dist que ilz n'avoyent pas assez couppee pres[7] la langue de Christine, sy luy couppassent si pres que tant ne peust parler a [fol. 161v a] son Crist. Sy luy errachierent la langue a croc de fer[8] et luy coupperent jusques au gavion.

"Et celle cracha le coupon de sa langue au visaige[9] du tirant et luy en creva l'ueil, et luy dist, aussi sainement que oncques mais: 'Mauvais tirant,[10] que te vault avoir couppee ma langue affin que elle ne beneisse Dieu quant mon esperit a tousjours mais[11] le beneistra? Et le tien demourera perpetuel en maleisson. Et pour ce que tu ne congnois ma parolle, c'este bien raison que ma langue t'ait aveuglé.'

"Adonc elle,[12] qui ja veoit Jhesucrist seant a la destre de son Pere, fina son martire par deux fleches qui lui furent lanciees: l'une au costé, l'autre vers le cuer.

---

[1] Et le juge] Le juge
[2] les merveilleux signes] le mistere divin
[3] luy dist] respondi
[4] d[i]vines : *davines* benoissoit] divines et beneissoit
[5] et Il luy pleust a parfaire la couronne de son martire et la recevoir vers lui. Et adonc] que Il lui pleust a la recevoir vers lui, et que la couronne de son martire fust achevee. Adont
[6] dist] disoit
[7] couppee pres] pres coppé
[8] errachierent la langue a croc de fer] esracherent hors la lengue
[9] au visaige] jusques au visage
[10] 'Mauvais tirant . . .'] 'Tirant . . .'
[11] tousjours mais] tousjours
[12] elle] celle

"And the juge, blynded with the devyll so as he perceyved not the mervayllous sygnes, sayd unto Christine: 'Thou hast ynoughe shewed thy wytche craftes.'

"And she sayd to hym: 'Thou man out of wytte! Yf thyne eyen wolde se the vertues of God, thou sholdest byleve them.'

"And then he, beynge passynge wrothe, made to drawe her pappes out of her body, and anone there came out mylke [X1r] instede of blode. And for that that she without seasynge named the name of Our Lorde Jhesus, he made to cutte off her tonge but she spake better and clerer after then she dyde before, and blessyd God in thankynge Hym of His grete benefeytes that He dyde to her, and began to make her oryson unto God that it myght please Hym to perfourme the crowne of her martyrdome and to receyve her to Hym.

"And then there was herde a voyce frome heven, sayenge: 'Christine, pure and clene, the hevens ben open for thee and the reygne without ende redy. And all the company of sayntes blesseth God for thee, for thou hast fro thy youthe susteyned the name of Cryste.'

"And then she praysed and gloryfyed God, the eyen towarde heven. The voyce was herde agayne, whiche sayd: 'Come, Christine, My ryght welbyloved and chosen doughter, and receyve the palme and perdurable crowne and the rewarde of thy passyonable lyfe in the confessyon of My name.'

"And the false Julyan that herde this voyce blamed the tourmentoures that they had not cutte the tonge of Christine more nerer. So they cutte it so nyghe that she sholde not speke so moche as she dyde of Our Lorde Jesu Cryst, for they toke an yron hoke and pulled out the tonge and cutte it anone to the throte.

"And she toke the culpen of the tonge and threwe it to the vysage of the tyraunt and smote out his eye, and sayd to hym as holely as ever she spake before: 'Thou cursed tyraunt, what avayleth thee to cutte off my tonge to the entente that it sholde not worshyp [X1v] God, when my spyryte shal alway worshyp Hym? And thy spyryte shall dwell alway in cursednesse. And for that thou knowest not my worde, it is good reason that my tonge hathe made thee blynde.'

"Then she, whiche that sawe Jhesu Cryste syttynge in the ryght syde of His Fader, ended her martyrdome by two arowes that were shotte at her: one in the

Et un sien par[e]nt,¹ que elle avoit converti, enseveli le dit corps et escript [fol. 161v b] sa² glorieuse legende."

O benoite Christine, vierge beneuree et de Dieu tres elicte,³ vueilles par la saincteté dont Dieux t'a faicte digne, prier pour moy, pecharresse, nommee de⁴ ton nom, et me soyes propice et piteuse marraine. Sy voir que je m'esjouÿs d'avoir cause de exet⁵ et metre ta saincte legende en mes escriptures, laquelle pour ta reverence ay recordee⁶ au long, ce te soit agreable, et a toutes femmes cause de bon exemples.⁷

## Chapitre 11    De plusieurs saintes, qui virent martirer leurs enfans devant elles

"O, quelle est ou monde plus tendre chose que mere a son enffant, ne plus grant douleur que son cuer seuffre quant mal luy voit soffrir?⁸ Mais par ce que je voy foy est encores⁹ [fol. 162r a] plus grant chose comme il y paru a maintes vaillans femmes qui pour l'amour de Jhesucrist offroyent leurs propres enffans au tourment, si comme la benoite Felix, qui vit ses sept enffans¹⁰ qui estoyent tres biaulx jouvenciaulx martirer devant elle, et les¹¹ reconfortoit et admonnestoit de paciense par parolles de mere d'estre fermes en la foy, et pour l'amour de Dieu avoit oublié couraige maternel quant au corps. Et puis après, quant tous les ot offers au sacrefice, elle voulst estre sacrefiee au martire après.¹²

---

¹ par[e]nt : *parant*
² le dit corps et escript sa] le saint corps et escript la
³ beneuree et de Dieu tres elicte] digne et beneuree de Dieu, tres eslicte martire glorieuse
⁴ de] par
⁵ exet] enexer
⁶ recordee] recordee assez
⁷ et a toutes femmes cause de bon exemples] pries pour toutes femmes auxquelles ta sainte vie soit cause par bon exemple de bien finer leur vie Amen. *See annotations for additional passage*
⁸ soffrir] endurer
⁹ foy est encores] ancores est foy
¹⁰ enffans] filz
¹¹ et les] et la tres bonne mere les
¹² par parolles de mere d'estre fermes en la foy, et pour l'amour de Dieu avoit oublié couraige maternel quant au corps. Et puis après, quant tous les ot offers au sacrefice, elle voulst estre sacrefiee au martire après] et de estre fermes en la foy. Si avoit ceste bonne dame oublié courage maternel quant au corps pour l'amour de Dieu. Et puis après, quant au sacrefice les ot tous offers, elle volt estre sacrifiee et vint au martire

syde, that other towarde the herte. And a cosyne of hers, whiche was converted by her, buryed her body and wrote her gloryous legende."

O blessyd Christine, and holy mayden and chosen of God, I praye thee by the holynesse wherof God hath made thee soo worthy to praye for me, a synner named of thy name. And have pyte on me, blessyd godmoder, whiche haste rejoyced me to have cause to put thyne holy legende in my wrytynges, the whiche at th[y]¹ reverence I ha[ve]² recorded a longe that it myght be agreable to thee, and to all women cause of good ensample.

## Chapter 11   Of dyvers sayntes, whiche that sawe theyr chyldren martyred before them

"O, what thynge in the worlde is more tendre to a moderly herte than to se her chylde to suffre payne? But for that that I se, faythe is yet the grettest thynge as it appered to many worshypfull women, whiche for the love of Jhesu Cryste offred theyr owne chyldren to tourment as this blessyd [X2r] Felyx, whiche sawe her [.vii.]³ chyldren whiche were ryght fayre yonglynges martyred before her, and comforted and counsayled them of pacyence by moderly wordes to be stable in the faythe; and for the love of God, she had forgoten all womanly courage as to the body. And after that, when she had offred them all in sacrefyse to God, she wolde be sacrefyed herselfe unto God by martyrdome.

---

¹ th[y] : *the*
² ha[ve] : ha=
³ [.vii.] : *.viii.*

"*Item*, semblablement[1] la benoite Julite, qui avoit un filz nommé Tir, celle aussi[2] comme elle luy bailloit nourriture corporelle aussi faisoit elle spirituelle.[3] Car sans [fol. 162r b] cesser l'introduisoit en la foy tellement que luy, tres petit[4] enffant, ne pot oncques estre vaincu des martireur, ne par blandisses ne[5] par tourmens que il reniast le nom de Jhesucrist,[6] ains quant on le tourmentoit disoit de sa petite chere voix,[7] 'Je suis crestien! Je suis crestien! Je te rens graces, Nostre Sire[8] Dieux,' et parloit sy appertement[9] que homme de .xl. ans peust faire. Et sa[10] bonne mere le reconfortoit, laquelle fu aussi durement tourmenté. Et celle sans cesser louoit Dieu, et reconfortoit les autres martirs et parloit de la joye celestielle que ilz attendoyent et que ilz n'eussent paour.[11]

"*Item*, que pourrons nous dire de la merveilleuse constance et force que ot la benoite Blandine? Elle vit [fol. 162v a] tourmenter et martirier devant elle sa fille de l'aage[12] de quinze ans, que elle reconfortoit joyeusement. Et aprés elle, aussi joyeusement[13] que femme va a espoux, se ala mettre en[14] tourment et fu tant tourmenté par multitude de martirs que les martireurs se lasserent sur elle. Elle fu mise sur[15] un gril et rostie, detrenchee de pignes de fer; et tousjours elle gloriffioit Dieu, et ainsi pe[r]severa[16] jusques a la fin.

"Que t'en diroye pour emplir nostre cité et peupler de tel maigniee? Viengne sainte Ourse a tout ses .xi.^m vierges benoites martires pour le nom de Jhesucrist, toutes decoulees que comme elles fussent envoyees pour estre mariees. Et elles s'embatissent en terre de mescreans, et on les voulsist contraindre de [fol. 162v b] renoncier a la foy de Dieu: plus tost eslurent la mort que renoncier a Jhesucrist, leur Sauveur."[17]

---

1  semblablement] pareillement
2  celle aussi] celle dame tout aussi
3  faisoit elle spirituelle] bailloit espirituelle
4  tres petit] petit
5  ne par blandisses ne] ne
6  Jhesucrist] Jhesus
7  disoit de sa petite chere voix] il cryoit tant comme il pouoit de sa petite clere voix
8  Sire] Seigneur
9  appertement] tres appertement
10  Et sa] Sa
11  paour] point de paour
12  fille de l'aage] fille que elle tant amoit de l'aage
13  joyeusement] liement
14  en] ou
15  sur] sus
16  pe[r]severa : *pesevera*
17  *R moves last paragraph to end of chap. 10*

"Also the blessyd Julytte in the same wyse, whiche had a sonne named Cyrycus, she nourysshed hym not onely with bodely fode but also with spyrytuall for without seasynge she enfourmed hym in the faythe in suche wyse that he, beynge ryght lytell and yonge, myght never be overcome with tourmente ne by fayre wordes that he sholde forsake the name of Jhesu Cryste. But when he was tourmented he sayd with his lytell clere voyce: 'I am a Crysten man! I am a Crysten man! I thanke Thee, Our Lorde Jhesu Cryste!' And he spake so openly as it hadde ben a man of .xl. yeres of age. And his good moder comforted hym, the whiche was also ryght cruelly tourmented. And she without seasynge praysed Our Lorde, and comforted other martyres and spake of the hevenly joye that they dyde abyde, and that they sholde have noo drede.

"Also what shall we nowe saye of the mervayllous constaunce and strengthe that the blessyd Blandyne had? She sawe tourmented and martyred before her her doughter, whiche was of the age of .xv. yeres, whom she comforted joyously. And after as a [X2v] woman sholde go to her spouse, she wente to put her in tourmente and was soo moche tourmented by multytude of martyrdomes that the tourmentoures were wery of her, and put her on a grydyren and rosted her, and was alwaye prycked with pynnes of yron. And she alwaye gloryfyed Our Lorde God, and so she contynued anone to the dethe.

"What sholde I saye to thee for to fulfyll our cyte of suche meyny? Come on Saynt Ursula, with all thy .xi. thousande vyrgynes and blessyd martyres for the name of Jhesu Cryst, all theyr heedes smyten off so as they were sente to be maryed. And they aryved in a londe of myscreauntes whiche wolde constrayne them to forsake the faythe of God, and they chose rather to dye than to forsake the name of theyr Savyoure Jhesu Cryst."

## *Chapitre 12*    De[1] sainte Marine, vierge

"Des martires vierges se pourroit raconter a grant nombre, et pareillement d'autres qui vesquirent en religion et en maintes guises moult saintement. Et de deux te diray dont l'ystoire est moult belle.[2]

"Un homme seculier avoit un[e] seulle fille[3] petite nommee Marine. Si la mist en garde a un sien parent, et entra en religion, et moult menoit sainte vie. Et non pour tant, Nature le tiroit a sa fille, dont la paine luy donnoit[4] grant moleste. Sy estoit moult pensif, dont[5] l'abbé luy demanda la cause de son marrement tant que il luy dist que sa pensee estoit moult [fol. 163r a] durement[6] occuppee pour un petit[7] filz que il avoit laissié au siecle, que il ne pouoit oublier. L'abbé luy dist que il l'alast querre et le meist[8] en la religion avec luy. Si fu celle vierge avec[9] son pere vestue comme un petit[10] moine; et bien se savoit celler, et moult fu de bonne discipline. Et quant elle vint en l'aage de .xviii. ans, tousjours perseverant[11] de mieulx en mieulx, le pere qui moult saintement l'avoit introduite trespassa. Et elle demoura seulle en la celle de son pere en sainte vie si que l'abbé et tous louoyent sa sainte conversacion, et tenoyent que homme fust.

"Celle abbaye estoit a trois mille pres d'une ville ou avoit marchié. Si couvenoit aucuneffoiz que les moins alassent au dit marchié pour [fol. 163r b] achaster leurs neccessitees;[12] donc il advenoit aucuneffoiz quant il leur adnuytoit en yver,[13] selonc les affaires que ilz avoient, que ilz demourassent au giste en la ville. Et Marine, qui estoit nommé Frere Marin, aucuneffoiz demouroit a son tour[14] en la ville en certaine hostelerie ou communement se logoit.[15] Avint en ce temps que la fille de l'oste fu ençainte, et comme elle fust par ces[16] parens contrainte de dire de qui ce estoit, elle le mist assus a Frere Marin, de quoy les parens s'en[17] vindrent

---

[1]   De] Ci dit de
[2]   l'ystoire est moult belle] les legendes sont moult belles en approuvant tousjours le propos de constance de femme
[3]   Un homme . . . un[e] seulle fille : *une homme . . . un seulle fille*
[4]   donnoit] faisoit
[5]   dont] par quoy
[6]   moult durement] durement
[7]   petit : *petite*
[8]   meist] menast
[9]   avec luy. Si fu celle vierge avec] avecques lui. Si fu celle vierge avecques
[10]  petit : *petite*
[11]  perseverant] perseveroit
[12]  achaster leurs neccessitees] acheter leurs neccessaires
[13]  quant il leur adnuytoit en yver] en yver quant il leur anuitoit
[14]  demouroit a son tour] a son tour demouroit
[15]  logoit] logioyent
[16]  ces] ses
[17]  s'en] se

*Chapter 12*      Of Saynt Maryne, the holy vyrgyne

"Of vyrgynes martyred one myght tell a grete nombre, and the same wyse of others that lyved in relygyon and in many other holy guyses. And I shall tell thee of twayne of whom the hystory is ryght fayre.

"A seculer man had one onely doughter, lytell and yonge, named Maryne. So he put her in the warde of a cosyne of his owne, and entred in relygyon, and ledde ryght an holy lyfe. And not for that, Nature drewe hym to thynke on his doughter, wherof his payne made hym to be [X3r] hevy. So he was ryght pensyfe, and the abbot demaunded hym the cause of his hevynes so moche tyll he tolde hym that all his thought was upon a doughter of his whiche he had lefte in the worlde, whiche he myght not forgete. The abbot bad hym that he sholde go to fetche her and that she myght be put into relygyon with hym. So was this mayde with her fader clothed as a lytell monke and coude well kepe her close, and she was of ryght good dyscyplyne. And when she came to the age of .xviii. yeres, alwaye perseverynge frome good to better, the fader whiche had taught her this holy lyfe passed out of this worlde. And she abode alone in her fader's celle in holy lyvynge so that the abbot and all other praysed her holy conversacyon, and wyst none other but that she was a man.

"This abbay was but .iii. myles frome a market towne, so it fortuned that the monkes must of necessyte go other whyles unto the foresayd market for to bye theyr necessaryes. Wherof it happened dyvers tymes that they were nyghted in theyr comynge homewarde in the wynter season after that they hadde done theyr busynes, so that they must nedes lye in the towne. And Maryne, whiche was named Frere Maryne, dyvers tymes abode at his course in the foresayd towne in a certayne hostery where he lodged commonely when he came to the towne. So it happe in that tyme that the doughter of the hoste was with chylde, and as she was constrayned by her fader and moder to tell [X3v] whos it was, she put it upon Frere Maryne. Wherof the fader and moder came and complayned to the

plaindre a l'abbé, qui le fist appeller et moult fu dollent de ceste chose. Et la
sainte vierge ot plus chier prendre la coulpe sus elle que s'en excuser et[1] s'agenoilla
en plourant, disant: 'Pere, j'ay pechié: pries pour moy, je feray penitence.' [fol. 163v
a] Adonc l'abbé, couroucié, le fist batre et tourmenter,[2] et le mist hors du moustier
et deffendi l'entree. Et il se mist a terre devant le moustier,[3] et la gisoit en penitence, et demandoit aux freres un seul morcel de pain. Et la fille du tavernier enf-
fanta un filz que la mere d'elle apporta a Marin devant le moustier, et le laissa
illec. Et la vierge le receut, et de ce morcel de pain que les entrans lui donnoient
nourrissoyt cel enffant comme se il fust sien propre.

　　"Et un temps aprés ce les freres, meuz de pitié, prierent l'abbé que il receust
Frere Marin a misericorde et a paines luy contraignierent; et il avoit ja esté[4] cinq
ans en celle penitence devant la porte.[5] Et quant il fu entrez ou moustier, l'abbé
luy commenda[6] a faire tous les ors et [fol. 163v b] vilz offices de leans, et que il
apportast l'eaue a nettoyer tous leurs neccessaires, et que il servist a tous. Et la
sainte vierge le faisoit humblement et voulentiers.

　　"Et pou de temps aprés, elle s'endormi a Nostre Seigneur. Et quant les freres
l'ores[7] denoncié a l'abbé, il leur dist: 'Veez que son pechié fu tel que il n'en a pas
desservy pardon. Lavez le, touteffoiz, et l'enssevelissez loing du moustier.' Et si
comme ilz l'eurent despoillé, et ilz virent que c'estoit une femme, ilz si[8] commencierent a batre, et a crier, et moult estre dollens du mal et grief[9] que on avoit
fait a tant sainte creature, sans cause, de laquelle conversacion trop avoient grant
merveille. Ceste chose [fol. 164r a] nonciee a l'abbé, affouy la[10] et se laissa cheoir
aux piez du sainte[11] corps en moult grant pleur, batant sa coulpe et luy criant[12]
mercis et requerant pardon, et ordena sa sepulcure en une chappelle dedens le
moustier.

　　"La vindrent tous les moines, dont un[13] qui n'avoit que un oueil s'enclina
sur le corps, le baisant par grant devocion. Et tantost sa veue luy fu restituee ce
mesmes jour. Celle qui avoit eu l'enffant devint hors du scens et crioit son pechié,

---

　　[1] sus elle que s'en excuser et] sur elle que magnifester que elle fust femme pour soy
excuser si

　　[2] batre et tourmenter] batre durement

　　[3] le moustier] la porte

　　[4] contraignierent; et il avoit ja esté] condescendirent et ja avoit esté

　　[5] penitence devant la porte] penitence

　　[6] commenda] commanda

　　[7] l'ores] l'orent

　　[8] si] se

　　[9] et moult estre dollens du mal et grief] comme dolens et confus du mal

　　[10] affouy la] il affuy celle part

　　[11] sainte] saint

　　[12] et luy criant] cryant

　　[13] un : *une*

abbot, whiche made hym to be sente for and was ryght sorowfull of this thynge. And the holy mayden had lever take the blame upon her than to excuse her. And she kneled, wepynge, and sayd, 'Fader, pray for me: I have synned, and I shall do penaunce.' And then the abbot beynge ryght wrothe made hym to be beten and tourmented, and put hym out of the monastery, and defendynge hym the entrynge agayne. And he set hym on the erthe before the abbay and lay there in penaunce, and asked of his bretherne one morsell of brede ones a day. And the doughter of the hosteler was delyvered of a sone, and the moder of her brought this chylde to Maryne before the abbay and there lefte it. And the holy mayden receyved hym, and with the morselles of brede that men goynge in and out gave hym, nourysshed this chylde as thoughe it had ben his owne.

"And on a tyme after that the bretherne, moved with pyte, prayed the abbot that he wolde receyve agayne Frere Maryne to mercy, and with grete payne they constrayned hym at theyr prayer. And she had ben then .v. yeres in that penaunce before the gate of the monastery. And when he was entred in the abbaye, the abbot commaunded hym to do all the foule offyces of within, and that he sholde bryn[ge][1] in water to wasshe al theyr necessaryes, and that he sholde serve all the people of the place. And the holy vyrgyne dyde it humbly, and with a good wyll. [X4r]

"And within a whyle after, she passed to Our Lorde. And when the bretherne had tolde this to the abbot, he sayd to them: 'Se ye that his synne was suche that he deserved no pardon. Neverthe111esse, wasshe hym and bury hym ferre from the abbay.' And so, as they dyde off his clothes suche as he ware, they sawe that it was a woman. Then they began to crye and were passynge sory for the grete evyll and grevaunce that was done to soo holy a creature without cause, of the whiche conversacyon they had grete mervayle. This thynge tolde to the abbot, he was astonyed gretely. And anone he fell downe at the feete of the holy body in grete wepynge, betynge his brest for his blame, and cryenge mercy and requyrynge pardon, and ordeyned her sepulture in a chapell within the monastery.

"Thyder came al the monkes, amonge the whiche there was one that hadde but one eye, whiche kne[l]ed[2] downe and kyssed the holy body by grete devocyon. And anone his syght was restored to hym the same daye. And the woman that bare the chylde became out of her wytte and cryed on her synne, and then

---

[1] bryn[ge] : *bryn*
[2] kne[l]ed : *kneced*

et elle fu menee au saint corps et recouvra sa santé.[1] Et pluseurs miracles fist et encore[2] fait ou dit leeu."

## *Chapitre 13*     De[3] la benoite Euffrasine, vierge

"Pareillement en Alixandrie ot une vierge nommee [fol. 164r b] Euffrasine, laquelle Dieu avoit donnée a Paffousien son pere, homme de grant richesce, par les prieres d'un[4] saint abbé et d'un couvent de moines qui pres de lui estoit. Quant[5] ceste fille fu grande, le pere marier la voult. Mais elle, qui ce[6] estoit donnee a Dieu en propos de garder sa virginité, s'en fouy vestue en guise d'omme et requist que elle fust receu[7] en la dicte abbaye, et faisoit a croire que elle estoit un jouvencel de la court de l'empereur qui devocion avoit d'estre rendu leans. L'abbé, qui vit sa grant devocion, le[8] receut voulentiers. Quant le pere ne pot trouver sa fille,[9] il ot douleur a merveilles. Si vint a l'abbé dire sa grant douleur pour y trouver reconfort, et luy prier que luy et le couvent [fol. 164v a] priassent Dieu que aucune nouvelle en peussent ouÿr. L'abbé le reconforta et dist que il ne pourroit croire que fille donnee de Dieu par oroison fust perie. Longuement l'abbé et le couvent pria Dieu pour ceste chose. Et comme il n'en peust ouÿr aucune nouvelle, et le bon homme tousjours revenist a refuge a luy en sa grant tribulacion, un jour luy dist l'abbé:

"'Vrayement, je ne cuide point que ta fille soit mal alee car se ainsi fust,[10] je tiens que Dieux le nous eust revellé. Mais se tu veulz, parler a un filz de devocion et d'oroison que nous avons ceans qui ça vint de la court de l'empereur, et lui a Dieu donné[11] tant de grace que tout personne qui a luy parle se treuve reconforté.'[12]

"Paffoussien requist que pour Dieu il luy [fol. 164v b] parlast, et l'abbé[13] fist mener le pere a sa fille que il ne congnut, mais la fille bien congnut[14] le pere. Si fu

---

[1]  sa santé] santé
[2]  encore] ancores
[3]  De] Ci dit de
[4]  d'un] du
[5]  Quant] Et quant
[6]  ce] toute
[7]  fust receu] fu vestue
[8]  devocion le] affection la
[9]  sa fille] sa fille que il tant amoit
[10]  fust] estoit
[11]  Mais se tu veulz, parler a un filz de devocion et d'oroison que nous avons ceans . . . et lui a Dieu donné] Mais nous avons ceans un filz d'oroison . . . a qui Dieux a donné
[12]  reconforté] reconfortez; si peus parler a lui, s'il te plaist
[13]  requist que pour Dieu il luy et l'abbé] en requist que pour Dieu il y parlast, et adont l'abbé
[14]  congnut] recongneut

she was brought unto the holy body and there she recovered helthe. And syth Almyghty God dyde many myracles for her in the sayd place."

## Chapter 13    Of the moost holy and blessyd vyrgyne Eufrasyne [X4v]

"There was a mayde [o]f[1] Alexandre named Eufrasyne, the whiche God had gyven to her fader Paffousyen, a man of grete rychesse, by the prayers of an holy abbot and of a covent of monkes that was nyghe hym. When this doughter was waxen moche, the fader wolde have maryed her. But she that was gyven in purpose to kepe her vyrgynyte fled clothed in the guyse of a man, and requyred the abbot that she myght be receyved into the sayd abbaye, and made hym to byleve that she was a yonge man of the emperoures courte whiche had devocyon to be rendred into that relygyon. The abbot, whiche sawe his grete devocyon, receyved hym with good wyll.

"And when the fader myght not fynde his doughter, he had mervayllous sorowe. So he came to the abbot to tell his grete sorowe to fynde some comforte, and prayed hym and his covente to praye to God that he myght have some tydynges of her. The abbot comforted hym and sayd that he myght not byleve that a chylde gyven of God by prayer sholde be peryssshed. Longe the abbot and the covent prayed to God for this thynge, and as this good man myght here no tydynges came every day to the abbot to have some comforte in his trybulacyon, the abbot sayd to hym on a day:

"'Truely, I wene not that thy doughter is evyl gone, for yf it were so I deme that God wolde have shewed it unto us or this tyme. But and yf thou wylte, speke to a chylde of devocyon and prayer the whiche [X5r] we have here within, whiche came hyder frome the emperour's courte. And God hathe gyven hym so moche of grace that every persone that speketh with hym fyndeth hym ryght well comforted.'

"Paffousyen prayed hym that for Goddes love he myght speke with hym, and the abbot made the fader to be brought to the doughter, whiche he knewe not, but the doughter knewe well the fader. So she was anone full of teeres and

---

[1] [o]f : ƒ

tantost reamplie toute[1] de larmes et se tourna d'autre part si comme se il finast
quelque oroison, et[2] la biauté et frescheur de son vilz estoit ja moult flestrie pour
l'aspiece de l'astinence que elle faisoit.[3] Aprés elle parla a son pere et le reconforta
moult, et lui acertena que ains que il mourust que il verroit sa fille, et point ne
se doubtast que elle estoit ou service de Dieu ou que elle fust,[4] et qu'encore aroit
grant joye d'elle. Le pere, qui cuida que il le sceust par vertu divine, s'en parti
moult consolez et dist a l'abbé que oncques puis que sa fille estoit partie n'avoit
trouvé a son courage [fol. 165r a] autant de reconfort:[5] 'Et suis,' dist il, 'auss[i][6] lié
en la grace de Dieu que se je eusse trouvee ma fille.' Et en se recommandant a
l'abbé et aux oroisons des freres s'en parti. Mais ne se pouoit tenir de souvent
revenir et visiter[7] le saint frere, ne n'avoit bien fors tant que il devisoit avec luy.[8]

"Et ainsi dura par si long temps que ja avoit acompli celle[9] fille, qui Frere
Synaroch se faisoit appeller,[10] .xxxviii. ans dedens sa selle. Adonc la voult Dieu
appeller a soy, et maladie la prist.[11] Le bon homme de ce moult dolent vint la,
et quant il vit que Synaroch se mouroit il commença a crier, 'Las, ou sont tres[12]
doulces parolles et les promesses que tu m'avoyes faictes que je verroye ma fille?'

"Ainsi trespassa [fol. 165r b] Sinaroch en Dieu, et n'y estoit point[13] le pere
quant il trespassa. Un escript tenoit en sa main que nul ne luy pouoit oster: l'abbé
et tout le couvent s'i vint essaier, mais riens n'y faisoyent sur cella. Vint le pere
a grans plours et a grans cris pour son bon amy qu'il trouva mort, ou quel estoit
tout son reconfort. Et aussi tost que il s'aproscha du corps pour le baisier, devant
tous il ouvry la main et luy bailla l'escript. Et cil le prist et lut[14] dedens comment
elle estoit sa fille, et que nul ne touchast son corps pour l'ensevelir fors luy. Ceste
chose fu merveillable a luy, a l'abbé, et a tout le couvent, qui moult louerent sa

---

[1]  reamplie toute] toute remplie

[2]  et] et ja estoit

[3]  son vilz estoit ja moult flestrie pour l'aspiece de l'astinence que elle faisoit] son vis
moult flestrie pour l'asprece de l'abstinence

[4]  que ains que il mourust que il verroit sa fille, et point ne se doubtast que elle estoit
ou service de Dieu ou que elle fust] que sa fille estoit en bon lieu ou service de Dieu, et
que ains que il mourust que il la verroit

[5]  sa fille estoit partie n'avoit trouvé a son courage autant de reconfort] puis que il
avoit perdu sa fille n'avoit trouvé en son cuer autant de repos

[6]  auss[i] : *aussu*

[7]  pouoit tenir de souvent revenir et visiter] tenoit mie de souvent venir visiter

[8]  ne n'avoit bien fors tant que il devisoit avec luy] ne bien n'avoit fors tant que il
devisoit avecques lui

[9]  celle] ceste

[10]  Frere Synaroch se faisoit appeller] se faisoit appeller Frere Sinaroch

[11]  et maladie la prist] si la prist maladie

[12]  tres] tes

[13]  Sinaroch en Dieu, et n'y estoit point] en Dieu Sinaroch, et n'y estoit pas

[14]  lut] list

tourned her a parte so as thoughe she wolde ende some maner of oryson, and the beaute and the fresshnesse of her vysage was gretely empayred by the grete abstynence that she dyde. After she spake to her fader and comforted hym, and made hym certayne that he sholde se his doughter or he dyed, and that he sholde not doubte but that she was in the servyce of God wherever she were, and that yet he sholde have grete joy of her. The fader trowed that he knewe that by dyvyne vertue and departed thens ryght well comforted, and sayd to the abbot that ever syth his doughter departed he had not founde to his courage so moche of comforte. 'And I am,' sayd he, 'fulfylled with the grace of God syth that I shall have tydynges of my doughter.' And with that, recommendynge hym to the abbot and to the prayers of the bretherne, he departed. But he myght not holde hym but that he must often tymes come agayne to vysyte the holy brother, and he dyde nothynge but by his counsayle.

"And thus it endured by so longe tyme that this doughter, whiche named herselfe Synaroch, [X5v] had complete[d][1] the space of .xxxviii. yere within her celle. And than it pleased God to call her to Hym, and sykenes toke her. The good man, of that ryght sorowfull, came thyder. And whan he sawe that Synaroche sholde dye, he began to crye: 'Alas, where be those swete wordes and those promyses that thou hast made to me that I sholde se my doughter?'

"Synaroche passed to God, and the fader was not there when he passed. He helde a wrytynge in honde whiche no man myght take out: the abbot and all the covent came to assaye, but they dyde nothynge. Upon this the fader came thyder with grete cryenge and grete wepynge for this good frende whiche he founde dede, on whome was all his comforte, and as sone as he approched the corpes to kysse it, before all he opened the hande and toke to hym the wrytynge. And he toke it and redde within that it was his doughter, and that none sholde touche her body to bury it but onely he. This thynge was grete mervayle to hym, to the abbot, and to all the covent, whiche gretely praysed her holy stablenes in vertue, and to the fader doubled the wepynge in consolacyon of his

---

[1] complete[d] : *complete*

sainte constance et vertu. Et au pere redoubla le pleur en consolacion de sa vie,[1]
si vendi quanque il avoit, leans se rendi, [fol. 165v a] et la fina sa vie.

"Or t'ay dist de plusieurs vierges. Sy te diray d'autres dames martires tres
glorieuses et de sainte vie."[2]

## *Chapitre 14*      De la benoite dame Anastaise, et de ses compaignes[3]

"Ou temps de la grant persecucion des crestiens[4] estoit a Romme, ou temps de
Diodocien l'empereur, avoit en la cité une moult belle dame noble[5] et de grant
richesce et des plus auctorisees qui y fust,[6] qui avoit nom Anastaise. Celle dame
avoit a merveilles grant compassion du tourment que elle veoit faire chacun jour
aux[7] benois martirs, et pour les reconforter et viseter se vestoit chacun jour[8] en
habit d'une povre femme, et aloit a tout une pucelle es chartres ou ilz estoient,
et les reconfortoit de vins precieux et [fol. 165v b] de[9] viandes et de ce que elle
pouoit. Elle lavoit et torchoit leurs playes et oygnoit de precieux oignemens. Et
tant continua ainsi que celle[10] fu accusee a Publien, qui estoit un noble homme
de Romme qui la vouloit avoir a femme, qui moult s'en courouça et y mist telles[11]
gardes que plus n'osoit yssir hors de la maison. Adonc avoit en la chartre entre
les autres martirs sainte Grisogone, homme de grant excellence, qui moult avoit
souffert de griefs martirs. Et il estoit soustenuz des biens de la visitacion de celle
sainte Dame Anastaise, a laquelle celluy saint envoya par une bonne dame crestienne celeement plusieurs epistres la admonnestant de pacience, et pareillement
[fol. 166r a] luy en envoya elle par ycelle.[12] A la parfin, si que Dieu voult, celluy qui
si courte la tenoit mourut, et elle vendi tout quanque elle avoit et tout emploioit
en la visitacion et soustenance des martirs.

"Celle noble dame avoit moult grant suite de dames et de pucelles crestiennes, et entre les autres y avoit .iii. vierges seurs de noble lignee qui moult estoyent ses familieres. L'une de ses suers avoit nom Agappe, l'autre Thionne, et la

---

[1] en consolacion de sa vie] en pitié et consolacion de sa sainte vie
[2] martires tres glorieuses et de sainte vie] martires
[3] et de ses compaignes] *omitted*
[4] Ou temps de la grant persecucion des crestiens] Lors que la grant persecucion
estoit a Romme
[5] belle dame noble] noble dame
[6] fust] fussent
[7] chacun jour aux] tous les jours aux crestiens
[8] se vestoit chacun jour] chacun jour se mettoit en abit
[9] et de] de
[10] continua ainsi que celle] le continua ainsi que elle
[11] telles] tieulx
[12] ycelle] ycelle bonne dame

lyfe. So he solde all that ever he had, and rendred hym into the same abbaye, and there he ended his lyfe.

"Nowe I have tolde thee of dyvers vyrgynes. So I shall tell thee of other ladyes martyres ryght gloryous and of holy lyfe."

*Chapter 14*      **Of the blyssed Lady Anastase and her felowes** [X6r]

"There was in the tyme of the grete persecucyon of the Crysten people in Rome, in the tyme of Dyoclutan the emperoure, there was in that cyte ryght a noble lady of grete rychesse and of grete auctoryte whiche was named Anastase. This lady had mervayllous grete compassyon of the tourment that she sawe done everyday to the martyres, and for to comforte them and vysyte theym she clothed her in the habyte of a poore woman and wente with one mayden unto the prysons where they were, and comforted theym with precyous meetes and drynkes and of suche as she myght. She wasshed and wyped theyr woundes and anoynted them with ryght precyous oyntementes.

"And she contynued soo longe tyll she was accused to Publyen, whiche was a noble man of Rome whiche that wolde have had her to wyfe, whiche waxed wrothe with it; and he made suche awaytes on her that she durst not come oute of her house. And then amonge other martyres in the pryson there was Saynt Grysogone, a man of ryght grete excellence, the whiche hadde suffered many dyvers tourmentes. And he was susteyned of the goodes and the vysytacyons of that good and gracyous Lady Anastase, unto whome the foresayd Saynt Grysogone sent covertely dyvers epystles by a good, vertuous Crysten woman counsaylynge her of pacyence; and in the same wyse she sente unto hym by the [X6v] sayd woman. And at the last so as God wolde, he that helde her so shorte dyed, and she solde al that she had and employed it all in the vysytacyon and sustenaunce of martyres.

"This noble lady hadde grete suyte of ladyes and of maydyns crystened, and amonge the others there were .iii. maydens systers of noble lygnage whiche were ryght famylyer with her. One of these systers was called Agappe, that other

tierce Hirene. Sy vint a congnoissance a l'empereur que ses[1] .iii. nobles suers estoient crestiennes: il les manda et leur promist grans dons et que haultement les marieroit mais que elles renonçassent [fol. 166r b] Jhesucrist. Et comme elles ne feissent de tout ce nul compte, il les fist batre et puis mettre ou[2] dure chartre, en laquelle les visitoit leur sainte amie Anastaise, qui ne s'en partoit ne nuit[3] ne jour, et prioit a Dieu qui[4] la laissast tant vivre que ses biens dureroyent affin que elle les peust tous employer ou[5] celle sainte eouvre.

"L'empereur commanda a Dulcicion, son prevost, que tous les crestiennes qui estoient es chartres fussent contrains par tourmens de[6] adourer les ydolles. Si les fist le dit prevost tous admener devant luy, entre lesquelz estoient les trois benoites seurs. Quant le mauvais provost les vit, il les couvoita pour leur biauté, et les admonnesta en secret [fol. 166v a] par belles parolles et promesces[7] que elles s'accordassent a lui, et il les delivreroit. Mais comme elles fussent de tout ce reffusant,[8] il les bailla a garder a un sien familier et mener en sa maison, et se penssa que bon gré ou mal gré il les aroit. Quant vint la nuit, il ala seul et sans lumiere en l'ostel ou les pucelles fait mener les avoit.[9] Et si comme il vouloit aler au lieu ou il oyoit leurs voix, qui tout la nuit[10] disoient louenges[11] a Dieu, il passa par le lieu ou tous les vaissiaux de la cuisine estoyent. Et adonc luy, plain du diable, de l'esperit de luxure aveuglé si que Dieu voulst, prist a acoller et baisier estroictement puis l'un, puis l'autre de ses vaissiaulx et cuidoit estre avec les [fol. 166v b] pucelles, et tant ala ainsi faisant que il fu forment lassé.

"Et quant il fu jour, il s'en yssi a ses gens qui dehors l'attendoyent, lesquelz quant ainsi le virent, ce leur sembla la figure d'un diable, tant estoit souillié, gras et charbonné, et sa robe derouté et trainant par palletiaulx. Sy s'enfuyrent tous effrayez. Et quant il les vit ainsi fouir et que ilz le despitoient, a merveilles se esbahy pour quoy ce estoit.[12] Sy se penssa qu'il s'en yroit tout droit plaindre a l'empereur de ce que chascun par ou il passoit se mouquoyent escharnissoit.[13] Et quant il fu entrez ou palais ou plusieurs attendoyent au matin, adonc commença sur luy grande la huerie ou l'un le batoit de verges, l'autre [fol. 167r a] le poussoit

---

[1] ses] ces
[2] ou] en
[3] ne nuit] nuit
[4] qui] qu'il
[5] ou] en
[6] de] a
[7] promesces] par promesses
[8] reffusant] reffusantes
[9] les pucelles fait mener les avoit] l'ostel ou avoit fait mener ycelles
[10] oyoit leurs voix, qui tout la nuit] ouoyt les voix des vierges qui toute nuit
[11] louenges] louange
[12] a merveilles se esbahy pour quoy ce estoit] il s'esbahi a merveilles pour quoy c'estoit. Et si comme il aloit par la rue chacun qui l'encontroit l'escharnissoit
[13] se mouquoyent escharnissoit] l'escharnissoit

Thyonne, and the thyrde Hyrene. So it came to the knowlege of the emperour that these noble systers were crystened. He sente for them and promysed them grete gyftes and that he wolde marye them hyghly yf they wolde forsake the name of Jhesu Cryst. And as they made therof no charge, he made them to be beten and after to be put in harde pryson, in the whiche pryson theyr holy frende Anastase vysyted them, not sparynge nyght and day, and prayed God that he wolde suffre her to lyve whyle her goodes endured to the entente that she myght employ them al in that holy werke.

"The emperoure commaunded Dulcycyon, his provost, that all the Crysten people that were in the prysons sholde be constrayned by tourmentes to worshyp the ydolles. So the sayd provost made them for to be brought before hym, amonge whiche were the .iii. systers. And when the cursed juge sawe them, he coveyted them for theyr beaute, and counsaylled them in secrete wyse by fayre wordes and promyses that they sholde accorde to hym and he sholde delyver theym. [Y1r] But as they were all that refusynge, he put them into the warde of one that was famy-lyer with hym. And he made them to be ledde into his house, and he thought to have them agaynst theyr wyll or with theyr wyll. And when the nyght came, he wente alone without lyght to the house where he made them to be brought. And as he wolde goo to the place where he herde theyr voyce, whiche all the nyght dyde no thynge but prayse God, he passed by the place where all the vesselles of the kechyne were kepte. And then he, full of the devyll and blynded with the spyryte of lechery, so as God wolde, he toke them by the necke and kyssed them straytely, syth one and syth another, and trowed that it had ben the maydens. And so moche he wente thus doynge that he was verely wery.

"And when it was daye, he wente to his people whiche abode hym without, whiche when they sawe hym, he semed a fygure of the devyll so moche he was soylled with fatte and coles, and his gowne rente and traylynge in the dyrte. So they fledde from hym, all aferde. And when he sawe them fle thus and that they despysed hym, he was mervayllously abasshed wherfore it was. So he thought hym that he wolde go and complayne to the emperoure of that that every man mocked hym there as he wente and scorned hym. And when he was entred into the palas where many abode hym in the mornynge, then there began a grete crye upon hym, where some bete hym with roddes, some shoved hym abacke,

arriere, disant: 'Va de la, maleureux abominable! Tu pus tout!' L'autre luy crachoit
ou visaige, et les autres s'en rioyent. Si estoit tant esmerveillié[1] que ce pouoit estre
que a pou forcenoit, et le diable luy avoit si cloz les yeulx que il ne se pouoit apper-
cevoir; si s'en tourna ainsi en son hostel,[2] moult afelonnuy.

"Un autre juge fu mis en son lieu qui fist venir devant luy les trois benoites[3]
vierges, et leur voulst faire aourer les ydolles. Et pour ce que riens n'en vouldrent
faire, il les commanda estre despoullees toutes nues et batues. Mais oncques pour
tout leur puissance ne les peurent depoullier, et furent leurs robes sy aherses a
elles que on ne les[4] pot [fol. 167r b] oster. Sy les fist bouter en un feu tres ardent,
qui[5] riens ne leur grevoit. Mais elles requirent a Dieu que la finassent leur vie,
si[6] luy plaisoit, sy trespasserent glorieusement. Mais pour monstré[7] que de leur
voulenté estoit, oncques le feu ne brusla cheveul ne vestement que elles eussent.
Et quant le feu fu degasté, les corps d'elles furent trouvez, les mains jointes, aussi
entieres et fresches[8] que se elles dormissent. Et la benoite Dame Anastaise, qui
d'elles prenoit[9] garde, les enseveli."

## *Chapitre 15*     De sainte Theodorie, vierge[10]

"Une autre noble compaigne avoit Anastaise qui estoit nommee Theodorie,
laquelle avoit trois petis enffans.[11] Celle dame,[12] pour ce que elle reffusa a mariage
le [fol. 167v a] conte Leucadien, et que elle ne voulst sacrefier aux ydolles, plusieurs
tourmens luy furent faiz. Et pour mieulx la contraindre par pitié de mere, on
fist tourmenter l'un de ses filz. Mais par la vertu de foy qui passoit nature, elle
le reconfortoit, disant: 'Filz, ne doubtes point ses[13] tourmens, car par eulx tu yras
en gloire.' Celle dame,[14] elle fust emprisonnee. Un filz du diable vint a elle pour
violler sa chasteté, mais soubdainement[15] prist tres fort a seigner du nefz, si s'escria

---

[1]   esmerveillié] esbahi
[2]   ainsi en son hostel] ainsi
[3]   benoites] beneurees
[4]   les] leur
[5]   qui] mais
[6]   si] s'il
[7]   monstré] demonstrer
[8]   et fresches] et les visages aussi fres
[9]   Dame Anastaise, qui d'elles prenoit] Anastaise qui d'elles se prenoit
[10]  De sainte Theodorie, vierge] De la benoite Theodorie
[11]  enffans] filz
[12]  dame : *dames*
[13]  ses] ces
[14]  dame] dame, comme
[15]  soubdainement] incontinent

sayenge: [Y1v] 'Go out of the waye, thou unhappy and abhomynable persone! Thou stynkest all aboute!' Some scratched hym in the vysage, and some laughed hym to scorne. Soo he was greately admervaylled what that it myght be that he was almoost out of his wytte, for the devyll had closed soo his eyen that he myght no perceyve it; so he tourned hym home agayne unto his house, ryght foule ashamed.

"And then another juge was put in his place whiche made these thre blessyd vyrgynes to come before hym, and he wolde make them to worshyppe the ydolles. And for that that they wolde do nothynge as his byddynge was, he commaunded them to be dyspoyled all naked, and soo to be beten. Yet for all theyr myght, they myght not despoyle theym, for theyr clothes were so clevynge to them that there myght no man put them off. So he made them to be put in a fyre ryght hote brennynge, whiche greved them nothynge. And then they prayed to God that they myght ende theyr lyves, yf it pleased Hym; so they passed anone to Our Lorde ryght gloryously. But for to showe that it was theyr wyll to dye, the fyre never brente them, nor none of theyr clothes. And when the fyre was wasted, the bodyes of them were founde, the handes joyned, as hole and fresshe as thoughe they had slepte. And the blessyd Lady Anastase whiche toke good hede of them buryed them."

*Chapter 15*      Of Saynt Theodore the vyrgyne [Y2r]

"Another noble felawe had this good Anastase whiche was named Theodory, the whiche had .iii. yonge chyldren. This lady, for that that she refused maryage of the Erle Lencadyne and that she wolde not do sacrefyse to the ydolles, there was made many tourmentes for her, and to constrayne the better by moderly pyte made to tourment one of her sones. But by the vertue of the faythe whiche passed nature she comforted hym, sayenge: 'Sone, ne doubte thou not these tourmentes, for by them thou shalte go to joye everlastynge.' And then the lady was put in pryson. A sone of the devyll came to her to defoule her chastyte but sodeynly he began to blede at the nose, and he cryed and sayd that a yonge felawe had smyten

que un jouvencel qui estoit avec elle luy avoit donné du poing sus[1] le nefz. Sy fu de rechief tourmentee, et a la parfin occise luy et[2] ses trois fi[l]z,[3] qui rendirent[4] leurs benois esperis gloriffians Dieu, [fol. 167v b] et la benoite[5] Anastaise les enseveli.

"Ja avoit celle sainte[6] Anastaise tant frequenté la visitacion des martirs que elle fu detenue en la chartre, sy ne pot plus visiter les sains de Dieu, ne[7] n'avoit que boire ne que mengier. Mais Dieu, qui ne voulst pas que celle qui tant diligemment avoit conforté et repeuz ses benois membres eust souffrette, envoya vers elle l'esperit de sa benoite compaigne Theodorie avec grant lumiere, qui luy mist la table et apporta diverses precieuses reffeccions, et l'acompaigna ainsi par trente jours que on ne luy avoit livré quelconques chose a mengier et cuidoit on que elle fust mort de fain.

"Si fu trouvé toute [fol. 168r a] vive, et mené devant le prevost, qui grant dueil en ot. Et pour ce que plusieurs gens pour le miracle[8] se convertissoyent, il la fist mettre en une nef avec pluseurs malfaicteurs, qui estoient condempnez a mourir. Et quant ilz furent ou[9] haulte mer les maronniers, pour obeir ad ce que leur estoit commandé,[10] rompirent leur nef et[11] entrerent en un[e][12] autre vaissel. Adonc la benoite Theodosine[13] s'apparut a eulx, et les convoya par la mer un[e][14] nuit et un jour aussi seurement que se sur plaine terre fust, tant que elle les mist en l'isle de Palme, en laquelle moult d'evesques et de sains hommes avoyent esté envoyez en exil. Si furent la receuz a louenges a Dieu et a grant joye, et ceulx [fol. 168r b] qui estoyent eschappez avecques[15] Anastaise furent baptisiez et crurent en Dieu. Ceste chose, après venue a la congnoissance de l'empereur, les envoya tous querre qui estoyent, que hommes, que femmes, qu'enffans, plus de trois cens que il fist tous mourir par tourmens. Et la benoite Anastaise, après plusieurs grans argus que elle fist a l'empereur et divers tourmens que elle reçut, fu couronnee par martire."

---

[1] sus] sur
[2] occise luy et] occise et
[3] fi[l]z : *fisz*
[4] qui rendirent] aussi, qui rendirent a Dieu
[5] benoite] glorieuse
[6] sainte] benoite
[7] ne] et elle
[8] gens pour le miracle] plusieurs pour ce miracle
[9] ou] en
[10] commandé] ordonné
[11] leur nef et] la nef
[12] un[e] : *un*
[13] Adonc la benoite Theodosine] dont la benoite Theodorie
[14] un[e] : *un*
[15] avecques] avec

hym on the nose with his fyst whiche was with her in the pryson. So this lady was tourmented, and at the laste they slewe her and her .iii. sones whiche yelded theyr blessyd spyrytes, gloryfyenge God; and the blessyd Anastase buryed them.

"Then this holy Anastase had so moche haunted the vysytacyon of martyres that at the last she was taken and emprysoned, so she myght no more vysyte the sayntes of God, ne had no mete nor drynke. But God, whiche wolde not that she whiche so dylygently hadde comforted and refresshed his holy servauntes to suffre more, He sente unto her the spyryte of her blessyd felawe Theodorye with a grete lyght, the whiche set before her a table. And she brought [Y2v] with her dyvers precyous refeccyons and kepte company with her .xxx. dayes, in the whiche tyme was never delyvered to her mete nor drynke, and they trowed that she had ben deed for hongre.

"So she founde all alyve and brought before the provost, whiche had grete sorowe and for that that dyvers people were converted by the myracle, he made her to be put in a shyp with other trespassours that were condempned to dethe. And when they were in the hyghe see, the maryners to obey that that they were commaunded brake the shyp and wente into another vessell. And then the blessyd Theodosyne appered to them and conveyed them by the see a nyght and a daye as surely as they had ben upon the playne erthe, so moche that she set them in the Ile of Palme, in the whiche ile there were many bysshoppes and holy men put in exyle; so they were receyved there with praysynges to God and with grete joye. And those that were escaped with Anastase were baptysed and byleved in God. This thynge after come to the knowlege of the emperoure, he sente to fetche theym all—bothe man and woman and chylde, aboute the nombre of thre hondred—whiche he made all to dye by dyvers tourmentes. And the blessyd Anastase, after many grete argumentes that she made to the emperoure, and after dyvers tourmentes that she had, was crowned by martyrdome."

## *Chapitre 16*     De la noble Natalie[1]

"Natalie, la noble femme de Adrien, princes[2] de la chevalerie de l'Empereur
Maximien, comme elle fust crestienne secretement ou temps que plusieurs
crestiennes estoient martiriez, elle ouÿ dire que Adrien son mary, pour lequel
elle prioit Dieu sans cesser, estoit soubdainement [fol. 168v a] convertis en regardant les martirs tourmenter, et avoit confessé le nom de Jhesucrist. Pour[3] quoy
l'empereur, de ce tres aÿré, l'avoit faicte mettre en tres dure prison. La bonne
dame, tres resjouÿe de la conversion de son mary, s'en ala tantost a[4] la chartre
conforter ycelluy, et prier[5] que il vousist perseverer en ce que il avoit commensié;
et baisoit les liens dont il avoit esté[6] liez, en plourant de pitié et de joye, et moult
l'amonnestoit que il n'eust nul regart[7] aux terriennes joyes qui pou durent ains
eust devant les yeulx la grant gloire qui luy estoit appareillee. La fu longuement
ceste sainte dame reconfortant[8] luy et tous les autres martirs, priant Dieu que elle
fust[9] de leur compagnie, et moult leur pria que ilz reconfortassent [fol. 168v b] son
mary, duquel elle se doubtoit que par la force des tourmens il ne chancellast en la
fermeté de la foy. Elle le visitoit par chascun jour, et tousjours le sermonnoit de
fermeté avoir, et[10] moult de belles parolles luy disoit. Maiz pour ce que elle et plusieurs dames visitoyent les sains martirs, l'empereur fist deffendre que homme[11]
n'y entrast; et pour ce, elle se vesti en guise d'omme. Et quant vint au jour de son
derrain martire, elle fu presente et ses playes luy torchoit et baisoit son sanc,[12] et
luy prioit que il priast Dieu pour elle. Et ainsi le benoit Adrien trespassa.[13] Et
l'un[e][14] de ses mains qui luy avoit esté couppee elle retint et eveloppa chierement
comme sainte relique.

"Celle sainte dame, aprés la mort de son [fol. 169r a] mary, on voulst contraindre de marier pour ce que elle estoit de haulte lignee, et belle, et riche. Sy
estoit ades en oroisons, priant Dieu qui[15] la vousist tirer des mains de ceulx qui
contraindre la vouloyent. Et lors luy apparut en dormant l'esperit de son mary,

---

[1]  noble Natalie] noble et sainte Nathalie
[2]  princes] prince
[3]  Pour] Par
[4]  a] en
[5]  et prier] priant
[6]  avoit esté] estoit
[7]  nul regart] mie regrait
[8]  reconfortant] confortant
[9]  fust] fust bien brief
[10]  avoir et] et
[11]  homme] femme
[12]  sanc] sanc, plourant par devocion
[13]  trespassa] trespassa et elle l'enseveli moult devotement
[14]  un[e] : *un*
[15]  qui] que

*Chapter 16*     Of the noble Natalye [Y3r]

"Natalye, the noble wyfe of Adryan, prynce of the chevalry of the Emperoure
Maxymyan, as she was crystened secretly in the tyme that dyvers Crysten people
were martyred, she herde saye that Adryan her housbande, for whom she prayed
God without seasynge, was sodaynly converted in beholdynge the martyres tourmented and had confessed the name of Jhesu Cryst, wherfore the emperour, of
that ryght wrothe, made hym to be put in ryght an harde pryson. The good lady,
ryght joyous of the conversyon of her housbande, wente anone to the pryson to
comforte hym and to praye hym to persever in that he had begon, and kyssed
the chaynes with whiche he was bounde, wepynge for pyte and joye, and counsayllynge hym gretely that he wolde have no respecte to these erthely joyes that
endured but a whyle, but that he sholde have before his eyen the grete glory that
was ordeyned for hym. This holy lady was there longe comfortynge hym and
all the other martyres, praynge God that she myght be of theyr company, and
prayed them gretely that they sholde comforte her housbande, of whome she
doubted her that by force of tourmentes he sholde not chaunge in the stablenesse of the faythe. She vysyted hym every daye, and every daye preched hym
to have stablenesse, and many a fayre worde she spake to hym. But for that that
she and dyvers other ladyes vysyted the holy martyres, the emperoure made to
[Y3v] defende that no woman sholde come in to them, and therfore she clothed
her in the guyse of a man. And when it came to the daye of his last martyrdome,
she was presente and wyped his woundes and kyssed his blode, and prayed hym
that he wolde pray to God for her. And thus passed the blessyd Adryan. And she
toke with her one of his handes that was cutte off, and wrapped it full derely in
a coverchefe as a relyke.

"This holy lady after the dethe of her housbande one wolde constrayne her
to be wedded bycause she was of hyghe lygnage, fayre, and ryche. So she was
alway in oryson, prayenge God that He wolde drawe her out of the handes of
them that wolde constrayne her to be wedded. And then there appered to her in

qui reconforta[1] et luy dist que elle alast en Costantinoble ensevellir les corps de
moult de martirs qui la estoyent, et elle le fist. Et quant la[2] ot esté une piece ou
service divin en visitant les sains martirs enchartrez,[3] son mary de rechief s'aparu
a elle et luy dist: 'Suer et amie, chamberiere de Jhesucrist, vien t'en en gloire pardurable, car Nostre Seigneur t'appelle.' Et adonc celle s'eveilla et tantost aprés
trespassa." [fol. 169r b]

*Chapitre 17*      **De sainte Affre, qui fu folle femme**[4]

"Affre fu femme follieuse convertie a la foy de Jhesucrist et fu accusee au juge,
qui lui dist: 'Il ne te souffist mie la deshonnesteté de ton corps, se tu ne peches en
erreur de aourer Dieu estrange! Sacreffiez a noz dieux, si qu'ilz te pardonnent.'

"Et Affre respondi: 'Je sacrefieray a mon Dieu, Jhesucrist,[5] qui descendi
pour les pecheurs. Car son euvangille dist que une femme pecharesce luy lava les
piez de ses larmes et recut pardon. Et Il ne dispita oncques les folles femmes, ne
les pecheurs publiquans, ains les laissoit mengier avecques luy.'

"Le juge luy dist: 'Se tu ne sacrefiez, tu ne seras pas amee de tes ribaux, ne
ne recevras de eulx nulz dons.'[6]

"Elle respondi: 'Jamais ne recevray dons excommeniez,[7] et ceulx que j'ay
injustement guaignez[8] [fol. 169v a] j'ay prié aux povrez que ilz les veullent prendre
et prier pour mes pechiez.'[9]

"Le juge donna sa sentence: puis que Affre[10] sacriffier ne vouloit, fust arse. Et
quant elle fu livree au tourment, elle adourant disant:[11] 'Sire Dieux, tout puissant
Jhesucrist, qui appellas les pecheurs a penitence, reçoy en bon gré mon martire
en ceste heure de ma passion, et me delivre du feu pardurable par ce feu corporel,
qui est appareillé a mon corps.' Et celle, avironnee[12] du feu, disoit: 'Sire Jhesucrist, daignes recepvoir moy, povre pecharresce, a sacrefice[13] pour ton saint nom,

---

[1] Et lors luy apparut en dormant l'esperit de son mary, qui reconforta] Et son mari
lui apparut en dormant et la reconforta
[2] fist. Et quant la] fist voulentiers. Et quant elle
[3] enchartrez] en chartres
[4] femme] femme convertie
[5] Dieu, Jhesucrist] Dieu
[6] ne ne recevras de eulx nulz dons] ne de eulx ne recevras dons. Et
[7] dons excommeniez] don escommenié
[8] guaignez] receus
[9] mes pechiez] moy
[10] sentence: puis que Affre] sentence que Affre puis que
[11] disant] disoit
[12] avironnee] toute avironné
[13] a sacrefice] sacrifiee

slepynge the spyryte of her housbande whiche comforted her, and sayd unto her that she sholde goo into Co[n]stantynoble[1] to burye the bodyes of many martyres that were there; and she dyde soo. And when she had ben there a whyle in Goddes servyce in vysytynge the holy martyres emprysoned, her housbande appered unto her agayne and sayd to her: 'Syster and frende, chambere of Jhesu Cryste, come on into glorye perpetuall, for Our Lorde calleth thee.' And then she awoke, and anone after she passed to Our Lorde."

## *Chapter 17*    Of the holy and blessyd Saynt Affra [Y4r]

"Affra was a woman that lyved folyly converted to the fayth of Jhesu Cryst and was accused to the juge, whiche sayd to her: "It suffyseth not thee the dyshonestye of thy body, but that thou muste fall in erroure to worshyp a straunge God! Do sacrefyse to our goddes, that they maye pardon thee."

"And Affra answered, 'I shall doo sacrefyse to my God Jhesu Cryste, that came downe for synners. For His gospell sayth that a woman, a synner, wasshed His feete with her teres and had forgyvenesse. And He despysed never folyly lyvynge woman ne the publycanes synners, but He lete them ete with Hym.'

"The juge sayd unto her, 'If thou do no sacrefyse, thou shalte not be loved of thy rybaudes, ne tho[u][2] shalte receyve no gyftes of them.'

"She answered, 'I shal never receyve cursed gyftes. And those that I have goten untruely, I have prayed to the poore people that they wyll take them and pray for my synnes.'

"The juge gave his sentence that Saynt Affra sholde be brente syth that she wolde not do sacrefyse. And when she was delyvered to tourmente, she worshypped God and sayd: 'Lorde God Almyghty, Jhesu Cryst, whiche callest synners to penaunce, receyve my martyrdome in good[3] entente in the houre of my passyon, and delyver me fro everlastynge fyre by this corporall fyre that is arayed to my body.' And the fyre beynge aboute her, she sayd: 'Lorde Jhesu Cryst, pleaseth Thee to receyve me, a pore synner, in sacrefyse of Thy holy name, Thou that

---

[1] Co[n]stantynoble : *Coustantynoble*

[2] tho[u] : *thon*

[3] good : *goood*

Tu qui t'es[1] offert seul, sacrefié[2] pour tout le monde, et fu mis juste en la croix pour les nonjustes, et bon pour les mauvais, benoite[3] [fol. 169v b] pour les maudis, doulx pour les amers, net et ingnocent de[4] pechié pour leur les pecheur[s].[5] A toy [o]ffre[6] le sacrefice de mon corps, qui viz et raignes avec le Pere et le Saint Esperit, par tout le siecle des siecles.' Et ainsi fina la benoite Affre, pour quoy[7] Nostre Seigneur monstra[8] puis moult de miracles."

*Chapitre 18*     **Dit Justice que[9] plusieurs nobles dames qui servirent et h[o]stellerent[10] les apostres et autres sains**

"Que veulz tu que plus je t'en die, belle amye Christine? Sans cesser te pourroye ramentevoir telz exemples. Mais pour ce que tu t'es[11] esmerveillé sy que[12] tu as dit cy devant, que aucques tous aucteurs tant blasment les femmes, je te dis que quoy que tu ayes trouvé es escriptures[13] [fol. 170r a] des aucteurs payens, je croy que ad ce propos[14] pou trouveras es saintes legendes et es hystoires de Jhesucrist, et de ses apostres. Et meesmement de tous les sains, sy que tu puez veoir, ainsi merveilleuses constances[15] a grant nombre y trouveras par grace de Dieu en femmes, les biaulx serviteurs, les grans charites que elles sans recreandise faisoient par grant voulenté[16] aux sers de Dieu: les hospitalitez et les autres biens,[17] ainsi que il est escript de Drusienne, qui estoit une bonne dame vesve qui recevoit a hostes[18] saint

---

[1] t'es] es
[2] sacrefié] a sacrefice
[3] benoite] benoit
[4] de] du
[5] pecheur[s] : *pecheur*
[6] [o]ffre : *Affre*
[7] quoy] qui
[8] monstra] demonstra
[9] que] de
[10] h[o]stellerent : *hestellerent*
[11] t'es] es
[12] sy que] si comme
[13] escriptures] escrips
[14] ad ce propos] a propos de blasme de femme
[15] constances] constances et vertus
[16] les biaulx serviteurs, les grans charites que elles sans recreandise faisoient par grant voulenté] O! les beaulx services, les grans charitez que elles par grant cure et solicitude faisoient sanz recreandise
[17] biens] biens font ycestes choses point a peser? Et se aucuns folz hommes les vouloient tenir a frivoles, nul ne peut nyer que tieulx oeuvres selon nostre foy, ne soient les escheles qui mainent ou ciel
[18] hostes] hostel

offred Thyselfe in [Y4v] sacrefyse for all the worlde. And Thou, ryghtfull, were put on the crosse for the unryghtfull, and good for the evyll doers, blessyd for the cursed, swete for the bytter, clene and innocent from synne to delyver the synners. To Thee I offre the sacrefyse of my body, whiche lyveth and reygneth with the Fader, and the Holy Ghost, by all the worlde of worldes.' And thus ended the blessyd Affre, for whome Our Lorde hath shewed syth many myracles."

*Chapter 18*    **Here telleth Justyce of dyvers ladye[s]¹ whiche served and lodged the appostles and other sayntes**

"What woldest thou that I saye to thee more, fayre Christine? I myght brynge to remembraunce suche ensamples without nombre. But for that that thou arte admervaylled, so as thou haste sayd here before that wherfore all auctours blame women, I saye to thee that thoughe that thou hast founde it in the wrytynges of auctours paynymes, I trowe that to that purpose thou shalte fynde but fewe in holy legendes and in the hystoryes of Jhesu Cryst and of His appostles, and the same wyse of all the sayntes so as thou mayst se. But a grete nombre thou shalte fynde of mervayllous constaunce by the grace of God in women and good servyces, grete charytees that they have done and do, without faynynge and by good wyll [Z1r] to the servauntes of God, bothe hospytalytees and other good dedes, so as it is wryten of Drucyane, whiche was a good lady and a² wydowe whiche

---

¹ ladye[s] : *ladyed*
² and a : *and a a*

Jehan l'Euvangeliste, et le servoit et lui administroit son vivre. Et quant le dit saint Jehan recepvoit a son exil,[1] et ceulx de la cité luy firent[2] grant feste, [fol. 170r b] l'en portoit Drusienne en terre, qui mort estoit de dueil de ce que il demouroit tant.[3] Et les voisins luy disdrent: 'Jehan, voy cy Drusienne ta bonne hostesse, qui est morte pour l'annuy de ta demouree. Elle ne te servira plus.' Adonc saint Jehan luy dist, 'Drusienne, lieve sus, et va en ta maison et m'apreste ma refeccion.' Et celle resuscita.

"*Item*, une vaillant et noble dame de la cité de Limoges, nommee Susane: celle fu[4] la premiere qui hostella saint Marcial, qui la estoit envoyé par saint Pierre pour convertir le paÿs, et moult de bien luy fist.[5]

"*Item*, la bonne dame Maximille ensevelli saint Andry et le osta de la croix, et en ce faisant, se exposa[6] en peril de mort.

"*Item*, la sainte vierge Apingene [fol. 170v a] fuyuoit[7] par devocion saint Mathieu l'Euvengeliste,[8] et aprés sa mort luy fist ediffier une eglise.

"*Item*, une autre bonne dame estoit tant esprise de la saint amour de saint Pol l'Apostre[9] que elle le suivoit partout, et le servoit par grant diligence.

"*Item*, en cellui temps des apostres, une noble royne appellee Helaine, et ne fu pas celle qui fu mere de Constantin, mais une autre royne de Obbigois, qui ala en Jherusalem, ou quel lieu avoit tres grant chierté de vivres pour la famine qui y estoit. Et quant elle sçot que les sains de Nostre Seigneur qui estoient en la cité pour prescher et convertir le peuple mouroient de fain, elle fist achater tant de vivres que ilz en furent pourveuz tant que la famen dura.

"*Item*, quant on [fol. 170v b] menoit saint Pol pour le decoller[10] par le commandement de Noiron, une bonne dame qui avoit nom Paucille, qui avoit acoustumé de le aminstrer, luy vint a l'encontre[11] moult fort plourant. Et saint Pol luy demanda le cueuvrechief que elle avoit sur son chief, et elle luy bailla dont les mauvais qui la estoient se[12] mouquoyent, disant pour ce que moult estoit bel que tant perdoit elle. Saint Pol luy meysmes en banda ses yeux, et puis quant il fu mort, les anges le rendirent a la femme, tout plain de sanc, dont elle le tint moult

---

    [1] lui administroit son vivre. Et quant le dit saint Jehan recepvoit a son exil] administroit son vivre. Dont il advint, quant le dit saint Jehan s'en revenoit de son exil
    [2] firent] fasoient
    [3] demouroit tant] tant demouroit
    [4] celle fu] fu
    [5] bien luy fist] biens lui fist celle dame
    [6] exposa] mist
    [7] fuyuoit] suivoit
    [8] l'Euvengeliste] l'Euvangeliste et le servoit
    [9] Pol l'Apostre] Paul
    [10] le decoller] decoler
    [11] vint a l'encontre] vint au devant
    [12] se] s'en

receyved to host Saynt Johan the Evangelyst. She served hym of his mete and his drynke; and whan the sayd Saynt Johan sholde be receyved fro his exyle and those of the cyte made hym a grete feest, Drucyane was borne to be buryed, whiche was deed for sorowe that he taryed so longe. And her neyghboures sayd to hym: 'Johan, see here Drucyane thy good hostesse, whiche is deed for sorowe for thy longe taryenge. She shal serve thee no more.' And than Saynt Johan sayd to her: 'Drucyane, ryse up and go into thy house, and make redy my refeccyon.' And she rose frome dethe to lyfe.

"Also another of the cyte of Lymoges, named Susanne, she was the fyrst that harboured Saynt Marcyall, whiche was sente thyder by Saynt Peter to converte the countre, and dyde hym ryght moche good.

"Also the good Lady Maxymylle buryed Saynt Androwe, and toke hym frome the crosse; and doynge this, she put herselfe to the peryll of dethe.

"Also the holy mayde Euphygene folowed by devocyon Saynt Mathewe the Evangelyst. And after his dethe, she made to edefye for hym ryght a fayre chyrche.

"Also another good lady was so moche taken with the love of Saynt Poule the Apostle that she folowed hym all aboute, and served hym by grete dylygence.

"Also in that tyme of the apostles a noble quene called Helyn (and it was not she that [Z1v] was moder of Constantyne, but another quene of Oblygoys) whiche wente to Jherusalem in the whiche there was grete scarcete of vytaylles for the famyne that was there. And when she knewe that the sayntes of Our Lorde that were in the cyte to preche and to converte the people dyed for hongre, she made to bye so moche vytaylles for them that they were pourvayed as longe as the derthe lasted.

"Also when one lydde Saynt Poule to be heeded by the commaundement of Nero, a good lady whiche was called Pautylle, that was acostomed to serve hym, came ayenst hym, wepynge gretely. And Saynt Poule asked of her a coverchefe that she had upon her heed, and she toke it hym. Wherof the shrewde people that were there mocked hym, sayenge for that it was fayre that so moche she had loste. Saynt Poule hymselfe wyped his eyen, and after when he was deed, he sente it agayne to the woman, full of blode, wherfore she kepte it ryght rychely. And

chierement. Et saint Pol s'aparut a elle et luy dist que pour ce que elle luy avoit faicte service en terre,[1] que il luy feroit ou ciel en priant pour elle. D'assez d'autres en cas pareulz [fol. 171r a] te pourroye dire.

"Noble dame fu Baxelice en la vertu de charité. Celle[2] fu mariee a saint Julien, et des la nuit de leurs noces vouerent d'une[3] accort virginité. Et nul ne pourroit pensser la sainte conversacion de celle vierge, ne la multitude de femmes de[4] viergez qui par sa saint monicon furent sauvees et tirees a sainte vie. A brief dire, tant deseu[5] de grace par la tres grant charité qui estoit en elle que Nostre Seigneur parla a elle a son trespassement.

"Je ne sçay que plus t'en diroye, Christine, amie chiere.[6] Sans nombre pourroye compter de dames de divers estaz, tant vierges comme vesves ou mariees, en qui Dieux a demonstré ses vertus par merveilleuse force et constance. Si te suffise a tant, car bien [fol. 171r b] et bel sy qu'il m'est vis me suis acquitee de mon office en parfaisant les haulx combles de ta cité et la te peupler de excellens dames, si que je te promis.[7] Et non obstant que je ne nomme, ne nommer, ne pourroye fors a paines toutes les saintes dames par noms qui ont esté, qui sont, et qui seront, toutes puent[8] estre comprises en ceste Cité des Dames, de laquelle se puet dire: *Gloriosa dicta sunt de te civitas dei.* Si la te rens close, parfaicte, et bien ferment[9] si que je te promis. A Dieu te di la paix du Souverain soit permanent avec[10] toy."

## *Chapitre 19*     La fin du livre parle Christine aux dames

Mes tres redoubtes dames, Dieux soit loués: or est du tout achevee et parfaicte nostre cité, en laquelle a grant honneur vous toutes, celles qui amez [fol. 171v a] gloire, vertu, et loz pouez estre hebergees, tant les passees dames comme les presentes et celles a advenir, car pour toute dame honnourable est faite et fondee.

Et mes tres chieres dames, chose est naturelle[11] a cuer humain de soy esjouÿr quant il se treuve avoir victoire d'aucun[e][12] emprise, et que ses annemis soyent

---

[1]   en terre] en ce terre
[2]   Celle] Elle
[3]   vouerent d'une] eulx .ii. vouerent d'un
[4]   de] et de
[5]   A brief dire, tant deseu] Et a brief dire, tant desservi
[6]   Christine, amie chiere] Christine
[7]   promis] promis; et cestes derrenieres serviront de portes et de clostures en nostre cité
[8]   ne pourroye fors a paines toutes les saintes dames par noms qui ont esté, qui sont, et qui seront, toutes puent] pourroye fors a peines les saintes dames qui ont esté qui sont, et qui seront, elles peuent toutes
[9]   ferment] fermee
[10]   avec] avecques
[11]   est naturelle] naturelle est
[12]   d'aucun[e] : *d'aucun*

Saynt Poule appered to her and sayd that for so moche that she had done hym servyce in heven in prayenge for her. Ynoughe of others in lyke case I myght tell thee.

"Vaxyllete was a noble lady in the vertue of charyte. This lady was maryed to Saynt Julyan, and in the nyght of theyr weddynge of one acorde they vowed vyrgynyte. And none myght thynke the holy conversacyon of this woman, ne the multytude of women and maydens that were saved and drawne to holy lyfe by her holy monycyon. To saye shortely, [Z2r] so moche she had of grace in her that Our Lorde spake to her as she was in dyenge.

"I wote not what I sholde saye more, Christyne, my dere love. I myght tell thee without nombre of ladyes of dyvers estates, as well vyrgynes as wydowes or maryed women, in whome God hath shewed His vertues by mervayllous strengthe and constaunce. So be thou suffysed as nowe, for ryght well and fayre as it semeth me I have wel quytte me of myne offyce in perfourmynge of the hyghe bataylementes of thy cyte, and I have peopled it with excellente ladyes, so as I promysed thee. And nothwithstandynge that I name not, ne maye not name all the holy ladyes by theyr names whiche that hathe ben, whiche that ben, and whiche that shal be, all maye be comprehended in this Cyte of Ladyes, of the whiche one maye saye: *Gloriosa dicta sunt de te civitas dei.* That is to say, *Gloryous thynges ben sayd of thee, thou Cyte of God.* So I yelde it to thee as a parfyte thynge wel and stably, so as I promysed thee. Nowe I betake thee to God, and the peas of Oure Hyghe Soverayne be everlastyngely with thee." AMEN

*Chapter 19*     **Here Christine speketh unto the ladyes in the ende of the boke** [Z2v]

Mi ryght redoubted ladyes, worshypped b[e] God![1] Nowe is our cyte well accheved and made parfyte, in the whiche all ye that loveth honoure, vertue, and praysynge may be lodged with grete worshyp, as wel those that are past as those that ben nowe and those that be to come, for it is founded and made for every woman of worshyp.

And my ryght dere ladyes, it is a thynge natural to mannes herte to rejoyce hym when he fyndeth hym that he hathe the vyctory of ony entrepryse, and

---

[1] b[e] : *by*

confonduz. Sy avés cause orendoit, mes dames, de vous esjouÿr vertueusement en Dieu et bonnes meurs par ceste nouvelle cité veoir perfaicte, qui puet estre non mie seullement le reffuge de vous toutes, c'est a entendre des vertueuses, mais aussi la deffense et garde contre voz annemis et assaillans, se bien la gardez. Car vous pouez veoir que la matiere dont elle est toute est[1] de vertu [fol. 171v b] voire sy reluisant que toutes vous y pouez mirer, et par especial es combles de ceste derreniere partie, et semblablement en ce qui vous puet touchier des autres.

Et mes chieres dames, si ne vueillez mie user de ce nouvel heritage si comme[2] les arrogans qui deviennent orguilleux quant leur prosperité croist et leur richesce monte,[3] ains par l'exemple de vostre Royne la Vierge souveraine, qui aprés si grant honneur que on luy adnonçoit comme d'estre mere du Filz de Dieu, elle tant plus s'umilia en se appellant Chamberiere de Dieu. Ainsi, mes dames, comme il soit voir que les vertus plus sont grandes en creature plus la rendent humble et benigne vous soit cause [fol. 172r a] ceste cité d'amer[4] bonnes meurs et estre vertueuses et humbles.

Et n'ayes point, vous dames qui estes mariees,[5] a despit d'estre tant subgectes a voz mariz, car n'est pas aucunes foiz le meilleur a creature d'estre franche. Et ce tesmoigne ce que l'ange de Dieu dist a Edras. Ceulx, dist il, qui userent de leur franche voulenté churent en pechié, et despirent Nostre Seigneur, et defoulerent les justes, et pour ce furent periz.[6] Sy soiés[7] humbles et pacientes, et la grace de Dieu en croistra en vous, et au monde louenge[8] vous sera donnee car dit saint Gregoire que pacience est entree de paradis et la voye de Jhesucrist.

Et entre vous vierges en l'estat de pucellage, [fol. 172r b] soyés pures, simples, coyes, et[9] sans vagueté car les las des mauvais sont tenduz contre vous. Sy soies armees de vertueuse force contre leur cautelles par eschever leur frequentacion.[10]

---

¹ toute est] est toute

² si comme] si comme font

³ monte] multiplie

⁴ d'amer] d'avoir

⁵ Et n'ayés point, vous dames qui estes mariees] Et entre vous dames qui estes mariees, n'ayés point

⁶ *R admonition to wives revised, expanded; see annotations*

⁷ si soiés] Ainsi mes dames soiés

⁸ en croistra en vous, et au monde louenge] croistra en vous et louange

⁹ coyes, et] et quoyes

¹⁰ tenduz contre vous. Sy soies armees de vertueuse force contre leur cautelles par eschever] contre vous, voz regars soient bas, pou de paroles en voz bouches, cremeur soit en tous voz fais, et soiez armees de vertueuses force contre les cautelles des deceveurs, et eschevez

that his enemyes be confounded. So have ye cause, all ye my ladyes, to rejoyce you nowe vertuously in God and in good condycyons by this newe cyte to se it parfyte, whiche may not be onely the refuge of al you, that is to understande of vertuous women, but also the defence and warde ayenst your enemyes and assa-yllers, yf ye kepe it well. For ye may se that the matter wherof it is made is all of vertue, and so truely shynynge that all ye maye beholde therin and specyally in the emfrytaylynge of this laste partye, and the same wyse in that whiche may touche you of other partyes.

And my dere ladyes, soo use ye not of this newe herytage as these proude people whiche become so full of pryde when theyr prosperyte encreaseth and are mounted in rychesse, but by the ensample of your quene the Soverayne Vyrgyne, whiche after so grete worshyp that the aungell brought to her as to be the moder of the Sone of God, she [Z3r] so moche more meked her, in callynge her the hande mayden of God. So my ladyes, as be it true that the more the vertues ben, the more ye ought to yelde you humble and benygne, and this cyte be cause unto you to love good maners and to be vertuous and humble.

And have ye not in despyte, ye ladyes that ben maryed, to be so subjectes to your housbandes, for it is not sometymes beste to a creature to be free out of subjeccyon. And that wytnesseth the tonge of Our Lorde God where He sayth to Esoras the prophete: 'Those,' He sayth, 'that use theyr free wyll falleth in synne and despyse theyr Lorde, and defouleth the juste people, and therfore they per-ysshe.' So be ye humble and pacyente, and the grace of God shall encreace in you, and ye shal be gyven in praysynge to the worlde. For Saynt Gregory sayth that pacyence is the entrye of paradyse and the way of Jhesu Cryst.

And amon[ge][1] you vyrgynes in the state of maydenhode, be ye clene, sym-ple, coye, and without ydelnesse, for the gynnes of evyll men ben set agaynst you. So be ye armed with vertuous strengthe agaynst theyr cauteyles to eschewe theyr frequentacyon.

---

[1] amon[ge] : *amon*

Et aux vesves dames, soit honnesteté en habit, et maintien,[1] et parolle; devocion en fait et en conversacion; prudence en gouvernement; pacience qui besoing
leur a humilité et charité.[2]

Et toutes generaument—grandes, moyennes, et petites—vueillez estre avisees en deffense contre les annemis de vostre honneur et chasteté.[3] Voyés, mes
dames, comment ces hommes vous acusent[4] faictes tous menteurs ceulx qui vous
blasment. Et deboutes arrieres les lousengiers[5] qui par divers attraiz [fol. 172v a]
taschent[6] a soustraire ce que tant[7] devez garder, c'est assavoir voz honneurs. O,
la folle amour, dont ilz vous admonnestent: fuiez la, pour Dieu, fuiez! Car soyés[8]
certaines quoy que les aluchemens et les semblans[9] en soyent decevables, que
tousjours en est la fin a voz prejudices. Et ne croyés la contraire, car autrement
ne puet estre. Souvengne vous que ilz vous appellent frailles et fausses, et toutevoyes ilz quierent[10] engins estranges et decepvables a grans painnes et travaulx
pour vous prendre, si que on fait les bestes sauvaiges[11] aux laz. Fuyez, fuyez, mes
dames, telz[12] acointances soubz lesquelz ris sont enveloppez venins tres angoisse-
seux et qui livrent a mort. Et ainsi vous plaise, mes tres redoubtés, [fol. 172v b]
par[13] les vertuz attraire, et fouir les vices, acroistre et mouteplier nostre cité vous
resjouir et bien faire. Et moy, vostre servant[e],[14] vous soit recommandee en priant

---

    [1]  et maintien] maintien
    [2]  besoing leur a humilité et charité] bien besoing y a; force et resistence en tribu-
lacions et grans affaires; humilité en cuer, contenance, et paroles; et charité en oeuvres
    [3]  toutes generaument—grandes, moyennes, et petites—vueillez estre avisees en
deffense contre les annemis de vostre honneur et chasteté] briefment toutes femmes—soient grandes, moyennes, ou petites—vueillez estre sur toute riens avisees et caultes en deffence contre les ennemis de voz honneurs et de vostre chasteté
    [4]  acusent] accusent de tant de vices et de toutes pars
    [5]  faictes tous menteurs ceulx qui vous blasment. Et deboutés arrieres les lousengiers]
Faites les tous menteurs par monstrer vostre vertu et prouvez mençongeurs ceulx qui vous
blasment par bien faire en telle maniere que vous puissiés dire avec le psalmiste. La felonnie des mauvais cherra leur teste. Si deboutez arriere les losangeurs decevables
    [6]  taschent] tachent par mains tours
    [7]  tant] tant souverainement
    [8]  O, la folle amour, dont ilz vous admonnestent: fuiez la, pour Dieu, fuiez! Car
soyés] et la beauté de vostre loz. O mes dames, fuyez, fuyez la fole amour dont ilz vous
admonnestent. Fuyez la, pour Dieu, fuyez. Car nul bien ne vous en peut venir, ains soiés
    [9]  les aluchemens et les semblans] les aluchemens
    [10]  vous que ilz vous appellent frailles et fausses, et toutevoyes ilz quierent] vous,
cheres dames, comment ces hommes vous appellent fraisles, legieres, et tost tournees, et
comment toutevoyes ilz quierent tous engins
    [11]  bestes sauvaiges] bestes
    [12]  mes dames, telz] et eschevez tieulx
    [13]  par] pour
    [14]  servant[e] : *servant*

And to ladyes wedowes, be honest in habyte, and countenaunce, and in worde; devoute in dede and in conversacyon; prudente in governaunce; pacyente in that where nede is, in mekenesse and in charyte.

And to all generally—grete, meane, and lytel—wyll ye alway to be set in defence agaynst the enemyes of your worshyp and chastyte. Se, my ladyes, [Z3v] howe these that accuseth you maketh all them lyers that blameth you. And put abacke these losengyers, whiche by dyvers draughtes hurteth and withdraweth that that ye ought to kepe so well, that is to understande your worshyppes. O, the lewde love of whiche they counsayle you, and styreth you therto: fle it, for Goddes love, fle it! For be ye certayne thoughe that the semblaunt be fayre, it is deceyvable, that at all tymes the ende of it is prejudyce to you. And thynke not the contrary, for otherwyse it maye not be. Remembre howe they call you frayle and false, and alwaye they seke engynes ryght straunge and deceyvable with grete payne and travayle for to take you so as one dothe to take wylde beestes. Flee theyr gynnes, my ladyes, flee theyr acquayntaunce under laughynge of whome is lapped venyme ryght full of anguysshe, whiche bryngeth one lyghtly to the dethe. And thus that it please you, my ryght redoubted ladyes, to drawe to the vertues and flee vyces, to encreace and multeplye our cyte, and ye to rejoyce in well doynge. And me, your servaunt, to be recommended unto you in praynge

Dieu, qui par Sa grace en cestuy monde me doint vivre et perseverer en Son saint service, et a la fin soit piteable a mes grans deffaulx, et m'otroit la joye qui a tousjours dure qui ainsi le vous occroit.[1] A M E N.

**Explicit la troisiesme et derreniere partie du *Livre de la Cité des Dames***

---

[1] qui ainsi le vous occroit] ainsi par sa grace vous face. Amen.

God, whiche by his grace in this worlde graunte me for to lyve and persever in His holy servyce, and at the ende to be pyteous to my grete defautes, and graunte bothe unto you and me the joye whiche endure[th][1] evermore. A M E N. *Finis.*

By Permission of the Folger Shakespeare Library

---

[1] endure[th] : *endure=*

# Textual Annotations

Unless otherwise noted, identifications of character and place names follow those given in Rosalind Brown-Grant's *City of Ladies* (1999), 244–79. Variations between Christine's French (C) and Anslay's English (A) are noted, but not in the case of minor word order changes, or the common contemporary practice of substituting two similar words for one, or vice versa. Modern translations (RBG, EJR) and editions (*Ri, Cu, La*) have been consulted extensively, as have the notes accompanying Virginia Brown's edition and translation of Boccaccio's *On Famous Women* (*FW*). Details for other references can be found in the bibliography, including *The Oxford Classical Dictionary, Oxford Dictionary of National Biography, Oxford Dictionary of Saints*, and *Oxford English Dictionary*.

## Manuscripts

L    Ms., London, British Library Royal Manuscript 19.A.xix

F    Ms., Paris, Bibliothèque nationale de France fr. 826
     facsimile: http://gallica.bnf.fr/ark:/12148/btv1b8448966h

R    Ms., London, BL Harley 4431, Queen's Manuscript ("la reine")
     facsimile: http://www.pizan.lib.ed.ac.uk/gallery/index.html
     *Making of the Queen's Manuscript* xml transcription:
     http://www.pizan.lib.ed.ac.uk/xmlfinal/cdam.xml

## Editions

*Ri*    Earl Jeffrey Richards, second edition, 1998: based on *R*

*Cu*    Maureen Cheney Curnow, 1975: based on Ms., Paris, BnF fr. 607

*La*    Monika Lange, 1974: based on *R*

*FW*    Virginia Brown, ed. and trans., *De claris mulieribus* (*On Famous Women*), 2001

## Modern English Translations

RBG    Rosalind Brown-Grant (Penguin Classics, 1999; Penguin Books 2005)

EJR    Earl Jeffrey Richards (Persea, 1982; rev. ed. 1998)

## Printer's Prologue

Discussed in *History of English Poetry* (1781), 3:79–80. Printed in Ritson, *Biblio-graphica Poetica* (1802), 115–16; Hartshorne, *Book Rarities in Cambridge* (1829), 175 [first seven lines only]; Furnivall, *Notes and Queries* (1876): 367–68; Wogan-Browne, *Idea of the Vernacular* (1999), 304–10; Summit (2000), 95–96; Coldiron (forthcoming).

**every gentylman**—Summit, *Lost Property*, 96–97, reads prologue as usurping Christine's voice to reinforce patrilineal hegemony, noting statement that work is "*by* Bryan Anslay" [emphasis added]. View repeated by Downes, "Fashioning Defences," 71–81; Ferguson, *Dido's Daughters*, 222–23; Warren, "French Women and English Men," 434–36 and *Women of God and Arms*, 82–85. But Coldiron writes that "in any language, the *City of Ladies* directly challenges aspects of patriarchy and their literary and social consequences"; see *English Printing, Verse Translation, and the Battle of the Sexes*, 36.

**bokes olde**—Christine's *Cité* (1405) and Boccaccio's *FW* (ca. 1361) both old by 1521; legends of Troy, Greece, Rome add patina of antiquity.

**in my custodye**—pre-existence of translation implies that Pepwell, Gray did not commission it. No manuscript version survives.

**fautes for to amende**—modesty topos common in medieval, early modern writing.

# PART I

## Chapter 1

**After the maner . . .**—convoluted syntax feature of original text; here, prose complexity complements description of studiousness.

**Matheolus**—Mathieu de Boulogne (*d.* 1320), author of *Liber Lamentationum Matheoli* (ca. 1295), translated into French by Jean Le Fèvre (ca. 1371–1372); he also wrote *Le Livre de Leësce*, of debatable intent. See Blumenfeld-Kosinski, "Jean Le Fèvre's *Livre de Leësce*: Praise or Blame of Women?"; also Margolis, *Introduction*, 70, 139, 183, 186. Pair owned by George Boleyn in 1526, became part of Royal Library as Ms. Westminster 278; Carley, *Libraries*, 73.

**not speke well of the reverence of women**—true, but C says opposite: "cellui parloit bien a la reverence des femmes." See Reno, "Feminism and Irony," 131.

**my good moder**—see Ribémont, "La figure de la mère"; Arden, "Her Mother's Daughter." C praises domestic arts later in Part I.

**by one mouthe**—misogynist discourse was prevalent, but Christine found supporters, notably Jean Gerson,˙chancellor of the University of Paris, who sided with her in the *querelle de la Rose* (1401–1404). See Nathalie Nabert, "Christine de Pizan, Jean Gerson et le gouvernement des âmes"; Richards, "Christine de Pizan and Jean Gerson: An Intellectual Friendship"; Walters, "The Figure of the 'Seulette' in the Works of Christine de Pizan and Jean Gerson." Blamires, *Medieval Case for Women*, writes of pro-feminine writing by men more broadly.

**grete foyson of dyttyes and proverbes**—see Smith, *Oxford Dictionary of English Proverbs*, 723–26; Stevenson, *Macmillan Book of Proverbs*, 2555–87; Whiting, *Proverbs, Sentences, and Proverbial Phrases*, 658–63. Regarding Christine's own proverb collection and its circulation in England, see Coldiron, "Taking Advice from a Frenchwoman."

**wytnesse of many is for to byleve**—Deuteronomy 17:6.

**receyveth leest . . . leest is bounde**—Luke 12:48.

## Chapter 2

**upon my lappe a stremynge of lyght**—for discussion Kolve, "Annunciation to Christine," 179–81.

**waked of a dreme**—dream vision genre altered: this is no "fantasye." Noted by Blumenfeld-Kosinski, "Misogynistic Tradition," 279.

**neyther man nor woman with me**—added by A. On the Boethian parallels see Margolis, *Introduction*, 70–71.

**Dere doughter, drede thee nought**—language of endearment and preferment (and cf. Luke 1:30); virtues themselves called daughters of God.

**golde proveth hym in the fornayse**—Proverbs 17:3, 27:21; Isaiah 48:10.

*Boke of Metaphisike*—written ca. 335–322 BC by Aristotle; defines *Metaphysics* as "science of being as being."

**Arystotle . . . Plato**—Aristotle (384–322 BC), student of Plato (ca. 429–347 BC), who in turn was a student of Socrates (see note II.21, below). Differences in their views support Reason's assertion that philosophers need not agree. Neo-Platonism (first century AD) influenced early Christian authorities, including Augustine. Known in Middle Ages through commentaries of Macrobius, Chalcidius; humanists sought to recover study of Greek and Hebrew texts in their original languages.

**Saynt Austyne**—Augustine (AD 354–430), bishop of Hippo. Christine's title, *Cité des dames*, echoes *De civitate dei*. Story of his conversion in I.10; feast day 25

August. See Holderness, "Christine, Boèce et saint Augustin: la consolation de la mémoire"; Walters, "La réécriture de saint Augustin par Christine de Pizan: De *La Cité de Dieu* à la *Cité des dames*"; Margolis, *Introduction*, 70, 152.

**antyphrasys**—rhetorical strategy explained in text by Reason; an example is C's opening assertion that Matheolus speaks well of women.

**and shame to hym that sayth it**—change in A; "la vituperacion" begins complex new sentence in C.

*Romaunce of the Rose*—popular allegorical poem by Guillaume de Lorris (*fl.* 1230), Jean de Meun (*d.* ca. 1305); survives in roughly 300 MSS. Henry VIII owned at least five copies, including Vérard's print edition (Carley, *Libraries*, 22, 98–99). Chaucer's English translation appeared in editions of his *Works*, 1532–1602For *querelle de la Rose* (ca. 1400–1404) overview, see Hicks, "Situation du débat sur le *Roman de la Rose*"; McWebb and Richards, "New Perspectives on the Debate about the *Roman de la rose*"; Margolis, *Introduction*, 61–66. Selected letters in McWebb edition, *Debating the Roman de la Rose: A Critical Anthology*, 107–40. Regarding this scene, specifically, see Smith, "Jean de Meun in the 'Cité des Dames'," 134–37.

**evyll saynges generally of women hurteth the sayers and not the women**—cf. Christine's *Proverbes moraulx*, trans. Anthony Woodville (Caxton, 1478): "Hit sitteth not a woman to diffame | For vpon him self shal retorne the blame."

## Chapter 3

**Title:** abbreviation for Christ (chi-rho) used for Christine's name; see Oestreich, "Paradigmatic Participation and Eschewal," 256–58. Concerning Christine's self-representation, see Brownlee, "Le projet 'autobiographique'"; Gibbons, "Christine's Mirror"; Paupert, "Name of the Author"; Tarnowski, "Christine's Selves"; Zühlke, "Le 'moi' dans le texte et l'image."

**but that I sholde have been deceyved**—added by A.

**And she of the lesse auctoryte**—original litotes lost; C says Justice *not* the least authoritative; depicts her as the most formidable of the three. A's reading suggests even the least of the three women was intimidating.

**cometh not us to estable, thoughe that we knowe**—A mistakes minims of "vuit" [empty] for "vint" [come], and subjunctive of "to be" translated "to know."

**myroure**—Forhan, "Reflecting Heroes," discusses mirror genre; see also Mühlethaler, "'Traictier de vertu au proufit d'ordre de vivre'". For Reason as allegorical figure, see Quilligan, *Allegory*, 55–59; Tuve, *Allegorical Imagery*, 158, 234, 237–38, 260–61, 267; Wimsatt, *Allegory and Mirror*, 91–116.

**longe and contynuall studye**—Christine's scholarly training described in *Chemin de longue estude* (ca. 1402–1403), *L'Advision Cristine* (1405). Numerous source studies exist; more broadly, see Bell, "Humanism and the Problem of a Studious Woman" and Fenster, "'Perdre son latin': Christine de Pizan and Vernacular Humanism"; also Margolis, *Introduction*, 136–37.

**without fyndynge of ony champyon**—Martin le Franc (ca. 1410–1461) would dedicate *Le Champion des Dames* to Philip the Good (1396–1467). Printed in Lyons, ca. 1488 and Paris, 1530. Henry VIII probably owned a manuscript copy (Carley, *Libraries*, 26–27). For recent scholarship on Martin le Franc and transmission of his writing, see Swift, *Gender, Writing, and Performance: Men Defending Women in Late Medieval France*, 18–21, 68–90, 100–31.

**so unjuste a cause**—*L* and *F* read "si juste"; regarding contemporary legal discourse, see Curnow, "Legal-Judicial Content"; Richards, "Medieval Jurisprudence."

**out of the handes of Pharao**—compares Christine to Moses delivering Jewish people from Egyptian slavery (Book of Exodus; 2 Kings 17:7).

**onely ladyes of good fame**—marked difference from Boccaccio's *FW*; see Kolsky, *Geneaology of Women*, 7–15. McLeod, *Virtue and Venom*, discusses catalog genre; Blamires, *Medieval Case for Women*, examines pro-feminine tradition. See also Cowen, "Women as Exempla"; Brown-Grant, *Moral Defence*; Laird, "Good Women and *Bonnes Dames*"; Meale, "Legends of Good Women."

# Chapter 4

**to make and fortefye the Cyte of Ladyes**—regarding architectural metaphor, see Kellogg, "Reconfiguring Knowledge and Reimagining Gendered Space"; Wagner, "A Monumental (Re)construction of, by, and for Women of All Time."

**thou shalte receyve of us thre wyne and water**—translator, officer of royal cellars, adds "wyne" to original "eaues comme en fontaines cleres."

**Troye**—legendary city identified with modern Hisarlik near Hellespont; for its ideological importance, see Federico, "New Troy," xvii; Brumble, *Myths*, 326–29.

**Appolo, Mynerve, and Neptune**—Phoebus Apollo, Greek and Roman sun god associated with music, poetry, prophecy; Minerva, Roman goddess of wisdom (Pallas Athena, Greek); Neptune (Poseidon, Greek), god of seas. Story untold in *FW, Cité* but added to Minerva's life in an anonymous English adaptation of *FW* (ca. 1440), Ms. BL Add. 10304; see Cowen, "English Reading of Boccaccio" and "Woman's Wit" for MS discussion. See Brumble, *Myths*, 28–32, 218–22, 242–44 respectively.

**Cadmus founded the cyte of Thebes**—Cadmus, brother of Europa, legendary founder of Thebes. Christine recounts its fall in *La Mutacion de Fortune* (1403), discussed by Régnier-Bohler, "La tragédie thébaine." Account known to medieval readers through Statius' *Thebaid*. See Brumble, *Myths*, 318–20, 59–60. See II.60 for Jocasta.

**verray sybylle**—embodiment of female wisdom for Christine; stories told in II.1–3. For discussion, see Quilligan, *Allegory*, 105–16; Weinstein, "Sibylline Voices of Christine de Pizan," 6, 11–34; Brumble, *Myths*, 309–11.

**maulgre all his envyous enemyes**—military metaphor expressed in conflicting terms: "cité" feminine noun; in A, besieged city masculine: "*his* envyous enemyes . . . *he* be fought withall," concludes with feminine: "so *she* shal never be taken ne overcome." Brown-Grant discusses Christine's noun, pronoun use in "Feminist Linguist *avant la lettre*?" and "Writing Beyond Gender."

**Amosonye**—discussed by Johnston, "Redressing the Virago" and Zhang, "L'ancien royaume féminin et la nouvelle communauté des femmes." For legend's history, see DiMarco, "The Amazons and the End of the World"; Diner, *Mothers and Amazons*; DuBois, *Centaurs and Amazons*; Tyrrell, *Amazons: A Study in Athenian Mythmaking*; Brumble, *Myths*, 20–23.

**take the more credence**—in C, credibility assured by Reason's name; in A, source of trust in mission is God ("causes of our comynge").

**mynystresse in thy nede to do that thou myght not yestereven**—"errer" read "hier" [yesterday], creative allusion to opening chapter.

## Chapter 5

**Ryghtwysnesse**—Rectitude, infrequently allegorised; Quilligan identifies first instance in Philippe de Mézière's *Songe du Vieil Pèlerin*, 1387 (*Allegory*, 104–5).

**to every man that that is his**—Justinian, *Digest* I.1.10pr.; C, "chascun ce qui est sien."

**to measure the buyldynge**—cf. Revelation 21:15–16.

## Chapter 6

**Justyce**—one of four cardinal virtues with temperance, fortitude, prudence. Allegorized by Bernard of Clairvaux; see *Serm. in Festo Annun.* I.1–10 (*PL* 183.383); see also Schiller, *Iconography of Christian Art*, 1:11.

**to do to another**—cf. Matthew 7:12; Luke 6:31.

# Chapter 7

**Saynt Thomas**—one of Christ's apostles (Matthew 10:3; Mark 3:18; Luke 6:15; John 11:16, 14:5, 20:25–29; Acts 1:13). Gnostic work dating before AD 220 recounts travels to India, conversion of King Gundafor following miraculous events. Story repeated in writings of Ambrose, Jerome; see *Catholic Encyclopedia*.

**impossyble**—Luke 1:37.

# Chapter 8

**syth that I fele nowe that it is of wronge**—omits reference to Reason: "puis que je sens des ja *de vous* que c'esté a tort . . ."

**to gyve thee way**—C reads "te donner voye" but English syntax makes "the way" more natural than "thee."

**dyvers and indyfferent**—A alters C "diverses et differenciees" [various and distinct].

**entente jugeth the man**—Thomas à Kempis writes, "Man considers the actions, but God weighs the intentions," *De imitatione Christi*, bk. 2, chap. 6; cited in Knowles, *Oxford Dictionary of Quotations*, 805. See also Chaucer's "Th'entente is al," *Troilus and Criseyde*, bk. 5, line 1629.

**in thy sayenges**—*Le Débat de deux amans* (ca. 1400) argues all good things can be misused: "Ne peut on pas de toute chose bonne | Tres mal user?" (ll. 1393–1394).

**Ne blasment ne diffament . . .** —R "*ne blasment ne diffament hommes ne femmes. Les vices heent et les blasment on general, sanz nullui encoulper ne chargier, conseillent fuyr le mal, suivre les vertus, et aler droite voye.*"

**defaute of theyr owne ladyes**—departure from C, where their own bodies [*corps*] are to blame.

**grete age**—A exchanges C "vilté" for "vieillesse."

# Chapter 9

**Ovid**—Publius Ovidius Naso (43 BC–AD 17), Roman poet; died in exile, contrary to C's account. Work known through *Ovide moralisé*, early fourteenth-century verse adaptation; for Christine's use, see Kellogg, "Transforming Ovid"; Paupert, "'Pouëte si soubtil'." Also Margolis, *Introduction*, 189, 268 (index). Single copy of Caxton's prose translation, *Ovid Moralised* (ca. 1480), survives in Ms. Cambridge, Magdalene College, Old Library F.4.34 (Vol. I) and Ms.

Cambridge, Pepys Library 2124 (Vol. II). Latin-English study translation of *Ars Amatoria* printed by De Worde, 1513 (*STC* 18934).

**Vyrgyle**—Publius Vergilius Maro (70–19 BC), highly respected author among medieval readers. See Margolis, *Introduction*, 158, 189. Also Brumble, *Myths*, 347–49. *Aeneid* retold repeatedly, including Caxton's *Eneydos*, 1490 (*STC* 24796) and Gavin Douglas' *Eneados*, which faults inaccuracy of Caxton's version; MS completed 1513, printed W. Copland, 1553 (*STC* 24797).

**Ceco d'Astoly**—Cecco d'Ascoli or Francesco Stabili (ca. 1269–1327), astrologer, alchemist, and poet who wrote *L'Acerba*; executed as heretic 16 September 1327. See Rice, "A Note on Christine de Pisan and Cecco d'Ascoli," using Anslay translation; Margolis, *Introduction*, 164.

*Secrete of Women*—*De secretis mulierum*, late thirteenth-century gynaecological treatise often attributed to Aristotle, sometimes to Albertus Magnus; bound with Pseudo-Aristotle's *Secretum secretorum* in Sorbonne Ms.; see Green, "From 'Diseases of Women' to 'Secrets of Women'," 18, 22 and "'Traittié tout de mençonges'," 146–58, 163–70.

**the shap of man and woman**—creation of Adam and Eve described in Genesis 2.

**de l'une de ses costes . . .** — *R* "*de l'une de ses costes en significance que elle devoit estre coste lui et non mie à ses piez comme serve, et aussi que il l'amast comme sa propre char.*"

**Tullyus**—Marcus Tullius Cicero (106–43 BC), Roman orator, important medieval rhetorical authority. See Margolis, *Introduction*, 166–67.

*Response*: "**Eureux est cil . . .** — *R* "*Cellui ou celle en qui plus a vertus est le plus hault, ne la haulteur ou abbaissement des gens ne gist mie es corps selon le sexe, mais en la perfeccion des meurs et des vertus, et cellui est eureux qui sert à la Vierge.*"

**He is happy that serveth the Vyrgyne**—Mary, mother of Jesus, empress of the City of Ladies (III.1). On Christine's devotional writing, see Richards, "Les enjeux du culte marial."

**one of the Cathons**—Marcius Porcius Cato (234–149 BC), Roman censor, statesman, soldier, orator; in Middle Ages, thought to be author of proverb collection *Disticha Catonis*.

**trespace . . . had not ben**—cf. "O felix culpa" from *Exultet* of Easter vigil.

**lyfte up themselfe from that defaute**—(a) *L* "lever" [to lift] instead of "louer" [to praise], followed by "et" instead of "par." A reads "honneur" as verb:

> *L:* "Si se doit lever homme et femme de celle mesprison, et qui telle honneur lui est ensuivie" A: "So bothe man and woman ought to lyfte up themselfe from that defaute, and he that worshyppeth woman worshyppeth hymselfe."

*F:* "Sy se doit louer homme et femme de celle mesprison, par qui telle honneur luy est ensuivier"; see also RBG, 23, EJR, 24.

(b) second "creature" reads "createur" in other MSS (incl. *F* ):

*L:* "Car de tant comme nature humaine trebucha plus bas par creature, a elle esté relevee plus hault par creature" A: "For of so moche as mannes nature fell more lower by suche a creature as woman, by woman she is lyfte up agayne more hygher."

"For as low as human nature fell through this creature woman, was human nature lifted higher by this same creature." (EJR, 24)

"If human nature is fallen, due to the actions of one of God's creatures, it has been redeemed by the Creator Himself." (RBG, 23)

## Chapter 10

**the same Caton**—A correctly omits "Uticensis," error by C; Uticensis refers to his great-grandson, 95–46 BC.

**that Nature gyveth may not be taken away**—proverb appears in Richard Hill's commonplace book, Ms. Oxford, Balliol College 354 (early sixteenth century). C repeats in II.36 regarding women's aptitude for education.

**For so as the gospell recordeth**—Matthew 18:3.

**wepe, speke and spynne / God hath put in woman**—rewriting of pejorative Latin proverb: *Fallere, flere, nere, dedit Deus in muliere*; see *Oxford Dictionary of Proverbs*, 726. Used in Chaucer's *Wife of Bath's Prologue* (ca. 1386): "Deceit, weping, spinning God hath yive to wommen kindely" and Lydgate's *Of Deceitful Women* (ca. 1430). On Christine's version, see Angeli, "Encore sur Boccace et Christine de Pizan." For modern teaching approach, see Dawson, "Weeping, Speaking, and Sewing."

**wepe for . . . Lazare, whiche he raysed from the dethe**—John 11:33–44.

**teeres of the foresayd Mary Magdaleyne**—Luke 7:37–50. Greek tradition distinguished three Marys: (a) sinner whose demons were cast out by Christ; (b) Mary of Bethany, sister of Lazarus; (c) Mary Magdalene at the foot of the cross, witness to Christ's Resurrection. Treated as one person by Latin Fathers since Gregory the Great; see *Homiliae in Evangelia* 2.25, *PL* 76.1189AB. See also K. L. Jansen, *The Making of the Magdalen* (Princeton: Princeton University Press, 2000).

**teeres of the wydowe**—Luke 7:12–15.

**was not Saynt Austyne . . . converted to the fayth bycause of the wepynge of his moder?**—Monica (AD 333–387) followed her son Augustine to Italy where he

was baptised by Ambrose of Milan in 387. Comment by unnamed bishop, not Ambrose as Christine implies; cf. *Confessions* 8.3 (*PL* 32.751).

**my Lady Reason sayd**—A changes Ambrose's speech to observation by Reason.

**Ressureccyon**—Mary Magdalene reports Christ's Resurrection in Matthew 28:1–10, John 20:1–18; in Mark 16:1–8, women keep silent out of fear; in Luke 24:1–11, women are disbelieved.

**se bien y avisassent . . .** —*R* adds: *"Voire, dame," dis je, "mais je me soubsry d'une folie que aucuns hommes dient—et mesmement me souvient que je l'ay ouy prescher à aucun folz sermonneurs—que pour ce s'apparut Dieux à femme premierement, pour ce que il scet bien que elle ne se scet taire, affin que plus tost fust sa ressurrection publiees.» Response. «Fille, tu as bien dit, qui folz as appellez ceulx qui se dient. Car ne leur souffit pas de blasmer les femmes, se ilz n'imposent meismes à Jhesucrist tel blaseme, comme de dire que par un vice il eust voulu reveller si grant perfeccion et humilité, et ne sçay comment homme l'ose dire! Et quoy que ilz le dient par bourde, Dieu ne se doit pount mettre en chose de moquerie. Mais ancore aux premier propose . . ."*

**Have mercy on me, Lorde, for my doughter is syke!**—Matthew 15:22–28. Not only is Canaanite praised, Jesus miraculously cures girl, supporting case that daughters are valuable (II.8–11).

**woman Samarytane**—John 4:7–26.

**dysdayned not the devoute kynde of women**—A omits C's reproach: "Dieux, a quans coups noz pontificaux d'aujourd'ui daingneroient tenir parole, mesmes de son sauvement, à une si simple femmellette?" See RBG, 28; EJR, 30.

**that women may not byleve so soone, yet she spake at that tyme**— c/t confusion, reading "craire" [believe] for "taire" [keep quiet].

**Blessyd be that wombe**—Luke 11:27–28.

**spynne**—praised for utility, cleverness, artistry through Minerva (I.34), Arachne (I.39), Pamphile (I.40). For Arachne see Brumble, *Myths*, 32–33.

## Chapter 11

*Boke of Problemes*—Aristotle's *Problemata*; see De Leemans and Goyens for transmission, associated commentaries; also Margolis, *Introduction*, 159–60.

*Boke of Propryetees of Thynges*—Aristotle's *Categoriae*, as noted by RBG and EJR; title could also call to mind Jean Corbichon's translation for Charles V (1372) of popular thirteenth-century encyclopedia *De proprietatibus rerum* by Bartholomaeus Anglicus, *Le Livre des proprietes des choses*, title same as in C; Eng.

trans. by John Trevisa (ca. 1398), printed by De Worde for Caxton, 1495 (*STC* 1536); Berthelet, 1535 (*STC* 1537). See Margolis, *Introduction*, 127, 161.

**mannes nature**—C, gender neutral "nature humaine."

**gyven them understandynge**—A omits "et moult grant de telles y a" ["there are many such women," EJR, 31]. See also RBG, 29.

## Chapter 12

**Empresse Nychole**—Nicaula, legendary ruler born ca. 960 BC, also known as Queen of Sheba; identified as such by Boccaccio (*FW* chap. 43) but not Christine, who writes of Sheba separately (II.4); see Kellogg, "Christine de Pizan and Boccaccio," 125–26; Brown-Grant, "Décadence ou progrès?" 298–99; Angeli, "Encore sur Boccace," 118–19.

**Arabee . . . Ethyope . . . Egypte**—Arabian Peninsula, Ethiopia (Eastern Africa) and Egypt (Northern Africa). For discussion, see Clark-Evans, "The Defense of the African and Asian Ladies" and "Nicaula of Egypt and Arabia."

**Ile Maromye**—Meroë, in present-day Sudan, prospered from sixth century to early fourth century BC.

**Holy Scrypture speketh of her**—1 Kings 10; 2 Chronicles 9.

## Chapter 13

**Quene of Fraunce Fredegonde**—(*d.* AD 597), married to Chilperic I, mother of Clotar II; see Blumenfeld-Kosinski, "Christine de Pizan and the Mysogynistic Tradition," 291–92. On French women as *exempla*, see Cropp, "Les Personnages féminins tirés de l'histoires de la France."

**Kynge Charles**—Chilperic I (ca. 537–584), Fredegunde's husband. Concerning their ecclesiastical patronage, see Halfond, *"Sis Quoque Catholicis Religionis Apex."*

**grete prowesse**—C, "grant savoir."

**Clotharye**—Clotar II (AD 584–629), their son.

**Blaunche, moder onto Saynt Lowes**—(1188–1252) daughter of Alphonso VIII of Castile and Eleanor of Aquitaine; married Louis VIII in 1200, became regent in 1226 for Louis IX (1214–1270) during his minority; see also II.65.

**Jane, wedowe of Kynge Charles the Fourth**—Jeanne of Evreux (*d.* 1371), became third wife of Charles IV (the Fair) in 1325; he died two years later.

**wedded to the duke of Orlynaunce**—Blanche of France (1327–1392), daugher of Jeanne of Evreux ("sa noble fille"); wife of Philip, duke of Orléans, fifth son of Philip VI.

**Blaunche, whiche was wyfe to Kynge Johan**—Blanche of Navarre (*d.* 1398) second wife of Philip VI (1293–1350), not his son John II (1319–1364), who married Bonne of Luxembourg (1315–1349).

**duchesse of Anjou**—Marie of Châtillon-Blois (*d.* 1410), daughter of Charles of Blois, duke of Brittany, wife of Louis I, duke of Anjou.

**... nobles engans tant comme ilz furent petis**—*R* adds: "*O, com grandement fait à louer ceste dame en toutes vertus! En sa jeunece fu de si souveraine beauté que elle passa toutes autres dames, et de tres parfaicte chasteté et sagece en son parfaict aage, de tres grant gouvernement et souveraine prudence, et force et constance et courage, comme il y paru. Car aprés là mort de son seigneur, qui mourut en Ytalie, auques toute sa terre de Prouvence se rebella contre elle et ses nobles enfans. Mais ceste noble dame fant fist et tant pourchaça, que par force que par amours, que elle la remist toute en bonne obedience et subgecion. Et si bien la maintint soubz ordre de droit que oncques clameur ne plainte ne fu ouye de injustice qu'elle feist. D'autres dames de France, unes et autres, qui bien et bel en leur vesveté gouvernerent, elles et leurs juridicions, assez te pourroye dire...*"

**countesse de la Marche**—Catherine of Vendôme (*d.* 1411) inherited land after brother's death; John of Bourbon's wife, mother of Anne (II.68).

**Vandome and of Castres, whiche yet is on lyve**—A omits "grant terrienne" [great landowner].

**as well loved of theyr subjects, and better**—suggests queens' popularity sometimes greater than kings'; modern translators interpret "mieulx" as alluding to additional examples of good queens (RBG, 33; EJR, 35).

**ne pronounce the causes of partyes**—A keeps "dede of jugement" [fait de jugier] but omits *L* "ne jugier," consistent with *F*.

## Chapter 14

**Certes, madame, ye say ryght wel**—consistent with *F* ("Certes, Dame, bien dittez"); *L* omits "dame," relies on rubric to identify speaker ("Christine à Raison").

**and that that thou folowest it**—C context suggests "and thus" or "consequently."

**than that she hath berafte her**—female pronouns in A; examples in C (Aristotle, Alexander) demonstrate relevance to men.

**thoughe he had a body lyke unto Absolon**—Absalom, David's son, famed for physical beauty (2 Samuel 13–19).

**Alexandre**—Conquering Macedonian king (356–323 BC) who founded Alexandria (331 BC); student of Aristotle: see I.19, II.29. Cropp, "Christine de Pizan and Alexander the Great" and "The Exemplary Figure of Alexander the Great" discusses her approach to legend on its circulation see Ashurt, "Alexander the Great," and *A Companion to Alexander Literature*, ed. Zuwiyya. A simply says "lytell of body"; C reads "tres lait, petit, et de chetif cors."

**that is gyven of God**—A appears to read "don" [gift] as "donné" [given] and long *s* of "giste mucié" as *f*, "gyfte."

**soules of man**—simplified from C "les ames de plusieurs des plus fors."

**Nowe take thy truell and thy plumbe with thy lyne**—A reads "la truelle de ta plume" [pen] as a trowel and plumb line.

**sygnes of astrologye**—see Willard, "Christine de Pizan: The Astrologer's Daughter"; Ribémont, "Christine de Pizan, Isidore de Séville et l'astrologie."

**I shall cast hym on**—feminine pronoun in C.

## Chapter 15

**Semyramys**—in Augustine's *De civitate dei*, XVIII, chap. 2, husband Ninus contemporary with Abraham, first biblical patriarch (ca. 1900 BC); in *FW* chronology, she follows Eve; see Dulac, "Un mythe didactique chez Christine de Pizan: Sémiramis ou la veuve héroïque," for analysis. Cf. Brumble, *Myths*, 307–9.

**conquered with the swerde**—A omits "de leur proper" [*of their own*, i.e., in person].

**into Inde**—India, emblematic of medieval Far East, though Marco Polo travelled beyond to China.

**never man approched to make them warre**—Justin and Orosius, Boccaccio's sources, report that Semiramis, Alexander only conquerors to invade India; since Semiramis came first historically, feat was unprecedented.

**enforced and made agayn**—"against" probably typographical error; emended to continue idea of conquest, rebuilding [*reffist*, "made again"].

**Nembroche**—Nimrod, ancient king, descendant of Noah; Genesis 10:8–12; 1 Chronicles 1:10.

**Felde of Semyaar**—Plains of Shinar, where Tower of Babel was built; see Genesis 11:1–8, 14:1; Daniel 1:2; Zechariah 5:11.

**So she lyfted up herself**—cumbersome translation of C, in which she rises hastily, but consistent with lifting up her statue "upon an hyghe pyller."

Yet was this cause the gretter—C "Mais de ceste erreur, qui trop fu grande" becomes in A evaluation of most convincing argument. On C's stance, see Semple, "L'erreur et la morale: le dualisme de la 'loi païenne'."

## Chapter 16

grete see that holdeth in all the worlde—Mediterranean Sea; see Harrison, *Medieval Space*, Tomasch and Gilles, eds., *Text and Territory*, on contemporary concepts of geography. See also Edson, *Mapping Time and Space*, for discussion of medieval cartography.

Syche or Sychye—Scythia, today North Eastern Europe, borders the Black Sea not the Mediterranean. Boccaccio's *Cyrii* an abbreviation of *Themiscyrii*, a city in Pontus; noted by V. Brown, *FW*, 483.

yf they were delyvered of ony sons—Christine embraces but does not invent practice, as implied by Quilligan, "Translating Dismemberment," 259. Follows tradition of Benoît de Sainte-Maure's *Roman de Troie* (ca. 1160), Guido delle Colonne's *Historia destructionis Troiae* (1287), offering civilized depiction of Amazons. *The Book of John Mandeville* (ca. 1357), ed. Kohanski and Benson, based on Ms. London, British Library Royal 17.C.xxxviii: "And if they have knave chyldren, they sendeth hem to her fadres when they con eete, go, and speke." But Warner's edition, based on Ms. London, British Library Egerton 1982, reports violent alternative: "if any of tham be with childe and hafe a son, thai kepe it till it can speke and ga and ete by it self and than sendez it to the fader, or elles slaez it."

to perfourme theyr ordynaunce. Then they chose—so punctuated by A; following *L*, sentence division would read: *nourysshe them themselfe. To performe theyr ordynaunce, then they chose . . .*

Lampheto, that other Marpasye—*FW* chap. 11 says they were sisters; C does not.

they avenged the dethe of theyr frendes full notably—"frendes" for "amis" is broad enough to encompass all who were killed; BnF f.fr. 607 says "leurs maris" [husbands]; BL Harley 4431 reads "annemis" [enemies]; see *Ri*, 517 for selected variants.

were called Amozonnes, that is as moche to say as unpapped—V. Brown notes *Amazon* supposedly derived from the Greek, meaning "without a breast" (*FW*, 483).

as I have here before touched—see I.4.

Ephese—Ephesus; ruins in modern-day Turkey on the coast of Asia Minor.

**Synoppe**—not among *FW* Amazons; Sinope of Greek mythology lived near Black Sea; included among female warriors in Jean Le Fèvre's *Livre de Lëesce* and by Eustache Deschamps (1346–1406) among "Neuf Preuses," building upon popular medieval concept of (male) Nine Worthies; for discussion, see Cassagnes-Brouquet, "Penthésilée, reine des Amazones et Preuse."

**wasted all the lande and conquered**—omits C allusion to additional conquests.

## Chapter 17

**yf ryght worshyppful ladyes**—not conditional in C; perhaps misprinted "of."

**Thamarye**—Thamaris; not Amazon in *FW* chap. 49. Quilligan argues Christine's version closer to *Histoire Ancienne*; see "Dismemberment," 259.

**Cyrrus**—Cyrus the Great (*d.* 530 BC) conqueror of Medes and Babylonia, founding Persian empire; mentioned in 2 Chronicles, Ezra, Isaiah, Daniel. See Huber, "[É]tude comparative des récits sur Cyrus."

**And then she wente**—A reads "a loy" as a form of *aler* [to go].

**for one of her maydens**—death of her son [un sien filz] precipitates vengence in *FW* and *Cité*. A misses Christine's point that Amazons love their sons.

*Mutacyon of Fortune*—(1403) survives in 11 MSS; famously, Christine's persona copes with misfortune by transforming into a man. See Griffin, "Transforming Fortune"; Kiehl, "Christine de Pizan and Fortune: A Statistical Survey"; Tarnowski, "Maternity and Paternity in 'La Mutacion de Fortune'." Also Margolis, *Introduction*, 88–93, 262 (index).

*Epystle of Othéa*—(ca. 1400) survives in almost 50 MSS and multiple print editions in French and English; interprets story of Thamaris (chap. 57) as lesson in humility.

## Chapter 18

**Title: almoost overcome them**—abbreviation of C rubric.

**dredde and doubted anone to the londe [of] Grece**—departure from *FW* chap. 19–20, where Greeks easily overcome Amazons.

**howe they [were unable] to withstande theyr enemyes**—words seem to be lost at line break in *STC* 7271; intended phrase uncertain. *L* reports no army could resist the Amazons: "comment il n'estoit force qui peust resister a la leur"; emendation roughly consistent if "they" (neighboring lands) were unable to resist "theyr enemyes" (Amazons).

**Hercules**—Greek hero charged with completing twelve labors; C changes motive from heroic quest, to fear of conquest. Hercules later married Deianira (II.60). See Brumble, *Myths*, 154–66.

**Sampson le Forte**—Judges 13–16, Biblical figure famed for strength.

**go upon them fyrst**—so A translates "envair"; "invade" newly coined verb, earliest *OED* example dating from 1494.

**Theseus**—Athenian hero famed for defeating the Minotaur with Ariadne's help, not told by C. Text spells name "Thesens" except in rubric and this line. See Brumble, *Myths*, 320–22.

**soo many hystoryes**—for Amazons in history and literature, see DiMarco, Diner, DuBois, Hamaguchi, Kleinbaum, Schwarz, Tyrrell; also Brumble, *Myths*, 20–23.

**so many worshypfull men overcome by women**—C recognizes potential disbelief that Hercules would fear the Amazons.

**In the meanetyme**—C "En peu d'eure" [quickly].

**Orthya**—in *FW* chap. 19–20 daughter of Marpasia, co-regnant with Antiope; here Antiope, Orithya reign in succession, extending the empire's longevity.

**Quene Pantasylya**—see I.19.

**avenged upon theyr male talent**—not a gendered statement originally: "male talant," *displeasure* or *anger* in modern English. *Talent* used as English word for "disposition" since twelfth century; *male* as sex designation from late fourteenth century, as attested by *OED*.

**Manalyppe**—in *FW* chap. 19–20, sister of Antiope and Hippolyte ransomed in exchange for belt required as part of Hercules' ninth labor.

**Ipolyte**—legendary Amazonian queen, owner of belt Hercules sent to retrieve; appears in Chaucer's *Knight's Tale* and Shakespeare's *Midsummer Night's Dream* as wife of Theseus; see Hamaguchi, "Domesticating the Amazons," for discussion.

**wrathe**—A omits "et de maltalent" here.

**eche of theym bete theyr knyght**—omits (same as title) how horses were knocked down by ferocious blow: "chascune abati son chevalier, cheval et tout en un mont."

**So they helde them in theyr shyppes with them**—"retrairent" understood "returned to their ships" by RBG, 42; EJR, 46. Anslay perhaps had "tenir" in mind since Greeks hold two Amazons hostage.

**had well employed theyr wyll**—omits "les dames moult honnourerent."

**they kepte them with grete joy and pleasaunce**—"regardoient" [gazed at them] interpreted as form of *garder*.

**make a small peas with them**—"small" added by Anslay, perhaps anticipating Penthesilea's battle against Greeks a generation later, in the next chapter.

**for he was smyten with grete love**—in other versions, Hippolyta claimed as a prize of war, raped, abducted; see Hamaguchi, "Domesticating the Amazons."

**Ipolytus**—Hippolytus, hero of plays by Euripides, Seneca; that his name echoes his mother's might have interested Christine, but she does not follow their stories after Hippolyta leaves Scythia. See Brumble, *Myths*, 170–71.

## Chapter 19

**Pantassylle**—Penthesilea, also in *Othéa* (chap. 15). Boccaccio (*FW* chap. 32) says parentage unknown, but Christine makes her daughter of Orithya, favoring hereditary lineage over election of leaders in traditional legend. See Brownlee, "Hector and Penthesilea in the *Livre de la Mutacion de Fortune*," another context.

**grete warre of the Grekes agaynst the Troyans**—Dares the Phrygian and Dictys of Crete used as sources on war by Geoffrey of Monmouth, Guido delle Colonne. See I.4.

**Ector of Troy**—Hector considered foremost among Trojan heroes, founder of French royalty; see Abray, "Imagining the Masculine: Christine de Pizan's Hector"; Brumble, *Myths*, 151–52.

**porte of Troy**—translated as place rather than form of verb *porter*.

**Achylles**—Greek hero; in other accounts, kills and falls in love with Penthesilea at same time. In *FW*, she wants to bear Hector's child, fights to impress him. Christine follows different version in which Penthesilea arrives after Hector's death. See Brumble, *Myths*, 3–5.

**Kynge Pryamus . . . Quene Eccuba**—Priam and Hecuba of Troy, parents of Hector, Paris, Troilus, Cassandra (II.4), Polyxena (II.60). See Brumble, *Myths*, 152 for Hecuba.

**The grounde . . . of all worthynesse**—C "Le sommet" [pinnacle, summit].

**to stretche a swerde**—"ceindre" seemingly confused with *estendre*, but translated "gurde" elsewhere.

**my fortune**—A reads "ma fortune"; *R* "m'a Fortune tant esté."

**If I had ben there**—A seems to read "ja" as "je," "a venu" [had come] instead of "avenu" [happened]; C reads "Ja ce ne fust avenu"; see RBG, 44; EJR, 49.

**yet and [h]e were on lyve**—A reads "ye," but if Hector were still alive, there would be no need to avenge his death. His assailant must be implied subject: "if he were alive," that is, Achilles.

**lordes and ladyes of the chevalrye**—could be interpreted as an audience of male and female knights; C indicates courtly audience of barons, ladies, and knights.

**whiche semed you well in your lyfe**—interrogative "quel" introduces rhetorical question in French, becomes relative clause in A.

**So she wolde not tourne homewarde**—C suggests invading Greeks would never return home, had she lived longer.

**Pyrrus**—son of Achilles, who ordered Polyxena's execution (II.60).

**.viii. hondred yeres**—Amazons continued to fascinate early modern Europeans. Amazon river in South America so named after Spanish expedition reportedly saw female warriors there (1542); map by Abraham Ortelius (1570) locates Amazons amid the unexplored interior of the African continent.

**into that royalme**—Alexander's visit to the Amazons is in the late antique and medieval *Alexander* romances. For essays on the Alexander tradition, see Zuwiyya, *A Companion to Alexander Literature*.

## Chapter 20

**valyaunt Cenobye**—Cenobye, or Zenobia, ruled Palmyra from AD 267 to 272; story recounted in *FW* chap. 100, Chaucer's *Monk's Tale*, and Lydgate's *Fall of Princes* as victim of Fortune. Walker reads Zenobia in Elyot's *Defense of Good Women* (1545) as veiled reference to Catherine of Aragon; see also O'Brien, "Warrior Queen"; Wayne, "Zenobia in Medieval and Renaissance Literature."

**Palmurenes**—Palmyra, territory within Syria.

**Ptholomees**—dynasty named after Ptolemy (367/6–282 BC), Macedonian general who governed Egypt for Alexander until conqueror's death (323 BC), then ruled independently, succeeded by his descendants.

**to sle the wylde beestes**—echoes youthful exploits of Hercules (I.18); similar feats attributed to Camilla (I.23).

**Valeryan Auguste**—Valerian I, or Licinius Valerianus (AD ca. 200–260), Roman emperor from AD 253 to 260.

**Sapore**—Sapor I (Shabuhr), ruler of Persia from AD 240 to 272, captured Valerian.

to suffre the travayle of armes with her housbande — foreshadowing theme regarding great love of wives toward husbands; Hypsicratea (II.14) also praised for accompanying husband on military campaigns.

Ordonet . . . Herode — Septimius Odaenathus (*d.* 267), king of Palmyra, part of Roman empire; Herod, son of Odaenathus by another wife; assassinated with his father.

Mesopotame — Mesopotamia, from Greek meaning "between two rivers" (Tigris, Euphrates).

with his concubynes — interesting detail in book about women; capitalized "Concubines" in *STC* 7271 particularly draws attention.

Mais la dame de noble courage prist — *R "Mais riens ne lui val car la dame de noble courage bien l'en garda, car comme vaillant et preux prist."*

Galeryan and Claudyan, emperoures of Rome — Gallienus (Licinius Egnatius Gallienus, reigned AD 253–268), son of Valerian, and Claudius II (Marcus Aurelius Claudius II Gothicus, reigned AD 268–270) led Rome while facing pressure from Visigoths. Aurelian (Lucius Domitius Aurelianus, reigned AD 270–275), defeated Zenobia, as noted in *FW*; omitted by Christine. See Quilligan, *Allegory*, 93–94.

Armony — Armenia, region stretching across Turkey as far east as Georgia in classical and medieval times. Lesser Armenia, also known as Kingdom of Cilicia, bordered Mediterranean, important geographically for the Crusades and eastern trade routes. In 1375, Egyptians conquered Cilicia; last king of Lusignan dynasty fled to France.

and medle no ferther — added by A.

made her armure to be ledde in charyot — preceding description of "her harnoys on her backe and her helme on her heed" taken as the antecedent for the phrase, "se faisoit porter"; possibly long *s* has been confused with *l*. Phrase should be a reflexive construction: see RBG, 48; EJR, 53.

Longyne — Cassius Longinus (AD ca. 213–273) philosopher, rhetorician, and political advisor; executed by Aurelian after Zenobia's defeat.

her chyldren that she nourysshed — omits "en grant discipline" ["whom she had brought up very strictly," RBG, 49]. Zenobia's story left *in medias res*, her children continuing her noble lineage; notably, writes "all her hystoryes" by her own hand.

## Chapter 21

**Lylye . . . Thyerrys**—Lilia, mother of Gothic King Theodoric (reigned AD ca. 474–526), from *Grandes chroniques de France*; see Blanchard, "Compilation and Legitimation," 237–38; Quilligan, *Allegory*, 92–93.

**emperour of Constantynoble**—Zeno (reigned AD 474–491), Byzantine emperor during Theodoric's youth. Constantinople named after Constantine I (Flavius Valerius Constantinus, reigned AD 306–337), founded on site of Byzantium.

**Odonatre**—Odoacer, king of Italy, deposed last Western Roman Emperor Romulus Augustulus in AD 476; killed by Theodoric in AD 489.

**Ravenne**—Ravenna, Italian city on the Adriatic Sea.

## Chapter 22

**Fredegonde, of whom I spake before**—I.13. According to Phillippy, Medea, Dido, and Griselda "are the only divided biographies in the *Cité des dames*"; from "Establishing Authority," 160. Other two-part *exempla*: Artemisia (I.25, II.16), Nicostrata (I.33, II.5), Lucrece (II.44, II.63).

**they wolde laboure it**—*L* reads "laboureroient"; *F* and later redactions have "l'obeiroient," i.e., the barons would obey Fredegunde.

**al the bataylles sewynge by fayre ordre**—adds "al," omits "des chevaliers les suivoient."

## Chapter 23

**Camylle**—Camilla, Volscian warrior in Vergil's *Aeneid* (VII, XI); exemplar of self-restraint in *FW* chap. 39.

**Machabyus**—Metabus, Camilla's father and exiled king of the Volsci.

**trayled easely this vessell after hym**—A initially translates "escorces" as "ryndes of trees"; when tree bark becomes a boat, translated here as "vessell." "Bark" or "barque," meaning "small boat," entered English from French late in fifteenth century; word for tree bark has separate etymology of Scandinavian origin.

**warre with wylde bestes**—compare with Hercules (I.18) and Zenobia (I.20).

**Turnus agaynst Eneas**—king of Rutulians, Lavinia's unsuccessful suitor; according to Vergil, Camilla sided with Turnus and died during his war against Aeneas.

## Chapter 24

**Capadoce**—Cappadocia, in central Anatolia, part of modern-day Turkey.

**Veronycle**—Veronica, Latin form of Greek "Berenice"; Christine follows *FW* chap. 72 in combining two historical women: (a) Berenice (*b.* ca. 280 BC), second wife of Antiochus II (ca. 287–246 BC), assassinated with son by estranged wife, Laodice; (b) Laodice (*fl.* ca. 120 BC), whose husband Ariarathes VI was murdered by her brother, Mithridates VI Eupator Dionysus (120–163 BC). "Vernycle" in Middle English refers to an image of Christ, from legend of St. Veronica, whose handkerchief was used by Christ to wipe his face on the way to Calvary.

**Kynge My[t]rydaces**—Mithridates V Euergetes (152/1–120 BC), king of Pontus.

**Aryaraces**—Ariarathes VI (ca. 130–116 BC), husband of Laodice.

## Chapter 25

**Title: Chapter 25**—Christine reorganised later redactions, Artemisia following the Amazons (I.16–19) and Zenobia (I.20). *L's* table of contents develops inconsistencies at I.21; see introduction.

**Archemyse**—following *FW* chap. 57, conflates stories of two women: (a) Artemisia I (*fl.* 480 BC), who supported Xerxes at Battle of Salamis; (b) Artemisia (*fl.* 353 BC), who built memorial for Mausolus. Boccaccio discusses whether they might be two women, commending their achievements either way.

**Kynge Mansole**—Mausolus, king of Caria from 377 to 353 BC, husband of Artemisia. Spelled "Mansole" in *STC* 7271.

**in tyme and place hereafter**—II.16.

**Rodes**—Rhodes, island in Aegean Sea, site of major siege by Turks, who were ultimately successful in Anslay's time.

**and made [theyr] waye towarde the cyte**—pronoun confusion: invaders, not Artemisia, made their way ["leur chemin"] toward Halicarnassus. Unlikely but possible "her" third person plural pronoun; "theyr" commonly used in A.

**Dalycarnase**—Halicarnassus, ancient city on Caria's coast, now Bodrum in Turkey.

**them of the cyte whiche were good and trewe**—A combines two groups: "ceulx de la cité, et a aucuns bons et feaulx"; see RBG, 50; EJR, 56.

**retourned by the grete gate**—"grant port et prist le naivre"; probably city's main sea port rather than small cove used for departure, or city gates described earlier.

**two ymages of brasse**—foreshadows building of monument for her husband (II.16); *Cyte* contains other memorials to women: Semiramis—Babylon (I.15); Cloelia—Rome (I.26); Sappho—Lesbos (I.30); Minerva—Athens (I.34).

**Exerse, the kynge of Perse**—Xerxes I, king of Persia (reigned 486–465 BC); modern scholars believe the Biblical Esther (II.32) was his wife.

**Macedonyes**—Christine means Lacedaemonia, region of Greece near Sparta; Macedonia, home to Alexander the Great, is mountainous, landlocked.

**Grekes whiche had made alyaunce with this Lady Archemyse**—historically, and in Boccaccio's version, Artemisia fights with Xerxes against the Greeks. Christine casts her as rescuing, not attacking them. Ms. BL Add. 10304 also depicts Artemisia siding with Greeks; see Cowen, "English Reading of Boccaccio," 138–40. Another possibility is that anonymous English writer knew Christine's version.

**Salemyne**—Salamis, island near Athens, site of a major battle in 480 BC.

**dyscomfyted them**—C refers to Xerxes, singular, but implies his army and armada through synecdoche.

**thus she had people innumerable**—A construes "gens innombrables" as belonging to Artemisia; in C, they are the routed opposition.

**taryed theym**—A envisions rivers so clogged with ships they could hardly move.

## Chapter 26

**Cleolis**—Cloelia, Roman girl; *FW* chap. 52.

**certayne covenauntes**—after Tarquin was expelled for son's rape of Lucretia (II.44), Porsenna, king of the Etruscans, fought on his behalf, ultimately made peace with Romans, guaranteed by hostages (male and female).

**gretely praysed of them of Rome**—according to *FW*, Roman Senate sends Cloelia back to Porsenna, king frees her with other hostages; in C, Cloelia leads hostages to safety during initial escape.

**Nowe we must lyfte up the hyghe walles all aboute**—Christine's allegory follows a structured building plan: seven introductory chapters (I.1–7) followed by seven occupied with excavation work (I.8–14) and twelve setting foundation stones (I.15–26). Construction of the city walls (I.27–48) and interior buildings (II.1–11) produces a 2:1 ratio of outer circumference to inner structures in 33 chapters total, number associated with mastery and experience, being the age of Christ at His crucifixion; for general discussion, see Hopper, *Medieval Number Symbolism*.

## Chapter 27

**Title:** *L* gives I.28 title. *F* reads: "Demande Christine à Raison se diex voult oncquez anoblir aucun entendement de femme de la haultesse de sciencez, et responce de Raison." *R* concludes "et la response que Raison fait." *STC* 7271 rubric omits phrase about Reason's response entirely.

**they haunte not so many dyvers places** — added by A.

**nothynge that techeth . . . as dothe the experyence** — proverbial; see Knowles, *Oxford Dictionary of Quotations*, 631, 787; Stevenson, *Macmillan Book of Proverbs*, 1252.

**as I have sayd to thee before** — I.11.

## Chapter 28

**Title:** shorter than C, perhaps due to space constraints (sig. Kk 6r). *L* refers to "la royne Cornifie" (I.28); A "the noble mayde Cornyfye" correct.

**Cornyfye** — Cornificia, *FW* chap. 86, discussed Bell, "Humanism," 176–77; Phillippy, "Establishing Authority," 178. Boccaccio reports that her epigrams survived to the time of Jerome (AD ca. 340–420) but later survival unknown.

**by her fader** — A changes "ses parens."

**Cornyfycyen** — Quintus Cornificius, poet, rhetorician and governor of Africa Vetus, received letters from Cicero between 45 and 43 BC.

**Saynt Gregory** — became pope AD 590, one of four church fathers. Boccaccio cites Jerome, an earlier church father.

**Bocace** — Christine cites Boccaccio, her main *auctor*, for first time here in chapter about women illuminated by learning, despite already adapting numerous stories from *FW*, as noted by Quilligan, *Allegory*, 96.

**sayth in his boke** — see V. Brown's ed. and trans., sec. 3, 354–55.

**"Nowe ben they ashamed," sayth he, "as these slowe women"** — omitted from later *Cité* redactions.

## Chapter 29

**Probe the Romayne** — Faltonia Betitia Proba (*fl.* AD 351); differences from *FW* chap. 97 discussed by Quilligan, *Allegory*, 96–98; Blanchard, "Compilation and Legitimation," 239–40; Phillippy, "Establishing Authority," 179.

**Adelphe** — Clodius Celsinus Adelphius (*fl.* AD 351), Roman prefect.

**the whiche**—in lieu of C "Lesquelz livres et lesquelz dictiez."

**not without mervayle**—parallel with subsequent phrase; C reads "admiracion."

**and ryght a grete mervayle**—lacks C comparative "plus merveilleuse."

*Bucolyques . . . Eneydos . . . Georgykes*—see note on Vergil, I.9.

**sendynge of the Hol[y] Ghost to the apostles**—Proba's text, as it survives today (*PL* 19.803), ends at Feast of the Ascension rather than Pentecost; noted by V. Brown, *FW*, 500.

**the whiche boke was knowne**—C says her knowledge of Scripture was so comprehensive that most great medieval clerks and theologians could not equal it.

*Centonyas*—Proba's *Cento Vergilianus* printed ca. 1514, 1576, 1578; for modern ed. and trans. see Clark and Hatch, *The Golden Bough, the Oaken Cross*. Christine confuses "cento" [patchwork] with "centum" [a hundred].

**Omerus the poete**—Homer, author of *Iliad* and *Odyssey*; not read directly during the Middle Ages; Homeric *cento* by Proba doubtful (V. Brown, *FW*, 500). There was an actual Homeric cento by a woman author, the empress Eudocia (AD ca. 400–460).

## Chapter 30

**Title: Of Sapho, poete and phylosophre**—Sappho, born ca. 612 BC. For Christine's use of *FW* chap. 47, see Brown-Grant, "Décadence ou progrès?," 299. Title shorter than C, fits on one line (sig. Ll2r).

**cyte of Mylycene**—Mytilene, city on Greek island of Lesbos.

**Pernaso**—Mount Parnassus, north of Delphi, associated with Apollo and muses; site of Helicon well.

**.ix. muses**—A adds number; they are Calliope (eloquence, epic poetry), Clio (history), Erato (love poetry), Euterpe (music), Melpomene (tragedy), Polyhymnia (mimesis), Terpsichore (lyric poetry and dance), Thalia (comedy), Urania (astronomy). See Brumble, *Myths*, 225–31.

**braunches of vertue, and floures of dyvers colours**—A translates "verdure" [greenery] as "virtue."

**Grammer, Logyke, and the noble Rethoryke**—grammar, logic, and rhetoric formed the *trivium*, first part of medieval liberal arts education.

**Geometry, Arysmetryke . . . Musyke**—arithmetic, geometry, music, astronomy constitute the *quadrivium*. See Ribémont, "Christine de Pizan et les arts

libéraux: un modèle a géometrie variable." Boccaccio, Christine stop short of ascribing to her astronomy, most advanced discipline.

**Appolyne**—Apollo; see I.4.

**Castolyo**—Castalian spring, Muses' haunt.

**wrest of the harpe**—C "plestren" translated "plectrum" (RBG, 61; EJR, 67), but its meaning has changed since Middle Ages. "Plectrum" in fourteenth-through sixteenth-century English "a device for tightening the strings of a harp. Cf. *wrest.*" By seventeenth century, "plectrum" shifts in meaning to a device for plucking stringed instruments.

**sentences ben stronge to knowe**—"fortes a savoir"; *strong* could mean "obscure, difficult" (*MED*), or "having a powerful effect on the mind or will" (*OED*).

**And the scole . . . endureth unto this day**—continued study of her poems (*estude*), style of writing (*scole*).

**complayntes, and straunge lamentacyons of love**—Boccaccio dwells on Sappho's unhappiness in love; Christine does not. Phillippy, "Establishing Authority," 139–40.

*Saphyse*—for description and use of sapphic through history, see American Academy of Poets: http://www.poets.org/viewmedia.php/prmMID/5790.

**Crassus**—*L* appears to read "crasse" instead of "orasse." Marcus Licinius Crassus (*d.* 53 BC) was a wealthy Roman military leader who defeated Spartacus; Horace (65–8 BC) wrote *On the Art of Poetry*, odes, satires.

**wrytynges of Sapho**—not in *FW*; Christine conflates Sappho with Sophron, a later (male) poet from fifth century BC.

**of dyademes and of crownes**—omits "des roys" [of kings].

**Leonte**—Leontium, third century BC; see Phillippy, "Establishing Authority," 180–81.

**Theophrast**—Theophrastus (ca. 371–287 BC), philosopher, contemporary and successor of Aristotle; memory preserved in Jerome's *Adversus Jovinianum*. Inspired *Letter of Valerius to Ruffinus* (ca. 1180). Christine also mentions Theophrastus in II.13–4, II.19.

## Chapter 31

**Of the mayde Manthoa**—Manto, daughter of Tiresias, *FW* chap. 30. *F:* "Ci dit de la pucelle Manthoa." *L* rubric repeats previous chapter title.

**olde lawe of paynymes**—compare Semiramis, I.15.

**Thyryfye**—Tiresias, seer who foretells Oedipus' fate. See Brumble, *Myths*, 322–24.

**Kynge Edyppus**—Oedipus, subject of Sophocles' Greek tragedy; unknowingly kills his father, marries mother Jocasta (II.60), blinds himself upon discovering truth. Known to medieval readers through Statius, *Thebaid* (ca. AD 80–92). See Brumble, *Myths*, 245–46.

**Caldee**—Chaldea, region of southern Mesopotamia on Persian Gulf.

**Nembroche**—see I.15.

**Thebes was destroyed**—see also I.4, II.60.

**Manthoa**—Mantua, city in northern Italy.

## Chapter 32

**Medea**—*FW* chap. 17; for analysis of Christine's sympathetic depiction see Caraffi, "Il mito di Medea"; Kellogg, "Christine de Pizan and Boccaccio," 127; Phillippy, "Establishing Authority," 176–77; Stecopoulos, "Reconstruction of Myth," 53–55. See Morse, *Medieval Medea*, 230–35, for comparison with other medieval depictions; also Brumble, *Myths*, 186–89. Regarding Chaucer's *Legend of Good Women* in particular, see Laird, "Good Women and *Bonnes Dames*," 64–65; Meale, "Legends of Good Women," 60–65.

**Othes, kynge of Coloos**—Aeëtes, legendary king of Colchis, country on eastern shore of Black Sea.

**Perce**—Christine follows *FW* chap. 17 in naming ocean nymph Perse as Medea's mother. In *FW* chap. 38, Perse mother of Circe, sister of Aeëtes, therefore her aunt.

**in her tyme**—added by A.

**made Jason to conquere the golden fleece**—story continues in II.55.

**Cyrces . . . countree upon the see**— Circe, *FW* chap. 38; Boccaccio says area in southwest Italy named *Circeo* after her; omitted by Christine. See Brumble, *Myths*, 73–75.

**Ulyxes . . . Troy**—Ulysses, Greek hero in the Trojan war; wife Penelope (II.41) considered paradigm of faithfulness; Troy's foundation (I.4) and Trojan war (I.19) mentioned previously. See Brumble, *Myths*, 331–33, 264–65.

**not take the lande without lycence**—compare with cautiousness of Hercules (I.18), Aeneas (II.54).

**Ulyxes wente anone to her**—C omits *FW* assertion that she relented only when threatened with death, and that Ulysses lived with her a year, fathering a son.

**Dyomede**—Diomedes, king of Argos; Venus transformed his men, not Circe. See Brumble, *Myths*, 103–4.

## Chapter 33

**Nycostrate . . . called Carmentis**—Nicostrata, nymph and mother of Evander (*Aeneid* VIII); praised in *FW* chap. 27.

**Archadye**—Arcadia, mountainous region in middle of the Peloponnese.

**Pallent**—Pallas, Nicostrata's father in C; Bocaccio says King Ionius was her father, Pallas either husband or father-in-law.

**gyven of God**—A reads "donee" [given] instead of "douee" [endowed].

**Mercuryus**—Roman god Mercury (Hermes, Greek), quick-witted, fleet-footed messenger. See Brumble, *Myths*, 213–16.

**Tybre**—Tiber river, among longest in Italy.

**Mounte Palentyne**—Palatine Hill, site where Romulus and Remus built Rome, according to legend (II.33). See Brumble, *Myths*, 205 (s.v. "Mars").

**founded a fayre castell**—A adds "fayre"; in *FW* Evander, not Nicostrata, builds town of Pallanteum. Discussed by Stecopoulos, "Reconstruction of Myth," 51, 56–57; Walters, "Christine de Pizan as Translator," 26–29.

**al bestysshe and rude**—reminiscient of Nicaula, I.12; foreshadows Minerva (I.34), Ceres (I.35), Isis (I.36), credited with civilizing humanity. See Brown-Grant, "Décadence ou progrès?"; Kellogg, "Reconfiguring Knowledge," 136; Semple, "L'erreur et la morale: le dualisme de la 'loi païenne'."

**by ordre of ryght and reason after justyce**—echoes Christine's three mentors: Reason, Ryghtwysenesse, and Justice.

**carectes straunge**—see Quilligan, *Allegory*, 99–100.

**that this woman founde**—omits "ne dont petit gré lui doye estre sceu." See RBG, 65; EJR, 72 for modern translation; Brown-Grant, "Christine de Pizan as a Defender of Women," 93–94 for discussion.

**(that is to say in Frensshe *ouy*, and in Englysshe *ye*)**—A adds English.

**it endureth yet**—no longer stands.

## Chapter 34

**Mynerve**—Minerva; see I.4. Also in *FW* chap. 6; discussed by Benkov, "Coming to Writing: *Auctoritas* and Authority in Christine de Pizan," 37–38; Kellogg, "Christine de Pizan and Boccaccio," 126; Phillippy, "Establishing Authority," 182.

**so as thou haste wryten in other places**—in *Othéa* (chap. 13), figure of military prowess; invoked again at the outset of *Faits d'armes et de chevalerie* (1410).

**her surname was Pallas**—gloss to *Othéa* associates "Minerva" with knightly achievements, "Pallas" with wisdom.

**carectes**—Greek as well as Latin writers owe the invention of their language to women, according to Christine.

**abrevyacyons**—characteristic of the Greek hands of the fifteenth and sixteenth centuries that Renaissance westerners would have seen.

**she founde fyrst that ever was advysed to shere shepe**—"founde" should be in preceding phrase; see RBG, 66; EJR, 73. See also I.39.

**instrumentes of mouthe**—wind instruments bore martial association from the time of Pythagoras at least (ca. 500 BC).

**Wulcan**—Vulcan, Roman god of fire (Hephaestus, Greek) craftsman god married to Venus, Roman goddess of love (Aphrodite, Greek). See Brumble, *Myths*, 349–52.

**had her in grete reverence**—omits worship as goddess: "orent en si grant reverence ceste pucelle que ilz l'aourient comme deese."

**sygnyfyed wysdome and knyghthode**—Boccaccio notes wisdom only; Christine adds chivalric interpretation for each aspect of the statue; for context of *translatio studii et imperii*, see Stecopoulos, "Reconstruction of Myth," 55–56.

**ben brought and made open**—"apportes" [brought] read "appertes" [open].

**Gorgon**—here, serpent; in II.60, described as mesmerisingly beautiful. See Brumble, *Myths*, 142–43.

**as for kepe it**—awkward translation of "comme pour la garder."

**that men calleth a choughe**—"chuete" or "chouette" is an owl; "chough" is a jackdaw. See Introduction. Hodapp, "Minerva's Owl," notes allusion to bird by Charles d'Orléans. "Jackdaw" associated symbolically with noisy, prattling gossips; see "jay" in Badke, *Medieval Bestiary*, http://bestiary.ca/beasts/beast543.htm.

## Chapter 35

**Title: ryght noble Quene Seres**—Ceres, Roman goddess of harvests (Demeter, Greek); see Brumble, *Myths*, 69–70. *STC* 7271 adds "ryght noble," omits reference to agriculture in rubric.

**Syculyens**—inhabitants of Sicily.

**bytwene .ii. harde stones**—A specifies two.

**acornes, and hawthorne buryes, and wylde apples**—C "de glans et de blef sauvages, de pommes et de ceneles"; RBG: "acorns, wild grasses, apples and holly berries" (68); EJR: "acorns, wild grains and haws" (76).

**in wylde places and voyde as beestes**—A seems to translate "voyde" as referring to "wylde places"; in C, "vagans" describes nomadic people.

**brought out of beestysshnesse**—Christine strongly commends the merits of civilization, while Boccaccio *FW* chap. 5 laments humanity's loss of self-reliance. Brown-Grant provides analysis in "Décadence ou progrès?" See also Kellogg, "Christine de Pizan and Boccaccio"; Semple, "L'erreur et la morale: le dualisme de la 'loi païenne'"; Stecopoulos, "Reconstruction of Myth," 51–53.

**her doughter was ravysshed by Pluto, god of helle**—Roman goddess Proserpina (Persephone, Greek) appears as queen of faeries and wife of Pluto (Hades, Greek) in Chaucer's *Merchant's Tale*; relevant scholarship noted in *Riverside Chaucer*, 889. Henryson makes similar association in *Orpheus and Eurydice*; see Mills, "Romance Convention," 55. Christine links Proserpina with Orpheus myth in *Othéa* (chap. 70). See also Brumble, *Myths*, 281–84.

## Chapter 36

**Title: Ises**—"noble quene" added by A; Isis, legendary wife of Osiris, mother of Horus.

**transfourmed her into a cowe**—Christine, Boccaccio (*FW* chap. 8) conflate Isis with Io, whose story is told in Ovid's *Metamorphoses*. Jupiter turns her into a cow, attempting to hide the affair from Juno, who is not deceived, places cow under hundred eyes of watchful Argus. See Brumble, *Myths*, 179–80, 181–83. On Christine's Io, see Chance, "Re-Membering Herself."

**in thy Boke of Othéa**—in *Othéa* chap. 25, Isis is associated allegorically with the Virgin's conception of Christ by the Holy Spirit.

**founde dyvers maners of letters**—as with Nicostrata (Latin) and Minerva (Greek), Isis credited with inventing improved alphabet for Egyptians.

**doughter of I[n]achus**—Inachus, ancestor of the Argos royal line.

**Phoroneus, which was ryght a wyse man**—king of Argos, Io's brother.

**Aprys**—Osiris/Apis, combining an Egyptian god and king of Argos, respectively, counterpart of Isis/Io.

**Nyo[b]e**—Niobe, queen of Thebes. In Ovid's *Metamorphoses*, Niobe boasts that she is more worthy of sacrifices than Latona; in vengeance, her children are killed and she turns to stone, weeping still; offered as cautionary tale against pride in *FW* chap. 15. See Brumble, *Myths*, 244.

## Chapter 37

**Title: by dyvers ladyes**—C "ycelles" refers specifically to ones just mentioned.

**que leur savoir est comme chose de nul pris.**—*R* : *"Et est un reproche, que on dit communement quant on raconte de quelque folie, de dire c'est savoir de femme. Et à bref dire, l'oppinion et dit des hommes communement est que elles n'ont servy au monde ne servent fors en porter enfans et de filler." Response. "Or peus tu congnoistre la grant ingratitude de ceulx qui ce dient, et ilz sont comme ceulx qui vivent des biens et ne scevent dont ilz leur viennent . . ."*

**they yelde no thankynges to them from whom they come**—implies ingratitude towards mothers, from whom all men come; in C, antecedent is the good [bien] which has come to the world through women: "la grant ignorance <u>dont il leur vient</u>, ne graces n'en rendent <u>a nullui</u>"; see RBG, 70; EJR, 77.

**He dysprayseth not the woman kynde, ne thoughe that He considereth**—difficulty with "ne le leur quant il lui a pleu conceder." Christine says God did not disdain the feminine sex more than "le leur" (masculine sex) when he deigned to allow them such great understanding [il lui a pleu conceder].

**Carmentes**—see I.33.

**letters of Ebrue and of Grewe**—Latin alphabet superseded Hebrew and Greek, C argues; these languages gained renewed attention during sixteenth century.

**excellens gloires de Dieu, les sciences et les ars.**—*R* adds: *"Et que on ne die que ycestes choses te die par faveur: ce sont les propres paroles de Bocace, desquelles la verité est nottoire et magnifeste."*

## Chapter 38

**Christine and I sayd to her: "Ha, madame!"**—MSS signal change to Christine's voice: *L* <u>Christine:</u> | *Et je dis adonc a elle, "Ha da\me or aperçoy [. . .]"* (fol. 58r); *F* <u>Christine</u> *Et je diz a celle | dame, «Or appercoy [. . .]»* (fol. 29r). *STC* 7271 punctuation (sig. Nn1v) is almost certainly an error, but as it stands, the reader hears the

translator standing by Christine here. Compare Jean Dupré, writing to Marguerite de Navarre, who allies himself with pro-feminine cause: "defendre la querelle des honnestes femmes et mienne" (quoted by Swift in *Gender, Writing, and Performance: Men Defending Women in Late Medieval France*, 192–93).

**there is cause ynoughe of praysynge of them** — positive turn of Christine's reproof: "assez cause souffisant y avoit de non les blasmer"; see also I.37.

**Nowe lette them holde theyr peas** — A translates once; *L* and *F* repeat the phrase: "Or se taisent, or se taisent."

**and other suche** — C "et tous leurs complices" refers to those who support or sympathise with misogynists; see RBG, 72; EJR, 80.

**hath taught them . . . suche a lesson** — A omits C aside, "ce ne peuent ilz nier" [this they cannot deny].

**Yet what shall these nobles and knyghtes say to this thynge, so moche agaynst ryght, that saythe evyll generally of all women?** — rephrasing by A turns criticism of knights into an appeal for them to champion women against detractors. For concurring stance by other male writers, see Blamires, *Case for Women in Medieval Culture*; Swift, *Gender, Writing, and Performance: Men Defending Women in Late Medieval France*.

**all is come to them by women** — "d'une femme," i.e., Minerva.

**that lyveth in cytees and townes** — omits "civilement," adds "and townes."

**and goodnesses whiche they have done for them** — added by A.

**These thynges ben wel appeased without fayle, madame** — "appeased" [satisfied] different from "a peser" [to weigh, consider]. Speech belongs to Christine's persona; redactions after *L* clarify shift in voice to Reason; see RBG, 73.

## Chapter 39

**Title: the crafte to shere sheepe, to dresse the wolles and to make clothe** — C title not given in full, despite space in *STC* 7271 for complete rubric. Wool trade particularly important to English economy. See also I.34.

**Arenye, doughter of Ydmuete Cholophone** — Arachne (*FW* chap. 18), and her father, Idmon of Colophon. See Willard, "Arachne's Metamorphoses"; Brumble, *Myths*, 32–33.

**clothes of hyghe lyst** — finely-woven tapestries; scenes from C's *Cité* depicted this way. See Bell, *Lost Tapestries*.

**whiche became a flee**—Pallas Athena actually transformed Arachne into a spider. See Introduction.

**and maner of werkes to make lynnen clothe**—A side-steps Christine's technical list: "cultiver, ordener, roir, teiller, cerancer, et filer a la conoille et faire toilles"; see RBG, 73; EJR, 82.

**lyved not but with hawes and acornes**—Christine repeatedly repudiates idea of rustic "golden age"; see Brown-Grant, "Décadence ou progrès?"; Semple, "L'erreur et la morale: le dualisme de la 'loi païenne'."

**yf ony creature use evyll of well**—see I.8.

**and woman His owne body**—no women were recorded as present at the Last Supper, but Christine emphasizes that communion is received by both sexes.


## Chapter 40

**Title**: abbreviated; C adds that Pamphile discovered how to dye thread, make silk cloth.

**Pamphyle**—V. Brown translates "bombicem" (*FW* chap. 44) as cotton plucked off plants; here, "soye" [silk]. Burns, *Sea of Silk*, discusses literary references in Middle French. *OED* defines "bombyx" from time of Trevisa as being associated with silkworms.


## Chapter 41

**Title**: A omits reference to Marcia; "Mantoa" in *L*.

**Thamar**—according to Pliny, Thamaris or Timarete became a painter in ancient Greece, following her father's profession.

**as Bocace sayth**—*FW* chap. 56; Christine adds description of Olympic games.

**Nyton**—Micon, Athenian artist, fifth century BC.

**in that tyme of Olympe**—A omits "nonentiesme" [ninetieth].

**dyvers playes**—bodily exercise, not drama.

**when Archylans reygned upon the Macedonyes**—Archelaus (413–399 BC) ruled Macedonia before Alexander the Great.

**Ephese**—Ephesus; according to legend, founded by Amazons (I.16).

**Dyane**—Diana, Roman goddess of the moon (Artemis, Greek). See Brumble, *Myths*, 98–101.

**Irane**—Irene, a legendary Greek artist; *FW* chap. 59.

**Cracyne**—Crateuas (*fl.* ca. 100 BC), physician to Mithridates VI, illustrator of pharmacological books; Boccaccio, following Pliny, says Irene was his daughter and student; Christine says only that Irene studied with him.

**Marcya the Romayne**—(*fl.* 50 BC), Iaia of Cyzicus, Greek artist; *FW* chap. 66.

**Gaye and Spolyn**—Dionysius and Sopolis, supposedly contemporary with Marcia.

**Anastase**—Anastasia, illuminator contemporary with author; regarding C's illuminated MSS, see Ouy and Reno, *Album Christine de Pizan*.

**that there is mencyon made of ony werkeman in the towne of Parys**—translation dampens C's boast that the best artisans work in Paris.

**maketh flourysshynges as she dothe**—A omits description of high-caliber work on valuable manuscripts: "ne de qui on ait plus chier la besoingne, tant soit le livre riche ou chier, que on a d'elle qui finer en puet"; see RBG, 77; EJR, 85.

## Chapter 42

**Semproyne**—Sempronia (second century BC), daughter of Cornelia and Tiberius Sempronius Gracchus (*fl.* 177 BC), wife of Roman soldier and statesman Scipio Aemilianus Africanus Numantinus (185/4–29 BC); *FW* chap. 76.

**whiche she had so redy**—*L* "si tres prōt" read "prompt"; *R* "si tres grant."

**to sorowe**—A omits anger, "a yre vouloit."

## Chapter 43

**in subtyll thynges and scyences as others ben**—A seems to imply that women are as clever as men; modern translators take "tant en sciences comme aultres" to mean other disciplines; see RBG, 78; EJR, 87.

**thynges that prudence techeth**—Othéa, goddess of prudence, instructs Hector in *Epistre Othéa*; see Rouse and Rouse, "Prudence, Mother of Virtues," for connections between *Chapelet des vertus* and C's writing.

**she dothe so moche that naturally they ben prudent**—C syntax challenging; see RBG, 78; EJR, 87 for other possible translations.

**naturall wytte without scyence goten than goten with scyence**—clarified in later *Cité* redactions: *Ri*, 196; RBG, 79; EJR, 88.

grete annoyaunce to them that they busy them so moche—second "them" unclear; if "busy them" reflexive, slothful husbands resent wives bustling about; or, husbands (them) resent being nagged to do what they ought without being asked.

## Chapter 44

**Who shall fynde**—Proverbs 31:10–31 (with inserted comments).

**of all good**—double meaning of material security and pleasure from good deeds.

**And she shall yelde her fruyte**—"He" in C, i.e., God will reward her.

## Chapter 45

**Quene Gay Cyryle**—Tanaquil, wife of Lucius Tarquinius Priscus (616–579 BC), fifth king of Rome; *FW* chap. 46. "Gaia" name of earth goddess.

**Constaunce**—should read "Touscane," Tuscany.

**maryed to a kynge of the Romaynes**—A omits "Tarquin."

**in especyall**—added by A, emphasizing special attention to those in service to the queen.

## Chapter 46

**This Dydo was fyrst named Elyxa**—Dido, legendary founder of Carthage; her tragic love story (II.54) also recounted in Chaucer's *Legend of Good Women* and Gower's *Confessio Amantis*. *FW* chap. 42 notes that Dido and Aeneas were not historical contemporaries, could not have been lovers. For discussion, see Desmond, *Reading Dido*, 195–224; also Brumble, *Myths*, 101–3.

**a cyte in the lande of Auffryke named Cartage**—Carthage, city on the north coast of Africa (modern-day Tunisia). Foundation traditionally dated to 814 BC, becoming an empire rivalling Rome. Hannibal (*b.* 247 BC) its most famous general; see II.66 for his victory at Cannae during the Punic Wars.

**Fenyce**—Phoenicians, an ancient civilization of maritime traders (1500–300 BC) who lived on the eastern shore of the Mediterranean.

**Syrye**—Assyria; I.15 describes empire ruled by Semiramis (ca. 1900 BC).

**Agenor**—legendary Phoenician king, father of Cadmus (I.4) and Europa (II.60).

**Beel**—Belus, father of Dido; regarding her parentage in Vergil's *Aeneid*, see Mackie, "A Note on Dido's Ancestry."

**Cypre**—Cyprus, conquered by Richard I during the Third Crusade. Remained under Western governance in Anslay's time; seized by Ottoman empire in 1571.

**Pygynalyon**—Pygmalion, son of Metten I, inherited Phoenician throne as an infant; regency administered by Sychaeus, high priest married to his sister.

**Acerbe Cyte, or Cytens**—Sychaeus, husband of Elissa.

**they letted her not**—supplication in C that they should not hinder her; see RBG, 83; EJR, 93.

**and [to] those that knewe wel . . .** —perhaps Elissa's argument to the envoys; in C, thought process of the sailors, desiring to appease both sides; RBG, 83–84; EJR, 93.

**Grece . . . Cecyll . . . Mesulye**—landmarks during Elissa's voyage; in C "Crete," not "Grece." Sicily followed by Massylia, territory on north African coast.

**the manere and what people they were**—"manere" instead of "navire" [ship].

**when they sawe the lady and her people**—in C, welcomed after peaceful intent ascertained.

**by the crye and the flyght of byrdes**—divination previously established as credible branch of learning; see Manto (I.31), Medea (I.32).

**men of warre and wyse in armes**—explains perhaps A's omission of "peaceful" when describing her people.

**opened her treasoure**—unlike brother, Dido not avaricious, awarding treasure as befits a good leader; generosity proven again towards Aeneas (II.54).

**Dydo . . . virago**—Elissa renamed at very end, once her new kingdom has been named. Boccaccio praises women for acting like men; for Christine, "masculine" behavior is within the compass of natural female abilities.

**so as hereafter in tyme and place I shall tell thee**—her sister Ryghtwysnesse narrates Dido's love story (II.54).

## Chapter 47

**Opys or Ops**—Ops (Rhea, Greek), goddess of plenty, mother of Juno (II.60). Cf. Brumble, *Myths*, 190–92.

**Urane**—Uranus, Greek god of sky (Caelus, Roman) and father of Titans, including Kronos (Saturn, Roman), who eventually overthrew him. See Brumble, *Myths*, 334–35, 324.

**Vesta his wyfe**—Roman goddess of the hearth (Hestia, Greek), daughter of Opis and Saturn, sister of Jupiter (Zeus, Greek); traditionally, chose to remain a virgin. See II.10, II.47 regarding Vestal virgins. C follows *FW* chap. 3, with Livy, Lactantius as sources. See Brumble, *Myths*, 346–47.

**Saturnus, the kynge of Crete**—Lactantius, Christian apologist, insists that Saturn had an earthly kingdom; see L. Swift, "Lactantius and the Golden Age," 149. C follows *FW* in locating Greek gods on Crete. See Brumble, *Myths*, 299–304.

**Jupyter, Neptunus, and Pluto**—Jupiter overthrows Saturn to become supreme god; brothers Neptune (Poseidon, Greek), Pluto (Hades, Greek) rule the seas and underworld, respectively. See Brumble, *Myths*, 192–96, 276–77.

## Chapter 48

**Lavyne**—Lavinia, Aeneas' last wife. According to legend, their descendants were destined to found Rome (*FW* chap. 41); heroine of twelfth-century *Roman d'Eneas*.

**doughter of the Kynge Latyn**—Latinus, epynonymous king of Latium; see I.33. A omits "et puis mariee fust"; later *Cité* redactions read "et puis mariee a Eneas" (*Ri*, 212).

**Turnus, the kynge of Turylyens**—Rutulians lived southwest of Rome.

**notwithstandynge that his wyfe laboured the contrary**—in II.36, Christine tells how her mother opposed father's academic plans for her.

**Turnus moved warre agaynst Eneas**—Camilla supported Turnus (I.23).

**Astanyus**—Ascanius, son of Aeneas and his first wife, Creusa; Nennius reports that he fathered Brutus, after whom Britain was named.

**Julyus Sylvyus**—Julius Silvius; according to Geoffrey of Monmouth father of Brutus.

**sone-in-lawe**—her stepson, Ascanius.

**Alba**—Alba Longa, ancient city of Latium about twelve miles southeast of Rome.

**Remus and Romulus**—legendary founders of Rome; see II.33.

**an ende by them**—in C "par toy," referring to Christine.

# Part II

## Chapter 1

**Nowe take thy toles**—building metaphor reprised as Ryghtwysnesse exhorts narrator to "tempre thy morter" and secure the structure with the "foote of thy penne" (i.e., its base, the writing nib); A omits promise in C that they shall finish soon.

**whyle my syster Reason and you have ben busy**—A adds "my syster"; writes "busy" in lieu of "building" [bastissiez].

**were .x. by nombre**—*FW* chap. 21 mentions ten sibyls without naming them; C's list in tradition of Varro's *Res divinae* (second century BC), known through Lactantius in the Middle Ages. See Quilligan, *Allegory*, 105–17, on sibyls in *Cité*. Also Brumble, *Myths*, 309–11.

*sybelle* **is to say as "knowynge the thought of God"**—Boccaccio gives etymology from Aeolian dialect: *sios* [God] + *byles* [mind].

**Persya**—Persica of Persia.

**Lybcya**—Libica of Libya.

**Delphyca**—Delphica of Delphi; Ovid writes most famously of Almathea of Deiphebe, the Cumaean sibyl (II.3).

**Symerya**—Cimmeria, a place in Italy, according to Homeric tradition; also the name of an area near the Black Sea.

**Erophyle**—Herophile or Erythraea (II.2).

**Erytell**—Erythrea, peninsula in Asia Minor, north of Samos.

**Samya**—Samia, from the Greek island of Samos; Aesop, Epicurus, and Pythagoras associated with Samos as well.

**Cunyana**—Cumaean sibyl; A seems to read the minims of "m" as "ni."

**Elespontyne**—Hellespontina, named after Hellespont, narrow passage between Europe and Asia where Black Sea, Aegean meet; called Dardanelles today.

**in the temple of the noble auctores Solyn and Tyry**—*L* "temple" should read "temps"; in the time of Cyrus the Great (I.17) and Solon (ca. 640–560 BC), Athenian philosopher.

**Frygyca**—sibyl of Phrygia, in Asia Minor.

**Tyburtine**—Tiburtina or Albunea; mentioned in Vergil's *Eclogues*, believed during the Middle Ages to foretell the coming of Christ.

## Chapter 2

**Eryte**—Erythraea or Herophile, *FW* chap. 21.

**Jhesus Ceytos Cenyos Sother**—Scribes struggled with Greek phrase from Augustine, *De civitate dei*, XVIII, chap. 23. Select manuscript variants given in *Ri* (519):

Arsenal 2686  Jhus Ceyrob Ceuy Yos Sother

BnF f.fr. 607  Jhus Ceytos Ceuy Yos Sother

Harley 4431  Jhus Crytos [Ceytos?] Ceuy Yos Sother

BnF f.fr. 1178 Jhus Ceycos [Ceutos?] Ceuy Yos Sother

Two more manuscripts appear to read:

L              Jhesus cetos cenyos sother (fol. 72r)

F              Jhūs Ceyrob . Ceuy yos sother        (fol. 38v)

EJR uses Greek letters (101); RBG writes *Jesus Christos Theon nios soter* (93), Quilligan "Jesus Xristos theou uios soter" (*Allegory*, 113).

**whiche was to say in Englysshe**—"c'estoit à dire en latin, 'Jhesucrist, Filz de Dieu, Sauveur'." Preceding phrase is Greek, not Latin; A sidesteps issue by translating "in Englysshe" without C's reference to Latin.

**that is to say, the Day of J[u]gement**—A reads "c'est dist" instead of "ceste dist" i.e., "she said" (*Ri*, 224).

**fyre shal brenne bothe see and lande . . .**—consistent with *L*, *F*; passage abbreviated in later redactions.

**.xxvii. verses that this sybylle made**—Augustine, *De civitate dei*, XVIII, chap. 23, writes that the Greek phrase is an acrostic from twenty-seven lines of the *Sibylline Oracles*, collected and consulted from 496 BC to AD 363.

## Chapter 3

**Almethea**—Almathea or Deiphebe, the Cumaean sibyl; *FW* chap. 26.

**Champayne, which is nyghe Rome**—Campania, a region around Naples, 200 km or 124 mi from Rome.

**Tarquyne the Proude**—Tarquinius Superbus (reigned 534–510 BC), son of Tarquinius Priscus, mentioned in I.45 as Tanaquil's husband; see also Lucretia (II.44).

**some poetes fayned that [she] was loved of Phebus**—Ovid's *Metamorphoses*, XIV recounts how the Cumaean sybil asked Apollo for an extraordinarily long life but forgot to ask for eternal youth: all that was left of her eventually was a voice.

**God the sone**—Christine offers a Christian reading of the pagan story. The English homonym sun/son is not replicated in French [soleil/filz]. Here Christine writes "Dieu, soleil de sapience," from the fact Phoebus Apollo was the Greco-Roman sun god.

**ryvage of Bayoule**—ancient city of Baiae now mostly submerged in the Bay of Naples, not far from Lake Avernus ("lake of helle").

**ledde Eneas to helle and brought hym agayne**—Vergil's *Aeneid*, VI; Ovid's *Metamorphoses*, XIV.

**.ix. bokes**—demanded price, Tarquin's response told in *FW* chap. 26.

**And thou as a fole not longe ago**—I.1.

**she ended her dayes**—A omits location, "Siché," or Scythia, homeland of the Amazons (I.16). Changed, logically, to "Sicily" by RBG, 95; EJR, 104.

## Chapter 4

**Title: Of dy[v]ers ladyes prophetes**—"prophetes," while in the internal rubric, is omitted from the table of contents. Women were prohibited from preaching in the Catholic tradition.

**Delborra**—Deborah, leader of the Israelites (ca. 1200 BC).

**kynge of Canaan**—on Jabin's oppression of the Israelites, see Judges 4:2–3; A omits "par son sens" [*foresight* RBG, 96; *intelligence* EJR, 104].

**Elysabeth**—Elizabeth, cousin of Virgin Mary, mother of John the Baptist. Feast days: 8 September (Greek), 5 November (Roman).

**she sayd to the Blessyd Mayden**—Luke 1:41–45.

**Also, my frende, the good Lady Anne** –"Anne" possibly taken as "amie" and not cancelled. Present during presentation of the infant Christ (Luke 2:36–38).

**Symeon**—Simeon, prophet who proclaimed Christ's identity (Luke 2:25–35).

**Candelmasse Day**—2 February, forty days after the birth of Christ, when Mary's purification was complete and her infant was presented at the temple.

**quene of Saba, of whome Holy Scrypture maketh mencyon**—see 1 Kings 10 and 2 Chronicles 9. Queen of Sheba identified as Nicaula by Boccaccio (*FW* chap. 43), but not Christine (I.12).

**Salamon**—King Solomon; see also I.44.

**rode by the londe of Othyope**—Sheba's pilgrimage leads from Ethiopia and Egypt (I.12) across the Red Sea, through Arabian deserts to Jerusalem; distant pilgrimage to meet Solomon reminiscent of Penthesilea's lengthy travels to meet Hector (I.19).

**lytell trees**—legendary cedars of Lebanon.

**nyghe a water called Allephater**—Dead Sea, previously Lake Asphaltites.

**gave hym many precyous jewelles**—liberality as seen in Dido's story; metaphorically fitting as well: "for wisdom is more precious than rubies" (Proverbs 8:11).

**she sawe a longe borde**—recognition of the True Cross told in Jacobus de Voragine's *Legenda aurea* (ca. 1275), translated anonymously into English as the *Gilte Legende* (1438), again by Caxton (1483), reprinted repeatedly in England (*LA* hereafter).

**the body rested**—"s'arresta" as "rested"; see also I.18; I.22.

**They helde this worde but for a scorne or a jape**—C says opposite, "Ceste parole en tindrent mie a truffe les Juifs," i.e., prediction taken seriously and they worked (in vain) to prevent its fulfilment.

## Chapter 5

**Nycostrate, of whom mencyon was made before**—I.33.

**where hystoryes ynowe maketh mencyon**—RBG and EJR translate "duquel" as *whom*, referring to Evander; A's *where* perhaps influenced by references to Tiber River (I.26, I.33, II.62), Mount Palatine (I.33), Nicostrata's foreknowledge of Rome.

**Cassandra**—*FW* chap. 35, following classical sources, reports that Cassandra received gift of prophecy from Apollo but when she spurned his advances, he added a curse that no one would believe her; C omits Apollo's role. Cf. Brumble, *Myths*, 64–65.

**Pryamus of Troye**—Priam, introduced in I.19 as Hector's father.

**worshypfull Hector**—see I.19.

**was also a prophete**—in C, rhetorical question: "ne fu elle autressi . . . ?"

**counsayled . . . to make peas**—omits "pour dieu"; unclear whether she swears by a pagan deity or Christian God who enlightens all prophets.

**Basyne**—Basine, wife of Childeric I (AD ca. 436–481), mother of Clovis (466–511).

**kynge of Thorynge**—Thuringia, central Germany, overthrown by Franks in 531.

**Chylderyke, the .iii. kynge of Fraunce**—Childeric, third in the Merovingian line, allied with the Romans; see E. A. R. Brown, "France, 2: The Merovingian Dynasty," *ODMA* 2:652.

**grete bestes [. . .] and lytell beestes**—animals often figure in prophetic visions; "The Prophecies of Merlin" mention dragons, boars, and lions among many others. Basine's list descends from large, noble beasts to quotidian dogs, "eche of theym dyspysnyge other." See *Medieval Bestiary*, an illustrated online guide to animal lore: http://bestiary.ca/index.html.

## Chapter 6

**Justynyan**—Flavius Petrus Sabbatius Justinianus, or Justinian (reigned 527–565); his legal code was still studied in the Middle Ages. See *ODB* 2:1083–84.

**Emperoure Justyne**—Justin I (reigned 518–527). See *ODB* 2:1082.

**Anthony**—woman named mistakenly by C as Justinian's lover; in fact, it was Theodora who became his empress after changing law to allow high-born men to marry women from a lower class; for her sister Antonina, see II.29.

**when the houre of nyght was come**—in C, mid-day siesta "quant l'eure de midi fut venue" ["at noon," RBG, 99].

**a grete egle**—imperial Roman eagle, easily recognisable and important heraldic emblem in the Middle Ages.

**Justynyan answered**—Theodora's speech reported through direct discourse, while Justinian's side is narrated indirectly.

**to go upon them of Perce**—Persia; the two empires repeatedly fought each other during 502–532; 540–545; 572–591.

**they chose Justynyan to be emperour, the whiche slewthed not**—A translates "ne songia mie" as taking immediate action. Justinian never dreamed of being emperor (though he was the one who slept): Theodora's watchful prophecy proves true.

**wanne that batayle**—Belisarius (II.29), a general, is historically credited with winning the battle of Dara against the Persians in 530; see *ODB* 1:278. See note, I.39, for second Belisarius example added to later redactions.

**the emperoure sawe well that he was taken by his wordes**—particularly satisfying here considering Justinian's legal fame.

## Chapter 7

**dyssolute lyfe**—*L*, *F* add "des brigues et noises que ilz font"; *Ri* "aspres et ameres de brigues et riottes," 240 ["getting into nasty fights and vicious brawls," RBG, 102].

**Beholde how many sones**—*L*, *F* read "Et pour ce que tu demandes se plus treuvent d'amour es filz que es filles" ["And since you asked whether one finds greater love among sons than daughters"]; omitted by later redactions and A.

**thou shalte fynde them but thynne sowne**—A omits: "non obstant qu'il en ait esté et soit maint mais c'est à tart" ["although there are and have been many who have helped when it was too late," EJR, 111; see also RBG, 102].

**leurs filz comme leur dieu, et ilz sont ja grans devenus**—*R* adds: *"et par le pourchas du pere et par leur faire apprendre science ou mestier, ou par quelque bonne fortune, sont riches et plains, et leur viel pere soit devenu par aucune mesaventure povre et dechoit . . ."*

**ilz desirent sa mort pour avoir le sien**—*R* continues: *"O, Dieux scet quans filz de grans seigneurs et de riches hommes desirent la mort de leurs parens pour avoir leurs terres et leur avoir! Et de ce bien dit voir Petrac, qui dist: 'O, fol homme, tu desires avoir enfans, mais tu ne peus avoir nulz si mortieulx ennemis. Car se tu es povre, ilz seront tanez de toy et desireront ta mort pour en estre deschargez. Et se tu es riche, ilz ne la desireront pas moins pour avoir le tien.' Je ne vueil mie dire que tous soient tieulx, mais maint en y a. Et se ilz sont mariez . . ."*

**deussent reconforter et estre le baston et port de leur viellece**—*R:* ". . . *elles, qui tant les ont cheris et mignotement nourris, en sont bien guerredonnees, car il semble aux mauvais enfans que tout doit estre leur. Et se elles ne leur baillent tout ce qu'ilz veulent avoir, ilz ne les espargnent mie de leur dire du desplaisir assez. Et Dieux scet comment reverence y est gardee. Et pis y a, car les aucuns ne se feront ja conscience de mouvoir contre elles plait et proces; et c'est le guerredon que plusieurs ont quant ilz se sont toutes leurs vies pour acquerir ou mettre avant leurs enfans."*

## Chapter 8

**Drypetrue, quene of Laodocye**—Drypetina, queen of Laodicea, ancient city in Asia Minor named after Laodice, wife of Antiochus II (ca. 260 BC); see Berenice (I.24).

**Kynge Mytrydaces**—Mithridates VI, husband of Hypsicratea, father of Drypetina.

**she folowed hym in all bataylles**—compare Zenobia (I.20), Hypsicratea (II.14).

**a double rewe of tethe**—Boccaccio discusses this in *FW* chap. 75.

**the grete Pompee**—Gnaeus Pompeius Magnus, better known as Pompey the Great (106–48 BC), Roman general; husband of Julia (II.19), then Cornelia (II.28).

## Chapter 9

**Isyphyle**—Hypsipyle of Lemnos; *FW* chap. 16.

**Thoant . . . kynge of Levydynyens**—Thoas, king of Lemnos; English translation turns minims of "m" into "ui."

**countre rebelled ayenst hym**—Boccaccio says women made a pact to kill all men but Hypsipyle spared her father and smuggled him to safety.

**she reygned peasybly upon them**—C omits liaison with Jason when Argonauts stopped at Lemnos en route to Colchis (II.55).

**untrue cytezyns**—in *FW*, Hypsipyle has twin sons by Jason; because men cannot stay, she sends them to be raised by their grandfather. Her people thus learn of her original deception and force her into exile, where she suffers further hardships.

## Chapter 10

**Claudyne**—Claudia Pulchra, *FW* chap. 62; her father, Appius Claudius Pulcher, was a Roman consul from 143 BC.

**goddes [V]esta**— goddess also mentioned I.47, II.46 where her name is spelled with a *V*. See Brumble, *Myths*, 346–47.

**praysed gretely this mayden**—Cicero, *Pro Caelio*.

## Chapter 11

**Grete love also had a woman of Rome to her moder**—*FW* chap. 65. With the characters a daughter and her imprisoned father instead, this is the iconography known as "Caritas Romana," from Valerius Maximus, *Dict.* 5.4. ext.1.

**of manly compassyon**—C, "humaine compassion."

**Grysylde . . . of whome I shall telle hereafter**—II.50.

## Chapter 12

**stronge buyldynges of dongeons**—"fort edifies" in C refers to well-constructed palaces as well as towers [Fr., *dongeons*].

**tyme to people it**— in number symbolism, twelve significant because of the twelve tribes of Israel (Old Testament), apostles of Christ (New Testament), foundations of New Jerusalem (Book of Revelation); Christine also initiates her series of exemplary stories in I.12.

**by straungers** —in C, "estranges ostes" [foreign armies] cannot dislodge its inhabitants.

**nowe there is a newe femenyne royalme bygon**—recalls prophecy by Reason (I.4); Amazon empire becomes a point of origin for Christine's project along with Troy.

**this is the destyne of them**—later *Cité* redactions omit these lines.

## Chapter 13

**maryage be to men hevy**—on misogamous literature, see McLeod and Wilson, "A Clerk in Name Only."

**importunyte of women and of theyr ravenous grefe**—in C, "impetuosité des femmes et de leur rancuneuse moleste" ["because of women's faults and impetuosity, and because of their rancorous ill-humor, " EJR 118].

**Walere wryteth to Ruphyn**—Walter Map's *Letter of Valerius to Ruffinus*, part of *De nugis curialium* (ca. 1180), survives independently in more than fifty manuscripts; frequently misattributed to Valerius Maximus, author of *Factorum et dictorum memorabilium libri*, source used by Boccaccio and Christine; see Fenster, "Vernacular Humanism," 91, 98–100.

**Theophrastus in his boke sayth**—see I.30.

**thyselfe hath sayd somtyme**—Reason raises this point in I.3.

**bokes that so sayth, women made them not**—Wife of Bath makes a similar charge.

**esclaves amonge the Sarazynes**—Moslems, Crusaders' opponents, cast as enemies in romance literature; significant slave traders during the Middle Ages.

**whiche all crye not out an harowe**—modern English has lost the double sense of "harowe" as a cry for help, and "to cry harrowe" = to denounce someone's wrongful behavior.

**dye for hungre and for mysease**—A omits reference to their children.

**batues au retourner, et ce sera leur soupper.** —Rectitude continues in *R* : *"Qu'en dis tu, mens je? En veis tu oncques nulle de tes voisines ainsi atournees?' Et je à elle: 'Certes, dame, si ay fait mainte, dont grant pitié avoie.' Je t'en croy! . . .'"*

**thou haddest suche one**—Estienne de Castel died ca. 1389/90; Christine never remarried.

**Theofrastus**—see I.30.

**one shal not fynde but fewe suche servauntes**—C "point de tel serviteur" [not any]; A allows possibility of dedicated servants such as himself, though rare.

## Chapter 14

**Hypsytrace**—Hypsicratea, wife of Mithridates VI.

**Kynge Mytrydaces**—see also I.24, II.8.

**Romaynes moved ryght harde warre agaynst hym**—Pompey the Great eventually defeated Mithridates after three wars.

**smyte off her yelowe heres as golde**—compare to Zenobia (I.20). Hair cutting also a drastic measure in the stories of Saints Martina (III.6), Christine (III.10).

**stretchynge a swerde**—see note I.19 on "ceindre espee"; A omits "en lieu de riches conroies" ["no elegant girdle," RBG, 111; see also EJR, 121].

**Bocaca**—Boccaccio.

**Pompee**—see II.8.

## Chapter 15

**Empresse Tryayre**—Triaria, wife of Lucius Vitellius the Younger ("Lucyan Urylyan"), not emperor but brother of Aulus Vitellius (reigned AD April—December 69), whom Christine includes in her list of dissolute Roman emperors (II.49). Story from *FW* chap. 96, in turn from Tacitus.

**Vaspasyan**—Titus Flavius Vespasianus (reigned AD 69–79), or Vespasian, succeeded Aulus Vitellius as emperor.

**a cyte of Volques**—*FW* identifies as Terracina, in central Italy. Boccaccio condemns her cruelty; Christine lauds her bravery. See also Camilla (I.23), a Volscian warrior, and Veturia's son Coriolanus (II.34), who seized a Volscian stronghold.

## Chapter 16

**Archemyse . . . Mansole**—see I.25.

**put them in a vessell of golde**—compare to Argia (II.17), Ghismonda (II.58).

**Scope, Bryaxe, Thymothe, and Leothayre**—sculptors employed by Artemisia (fourth century BC); *FW* chap. 57 reports they were responsible for the four sides of the mausoleum: Scopas (E), Bryaxis (N), Timotheus (S), Leochares (W).

**Elycarnase . . . mayster cyte of Carye**—Halicarnassus; see note I.25.

**the [fyfte] werkeman . . . called Itrayre**—A reads "fyrst"; in fact, it should be the fifth; spelling of "fyfte" adopted from the list of sibyls. "Yteron" included by Boccaccio among artisans, but V. Brown notes that in Pliny, "pteron" means "colonnade" and is not a person's name. Brown-Grant writes that if another person were to be named, it should be Satyrus, a Greek architect.

**the syxte werkeman, named Pychys**—Pythius, Greek architect who designed the mausoleum with Satyrus.

**.vii. mervayles of the worlde**— idea traced back to Herodotus (fifth century BC) conceptually, though it continued to evolve through the Middle Ages and remains a point of debate today: Seven Wonders of the ancient world are the great pyramid of Giza, the hanging gardens of Babylon, the statue of Zeus in Olympia, the Ephesian temple of Artemis, the mausoleum at Halicarnassus, the Colossus of Rhodes, and the lighthouse of Alexandria; only the Great Pyramid remains standing. Mausoleum sculptures are preserved in the British Museum.

**mansolees**—*Speculum Sacerdotale* (ca. 1425) first *OED* quotation for "mausoleum."

# Chapter 17

**Argyne**—Argia, daughter of Adrastus, king of Argos ["Arge"] in East Peloponnese.

**Polymy[t]e**—Polynices, son of Oedipus, Argia's husband.

**Ethyocles**—Eteocles, brother of Polynices, who refuses to abide by power-sharing agreement; tragic end mentioned in reference to their mother, Jocasta (II.60). Cf. Brumble, *Myths*, 318–20.

**thyrde parte of his people**—*L* appears to read "ne demoura de tout l'ost en vie fors le dit roy Adrastus sur .iii.ᵉ de gent"; *F*: "fors le Roy adrast<u>us</u> luy .iii.e de ge<u>n</u>t" (fol. 48r); *Ri*, 264: "lui et iijᶜ de gent"; EJR, 125: "King Adrastus and three hundred soldiers"; RBG, 114: "King Adrastus, the only one of the three princes who survived."

**Bacace**—*FW* chap. 29, using *Thebaid*; Antigone recovers corpse in play by Sophocles. Cf. Brumble, *Myths*, 27–28.

**whiche after the lykenesse of dyvers fowles flyeth aboute deed bodyes**—"fols oppinent" [fools believe] mistaken for fowls, sustaining imagery of carrion birds.

**Kynge Creonce**—Creon, who ruled Thebes after deaths of Eteocles, Polynices.

adventure her body to the dethe—consistent with *F*, *R*: "exposer son corps a mort." *L* reads "espouser" for "exposer." Ensuing vengeance, not in *FW*, recalls Amazons (I.16).

## Chapter 18

Egryppyne—Vipsania Agrippina (ca. 14 BC to AD 33), *FW* chap. 90. Her daughter, also named Agrippina, was Nero's mother (II.48).

doughter of Marke Egryppyne and of Julye—Marcus Agrippa (ca. 62–12 BC), Roman general, and Julia (39 BC to AD 14).

Emperour Octavyan—Gaius Julius Caesar Octavianus, or Octavian (63 BC to AD 14), Julius Caesar's heir and first Roman Emperor to bear the title "Augustus."

Bermanyce—Germanicus Julius Caesar (ca. 15 BC to AD 19), Roman general and Agrippina's husband. Lower-case "g" graph clear in *L*, distinct from "b."

Tybere the Emperour—Tiberius Julius Caesar Augustus (42 BC to AD 37), Octavian's successor; C names him among tyrants (II.47).

she withdrewe not to say grete vylanyes—A appears to follow *L*, which reads "traisoit" instead of "taisoit" (*Ri*, 268).

## Chapter 19

Matheolus and all other janglers—I.1.

Phylostratus—Theophrastus; see I.30; II.13.

Julye—Julia (ca. 73–55 BC), daughter of Julius Caesar.

Julyus Cesar—Gaius Julius Caesar (ca. 100–44 BC), not emperor but "dictator," as noted in the title of *FW* chap. 81.

Cor[n]ylle—Cornelia, daughter of Lucius Cornelius Cinna, Roman consul.

Pompee—II.8; II.14.

the see and caves—appears to read "eaues" [waters] as "caues."

the grete werre—Caesar defeated Pompey 48 BC, ruled as dictator until 15 March 44 BC; in II.25, II.28, C posits they might have lived, had they heeded advice from their wives.

## Chapter 20

**Tyerce Emulyene**—Tertia Aemilia, daughter of a Roman consul, wife of Scipio Africanus the Elder. See Rouillard, "'Faux Semblant'," 22–23.

**Scypyon the fyrste Affrycan**—Scipio Africanus the Elder (236–183 BC), victorious over Hannibal in the Second Punic War; see I.46, ll. 2331–32, 2421.

**to make mencyon therof to ony other**—omits "encore pis" [even worse].

**wolde not saye, thoughe they knewe well**—A emphasizes discretion, adding "wolde not saye."

**a lady of Brytayne . . . countesse of Coemen**—unidentified; might refer to Comines, in north of France. Tour Coetquen was built at Dinan in NE Brittany by John V, count of Montfort. His first two wives, Mary Plantagenet (*d.* 1362) and Joan Holland (*d.* 1384), "lyved but late" when Christine was writing (1405); both ladies from Britain as well as Brittany, potentially of interest to English readership.

## Chapter 21

**Vancyppe**—Xanthippe, wife of Socrates, not in *FW*. Traditionally maligned as a shrew, as in *Wife of Bath's Prologue*; C rehabilitates as devoted wife.

**so she had to husbande . . . Socrates**—Socrates (ca. 469–399 BC) was a Greek philosopher and Plato's teacher; see I.2, l. 116.

## Chapter 22

**Seneke**—Seneca the younger (ca. 4 BC to AD 65), Roman philosopher and playwright who was Nero's tutor before exile in AD 41; his father, Seneca the Elder (ca. 60 BC to AD 37), was a rhetorician. See also Brumble, *Myths*, 309.

**byloved of his wyfe, fayre and yonge**—C challenges long-standing literary convention of unhappy marriages between old and young partners as in the *Merchant's Tale*, the *Wife of Bath's Prologue*.

**Pompee Paulyne**—Pompeia Paulina; *FW* chap. 94, based on Tacitus.

**tyraunt Emperour Nero**—Nero Claudius Caesar (AD 37–68), infamous for killing his mother. See Cropp, "Nero, Emperor and Tyrant"; see also II.27, II.48.

**noble doughter of one of the grete barons of Brytayne**—Jeanne of Laval, whose father was John of Laval, lord of Châtillon in western Loire valley, near Brittany.

**Syr Bertram Claquyn**—Bertrand du Guesclin, count of Longueville, French military leader during the Hundred Years' War; married Jeanne of Laval in 1374.

## Chapter 23

**Sulpyce**—Sulpicia praised in *FW* chap. 85 for fidelity shown to her husband, Lentulus, during a proscription; see also Curia (II.26; *FW* chap. 83).

**Lentylyus Consulyennole, a man of Rome** –Lucius Cornelius Lentulus Crus, or Cruscellio, Roman praetor (first century BC). *L* omits *b* from "noble" after a line break.

**her frendes have lefte it to make a proffe therof**—A suggests they leave her; in modern translations, relatives have the ill husband examined for her sake; see RBG, 121; EJR, 132.

## Chapter 24

**Of many women also in the same wyse**—*FW* chap. 31; "together" [*ensemble*] would be more accurate than "also": women work collaboratively to free their husbands.

**Jason had ben in Coltos to gete the golden fleece**—see also I.32, II.9, II.55.

**a countre of Grece that is called Menudye**—Orchomenos, in Boetia.

**Lacedemonye**—Lacedaemonia, in the Peloponnese; see I.25.

**and so they dyde**—A addition.

**this was theyr conclusyon**—omits "que toutes ensemble" [that all together].

## Chapter 25

**Mayster Johan de Meun**—see I.2. For the *Rose* debate, see Introduction; see also Margolis, *Introduction*, 61–66, 180. Smith discusses this scene, "Jean de Meun in the 'Cité des Dames'," 137–38.

**for dyscrecyon and secretenesse are to be commended in ony persone**—A addition.

**there was late a man in Rome ryght notable named Brutus**—A omits "n'ot mie celle oppinion," changes *noble* to more ambivalent "notable."

**a gentylwoma[n] named Porcya**—Portia (*d.* ca. 42 BC), daughter of Cato Uticensis "Chaton the Lesse"; "gentylwoman" added by A.

**nevewe to Grete Chaton**—Cato the Elder, or Marcius Porcius Cato; see I.9. Cato Uticensis was his great-grandson, not nephew.

**Cassyen**—Cassius, or Gaius Cassius Longinus, conspired in the assassination.

## Chapter 26

**Curya**—Curia, whose husband was subject to the same proscription in 43 BC as Sulpicia's (II.23); name alternatively spelled "Turia."

**Quyntus Lucrecyus**—Quintus Lucretius Vespillo, Roman counsul (48 BC) before triumviral proscription.

**"For my desyre is to be felawe with hym . . . "**—A turns into direct discourse.

**delyvered hym**—eventually pardoned, became consul again (19 BC).

## Chapter 27

**In the tyme that Nero . . . reygned in Rome**—(AD 54–68); see II.22; II.48.

**one woman in the whiche they trusted**—*FW* chap. 93 follows Tacitus in naming her Epicharis, a freedwoman.

**they kepte them not wysely fro spekynge**—she is a willing conspirator in *FW*, unwisely trying to enlist someone who hands her over to Nero.

**that conspyred thus the dethe of the emperour**—added by A.

**nor by force of tourmentes**—*FW* reports after she was weakened physically, she hanged herself to avoid disclosing information if tortured further.

## Chapter 28

**yf Brutus had byleved Porcya**—II.25.

**Julyus Cesar, of whome we have spoken**—II.19, II.25; Calpurnia is the unnamed wife here. Not named in *FW*, but accounts by Lucan were known and used in the medieval period; see Crosland, "Lucan in the Middle Ages."

**Pompe that had wedded Julye . . . as I have sayd before**—II.19.

**Cornelya**—widow of Publius Licinius Crassus; married Pompey 52 BC.

**dyscomfyted by Julyus Cesar**—see II.19.

**Tholomee**—Ptolemy XIII (63–47 BC), king of Egypt.

**nor do by her counsayle**—phrase not in C; A omits "elle a qui de cuer n'en disoit nul bien" ["she suspected deep down that something was amiss," RBG, 127; see also EJR, 138].

**Ector of Troye**—see I.19, II.5.

**A[n]dromatha**—Andromache, daughter of Eetion. Cf. *Iliad* 6.480–520.

as it is sayd before—Hector killed by Achilles in Trojan War; Andromache given as prize to Pyrrhus, Achilles' son, against whom Penthesilea fights to avenge Hector's death (I.19).

## Chapter 29

**Emperoure Justynyan, of whome it is sayd before**—see II.6.

**Bellyfere**—Belisarius (500–565), Roman general. For the medieval "Romance of Belisarius," see *ODB* 1:278.

**Voendres**—Vandals, Germanic tribe that conquered parts of Western Europe in fourth and fifth centuries.

**whiche was called Antonye**—Antonina, sister of Justinian's wife Theodora.

**ye shal assemble**—omits Antonina's participation; see RBG, 129, EJR, 140.

**And I tell you**—A seems to read "j'en dis" instead of "tendis" [while].

**destroy all that they fynde**—should be first person plural.

**toke the kynge of Voendres**—Gelimer, king 530–533; Belisarius won the battle of Tricamarum, reclaiming Carthaginian territory in North Africa.

**l'ama mieulx que oncques mais**—*R "Item, une autre fois advint que par le faulx rapport des envieux cellui Belisaire decheut de la grace de l'empereur telement que il fu du tout mis hors de l'office de la chevalerie. Mais sa femme le reconfortoit et donnoit esperance. Si avint que l'empereur mesmement fu deposé de l'empire par les diz envieux. Mais Belisaire, par le conseil de sa femme, à tele puissance comme il pot avoir, fist tant, non obstant que l'empereur lui eust fait grant tort, que il le remist en son siege, et ainsi esprouva l'empereur la loyauté de son chevalier et la trahison des autres, et tout par le sens et bon conseil de la sage dame."*

**Kynge Alexander**—Alexander the Great; see I.14, I.15, I.20.

**the quene his wyfe**—Barsine, Alexander's second wife or concubine. Anecdote from the *Alexander Romance*.

**Dayre, kynge of Perse**—Darius III, king of Persia (ca. 336–330 BC), territory conquered by Alexander the Great.

## Chapter 30

**I have proved to thee**—Reason narrates tales of innovative women who "brought to the worlde scyences and craftes" (I.27–42).

**as I have sayd to thee before**—Reason praises the Virgin Mary in I.9; Justice honors her as well in III.1.

**and to all the worlde**—A translates "et a tout le moins" as the whole world [*monde*] rather than "at the very least."

**Moyses**—Moses, Old Testament leader of the Jewish people who led them out of captivity in Egypt; see I.3.

**there sholde a man be borne of the Ebrues**—Exodus 1:1–22; 2:1–10.

**defende**—"tireroit le peuple" ["lead," EJR, 142; "deliver," RBG, 130].

**as God wolde that he sholde be saved**—compare II.4, regarding the True Cross: "But that that God wyll have kepte is well saved."

**Chermyche**—Thermutis, name given to Pharaoh's daughter by Josephus (ca. AD 37–101).

**to save**—C "savoir" [know].

## Chapter 31

**Judyth**—Judith, widow who delivered the city of Bethulia from a siege; Book of Judith found in the Septuagint and the Vulgate Bible. For the story's origins and Christine's revision, see Case, "Judith: Some Sequels."

**seconde Nabugodonosor**—Nabuchodonosor II ruled Babylonian Empire ca. 605–562 BC.

**Holophernes**—Holofernes, Assyrian general.

**thyrde parte of the nyght**—night watches were traditionally marked in three-hour increments: 6–9 pm, 9pm-12 am, 12–3 am, 3–6 am. Thus Judith's promise to come at midnight corresponds with the third part of the night. C "a la .iii.e nuytee" translated "third night" by RBG 132; EJR 144.

**no man knewe the way**—"joye" perhaps confused with *voy*.

## Chapter 32

**Quene Hester**—Esther, Jewish wife of Ahasuerus, king of Persia.

**Kynge Assuere**—thought by modern scholars to be Xerxes I; see I.25.

**Naman**—Haman, prime minister who bore a grudge against Mordecai, ordered execution of the Jews. Syntax is convoluted both in A and C: "que" and "qui" are repeated several times.

**Mardocheus**—Mordecai, Esther's uncle, appointed to Haman's position once the king learns about his plot against the Jews.

**with her woman**—in C, plural: "ses femmes."

**Delborra, of whom I have spoken above**—II.4.

## Chapter 33

**Remus and Romulus**—legendary twin sons of Mars, abandoned then nursed by a wolf; founders of Rome, as mentioned in the story of Lavinia (I.48).

**Romulus had peopled the cyte**—Romulus kills Remus during an argument, becomes sole king of Rome, named after himself.

**kynge of Sabyne**—the Sabini were an ancient tribe living across the Tiber River, near Rome.

**to make knyghtes**—C "de faire chevaleries" [chivalric deeds].

**taken awaye with strengthe**—Augustine (*De civitate dei*, II, ch. 17) condemns the Romans for seizing the Sabine women by force; see Wolfthal, "'Douleur'," 60, 67.

**this thynge was gretely sorowed of the ladyes of the cyte**—A addition.

**Romulus**—C "les Romains" [Romans].

**that is to say, without faders**—addition by A.

**and let us no longer lyve**—embellishment by A.

**they were gretely abasshed and dysmayde**—i.e., the husbands; *L* erroneously reads "parmi elles."

## Chapter 34

**Vetury**—Veturia, Roman matron, mother of Coriolanus; *FW* chap. 55.

**Marcyan**—Gnaeus Marcius Coriolanus, of doubtful historicity. See Lehman, "Coriolanus Story in Antiquity," for use by classical authors; Shakespeare would also write a play about Coriolanus.

**Coryens**—Coriolans, of ancient Latium city of Corioli.

**Volques**—see II.15.

**ryght daungerous to governe the people**—compare Camilla (I.23), Hypsipyle (II.9), Claudia (II.10). Coriolanus wanted relief for the masses to be conditional upon increased aristocratic power, reported *FW*, not C.

**noblest ladyes of the towne**—In *FW*, envoy included the mother, wife, and children of Coriolanus; C focuses on Veturia.

**as a good knyght**—A's interpretation of "comme bon et humain."

## Chapter 35

**Crotylde**—Clotilde (ca. 474–545), daughter of Chilperic II, king of Burgundy.

**Clodonne, kynge of Fraunce**—Clovis I (ca. 466–511), Merovingian king, son of Childeric I and Basine (II.5).

**she was a good lady and an holy**—venerated as a saint; feast day 3 June.

**kynge of Almaunce**—the Alemanni, group of Germanic tribes overcome by the Franks (AD 496).

**with grete comforte and joye, and receyved baptyme with the quene**—phrases reorganised in A; queen, already Christian, would not need baptism. King's safe return and baptism cause joy for the king and queen in C.

**soo plenteously on us**—"us" referring to French.

**worshypped by God**—C, "thanks be to God" [*Dieu merci*].

**holy martyrs**—see III.18.

**not onely the martyres**—A omits "Que dis je?"

**appostles**—the original Twelve Apostles are Peter, Andrew, James, John, Philip, Bartholomew, Thomas, Matthew, James son of Alphaeus, Judas Thaddeus, Simon, and Judas Iscariot (Matthew 2:2–4, Mark 3:13–19, and Luke 6:14–16). Matthias was later chosen to replace Judas.

**Saynt Denys**—Denis, bishop of Paris, patron saint of France; beheaded during persecution by Decius (ca. AD 275). Recorded in the late sixth century with Rusticus, Eleutherius in *Passio SS. Dionsyii, Rustici et Eleutherii*; three traditionally named together.

**ryver of Sayne**—the Seine, in Paris.

**Catule**—Catulla, legendary matron who buried Denis and his companions.

**Gevenyene**—Genevieve (ca. 420–540); in *LA*, but not among saints' lives in Part III.

**Dangobert**—Dagobert I (ca. 608–638), son of Clotar, grandson of Fredegunde (I.13, I.22). Founded St. Denis Basilica (ca. 624), royal burial place restored in nineteenth century.

# Chapter 36

**scyences of sorcery** — Medea, Circe (I.32) held to different standard.

**Quintus Ortencyus** — Quintus Hortensius Hortalus (114–49 BC), Roman orator and consul; contemporary of Cicero.

**Hortence** — Hortensia, daughter of Hortensius.

**as Bocace sayth** — *FW* chap. 84.

**governed by thre men** — second triumvirate: Octavian (II.18), Mark Antony (II.42), Lepidus (Marcus Aemilius Lepidus, *d.* 12 BC).

**Johan Andry, a solempne legyster of Boloyne la Grace** — Giovanni Andrea (1275–1347), authority on canon law, author of *Novella super Decretalium*, who taught at the University of Bologna. A, writing in 1521, omits "n'a mie .lx. ans."

**Thy fader** — Tommaso da Pizzano (*d.* 1387) moved his family to Paris in 1368 for a position in Charles V's court.

**thou were taryed** — in later redactions, C adds: "Rather, it was because your mother, as a woman, held the view that you should spend your time spinning like the other girls, that you did not receive a more advanced or detailed initiation into the sciences" (RBG, 141); see also EJR, 154–55. Passage in French:

> *R:* "*Si ne sont mie tous hommes, et par especial les plus sages, de la sus dicte oppinion que mal soit que femmes sachent letrés, mais bien est voir que plusieurs qui ne sont pas sages le dient, pour ce que il leur desplairoit que femmes sceussent plus que eulx. Ton pere, qui fu grant naturien et philosophe, n'oppinoit pas que femmes vaulsissent pis par science, ains de ce que encliné te veoit aux letrés, si que tu scez, y prenoit grant plaisir. Mais l'oppinion femenine de ta mere, qui te vouloit occupper en fillasses selon l'usage commun des femmes, fu cause de l'empeschement que ne fus en ton enfance plus avant boutee es sciences et plus en parfont. Mais si que dit le proverbe [. . .]*"

**But as the proverbe saythe** — see I.10. Passage cited by Sophia Jex-Blake, "Medicine as a Profession for Women" (1869; repr. 1886), at 98: "That this controversy is no new one may be proved by reference to a very curious black-letter volume now in the British Museum, wherein the writer protests: 'I mervayle gretely of the opynyon of some men that say they wolde not in no wyse that theyr doughters or wyves or kynneswomen sholde lerne scyences, and that it sholde apayre their cōdycyons. This thing is not to say ne sustayne. That the woman apayreth by connynge it is not well to beleve. As the proverbe saythe, "that nature gyveth maye not be taken away".'" Also cited in 1913 by John Augustine Zahm, *Woman in Science*, discussing C's career, 106–10, at 106. He adds, "It is to be hoped that some enterprising English publisher will soon favor us with a reprint of the quaint old, but none the less valuable, volume, *The Boke of the Cyte of Ladyes*" (107).

## Chapter 37

**Susanne**—Susanna, from an apocryphal chapter in the Book of Daniel; *Pistel of Swete Susan* (late fourteenth century) tells story in Middle English verse.

**Joachym**—Joachim, wealthy Jew of Babylon married to Susanna.

**envyronned with anguysshe in every parte**—in C, part of Susanna's speech; here, narrative description.

**Danyel**—Daniel, one of five major Old Testament prophets: Isaiah, Jeremiah, Baruch, Ezekiel.

## Chapter 38

**Sarra**—Sarah, wife of Abraham, mother of Isaac.

**aboute the .xx. chapytre of Genesis**—A adds name of book (Genesis 12:10–20); similar story tells how Abimelech, king of Gerar, was cursed until he restored Sarah to Abraham (Genesis chap. 20); a third version involves Abimelech, Isaac, and Rebecca (Genesis 26: 1–11).

**Abraham**—first biblical patriarch (Genesis 11:26 to 25:18).

**desyred of God that she loved soo tenderly**—C says that her goodness made her well-loved of God, who preserved her; A construes "lui empetra" as a petition, adding: "And Almyghty God, herynge her petycyon."

## Chapter 39

**Rebecca**—wife of Isaac, mother of Jacob and Esau.

**Our Lorde Jhesu**—C "Dieu"; Old Testament story precedes the incarnation of Christ in human chronology, but God exists in all times theologically.

**notwithstandynge she was olde and barayne**—Rebecca was barren until Isaac prayed for children; he was sixty when the twins Esau and Jacob were born (Genesis 25:21–26). His mother Sarah's barrenness was even more remarkable: she gave birth to Isaac when she was ninety (Genesis 17:17–21; 18:9–15; 21:1–7).

**Jacob and Esau**—twin brothers; though Jacob was younger, he tricked Esau out of his birthright and blessing (Genesis 25:27–34; 27:1–40).

**lygnages of Israell**—Jacob's twelve sons founded twelve tribes of Israel; Esau's descendants are known as Edomites.

## Chapter 40

Ruth—a Moabite woman who married the Hebrew son of Naomi; after his death, she followed her mother-in-law back to Bethlehem; the Book of Ruth is set in the time of the Judges (ca. 1200–1050 BC).

Davyd—second king of Israel (tenth century BC), believed to have written the Psalms, revered as an ancestor of Jesus.

this noble lady was so good and chaste—Christine, herself a widow, does not mention Ruth's remarriage to a relative of her husband, Boaz (Ruth 4:9–13). Catherine of Aragon's first marriage to Henry VIII's older brother became a central point of contention in their divorce proceedings.

## Chapter 41

Penolope, the wyfe of Prynce Ulyxes—Penelope, Ulysses' faithful spouse; Brumble, *Myths*, 264–65.

Troye—mentioned I.4, I.19, I.32, II.5, II.28.

devoute to her goddes—A specifies "her" deities, clarifying shift from Old Testament to classical story.

his yonge sone Thelomachus—"yonge" added by A. Telemachus, young when Ulysses left, was "parfytely growne" by the time he returned.

## Chapter 42

Maryamyre . . . Kynge Arystobolus—Mariamme (*fl.* 37 BC), beautiful Hebrew woman, granddaughter of Aristobulus; *FW* chap. 87.

Kynge Anthony of Egypte—Mark Antony (ca. 82–30 BC), member of the second triumvirate (II.36), Cleopatra's lover, father of Antonia (II.43). Defeated by Octavian's general, Marcus Agrippa (II.18) in 31 BC.

Herode Anthypater—Herod the Great (ca. 73–4 BC), son of Antipater, appointed by Mark Antony to govern Galilee. Villain of nativity plays for ordering the death of male infants in Bethlehem (Matthew 2:1–8, 16–18).

broder of this good lady—Aristobulus III, drowned on Herod's orders.

## Chapter 43

Title: broder of the noble Emperoure Nero—Added by A: "Nero" here refers to Tiberius (II.18), not infamous Nero born generations later (II.22, II.27, II.48).

**Anthony**—Antonia Minor, daughter of Mark Antony, mother of Germanicus (II.18) and Claudius (II.47).

**Druse Thybere**—Drusus I (38–9 BC), stepson of Octavian (II.18).

**as Bocace saythe**—*FW* chap. 89.

**quoy que les mauvaises gens dient.**—*R*: *"Mais je ne cuide mie qu'en tous les temps passéz fussent ne courussent au tant de mauvaises lengues comme il est au jour d'uy, ne que tant fussent hommes enclins à mesdire de femmes sanz savoir achoison qu'ilz font ores. Et fois doubte que, se ycelles bonnes et belles, dont je t'ay parlé, vivient ou temps de maintenant, qu'en lieu de loz que les ancians leur donnerent, leur seroient par envie mis sus mains blasmes. Mais à retourner à nostre matiere, ancore d'icelles bonnes et chastes . . ."*

**Valery**—Valerius Maximus; see II.13.

**Lady Sulpyce**—Sulpicia, daughter of Servius Paterculus and wife of Fulvius Flaccus, consul (*d.* 205 BC); chosen to consecrate a statue of Venus Verticordia (*FW* chap. 67); here, Valerius Maximus *Fact.* 8.15.12. Different Sulpicia (*FW* chap. 85) lived first century BC; see II.23.

## Chapter 44

**Lucres**—Lucretia, legendary character whose rape precipitated the deposition of the last Roman king, foundation of Republic (sixth century BC); see also II.64. Cf. Brumble, *Myths*, 201–3.

**Tarquyne Collatyn**—Lucius Tarquinius Collatinus, consul (509 BC), Lucretia's husband; great-nephew of Tarquinius Priscus, fifth king of Rome and Tanaquil's husband (I.45).

**Tarquyne the Prowde, sone of the kynge**—legend centers on Sextus Tarquinius, son of Tarquin the Proud (II.3).

**convenable and juste**—omits "et saincte" [holy]. For English legal history, see Corinne Saunders, *Rape and Ravishment in the Literature of Medieval England*, 33–75.

## Chaper 45

**quene and wyfe of Orgyagontes, kynge of Gausegres**—rulers of Galatia in the second century BC; the queen is unnamed here and in *FW* chap. 73; Plutarch (ca. AD 50–120), in *Moralia*, calls her Chiomara.

**taken by the sayd Romaynes in a batayle**—Gnaeus Manlius Vulso defeated the Galatians in 189 BC.

**he left off and spake no more**—A's phrasing.

## Chapter 46

**Sysponne**—Hyppo, Greek woman; *FW* chap. 53.

**Sycambres (whiche nowe ben called Frensshmen)**—*FW* chap. 80.

**Vesta**—see I.47, II.19.

**Vyrgyne**—Virginia (fifth century BC), daughter of Virginius, in *FW* chap. 58, *Roman de la Rose*, Chaucer's *Physician's Tale*, Gower's *Confessio Amantis*, Lydgate's *Fall of Princes*.

**the false juge Claudyen**—Appius Claudius, a Roman magistrate who sought to seize Virginia with assistance from Marcus Claudius; Virginius thwarts their plan by killing his daughter. Boccaccio and Gower recount this as a surprise move; Chaucer relates a discussion first between father and daughter, ending with her compliance; Christine says it was her preference to die.

**there was a cyte taken in Lombardy**—Lombardy, in northern Italy, has been economically important for centuries; three of its medieval cities are Pavia, Brescia, and Mantua (I.31). Episode taken from *Les Grandes Chroniques de France*.

**they sholde be solde to be ravysshed**—A translates "vendroit" as a form of "vendre" [to sell].

**toke the flesshe of chekyns rawe**—same ruse appears in Pierre de la Cépède's *Paris et Vienne*, which was translated and printed by Caxton, 1485:

> fro whom yssued soo grete a stenche / that vnnethe they myght suffre and endure it / whiche sauour came fro vnder hyr arme holes of the two quarters of the henne / whiche were roten / (sig. d1v)

## Chapter 47

**bowynge as chyldren**—omits final phrase, that they have no constancy at all.

**lytell mote . . . grete beme**—Matthew 7:3–5; Luke 6:41–42; see also II.65.

**they laboure so moche to the women**—A seems to read "cuerent" [*cuirier*, to distress] as "ovrerent" ["laboure"]. Christine expanded this passage significantly in later redactions; for translation, see RBG, 151, EJR, 165.

**que femmes par nature sont moult fresles**—*R*, changes in italic: *"Et puis que ilz accusent de fragilité les femmes, il est à presupposer que ilz se reputent estre constans, ou à tout le moins que les femmes ne le soient pas si comme eulx. Et il est voir toute-voyes que* ilz demandent aux femmes trop plus grant constance que ilz mesmes ne scevent avoir, car eulx, qui se dient tant estre fors et de noble condicion, ne se peuent tenir de cheoir en plusieurs tres grans deffaulx et pechéz, *non mie tous par*

*ignorence, mais par pure malice, ayant congnoissance* que ilz mesprennent, *mais de tout ce ilz s'excusent et dient que c'est humaine chose que de pecher. Mais quant il avient* que aucunes cheent en aucune defaillance, *et* dont eulx mesmes sont cause par *leur grant pourchas de longue main, adont c'est toute fragilité et inconstance selon leurs diz. Mais comme il me semble à droit juger,* puis que tant fraisles les reputent, ilz deussent aucunement supporter leur fragilité, et *non pas reputer à elles estre grant crisme ce que ilz tiennent à eulx estre petit deffault. Car il n'est tenu en loy ne trouvé en nulle escripture que il leur loise à pecher ne que aux femmes, ne que vice leur soit plus excusable. Mais de fait ilz se donnent tele auctorité que* ilz ne veulent supporter *les femmes,* ains leur font et dient, *plusieurs en y a,* moult *d'oultrages* et de griefs . . ."

*Pystle of the God of Love—Epistre au dieu d'Amours* (1399), in verse, translated and adapted by Hoccleve without attribution to Christine. Edited together by Fenster and Erler; see also Ellis, "Letter of Cupid." Also, Margolis, *Introduction,* 48–50.

**Emperour Claudyen**—Claudius (Nero Germanicus Tiberius Claudius, 10 BC to AD 54), son of Drusus I and Antonia Minor (II.43).

**Tybere . . . what was he more wrothe?**—Tiberius; "wrothe" [wrathful or evil] appropriate in context; transposing r/o, "worthe," better translation of C: "de combien valu il mieulx?" See also II.18, II.43.

## Chapter 48

**Nero**—see II.22; Curnow identifies Boccaccio's *De casibus virorum illustrium* and Vincent of Beauvais' *Speculum historiale* as Christine's chief sources on emperors' misdeeds.

**and slepte the day**—A addition, though logical consequence of night activities.

**dethe of his fader and of his moder**—C reports father killed, then his mother; listed together by A.

**Octovyene**—Octavia (Claudia Octavia, AD *b.* ca. 40), daughter of Claudius and his third wife, Valeria Messalina. Nero divorced Octavia in AD 62, banished her, then ordered her execution.

**and toke another**—Poppaea Sabina (AD *d.* 65), Nero's second wife; *FW* chap. 95 reports she was behind Octavia's divorce, exile, and execution; according to legend, Nero kicked her while she was pregnant with their second child, causing her death.

**a kynneswoman of his owne**—Claudia Antonia (AD *fl.* 41), whose husband Faustus Cornelius Sulla was executed on Nero's orders; she too was later put to death.

**his lytell doughter**—Nero's sole child, Claudia Augusta, died as an infant (AD 41).

**Seneke**—Seneca; see II.22.

**ne gathered togyder the crueltees of hym**—C "en comble de tout" perhaps read "en semble."

**made grete joye**—omits "de beaulté de la flamme" [of the flame's beauty].

**Saynt Peter and Saynt Poule, and many other martyres**—fire in Rome blamed on Christians, according to the *Catholic Encyclopedia*, and was followed by the Neronian persecution; Peter and Paul were martyred in AD 67. See also III.18.


## Chapter 49

**Galba**—Servius Sulpicius Galba (3 BC to AD 69), whose reign lasted a matter of months. Name appears in C rubric but not printed in A chapter heading.

**Othomy**—Marcus Salvius Otho (AD 32–69), emperor quickly deposed by Vitellius.

**Vyncylyen**—Aulus Vitellius (AD 15–69), son of Lucius Vitellius; see II.15.

**Trayane and Tytus**—Trajan (Marcus Ulpius Traianus), reigned AD 98–117; Titus (Titus Flavius Vespasianus), emperor from AD 71 to 81.

**Constantyne**—Constantine I (Flavius Valerius Constantinus) became Roman Emperor at Eboracum (York) in AD 306. Christianity became empire's official religion during his reign; see note I.21.

**yf the worlde be in amendynge**—compare to Christine's argument against a lost "golden age" in I.38.

**I shall say to thee more**—argument continues despite C "plus ne t'en diray."

**after the ymage of God**—i.e., women as well as men; see I.9. *R*, changes in italic:

*"Et à tout dire, que c'est inconstance ou varieté?* Autre chose *proprement* n'est ne mais faire contre ce que raison *commande, car elle ennorte à bien faire toute* creature *de bon entendement. Et quant l'omme ou femme laisse vaincre à sensualité le regart de raison, c'est fragilité et inconstance, et de tant que la personne chet en plus grant deffaulte ou pechié, de tant est en lui la fragilité plus grande, car elle est plus loing du regart de raison. Or est il ainsi, selon ce que les histoires accordent—et l'experience, je croy, ne le contredit—que,* quoy que philosophes et *autres* aucteurs *dient de la variacion des femmes . . ."*

**in Holy Scrypture**—"en nulle escripture" means any writing, though ensuing example is from the Bible.

**Athalys and Jesobell her moder, quenes of Jherusalem**—Athaliah reigned ca. 843–837 BC after killing rival family members (2 Kings 11); Jezebel maligned for encouraging idolatry (1 Kings 16–21; 2 Kings 9), sexual promiscuity (Revelation 2:20–23).

**Brunehent, quene of Fraunce**—Brunhilde (ca. 550–613), wife of King Sigibert, who fought Fredegunde over the Frankish succession (I.13; I.22).

**Judas**—Judas Iscariot, apostle who betrayed Jesus (Matthew 26:14–16, 47–50; Mark 14:10–11, 43–45; Luke 22:3–6, 47–48; John 13:26–30, 18:2–3). Revised, in *R*: "*. . . qui tant de biens lui avoit faiz, la durté et cruaulté des Juifs et du peuple d'Israel, qui n'occirent pas tant seulement Jhesucrist par envie, mais aussi plusieurs sains prophetes qui devant lui furent, les uns sierent par mi, les autres assommerent et diversement occirent. Et me prens aussi Julien l'Appostat, lequel, pour sa grant perversité, aucuns reputent avoir esté l'un des antecrists, Denis, le faulx tirant de Cecile, qui tant estoit detestable que deshonneste chose est de lire sa vie—avec ce . . .*"

**Julyan the apostata**—Flavius Claudius Julianus, Roman Emperor (reigned 361–63) tried to reinstate pagan beliefs. See *ODB* 2:1079.

**Denys the tyraunt**—Dionysius I of Syracuse (ca. 430–367 BC), despot of Sicily.

**antecrystes also**—omits "qui doivent estre" ["who are yet to come," RBG, 156; "who must come," EJR, 170].

**by ensamples of the dedes of them**—A omits "et pour contredire," interprets phrase as referring to "frail" men; Christine looks ahead to examples of resolute women.

## Chapter 50

**marquys of Saluce**—the title "marquess of Saluzzo," dating from the twelfth century, applies to a city in the Piedmont area of western Italy.

**Gautyre sans Pere**—Gualtieri in Boccaccio's version; Walter in Chaucer's *Clerk's Tale*. Emphasis here on his power: commonly identified as "marquys," not by name.

**Janycle**—Janicle, or Guiannucolo; see also II.11.

**Grysylde**—Griselda (II.11), famed for her patience; story told in Boccaccio's *Decameron* (X.10), composed between 1348 and 1351; tale translated by Petrarch into Latin, retold in French, English; see Bornstein, "An Analogue to Chaucer's *Clerk's Tale*," and Waugh, "A Woman in the Mind's Eye (and Not): Narrators and Gazes in Chaucer's *Clerk's Tale* and in Two Analogues." In 1558, William Forrest dedicated the *History of Grisild the Second* about Catherine of Aragon to her daughter, Mary I.

**all the people loved her**—popular opinion is fickle in Chaucer's version; Christine shows this elsewhere (I.23, II.9, 10); here, populace constant in their support for Griselda.

**Boloyne la Grace**—Bologna, in Northern Italy, site of famous medieval university where Giovanni Andrea taught law (II.36).

**Payngo**—Panico, about twenty miles south of Bologna.

**the fade[r] receyved it with grete joye**—A adds "father"; Christine only says that Griselda bore a son, "who was joyfully received" (EJR, 172).

**by his knyghtes and his squyers**—C "de ses chevaliers et subgiez."

**answered Grysylde**—her oration demonstrates nobility of character, proving again women's ability to speak well (I.10).

**yet he overcame his courage**—omits "et portant de la chambre" so that Walter is present for her public disrobing.

**that his lorde sholde be full every daye**—"son seigneur" viewed from Janicle's perspective by A and RBG (159); EJR chooses "her lord," referring to Griselda (174).

**she shall not suffred**—"shall" instead of "be able" [*ne pourroit pas souffrir*]. A's "paradventure" leaves open whether she would or would not endure testing due to ability or choice.

**without sayenge the contrary**—omits C "sans aucune desserte d'elle" ["so undeservedly," EJR, 175].

**my true spouse**—double meaning versus C "loial."

**this lady, herynge the wordes of her lorde the marquys**—C identifies Griselda here by title, "la marquise."

**There was she greued**—Griselda grew to greater pre-eminence, consistent with C, but "grieved" consistent with preceding sentence, perspective.

**and of the comunes also**—added by A; C mentions only barons.

## Chapter 51

**I have sayd to thee. Nowe I shall telle thee**—"assez l'en retray" understood as "to tell or say," one meaning of *retraire*; another meaning is "to resemble" ["Florence . . . greatly resembled Griselda," EJR, 176].

**Florence, empresse of Rome**—legendary character from *Les Miracles de Nostre Dame* (l. 4492), compiled by Gautier de Coinci, ca. 1218–1236. The story found

its way into other Romance languages. See J. K. Moore, *Libro de los huéspedes*, MRTS 349 (Tempe: ACMRS, 2008), 207 n. 1.

**he put her in pryson**—in C, she imprisoned him, somewhat odd since the brother is empowered with guardianship of queen and country.

**that she sholde kepe the countre whyle he wolde go ayenst his broder**—in C, Florence lets the prisoner out to welcome his brother home, never suspecting that he would turn the king against her. "Arry[vy]nge" matches C "lui arrive," but "arrynge" could be read that the emperor was in error for believing false rumours about his wife.

**at all tymes**—C, "a toutes fins" [no matter what].

**good for evyll**—cf. Romans 12:21.

## Chapter 52

**Bocace . . . *Boke of Cent Nouvelles***—Boccaccio's *Decameron* (II.9) names the wife as Zinevra; for an analysis of Christine's use of the story, see Brownlee, "Canonical Authors," 249–52. Similar tale found in Gerbert de Montreuil's *Roman de la violette* and anonymous *Roman du comte de Poitiers*, both from the thirteenth century. Boccaccio's story inspired *Frederyke of Jennen*, printed in English by De Worde (ca. 1517), Dusborowghe (1518), and W. Copland (ca. 1560); Shakespeare's *Cymbeline* offers another version of the tale.

**Lombardes**—see II.46.

**Janevoys**—from Genoa, south of Lombardy on the Ligurian seacoast.

**Ambrose**—Ambrogiuolo in *Decameron*.

**floryns**—gold currency first minted in the thirteenth century.

**Gene**—Genoa; see above.

**that repayred ofte**—lived there, RBG, 164; EJR, 179.

**wente prevyly out of the cofre**—A addition (implied by C).

**wente to Parys agayne**—A adds city name.

**this woman**—A addition.

**good woman**—"good" added by A.

**dyde so moche whiche was so good and so fayre**—C seems to describe woman as "bonne et belle"; in A, describes her actions.

**Cateloyne**—Catalonia, on Mediterranean coast, part of medieval Aragon.

**for he founde never so good a servaunt**—another subtle salvo against the claim that men should rely on servants rather than women; see II.13.

**Alexandre**—Alexandria; see I.14.

**sowdan of Babylone**—sultan of Babylon (Cairo); Ottoman Empire overthew the Mamluk Egyptian royalty early in the sixteenth century, thus contemporary event for A's readers.

**I shall tell you howe I gate it**—A addition. Sagurat has shifted to "thou," but Ambrose, observing their difference in rank, still uses "you."

**moreover, besyde that I gate fyve thousand floryns of good golde**—A translates more freely than usual, adding "good golde."

**Then knewe Sagurat the cause of the wrathe of her housbande**—A names her while Christine writes "la dame"; feminine gender is restored after Ambrose's revelation.

**And to make the tale shorte, when he was come into that countre**—A addition.

**But or he came**—transition added by Anslay.

**he had wel enfourmed . . . and she prayed hym also**—Christine refers to Sagurat here with masculine "il"; A adds feminine pronoun.

**without makynge thee to be tourmented**—*L* repeats "dis la verité" after a line break; written once in *F*, *R* and *STC* 7271. A omits accusation at end of this phrase: see RBG, 168; EJR, 183.

**And ryght so**—A adds: "and there they lyved together longe tyme after in prosperyte and joye."

## Chapter 53

**Title: my Lady Christine**—C simply gives Christine's name.

**Loonce**—Leaena (sixth century BC), Greek woman who refused to give information about a plot against the tyrant Hipparchus (*FW* chap. 50); see Quilligan, "Dismemberment," 261–62.

**a toy reservee, et non mie a elles**—expanded in *R*: ". . . *car par leurs oeuvres estoient assez les femmes louees aux gens de bon entendement et de consideracion vraye, sanz ce que autre escript elles en feissent. Et quant à la longueur du temps passé sanz estre contrediz leurs accuseurs et mesdisans, je te di que toutes choses viennent bien à point . . .*"

**whiche yet endureth**—*R*: "qui *à si grant peine en furent estirpees* et ancore durassent, qui ne les eust *contredictes et convaincues.*" See RBG, 169; EJR, 185. Different heresies a contemporary concern among sixteenth-century English readers.

**yet was one ryght evyll**—Judas Iscariot; see II.49. Later redactions note lack of good men in Nineveh (Book of Jonah), Sodom (Genesis 18:20–33, 19:1–29), remark by Jesus (John 8:7) that those without sin should cast the first stone:

*R: "... toutevoyes ne le sont elles mie toutes, ne meismes la plus grant partie." Response. "Que la plus grant partie ne le soient, c'est faulx. Et par ce que devant t'ay dit de l'experience que on peut chacun jour veoir de leurs devocions et autres charitables biens et vertus, et que par elles ne viennent pas les grans orreurs et maulx que on fait au monde continuellement, est assez prouvé. Mais que toutes ne soient pas bonnes, quel merveille! En toute la cité de Ninivé, qui estoit grande, ne fu pas trouvé un bon homme quant Jonas, le prophete, y ala de part Nostre Seigneur pour la confondre se convertie ne se fust. N'en fu il ancore moins en celle de Sodome, comme il y paru, quant Loth la delaissa que le feu du ciel l'ardi. Et nottes, qui plus est, que en la compaignie de Jhesucrist, ou n'estoient que .xii. hommes, si en y ot un tres mauvais homme. Et les hommes oseroient dire que toutes femmes deussent estre bonnes, ou celles qui ne le sont que on les doye tant lappider! Mais je leur prie que ilz regardent en eulx mesmes, et cellui qui sera sans pechié si giette la premiere pierre! Mais eulx mesmes . . ."*

**that the women shall folowe them**—Christine ends the chapter at this point in later redactions; next part of dialogue begins II.54. Lange argues that *L* preserves an early redaction partly based on this lack of division (lxi, lxvi-lxviii).

***Boke of the Crafte of Love***—Ovid's *Ars amatoria*; see I.9, II.41.

**to eschewe them**—similar to point in I.8.

**serpent . . . herbe**—classical reference to Vergil, *Eclogues* 3.93, implied reference to serpent in Eden.

***Epystle of the God of Love . . . Epystles upon the Romaunce of the Rose***—see note I.2, II.47. See also Smith, "Jean de Meun in the 'Cité des Dames'," 138–39.

**of whome it is spoken here above**—see I.46.

**as thyselfe hathe touched other tymes**—*Débat des deux amans* (ll. 1481 ff.), *Epistre au dieu d'Amours* (l. 445).


## Chapter 54

**Eneas fledde frome Troye**—see I.4, I.19, I.32, II.5, II.28, II.41; *FW* chap. 42 denounces Vergilian love story of Dido and Aeneas.

**to take londe without lycence**—similar caution exercised by Hercules when approaching the Amazons (I.18) and Ulysses, arriving on Circe's island (II.32).

**came agaynst hym**—non-confrontational: Dido welcomes Aeneas in person.

had not spared her goodes there as the herte was holly sette—reminiscent of Matthew 6:21, "For where your treasure is, there your heart will be also."

a grete fyre that she lete make—*FW* chap. 42 reports that Dido built pyre to honour her dead husband, Sychaeus, then killed herself to avoid remarrying.

others say that she slewe herselfe with the swerde of Eneas—often illustrated in medieval manuscripts; see Desmond, *Reading Dido*, 120, 146–48, 150.

## Chapter 55

Medea . . . whiche had so moche understandynge—see I.32; depicted as true lover in Christine's *Débat des deux amans* (l. 1455), *Livre des Trois jugemens* (l. 885), *Epistre au dieu d'Amours* (l. 437).

And that he myght—Medea, not Jason in C; see RBG, 174; EJR, 190.

fell in suche dyspayre—C omits gruesome aspects of the legend, in which she kills her brother and two young children (cf. Brumble, *Myths*, 187–89).

## Chapter 56

Ovyde telleth—C answers Ovid's criticism of women (II.53) with selection of heroines found in his writing: Dido (II.54; *Heroides* VII), Medea (II.55; *Metamorphoses* VII), Thisbe (II.56; *Metamorphoses* IV); Hero (II.57, *Heroides* XVIII-XIX).

Pyramys . . . Tysbe—Boccaccio *FW* chap. 13, Chaucer's *Legend of Good Women*, Gower's *Confessio Amantis* all tell the story of Pyramus and Thisbe; it reappears as a comic reprise in Shakespeare's *A Midsummer Night's Dream*. See Brumble, *Myths*, 292–93.

## Chapter 57

loved not moche lesse the Hander—*STC* 7271 reads "le hander" instead of "Lehander." See Brumble, *Myths*, 168–69.

than she sholde be blamed for hym—"celle" in *L* should read "celee" [hidden]; see RBG, 177; EJR, 192.

Herles—Hellespont; see II.1.

Habydon—Abydos; traditionally, Hero's city should be Sestos.

**for drede of whiche he doubted hym**—*L* mistakenly reads "pour" after first "il n'y alast" when it should only follow the second: "qui se doubtoit" refers to Hero in C, not Leander, changing lover's fear for his life into his fear of being thought a coward.

**good Hero**—C "povre" [poor, pitiable].

## Chapter 58

*Boke of Cent Nouvelles*—in Boccaccio's *Decameron*, Ghismonda's story exemplifies the theme of love ending unhappily (IV.1); Lisabetta (II.59) falls under the same topic (IV.5).

**a prynce of Salerne named Tancre**—Tancredi of Salerno, in southwestern Italy along the Mediterranean coast, near Naples; town famed in the Middle Ages for its medical university. A spells name "Cancre"; silently emended.

**Sysmonde**—Ghismonda in Italian. William Walter translated *Guystarde and Sygysmonde* (De Worde, 1532) *STC* 3188.5, from a Latin version of Boccaccio's tale by Philip Beroaldo; see A. S. G. Edwards, "William Walter," *Oxford DNB* 57:180–81.

**erle of Champayne**—Campania, Italian region near Naples; see II.3.

*un prince de Salerne [. . .] en tel maniere lui dist*—Revised opening in *R*:

*un prince de Salerne fu qui nommez estoit Tancré. Cellui avoit une moult belle fille courtoise, sage, et bien moriginée, laquelle avoit nom Sismonde. Le pere amoit celle fille de si grant amour que durer ne pouoit se il ne la veoit, et à trop grant peine quoy que il en feust moult pressez se volt accorder à la marier, toutevoyes fu donnée au conte de Campaigne. Mais comme elle ne demourast gueres en mariage le dit conte mort, le pere la reprist devers soy deliberant de jamais plus ne la marier. La dame qui estoit toute la joye de la viellece du pere, se sentoit belle et en la fleur de sa jeunesce souëvement, nourrie croy bien que n'avoit pas moult agréable d'ainsi user sa jeunece sanz mari. Mais au vouloir de son pere contredire n'osoit, ycelle dame si que elle estoit souvent en sale coste son pere va aviser entre les gentilz hommes de la court un escuier, lequel sur tous les autres quoy que grant foison de chevaliers et de nobles gens y eust, lui sembla bel et ancore mielx condicionné, et en toutes choses bien digne d'estre amé. Et à brief dire tant se prist garde de ses manieres que elle delibera pour passer sa jeunece plus joyeusement, et appaisier la gayeté de son jolis courage, que elle prendroit sa plaisance en cellui. Et toutevoies par longue piece ains que ceste chose descouvrist regardoit par chacun jour si que elle se sëoit à la table bien les meurs et contenances de cellui qui nommez Guiscart estoit. Mais plus s'en prenoit garde tant plus de jour en jour lui sembloit estre plus parfaict en toutes choses, par quoy quant assez y ot avisié le manda un jour vers elle et lui dist en tele maniere [. . .]*

**to take her pleasaunce**—*L* reads "en" but lacks "lui" [*in him*, i.e. the squire].

**Guyscart**—Guiscardo in Boccaccio's tale.

**ye . . . you . . . your**—Ghismonda changes to familiar "tu" at this point in C; A preserves formal address until Ghismonda declares her love.

**went alone into her chambre**—correct reading, although *L* lacks "chambre."

**myght not kepe hym but that he had departed them**—"ne lui courust sus" translated alternatively as "barely prevented him from rushing upon the stranger," EJR, 195; "he had to restrain himself from confronting her on the spot," RBG, 180.

**pryckynges whiche are to passe**—in C, difficult to pass.

**myne herte that he desyred**—"il" agrees with "mon cuer," not Guiscardo; Ghismonda instigated the affair.

**whiche is but donge**—later *Cité* redactions omit "que n'est que fiens."

**your owne blame consydered**—"que vous dites" in *L*, *F*; omitted by later redactions and here by A.

**to enjoy of that thynge that she loved moost**—omits "just as she had made him joyful in the one thing he had held most dear" (EJR, 198); see also RBG, 182.

**cruelte of that [one who] maketh me to see thee**—seems to be missing "cellui qui." A expands the next phrase: "Ye were alwaye present in myne herte, and the veray eyen of my thought."

**above all thynge**—A addition.

**a boxe**—"buirete" translated as a "small phial" (RBG, 183), or "small flask" (EJR, 199).

**cursed the fader**—A reads "maudirent" instead of "mandirent" [summoned].

**his doughter answered hym**—omits "si que elle pot" [to the extent she could]; see RBG, 183; EJR, 199.

**ryght straytely in her handes**—A addition.


## Chapter 59

**Messyne in Italy**—Messina, in Sicily.

**a yonge woman named Lyzabeth**—Lisabetta (*Decameron*, IV.5).

**whiche was named Laurence**—Lorenzo in Boccaccio's tale.

**unto a manere of theves**—"of theves" added by Anslay.

HOPE JOHNSTON

to theyr house—"ala Mesinee," i.e., Messina.

"What perteyneth it to thee to knowe?"—omits subsequent threat: "Se plus tu parles de lui, mal pour toy" ["If you talk about him any more, it will be worse for you," EJR, 200; see also RBG, 184].

that she founde there—sensible in context; L should read "apporté" [brought].

toke the body out of the erthe—A reads "recouvroy" as recovered, instead of cover again ["she covered up the body once more with earth and took only Lorenzo's head," RBG, 185].

to her house agayne—C "en la cité."

And thus she lete it passe—misreading of "ainsi la lasse" [the poor girl].

they made a songe—Boccaccio concludes tale by quoting opening of Sicilian folksong.

Of another also telleth Bocace—Guillaume de Roussillon's revenge told in Decameron (IV.9).

Lady of Fayllee . . . Castelayne of Coussy—Dame de Fayel unwittingly eats Châtelain's heart in romance by Jakemes (ca. 1280?), translated into English, William Copland, [1556?]), STC 24223. Coeur mangé is a recurrent folk motif. Regarding Châtelain (d. 1203) as historical trouvère, see Gaunt, "The Châtelain de Couci."

by too grete a love—Châtelaine de Vergy (ca. 1270?), another romance. L defective here; should read "la chastelaine du Vergi mourut par trop amer; sy fist Yseut, qui trop ama Tristan" (F, f.74r).

also Isoude, Trystram—tragic love story of Tristan and Isolde retold in verse and prose throughout the Middle Ages, in multiple languages, from Thomas and Béroul in the twelfth century through Malory in the fifteenth. See ODMA 4:1655.

Tyamere, whiche loved Hercules—Deianira, second wife of Hercules (I.18) unwittingly poisoned him; lovers found in Ovid's Metamorphoses and Heroides. See Brumble, Myths, 162–64.

## Chapter 60

Juno, doughter of Saturnus and of Opys—Roman goddess of marriage and childbirth (Hera, Greek); FW chap. 4. See Brumble, Myths, 190–92. For Saturn and Ops, see I.47.

**those madde people**—"saniens" in *L*, or *Samiens* (*Ri*, 404); people of Samos, large Aegean island where Juno was revered.

**for her stature**—*L* "estature"; "son ymage" in later redactions (*Ri*, 404).

**Europe that was doughter of Agenor, kynge of Phenyce**—Europa, *FW* chap. 9. Her brother Cadmus (I.4) visited the Delphic oracle (II.1), leading him to found Thebes. Christine names their father, Agenor, among Dido's famous ancestors (I.46).

**named the thyrde parte of the worlde after her name**—medieval "T-O" maps represented the world divided in three parts:

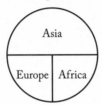

Asia fills the top half of the circle, with Europe and Africa on the bottom; such maps were common throughout the Middle Ages.

**Englonde of a woman that was called Angle**—Christine might be thinking of Albina material, which circulated in French and English; for a bibliography of ongoing research, see http://www.fordham.edu/frenchofengland/albina.html.

**Jocasta, quene of Thebes**—mother and wife of Oedipus, *FW* chap. 25. A gives confusing version of events: sons killed one another, "entre occire deux filz," rather than Oedipus being "slayne bytwene two sones that she had." See Brumble, *Myths*, 245–46.

**Meduse, or [G]argon . . . Kynge Porce . . . became a stone**—*FW* chap. 22 reports Medusa's riveting beauty, gold hair; see also I.34 (*FW* chap. 6), where her name is spelled with a "G." Phorcys traditionally sea-god and father of the Gorgons; C says she rendered people immobile, not other way around. See Brumble, *Myths*, 142–43.

**Helayne, wyfe of Menelaus**—Helen of Troy, wife of Menelaus, *FW* chap. 37.

**doughter of Tyndarus, kynge of Ceballe and of Leyda his wyfe**—Tyndareus, king of Sparta, son of Oebalus ("Ceballe"); traditionally Helen was conceived after Leda was ravished by Jupiter in the form of a swan. See Brumble, *Myths*, 153–54.

**ravysshynge that Parys made of her**—Paris, son of Priam, brother of Hector (I.19) and Cassandra (II.5).

**Polexene**—Polyxena, sacrificed on Achilles' tomb.

## Chapter 61

appostle Saynt Barthylmewe—Bartholomew, one of Christ's apostles (II.35); believed to have preached in Egypt, Mesopotamia, Persia. Martyred by flaying; feast day 24 August.

## Chapter 62

Claudyne—Claudia Quinta, *FW* chap. 77; chaste Roman woman who, according to legend, lived during the Second Punic War (218–201 BC). Story told by Valerius Maximus, Livy, Ovid, Pliny the Elder, and others.

Pyssemonde—statue of the Phrygian earth-mother goddess Cybele, from Pessinus, a city in Galatia (modern day Anatolia, in Turkey). Cf. Brumble, *Myths*, 85–87.

Tybre—see I.26, I.33.

## Chapter 63

Title: Howe they lye not—"ne doit pas" in *F* [how women should not be misjudged]. Title changed in later redactions; see *Ri*, 410; RBG, 190; EJR, 206.

Lucresse of whom I spake here above—II.44.

they began to speke of theyr wyves—compare with trouble that develops in the story of Sagurat (II.52); see also comments about harm of betting (II.8).

## Chapter 64

Quene Blaunche, moder of Saynt Lewes—Blanche, Louis IX; see I.13, l. 820.

erle of Champayne—Thibault IV (1201–1253), count of Champagne who became king of Navarre in 1234; lyrics attributed to him as a *trouvère* remain extant.

ne durst never warre ayenst hym after—in C, subject is his lovesickness for Blanche, not political outcome; see RBG, 191; EJR, 208.

she answered hym . . . when she doubted not—his reply, not hers.

soo she loved hym all his lyfe after—he declares love for her in C.

at Provynce and also at Troyes—Provins, Troyes are two towns in Champagne, about 105 miles southeast of Paris.

of the pleasaunce—in C, displeasure.

**seynge in me ony countenaunce of foly**—originally a question: "Do these men see . . .?" EJR, 208; RBG, 192.

**grete welthe of them**—C probably intends "le grant bien d'elles" in reference to virtue, but as the Wife of Bath discovers women (and men) might be sought for goods as well as good character.

## Chapter 65

**as I have sayd**—II.47.

**lovynge to spynne and carde**—A appears to read *aimer* for *amasser* ["take pleasure in storing up [. . .]," RBG, 192; EJR, 209].

**of that that sholde be to theyr worshyp**—later redactions clarify that women would give generously where it would be used wisely; see *Ri*, 416; RBG, 192.

**that sholde fynde theyr housholde**—reminiscent of anecdote (I.10) about drunkard and his wife.

**it appereth to almesse**—overly literal translation of "il appert aux aumosnes"; the sense of the passage is that women's habit of giving alms countermands charges of avarice.

**prysoners in the londe of the Sarazyns**—C refers to all prisoners, even among Saracens.

**lowe in the worlde**—alternatively, "in this world here below" (EJR, 210).

**confortez et secourus par les femmes et par leur avoir**—R adds: *Et je, Cristine, dis adont: "Certes, dame, à vostre propos il me souvient avoir veu de femmes moult honorables en discrette largece de ce que elles pouoient. Et scez et congnois au jour d'uy de eles qui plus grant joye ont quant elles peuent dire 'tien!,' là ou il est bien employé, que nul aver ne pourroit avoir de tirer à soy et mettre en coffre. Mais je ne sçay à quoy hommes vent tant disant que femmes sont tant escharces, car, quoy que on die que Alixandre fu, je vous di bien que oncques n'en vy point." Droitture se print adont à rire et dist: "Amie, certes ne furent pas escharces . . ."*

**the ladyes of Rome were not scarse**—as Curnow observes, difficult to identify specific corresponding historical event. Speech by Hortensia (II.36), as recorded by Appius, alludes to an earlier time during Punic Wars when Roman women donated jewelry; perhaps Christine had this in mind.

## Chapter 66

*Dedes of the Romaynes*—*Faits des Romains* (ca. 1213) and *Histoire Ancienne jusqu'à César* (ca. 1208–1213) both popular medieval sources for Roman material.

**Buyse or Paulyne**—Busa, or Paulina Busa, a wealthy woman in Canosa, allied with the Romans, who provided shelter to soldiers defeated by Hannibal; *FW* chap. 69.

**londe of Puylle**—Apulia, region in south-east Italy.

**Hanyball**—Hannibal, famous Carthaginian general; see notes I.46; II.20.

**Canes**—Cannae, in Apulia, where Hannibal defeated Roman army (216 BC).

**of ladyes I myght tell thee ynoughe**—A omits "de ton temps"; see also II.36. A retains "whiche is yet on lyve."

**lady de la Ryvere, named Margarete**—Marguerite de la Rivière (*d.* after 1405).

**Lorde Burell**—Bureau de la Rivière (*d.* 1400), Charles V's chamberlain from 1367 and counsellor of Charles VI; mentioned in Froissart's *Chroniques*, translated into English by John Bourchier, Lord Berners (Pynson, 1523), *STC* 11396.

**Syr Emenyon de Pomyners**—Amanieu de Pommiers, veteran of the Hundred Years War.

## Chapter 67

**Isabell de Bavere**—Isabeau of Bavaria (ca. 1370–1435), wife of Charles VI (1368–1422); first owner of the "Queen's Manuscript." Though politic to praise her virtue here, modern critics debate her standing. See Adams, "Female Regency," "Isabeau de Bavière et la notion de régence," "Recovering Queen Isabeau," and Delogu, *"Advocate et moyenne*: Christine de Pizan's Elaboration of Female Authority."

**duchesse of Berry, wyfe of Duke Johan**—Duchess Jeanne of Boulogne and Auvergne (*d.* ca. 1423), second wife of John, duke of Berry (1340–1416), owner of the "Duke's Manuscript" (ca. 1408), later divided in five parts: BnF f.fr. 835, 606, 836, 605, 607. As Christine notes, Charles V and his younger brothers John, duke of Berry and Philip the Bold (1342–1404), duke of Burgundy, were sons of John II (see I.13).

**duchesse of Orlyaunce, wyfe of Lewes**—Valentina Visconti (*d.* 1408), noblewoman from Milan ("Myllayne") married to Louis, duke of Orléans (1372–1407), younger son of Charles V; Orléans was assassinated in 1407.

**wyse of her behavoure**—omits "et en toutes choses tres vertueuse, et c'est chose notoire" ["and virtuous in all things—and all this is well known," EJR, 213; see also RBG, 196].

**duchesse of Burgoyne, wyfe of Duke Johan**—Marguerite of Bavaria (*d.* 1423), married to John the Fearless, duke of Burgundy (1371–1419) and heir of Philip the Bold. John the Fearless and Louis of Orléans served as co-regents for Charles VI, debilitated by mental illness; Burgundy then orchestrated Orléans' death. Christine's oldest son, Jean, received a place in the Burgundy household after several years in England with the earl of Salisbury and Henry IV; see Laidlaw, "Salisbury," 130–34, 136; Willard, *Life and Works*, 165–67.

**countesse of Cleremount, doughter of the duke of Berry**—Marie of Berry (*d.* 1434); her mother, Jeanne of Armagnac (*d.* 1387), was Berry's first wife. Marie's husband John, duke of Burgundy (1381–1434), was captured at Agincourt in 1415 and remained a prisoner to his death.

**duchesse of Holande and countesse of Heynaulte**—Marguerite of Burgundy (1374–1441), daughter of Philip the Bold, sister of John the Fearless. Her husband William (*d.* 1417) became count of Bavaria, Hainault, and Holland after father's death in 1404.

**duchesse of Burgon**—Anne of Auvergne (*d.* after 1416), duchess of Burgundy, wife of Louis II; parents of John, duke of Burgundy.

**countesse of Saynt Poule, doughter of the duke of Bar**—Bonne of Bar, countess of Saint-Pol, whose father Robert, duke of Bar was Charles VI's first cousin ["cosyn germayne of the kynge"]. She married Valeran of Luxembourg, count of Saint-Pol and Ligny.

**Anne, doughter somtyme of the erle of Marche**—Anne of Burgundy (*d.* after 1406), daughter of John, count of La Marche (1344–1393); brother Jacques assumed title. Married queen's brother, Louis of Bavaria, in 1402.

**nowe I have suffycently done myne offyce**—omits "comme il me semble" ["it seems to me," RBG, 197; EJR, 214].

## Chapter 68

**were made by me**—omits "for you."

**Nowe pray for me**—conclusion of Part II and relative brevity of Part III make it stand apart, much as Justice is distinguished from her sisters in their initial description (I.3).

# Part III

## Chapter 1

**moost excellent and blessyd Quene**—Virgin Mary, regularly used in pro-feminine discourse to counterbalance Eve; see Blamires, *Case for Women*, 96–125.

**make refuge**—misreading of "faire reffus" ["will not refuse to live in the City of Ladies," Brown-Grant, 201; see also EJR, 217].

**same salutacyon that the aungell brought to thee**—Luke 1:26–38 describes Gabriel's visit to Mary. Feast of the Annunciation celebrated 25 March; for Annunciation imagery, see also I.2.

**Nowe then come on our Hevenly Quene**—list of appellations for the Virgin Mary, whose veneration was widespread in the medieval period.

## Chapter 2

**blessyd systers . . . and Saynt Mary Magdaleyne**—John 19:25 reports that Mary stood at the foot of the cross with her sister, Mary the wife of Cleopas; this may be the same person referred to in Mark 15:40 and Matthew 27:56 as Mary, the mother of James and Joseph. Matthew writes that the mother of Zebedee's sons stood by the cross, who might be Salome, the companion named by Mark. All three accounts refer to Mary Magdalene, to whom Christ first appeared after his Resurrection; see I.10. Luke 23:49 does not give names for the women who witnessed the Crucifixion, nor does Christine, apart from Mary Magdalene.

## Chapter 3

**lyves ben of good ensample**—C's primary source is Vincent of Beauvais' *Speculum historiale*, trans. Jean of Vignay as *Le Miroir historial* (ca. 1333); see II.4. For discussion of martyrs in A's translation, see Long, "A Medieval French Book," 529–31.

**Katheryn**—Catherine of Alexandria, popular medieval saint whose emblem is the "Catherine" wheel. Joan of Arc, Christine's contemporary and subject of her last known work, reportedly heard Catherine's voice. Versions of Catherine's *vita* circulated in Anglo-Norman and Middle English; see editions of Reames, Winstead for more. Three of Henry VIII's six wives named Catherine (Aragon, Howard, and Parr).

**Kynge Costes of Alexandre**—Costus, legendary king and father of Catherine.

**notably she governed her and her herytage**—echoing C's theme of women as good leaders (I.13–26).

**Emperour Maxencyus**—Marcus Aurelius Valerius Maxentius, Roman emperor AD 307–312, whose defeat and death in battle against Constantine is ascribed by Eusebius to the miraculous intervention of Christ. RBG notes that Maxentius, historically, was tolerant of Christians.

**a grete clerke and had lerned scyences**—reprising theme of women's scholarly aptitude (I.27–32, II.36).

**that [she] was so fayre**—C mentions her beauty at this point; in A, speech might be attractive and just.

**phylosophres in all the londe of Egypte**—A omits "les plus sages . . . que on sceut" and "qui de philosophie adont moult estoit renommee"; see RBG, 204; EJR, 220. In Part I, Christine positions herself as debating eminent philosophers not just from her own time, but throughout history.

**they were all converted . . . by her they were put in the nombre of the blessyd martyrs**—formulaic element; emperor's wife converts and is likewise martyred, winning further converts in the process.

**suche a myracle God shewed**—body's incorruptibility considered a sign of saintliness; compare with description of three sisters who burn to death, III.14. Sweet odors, milk in lieu of blood are other bodily signs of holiness.

**tyraunte Maxencyus, whiche gretely coveyted the holy vyrgyne**—despots in the saints' lives recall earlier *exempla* of cruel emperors (II.47–49); lust contrasted with the virgins' purity time and again. On virgin martyrs, see Kelly, *Performing Virginity and Testing Chastity in the Middle Ages*, 40–62.

**without mete or drynke**—miraculous subsistence modelled on Jesus' fasting and temptation by hunger during forty days of trial (Matthew 4:1–4; alluding to Deuteronomy 8:3).

**drawe off her pappes**—mutilation another recurrent element of saints' lives; St. Agatha in particular can be identified this way.

**remembraunce of her passyon**—Catherine became patroness of philosophers and preachers. Feast day, 25 November, suppressed in 1969, restored in 2002.

**voyce came fro heven**—a heavenly voice and intercession by angels can be found in many saints' lives.

**Mounte Synay**—Mount Sinai, holy mountain in Exodus where Moses receives the Ten Commandments. St. Catherine's Monastery, founded by Justinian, exists there to this day.

## Chapter 4

**Saynt Margarete**—Margaret or Marina, virgin shepherdess whose cult flourished from the ninth century onwards. Traditionally thought to have been martyred during Diocletian persecution (AD 303–305), venerated as one of the Fourteen Holy Helpers with Catherine (III.3) and Barbara (III.9); all their lives are told in *LA*. See McInerney, "Rhetoric, Power, and Integrity," for discussion of Middle English *Seinte Margarete*.

**Antyoche**—Antioch in Asia Minor (modern-day Turkey) was one of the most important cities in the Roman Empire, along with Rome and Alexandria.

**Olybryus**—Olybrius, Roman prefect and governor of Antioch.

**an horryble serpente**—Margaret's iconic symbol is a dragon on a chain; miraculous escape from its belly seems to explain her association with childbirth, despite being a virgin.

**cryed with an hygh voyce, "Mercy!"**—defeat of demons, particularly those in idols, standard feature of saints' lives.

**aungelles of God**—singular, not plural in C.

**palme of the vyctory**—emblem of martyrdom; Christianity adopted the palm as a symbol of victory from pre-Christian Greek and Roman tradition.

**This false Olybryus also made to tourmente [. . .] Regyne**—Christine conflates the prefect in Margaret's legend with another, earlier Olybrius, who was a proconsul in Burgundy; Regina, born into a pagan family, converted to Christianity and was martyred in Autun after refusing to marry Olybrius.

## Chapter 5

**Saynt Luce**—Lucilla or Luceja, whose life is told in the seventh-century *Passio SS Lucillae et Florae*. D'Angelo, "Il dossier," traces medieval accounts primarily to Tuscany between the ninth and twelfth centuries; not in *LA*. Christine does not mention Flora, Lucilla's sister, traditionally abducted together.

**Kynge Aceya**—Eugegius or Aucejas, barbarian king converted by Lucilla, Flora.

**buylde a temple**—plural in C.

**.vii. kalenders of Jule**—*Acta Sanctorum* (July VII); according to classical practice, kalends was the first day of the month, and "seven kalends" would be seven days before = 25 June; see note RBG, 243; *Catholic Encylopedia* entry on "Dates and Dating."

## Chapter 6

**Martyne**—Martina, virgin martyred under Emperor Alexander Severus (reigned AD 222–235); not in *LA*.

**lyftynge up her joyned handes**—in C, lifts eyes, not hands.

**of the temple**—A addition.

**Emenyon**—Elagabalus (Marcus Aurelius Antoninus, reigned AD 218–222), cousin of Alexander; historically, Alexander became emperor after Elagabalus died in AD 222.

**wylde beestes**—other saints' lives feature fierce predators, poisonous snakes.

**slewe Emenyon**—historically, Elagabalus not mauled by a lion but beheaded after failed attempt to kill Alexander.

**heere of her heed sholde be cutte awaye**—Samson's great strength lost when Delilah cuts his hair (Judges 16:17–19); for importance of hair as a symbol of femininity, see II.14.

**as the apostle sayth**—1 Corinthians 11:15.

## Chapter 7

**Saynt Luce of Syracuse**—Lucy, virgin martyred during the Diocletian persecution (302–305); story also told in *LA*. A adds "Syracuse," a city in Sicily, to distinguish her from Lucilla (III.5); C rubric reads "another Saint Lucy."

**Saynt Agace**—Agatha, virgin martyred in Catania, Sicily during persecution of Decius (reigned 249–251); often depicted holding severed breasts, signifying one of her tortures. Feast day 5 February.

**Cathonyas**—Catania; see above.

**soule shal never be defouled without consente of the mynde**—for interpretative discussion, see Wogan-Browne, *Saints' Lives and Women's Literary Culture, 1150–1300*, 99–106.

**And at her passynge, she prophesyed that that was to come**—reminiscent of the Cumaean sibyl and other female prophets (II.1–6).

**Saynt Benet borne in Rome**—Benedicta, martyred by her father, a Roman senator, in Origny, France; not in *LA*. Her feast day, 8 October, was suppressed in 1969.

**by prechynge the Crysten relygyon**—see II.4.

**Saynt Fauste**—Fausta, fourteen-year old virgin tortured in Pontus during persecution of Diocletian, not Maximian ("Maxymyon").

**fro the houre of tyerce anone to the houre of noone**—i.e., for six hours. Romans measured the passage of time by tolling the hours of prime (6 am), terce (9 am), sext (12 pm), none (3 pm), adopted by Jews for the observance of set prayers, later known by Christians as the canonical hours; see D. Hiley, "Divine Office," *ODMA* 2:508.

**hevens open**—cf. Acts 7:56.

**when Saynt Fauste was in**—in C, put [*mise*] in cauldron.

**assembled in My name**—Matthew 18:20.

## Chapter 8

**Justyne borne in Anthyoche**—Justine or Justina, virgin of Antioch, who became an abbess before her martyrdom; story recounted at greater length in *LA*. Died in Nicomedia with Cyprian during the Diocletian persecution, on 26 September 304, which became their feast day.

**wente his waye, confused**—"s'en ala confus" might be more appropriately understood as "confounded" or "conquered."

**Cypryen**—saint and bishop who was a necromancer before his conversion by Justine; martyred together (see above).

**Eulalye, borne in Spayne**—two Spanish saints named Eulalia died during the Diocletian persecution: one is the virgin of Merida, martyred 10 December 304, the other was martyred in Barcelona on 12 February 304. Similarities in their legends have raised arguments that they might be the same person. Not in *LA*.

**Matre**—Macra, virgin martyred during the Diocletian persecution and buried near Rheims ["Raynes"]; not in *LA*.

**Faythe**—Foy or Fides, virgin martyred during the third century in the town of Agen, in Aquitaine, France; her relics were moved to an abbey in Conques, France dating from the late eleventh or early twelfth century. Her cult spread to Spain and England, lasting into the sixteenth century. Not in *LA*. See Simon de Walsingham's "Saint Faith" in *Verse Saints' Lives Written in the French of England*, ed. and trans. D. W. Russell, MRTS 431 (Tempe: ACMRS, 2012).

**Our Lorde crowned her**—omits "à la fin a la veue du monde"; see RBG, 213–14; EJR, 230.

**Marcyenne**—Marciana, martyred in Caesarea on the north coast of Africa (modern-day Algeria) during the Diocletian persecution; not in *LA*.

**threwe hym to the grounde**—traditionally an idol dedicated to Diana.

**she ended her lyfe in her grete tourmente**—the standard representation of her in art shows the virgin being gored by a bull.

**Eufenye**—Euphemia, virgin martyred in Chalcedon, Bithynia (Asia Minor) during the Diocletian persecution; in *LA*.

**Prysens**—Priscus, Roman proconsul and governor of Bithynia.

**.xl. cubytes of hyght**—about sixty feet high.

**soo hyghe that all people praysed her**—confusion of "l'ouoyent" [heard] and *louer*, to praise.

**of ony wylde beestes**—in *F*, *Cité* ends at this point with a brief explicit, suggesting an incomplete exemplar.

## Chapter 9

**Theodosyne**—Theodosia of Tyre, martyred at Caesarea on 2 April 307; not in *LA*.

**And she sayd to hym**—reminiscient of curses spoken in parallel with the Beatitudes (Luke 6:24–26).

**God sente her a whyte cloude**—intervention to protect a virgin's modesty recurs in other saints' lives.

**Urban**—A adds "the juge," traditionally believed to have martyred Theodosia.

**Maxymyan the emperoure**—Marcus Aurelius Valerius Maximianus, or Maximian, Roman emperor from 286 to 305 with Diocletian.

**Barbara**—legendary saint, usually depicted with the tower in which she was confined. Feast day, on 4 December, suppressed in 1969; in *LA*.

**whiche serched anone bothe hym and his beestes**—RBG translates "secha" as "scorched to death" (216); EJR has "immediately was turned to stone" (232). *OED* defines "serch" as an obscure fifteenth-century word for worked stone, but A's verb holds some logic since the father is searching for her, and shepherd has just provided directions.

**that her heed sholde be smyten off**—omits preceding phrase in *L*, "que en la tast de devant luy"; *Ri* "que on l'otast de devant lui" (460) ["they took her back before the prefect," RBG, 216; see also EJR, 233].

**Dorothe**—Dorothy, legendary saint believed to have been martyred at Caesarea, Cappadocia ca. 300; feast day 6 February, surpressed 1969. Represented with a basket of roses; in *LA*.

**Theophylus**—Theophilus, lawyer converted by Dorothy at her execution according to legend.

**for it was wryten in the moneth of February**—A alters "car il estoit yver" ["for this took place during the winter, in the month of February" EJR, 234; see also RBG, 217].

**Saynt Cecyle, Saynt Agnes, Saynt Agace**—Cecilia, Roman virgin and patroness of music, often depicted with organ pipes, feast day 22 November; Agnes, virgin martyred in Rome, represented with a lamb, feast day 21 January. For Agatha, see III.7. All in *LA*.

*Hystoryal Myroure*—see III.3.


# Chapter 10

**Saynt Christine . . . of Syre**—Christine follows the usual practice of amalgamating two women: (i) Phoenician virgin from Tyre; (ii) Italian virgin from Bolsena, Tuscany. *LA* reports that she was born in Tyre, Italy; William Paris also assigns her birthplace to Italy in his late fourteenth-century English poem. Christine's feast day is celebrated 24 July. For more on Christine de Pizan's treatment of the legend, see Brownlee, "Saint Christine in the *Cité des dames*."

**Urban, mayster of the chevalrye**—according to tradition, Christine's father, Urban, was governor of Tyre.

**nor drynke**—added by A.

**manaced her with all tourmentes**—Christine's story includes a litany of torments and miraculous interventions on her behalf. Most are standard elements already seen, but amplification—for instance, facing three judges, instead of one—sets Christine's story apart.

**asked her fader alwaye yf he advysed her not**—father asks Christine, not vice versa; see RBG, 219; EJR, 235.

**overcome and confused**—"confus" as "vanquished" in this context; see III.8.

**dyed myschevously, and in the mornynge after she was founde prayenge in her fader's halle in a corner. And thus**—added by A.

**newe juge named Zyon**—Dyon, according to legend.

**by the heere of her heed**—regarding the importance of hair, see III.6.

**Julyan**—Julian, third judge as is traditional.

**and .iii. nyghtes**—A addition.

**other .ii. horryb[l]e serpentes** — omits "nommez guievres," translated as "vipers" by RBG (222) and EJR (238). *Guivre* in Middle English is *wyver*, or *wyvern*, a heraldic beast similar to a dragon.

**cutte off her tonge** — torture is frequently followed by a miracle; here Christine's ability to talk recalls both the opening argument about women who speak well (I.10) and the constancy of Leaena who bit off her tongue rather than betray the conspirators (II.53).

**Ce te soit agreable!** — Expanded in *R*: "*. . . Pries pour toutes femmes, aux quelles ta sainte vie soit cause, par bon exemple, de bien finer leur vie. Amen." "Que t'en diroye, belle amie, pour emplir nostre cité de tel mesgniee plus à grant flotte, viengne saint Ourse à tout ses .xi.m vierges benoites martires, pour le nom de Jhesucrist toutes decolees, que, comme elles fussent envoyees pour estre mariees et elles s'embatissent en terre de mescreans et on les voulsist contraindre de renoncier à la foy de Dieu, plus tost esleurent la mort que renoncier à Jhesucrist, leur Sauveur.*"

# Chapter 11

**O, what thynge in the worlde is more tendre to a moderly herte** — A compresses Christine's double observation that nothing is dearer than a child to a mother, nor more painful than to see it suffer. Christine and Reason discuss affinity between women and children in I.10.

**Felyx** — Gregory includes the story of Felicitas and her seven sons in his "Homiliæ super Evangelia" 1.3 (*PL* 76.1086–1089); feast is observed 23 November. Not in *LA*.

**Julytte . . . had a sonne named Cyrycus** — Julitta, mother of St. Cyricus (spelled Quirine in *LA*), martyred together in Tarsus during the fourth century.

**never be overcome with tourmente** — A reads "martireurs" as doubling for "tourmens" without referring directly to torturers; compare RBG, 224 and EJR, 241.

**Blandyne** — Blandina, slave converted to Christianity; martyred in Lyons during persecution of Marcus Aurelius; feast day 2 June. Not in *LA*.

**Ursula** — according to legend, British princess martyred in Cologne with eleven thousand virgins. Feast day 21 October; in *LA*. In later redactions, reference to Ursula appears at the end of St. Christine's life.

## Chapter 12

**A seculer man had one onely doughter**—Marina, virgin disguised as monk (Brother Marinus), thought to be based on Pelagia of Jerusalem, fourth-century virgin martyr whose name is "Marina" when translated from Greek to Latin. See *ODB* 2:1299. *L* confuses indefinite articles, referring to her father Eugenius as "une homme," his daughter as "un seulle fille." Gender confusion might stem at times from the story itself.

**upon a doughter of his**—in C, Eugenius dissembles that he is thinking of a son, concealing Marina's gender. In A, abbot seems to welcome Marina as a girl: "bad hym that he sholde go to fetche her, and that she myght be put into relygyon with hym," although later in A abbot unaware of gender ("wyst none other but that she was a man").

**Wherof the fader and moder came**—A gender-specific here versus C "les parens."

**ones a day**—A's interpretation.

**when he**—i.e., Marina.

## Chapter 13

**mayde [o]f Alexandre named Eufrasyne**—Euphrosyne (*d*. ca. 470) one of several virgins who chose an ascetic life by assuming the identity of a man; story appears among lives of the desert fathers (*Vitae Patrum*), available in print by the early sixteenth century. Feast day is 16 January (Roman), 25 September (Greek). Not in *LA*. A omits connection to previous chapter, "pareillement" [similarly].

**Paffousyen**—Paphnutius, wealthy father of Euphrosyne.

**syth that I shall have tydynges of my doughter**—more accurately, "I am as happy as if I had actually found my daughter" (RBG, 228). A misses C irony.

**whiche named herselfe Synaroch**—traditionally, the name is "Smaragdus."

## Chapter 14

**in the tyme of Dyoclutan the emperoure**—Diocletian (Gaius Aurelius Valerius Diocletianus, reigned 284–305); see also Margaret (III.4), Lucy of Syracuse and Fausta (III.7), Justine, Eulalia, Macra, Marciana, and Euphemia (III.8).

**Anastase**—Anastasia, noblewoman who, according to legend, was the daughter of Praetextatus, a notable Roman, and studied under St. Chrysogonus. She died

at Sirmium, southwest of the Danube, ca. 304. Her feast day was commemorated during the second mass on 25 December, and her life is related briefly in *LA*.

**she clothed her**—A omits "chacun jour" [every day].

**anoynted them with ryght precyous oyntementes**—recalls Mary's act of devotion to Jesus (John 12:3–8).

**Publyen**—Publius, Anastasia's pagan husband according to legend.

**Saynt Grysogone**—*L* and Caxton's translation of *LA* also spells name "Grysogone." Chrysogonus, spiritual guide of Anastasia; martyred during the Diocletian persecution in Aquileia, Italy; feast days on 16 April (Greek), 25 November (Roman).

**Agappe, that other Thyonne, and the thyrde Hyrene**—Agape, Chionia, and Irene, three sisters who were burned to death during Diocletian persecution, in 304; their feast day is 3 April. Not in *LA*.

**Dulcycyon**—Dulcitius, official who tries to rape the sisters but is divinely prevented from doing so; subject of play by Hrotsvitha.

**the .iii. systers**—omits "benoites" [blessed].

**wolde go and complayne**—omits "tout droit," i.e., straightaway, without taking time to make himself presentable.

**scratched hym**—should be "spat at" [crachoit].

## Chapter 15

**Title: Theodore the vyrgyne**—A follows the rubric of *L*, confusing her with the thirteen-year old virgin Theodora who died with her sisters in Alexandria during the Diocletian persecution; this is Theodota, mother of three children, who lived in Nicaea. *LA* recounts the life of St. Theodora of Alexandria from the time of Zeno; she was deceived by an incubus, then disguised herself as a monk before living a holy life in penance.

**Erle Lencadyne**—Leucatius, a Roman prefect.

**tourmented**—omits "de rechief" [again].

**Theodosyne**—see III.9.

**Ile of Palme**—Palmaria, off coast of Italy.

## Chapter 16

**Natalye ... Adryan**—Natalia, or Nicomedia, wife of Adrian or Hadrian, body-guard of Emperor Galerius, who persecuted Christians until his conversion. Adrian was martyred ca. 306; Natalia's story is told with his in *LA*.

**Maxymyan**— should be Diocletian.

## Chapter 17

**Affra**—Afra, repentant prostitute and Christian convert in Augsburg who sheltered Bishop Narcissus of Gerundum; feast day 5 August. The rubric of *STC* 7271 adds "holy and blessyd," omits "qui fu folle femme" [who was a prostitute].

**wasshed His feete with her teres**—see Luke 7:37–38; another validation of women's tears.

**He despysed never**—see Matthew 9:10–13; Mark 2:15–17.

**ryghtfull ... for the unryghtfull**—see 1 Peter 3:18; Romans 5:6–8.

**To The I offre**—*L* scribe appears to have written the saint's name "affre" instead of verb "offre."

## Chapter 18

**les hospitalitez et les autres biens**—continues in *R*: "*font ycestes choses point à peser? Et se aucuns folz hommes les vouloient tenir à frivoles, nul ne peut nyer que tieulx oeuvres, selon nostre foy, ne soient les escheles qui mainent ou ciel.*"

**Drucyane**—Drusiana, Ephesian woman unnamed in the Bible; *LA* recounts her story in life of St. John the Evangelist, author of the fourth gospel, feast day 27 December. Two Florentine chapels depict Drusiana's resurrection in artwork commissioned during the fourteenth and fifteenth centuries.

**receyved fro his exyle**—*L* "recepvoit" could be a misreading of "revenoit" (*Ri*, 494).

**another of the cyte of Lymoges, named Susanne**—Limoges, France; Susanna mentioned by *LA* in life of St. Marcial, telling how he was converted and commissioned as a missionary by St. Peter.

**Maxymylle buryed Saynt Androwe**—Andrew, apostle crucified in Patras ca. AD 60. Maximilla identified in *LA* as Christian wife of Ægeas, provost of Achaia who martyred Andrew.

**Euphygene**—Ephigenia, daughter of King Egippus, converted by Matthew; dedicated her life to Christ. The new king, Hirtacus, sought to marry her, but Matthew intervened and was martyred. King would have burned Ephigenia to death in her house with more than 200 virgins, but Matthew miraculously (and posthumously) intervened. Ephigenia's brother became the new king.

**ryght a fayre chyrche**—C says that she founded a church; A embellishes it.

**another good lady**—this is Thecla, Paul's disciple and traveling companion. See Stephen J. Davis, *The Cult of Saint Thecla: A Tradition of Women's Piety in Late Antiquity* (Oxford: Oxford University Press, 2001). Also Lydia, whose conversion, hospitality is recounted in Acts 16:13–15; Damaris, another woman, is listed among Paul's followers in Acts 17:34.

**Helyn . . . quene of Oblygoys**—Helen, queen of Adiabene; according to Josephus, provided assistance during a famine; not in Acts 11:28.

**Pautylle**—Plautilla or Lemobia, noblewoman and disciple of Paul's; in *LA*.

**wyped his eyen**—rather, "used the veil to blindfold himself" (RBG, 236).

**he sente it agayne**—C reports that "the angels gave" it to her (RBG, 236).

**she had done hym servyce in heven in prayenge for her**—*STC* 7271 suffers from omitted lines: "for having done him this service on earth, he would do her a service in heaven by praying for her soul" (RBG, 236); see also EJR, 253.

**Vaxyllete**—Basilissa, Egyptian noblewoman married chastely to Julian; martyred during the Diocletian persecution. Feast held 6 January. Not in *LA*.

**That is to say,** *Gloryous thynges ben sayd of thee, thou Cyte of God*—Psalm 87:3. Added by A; not translated in C.

## Chapter 19

**Worshypped b[e] God!**—In C, "Dieux soit loues." Erroneous "by God" in *STC* 7271 suggests women are blessed, chief topic of Part III.

**hande mayden**—Luke 1:38.

**Esoras the prophete**—Ezra, Hebrew prophet and leader; RBG identifies as Vulgate, 2 Esdras 8:56–58.

**Gregory**—*Hom. in Ezech.* 2.5, *PL* 76.993.

**[Advice to wives]**—*R* expansion shown in italics: "*Et celles qui ont maris paysibles, bons et discres et à elles de grant amour, loient Dieu de ce benefice, qui n'est pas petit, car plus grant bien au monde ne leur pouroit estre donné. Et soient diligentes de les servir, amer et cherir en la loyauté de leur cuer, si que elles doivent, gardant leur paix et priant*

*Dieu qu'il leur maintiengne et sauve. Et celles qui les ont moyens entre bons et mauvais, ancores doivent Dieu louer que elles n'ont des pires, et mettre peine de les amoderer en leur perversité et les tenir en paix selon leurs condicions. Et celles qui les ont divers, felons et reveches, mettent peine tele en endurans que elles puissent convaincre leur felonnie et les ramener, se elles peuent à vie raisonnable et debonnaire. Et se yceulx sont tant obstinéz que elles ne puissent, au moins y acquerront elles grant merite à leurs ames par la vertu de pacience, et tout le monde les benistra et sera pour elles.*

"*Ainsi mes dames*, soies humbles et pacientes, et la grace de Dieu croistra en vous et louange vous sera donnee *et le regne des cieulx*, car dit saint Gregoire que pacience est entree de Paradis et la voye de Jhesucrist. *Et ne soit nulle de vous ahurtee ne endurcie à oppinions frivoles, sanz fondement de raison, ne en jalousies, ne en perversitéz de testes, ne en haultainetez de paroles, n'en oeuvres oultrageuses, car ce sont choses qui bestournent le sens et rendent la personne comme forcenee, lesquelles manieres sont a femmes tres descouvenables et malseantes.*"

**Voyés, mes dames**—R: "*Voyez, mes dames, comment ces hommes vous accusent de tant de vices et de toutes pars. Faites les* tous menteurs *par monstre vostre vertu, et prouvez mençongeurs ceulx qui vous blasment par bien faire, en telle maniere que vous puissies dire avec le psalmiste, 'la felonnie des mauvais cherra sur leur teste.'* Si deboutez arriere les losangeurs *decevables* qui par divers attrais tachent *par mains tours* à soubtraire ce que tant *souverainement* devez garder, c'est à savoir voz honneurs *et la beauté de vostre loz. O mes dames, fuyez, fuyez* la fole amour dont ilz vous admonnestent! Fuyez la, pour Dieu, fuyez! *Car nul bien ne vous en peut venir. Ains* soies certaines [. . .]" Cf. Psalm 7:16.

**fle it, for Goddes love, fle it!**—critics have argued that Christine is parodying the *Roman de la Rose* here.

# Bibliography

## Manuscripts

Cambridge, St. John's College 208
London, British Library Additional 10304
———. Harley 838
———. Harley 4431
———. Royal 15.E.VI
———. Royal 19.A.xix
London, Public Record Office, PROB 11/25/360
———. PRO PROB 11/28/283
Longleat Wiltshire, 253
Paris, Arsenal 2686
Paris, Bibliothèque Nationale de France f.fr. 605–7
———. f.fr. 826
———. f.fr. 835–36
———. f.fr. 1178
———. f.fr. 1179
———. f.fr. 24293

## Early Printed Books

Christine de Pizan. *The Boke of the Cyte of Ladyes*, trans. Brian Anslay, *STC* 7271. London: Pepwell, 1521.

    Cambridge, King's College Library M.29.9.
    London, British Library C.13.a.18 [complete] and C.40.m.9.(12.) [fragment].
    Longleat House Library, Wiltshire, *STC* 7271.
    Oxford, Corpus Christi College Library Δ.3.7.
    Washington, D.C., Folger Shakespeare Library, *STC* 7271.

———. *The Boke of the Fayttes of Armes and of Chyualrye*, trans. William Caxton, *STC* 7269. Westminster: Caxton, 1489.
———. *The Booke Whiche is Called the Body of Polycye*, *STC* 7270. London: Skot, 1521.

———. *The .C. Hystoryes of Troye*, STC 7272. London: Wyer, [1549?].

———. *The Morale Prouerbes of Cristyne*, trans. Anthony Woodville, *STC* 7273. Westminster: Caxton, 1478.

Elyot, Sir Thomas. *The Defence of Good Women*, STC 7657.5, 7658. London: Berthelet, 1540, 1545.

Erasmus, Desiderius. *[Christiani hominis institutum in fide Jesu et in amore]*, STC 10450.3. London: Pepwell, 1620.

[Jean d'Outremeuse?]. *Boke of John Maundvyle*, STC 17246, 17247, 17249, 17249.5 (formerly 17248), 17250, 17251. London: Pynson, 1496; Westminster: De Worde, 1499; London, De Worde, 1503, [1510?]; London: East, 1568, [1582?].

[Laneham, Robert?] *A Letter*, STC 15190.5, 15191. [London: s. n., 1575, ca. 1585].

Vives, Juan Luis. *The Instruction of a Christen Woman*, trans. Richard Hyrde, *STC* 24856–24863. London: Berthelet, [1529?], [1531?], 1541, 1547; Powell, 1557; Wykes, [1567?]; Waldegrave, 1585; Danter, 1592.

## Editions, Translations, and Facsimiles

Augustine of Hippo, *De civitate dei*, trans. Marcus Dods. Buffalo, NY: Christian Literature Publishing, 1887; New Advent, 2009. http://www.newadvent.org/fathers/1201.htm.

Boccaccio, Giovanni. *Des Cleres et nobles femmes*, ed. Jeanne Baroin and Josiane Haffen. 2 vols. Annales Littéraires de l'Université de Besançon 498, 556. Paris: Belles Lettres, 1993–1995.

———. *Famous Women*, ed. and trans. Virginia Brown. I Tatti Renaissance Library 1. Cambridge, MA and London: Harvard University Press, 2001.

———. *Forty-Six Lives from Boccaccio*, trans. Henry Parker, Lord Morley, ed. Herbert G. Wright. Early English Text Society o.s. 214. London: Oxford University Press, 1943.

———. *Die mittelenglische Umdichtung von Boccaccio's* De claris mulieribus, ed. Gustav Schleich. Palaestra 144. Leipzig: Mayer and Müller, 1924.

Brewer, J. S., J. Gairdner, and R. H. Brodie, eds. *Letters and Papers, Foreign and Domestic, of the Reign of Henry VIII*. 22 vols. London: HMSO, 1920.

Capgrave, John. *The Life of Saint Katherine of Alexandria*, ed. Karen A. Winstead. Notre Dame: University of Notre Dame Press, 2011.

Carley, James P., ed. *The Libraries of King Henry VIII*. Corpus of British Medieval Library Catalogues 7. London: British Library, 2000.

Chaucer, Geoffrey. *The Riverside Chaucer*, gen. ed. Larry D. Benson. 3rd ed. Oxford: Oxford University Press, 1987.

Christine de Pizan. *The Boke of the Cyte of Ladyes*, trans. Brian Anslay. In *Distaves and Dames: Renaissance Treatises for and about Women*, ed. Diane Bornstein. Delmar, NY: Scholars' Facsimiles & Reprints, 1978.

————. *The Book of the City of Ladies*, trans. Rosalind Brown-Grant. New York and London: Penguin Classics, 1999; Penguin Books, 2005.

————. *The Book of the City of Ladies*, trans. Earl Jeffrey Richards. New York: Persea, 1982; rev. ed. 1998.

————. *The Book of Fayttes of Armes and of Chyualrye*, trans. William Caxton, ed. A. T. P. Byles. Early English Text Society o. s. 189. London: Oxford University Press, 1937.

————. *The Book of the Body Politic*, ed. and trans. Kate Langdon Forhan. Cambridge: Cambridge University Press, 1994.

————. *Le Chemin de longue estude*, ed. Andrea Tarnowski. Livre de Poche Lettres Gothiques 4558. Paris: Librairie générale française, 2000.

————. *Christine de Pizan in English Print, 1478–1549*, ed. A. E. B. Coldiron. MHRA Tudor and Stuart Translations 6. London: MHRA (forthcoming).

————. "Christine de Pizan's *Epistre à la reine* (1405)," ed. Angus J. Kennedy. *Revue des Langues Romanes* 92 (1988): 253–64.

————. *La Città delle dame*, trans. Patrizia Caraffi, ed. Earl Jeffrey Richards. 2nd ed. Biblioteca Medievale 2. Milan: Luni, 1998.

————. *Le Débat sur le Roman de la Rose*, ed. Eric Hicks. Paris: Champion, 1977.

————. *Le Ditié de Jehanne d'Arc*, ed. and trans. Angus J. Kennedy and Kenneth Varty. Medium Ævum Monographs n. s. 9. Oxford: Society for the Study of Mediæval Languages and Literature, 1977.

————. *The Epistle of Othéa*, trans. Stephen Scrope, ed. Curt F. Bühler. Early English Text Society o. s. 264. London: Oxford University Press, 1970.

————. *The Epistle of Othéa to Hector: A "Lytil Bibell of Knyghthod,"* trans. Anthony Babyngton, ed. James D. Gordon. Philadelphia: University of Pennsylvania Press, 1942.

————. *Epistre Othéa*, ed. Gabriella Parussa. Textes littéraires français 517. Geneva: Droz, 1999.

————. "*Livre de la cité des dames*, Kritische Textedition auf Grund der sieben überlieferten 'manuscrits originaux' des Textes," ed. Monika Lange. Ph.D. diss., University of Hamburg, 1974.

————. "The *Livre de la cité des dames* of Christine de Pisan: A Critical Edition," ed. Maureen Cheney Curnow. Ph.D. diss., Vanderbilt University, 1975.

————. *Le Livre de l'advision Cristine*, ed. Christine Reno and Liliane Dulac. Paris: Champion, 2001.

————. *The "Livre de la Paix" of Christine de Pisan*, ed. Charity Cannon Willard. 'S-Gravenhage: Mouton, 1958.

————. *Le Livre du corps de policie*, ed. Angus J. Kennedy. Études christiniennes 1. Paris: Champion, 1998.

————. *The Love Debate Poems of Christine de Pizan*, ed. Barbara K. Altmann. Gainesville: University Press of Florida, 1998.

———. *The Middle English Translation of Christine de Pisan's* Livre du corps de policie, ed. Diane Bornstein. Middle English Texts 7. Heidelberg: Carl Winter Universitätsverlag, 1977.

———. *Oeuvres poétiques de Christine de Pisan*, ed. Maurice Roy. 3 vols. Société des anciens textes français 23. Paris: Firmin Didot, 1886–1896.

———. *Poems of Cupid, God of Love*, ed. and trans. Thelma S. Fenster and Mary Carpenter Erler. Leiden: Brill, 1990.

Furnivall, Frederick J., ed. *Captain Cox, His Ballads and Books; or, Robert Laneham's Letter.* London: Ballad Society, 1871.

Jacobus de Voragine. *Legenda aurea*, trans. William Caxton, ed. F.S. Ellis. 7 vols. London: Dent, 1900. http://www.fordham.edu/halsall/basis/goldenlegend/index.htm.

Kirby, J. L., ed. *Calendar of Inquisitions Post Mortem: 1–6 Henry IV (1399–1405)*, 18:299. London: HMSO, 1987.

Kohanski, Tamarah, and C. David Benson, eds. *The Book of John Mandeville.* Kalamazoo: Medieval Institute Publications, 2007. http://www.lib.rochester.edu/camelot/teams/tkfrm.htm.

Kuin, R. J. P. *Robert Langham, A Letter.* Leiden: Brill, 1983.

Lytle, H. C. Maxwell, J. G. Black, and R. H. Brodie, eds. *Calendar of Patent Rolls*, vol. 1, *1485–1494*. London: PRO, 1914; repr. Nendeln, Liechtenstein: Kraus, 1970.

Plutarch. *Moralia*, ed. and trans. Frank Cole Babbitt. Loeb Classical Library 245. Cambridge, MA: Harvard University Press, 1931. http://penelope.uchicago.edu/Thayer/E/Roman/Texts/Plutarch/Moralia/Bravery_of_Women*/B.html.

Proba, Faltonia Betitia. *The Golden Bough, the Oaken Cross: The Vergilian Cento of Faltonia Betitia Proba*, ed. and trans. Elizabeth A. Clark and Diane F. Hatch. American Academy of Religion Texts and Translations Series 5. Chico, CA: Scholars Press, 1981.

Shakespeare, William. *King Lear*, ed. Grace Ioppolo. New York and London: Norton, 2008.

Vives, Juan Luis. *The Education of a Christian Woman: A Sixteenth-Century Manual*, ed. and trans. Charles Fantazzi. Chicago: University of Chicago Press, 2000.

Warner, George F., ed. *The Buke of John Mandeuill.* Westminster: Nichols & Sons, 1889. Repr. Ann Arbor: University of Michigan Digital Library Production Service, 2003. http://name.umdl.umich.edu/acd9576.

Wogan-Browne, Jocelyn, Nicholas Watson, Andrew Taylor, Ruth Evans, eds. *The Idea of the Vernacular: An Anthology of Middle English Literary Theory, 1280–1520.* Exeter: Exeter University Press, 1999.

## Secondary Sources

Abray, Lorna Jane. "Imagining the Masculine: Christine de Pizan's Hector, Prince of Troy." In *Fantasies of Troy: Classical Tales and the Social Imaginary in Medieval and Early Modern Europe*, ed. Stephen D. Powell and Alan Shepard, 133–48. Toronto: Centre for Reformation and Renaissance Studies, 2004.

Adams, Tracy. "Christine de Pizan, Isabeau of Bavaria, and Female Regency." *French Historical Studies* 32 (2009): 1–32.

———. "Isabeau de Bavière et la notion de régence chez Christine de Pizan." In Dulac et al., *Desireuse de plus avant enquerre*, 33–44.

———. "Recovering Queen Isabeau of France (c. 1370–1435): A Re-Reading of Christine de Pizan's Letters to the Queen." *Fifteenth-Century Studies* 33 (2008): 35–54.

Alexander, J. J. G. "Foreign Illuminators and Illuminated Manuscripts." In Hellinga and Trapp, *Cambridge History of the Book in Britain*, 3:47–64.

Allen, Prudence. *The Concept of Woman: The Early Humanist Reformation, 1250–1500*, vol. 2. Grand Rapids: W. B. Eerdmans, 2006.

Altmann, Barbara K., and Deborah L. McGrady, eds. *Christine de Pizan: A Casebook*. New York and London: Routledge, 2003.

*American Heritage Dictionary of Indo-European Roots*, ed. Calvert Watkins. 2nd ed. New York: Houghton Mifflin Harcourt, 2000.

Ames, Joseph. *Typographical Antiquities, or, The History of Printing in England, Scotland, and Ireland*, rev. William Herbert and Thomas Frognall Dibdin. 4 vols. London: William Miller, 1810–1819.

Angeli, Giovanna. "Encore sur Boccace et Christine de Pizan: Remarques sur le *De mulieribus claris* et *Le Livre de la cité des Dames* ('Plourer, parler, filer mist Dieu en femme' I.10)." *Moyen Français* 50 (2002): 115–25.

Arden, Heather. "Her Mother's Daughter: Empowerment and Maternity in the Works of Christine de Pizan." In Kennedy, *Contexts and Continuities*, 1:31–41.

Armstrong, Elizabeth. "English Purchases of Books from the Continent 1465–1526." *English Historical Review* 94 (1979): 268–90.

Ashley, Kathleen. "Material and Symbolic Gift-Giving: Clothes in English and French Wills." In *Medieval Fabrications: Dress, Textiles, Clothwork, and Other Cultural Imaginings*, ed. E. Jane Burns, 137–46. New York: Palgrave Macmillan, 2004.

Ashurst, David. "Alexander the Great." In *Heroes and Anti-Heroes in Medieval Romance*, ed. Neil Cartlidge, 27–41. Woodbridge: D. S. Brewer, 2012.

Attar, Karen. "Collectors and Collections at King's College Cambridge." M.A. thesis, University College London, 2001.

Aussems, Mark. "Christine de Pizan et la main X: quelques questions." In Dulac et al., *Desireuse de plus avant enquerre*, 209–19.

Autrand, Françoise. *Christine de Pizan: une femme en politique*. Paris: Fayard, 2009.

Badke, David, ed.*The Medieval Bestiary: Animals in the Middle Ages*. http://bestiary.ca/index.html.

Bayne, Diane Valeri. "*The Instruction of a Christian Woman*: Richard Hyrde and the Thomas More Circle." *Moreana* 45 (1975): 5–15.

Bell, Susan Groag. "Christine de Pizan (1364–1430): Humanism and the Problem of a Studious Woman." *Feminist Studies* 3–4 (1976): 173–84.

———. *The Lost Tapestries of the* City of Ladies: *Christine de Pizan's Renaissance Legacy*. Berkeley and London: University of California Press, 2004.

Benkov, Edith Joyce. "Coming to Writing: *Auctoritas* and Authority in Christine de Pizan." *Moyen Français* 34–35 (1994–1995): 33–48.

Benson, Pamela Joseph. *The Invention of the Renaissance Woman: The Challenge of Female Independence in the Literature and Thought of Italy and England*. University Park, PA: Pennsylvania State University Press, 1992.

Besnardeau, Wilfrid. "La représentation des Anglais dans le *Ditié de Jehanne d'Arc* de Christine de Pizan." In Dulac et al., *Desireuse de plus avant enquerre*, 45–56.

Birrell, T. A. *English Monarchs and Their Books: From Henry VII to Charles II*. London: British Library, 1987.

Blamires, Alcuin. *The Case for Women in Medieval Culture*. Oxford: Clarendon Press, 1997.

Blanchard, Joël. "Compilation and Legitimation in the Fifteenth Century: *Le Livre de la Cité des Dames*," trans. Earl Jeffrey Richards. In Richards, *Reinterpreting Christine de Pizan*, 228–49.

Blayney, Peter W. M. *The Stationers' Company and the Printers of London, 1501–1557*, 2 vols. Cambridge: Cambridge University Press, 2013.

Blumenfeld-Kosinski, Renate. "Christine de Pizan and Classical Mythology: Some Examples from the 'Mutacion de Fortune'." In Zimmermann and De Rentiis, *City of Scholars*, 3–14.

———. "Christine de Pizan and the Misogynistic Tradition." *Romanic Review* 81 (1990): 279–92.

———. "Christine de Pizan and the Political Life in Late Medieval France." In Altmann and McGrady, *Christine de Pizan: A Casebook*, 9–24.

———. "'Femme de Corps et Femme par Sens:' Christine de Pizan's Saintly Women." *Romanic Review* 87 (1996): 157–75.

———. "Jean Le Fèvre's *Livre de Leësce*: Praise or Blame of Women?" *Speculum* 69 (1994): 705–25.

Boffey, Julia. "Lydgate's Lyrics and Women Readers." In Smith and Taylor, *Women, the Book and the Worldly*, 139–49.

———. "Women Authors and Women's Literacy in Fourteenth- and Fifteenth-Century England." In Meale, *Women and Literature in Britain*, 159–82.

Bornstein, Diane. "An Analogue to Chaucer's *Clerk's Tale.*" *Chaucer Review* 15 (1981): 322–31.

———. "Anti-Feminism in Thomas Hoccleve's Translation of Christine de Pizan's *Epistre au Dieu d'Amours.*" *English Language Notes* 19 (1981): 7–14.

———. "French Influence on Fifteenth-Century English Prose as Exemplified by the Translation of Christine de Pisan's *Livre du corps de Policie.*" *Mediaeval Studies* 39 (1977): 369–86.

Bossy, Michel-André. "Arms and the Bride: Christine de Pizan's Military Treatise as a Wedding Gift for Margaret of Anjou." In Desmond, *Categories of Difference*, 236–56.

Bowers, Fredson. "Notes on Theory and Practice in Editing Texts." In *The Book Encompassed: Studies in Twentieth-Century Bibliography*, ed. Peter Davidson, 244–57. Winchester: St. Paul's Bibliographies and Newcastle, DE: Oak Knoll Press, 1998.

Brabant, Margaret, ed. *Politics, Gender, and Genre: The Political Thought of Christine de Pizan.* Boulder, CO: Westview Press, 1992.

———, and Michael Brint. "Identity and Difference in Christine de Pizan's *Cité des Dames.*" In Brabant, *Politics, Gender, and Genre*, 207–22.

Brown, Cynthia J. "The Reconstruction of an Author in Print: Christine de Pizan in the Fifteenth and Sixteenth Centuries." In Desmond, *Categories of Difference*, 215–35.

Brown-Grant, Rosalind. "Christine de Pizan as a Defender of Women." In Altmann and McGrady, *Christine de Pizan: A Casebook*, 81–100.

———. *Christine de Pizan and the Moral Defence of Women: Reading Beyond Gender.* Cambridge: Cambridge University Press, 1999.

———. "Christine de Pizan: Feminist Linguist *avant la lettre?*" In Campbell and Margolis, *Christine de Pizan 2000*, 65–76.

———. "Décadence ou progrès? Christine de Pizan, Boccace et la question de 'l'âge d'or'." *Revue des Langues Romanes* 92 (1988): 297–306.

———. "Des hommes et des femmes illustrés: Modalités narratives et transformations génériques chez Pétrarque, Boccace, et Christine de Pizan." In Dulac and Ribémont, *Une Femme de lettres*, 469–80.

———. "Writing Beyond Gender: Christine de Pizan's Linguistic Strategies in the Defence of Women." In Kennedy, *Contexts and Continuities*, 1:155–70.

Brownlee, Kevin. "Christine de Pizan's Canonical Authors: The Special Case of Boccaccio." *Comparative Literature Studies* 32 (1995): 244–61.

———. "Discourses of the Self: Christine de Pizan and the *Romance of the Rose.*" In *Rethinking the* Romance of the Rose*: Text, Image, Reception*, ed. idem and Sylvia Huot, 234–61. Philadelphia: University of Pennsylvania Press, 1992.

———. "Hector and Penthesilea in the *Livre de la Mutacion de Fortune*: Christine de Pizan and the Politics of Myth." In Dulac and Ribémont, *Une Femme de lettres*, 69–82.

———. "Martyrdom and the Female Voice: Saint Christine in the *Cité des dames*." In *Images of Sainthood in Medieval Europe*, ed. Renate Blumenfeld-Kosinski and Timea Szell, 115–35. Ithaca: Cornell University Press, 1991.

———. "Le projet 'autobiographique' de Christine de Pizan: Histoires et fables du moi." In Hicks, *Au champs des escriptures*, 5–23.

———. "Rewriting Romance: Courtly Discourse and Auto-Citation in Christine de Pizan." In Chance, *Gender and Text*, 172–94.

Brumble, H. David. *Classical Myths and Legends in the Middle Ages and the Renaissance*. Westport, CT: Greenwood Press, 1998.

Bühler, Curt. "Sir John Fastolf's Manuscripts of the *Epitre d'Othéa* and Stephen Scrope's Translation of This Text." *Scriptorium* 3 (1949): 123–28.

Bullough, Geoffrey. "*King Lear* and the Anslay Case: A Reconsideration." In *Festschrift Rudolf Stamm zu seinem sechzigsten Geburtstag am 12. April 1969*, ed. Eduard Kolb and Jorg Hasler, 43–49. Bern: Francke, 1965.

Burns, E. Jane. *Sea of Silk: A Textile Geography of Women's Work in Medieval French Literature*. Philadelphia: University of Pennsylvania Press, 2009.

Burrow, Colin. "The Experience of Exclusion: Literature and Politics in the Reigns of Henry VII and Henry VIII." In *The Cambridge History of Medieval English Literature*, ed. David Wallace, 793–820. Cambridge: Cambridge University Press, 1999.

Butterfield, Ardis. "Chaucerian Vernaculars." *Studies in the Age of Chaucer* 31 (2009): 25–51.

———. *The Familiar Enemy: Chaucer, Language, and Nation in the Hundred Years War*. Oxford: Oxford University Press, 2009.

———. "France." In *Chaucer: Contemporary Approaches*, ed. Susanna Fein and David Raybin, 25–46. University Park, PA: Pennsylvania State University Press, 2010.

Callahan, Leslie Abend. "Filial Filiations: Representations of the Daughter in the Works of Christine de Pizan." In Hicks, *Au champ des escriptures*, 481–91.

Campbell, John, and Nadia Margolis, eds. *Christine de Pizan 2000: Studies in Honour of Angus J. Kennedy*. Amsterdam and Atlanta: Rodopi, 2000.

Campbell, P. G. C. "Christine de Pisan en Angleterre." *Révue de littérature comparée* 5 (1925): 659–70.

Caraffi, Patrizia. "Il mito di Medea nell'opera di Christine de Pizan." In *Magia, gelosia, vendetta: Il mito di Medea nelle lettere francesi*, ed. L. Nissim and A. Preda, 57–70. Milan: Cisalpino, 2006.

———. "Medea sapiente e amorosa: Da Euripide a Christine de Pizan." In Hicks, *Au champ des escriptures*, 133–47.

———. "Silence des femmes et cruauté des hommes: Christine de Pizan et Boccaccio." In Kennedy, *Contexts and Continuities*, 1:175–86.

Carley, James P. *The Books of King Henry VIII and His Wives*. London: British Library, 2004.

Case, Ellen. "Judith: Some Sequels. How a Biblical Heroine is Reconstructed in a Medieval Story and a Sixteenth-Century Play." In *Transitions: prospettive di studio sulle trasformazioni letterarie e linguistiche nella cultura italiana*, ed. Kevin B. Reynolds, Dario Brancato, Paolo Chirumbolo, and Fabio Calabrese, 133–41. Florence: Cadmo, 2004.

Case, Mary Anne C. "Christine de Pizan and the Authority of Experience." In Desmond, *Categories of Difference*, 71–87.

Casebier, Karen. "Re-Writing Lucretia: Christine de Pizan's Response to Boccaccio's 'De Mulieribus Claris'." *Fifteenth-Century Studies* 32 (2007): 35–52.

Cassagnes-Brouquet, Sophie. "Penthésilée, reine des Amazones et Preuse, une image de la femme guerrière à la fin du Moyen Âge." *Clio* 20 (2004). http://clio.revues.org/document1400.html.

Cerquiglini-Toulet, Jacqueline. "Christine de Pizan and the Book: Programs and Modes of Reading, Strategies for Publication." *Journal of the Early Book Society for the Study of Manuscripts and Printing History* 4 (2001): 112–26.

Chance, Jane, ed. *Gender and Text in the Later Middle Ages*. Gainesville: University Press of Florida, 1996.

———. "Gender Subversion and Linguistic Castration in Fifteenth-Century English Translations of Christine de Pizan." In *Violence against Women in Medieval Texts*, ed. Anna Roberts, 161–94. Gainesville: University Press of Florida, 1998.

———. "Re-Membering Herself: Christine de Pizan's Reconfiguration of Isis as Io." *Modern Philology* 111 (2013): 133–57.

Christianson, C. Paul. "The Rise of London's Book-Trade." In Hellinga and Trapp, *Cambridge History of the Book in Britain*, 3:128–47.

Clark-Evans, Christine. "Christine de Pizan's Feminist Strategies: The Defense of the African and Asian Ladies in the *Book of the City of the Ladies*." In Dulac and Ribémont, *Une Femme de lettres*, 177–93.

———. "Nicaula of Egypt and Arabia: *Exemplum* and Ambitions to Power in the *City of Ladies*." In Kennedy, *Contexts and Continuities*, 1:287–300.

Coldiron, Anne E. B. *English Printing, Verse Translation, and the Battle of the Sexes, 1476–1557*. Farnham and Burlington, VT: Ashgate, 2009.

———. "French Presences in Tudor England." In *A Companion to Tudor Literature*, ed. Kent Cartwright, 246–60. Oxford and Malden, MA: Wiley-Blackwell, 2010.

———. "Taking Advice from a Frenchwoman: Caxton, Pynson, and Christine de Pizan's Moral Proverbs." In *Caxton's Trace: Studies in the History of English Printing*, ed. William Kuskin, 127–66. Notre Dame: University of Notre Dame Press, 2006.

———. "Translation's Challenge to Critical Categories: Verses from French in the Early English Renaissance." *Yale Journal of Criticism* 16 (2003): 315–44.

———. "William Caxton." In *The Oxford History of Literary Translation in English*, vol. 1: *to 1550*, ed. Roger Ellis, 160–69. Oxford: Oxford University Press, 2008.

———. "Women in Early English Print Culture." In *The History of British Women's Writing, 1500–1610: Volume Two*, ed. Caroline Bricks and Jennifer Summit, 60–83. New York and Basingstoke: Palgrave Macmillan, 2010.

Collette, Carolyn. "Aristotle, Translation, and the Mean: Shaping the Vernacular in Late Medieval Anglo-French Culture." In *Language and Culture in Medieval Britain: The French of England*, ed. Wogan-Browne et al., 373–85.

Costomiris, Robert. "Christine de Pisan's Boke of the Cyte of Ladyes in its Henrician Setting." *Medieval Perspectives* 18 (2003 [2011]): 79–93.

———. "William Thynne, Editor of Chaucer." *The Library*, 7th ser., 4 (2003): 3–15.

Cowen, Janet. "An English Reading of Boccaccio: A Selective Middle English Version of Boccaccio's *De Mulieribus Claris* in British Library MS Additional 10304." In *New Perspectives on Middle English Texts: A Festschrift for R. A. Waldron*, ed. Susan Powell and Jeremy J. Smith, 129–40. Cambridge: D. S. Brewer, 2000.

———. "The Translation of Boccaccio's *De Mulieribus Claris* in British Library MS Additional 10304 and *The Forty-Six Lives* Translated from Boccaccio by Henry Parker, Lord Morley." *Notes and Queries* 45 (1998): 28–29.

———. "Woman's Wit in the Middle English Translation of Boccaccio's *De Mulieribus Claris*: British Library MS Additional 10304." In *Lexis and Texts in Early English: Studies Presented to Jane Roberts*, ed. Christian J. Kay and Louise M. Sylvester, 89–104. Costerus New Series 133. Amsterdam and Atlanta: Rodopi, 2001.

———. "Women as Exempla in Fifteenth-Century Verse of the Chaucerian Tradition." In *Chaucer and Fifteenth-Century Poetry*, ed. Julia Boffey and Janet Cowen, 51–63. London: King's College London Centre for Late Antique and Medieval Studies, 1991.

Cropp, Glynnis M. "Christine de Pizan and Alexander the Great." In Campbell and Margolis, *Christine de Pizan 2000*, 125–34.

———. "The Exemplary Figure of Alexander the Great in the Works of Eustache Deschamps and Christine de Pizan." In Kennedy, *Contexts and Continuities*, 1:301–13.

———. "Nero, Emperor and Tyrant, in the Medieval French Tradition." *Florilegium* 24 (2008): 21–36.

———. "Les Personnages féminins tirés de l'histoires de la France dans le *Livre de la Cité des Dames*." In Dulac and Ribémont, *Une Femme de lettres*, 195–208.

Crosland, Jessie. "Lucan in the Middle Ages: With Special Reference to the Old French Epic." *Modern Language Review* 25 (1930): 32–51.

Curnow, Maureen Cheney. "*The Boke of the Cyte of Ladyes*, an English Translation of Christine de Pisan's *Le livre de la cité des dames*." *Bonnes Feuilles* 3
(1974): 116–37.

———. "'La Pioche d'Inquisicion': Legal-Judicial Content and Style in Christine
de Pizan's *Livre de la Cité des Dames*." In Richards, *Reinterpreting Christine
de Pizan*, 157–72.

D'Arcens, Louise. "'Je, Christine': Christine de Pizan's Autobiographical Topoi."
In *The Unsociable Sociability of Women's Lifewriting*, ed. Anne Collett and
Louise D'Arcens, 18–36. New York and Basingstoke: Palgrave Macmillan,
2010.

D'Angelo, Edoardo. "Il dossier delle sante Flora e Lucilla e la 'Argumentatio
passionis' (BHL 5021c)." *Hagiographica* 8 (2001): 121–64.

Davis, Stephen J. *The Cult of Saint Thecla: A Tradition of Women's Piety in Late
Antiquity*. Oxford: Oxford University Press, 2001.

Dawson, Maureen G. "Weeping, Speaking, and Sweing: Teaching Christine de
Pizan's 'The City of Ladies'." *Studies in Medieval and Renaissance Teaching*
n.s. 12 (2005): 5–26.

Delany, Sheila. "History, Politics, and Christine Studies: A Polemical Reply." In
Brabant, *Politics, Gender, and Genre*, 193–206.

———. "'Mothers to Think Back Through': Who Are They? The Ambiguous
Example of Christine de Pizan." In *Medieval Texts and Contemporary Readers*, ed. Laurie A. Finke and Martin B. Shichtman, 177–97. Ithaca and London: Cornell University Press, 1987.

———. "Rewriting Woman Good: Gender and the Anxiety of Influence in Two
Late-Medieval Texts." In *Chaucer in the Eighties*, ed. Julian N. Wasserman and
Robert J. Blanch, 75–92. Syracuse: Syracuse University Press, 1986.

Delogu, Daisy. "*Advocate et moyenne*: Christine de Pizan's Elaboration of Female
Authority." In Dulac et al., *Desireuse de plus avant enquerre*, 57–67.

Desmond, Marilynn, ed. *Christine de Pizan and the Categories of Difference*.
Medieval Cultures 14. Minneapolis and London: University of Minnesota
Press, 1998.

———. "Christine de Pizan: Gender, Authorship and Life-writing." In *The
Cambridge Companion to Medieval French Literature*, ed. Simon Gaunt and
Sarah Kay, 123–35. Cambridge: Cambridge University Press, 2008.

———. *Reading Dido*. Medieval Cultures 8. Minneapolis: University of Minnesota Press, 1994.

———, and Pamela Sheingorn. *Myth, Montage, and Visuality in Late Medieval
Manuscript Culture: Christine de Pizan's Epistre Othéa*. Ann Arbor: University of Michigan Press, 2003.

*Dictionnaire du Moyen Français*, version 2010. Analyse et Traittement Informa-
tique de la Langue Française (ATILF), Centre National de la Recherche
Scientifique, Université Nancy. http://www.atilf.fr/dmf.

DiMarco, Vincent J. "The Amazons and the End of the World." In *Discovering New Worlds: Essays on Medieval Exploration and Imagination*, ed. Scott D. Westrem, 69–90. New York and London: Garland, 1991.

Diner, Helen. *Mothers and Amazons: The First Feminist History of Culture*, trans. J. P. Lundin. New York: Julian, 1965.

Dowling, Maria. *Humanism in the Age of Henry VIII*. London: Croom Helm, 1986.

Downes, Stephanie. "A 'Frenche Booke Called the Pistill of Othea': Christine de Pizan's French in England." In Wogan-Browne et al., *Language and Culture in Medieval Britain: The French of England*, 457–68.

———. "Fashioning Christine de Pizan in Tudor Defences of Women." *Parergon* 23 (2006): 71–92.

Driver, Martha W. "Christine de Pisan and Robert Wyer: The *.C. Hystoryes of Troye*, or *L'Epistre d'Othea* Englished." *Gutenberg-Jahrbuch* 72 (1997): 125–39.

———. "'Me fault faire': French Makers of Manuscripts for English Patrons." In Wogan-Browne et al., *Language and Culture in Medieval Britain: The French of England*, 420–43.

———. "Mirrors of a Collective Past: Reconsidering Images of Medieval Women." In *Women and the Book: Assessing the Visual Evidence*, ed. Jane H. M. Taylor and Lesley Smith, 75–93. London and Toronto: British Library and University of Toronto Press, 1996.

DuBois, Page. *Centaurs and Amazons: Women and the Prehistory of the Great Chain of Being*. Ann Arbor: University of Michigan Press, 1982.

Duff, E. Gordon. "A Bookseller's Accounts, *c.* 1510." *The Library*, n. s. 8 (1907): 256–66.

———. "Notes on Stationers from the Lay Subsidy Rolls of 1523–4." *The Library*, n. s. 9 (1908): 257–66.

———. "The Stationers at the Sign of the Trinity." *Bibliographica* 1 (1895): 93–113; 175–93.

Dulac, Liliane. "Un mythe didactique chez Christine de Pizan: Sémiramis ou la veuve héroïque." In *Mélanges de philologie romane offerts à C. Camproux*, ed. Robert Lafont et al., 2:315–43. 2 vols. Montpellier: Centre d'Estudis Occitans, 1978.

———, Anne Paupert, Christine Reno, and Bernard Ribémont, eds. *Desireuse de plus avant enquerre . . .: Actes du VIᵉ Colloque international sur Christine de Pizan (Paris, 20–24 juillet 2006)*. Études Christiniennes 11. Paris: Champion, 2008.

———, and Bernard Ribémont, eds. *Une Femme de lettres au moyen âge: Études autour de Christine de Pizan*. Orléans: Paradigme, 1995.

Edson, Evelyn. *Mapping Time ad Space: How Medieval Mapmakers Viewed Their World*. London: British Library, 1997.

Edwards, A. S. G., and Carol M. Meale. "The Marketing of Printed Books in Late Medieval England." *The Library*, 6th ser., 15 (1993): 95–124.

Ellis, Roger. "Chaucer, Christine de Pizan, and Hoccleve: The Letter of Cupid." In *Essays on Thomas Hoccleve*, ed. Catherine Batt, 19–54. Turnhout: Brepols, 1996.

Erler, Mary C. "Wynkyn de Worde's Will: Legatees and Bequests." *The Library*, 6th ser., 10 (1988): 107–21.

Federico, Sylvia. *New Troy: Fantasies of Empire in the Late Middle Ages*. Medieval Cultures 36. Minneapolis and London: University of Minnesota Press, 2003.

Fenster, Thelma. "Did Christine Have a Sense of Humor? The Evidence of the *Epistre au dieu d'Amours*." In Richards, *Reinterpreting Christine de Pizan*, 23–36.

———. "'Perdre son latin': Christine de Pizan and Vernacular Humanism." In Desmond, *Categories of Difference*, 91–107.

———. "Possible Odds: Christine de Pizan and the Paradoxes of Woman." In Kennedy, *Contexts and Continuities*, 2:355–66.

Ferguson, Margaret W. *Dido's Daughters: Literacy, Gender, and Empire in Early Modern England and France*. Chicago and London: University of Chicago Press, 2003.

Ferrante, Joan M. *Woman as Image in Medieval Literature: From the Twelfth Century to Dante*. New York: Columbia University Press, 1975; repr. Durham, NC: Labyrinth Press, 1985.

Finke, Laurie A. "The Politics of the Canon: Christine de Pizan and the Fifteenth-Century Chaucerians." *Exemplaria* 19 (2007): 16–38.

Ford, Margaret Lane. "Importation of Printed Books into England and Scotland." In Hellinga and Trapp, *Cambridge History of the Book in Britain*, 3:179–201.

Forhan, Kate Langdon. *The Political Theory of Christine de Pizan*. Aldershot: Ashgate, 2002.

———. "Reflecting Heroes: Christine de Pizan and the Mirror Tradition." In Zimmermann and De Rentiis, *City of Scholars*, 189–96.

Fox, Alistair. *Politics and Literature in the Reigns of Henry VII and Henry VIII*. Oxford: Blackwell, 1989.

Franklin, Margaret. *Boccaccio's Heroines: Power and Virtue in Renaissance Society*. Aldershot: Ashgate, 2006.

Furnivall, Frederick J. "Bryan Anslay." *Notes and Queries*, 4th ser., 6 (1870): 367–68.

Gaunt, Simon. "The Châtelain de Couci." In *The Cambridge Companion to Medieval French Literature*, ed. idem and Sarah Kay, 95–108. Cambridge: Cambridge University Press, 2008.

Gauvard, Claude. "Christine de Pizan et ses contemporains: L'Engagement politique des écrivains dans le royaume de France au XIV$^e$ et XV$^e$ siècles." In Dulac and Ribémont, *Une Femme de lettres*, 105–28.

Gaskell, Philip. *A New Introduction to Bibliography*. Winchester: St. Paul's Bibliographies and New Castle, DE: Oak Knoll Press, 1995. First published Oxford: Oxford University Press, 1972.

Gee, John Archer. "Margaret Roper's English Version of Erasmus' *Precatio Dominica* and the Apprenticeship behind Early Tudor Translation." *Review of English Studies* 13 (1937): 257–71.

Gibbons, Mary Weitzel. "Christine's Mirror: Self in Word and Image. " In Kennedy, *Contexts and Continuities*, 2:367–96.

Gibbs, Stephanie Viereck. "Christine de Pizan's *Epistre Othea* in England: The Manuscript Tradition of Stephen Scrope's Translation." In Kennedy, *Contexts and Continuities*, 2:397–408.

Gillespie, Alexandra. *Print Culture and the Medieval Author: Chaucer, Lydgate, and Their Books, 1473–1557*. Oxford: Oxford University Press, 2006.

Gillespie, Vincent and Susan Powell, eds. *A Companion to the Early Printed Book in England, 1476–1558*. Woodbridge: Boydell & Brewer, 2014.

Gillett, A. "Orosius." *ODMA* 3:1235.

González Doreste, Dulce Maria, and Francisca del Mar Plaza Picón. "À propos de la compilation: Du *De claris mulieribus* de Boccace à *Le Livre de la Cité des Dames* de Christine de Pisan." *Moyen Français* 51–53 (2002–2003): 327–37.

Goodrich, Jaime. "Thomas More and Margaret More Roper: A Case for Rethinking Women's Participation in the Early Modern Public Sphere." *Sixteenth Century Journal* 39 (2008): 1021–40.

Green, Karen. "Christine de Pizan: Isolated Individual or Member of a Feminine Community of Learning?" In *Communities of Learning: Networks and the Shaping of Intellectual Identity in Europe, 1100–1500*, ed. Constant J. Mews and John N. Crossley, 229–250. Turnhout: Brepols, 2011.

———. "What Were the Ladies in the City of Ladies Reading? The Libraries of Christine de Pizan's Contemporaries." *Medievalia et Humanistica* 36 (2010): 77–100.

Green, Monica H. "From 'Diseases of Women' to 'Secrets of Women': The Transformation of Gynecological Literature in the Later Middle Ages." *Journal of Medieval and Early Modern Studies* 30 (2000): 5–39.

———. "'Traittié tout de mençonges': The *Secrés des dames*, 'Trotula,' and Attitudes toward Women's Medicine in Fourteenth- and Early Fifteenth-Century France." In Desmond, *Categories of Difference*, 146–78.

Griffin, Miranda. "Transforming Fortune: Reading and Chance in Christine de Pizan's *Mutacion de Fortune* and *Chemin de long estude*." *Modern Language Review* 104 (2009): 55–70.

Griffiths, Jeremy, and Derek Pearsall, eds. *Book Production and Publishing in Britain, 1375–1475*. Cambridge: Cambridge University Press, 1989.

Gwara, Joseph J. "Three Forms of w and Four English Printers: Robert Copland, Henry Pepwell, Henry Watson, and Wynkyn de Worde." *Papers of the Bibliographical Society of America* 106 (2012): 141–230.

Gunn, Steven. "The French Wars of Henry VIII." In *The Origins of War in Early Modern Europe*, ed. Jeremy Black, 28–51. Edinburgh: Donald, 1987.

Hales, John W. *Notes and Essays on Shakespeare*. London: G. Bell, 1884.

Halfond, Gregory I. "*Sis Quoque Catholicis Religionis Apex*: The Ecclesiastical Patronage of Chilperic I and Fredegund." *Church History* 81 (2012): 48–76.

Hamaguchi, Keiko. "Domesticating the Amazons in the *Knight's Tale*." *Studies in the Age of Chaucer* 26 (2004): 331–54.

———. "Transgressing the Borderline of Gender: Zenobia in the *Monk's Tale*." *Chaucer Review* 40 (2005): 183–205.

Hanawalt, Barbara A. *The Wealth of Wives: Women, Law, and Economy in Late Medieval London*. Oxford: Oxford University Press, 2007.

Harrison, Dick. *Medieval Space: The Extent of Microspatial Knowledge in Western Europe during the Middle Ages*. Lund: Lund University Press, 1996.

Harrison, K. P. "Katherine of Aragon's Pomegranate." *Transactions of the Cambridge Bibliographical Society* 2 (1954): 88–92.

Hartshorne, Charles Henry. *The Book Rarities in the University of Cambridge*. London: Longman, 1829.

Hassell, James Woodrow. *Middle French Proverbs, Sentences, and Proverbial Phrases*. Subsidia mediaevalia 12. Toronto: Pontifical Institute of Mediaeval Studies, 1982.

Havely, Nick. "Britain and Italy: Trade, Travel, Translation." In *A Companion to Medieval English Literature and Culture, c.1350–c.1500*, ed. Peter Brown, 215–30. Oxford: Blackwell, 2007.

Hazlitt, W. C. *Hand-Book to the Popular, Poetical, and Dramatic Literature of Great Britain*. London: John Russell Smith, 1867.

———. *Bibliographical Collections and Notes*. 6 vols. London: Quaritch, 1876–1903.

Hellinga, Lotte. "Importation of Books Printed on the Continent into England and Scotland before c. 1520." In *Printing the Written Word: The Social History of Books, circa 1450–1520*, ed. Sandra Hindman, 205–24. Ithaca and London: Cornell University Press, 1991.

———. *William Caxton and Early Printing in England*. London: British Library, 2010.

———, and J. B. Trapp, eds. *The Cambridge History of the Book in Britain*, vol. 3, *1400–1557*. Cambridge: Cambridge University Press, 1999.

Hicks, Eric. "Situation du débat sur le *Roman de la Rose*." In Dulac and Ribémont, *Une Femme de lettres*, 51–67.

———, ed., with Diego Gonzalez and Philippe Simon. *Au champ des escriptures: IIIe Colloque international sur Christine de Pizan (Lausanne, 18–22 juillet 1998)*. Études Christiniennes 6. Paris: Champion, 2000.

Ho, Cynthia. "Communal and Individual Autobiography in Christine de Pizan's *Book of the City of Ladies*." *CEA Critic* 57 (1994): 31–40.

Hoche, Dominique T. "'Come Boece a Pavie': Christine de Pizan's Use of Boethius's *Consolation of Philosophy* in *The Book of the City of Ladies*." *Carmina Philosophiae* 13 (2004): 23–52.

————. "Interrogating Boundaries: Christine de Pizan and Her Influence in Late Medieval and Early Modern England." Ph.D. diss., Michigan State University, 2003.

————. *The Reception of Christine de Pizan's* Fais d'Armes *in Fifteenth-Century England: Chivalric Self-Fashioning.* Lewiston, NY and Lampeter: Edwin Mellen Press, 2007.

Hodapp, William F. "Minerva's Owl in Charles d'Orléans's English Poems: A Mythographic Note on Line 4765." *American Notes & Queries* 9 (1996): 3–7.

Hodnett, Edward. *English Woodcuts, 1480–1535.* Oxford: Oxford University Press, 1973.

Holderness, Julia Simms. "Buried Treasure: A Lost Document from the Debate on the Romance of the Rose." In *Collections in Context: The Organization of Knowledge and Community in Europe,* ed. Karen Fresco and Anne D. Hedeman, 64–74. Columbus: Ohio State University Press, 2011.

————. "Christine, Boèce et Saint Augustin: la consolation de la mémoire." In Dulac et al., *Desireuse de plus avant enquerre,* 279–89.

————. "Feminism and the Fall: Boccaccio, Christine de Pizan, and Louise Labé." *Essays in Medieval Studies* 21 (2004): 97–108.

Hopper, Vincent Foster. *Medieval Number Symbolism.* New York: Columbia University Press, 1938.

Hosington, Brenda M. "Translation, Early Printing, and Gender in England, 1484–1535." *Florilegium* 23 (2006): 41–67.

Huber, Franziska. "*L'Histoire ancienne jusqu'à César,* source du *Livre de la Mutacion de Fortune* de Christine de Pizan: étude comparative des récits sur Cyrus." In Hicks, *Au champ des escriptures,* 161–74.

Huguet, Edmond. *Dictionnaire de la langue française du seizième siècle.* 10 vols. Paris: Champion, 1925–.

Hume, Martin. *The Wives of Henry the Eighth.* London: Eveleigh Nash and Grayson, 1927.

International Genealogical Index. http://www.familysearch.org.

Jambeck, Karen K. "The Library of Alice Chaucer, Duchess of Suffolk: A Fifteenth-Century Owner of a 'Boke of le Citee de Dames'." *Profane Arts* 7 (1998): 106–35.

Johnston, Hope. "Catherine of Aragon's Pomegranate, Revisited." *Transactions of the Cambridge Bibliographical Society* 13 (2005 [2008]): 153–73.

————. "Desiderius Erasmus, *A deuoute treatise vpon the Pater noster.*" EEBO Introduction Series, http://eebo.chadwyck.com/intros/htxview?template=basic. htx&content=roper.htm.

————. "Redressing the Virago in Christine de Pizan's *Livre de la cité des dames.*" *CRMH* 24 (2012): 439–60.

Jones, Ann Rosalind, and Peter Stallybrass. "The Currency of Clothing." In *Fashion: Critical and Primary Sources,* ed. Peter McNeil, 1:315–41. Oxford and New York: Berg, 2009.

Jordan, Constance. "Feminism and the Humanists: The Case for Sir Thomas Elyot's *Defense of Good Women*." In *Rewriting the Renaissance: The Discourses of Sexual Difference in Early Modern Europe*, ed. Margaret W. Ferguson, Maureen Quilligan, and Nancy J. Vickers, 242–58. Chicago and London: University of Chicago Press, 1986.

———. *Renaissance Feminism: Literary Texts and Political Models*. Ithaca: Cornell University Press, 1990.

Kaufman, Peter Iver. "Absolute Margaret: Margaret More Roper and 'Well Learned' Men." *Sixteenth Century Journal* 20 (1989): 443–56.

Kellogg, Judith L. "Christine de Pizan and Boccaccio: Rewriting Classical Mythic Tradition." In *Comparative Literature East and West: Traditions and Trends*, ed. Cornelia N. Moore and Raymond A. Moody, 124–31. Honolulu: College of Languages, Linguistics and Literature, University of Hawaii and the East-West Center, 1989.

———. "The *Cité des dames*: An Archaeology of the Regendered Body Politic." In Kennedy, *Contexts and Continuities*, 2:431–41.

———. "*Le Livre de la cité des dames*: Reconfiguring Knowledge and Reimagining Gendered Space." In Altmann and McGrady, *Christine de Pizan: A Casebook*, 129–46.

———. "Transforming Ovid: The Metamorphosis of Female Authority." In Desmond, *Categories of Difference*, 181–94.

Kelly, Kathleen Coyne. *Performing Virginity and Testing Chastity in the Middle Ages*. Routledge Research in Medieval Studies 2. London and New York: Routledge, 2000.

Kelsall, David, Archivist of St. Alban's Cathedral. Personal correspondence, 22 Feb. 2006.

Kennedy, Angus J. *Christine de Pizan: A Bibliographical Guide*. London: Grant & Cutler, 1984; *Supplement I*, 1994; *Supplement II*, Woodbridge: Tamesis, 2004.

———. "Christine de Pizan's Crown of Twelve Stars." *Medium Ævum* 78 (2008): 279–92.

———, ed., with Rosalind Brown-Grant, James C. Laidlaw, and Catherine M. Müller. *Contexts and Continuities: Proceedings of the IV[th] International Colloquium on Christine de Pizan (Glasgow 21–27 July 2000)*. Glasgow: University of Glasgow Press, 2002.

Kiehl, Carole. "Christine de Pizan and Fortune: A Statistical Survey." In Kennedy, *Contexts and Continuities*, 2:443–52.

Kleinbaum, Abby Wettan. *The War Against the Amazons*. New York: McGraw-Hill, 1983.

Knowles, John. "How Shakespeare Knew King Leir." *Shakespeare Survey* 55 (2002): 12–35.

Kolsky, Stephen D. *The Genealogy of Women: Studies in Boccaccio's* De mulieribus claris. Studies in the Humanities 62. New York and Oxford: Peter Lang, 2003.

Kolve, V. A. "The Annunciation to Christine: Authorial Empowerment in *The Book of the City of Ladies.*" In *Iconography at the Crossroads*, ed. Brendan Cassidy, 172–96. Princeton: Princeton University Department of Art and Archaeology, 1993.

Kosta-Théfaine, Jean-François. "Les *Proverbes moraulx* de Christine de Pizan." *Moyen Français* 38 (1996): 61–77.

Laidlaw, James C. "Christine and the Manuscript Tradition." In Altmann and McGrady, *Christine de Pizan: A Casebook*, 231–49.

———. "Christine de Pizan: An Author's Progress." *Modern Language Review* 78 (1983): 532–50.

———. "Christine de Pizan: A Publisher's Progress." *Modern Language Review* 82 (1987): 35–67.

———. "Christine de Pizan, the Earl of Salisbury and Henry IV." *French Studies* 36 (1982): 129–43.

Laird, Edgar. "Christine de Pizan and Controversy Concerning Star-Study in the Court of Charles V." *Culture and Cosmos* 1 (1997): 35–48.

Laird, Judith. "Good Women and *Bonnes Dames*: Virtuous Females in Chaucer and Christine de Pizan." *Chaucer Review* 30 (1995): 58–70.

Larson, Wendy R. "Who Is the Master of This Narrative? Maternal Patronage of the Cult of St. Margaret." In *Gendering the Master Narrative: Women and Power in the Middle Ages*, ed. Mary C. Erler and Maryanne Kowaleski, 94–104. Ithaca and London: Cornell University Press, 2003.

Lebreton, Jules. "St. Justin, Martyr." *Catholic Encyclopedia.* http://www.newadvent.org/cathen/08580c.htm.

Leemans, Pieter de, and Michèle Goyens, eds. *Aristotle's Problemata in Different Times and Tongues.* Mediaevalia Lovaniensia, 1st ser., 39. Leuven: University of Leuven Press, 2006.

Lehman, Alan D. "The Coriolanus Story in Antiquity." *Classical Journal* 47 (1952): 329–36.

Lloyd, Christopher, and Simon Thurley. *Henry VIII: Images of a Tudor King.* Oxford: Phaidon Press, 1990.

Long, Mary Beth. "A Medieval French Book in an Early Modern English World: Christine de Pisan's *Livre de la Cité des Dames* and Women Readers in the Age of Print." *Literature Compass* 9 (2012): 521–37.

Loukopoulos, Halina D. "Classical Mythology in the Works of Christine de Pizan, with an Edition of 'L'Epistre Othéa' from the Manuscript Harley 4431." Ph.D. diss., Wayne State University, 1977.

Lysons, Daniel. *The Environs of London: Counties of Herts, Essex & Kent.* 4 vols. London: Strahan, 1796. http://www.british-history.ac.uk/report.aspx?compid=45488.

Mackie, C. J. "A Note on Dido's Ancestry in the 'Aeneid'." *Classical Journal* 88 (1993): 231–33.

Mahoney, Dhira B. "Middle English Regenderings of Christine de Pizan." In *The Medieval Opus: Imitation, Rewriting, and Transmission in the French Tradition*, ed. Douglas Kelly, 405–27. Amsterdam: Rodopi, 1996.

Malcolmson, Cristina. "Christine de Pizan's *City of Ladies* in Early Modern England." In *Debating Gender in Early Modern England, 1500–1700*, ed. eadem and Mihoko Suzuki, 15–35. New York: Palgrave Macmillan, 2002.

Mann, Jill. *Geoffrey Chaucer*. London: Harvester Wheatsheaf, 1991.

Margolis, Nadia. "From Chrétien to Christine: Translating Twelfth-Century Literature to Reform the French Court during the Hundred Years War." In *Shaping Courtliness in Medieval France*, ed. Daniel E. O'Sullivan and Laurie Shepard, 213–25. Woodbridge: D. S. Brewer, 2013.

———. *An Introduction to Christine de Pizan*. Gainesville: University Press of Florida, 2011.

———. "Modern Editions: Makers of the Christinian Corpus." In Altmann and McGrady, *Christine de Pizan: A Casebook*, 251–70.

McCutcheon, Elizabeth. "The Education of Thomas More's Daughters: Concepts and Praxis." In *East Meets West: Homage to Edgar C. Knowlton, Jr.*, ed. Roger L. Hadlich and J. D. Ellsworth, 193–207. Honolulu: Department of European Languages and Literature, University of Hawaii, 1988.

McGrady, Deborah. "Reading for Authority: Portraits of Christine de Pizan and Her Readers." In *Author, Reader, Book: Medieval Authorship in Theory and Practice*, ed. S. B. Partridge and E. Kwakkel, 154–77. Toronto: University of Toronto Press, 2012.

———. "What is a Patron? Benefactors and Authorship in Harley 4431, Christine de Pizan's Collected Works." In Desmond, *Categories of Difference*, 195–214.

McInerney, Maud Burnett. "Rhetoric, Power, and Integrity in the Passion of the Virgin Martyr." In *Menacing Virgins*, ed. Kathleen Coyne Kelly and Marina Leslie, 50–70. Newark, DE: University of Delaware Press, 1999.

McKendrick, Scot. "A European Heritage: Books of Continental Origin Collected by the English Royal Family from Edward III to Henry VIII." In *Royal Manuscripts: The Genius of Illumination*, ed. Scot McKendrick, John Lowden, and Kathleen Doyle, 43–65. London: British Library, 2011.

McKerrow, Ronald B. *An Introduction to Bibliography for Literary Students*. Winchester: St. Paul's Bibliographies and New Castle, DE: Oak Knoll Press, 1994. First published Oxford: Clarendon Press, 1927.

———. *Printers' and Publishers' Devices in England and Scotland, 1485–1640*. London: Bibliographical Society, 1949.

McKitterick, David. *Print, Manuscript, and the Search for Order, 1450–1830*. Cambridge and New York: Cambridge University Press, 2003.

McLeod, Glenda. *Virtue and Venom: Catalogs of Women from Antiquity to the Renaissance*. Ann Arbor: University of Michigan Press, 1991.

———, and Katharina Wilson. "A Clerk in Name Only—A Clerk in All but Name: The Misogamous Tradition and 'La Cité des Dames'." In Zimmermann and De Rentiis, *City of Scholars*, 67–76.

McWebb, Christine, ed. *Debating the Roman de la Rose: A Critical Anthology*. New York: Routledge, 2007.

———, and Earl Jeffrey Richards. "New Perspectives on the Debate about the *Roman de la rose*." In Dulac et al, *Desireuse de plus avant enquerre*, 103–16.

Meale, Carol M. "'. . . alle the bokes that I haue of latyn, englisch, and frensch': Laywomen and Their Books in Late Medieval England." In eadem, *Women and Literature*, 128–58.

———, and Julia Boffey. "Gentlewomen's Reading." In Hellinga and Trapp, *Cambridge History of the Book in Britain*, 3:526–40.

———. "Legends of Good Women in the European Middle Ages." *Archiv für das Studium der Neueren Sprachen und Literaturen* 229 (1992): 55–70.

———. "Patrons, Buyers, and Owners: Book Production and Social Status." In Griffiths and Pearsall, *Book Production, 1375–1475*, 201–38.

———. "Reading Women's Culture in Fifteenth-Century England: The Case of Alice Chaucer." In *Mediaevalitas: Reading the Middle Ages*, ed. Anna Torti and Piero Boitani, 81–101. Cambridge: D. S. Brewer, 1996.

———, ed. *Women and Literature in Britain, 1150–1500*. 2nd ed. Cambridge Studies in Medieval Literature 17. Cambridge: Cambridge University Press, 1996.

Mews, Constant J. "Latin Learning in Christine de Pizan's *Livre de paix*." In *Healing the Body Politic: The Political Thought of Christine de Pizan*, ed. Karen Green and idem, 61–80. Turnhout: Brepols, 2005.

Michaud-Fréjaville, Françoise. "'Fors nature': Dieu, le roi Charles et la Pucelle, ou Faut-il changer notre titre du Ditié de Jeahnne d'Arc?" *CRMH* 25 (2013): 545–58.

Miner, Dorothy Eugenia. *Anastaise and Her Sisters: Women Artists of the Middle Ages*. Baltimore: Walters Art Gallery, 1974.

Minnis, Alastair. *Translations of Authority in Medieval English Literature*. Cambridge: Cambridge University Press, 2009.

Mitchell, Christine M. "Classical, Christian, and Feminine Rhetorical Influences on Christine de Pizan's *Book of the City of Ladies*." Ph.D. diss., University of Southwestern Louisiana, 1999.

Moreau, Thérèse. "I, Christine, an Italian Woman." In *Displaced Women: Multilingual Narratives of Migration in Europe*, ed. Lucia Aiello, Joy Charnley, and Mariangela Palladino, 71–90. Newcastle upon Tyne: Cambridge Scholars, 2014.

Morini, Massimiliano. *Tudor Translation in Theory and Practice*. Aldershot and Burlington, VT: Ashgate, 2006.

Morse, Ruth. *The Medieval Medea*. Cambridge: D. S. Brewer, 1996.

———. "Problems of Early Fiction: Raoul Le Fèvre's *Histoire de Jason*." *Modern Language Review* 87 (1983): 34–45.

Mühlethaler, Jean-Claude. "Problèmes de réécriture: amour et mort de la princesse de Salerne dans le *Decameron* (IV.1) et dans la *Cité des Dames* (II.59)." In Dulac and Ribémont, *Une Femme de lettres*, 209–20.

———. "'Traictier de vertu au proufit d'ordre de vivre': relire l'oeuvre de Christine de Pizan à la lumière des miroirs des princes." In Kennedy, *Contexts and Continuities*, 2:585–601.

Nabert, Nathalie. "Christine de Pizan, Jean Gerson et le gouvernement des âmes." In Hicks, *Au champ des escriptures*, 251–68.

Nevile-Sington, Pamela. "Press, Politics and Religion." In Hellinga and Trapp, *Cambridge History of the Book in Britain*, 3:576–607.

Niederoest, Monique. "Violence et autorité dans *La Cité des dames* de Christine de Pizan." In Hicks, *Au champ des escriptures*, 399–410.

O'Brien, Dennis J. "Warrior Queen: The Character of Zenobia According to Giovanni Boccaccio, Christine de Pizan, and Sir Thomas Elyot." *Medieval Perspectives* 8 (1993): 53–68.

Oestreich, Donna J. "Christine de Pisan's *Book of the City of Ladies*: Paradigmatic Participation and Eschewal." In *Representations of the Feminine in the Middle Ages*, ed. Bonnie Wheeler, 253–75. Dallas: Academia, 1993.

Orme, Nicholas. "Schools and School-Books." In Hellinga and Trapp, *Cambridge History of the Book in Britain*, 3:449–69.

Ouy, Gilbert, Christine Reno, and Inès Villela-Petit. *Album Christine de Pizan*. Texte, Codex et Contexte 14. Turnhout: Brepols, 2012.

*Oxford Classical Dictionary*, ed. Simon Hornblower and Antony Spawforth. 3rd ed. Oxford: Oxford University Press, 1999.

*Oxford Dictionary of English Proverbs*, ed. William George Smith, rev. ed. Sir Paul Harvey. Oxford: Clarendon Press, 1957.

*Oxford Dictionary of National Biography*, ed. H. G. C. Matthew and Brian Harrison. 61 vols. Oxford: Oxford University Press, 2004.

*Oxford Dictionary of Quotations*, ed. Elizabeth Knowles. 7th ed. Oxford: Oxford Univeristy Press, 2009.

*Oxford Dictionary of Saints*, ed. David Hugh Farmer. 5th ed. Oxford: Oxford University Press, 2004.

*Oxford English Dictionary*, prepared by J. A. Simpson and E. S. C. Weiner. 2nd ed. 10 vols. Oxford: Oxford University Press, 1989.

Ouy, Gilbert, and Christine M. Reno. "Identification des autographes de Christine de Pizan." *Scriptorium* 34 (1980): 221–38.

———. "Les Hésitations de Christine: Etude des variantes de graphies dans trois manuscrits autographes de Christine de Pizan." *Revue des Langues Romanes* 92 (1988): 267–86.

Parker, Holt N. "Women and Humanism: Nine Factors for the Woman Learning." *Viator* 35 (2004): 518–616.

Parkes, Malcolm B. *Scribes, Scripts and Readers: Studies in the Communication, Presentation and Dissemination of Medieval Texts.* London: Hambledon Press, 1991.

Parmiter, Geoffrey de C. *The King's Great Matter: A Study of Anglo-Papal Relations 1527–1534.* London: Longmans, 1967.

Parussa, Gabriella. "Autographes et orthographe: quelques considérations sur l'orthographe de Christine de Pizan." *Romania* 117 (1999): 143–59.

———, and Richard Trachsler. "*Or sus, alons ou champ des escriptures.* Encore sur l'orthographe de Christine de Pizan: l'intérêt des grands corpus." In Kennedy, *Contexts and Continuities*, 3:621–43.

Patton, Elizabeth. "Second Thoughts of a Renaissance Humanist on the Education of Women: Juan Luis Vives Revises His *De institutione feminae Christianae.*" *American Notes & Queries* 5 (1992): 111–14.

Paupert, Anne. "Christine et Boèce: De la lecture à l'écriture, de la réécriture à l'écriture du moi." In Kennedy, *Contexts and Continuities*, 3:645–62.

———. "The Name of the Author: Self-Representation in Christine de Pizan's *Livre de la cité des dames.*" *Exemplaria* 4 (1992): 201–28.

———. "'La narracion de mes aventures,' des premiers poèmes à *L'Advision*: l'élaboration d'une écriture autobiographique dans l'oeuvre de Christine de Pizan." In Hicks, *Au champ des escriptures*, 51–71.

———. "'Pouëte si soubtil' ou 'grand deceveur': Christine de Pizan lectrice d'Ovide." In *Ovide métamorphosé: Les Lecteurs médiévaux d'Ovide*, ed. Laurence Harf-Lancner, Laurence Mathey-Maille, and Michelle Szkilnik, 45–68. Paris: Presses Sorbonne Nouvelle, 2009.

Pearsall, Derek. *The Life of Geoffrey Chaucer: A Critical Biography.* Cambridge, MA and London: Blackwell, 1992.

Pettegree, Andrew, Malcolm Walsby, and Alexander Wilkinson, eds. *French Vernacular Books.* 2 vols. Leiden: Brill, 2007.

Phillippy, Patricia A. "Establishing Authority: Boccaccio's *De Claris Mulieribus* and Christine de Pizan's *Le Livre de la Cité des Dames.*" *Romanic Review* 77 (1986): 167–94.

Phillips, Kim M. *Medieval Maidens: Young Women and Gender in England, 1270–1540.* Manchester: Manchester University Press, 2003.

Pinet, Marie-Josephe. *Christine de Pizan (1364–1430): Étude biographique et littéraire.* Paris: Champion, 1927. Reprint, Geneva: Slatkine, 2011.

Plant, Majorie. *The English Book Trade: An Economic History of the Making and Sale of Books.* London: Allen & Unwin, 1965.

Pollard, Graham. "The English Market for Printed Books." *Publishing History* 4 (1978): 7–48.

Praet, Joseph Basile Bernard van. *Recherches sur Louis de Bruges.* Paris: Du Bure, 1831.

Pratt, Karen. "The Strains of Defense: The Many Voices of Jean Le Fèvre's *Livre de Leësce.*" In *Gender in Debate from the Early Middle Ages to the Renaissance,* ed. Thelma S. Fenster and Clare A. Lees, 113–33. New York and Basingstoke: Palgrave, 2002.

Quilligan, Maureen. "Allegory and Female Agency." In *Thinking Allegory Otherwise,* ed. Barbara Machosky, 163–87. Stanford: Stanford University Press, 2010.

———. *The Allegory of Female Authority: Christine de Pizan's* Cité des Dames. Ithaca and London: Cornell University Press, 1991.

———. "Translating Dismemberment: Boccaccio and Christine de Pizan." *Studi sul Boccaccio* 20 (1991–1992): 253–66.

Rabil, Albert, Jr. "Geoffrey Chaucer, the Wife of Bath (ca. 1395) and Christine de Pizan, from the Letter of the God of Love (1399) to City of Ladies (1405): A New Kind of Encounter between Male and Female." In *Attending to Early Modern Women: Conflict and Concord,* ed. Karen Nelson and Amy M. Froide, 189–206. Newark, DE: University of Delaware Press, 2013.

Ramsay, Alison. "On the Link between Rape, Abduction, and War in Christine de Pizan's *Cité des dames.*" In Kennedy, *Contexts and Continuities,* 3:693–703.

Reames, Sherry L. *Middle English Legends of Women Saints.* Kalamazoo: Medieval Institute Publications, 2003.

Régnier-Bohler, Danielle. "La tragédie thébaine dans 'La Mutacion de Fortune'." In Zimmermann and De Rentiis, *City of Scholars,* 127–47.

Reno, Christine. "Christine de Pizan: 'At Best a Contradictory Figure'?" In Brabant, *Politics, Gender, and Genre,* 171–91.

———. "Christine de Pizan: Feminism and Irony." In *Seconda miscellanea di studi e ricerche sul Quattrocento francese,* ed. Jonathan Beck and Gianni Mombello, 125–33. Chambéry: Centre d'Etudes Franco-Italiens, 1981.

———. "Christine de Pizan's *Enseignemens moraux*: Good Advice for Several Generations." In *Christine de Pizan: The Making of the Queen's Manuscript* (2005): 1–15. http://www.pizan.lib.ed.ac.uk/morauxnov05.pdf.

———. "The Cursive and Calligraphic Scripts of Christine de Pisan." *Ball State University Forum* 19 (1978): 3–20.

———, and Gilbert Ouy. "X + X' = 1. Response to James C. Laidlaw." In Kennedy, *Contexts and Continuities,* 3:723–30.

Reynolds, Susan. "Medieval *Origines Gentium* and the Community of the Realm." *History* 68 (1983): 375–90.

Ribémont, Bernard. "Christine de Pizan et la figure de la mère." In Campbell and Margolis, *Christine de Pizan 2000,* 149–61.

———. "Christine de Pizan, Isidore de Séville et l'astrologie: compilation et 'mutacion' d'un discours sur les arts libéraux." In Dulac et al., *Desireuse de plus avant enquerre,* 303–14.

———. "Christine de Pizan et l'encyclopédisme scientifique." In Zimmermann and De Rentiis, *City of Scholars,* 174–85.

———. "Christine de Pizan et les arts libéraux: un modèle a géometrie variable." *French Studies* 63 (2009): 137–47.

———. "Christine et la nouveauté." In Kennedy, *Contexts and Continuities*, 3:731–45.

———. "Christine de Pizan, la justice et le droit." *Moyen Âge* 118 (2012): 129–68.

Rigby, Stephen H. "The Body Politic in the Social and Political Thought of Christine de Pizan: Part I, Reciprocity, Hierarchy and Political Authority." *CRMH* 24 (2012): 461–83.

———. "The Body Politic in the Social and Political Thought of Christine de Pizan: Part II, Social Inequality and Social Justice." *CRMH* 25 (2013): 559–79.

Ricci, Seymour de. *English Collectors of Books and Manuscripts, 1530–1930*. Cambridge: Cambridge University Press, 1930.

Rice, John P. "A Note on Christine de Pisan and Cecco d'Ascoli." *Italica* 15 (1938): 149–51.

Richards, Earl Jeffrey. "Christine de Pizan and Jean Gerson: An Intellectual Friendship." In Campbell and Margolis, *Christine de Pizan 2000*, 197–208.

———. "Christine de Pizan and Medieval Jurisprudence." In Kennedy, *Contexts and Continuities*, 3:747–66.

———. "Editing the *Livre de la cité des dames*: New Insights, Problems and Challenges." In Hicks, *Au champ des escriptures*, 789–816.

———. "Les enjeux du culte marial chez Christine de Pizan." In Dulac et al., *Desireuse de plus avant enquerre*, 141–65.

———. "Finding the 'Authentic' Text: Editing and Translating Medieval and Modern Works as Comparable Interpretive Exercises (Chrétien's *Charrette*, Christine de Pizan's *Cité des Dames*, and Diderot's *Neveu de Rameau*)." *L'Esprit Createur* 27 (1987): 111–21.

———. "Rejecting Essentialism and Gendered Writing: The Case of Christine de Pizan." In Chance, *Gender and Text*, 96–131.

———. "Where are the Men in Christine de Pizan's *City of Ladies?* Architectural and Allegorical Structures in Christine de Pizan's *Livre de la cité des dames*." In *Translatio Studii: Essays by His Students in Honor of Karl D. Uitti for His Sixty-Fifth Birthday*, ed. Renate Blumenfeld-Kosinski, Kevin Brownlee, Mary B. Speer, and Lori J. Walters, 221–44. Amsterdam and Atlanta: Rodopi, 2000.

———, ed., with Joan Williamson, Nadia Margolis, and Christine Reno. *Reinterpreting Christine de Pizan*. Athens, GA: University of Georgia Press, 1992.

Ritson, Joseph. *Bibliographica Poetica*. London: Roworth, 1802.

Rooks, John. "*The Boke of the Cyte of Ladyes* and Its Sixteenth-Century Readership." In *The Reception of Christine de Pizan from the Fifteenth through the Nineteenth Centuries*, ed. Glenda K. McLeod, 83–100. Lewiston, NY: Mellen, 1991.

Ross, Sarah Gwyneth. *The Birth of Feminism: Woman as Intellect in Renaissance Italy and England*. Cambridge, MA: Harvard University Press, 2009.

Rouillard, Linda. "'Faux Semblant ou Faire Semblant?': Christine de Pizan and Virtuous Artifice." *Forum for Modern Language Studies* 46 (2010): 16–28.

Rouse, Mary A., and Richard H. Rouse. "Prudence, Mother of Virtues: The *Chapelet des vertus* and Christine de Pizan." *Viator* 39 (2008): 185–228.

Roussos, Katherine. "Universalité et création féminine: le *Livre de la Cité des Dames* comme processus transcendant." In Dulac et al., *Desireuse de plus avant enquerre*, 329–43.

Salter, Elizabeth. *English and International: Studies in the Literature, Art and Patronage of Medieval England*, ed. Derek Pearsall and Nicolette Zeeman. Cambridge: Cambridge University Press, 1988.

Saunders, Corinne. *Rape and Ravishment in the Literature of Medieval England.* Cambridge: D. S. Brewer, 2001.

Scattergood, V. J. *Politics and Poetry in the Fifteenth Century.* London: Blandford, 1971.

Schiller, Gertrud. *Iconography of Christian Art.* 2 vols. London: Lund Humphries, 1971.

Schwarz, Kathyrn. *Tough Love: Amazon Encounters in the English Renaissance.* Durham, NC: Duke University Press, 2000.

Semple, Benjamin. "L'erreur et la morale: le dualisme de la 'loi païenne' selon Christine de Pizan." In Dulac et al., *Desireuse de plus avant enquerre*, 167–79.

Simpson, James. "Chaucer as a European Writer." In *The Yale Companion to Chaucer*, ed. Seth Lerer, 55–86. New Haven and London: Yale University Press, 2006.

———. "The Other Book of Troy: Guido delle Colonne's *Historia destructionis Troiae* in Fourteenth- and Fifteenth-Century England." *Speculum* 73 (1998): 397–423.

———. "The Sacrifice of Lady Rochford: Henry Parker, Lord Morley's Translation of *De claris mulieribus*." In *'Triumphs of English': Henry Parker, Lord Morley, Translator to the Tudor Court*, ed. Marie Axton and James P. Carley, 153–69. London: British Library, 2000.

Slerca, Anna. "Dante, Boccace, et le *Livre de la Cité des Dames* de Christine de Pizan." In Dulac and Ribémont, *Une Femme de lettres*, 221–30.

Smith, Geri L. "Jean de Meun in the 'Cité des Dames': Author versus Authority." *Fifteenth-Century Studies* 35 (2010): 132–42.

Smith, Hilda. "Humanist Education and the Renaissance Concept of Woman." In *Women and Literature in Britain, 1500–1700*, ed. Helen Wilcox, 9–29. Cambridge: Cambridge University Press, 1996.

Smith, Lesley, and Jane H. M. Taylor, eds. *Women, the Book and the Worldly.* Cambridge: D. S. Brewer, 1995.

Solente, Suzanne. *Christine de Pisan: Extrait de l'histoire littéraire de la France*, vol. 40. Paris: Klincksieck, 1969.

Solterer, Helen. *The Master and Minerva: Disputing Women in French Medieval Culture.* Berkeley: University of California Press, 1995.

*Southwell and Nottingham Church History Project*. University of Nottingham and Diocese of Southwell, http://southwellchurches.nottingham.ac.uk.

Starkey, David. *Six Wives: The Queens of Henry VIII*. London: Chatto and Windus, 2003.

Stecopoulos, Eleni, with Karl D. Uitti. "Christine de Pizan's *Livre de la Cité des Dames*: The Reconstruction of Myth." In Richards, *Reinterpreting Christine de Pizan*, 48–62.

Stevenson, Burton. *The Macmillan Book of Proverbs, Maxims, and Famous Phrases*. New York: Macmillan, 1987.

Strohm, Paul. *Hochon's Arrow: The Social Imagination of Fourteenth-Century Texts*. Princeton: Princeton University Press, 1992.

Summit, Jennifer. *Lost Property: The Woman Writer and English Literary History, 1380–1589*. Chicago and London: University of Chicago Press, 2000.

Sutton, Anne, and Livia Visser-Fuchs. *Richard III's Books*. Stroud: Sutton, 1997.

Swift, Helen J. *Gender, Writing, and Performance: Men Defending Women in Late Medieval France, 1440–1538*. Oxford: Clarendon Press, 2008.

Swift, Louis J. "Lactantius and the Golden Age." *American Journal of Philology* 89 (1968): 144–56.

Sylvester, Louise. "Reading Narratives of Rape: The Story of Lucretia in Chaucer, Gower, and Christine de Pizan." *Leeds Studies in English* 31 (2000): 115–44.

Tarnowski, Andrea. "Christine's Selves." In Dulac et al., *Desireuse de plus avant enquerre*, 181–88.

———. "Maternity and Paternity in 'La Mutacion de Fortune'." In Zimmermann and De Rentiis, *City of Scholars*, 116–26.

Taylor, Craig. "The Salic Law, French Queenship, and the Defense of Women in the Late Middle Ages." *French Historical Studies* 29 (2006): 543–64.

Taylor, Jane H. M. "Translation as Reception: Boccaccio's *De mulieribus claris* and *Des cleres et nobles femmes*." In *Por le soie amisté: Essays in Honour of Norris J. Lacy*, ed. Keith Busby and Catherine M. Jones, 491–507. Faux Titre 183. Amsterdam and Atlanta: Rodopi, 2000.

Thurley, Simon. *The Royal Palaces of Tudor England: Architecture and Court Life, 1460–1547*. New Haven and London: Yale University Press, 1993.

Tolhurst, Fiona. "The Great Divide?: History and Literary History as Partners in Medieval Mythography." *Historical Reflections* 30 (2004): 7–27.

Tomasch, Sylvia and Sealy Gilles, eds. *Text and Territory: Geographical Imagination in the European Middle Ages*. Philadelphia: University of Pennsylvania Press, 1997.

Travitsky, Betty S. "Reprinting Tudor History: The Case of Catherine of Aragon." *Renaissance Quarterly* 50 (1997): 164–74.

"Tudor Kitchens." Hampton Court Palace. Historic Royal Palaces, http://www.hrp.org.uk/Resources/Tudor Kitchens Factsheet2.pdf.

Tuve, Rosemond. *Allegorical Imagery: Some Medieval Books and Their Posterity.* Princeton: Princeton University Press, 1966.

Tyrrell, Blake. *Amazons: A Study in Athenian Mythmaking.* Baltimore: Johns Hopkins University Press, 1984.

Valentini, Andrea. "Gui de Mori: Misogyne ou allié de Christine de Pizan?" *Romanic Review* 101 (2010): 593–618.

Vines, Amy Noelle. "A 'Worldly Occupacioun': English Women's Readership and Patronage of Medieval Secular Literature, 1350–1500." Ph.D. diss., Brown University, 2006.

Wagner, Jill E. "Christine de Pizan's *City of Ladies*: A Monumental (Re)construction of, by, and for Women of All Time." *Medieval Feminist Forum* 44 (2008): 69–80.

Wakelin, Daniel. *Humanism, Reading, and English Literature, 1430–1530.* Oxford: Oxford University Press, 2007.

Walker, Greg. *Persuasive Fictions: Faction, Faith and Political Culture in the Reign of Henry VIII.* Aldershot: Scolar and Brookfield, VT: Ashgate, 1996.

———. *Writing Under Tyranny: English Literature and the Henrician Reformation.* Oxford: Oxford University Press, 2005.

Wallace, David. "Chaucer's Italian Influence." In Boitani and Mann, *Cambridge Companion to Chaucer,* 36–57.

Walters, Lori J. "Christine de Pizan as Translator and Voice of the Body Politic." In Altmann and McGrady, *Christine de Pizan: A Casebook,* 25–41.

———. "The Figure of the 'Seulette' in the Works of Christine de Pizan and Jean Gerson." In Dulac et al., *Desireuse de plus avant enquerre,* 119–39.

———. "The 'Humanist Saint': Christine, Augustine, Petrarch, and Louis IX." In Kennedy, *Contexts and Continuities,* 3:873–88.

———. "La réécriture de saint Augustin par Christine de Pizan: De *La Cité de Dieu* à la *Cité des dames.*" In Hicks, *Au champ des escriptures,* 197–215.

———. "'Translating' Petrarch: *Cité des dames* II.7.1, Jean Daudin, and Vernacular Authority." In Campbell and Margolis, *Christine de Pizan 2000,* 283–97.

Wandruszka, Nikolai. "Familial Traditions of the *de Piçano* at Bologna." In Kennedy, *Contexts and Continuities,* 3:889–906.

———. "The Family Origins of Christine de Pizan: Noble Lineage between City and *Contado* in the Thirteenth and Fourteenth Centuries." In Hicks, *Au champ des escriptures,* 111–30.

Warren, Nancy Bradley. "Christine de Pizan and Joan of Arc." In *The History of British Women's Writing, 700–1500: Volume One,* ed. Liz Herbert McAvoy and Diane Watt, 189–97. New York and Basingstoke: Palgrave Macmillan, 2012.

———. "French Women and English Men: Joan of Arc, Margaret of Anjou, and Christine de Pizan in England, 1445–1540." *Exemplaria* 16 (2004): 405–36.

———. *Women of God and Arms: Female Spirituality and Political Conflict, 1380–1600.* Philadelphia: University of Pennsylvania Press, 2005.

Watson, Nicholas. "Theories of Translation." In *The Oxford History of Literary Translation in English to 1550*, ed. Roger Ellis, 1:71–91. Oxford: Oxford University Press, 2008.

Waugh, Robin. "A Woman in the Mind's Eye (and Not): Narrators and Gazes in Chaucer's *Clerk's Tale* and in Two Analogues." *Philological Quarterly* 79 (2000): 1–18.

Wayne, Valerie. "Zenobia in Medieval and Renaissance Literature." In *Ambiguous Realities: Women in the Middle Ages and Renaissance*, ed. Carole Levin and Jeanie Watson, 48–65. Detroit: Wayne State University Press, 1987.

Weinstein, Jessica R. "The Sibylline Voices of Christine de Pizan." Ph.D. diss., Rice University, 2006.

West, Anne Marie. "'Doulce chose est que mariage': Exemplarity and Advice in the Works of Christine de Pizan." Ph.D. diss., Florida State University, 2009.

Whiting, Bartlett Jere. *Proverbs, Sentences, and Proverbial Phrases: From English Writings Mainly Before 1500*. Cambridge, MA: Belknap Press, 1968.

Wilkinson, Alexander S. "Lost Books Printed in French before 1601." *The Library*, 7th ser., 10 (2009): 188–205.

Willard, Charity Cannon. "An Autograph Manuscript of Christine de Pisan?" *Studi Francesi* 27 (1965): 452–57.

———. "Christine de Pizan and Arachne's Metamorphoses." *Fifteenth-Century Studies* 23 (1997): 138–51.

———. "Christine de Pizan: From Poet to Political Commentator." In Brabant, *Politics, Gender and Genre*, 17–32.

———. *Christine de Pizan: Her Life and Works*. New York: Persea, 1984.

———. "Christine de Pizan on the Art of Warfare." In Desmond, *Categories of Difference*, 3–15.

———. "Christine de Pizan: The Astrologer's Daughter." In *Mélanges à la mémoire de Franco Simone: France et Italie dans la culture européenne*, ed. J. Beck and Gianni Mombello, 95–111. Geneva: Slatkine, 1980.

———. "The Manuscript Tradition of the *Livre de trois vertus* and Christine de Pizan's Audience." *Journal of the History of Ideas* 27 (1966): 433–44.

———. "Pilfering Vegetius? Christine de Pizan's *Faits d'armes et de chevalerie*." In Smith and Taylor, *Women, the Book and the Worldly*, 31–37.

———. "Raoul de Presles's Translation of Saint Augustine's *De Civitate Dei*." In *Medieval Translators and Their Craft*, ed. Jeanette Beer, 329–46. Studies in Medieval Culture 25. Kalamazoo: Western Michigan University, 1989.

Wilson, Katharina M., and Elizabeth M. Makowski. *Wykked Wyves and the Woes of Marriage: Misogamous Literature from Juvenal to Chaucer*. Albany: State University of New York Press, 1990.

Wimsatt, James I. *Allegory and Mirror: Tradition and Structure in Middle English Literature*. New York: Pegasus, 1970.

Winter, Patrick M. de. "Christine de Pizan, ses enlumineurs et ses rapports avec le milieu bourguignon." In *Actes du 104e Congrès National des Sociétés Savantes Bordeaux 1979*, 335–76. Paris: Bibliothèque Nationale, 1982.

Wogan-Browne, Jocelyn. "'Cest livre liseez . . . chescun jour': Women and Reading *c*.1230-*c*.1430." In Wogan-Browne et al., *Language and Culture in Medieval Britain: The French of England*, 239–53.

———— et al., eds. *Language and Culture in Medieval Britain: The French of England c.1100-c.1500*. Woodbridge and Rochester, NY: York Medieval Press, 2009.

Wolfthal, Diane. "'Douleur sur toutes autres': Revisualizing the Rape Script in the *Epistre Othéa* and the *Cité des dames*." In Desmond, *Categories of Difference*, 41–70.

Yeager, Robert F. "Books and Authority." In *A Concise Companion to Chaucer*, ed. Corinne Saunders, 51–67. Oxford and Malden, MA: Blackwell, 2006.

Yenal, Edith. *Christine de Pizan: A Bibliography*. 2nd ed. London: Scarecrow, 1989.

Zhang, Xiagyun. "L'ancien royaume féminin et la nouvelle communauté des femmes." In Dulac et al., *Desireuse de plus avant enquerre*, 357–70.

Zimmermann, Margarete. "L'Oeuvre de Christine de Pizan à la croisée des cultures." In Dulac et al., *Desireuse de plus avant enquerre*, 427–39.

————, and Dina De Rentiis, eds. *The City of Scholars: New Approaches to Christine de Pizan*. European Cultures Series: Studies in Literature and the Arts 2. Berlin and New York: Walter de Gruyter, 1994.

Zühlke, Bärbel. "Christine de Pizan—le 'moi' dans le texte et l'image." In Zimmermann and De Rentiis, *City of Scholars*, 232–41.

Zuwiyya, A. David, ed. *A Companion to Alexander Literature in the Middle Ages*. Leiden and Boston: Brill, 2011.

## *Oxford DNB* Entries

"Adela, Countess of Blois (*c.* 1067–1137)." Lois L. Huneycutt. 1:336–37. doi:10.1093/ref:odnb/161.

"Anne [Anne Boleyn] (*c.* 1500–1536)." E. W. Ives. 2:181–88. doi:10.1093/ref:odnb/557.

"Anslay, Brian (*d.* 1536)." Retha M. Warnicke. 2:258–59. doi:10.1093/ref:odnb/573.

"Beaufort, John, Marquess of Dorset and Marquess of Somerset (*c.* 1371–1410)." G. L. Harriss. 4:637–38. doi:10.1093/ref:odnb/1861.

"Beaufort, Margaret, Countess of Richmond and Derby (1443–1509)." Michael K. Jones and Malcolm G. Underwood. 4:639–43. doi:10.1093/ref:odnb/1863.

"Brereton, William (*c.* 1487x90–1536)." E. W. Ives. 7:470–71. doi:10.1093/ref:odnb/70865.

"Copland, Robert (*fl.* 1505–1547)." Mary C. Erler. 13:334–36. doi:10.1093/ref:odnb/6265.

"Cox, Captain, of Coventry (*fl.* 1575)." A. H. Bullen, rev. Elizabeth Goldring. 13:831. doi:10.1093/ref:odnb/6517.

"Cromwell, Thomas, Earl of Essex (*b.* in or before 1485, *d.* 1540)." Howard Leithead. 14:366–86. doi:10.1093/ref:odnb/6769.

"Edward IV (1442–1483)." Rosemary Horrox. 17:849–59. doi:10.1093/ref:odnb/8520.

"Edward VI (1537–1553)." Dale Hoak. 17:861–72. doi:10.1093/ref:odnb/8522.

"Elizabeth [Elizabeth of York] (1466–1503)." Rosemary Horrox. 18:82–85. doi:10.1093/ref:odnb/8635.

"Elizabeth I (1533–1603)." Patrick Collinson. 18:95–130. doi:10.1093/ref:odnb/8636.

"Fisher, John [St. John Fisher] (*c.* 1469–1535)." Richard Rex. 19:685–93. doi:10.1093/ref:odnb/9498.

"Forrest, William (*fl.* 1530–1576)." Peter Holmes. 20:386–87. doi:10.1093/ref:odnb/9892.

"Grey, Richard, Third Earl of Kent (*b.* in or before 1478, *d.* 1524)." G. W. Bernard. 23:877–78. doi:10.1093/ref:odnb/58355.

"Hawkins, Nicholas (*c.* 1495–1534)." D. G. Newcombe. 25:933–34. doi:10.1093/ref:odnb/12678.

"Henry I (1068/9–1135)." C. Warren Hollister. 26:421–34. doi:10.1093/ref:odnb/12948.

"Henry II (1133–1189)." Thomas K. Keefe. 26:434–49. doi:10.1093/ref:odnb/12949.

"Henry VI (1421–1471)." R. A. Griffiths. 26:497–510.

"Henry VII (1457–1509)." S. J. Gunn. 26:510–22. doi:10.1093/ref:odnb/12954.

"Henry VIII (1491–1547)." E. W. Ives. 26:522–51. doi:10.1093/ref:odnb/12953.

"Katherine, Duchess of Lancaster (1350?–1403)." Simon Walker. 30:888–90. doi:10.1093/ref:odnb/26859.

"Katherine [Catalina, Catherine, Katherine of Aragon] (1485–1536)." C. S. L. Davies and John Edwards. 30:892–901. doi:10.1093/ref:odnb/4891.

"Katherine [*née* Katherine Howard] (1518x24–1542)." Retha M. Warnicke. 30:906–10. doi:10.1093/ref:odnb/4892.

"Katherine [Katherine Parr] (1512–1548)." Susan E. James. 30:901–6. doi:10.1093/ref:odnb/4893.

"Langham, Robert (*c.* 1535–1579/80)." H. R. Woudhuysen. 32:481–82. doi:10.1093/ref:odnb/16002.

"Leland, John (*c.* 1503–1552)." James P. Carley. 33:297–301. doi:10.1093/ref:odnb/16416.

"Lydgate, John (*c.* 1370–1449/50?)." Douglas Gray. 34:843–48. doi:10.1093/ref:odnb/17238.

"Mandeville, Sir John (*supp. fl. c.* 1357)." M. C. Seymour. 36:406–7. doi:10.1093/ref:odnb/17928.
"Marie (*fl. c.* 1180–*c.* 1189)." Tony Hunt. 33:666. doi:10.1093/ref:odnb/52460.
"Mary (1496–1533)." David Loades. 37:68–71. doi:10.1093/ref:odnb/18251.
"Mary I (1516–1558)." Ann Weikel. 37:111–24. doi:10.1093/ref:odnb/18245.
"Matilda (1102–1167)." Marjorie Chibnall. 37:321–29. doi:10.1093/ref:odnb/18338.
"Montagu, John, Third Earl of Salisbury (*c.* 1350–1400)." Anthony Goodman. 38:741–42. doi:10.1093/ref:odnb/18995.
"More, Sir Thomas (1478–1535)." Seymour Baker House. 39:60–76. doi:10.1093/ref:odnb/19191.
"Neville, William (*b.* 1497, *d.* in or before 1545)." A. S. G. Edwards. 40:548. doi:10.1093/ref:odnb/19968.
"Pelgrim, Joyce (*d.* 1526?)." Gordon Duff, rev. Anita McConnell. 43:457. doi:10.1093/ref:odnb/21785.
"Pepwell , Henry (*d.* 1539/40)." Alexandra Gillespie. 43:637–38. doi:10.1093/ref:odnb/21901.
"Roper [*née* More], Margaret (1505–1544)." Margaret Bowker. 47:718–19. doi:10.1093/ref:odnb/24071.
"Stephen (*c.* 1092–1154)." Edmund King. 52:408–16. doi:10.1093/ref:odnb/26365.
"Thynne, William (*d.* 1546)." Sydney Lee, rev. A. S. G. Edwards. 54:750–51. doi:10.1093/ref:odnb/27426.
"Tuke, Sir Brian (*d.* 1545)." P. R. N. Carter. 55:523–24. doi:10.1093/ref:odnb/27803.
"Vives, Juan Luis (1492/3–1540)." Charles Fantazzi. 56:569–73. doi:10.1093/ref:odnb/28337.
"Walter, William (*fl. c.* 1525–1533)." A. S. G. Edwards. 57:180–81. doi:10.1093/ref:odnb/28641.

# Selective Glossary

## A

**abrode,** *adv.* (i) widely, at large; (ii) out-stretched

**admervaylled,** *v.* amazed, marveled at, admired

**advyse,** *v.* to consider or devise

**advysyon,** *n.* meaningful vision, dream

**almesse,** *n.* charitable gifts

**anone,** *adv.* straightaway

**antentyke,** *a.* of old times

**apayre,** *v.* to make worse

**appetyte,** *n.* desire

**araymentes,** *n.* wealthy attire, adornments

**arguous,** *a.* devisive, disputable

**arrynge,** *n.* fault

**assotted,** *v.* infatuated

**assoyle,** *v.* refute

**assoyled,** *v.* cleared up, refuted

**attravers,** *adv.* crosswise

**avaunte,** *v.* boast

**awaytes,** *n.* ploy, ambush

## B

**bain,** *n.* bath or bath-tub

**barbaryne,** *n.* barbarian, uncivilized; non-Christian

**bastyled,** *v.* fortified

**basylycon,** *n.* basil

**bayned,** *v.* bathed

**berafte,** *v.* deprived

**blowen,** *v.* proclaimed

**bothomes,** *n.* silkworm cocoons; skeins of thread

**busshmentes,** *n.* concealed groups of fighters

**buxomnesse,** *n.* humility, complaisance

## C

**can,** *v.* to know or have skill

**caraynes,** *n.* carrion; dead bodies, corpses

**cautele,** *n.* strategem, cunning

**cauteylous,** *a.* deceitful, untrustworthy

**caytyvous,** *adj.* from "caitiff" vile, base, wretched

**chasynge,** *vbl. n.*, embossing, figures set in relief

**cell,** *n.* small room

**chaplettes,** *n.* circlets; headcoverings

**chaufed,** *v.* flushed, inflamed

**chere,** *n.* (i) countenance, appearance; (ii) precious items, goods

**clargye,** *n.* scholarship, learning

**clefte,** *v.* split

**clere,** *a* brightly shining

**colubres,** *n.* snakes

**comfortatyfe,** *a.* reviving

**compace,** *v.* measure

**conyes,** *n.* rabbits

**connynge,** *n.* knowledge, intelligence

**consayte,** *n.* faculty of understanding

**contentes,** *n.* contention, disagreement

**convenyent,** *a.* and *n.* congruous; agreeing with one's nature or character

**corne,** *n.* grain

**coude,** *v.* knew; + *inf.*, knew how, was able

**courage,** *n.* heart; spirit

**courtoysye,** *n.* (i) gracefulness; (ii) noblility

**covenable,** *a.* fitting, appropriate

**coye,** *a.* quiet, still

**culpen,** *n.* cut portion (as in "cut of meat")

**curious,** *a.* (i) fastidious, hard to please, (ii) clever, ingenious

**curyously,** *adv.* attentively

# D

**debatous,** *a.* contentious
**debonayrnesse,** *n.* graciousness
**delycate, delycatyfe,** *a.* dainty
**devoyre,** *n.* duty
**devyse,** *n.* contrivance
**dongeons,** *n.* great towers or keep at the
     centre of a castle
**doubted,** *a.* feared, respected
**doubtynge,** *vbl. n.* fearing, uncertain
**dredefull,** *a.* fearful
**dressynge,** *v.* to adjust, align
**dyke,** *v.* dug
**dyscuted,** *v.* discussed, investigated,
     examined
**dysporte,** *v.* to divert, amuse, entertain
     (oneself); *n.* entertainment
**dyspraysyng,** *n.* despite
**dystempered,** *v.* to disturb balance,
     unsettle
**dyversyte,** *n.* unagreeable, unfavourable

# E

**emfrytaylynge,** *n.* detailed work
**empropryed,** *v.* assigned as a prerogative
**encheson,** *n.* cause; because of
**endyte,** *v.* write, compose
**endytoure,** *n.* one who writes or creates
**endytynge,** *n.* writing, creating
**engrudgeth,** *v.* to vex mentally; envy
**ententyfely,** *adv.* intently, ernestly
**entremete,** *v.* concern oneself, interfere
**esclaves,** *n.* captives, oppressed individu-
     als; slaves
**estable,** *v.* to secure, fix firmly

# F

**faconde,** *n.* eloquence
**fardell,** *n.* packet, bundle of items
**faute, fauteth,** *v.* be absent, lacking
**fayne,** *v.* (i) to invent, relate as a fable; (ii)
     to feign, deceive
**fayne,** *adv.* gladly, willingly
**fayntly,** *adv.* deceitfully
**forbledde,** *v.* covered in blood
**fortakynge,** *vbl. n.* seizure, taking (away)

**forwepte,** *v.* exhausted from crying
**foundement,** *n.* foundation; beginning
**foyson,** *n.* abundance
**free,** *adj.* clear
**frendely,** *adv.* without hostility
**fynaunce,** *n.* settlement, ransom
**fynably,** *adv.* finally
**fynde,** *v.* support

# G

**garnysshed,** *a.* prepared for defence
**gate,** *v.* got, obtained, achieved
**gentyll,** *a.* well-born; generous, courteous
**glayves,** *n.* swords
**grave,** *v.* dug
**grees,** *n.* grease
**greued,** *v.* grew to eminence; prospered
**greves,** *n.* hardships
**guyse,** *n.* (i) habit, practice; (ii) fashion,
     style, appearance

# H

**happely, haply,** *a.* by chance
**hardely,** *adv.* boldly
**harnoys,** *n.* armour
**haunte,** *v.* (i) associate with regularly; (ii)
     use habitually
**hauntynge,** *n.* (i) practice, exercise; (ii)
     visitation
**hawberke,** *n.* coat of mail
**herbegage,** *n.* lodging
**holofaunt,** *n* elephant
**hyghe lyst,** *n.* fine fabric; tapestry

# I

**instaunce,** *n.* urging, solicitation

# J

**janglers,** *n.* chatterboxes; jesters, buffoons
**jape,** *n.* deceptive trick, joke
**journeys,** *n.* days

# K

**kynde,** *n.* natural condition

# L

**lanternesse,** *n.* lantern (female); a light to show the way

**large,** *a.* ample; *adv.* generous, lavish

**largenesse,** *n.* liberality

**latches,** *a.* remiss, negligent

**lawryere,** *n.* laurel

**lefe,** *a.* beloved

**lefte,** *v.* ceased

**lesynges,** *n.* lies

**lever,** *adv.* rather

**lewde,** *a.* ignorant; vulgar, base; poor, ugly

**liveray,** *n.* allotment (of provisions for servants, historically)

**lordeshyp,** *v.* to govern, rule over

**losengyers,** *n.* cunning liars, flatterers, deceivers

**loued,** *v.* lauded, praised

**lowynge,** *n.* praising

**lust,** *n.* delight

**lytell,** *a.* small

# M

**males,** *n.* bags, pouches

**male talent,** *n.* displeasure, ill-will

**malyce,** *n.* mischief, harmful action

**manased,** *v.* threatened

**marched,** *v.* bordered

**maulgre,** *prep.* in spite of

**may,** *n.* fresh greenery; hawthorn

**maystry,** *n.* superiority, achievement

**meane,** *a.* middle or intermediate

**meese,** *n.* portion of food

**meyne, meyny,** *n.* household

**mesell,** *n.* leper

**mete,** *n.* food

**modered,** *v.* held in check; moderated

**movynge,** *n.* motive

# N

**named,** *a.* famous

**nice,** *a.* (i) foolish; (ii) dissolute; (iii) finely dressed; (iv) particular

**nycetees,** *n.* foolish deeds

**noyed,** *v.* vexed; harmed

# O

**oblacyons,** *n.* offerings

**or,** *prep.* before

# P

**payne,** *n.* diligence, labour to accomplish something

**paynyme,** *n.* pagan

**peas,** *n.* peace

**perfourme,** *v.* build; complete, finish

**pervencle,** *n.* periwinkle blue

**playnte,** *n.* accusation, grievance

**plumbe,** *n.* device to establish a true vertical line

**pomell,** *n.* knob, protruding part of furniture

**pontyfycall,** *a.* dignified

**pourchaced,** *v.* brought about, obtained

**pourvey,** *v.* provide

**praty,** *a.* well-conceived, enjoyable

**prejudyable,** *a.* damaging, harmful

**preparate,** *a.* prepared

**processe,** *n.* legal proceeding, judicial case

**pryce,** *n.* value, esteem

**puissance,** *n.* strength

**pycoys,** *n.* pickaxe

# Q

**quycke,** *a.* lively, acute; *adv.* alive

**quyte,** *v.* paid

# R

**raced,** *v.* cut away

**rayments,** *n.* garments

**raynes,** *n.* loins (literally, kidneys)

**recke,** *v.* care

**recrayed,** *a.* cowardly, slothful

**redoubted,** *a.* respected, worthy of reverence

**redynge,** *n.* ordenance; advice, counsel

**requyre,** *v.* to ask for something

**rested,** *v.* refrained from action

**rowte,** *n.* troops in defeat and dissarray; chaotic group of people

**rubrysshe,** *n.* rubbish, refuse

**rybaude,** *n.* a wicked, licentious person of low social status

**ryvayle,** *n.* landing place, port, shore

# S

**sadde,** *a.* serious, sober; *n.* sobriety
**saluynge,** *n.* greeting, saluting
**scarse,** *adv.* avaricious, stingy
**scommers,** *n.* pirates, those who roam the seas
**seased,** *v.* take possession of a feudal holding
**seller,** *n.* (i) wine cellar; (ii) merchant
**semblaunt,** *n.* demeanor, outward appearance (with implied deceit)
**semble,** *a.* similar
**semed,** *v.* befitted
**sentences,** *n.* opinions on specific questions
**sewe,** *v.* pursue
**sewyngly,** *adv.* accordingly
**shalmes,** *n.* musical instruments, related to the oboe
**shrewe,** *n.* troublesome person, inclined to evil; hence *shrewdenesse, shrewdely,*
**slaw-strynge,** *a.* slow-stirring
**slewthed,** *v.* hesitated, held back
**slyppernesse,** *n.* slipperiness; instability
**smote,** *v.* struck
**socours,** *n.* aid; *v.* to help
**solace,** *n.* entertainment, pleasure, comfort
**somme,** *v.* add up, calculate
**sondre,** *adv.* apart
**sparcle,** *v.* scatter
**spedefulnesse,** *n.* success
**stabled,** *v.* confirmed; established, made steadfast
**stablements,** *n.* ordinances, regulations
**strayte,** *a.* narrow; *adv.* tightly, close
**supprysed,** *v.* seized with an emotion, overcome
**suretye,** *n.* safety
**syege,** *n.* (i) seat; (ii) siege
**sygnyouryes,** *n.* lordships, domains
**syth,** *a.* since, afterwards

# T

**table,** *n.* board, other surface used for a painting
**talent,** *n.* disposition, will

**targe,** *n.* light shield used by footmen, archers
**tatches,** *n.* blemishes
**tempre,** *v.* mix, prepare mortar for use
**travayle,** *v.* (i) to work; (ii) to trouble or weary oneself; (iii) to travel
**travayle,** *n.* (i) labour, toil; (ii) hardship
**travayllers,** *n.* labourers
**trowe,** *v.* believe
**trowynge,** *n.* intent or belief
**truell,** *n.* trowel for spreading mortar
**twayne,** *n.* two

# U

**unassoyled,** *v.* untested, unresolved
**unethes,** *adv.* not easily
**unkynde,** *a.* (i) ungrateful; (ii) unnatural

# V

**valure,** *n.* merit, worth
**verely,** *adv.* truly; **verray,** *a.* true
**visage,** *n.* face
**voulentees,** *n.* as one desires
**vyander,** *n.* one who offers hospitality; supplies provisions
**vytayles,** *n.* food

# W

**wanhope,** *n.* hopelessness
**wende,** *v.* believed, thought
**wolde,** *v.* desired, wanted
**woode,** *a.* insane; enraged
**woodnesse,** *n.* wildness, violence
**worshyp,** *v.* honour
**wrest,** *n.* device for tuning, plucking stringed instrument
**wyle,** *n.* sly trick
**wysele,** *adv.* cunningly
**wyte,** *v.* know

# Y

**y(e)oman,** *n.* attendant in a royal household of upper middle rank